The whole duty of a woman: or, an infallible guide to the fair sex. Containing, rules, directions, and observations, for their conduct and behaviour through all ages and circumstances of life, as virgins, wives, or widows. ...

ECCO

PRINT EDITIONS

The whole duty of a woman: or, an infallible guide to the fair sex. Containing, rules, directions, and observations, for their conduct and behaviour through all ages and circumstances of life, as virgins, wives, or widows. ...

Multiple Contributors, See Notes
ESTCID: T027551
Reproduction from British Library
Text is complete despite pagination. Pp. 33-40, 207, 529-540 and 687 misnumbered 41-48, 407, 527-538 and 487 respectively.
London : printed for T. Read, 1737.
[2],653,664-694p.,plates : ill. ; 4°

ECCO
ECCO

Eighteenth Century
Collections Online
Print Editions

Gale ECCO Print Editions

Relive history with *Eighteenth Century Collections Online*, now available in print for the independent historian and collector. This series includes the most significant English-language and foreign-language works printed in Great Britain during the eighteenth century, and is organized in seven different subject areas including literature and language; medicine, science, and technology; and religion and philosophy. The collection also includes thousands of important works from the Americas.

The eighteenth century has been called "The Age of Enlightenment." It was a period of rapid advance in print culture and publishing, in world exploration, and in the rapid growth of science and technology – all of which had a profound impact on the political and cultural landscape. At the end of the century the American Revolution, French Revolution and Industrial Revolution, perhaps three of the most significant events in modern history, set in motion developments that eventually dominated world political, economic, and social life.

In a groundbreaking effort, Gale initiated a revolution of its own: digitization of epic proportions to preserve these invaluable works in the largest online archive of its kind. Contributions from major world libraries constitute over 175,000 original printed works. Scanned images of the actual pages, rather than transcriptions, recreate the works *as they first appeared.*

Now for the first time, these high-quality digital scans of original works are available via print-on-demand, making them readily accessible to libraries, students, independent scholars, and readers of all ages.

For our initial release we have created seven robust collections to form one the world's most comprehensive catalogs of 18th century works.

Initial Gale ECCO Print Editions collections include:

History and Geography

Rich in titles on English life and social history, this collection spans the world as it was known to eighteenth-century historians and explorers. Titles include a wealth of travel accounts and diaries, histories of nations from throughout the world, and maps and charts of a world that was still being discovered. Students of the War of American Independence will find fascinating accounts from the British side of conflict.

Social Science

Delve into what it was like to live during the eighteenth century by reading the first-hand accounts of everyday people, including city dwellers and farmers, businessmen and bankers, artisans and merchants, artists and their patrons, politicians and their constituents. Original texts make the American, French, and Industrial revolutions vividly contemporary.

Medicine, Science and Technology

Medical theory and practice of the 1700s developed rapidly, as is evidenced by the extensive collection, which includes descriptions of diseases, their conditions, and treatments. Books on science and technology, agriculture, military technology, natural philosophy, even cookbooks, are all contained here.

Literature and Language

Western literary study flows out of eighteenth-century works by Alexander Pope, Daniel Defoe, Henry Fielding, Frances Burney, Denis Diderot, Johann Gottfried Herder, Johann Wolfgang von Goethe, and others. Experience the birth of the modern novel, or compare the development of language using dictionaries and grammar discourses.

Religion and Philosophy

The Age of Enlightenment profoundly enriched religious and philosophical understanding and continues to influence present-day thinking. Works collected here include masterpieces by David Hume, Immanuel Kant, and Jean-Jacques Rousseau, as well as religious sermons and moral debates on the issues of the day, such as the slave trade. The Age of Reason saw conflict between Protestantism and Catholicism transformed into one between faith and logic -- a debate that continues in the twenty-first century.

Law and Reference

This collection reveals the history of English common law and Empire law in a vastly changing world of British expansion. Dominating the legal field is the *Commentaries of the Law of England* by Sir William Blackstone, which first appeared in 1765. Reference works such as almanacs and catalogues continue to educate us by revealing the day-to-day workings of society.

Fine Arts

The eighteenth-century fascination with Greek and Roman antiquity followed the systematic excavation of the ruins at Pompeii and Herculaneum in southern Italy; and after 1750 a neoclassical style dominated all artistic fields. The titles here trace developments in mostly English-language works on painting, sculpture, architecture, music, theater, and other disciplines. Instructional works on musical instruments, catalogs of art objects, comic operas, and more are also included.

bibliolife
old books. new life.

The BiblioLife Network

This project was made possible in part by the BiblioLife Network (BLN), a project aimed at addressing some of the huge challenges facing book preservationists around the world. The BLN includes libraries, library networks, archives, subject matter experts, online communities and library service providers. We believe every book ever published should be available as a high-quality print reproduction; printed on-demand anywhere in the world. This insures the ongoing accessibility of the content and helps generate sustainable revenue for the libraries and organizations that work to preserve these important materials.

The following book is in the "public domain" and represents an authentic reproduction of the text as printed by the original publisher. While we have attempted to accurately maintain the integrity of the original work, there are sometimes problems with the original work or the micro-film from which the books were digitized. This can result in minor errors in reproduction. Possible imperfections include missing and blurred pages, poor pictures, markings and other reproduction issues beyond our control. Because this work is culturally important, we have made it available as part of our commitment to protecting, preserving, and promoting the world's literature.

GUIDE TO FOLD-OUTS MAPS and OVERSIZED IMAGES

The book you are reading was digitized from microfilm captured over the past thirty to forty years. Years after the creation of the original microfilm, the book was converted to digital files and made available in an online database.

In an online database, page images do not need to conform to the size restrictions found in a printed book. When converting these images back into a printed bound book, the page sizes are standardized in ways that maintain the detail of the original. For large images, such as fold-out maps, the original page image is split into two or more pages

Guidelines used to determine how to split the page image follows:

• Some images are split vertically; large images require vertical and horizontal splits.
• For horizontal splits, the content is split left to right.
• For vertical splits, the content is split from top to bottom.
• For both vertical and horizontal splits, the image is processed from top left to bottom right.

THE

CONTENTS.

a

The CONTENTS.

THE WHOLE
DUTY *of a* WOMAN:
Or, an infallible
GUIDE to the FAIR SEX.
CONTAINING,

RULES, DIRECTIONS, and OBSERVATIONS, for their Conduct
and Behaviour through all Ages and Circumstances of Life,

AS

VIRGINS, WIVES, or WIDOWS.

WITH

DIRECTIONS, how to obtain all Useful and Fashionable
Accomplishments suitable to the SEX. In which are comprised all Parts of
GOOD HOUSEWIFRY, particularly RULES and RECEIPTS in
every Kind of COOKERY.

1 Making all Sorts of Soops and Sauces.
2 Dressing Flesh, Fish, and Fowl; this last illustrated with Cuts, shewing how every Fowl, Wild or Tame, is to be trust for the Spit. Likewise all other Kind of Game.
3 Making above 40 different Sorts of Puddings.
4 The whole Art of Pastry in making Pies, Tarts, and Pasties.
5. Receipts for all Manner of Pickling, Collaring, &c
6 For Preserving, making Creams, Jellies, and all Manner of Confectionary.
7. Rules and Directions for setting out Dinners, Suppers, and Grand Entertainments.

To which is added,

BILLS of FARE for every Month in the Year, curiously
engraven on COPPER PLATES, with the Forms of Tables and Dishes,
and the Shapes of Pies, Tarts, and Pasties. With Instructions for Marketing.

ALSO

RULES and RECEIPTS for making all the choicest Cordials
for the Closet: Brewing Beers, Ales, &c Making all Sorts of *English* Wines,
Cyder, Mum, Mead, Metheglin, Vinegar, Verjuice, Catchup, &c. With
some fine Perfumes, Pomatums, Cosmeticks and other Beautifiers.

LONDON: Printed for T. READ, in *Dogwell-Court, White-Fryers, Fleet-Street.*
MDCCXXXVII.

THE WHOLE
DUTY *of a* WOMAN:
OR, AN
Infallible GUIDE
TO THE
FAIR SEX.

CHAP. I.
Of RELIGION.

S a very pious and ingenious Author has obferv-ed, That altho' the Female may be thought by fome, tho' fuie very unjuftly, to be inferior in their Intellectuals to the other Sex, yet, in the fublimeft Part of Humanity, no one can difpute their E-

quality;

quality; they have Souls of as divine an Original, as endless a Duration, and as capable of infinite Happiness. It ought then to be the first Care of the Fair Sex, as it is to all Mankind, the Matter of greatest Concern, to regard the Promises of another Life, nor is there any Thing that can make them easier or more amiable in this.

THE distinct and most principal Scenes in which a Woman can be supposed to be an Actor, are these three, VIRGINITY, MARRIAGE, and WIDOWHOOD, which as they differ widely from each other, so for the discharging their respective Duties, there are particular Cautions worthy to be observed.

VIRGINITY, or the Virgin State, is first in Order of Time, the grand Element essential to this State is Modesty, which, tho' necessary to all, is in a more eminent Degree required here. It is the very Characteristick of this Sex, as Courage is of the other; for as the great Mr. *Addison* observes, As a Man without Courage is said to be no Man, so a Woman without Modesty is as much out of Nature and Kind. Modesty in Virgins should appear in its highest Elevation: But as all Virtues are to be acquired by the Helps of Religion, and as none can be truly virtuous or happy without it, we shall, in the first Place, endeavour to give our Fair Readers an Idea of the true Spirit of the *Christian Religion*, which in every View and Design directly tends to make us easy with ourselves, kind and comfortable to one another here, and happy with God hereafter.

It is evident that our holy Religion is a wise Institution to every one, who considers that God is its Author, whose Wisdom appears in all his Works: Thus the Frame of

visible

visible Nature being agreeably set together, and having each Part of it suited to useful and proper Ends, demonstrates itself to be the Work of divine Wisdom; in like manner the whole Plan of pure Religion, having also its Parts suitable to each other, and every one of them agreeably set to the same good and great Design of the whole, does thereby prove itself to be the Contrivance of an All-wise God.

And hereby the Wisdom of the Christian Religion will particularly appear, because every Part of it tends to promote the unviersal Good of Mankind; for which Reason the divine Founder thereof was named JESUS, that is, SAVIOUR, because his only Design was to save us from the prevailing Power of Sin, and from those Miseries in which that evil Power would involve us.

Thus Temperance promotes our Health, Justice in our Dealings prevents us from sustaining the Revenges of the Injured, and gains us Trust among Men, with all the Benefits which arise from thence. Charity, by promoting the common Good of others, draws back their Love and Affection to ourselves, while Patience preserves Quiet within our own Breasts, and Self-Denial, by restraining our extravagant Appetites, establishes the just Power of Reason over us, thereby fitting us for all Conditions of Life; and thus the Law of Christ answers to the Character of Wisdom, by its Agreeableness to the best Design of God in the chief Good of Man: And upon this Account *Solomon* charactered the Idea of Religion under the Name of Wisdom.

Beside these moral Duties there are several Threats of God's Judgments and Promises of his Favour contained,

in

in Chrift's Inftitution, the former were wifely defigned to reftrain us from Immoralities, which are our greateft Follies; and the latter to engage us in the Practice of Virtue, which is our greateft Wifdom : The Threatnings prepare the Way for the Promifes, and qualify us to receive them; inafmuch as they fhake off our Affections from ill Objects, in order for the Promifes, to fix them upon good ones. We muft needs ceafe to do Evil before we can learn to do well.

Now, altho' a due Confideration of the divine Nature will carry us on to the Belief of a future State, in which he, who is in Perfection, the beft of all Beings, will diftinguifh the Good from the Bad by ample Rewards and juft Punifhments, yet, becaufe every one's Capacity may not be fufficient to make this wife Reflection, therefore Jefus Chrift was pleafed *to bring Life and Immortality to light*, as the Gofpel phrafes it, *i. e.* to give the World full Affurance of a future State, in which the juft God will diftinguifh Men hereafter in fuch a Manner as they fhall diftinguifh themfelves here ; and it is the Wifdom of every one to preferve this Belief in his Heart, and bear it always about him, becaufe it is the moft awful Monitor againft our committing Folly, and yields the ftrongeft Encouragement to Virtue

From what has been faid, we hope it may be feen, *Firft,* What is meant by *faving a Soul,* viz. to deliver it from vitious Habits and fearful Punifhments, the fatal Confequents of fuch Habits ; and by eftablifhing Virtue therein to recommend it to the Favour of God. And *Secondly,* That the Gofpel of Chrift was defigned to this very End, and its Tendency hereunto is its Wifdom. And *Thirdly,* From hence you alfo perceive in what Refpect Faith in

Jefus

Jesus Christ is said to save us, *viz.* because this Faith is our receiving the Christian Moral for the Rule of our Lives, and the Threats and Promises contain'd in the Gospel for the outward Motives of our Practice according to that Rule.

And from these three Considerations summ'd up together, you may examine all the various Pretences which differing Churches and Communions make to the Purity of the Christian Faith, so as to form a right Judgment of 'em, for that Communion which manifests itself to have no other Design than to assist its Members in saving their Souls from the Power of Sin, by the Moral and Motives aforemention'd, is certainly the purest Church.; and that Faith which has no other Tendency, is the purest Faith: So that if you form yourself upon this Principle, you may pass by all nice Speculations, or profound Mysteries which have no direct Tendency to improve your Morals, without any Hazard of Salvation.

Secondly, As the Christian Institution is wisely practical, so it is plain, or in other Words we may say, that as the Wisdom of the Christian Religion appears first by its being practical, so it appears secondly by being plain. The obscure Answers which were given out from the old Heathen Oracles, are now known to have proceeded from the Indirectness of a designing Priesthood; who, to maintain their Pretence of foretelling what shall come to pass, sent back all those who came to enquire after future Events with doubtful and uncertain Answers. And it has been the Observation of wise Men, that when any one affects to be dark and mysterious in his Conversation, either he has some indirect Design in so doing, or else, whilst he makes

an

an Oftentation of Wifdom, he does in reality but difcover his Folly.

Now the Wifdom of God cannot be conceived to aim at any other Defign in communicating itfelf to us, than the Information of our Minds in the Nature of Good and Evil, and this in order to direct our Choice; and all Inftructions muft of neceffity be plain, fince 'tis by Things eafy and familiar, fuch as at firft fight we may apprehend, whereby we can be led on to the Knowledge of Matters more remote and difficult; but obfcure and unintelligible Doctrines can have no Effect upon us befide unprofitable Amufement; and *whatfoever is by the Wifdom of God laid out of our Reach, can be no Part of our Concern.*

Farther, to what End did he give us intellectual Faculties? Surely not to amufe but to improve us, by enabling us throughly to underftand each Part of our holy Religion, which directly tends to this End, *viz.* our moral Improvement, as you will foon perceive, if you reduce the Chriftian Inftitution to its general Heads, which are thefe.

Firft, A Narration of Matters of Fact.

Secondly, A Declaration of moral Laws.

Thirdly, A Revelation of fuch Motives which are proper to inforce this Law upon our Minds. And *Fourthly,* Serious Exhortations to refrefh our Memories with our Duty, and earneftly to recommend it to our Practice.

Firft, The Reader fees, that the Matters of Fact contain'd in the four Gofpels, and the Acts of the Apoftles,

viz.

viz. the Travels and Tranfactions of Chrift and his Difciples, are fo plainly related, that you underftand the Relation as eafily as you read it. And *Secondly*, All Laws muft be plain, becaufe they are Directions. Now, obfcure Directions are but Delufions; and Laws which are dubious and difficult to be underftood, are Traps and Snares. And *Thirdly*, 'T is as neceffary that Motives fhould be very intelligible, becaufe their Defign is to work ftrongly upon our Wills, by convincing our Underftandings. Add to this *Fourthly*, That myftical and unintelligible Exhortations are ridiculous, upon which Account St. *Paul* forbad Religious Exercifes to be performed in an unknown Tongue.

Now as the four Gofpels and Acts of the Apoftles contain Matters of Fact, Laws, and Motives, fo the Epiftles contain Exhortations to Serioufnefs and Piety, arifing from the Laws, Facts and Motives before-mentioned: And thefe Books are fufficiently comprehenfive of the Inftitutions and Ordinances of *Jefus* Chrift; which ought indeed to be eafily intelligible, becaufe they concern the poor, weak, and unletter'd People as much as the Learned.

Nor can it be fuppofed that the Doctrine of Chrift was by him, or his Apoftles, deliver'd firft of all into the Hands of the Learned to be by them convey'd into the Minds of the Ignorant; but on the contrary, 'tis manifeft that our Saviour directed both his Difcourfes and Actions immediately to the common People as well as to the Scribe; and in like manner did his Difciples addrefs their Preachings and Writings.

From all this Difcourfe concerning the Clearnefs of Chrift's Inftitution, you may fpare yourfelf the needlefs

B

Trouble

Trouble of reading abftrufe and myfterious Points of Divinity. Nor need you fuffer yourfelf to be amus'd with the pretended deep Speculations of profound Men, when you have the plain Directions of a wife and a good God before you, in following whereof you fhall meet with great Reward.

Thirdly, The Chriftian Inftitution is fhort. True and genuine Religion has always been fumm'd up, and gathered together into a narrow Compafs, by thofe who beft underftood it. Thus *Micah* (vi. 8.) fpeaking of God, faith, *He hath fhewn thee, O Man, what is good; and what doth the Lord thy God require of thee, but to do juftly, to love Mercy, and to walk humbly with thy God.* And our Saviour fums up the whole Law in our Love to God, and our Neighbour. And in another Place includes the whole Scope of the Law and the Prophets, in this one Rule, *Whatfoever ye would that Men fhould do unto you, even fo do ye unto them*, hereby directing us to make a right Ufe of that Reafon which God eftablifh'd as his Oracle in our Breafts; to which we may at all times refort, and from whence we may be refolv'd in fuch Cafes as concern our Duty to one another.

For, as by confulting your own Reafon, you know wherein you are juftly dealt with, and wherein you receive Wrong; When you are kindly us'd, and when otherwife, fo from the fame Principle of Reafon you cannot but know when you deal juftly or wrongfully, and when you do kind or ill Offices to another: This one fhort comprehenfive Rule, taking for its Foundation the Equality of Mankind in refpect of their common Nature, renders Religion itfelf a Matter fenfible unto us.

For

For we can feel the Wound of a sharp slanderous Tongue as sensibly as that of a Sword; we can feel the Wrongs done to ourselves and Families, and are as much sensible of the Benefits we enjoy from the just and kind Dealings of those with whom we are concern'd, and hereby we are in the shortest and plainest way admonish'd of our Behaviour to others; and if this one short Rule were reduc'd to practice, the State of Paradise would be restor'd, and we should enjoy a Heaven upon Earth.

For hereby, *First*, All Persecutions for Conscience sake, which have occasion'd such violent Disorders and vast Effusion of Blood, would be at an End, because every one, who has any Conscience, would most willingly preserve it free from the Impositions of Men in the Worship of God. To compel Men by Fire and Faggot to partake even of a delicious Entertainment, is a savage sort of Hospitality.

Secondly, All Factions in any State would be at an End, if every Member thereof were contented that every one of his Fellow-Members, who was not an Enemy to the Government, might, having equal Pretence of Merit, enjoy equal Privileges with himself.

Thirdly, The Occasions of War and Law-Suits would be taken away; since nothing but manifest Wrong can be the just Cause of either.

And *Fourthly*, There would be no private Quarrels and Uneasiness among Neighbours, since by this Rule of doing as we would be done unto, all rash Censures, sharp Reflections, ungrounded Suspicions and Jealousies, which are the Seeds of private Animosities, are taken away. And hereby we may expect a plentiful Store of God's Blessings

among

among us, who will meafure out his Kindnefs to us in the
fame manner as we meafure out ours to one another.

The Reafon why Religion fhould be both a fhort and
plain Inftitution, will appear if you confider the common
Circumftances and Conditions of Men in this World. For
though many have Leifure enough to read and digeft whole
Volumes of ufeful Knowledge (if there are any fuch) yet
the greateft Part of Mankind being neceffarily employ'd
in making daily Provifions for themfelves and Families,
and difcharging the common Offices of Life, cannot attend to any religious Inftitution which is either difficult or
tedious.

'Tis certain, That the whole Life of Man is not sufficient for him to read all the Controverfies which have been
written upon pretence of Religion ; but 'tis as certain,
That God never lays on us a greater Task than what he
affords us both Abilities and Opportunities to perform ,
wherefore we may conclude, That fince the Duties of Religion are laid in common upon all, the poor Day-Labour-
er muft have Ability and Opportunity fufficient to inftruct
himfelf therein, without hindering the conftant Work of
his Calling. And in all this the Wifdom and Goodnefs
of God are made known, by adapting our Duties to our
Circumftances of Life.

From hence you may fave yourfelf the Trouble of reading the long and tedious Difputes which with fuch intem-
perate Zeal are always in Agitation among the feveral Parties of Chriftians. Indeed, the true Chriftian Inftitution
being fhort, it cannot admit of being fpun out into long
Controverfies : And tho' there are many Books of Contro-
verfial Divinity, there cannot be one Controverfy about the

Matter

Matter of meer Religion, as whether we should maintain in our Hearts a high Reverence and Veneration for Almighty God? Whether we ought to walk before him in Sincerity and Uprightness? Whether or no we should be thankful to him for all the Benefits which we have receiv'd from him? Whether we shall submit to his Will with Patience, and endeavour to govern our Passions, to bring them to a due Moderation and Temper, by making them subject to the Law of Reason? Whether we should be true to our Promises, just in our Dealings, charitable to the Poor, and sincere in our Devotions? Whether we should be temperate and sober, modest and chaste, and demean ourselves in an humble, civil, and agreeable manner towards those with whom we converse? Whether we should be heartily sorry when we come short of our Duty, and should be watchful in the Denial of our irregular Appetites, Passions, and evil Inclinations for the future? In short, it has not been disputed whether Justice, Benignity, Meekness, Charity, Moderation, Patience and Sobriety, should be receiv'd into our Affections; or whether we should love God and our Neighbour? Orthodoxy of Faith is made the Pretence of Controversy, but the one thing necessary is Orthodoxy of Practice.

In this Discourse upon the Subject of Religion, Devotion ought not to be left out, because Thankfulness is a necessary Part of Religion, and Prayer is the Preservative of the whole. A frequent Repetition of our Thanks for all the Benefits we enjoy, preserve in our Minds the Consideration of God as the greatest and best of Beings; and thereby nourishes Veneration and Gratitude. In like manner Prayer for Pardon of Sin, and Preservation of our

Persons,

Perfons, is a conftant Recognition of the Mercy and Bounty of God : But Prayer againft the Power of Sin is the
actual withdrawing of our Inclinations from Evil; and
Prayer for any Grace is an actual Application of our
Min 's, to attain the particular Virtue for which we pray.

Now altho' we would not advife againft fet Hours and
Forms of Devotion, either private or publick, yet, we
would rather recommend a fort of habitual and occafional
Devotion, as very proper to preferve the ftrongeft Impreffions of Religion upon your Mind.

It may be obferv'd, that many who are very punctual
in keeping to their exact Times and Forms of Devotion,
have fallen fhort of any vifible Improvement in Virtue.
The fame Pride, Frowardnefs, Falfhood, Covetoufnefs,
and Bitternefs of Spirit, have appear'd in many who have
been conftant Frequenters of the Publick as well as Clofet
Forms of Prayer, as if God had not been in all their
Thoughts. The Reafon whereof feems to be, becaufe their
formal Petitions fuperfede their habitual Endeavours. Men
are apt to think that fince they fpend in every Day fuch
a Portion of Time in Prayer, they have done all their
Part ; and fo they leave God Almighty to take care of the
Event : And this is indeed all we can do when we make
our Petitions to our Benefactors upon Earth, *viz.* offer up
our Requefts to them, either by Word or Writing, and
then only expect their Anfwer.

But 'tis otherwife with relation to God. Our Petitions
to him muft not take off from our conftant Endeavours to
perform that Work for which we pray his Enablement :
And this occafional Devotion, which we would recommend, is in its own Nature a conftant Endeavour after
Virtue,

Virtue, as well as a serious Petition for it: For it ariseth from a frequent Observation of ourselves in our particular occurring Circumstances, from which Observation suitable Desires will almost necessarily flow: As if at any Time we find that we have done an ill Thing, immediately upon the Discovery, we should beg God's Pardon, and resolve to make Recompence for the Ill we have done: Or if we have design'd any Evil in our Hearts, and presently beg Pardon of him who knoweth the Secrets thereof; in so doing we have given Check to its Progress. In like manner, if we have spoken slanderously, rashly, or injuriously, concerning any one, and upon Recollection thereof we ask Forgiveness of God, and desire that we may not do the like for the future; but on the contrary, that we may govern our Tongues better: In all this we are labouring to withdraw our Souls from Evil, and to form ourselves upon a Principle of Virtue.

Every Night and Morning are proper Times of Leisure to call to Mind the Preservation, Support, and Advantages we have receiv'd the Day or Night preceding: And this Recollection being accompany'd with Thankfulness to our great Preserver, is the actual Continuance and carrying on of our Gratitude to God. If we perceive Pride or Passion to arise in our Hearts, so that we are apt to put a great Value upon every thing we do, and despise others; or if we find ourselves eagerly concern'd for any little Worldly Advantage, or any small Punctilio of Honour, and hereupon we beg of God for an humble Spirit, and a heavenly Mind, we are herein endeavouring to expel the Poison of Sin by its proper Antidote.

We

We cannot but feel the Diforders of our Minds, as much as the Difeases of our Bodies; and the Caufes of a diforder'd Mind are much more eafily difcern'd, than the Caufes of a Bodily Diftemper: For either our Minds are troubl'd for Want or Loffes, or it may be for the Profperity of others, or want of a Revenge, or becaufe we cannot have our Will in what we defign'd. Upon thefe or fuch like Occafions, the proper Cure is Devotinal in begging God's Pardon for our Difcontent; and being defirous that our Wills fhould be fubmitted to his who has taught us that we fhould not return Evil for Evil, but that we fhould love our Neighbours as ourfelves This fort of Soliloquy, and occafional mental Addrefs to God, is a fure way to compofe the Diforders of our Thoughts. For the growing Power of any Sin is moft certainly fupprefs'd by introducing the oppofite Virtue into our Defires.

The fame Method may be ufed as to Sins of Omiffion. A ferious Perfon will obferve Neglects of common Duties, which refpect either God or Man. He cannot but take Notice how much he has neglected his Bufinefs, or his Health; how little he has confider'd God as his Owner, Governor and Benefactor; and how fmall a Portion of what God has blefs'd him with he has laid out upon the Good of his Fellow-Creatures. And if hereupon a Man is ferioufly defirous to become more dutiful to God, more ufeful to himfelf, and beneficial to others, he is therein actually bending his Mind to fupply his former Omiffions.

This cafual Devotion arifing from the Obfervation of ourfelves, under the common Circumftances of Life (al-tho' it can have no fet Times and Forms prefcrib'd to it) will be very effectual to produce, preferve, and increafe a

true

true Senfe of Religion within us. And if you are pleas'd to apply your Thoughts hereunto, as occafion fhall direct you, this Devotion will foon become habitual, cuftomary and eafy: And its Returns, which will be frequent and fhort, will be a continual Reftraint from evil-doing, and an actual Exercife of Virtue.

This Exercife is commonly referv'd to be perform'd all at once, in an actual Preparation before receiving the Sacrament of the LORD's SUPPER; which is ufually perform'd by help of an artificial Catalogue of Sins methodically collected out of the Ten Commandments, according to which Catalogue fet Forms of Confeffions are drawn up, which the Preparant is to take upon Content, and without any fort of Judgment or Difcretion of his own, he confeffes himfelf guilty of all the Sins therein mention'd, together with all their Aggravations, tho', it may be, many of them were of fuch a heinous Nature as never enter'd into his Heart to commit. And if thefe Catalogues and confeffional Forms are read over once a Quarter of a Year, or, it may be, once a Month againft the ufual Sacrament-Day, the Work of Preparation is thought to be well pafs'd over.

But fure it is better to keep a conftant cuftomary Watch over ourfelves, and upon the firft Difcovery of any evil Defign or Action, immediately to retract it within our own Hearts, as in the Prefence of God, and by mental Prayer, proper to the Occafion, arm ourfelves againft committing the like for the future. Hereby you difcharge a Duty in its proper Seafon, which is better than to delay it to a prefix'd Diftance of Time; for what is moft frefh in Memory will make the moft lively Impreffion upon us, but may

C

in

We cannot but feel the Diforders of our Minds, as much as the Difeafes of our Bodies; and the Caufes of a diforder'd Mind are much more eafily difcern'd, than the Caufes of a Bodily Diftemper: For either our Minds are troubl'd for Want or Loffes, or it may be for the Profperity of others, or want of a Revenge, or becaufe we cannot have our Will in what we defign'd. Upon thefe or fuch like Occafions, the proper Cure is Devotinal in begging God's Pardon for our Difcontent; and being defirous that our Wills fhould be fubmitted to his who has taught us that we fhould not return Evil for Evil, but that we fhould love our Neighbours as ourfelves. This fort of Soliloquy, and occafional mental Addrefs to God, is a fure way to compofe the Diforders of our Thoughts For the growing Power of any Sin is moft certainly fupprefs'd by introducing the oppofite Virtue into our Defires.

The fame Method may be ufed as to Sins of Omiffion. A ferious Perfon will obferve Neglects of common Duties, which refpect either God or Man. He cannot but take Notice how much he has neglected his Bufinefs, or his Health; how little he has confider'd God as his Owner, Governor and Benefactor; and how fmall a Portion of what God has blefs'd him with he has laid out upon the Good of his Fellow-Creatures. And if hereupon a Man is ferioufly defirous to become more dutiful to God, more ufeful to himfelf, and beneficial to others, he is therein actually bending his Mind to fupply his former Omiffions.

This cafual Devotion arifing from the Obfervation of ourfelves, under the common Circumftances of Life (altho' it can have no fet Times and Forms prefcrib'd to it) will be very effectual to produce, preferve, and increafe a
true

true Senſe of Religion within us. And if you are pleas'd to apply your Thoughts hereunto, as occaſion ſhall direct you, this Devotion will ſoon become habitual, cuſtomary and eaſy: And its Returns, which will be frequent and ſhort, will be a continual Reſtraint from evil-doing, and an actual Exerciſe of Virtue.

This Exerciſe is commonly reſerv'd to be perform'd all at once, in an actual Preparation before receiving the Sacrament of the LORD's SUPPER; which is uſually perform'd by help of an artificial Catalogue of Sins methodically collected out of the Ten Commandments, according to which Catalogue ſet Forms of Confeſſions are drawn up, which the Preparant is to take upon Content, and without any ſort of Judgment or Diſcretion of his own, he confeſſes himſelf guilty of all the Sins therein mention'd, together with all their Aggravations, tho', it may be, many of them were of ſuch a heinous Nature as never enter'd into his Heart to commit. And if theſe Catalogues and confeſſional Forms are read over once a Quarter of a Year, or, it may be, once a Month againſt the uſual Sacrament-Day, the Work of Preparation is thought to be well paſs'd over.

But ſure it is better to keep a conſtant cuſtomary Watch over ourſelves, and upon the firſt Diſcovery of any evil Deſign or Action, immediately to retract it within our own Hearts, as in the Preſence of God, and by mental Prayer, proper to the Occaſion, arm ourſelves againſt committing the like for the future. Hereby you diſcharge a Duty in its proper Seaſon, which is better than to delay it to a prefix'd Diſtance of Time; for what is moſt freſh in Memory will make the moſt lively Impreſſion upon us, but may

C

in

in a little time be forgotten. Besides, we are apt to turn Forms into Formalities, and a natural Discharge of religious Duties must be more improving than an artificial one.

A serious well-inclin'd Temper of Mind is certainly the best Preparation for the Lord's Supper, or any other of the Ordinances of Jesus Christ, that we may partake of 'em with Advantage and Delight.

David advises us to delight ourselves in the Lord, *i. e* in all his Ways and Ordinances; and there is no Reason that our Preparation for the Lord's Table, and Participation at it, should be accompany'd with greater Anxieties of Mind, than our communicating in any other holy Office; such as publick Prayer or Preaching. We expect the same Blessing of God in the Improvement of our Virtues from all of these Ordinances alike. And why with Terror upon our Minds we should use any of those Means which God has ordain'd for our Good, is not easy to be understood. A Man indeed ought to perform every religious Office seriously and soberly; but Fear, by amusing and distracting the Mind, is apt to render the Ordinance unprofitable.

Men ought likewise to be discourag'd from coming to Prayer, Preaching or Communicating at the Lord's Table, with a careless, or profane Temper of Mind; because such Unpreparedness does harden Men's Hearts, and renders the Ordinance unprofitable. Such as this was the Case of the *Corinthians*, who in celebrating the Lord's Supper, were so inconsiderate of what they came to do, that some were drunk at the Lord's Table, as you read, 1 *Cor.* xi. 21. *For in eating every one taketh before other his own Supper; and one is hungry, and another is drunken;*

and

and to this their prophane Behaviour, thofe Texts of Scripture do particularly relate, which affright fome Men from, and others in receiving the Sacrament: On this Account 'twas faid, by St. *Paul, That they were guilty of the Body and Blood of Chrift; and to eat and drink Damnation to themfelves, not difcerning the Lord's Body,* ver. 27, 29. *i. e.* by fuch a profane and unworthy Communicating, they call down God's Judgments upon themfelves; for fo the Word Damnation ought to be underftood, becaufe it refers to the Judgments fpecify'd in the following Verfe, where 'tis faid, that, *For this Caufe (viz.* of drunken Communicating*) many are weak and fickly among you, and many fleep,* i. e. *die,* ver. 30. Now to avoid thefe Judgments he exhorts them to examine themfelves, *i. e.* to confider with themfelves what was the meaning of that Duty which they were to perform at the LORD's TABLE, which Duty was this, *viz.* to call to mind the Death of Jefus Chrift. And this Commemoration is by St. *Paul* ftil'd, *Difcerning the Lord's Body.*

The vifible Signs of our Saviour's Death, which we difcern on the LORD's TABLE, do prepare our Minds to contemplate a divine Perfon, who for his great Charity to the ftupid World, fuffer'd the higheft Injuftice, with fuch an invincible Patience, and Heroick Fortitude, as was fuperior to the fharpeft Malice of his Enemies. Thereby fetting before us the brighteft Example of an unfhaken Refolution to do Good in fpight of all Difcouragements.

It is to be hoped that it may appear by this Difcourfe, that the Chriftian Religion is a wife, a plain, and a fhort Inftitution, the Belief whereof was defign'd to fave our Souls from the Power and Danger of Sin, by ingrafting

virtuous

virtuous Habits in our Minds. The Readers will likewise perceive, that it is neceſſary to keep a conſtant Watch over ourſelves, to repent as often as we perceive ourſelves to tranſgreſs, and by occaſional mental Devotion, incline our Hearts to obſerve the Law of Chriſt, and all this in order to build up a Habit of Virtue within us. They will alſo perceive, that the Contemplation of the Death of Chriſt, with all its Circumſtances, tends to the ſame admirable End.

And if theſe, or any other Means, ſhall work upon them to be generouſly juſt, to bear a good Will to all Men, to do what Good they can, and to be unconcern'd for the Events of Things which are not within their Power, they will be eaſy within themſelves, and ſatisfy'd in their own Conſciences, which is the Dawn of Heaven upon Earth, and they may chearfully communicate at any time.

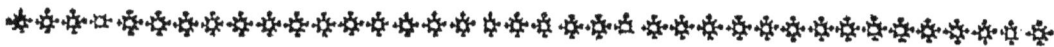

✤✤✤✤✤✤✤✤✤✤✤✤✤✤✤✤✤✤✤✤ ✤✤✤ ✤✤✤ ✤✤✤✤✤✤✤✤✤✤✤✤✤✤

C H A P. II.

Of M O D E S T Y.

HAVING ſaid all that we thought proper, and all that we believe will be neceſſary on the Head of Religion, we ſhall next ſpeak of that amiable Quality in the Fair Sex called, MODESTY, which is properly termed, *The Science of decent Motion*; being a Guider and Regulator of all decent and comely Carriage and Behaviour, it checks and controls all rude Exorbitances, and is the great

Civilizer

Civilizer of Converfations. It is indeed a Virtue of a general Influence, does not only ballaft the Mind with fober and humble Thoughts of ourfelves, but alfo fteers every Part of the outward Frame. It appears in the Face in calm and meek Looks, where it fo impreffes itfelf, that it feems thence to have acquired the Name of *Shamefac'dnefs.* Certainly, whatever the modern Opinion may be, there is nothing which gives a greater Luftre to a Feminine Beauty. For when Women have ftrain'd the Art of adorning themfelves to the higheft Pitch, an innocent Modefty, and native Simplicity of Look, fhall eclipfe their glaring Splendour, and triumph over their artificial Handfomenefs: On the other Hand, if Boldnefs be read in her Face, it blots all the Traces of Beauty, and, like a Cloud over the Sun, intercepts the View of all that was otherwife amiable, and renders its Blacknefs the more obfervable, by being placed near fomewhat that was apt to attract the Eyes.

But Modefty is not only confined to the Face, fhe is there only in Shadow and Effigy, but is in Life and Motion in the Words; whence fhe banifhes all Indecency and Rudenefs, all infolent Vauntings, and fupercilious Difdains, and whatever elfe may render a Perfon troublefome or ridiculous to Company. It refines and tunes the Language, modulates the Tone and Accents, not admitting the Intrufion of unhandfome, earneft, or loud Difcourfe; fo that the modeft Tongue is like the imaginable Mufick of the Spheres, fweet and charming, but not to be heard at a Diftance.

As Modefty prefcribes the Manner, fo it alfo does the Meafure of Speaking; it reftrains all exceffive Talkativenefs, for that, indeed, is one of the greateft Affumings

imaginable;

imaginable; and fo rude an impofing on Company, that there can fcaice be a greater Indecency in Converfation. This is ingenioufly expiefs'd by our divine Poet *Herbert.*

A civil Gueft
Will no more talk all, than eat all the Feaft.

He that ingroffes the Talk enforces Silence upon the reft, and fo is piefumed to look on them only as his Auditors and Pupils, whilft he magifterioufly dictates to them; which gave Occafion to *Socrates* to fay, *It is Arrogance to ſpeak all, and to be willing to hear nothing.* It is indeed univerfally an infolent unbecoming thing, but moft peculiarly fo in a Woman.

The ancient *Romans* thought it fo much fo, that they allowed not that Sex to fpeak publickly, tho' it were in their own neceffary Defence; infomuch that when *Amefia* ftood forth to plead her own Caufe in the Senate, they look'd on it as fo prodigious a thing, that they fent to confult the Oracle what it portended to the State. And tho' thefe firft Seveiities were foon loft in the Succeffes of that Empire, *Valerius Maximus* could find but two moie, whofe either Neceffity or Impudence perfuaded them to repeat this unhandfome Attempt.

Befides this affuming Sort of Talkativenefs, there is another ufually charged upon the Fair Sex, a meer chatting, prattling Humour, which maintains itfelf at the Coft of their Neighbours, and can never want Supplies as long as there is any body within the Reach of their Obfervation. This, it is to be hoped, is chiefly the Vice of the vulgar Soit of Women, the Education of the Nobler fetting them

above

above thofe mean Entertainments. Yet when it is remembered that St. *Paul* makes Tatling the Effect of Idlenefs, it may not unreafonably be feared, that where there is moft of the Caufe, there will be fome of the Effect. And, indeed, it would puzzle one to conjecture, how that Round of formal Vifits among Perfons of Quality fhould be kept up without this. That their Vifits fhould be only a dumb Shew, none will fufpect among Women; and when the unfafhionable Themes of Houfewifry, Piety, *&c.* are excluded, there will not remain many Topicks of Difcourfe, unlefs this be called in for a Supply, and this, indeed, is a moft inexhauftible Referve, it having fo many Springs to feed it, that it is fcarce poffible it fhould fail, yet how careful ought the Fair Sex to be of giving way to this Vice, which is not only *immodeft*, but directly oppofite to all the Obligations of Juftice and Charity, which are fcarce fo frequently violated by any thing, as by this Licentioufnefs of the Tongue.

Such a degenerate Age do we now live in, that every thing feems inverted, even Sexes, whilft Men fall into the Effeminacy and Nicenefs of Women, and Women take up the Confidence, the Boldnefs of Men, and this too under the Notion of good Breeding. A Blufh, which was formerly accounted the Colour of Virtue, is now looked on as worfe Manners than thofe Things which ought to occafion it. And not only the Air but Vices of Men are carefully copied by fome Women, who think they have not made a fufficient Efcape from their Sex, till they can be as daringly wicked as the other. A fober modeft Dialect is too effeminate for them; a bluftring ranting Stile is taken up, and, to fhew them Proficients in it, adorned

with

with all the Oaths and Imprecations their Memory or In-
vention can supply, as if they meant to vindicate their
Sex from the Imputation of Timeroufnefs by daring the
Almighty: And when to this a Woman adds the Vice of
Drunkennefs, nothing that is human approaches fo near the
Beaft. She who is firft Proftitute to Wine, will foon be
fo to Luft alfo: She has difmifs'd her Guards, difcarded all
the Suggeftions of Reafon, as well as Grace, and is at the
Mercy of any, nay, every Affailant: And unlefs her Vice
fecure her Virtue, and the Loathfomenefs of the one prevent Attempts on the other, it is fcarce imaginable a Woman who lofes her Sobriety fhould keep her Chaftity. If
we confider Modefty in this Senfe we fhall find it the moft
indifpenfable Requifite of a Woman; a Thing fo effential
and natural to the Sex, that every the leaft Declination
from it, is a Proportionable receding from Womanhood.
This Virtue is fo much an Inftinct of Nature, that tho'
too many make a fhift to fuppiefs it in themfelves, yet they
cannot fo darken the Notion in others, but that an impudent Woman is looked upon as a fort of Monfter, a thing
diverted and diftorted from its proper Form. That there is
indeed a ftrange Repugnancy to Nature, needs no other
Evidence, than the ftruggling and Difficulty in the firft Vi-
olations of Modefty, which always begin with Regrets
and Blufhes, and require a great deal of Self-Denial, much
of vicious Fortitude, to encounter with the Recoilings and
Upbraidings of their own Minds. Such are the Horrors
and Shames that precede thofe firft Guilts, that they muft
commit a Rape upon themfelves, force their own Reluctan-
ces and Averfions, before they can become willing Profti-
tutes to others. This their Seducers feem well to underftand,

stand, and upon that Score are at the Pains of so many preparatory Courtings, such Expence of Presents too, as if this were so uncouth a Crime, that there were no Hope to introduce it but by a Confederacy of some familiar Vices, their Pride or their Covetousness.

The best way to countermine the Stratagems of Men, is for Women to be suspiciously vigilant even of the first Approaches. The General who would defend a Fort must not abandon the Outworks, and she, who will secure her Chastity, must never let it come to too close a Siege, but repel the very first and most remote Insinuations of a Tempter. Therefore when we speak of Modesty in our present Notion of it, we are not to oppose it only to the grosser Act of Incontinency, but to all those Misbehaviours, which either discover or may create an Inclination to it; of which Sort is all Lightness of Carriage, wanton Glances, obscene Discourse, Things that shew a Woman so weary of her Honour, that the next Comer may reasonably expect a Surrender, and consequently be invited to the Assault: Yet is not this the only State of Danger; they who keep their Ranks, and tho' they do not provoke Assaults, yet stay to receive them, may be far enough from Safety. She who lends a patient Ear to the Praises of her Wit and Beauty, intends at first perhaps only to gratify her Vanity, but when she is once charmed with that Syren's Song, bewitched with that Flattery, she insensibly declines to a Kindness for that Person who values her so much; and when that Spark shall be blown up by perpetual Remonstrances of Passion, and perhaps little Romantic Artifices of pretending to die for her, with a thousand other Tricks, which Lust can suggest, it will soon grow to an

N° 2.　　　　　　　D　　　　　　　unquenchable

unquenchable Flame, to the Ruin both of her Virtue and Honour.

Let no Woman therefore prefume upon the Innocence of her firft Intentions, fhe may as well, upon Confidence of a found Conftitution, enter a Peft-Houfe, and converfe with the Plague, whofe Contagion does not more fubtily infinuate itfelf, than this Sort of Temptation: And as in that Cafe fhe would not ftay to define what was the critical Diftance, at which fhe might approach with Safety, but would run as far from it as fhe could; fo in this, it no lefs concerns her, to remove herfelf from the Poffibility of Danger, and (how unfafhionable foever it be) to put on fuch a fevere Modefty, that her very Looks fhould guard her, and difcourage the moft impudent Affailant · But perhaps that Sex may fear, that by putting on fuch a Strict-nefs, they fhall lofe the Glory of their Beauty, which is now eftimated by the Number of thofe who court and adore them　To this, in the firft Place, it may be faid, that they are miferable Trophies to Beauty that muft be built on the Ruins of Virtue and Honour; and fhe that to boaft the length of her Hair fhould hang herfelf in it, would but act the fame Folly in a lower Inftance.

But then fecondly, 'tis a great Miftake to think their Beauty fhall be lefs prized, fince it is incident to Man's Na-ture to efteem thofe Things moft that are at a Diftance, whereas an eafy and cheap Defcent begets Contempt. There is nothing like Refervednefs that can make their Beauty triumphant. Parly and Conqueft are the moft dif-tant Things, and fhe that defcends to treat with an Affail-ant, whatever he may tell her of his being her Captive, 'tis but in order to the making her his, which when fhe

once

once is, there is no State of Servitude half so wretched, nothing in the World being so slavishly abject as a proftitute Woman: For besides all the Interest of another Life, which she basely resigns, she sacrifices all that is valuable in this: Her Reputation she put wholly in his Power that has debauched her, and which is worse her Reformation too: If she should have a Mind to return to Virtue she dares not for fear he should divulge her former Strayings from it; so that like *Cataline*, she is engaged to further Evils to secure the past. She is subject not only to his Lust, but to all his Humours and Fancies, nay, even to all those who have been instrumental to their Privacies, none of them all being to be displeased for fear of blabbing: And when it is remembred, what Sort of Cattle they are, which are commonly the Engines in such Affairs, there can scarce be any thing more deplorable than to be within their Lash. Women who have abandoned their Virtue are in the most servile and wretched Condition whatever.

Let all those, therefore, who are yet untainted, and by being so, have their Judgments clear and unbias'd, consider soberly the Misery of the other Condition, and that not only to applaud, but secure their own; and whenever the outward Pomps and gaudy Splendors of a vitiated Woman seem, like that of *Cresus*, to boast their Happiness, let them look thro' that Fallacy, and answer with *Solon*, *That those only are happy who are so at their End.* Their most exquisite Deckings are but like the Garlands on a Beast design'd for Sacrifice; their richest Gems are but the Chains, not of their Ornament but Slavery; and their gorgeous Apparel, like that of *Herod*, covers, perhaps, a

putrid

putrid Body, (for even that doth not seldom prove their Fate) or, however, a more putrid Soul. They who can thus consider them, will avoid one great Snare; for 'tis not always so much the Lust of the Flesh, as that of the Eyes which betrays a Woman. 'Tis the known Infirmity of the Sex, to love Gaiety, and a splendid Appearance, which renders all Temptations of that Sort so connatural to them, that those who are not arrived to a more sober Estimate of Things, will scarce be secure. It will, therefore, be necessary for them to regulate their Opinions, and reduce all such Things to their just Value, and then they will appear so trifling, that they can never maintain any Competition with the more solid Interests of Virtue and Honour: For tho' those Terms seem, in this loose Age, to be exploded, yet, where the Things are visible, they extort a secret Veneration, even from those who think it their Concern publickly to deride them: Whereas, on the other Side, a Defection from them exposes to all the Contempt imaginable, renders them despis'd even by those who betray'd them to it, leaves a perpetual Blot upon their Names and their Family. For in the Character of a Woman, let Wit and Beauty and all Female Accomplishments stand in the Front, yet if Wantonness bring up the Rear, the Satyr soon devours the Panegyric, and, as in an Echo, the last Words only will reverberate, and her Vice will be remembred when all the rest is forgot.

What hath been already said, may be sufficient to convince every Woman how much it is her Concern to keep herself strictly within the Bounds of Modesty and Virtue.

In

In order to which, there is nothing more important than a judicious Choice of their Company.

Vice is contagious, and this especially has that worst Quality of the Plague, that 'tis malicious, and would infect others. A Woman that knows herself scandalous thinks she is reproach'd by the Virtue of another, looks on her as one that is *made to reprove her Ways,* as it is, *Wisd.* 11. 14. and therefore in her own Defence strives to level the Inequality, not by reforming herself, (that she thinks too hard a Task) but by corrupting the other. To this End such are willing to screw themselves into an Acquaintance, will be officiously kind, and by all Arts of Condescention and obliging, endeavour to ensnare a Woman of Reputation into their Intimacy: And if they succeed, if they can but once entangle her into that Cobweb-Friendship, they then, Spider like, infuse their Venom, never leave their vile Insinuations 'till they have poisoned and ruined her. But if, on the other Side they meet with one of too much Sagacity to be so entrapped; if they cannot taint her Innocence, they will endeavour to blast her Fame; represent her to the World to be what they would have made her: So that there is no conversing with them, but with a manifest Peril, either of Virtue or Honour, which should be a sufficient Dissuasive. It is true, it is not always in one's Power to shun the meeting with such Persons, they are too numerous, and too intruding to be totally avoided: But all voluntary Converse supposes a Choice, and therefore every body that will, may refrain that, may keep on the utmost Frontiers of Civility, without ever suffering any Approach towards Intimacy and Familiarity.

Were

Were this Distance to be duly observed, it might be of excellent Use, and seems very well to agree with the Sense of *Solon*, the wise *Athenian* Law-giver, who, besides that he shut the Temple Doors against them, interdicted them the sacred Assemblies, made it one of his Laws, that an Adultress should not be permitted to wear any Ornaments, that so they might in their Dress carry the Note of their Infamy. Should we have the like Distinction observed, it is to be feared that many of our gayest Birds would be unplumed: And tho' the same be not now an Expedient practicable, yet the former is, and might be of very good Use. For besides that already mentioned of securing the Innocent, it might, perhaps, have a good Effect on the Guilty, who could not but reflect with some Shame on themselves, if they were thus singled out and discriminated: Whereas, whilst they are suffered to mix with the best Societies, like hurt Deer in an Herd, they flatter themselves they are undiscernable.

But indeed the Advantage of this Course is yet more extensive, and would reach the whole Sex, which now seems to lie under a general Slander, for the Faults of particular Persons. We know any considerable Number of smutty Ears cast a Blackness on the whole Field, which yet were they apart, would, perhaps, not fill a small Corner of it; and in this uncharitable Age, Things are apt to be denominated, not from the greater, but worser Part: Whereas, were the Precious severed from the Vile, by some Note of Distinction, there might then a more certain Estimate be made. And we cannot be so severe to Womankind, as not to believe the scandalous Part would then make but a small Shew, which now makes

so

fo great a Noife: Befides this there can be but one more
Way fuggefted for Women of Honour to vindicate their
Sex, and that is, by making their own Virtue as illuftri-
ous as they can, and by the bright Shine of that, draw off
Mens Eyes from the worfer Profpect; and to this there
is required not only Innocence, but Prudence, to abftain
as from all real Evil, *fo from the Appearance of it too*; not
by any doubtful or fufpicious Action, to give Umbrage
for Cenfure, but, as the Apoftle fays, in another Cafe, *To
cut off Occafion from them that defire Occafion*; to deny
themfelves the moft innocent Liberties when any fcandalous
Inference is like to be deduc'd from them: And tho' perhaps no Caution is enough to fecure againft the Malicious
and the Jealous, tho' 'tis poffible fome black Mouth may
afperfe them, yet, they have ftill *Plato*'s Referve, who
being told of fome who had defam'd him, *'Tis no Matter*, faid he, *I will live fo that none fhall believe them*.
If their Lives be fuch, that they may acquit themfelves
to the Sober and Unprejudiced, they have all the Security
can be afpired to in this World; the more evincing Atteftation, they muft attend from the unerring Tribunal
hereafter, where there lies a certain Appeal for all injur'd
Perfons who can calmly wait for it.

But notwithftanding what has been faid of Modefty,
let not a Woman think that her whole Virtue depends
on that only, there are fome Women, who know no
other, and are perfuaded, that in this, they acquit all the
Duties of Society: They think they have a Privilege to
fail in all the reft, to be proud, arrogant, and to flander
with Impunity. *Anne* of *Bretagne* in *France*, was a
Princefs fo imperious and haughty, that fhe try'd very
much

much the Patience of *Lewis* XII This Prince used often to say, in complying with her Temper, *We must expect to pay for the Chastity of Woman.* Let not Women exact this Payment, but remember, that it is a Virtue which regards only themselves, and which loses its Lustre when unaccompany'd by others

Modesty ought to diffuse itself thro' all their Actions and embellish the whole Conduct of the Female Sex. It is fabled, that *Jupiter*, in composing the Passions, gave each its particular Residence. Modesty was forgotten in this Distribution, and presenting itself, he was at a Loss where to place it, and therefore permitted it to mingle with all the others: Since that Time, it is inseparable from them. It is a Friend to Truth, and betrays the Deceptions that presume to attack it, it is linked and united particularly to Love, is ever in his Company, and often discovers his Votaries; nay, he is divested of his Charms the Moment he is without it. In short, there is nothing so becoming, nothing gives a greater Grace to all Persons, than Modesty.

❖❖❖

CHAP. III.

Of MEEKNESS.

IN the next Place we may rank Meekness as a necessary Feminine Virtue, this even Nature seems to teach, which abhors Monstrosities and Disproportions, and therefore

fore having allotted to Women a more fmooth and foft Compofition of Body, infers thereby her Intention, that the Mind fhould correfpond with it. For tho' the Adulterations of Art can reprefent in the fame Face Beauty in one Pofition, and Deformity in another, yet, Nature is more fincere, and never meant a ferene and clear Forehead fhould be the Frontifpiece to a cloudy tempeftuous Heart. 'Tis, therefore, to be wifh'd they would take the Admonition, and, whilft they confult their Glaffes, whether to applaud or improve their outward Form, they would caft one Look inwards, and examine what Symmetry is there held with a fair Outfide, whether any Storm of Paffion darken and overcaft their interior Beauty, and ufe, at leaft, an equal Diligence to refcue that, as they would to clear their Face from any Stain or Blemifh.

But it is not Nature only which fuggefts this, but the God of Nature too, Meeknefs being not only recommended to all as a Chriftian Virtue, but particularly enjoin'd to Women as a peculiar Accomplifhment of their Sex, 1 *Pet.* iii. 4. where after the Mention of all the exquifite and coftly Deckings of Art, this one *Ornament of a meek and quiet Spirit,* is confronted to them, with this eminent Atteftation, that it is *in the Sight of God of great Price,* and, therefore, to all who will not enter difpute with God and conteft his Judgment, it muft be fo too. Now, tho' Meeknefs be in itfelf a fingle entire Virtue, yet, it is diverfify'd according to the feveral Faculties of the Soul, over which it has Influence; fo that there is a Meeknefs of the Underftanding, a Meeknefs of the Will, and a Meeknefs of the Affections; all which muft concur to make up the meek and quiet Spirit.

E

Firft,

First, The Meeknefs of the Underftanding confifts in a Pliablenefs to Conviction, and is directly oppofite to that fullen Adherence obfervable in too many, who judge of Tenets not by their Conformity to Truth and Reafon, but to their Prepoffeffions, and tenacioufly retain'd Opinions, only becaufe they, or fome in whom they confide, have once own'd them, and certainly fuch a Temper is, of all others, the moft obftructive to Wifdom. This puts them upon the Chance of a Lottery, and what they firft happen to draw determines them merely upon the Privilege of its Precedency: But whilft we decry this prejudicated Stiffnefs, we ought not to plead for its contrary Extreme, and recommend a too eafy Flexibility, which is a Temper of equal, if not more ill Confequence than the former. The adhering to one Opinion can expofe but one Error, but a Mind that lies open to the Effluxes of all new Tenets, may fucceffively entertain a whole Ocean of Delufions; and to be thus yielding, is not a Meeknefs, but Servilenefs of Underftanding.

A fecond fort of Meeknefs is that of the Will, which lies in its juft Subordination and Submiffion to a more fupreme Authority, which in divine Things is the Will of God; in Natural or Moral, right Reafon; and in human Conftitutions, the Command of Superiors: And fo long as the Will governs itfelf by thefe in their refpective Orders, it tranfgreffes not the Meeknefs requir'd of it. But Experience atteft, that the Will is now in its Depravation an imperious Faculty, apt to caft off that Subjection to which it was defign'd, and act independently from thofe Motives which fhould influence it. This, God knows, is too common in all Ages, all Conditions, and Sexes; but the Feminine

minine lies more especially under an ill Name for it: Whether that hath grown from the low Opinion conceived of their Reason, less able to maintain its Empire, or from the multiply'd habitual Instances, which, they themselves have given of unruly Wills, is not easy to determine; but, either Way, it is so great a Reproach as they should be very industrious to wipe off. And, truly, there can be no stronger Incentive to that Endeavour, than having a right Estimate of the Happiness, as well as Virtue, of a governable Will: How calmly do those glide thro' all, even the roughest, Events, that can but master that stubborn Faculty? A Will resigned to God's, how does it enervate and enfeeble any Calamity? Nay, indeed, it triumphs over it, and by that Conjunction with him that ordains it, may be said to command, even, what it suffers. It was a Philosophical Maxim, that a wise moral Man could not be injured, could not be miserable. But, sure it is much more true of him who has that divine Wisdom of Christian Resignation, that twists and inwarps all his Choices with God's, and is neither at the Pains nor Hazards of his own Elections, but is secure, that unless Omniscience can be deceived, or Omnipotence defeated, he shall have what is really best for him.

Proportionable, tho' not equal to this, is the Happiness of a Will regulated by Reason in things within its Sphere: It is the Dignity of human Nature, and that which distinguishes it from that of Beasts. And, even those grow the more contemptible in the Kinds, the farther they are removed from it.

. An ungovernable Will is the most precipitous thing imaginable, and, like the Devil in the Swine, hurries

E 2

headlong

headlong to Deftruction ; and, yet, deprives one of that poor Referve, that faint Comfort of the Miferable, Pity, which will not be fo much invited by the Mifery, as averted by that Wilfulnefs which caufed it : Nay, indeed, fo little can fuch Perfons expect the Compaffion of others, that 'twill be hard for them to afford themfelves their own : The Confcioufnefs that their Calamities are but the Iffues of their own Perverfnefs, being apt to difpofe them more to Hate than Pity. And, this is no fmall Accumulation of Wretchednefs, when a Man fuffers not only directly, but at the Rebound too ; reinflicts his Miferies upon him-felf, by a grating Reflection on his own Madnefs. Yea, fo great an Aggravation is it, that even Hell itfelf is en-hanced and compleated by it ; all the Torments there, being edg'd and fharpned by the woful Remembrance, that they might once have been avoided.

In the laft Place, a Will duly fubmiffive to lawful Supe-riors, is not only an amiable thing in the Eyes of others, but exceedingly happy to one's felf ; it is the Parent of Peace, and Order both public and private. A Bleffing fo confiderable, as is very cheaply bought with a little re-ceding from one's own Will or Humour : Whereas the con-trary Temper is the Spring and Original of infinite Con-fufions, the grand Incendiary which fets Kingdoms, Churches, Families, in Combuftion ; a flat Contradiction not only to the Word, but even the Works of God, a kind of anticreative Power, which reduces Things to that Chaos from whence God drew them. Our Age has given us too many and too pregnant Inftances of its mifchievous Effects, which may ferve to enhance the Value of that go-vernable and malleable Temper we would recommend.

And

And as a Will thus refigned to Reafon and juft Authority, is a Felicity all rational Natures fhould afpire to, fo efpecially the Feminine Sex, whofe Paffions being naturally the more impetuous, ought to be the more ftrictly guarded and kept under the fevere Difcipline of Reafon, for where it is otherwife, where a Woman has no Guide but her Will, and her Will is nothing but her Humour, the Event is fure to be fatal to herfelf, and often to others alfo.

And the Hazard of this renders that other Reftraint of the Will, *viz.* that of Obedience to Superiors, a very happy Impofition, tho', perhaps, it is not always thought fo; for thofe who refift the Government of Reafon, are not very apt to fubmit to that of Authority. Yet, fure God and Nature do atteft the particular Expediency of this to Women, by having placed that Sex in a Degree of Inferiority to the other. Nay, farther, 'tis obfervable, that as there are but three States of Life, thro' which they can regularly pafs, *viz.* Virginity, Marriage, and Widowhood, two of them are States of Subjection, the Firft to the Parent, the Second to the Husband, and the Third, as it is cafual, whether ever they arrive to it or no, fo if they do, we find it, by God himfelf, reckoned as a Condition the moft defolate and deplorable. If we fhould fay, this happens upon that very Score, that they are left to their own Guidance, the fad Wrecks of many would too much juftify the Glofs: But, however, it evinces, that God fets not the fame Value upon their being Mafterlefs, which fome of them do, whilft he reckons them moft miferable when they are moft at Liberty.

And

And since God's Assignation has thus determined Subjection to be the Women's Lot, there needs no other Argument of its Fitness, or for their Acquiescence: Therefore, whenever they oppose it, the Contumacy flies higher than the immediate Superior, and reaches God himself: And it is likely that there would not many of that timorous Sex dare so far, were it not for some false Punctillio's of Honour, which, like those among our Duellists, they have imposed upon themselves. These represent Meekness and Submission as a silly sheepish Quality unfit for Women of Breeding and Spirit; whilst an imperious Obstinacy passes for Nobleness and Greatness of Mind: But, alas! they are wofully mistaken in their Notion of a great Spirit, which consists in scorning to do unworthy and vile Things, and couragiously encountring the adverse Events of Life, not in spurning at Duty, or seeking to pull themselves from that Sphere where the divine Wisdom has placed them. No sure, Stubbornness is the Mark only of a great Stomach, not of a great Mind; and the Cruelty of a Coward may as well denominate him valiant, as the Ungovernableness of a Woman can speak her generous.

This may be presumed to be the common Sense of all, for what Value soever they put upon themselves, nothing renders them less acceptable to others; an imperious Woman being a Plague to her Relatives, and a Derision to Strangers, yea, and a Torment to herself; every the least Contradiction, which a meek Person would pass over insensibly, inflaming such an unruly Temper, and transporting her to such Extravagancies, as often produce very mischievous Effects.

On

On the other fide, if fhe be humour'd and complied with, that ferves only to make her more infolent and intoleiable, makes her Humours grow to fuch an height, that fhe knows not herfelf what would pleafe her, and yet expects that others fhould; fo that to fuch a one, we may apply what *Hannibal* faid of *Marcellus, That if he were vanquifhed, he never gave Reft to himfelf, nor if he were victorious, to others.* Certainly the Uneafinefs of a perverfe Spirit is fo great, that could fuch come but to compare it with the Calm and happy Serenity of Meeknefs and Obedience, there would need no other Lecture to commend them to their Efteem or Practice

The laft Bianch of Meeknefs is that of Affections, and confifts in reducing the Paffions to a Temper and Calmnefs, not fuffering them to make Uproars within to difturb one's felf, nor without to the difquieting of others; and to this Regulation Meeknefs is generally fubfervient. The correcting fome particular Paffions are more immediately affignable to other Virtues; but that on which this has a more direct and peculiar Influence is Anger, a two-edged Paffion, which whilft it deals its Blows without, yet wounds more fatally within. The Commotion and Vexation which an angry Man feels, is far more painful than any thing he can ordinarily inflict upon another; herein juftifying the Epithet ufually given to Anger, that it is a fhort Madnefs, for who that were in his right Wits would incur a greater Mifchief to do a lefs? It is, indeed, fo great a Diftemper of the Mind, that he that is poffefs'd with it is incompetent for any fober Undertaking, and fhould as much be fufpended from acting, as one in a Phrenzy or Lunacy. This was the Judgment and Practice too of *Plato,* who going

to

to chaftife a Servant, and finding himself grow angry, ftopt his Correction, a Friend coming in and asking what he was doing? *Punifhing*, replies he, *an angry Man*, as thinking himself unfit to difcipline another, till he had fubdued his own Paffion. Another Time his Slave offended him, *I would beat thee*, faid he, *but that I am angry*. It were endlefs, indeed, to recite the black Epithets given by all Moralifts to this Vice. It may fuffice to take the Suffrage of the Wifeft of Men, one who had acquainted himfelf *to know Madnefs and Folly*. *Eccle.* i. 17. And we find it his Sentence that *Anger refts in the Bofom of Fools*. *Eccle.* vii. 9.

And what is thus univerfally unbecoming to human Nature, cannot fure be lefs indecent for the gentler Sex: It is rather more fo, every thing contracting fo much more of Deformity, by how much it recedes from its proper kind. Now Nature hath befriended Women with a more cool and temperate Conftitution, put lefs of Fire, and confequently of Choler, in their Compofitions; fo that their Heats of that kind are adventitious and preternatural, raifed often by Fancy or Pride, and fo both look more unhandfomely, and have lefs of Pretence to veil and cover them. Befides, Women have a native Feeblenefs, unable to back and affert their Angers with any effective Force, which may admonifh them 'twas never intended they fhould let loofe to that Paffion, which Nature feems by that very Inability to have interdicted them: But when they do it, they render themfelves at once defpis'd and abhor'd; nothing being more ridiculoufly hateful, than an impotent Rage.

But as the moft feeble Infect may fometimes difturb, tho' not much hurt us, fo there is one Feminine Weapon,
which

which as 'tis always ready, so proves often troublesome, *viz.* the Tongue, which, tho' in its loudest Clamours can naturally invade nothing but the Ear, yet, even that is a Molestation. The Barking of a Dog, tho' we are secure he cannot bite, is a grating unpleasant Sound, and while Women seek that way to vent their Rage, they are but a sort of speaking Brutes, and should consider whether that do not reflect more Contempt upon themselves, than their most virulent Reproaches can fix upon others.

But some Things have had the Luck to acquire a Formidableness no body knows how: And, sure, there is no greater Instance of it than in this Case. A clamorous Woman is look'd upon, tho' not with Reverence, yet with much Dread; and we often find Things done to prevent or appease her Storms, which would be denied to the calm and rational Desires of a meeker Person. And, perhaps, such Successes have not been a little accessory to the fomenting the Humour: Yet, sure it gives them little Cause of triumph, when they consider how odious it makes them, how unfit, yea, intolerable, for human Society: *It is better,* saith *Solomon, to dwell in a Corner of a House Top, than with a brawling Woman in a wide House.* Nor does the Son of *Sirac* speak less sharply, tho' more ironically, *A loud crying Woman and a Scold, shall be sought out to drive away the Enemy :* And tho' he taxes the Feminine Vices impartially enough, yet, there is scarce any of them which he more often and more severely brands, than this of Unquietness: It seems it was a thing generally look'd upon as very insufferable, as appears by *Socrates,* who, when he designed to discipline himself to perfect Patience and Tolerance, knew no better Way of

F

Exercise,

to chaſtiſe a Servant, and finding himſelf grow angry, ſtopt his Correction; a Friend coming in and asking what he was doing? *Puniſhing*, replies he, *an angry Man*, as thinking himſelf unfit to diſcipline another, till he had ſubdued his own Paſſion. Another Time his Slave offended him, *I would beat thee*, ſaid he, *but that I am angry*. It were endleſs, indeed, to recite the black Epithets given by all Moraliſts to this Vice. It may ſuffice to take the Suffrage of the Wiſeſt of Men, one who had acquainted himſelf *to know Madneſs and Folly*. *Eccle.* i. 17. And we find it his Sentence that *Anger reſts in the Boſom of Fools*. *Eccle.* vii. 9.

And what is thus univerſally unbecoming to human Nature, cannot ſure be leſs indecent for the gentler Sex: It is rather more ſo, every thing contracting ſo much more of Deformity, by how much it recedes from its proper kind. Now Nature hath befriended Women with a more cool and temperate Conſtitution, put leſs of Fire, and conſequently of Choler, in their Compoſitions; ſo that their Heats of that kind are adventitious and preternatural, raiſed often by Fancy or Pride, and ſo both look more unhandſomely, and have leſs of Pretence to veil and cover them. Beſides, Women have a native Feebleneſs, unable to back and aſſert their Angers with any effective Force, which may admoniſh them 'twas never intended they ſhould let looſe to that Paſſion, which Nature ſeems by that very Inability to have interdicted them: But when they do it, they render themſelves at once deſpis'd and abhor'd; nothing being more ridiculouſly hateful, than an impotent Rage.

But as the moſt feeble Inſect may ſometimes diſturb, tho' not much hurt us, ſo there is one Feminine Weapon, which

which as 'tis always ready, ſo proves often troubleſome, *viz.* the Tongue, which, tho' in its loudeſt Clamours can naturally invade nothing but the Ear, yet, even that is a Moleſtation. The Barking of a Dog, tho' we are ſecure he cannot bite, is a grating unpleaſant Sound, and while Women ſeek that way to vent their Rage, they are but a ſort of ſpeaking Brutes, and ſhould conſider whether that do not reflect more Contempt upon themſelves, than their moſt virulent Reproaches can fix upon others.

But ſome Things have had the Luck to acquire a Formidableneſs no body knows how: And, ſure, there is no greater Inſtance of it than in this Caſe. A clamorous Woman is look'd upon, tho' not with Reverence, yet with much Dread; and we often find Things done to prevent or appeaſe her Storms, which would be denied to the calm and rational Deſires of a meeker Perſon. And, perhaps, ſuch Succeſſes have not been a little acceſſory to the fomenting the Humour: Yet, ſure it gives them little Cauſe of triumph, when they conſider how odious it makes them, how unfit, yea, intolerable, for human Society: *It is better*, ſaith *Solomon, to dwell in a Corner of a Houſe Top, than with a brawling Woman in a wide Houſe.* Nor does the Son of *Sirac* ſpeak leſs ſharply, tho' more ironically, *A loud crying Woman and a Scold, ſhall be ſought out to drive away the Enemy :* And tho' he taxes the Feminine Vices impartially enough, yet, there is ſcarce any of them which he more often and more ſeverely brands, than this of Unquietneſs: It ſeems it was a thing generally look'd upon as very inſufferable, as appears by *Socrates,* who, when he deſigned to diſcipline himſelf to perfect Patience and Tolerance, knew no better Way of

F

Exerciſe,

Exercife, than to get a Shrew to his Wife, an Excellence, that may, perhaps, again recommend a Woman, when we fall to an Age of Philofophers; but, at prefent, it will be hard for any of our *Xantippes* to find a *Socrates*; and, therefore, that Quality is as deftructive to their Interefts in getting Hufbands, as it is to the Hufband when he is got. Much more need not be faid of this Fault if we were to fpeak only to Gentlewomen, for if neither moral nor divine Confiderations have prevented it, yet probably Civility and a genteel Education hath: A Scold being a Creature to be look'd for only in Stalls and Markets. Yet if there be any, among Women of Fafhion, who have defcended to fo fordid a Practice, they have fo far degraded themfelves, that they are not to wonder if others fubftract that Refpect, which upon other Accounts they might demand.

To fuch the ufual Method of Phyfic fhould be recommended, which is to cure by Revulfion: They fhould let that fharp Humour which fo habitually flows to the Tongue, be taught a little to recoil and work inward; and inftead of reviling others, difcipline and correct themfelves; let them upbraid their own Madnefs, that to gratify an impotent, nay, a moft painful Paffion, have degenerated from what their Nature, their Qualities, their Education, defign'd them: And if they can thus reverfe their Difpleafures, 'twill not only fecure others from all their indecent Affaults, but it will at laft extinguifh them. For Anger is corrofive, and if it be kept only to feed upon itfelf, muft be its own Devourer, if it be permitted to fetch no Forage from without, nor to nourifh itfelf with Sufpicions and Surmifes of others, nor to make any Sallies at the Tongue, it can not long hold out.

How

How much they will herein confult their Intereft and their Reputation too, may be taught by *Solomon,* who makes it the diftinctive *Sign of a foolifh Woman, to be clamorous. Prov.* IX. 13. Whereas when he gives the Character of his excellent Woman, he links Wifdom and Gentlenefs together, *She openeth her Mouth with Wifdom, and in her Tongue is the Law of Kindnefs. Prov.* XXXI. 26. If this Verdict may be admitted, as fure it ought, whether we confider his Wifdom, or dear bought Experience in Women, it will confute the common Plea of querulous Spirits, who think to feem infenfible of any the leaft Provocation, is to appear filly and ftupid; tho' truly if it were fo, it would be full as eligible as to appear mad and raving, as they commonly do in the Tranfport of their Fury.

To conclude. Meeknefs is fo amiable, fo endearing a Quality, and fo peculiarly embellifhing to Women, that did they but all confider it with half the Attention they do their more trivial exterior Ornaments, it would certainly be taken up as the univerfal Mode, in all the feveral Variations of it mention'd in this Chapter.

C H A P. IV.

Of COMPASSION.

Compaffion and Mercy are of near Affinity to the Virtue of Meeknefs, and, indeed, can fcarce thrive in any Place where the latter hath not prepared the Soil: An-

ger

ger and Obſtinacy being like that rough Eaſt Wind which
brought the *Egyptian* Locuſt, *Exod* x. 13. to eat up every green Thing in the Land.   A Mind haraſſed with its
own Impatiency, is not at leiſure to obſerve, much leſs to
condole the Calamities of others : But as a calm and clear
Day befriends us with a more diſtinct Proſpect of diſtant
Objects ; ſo when all is quiet and ſerene within us, we can
then look about us, and diſcern what Exigencies of others
invite our Pities.

Much need not be ſaid to raiſe an Eſtimate of this Virtue, ſince 'tis ſo eſſential to our Nature, ſo interwoven in
the Compoſition of Humanity, that we find in Scripture
Phraſe, Compaſſion is generally ſeated in the moſt inward
ſenſible Part of our Frame and Bowels So *Col.* iii. 12.
Put on therefore Bowels of Mercy ; and *Phil.* ii. 1. *Bowels
and Mercies* : So that a cruel ruthleſs Perſon unmans himſelf, and is by the common Vote of Mankind to be liſted
among Brutes, nay, not among the Better, but only the
more hateful, noxious Sort of them.

But this is yet more unnatural in the Female Sex, which
being of ſofter Mold, is more pliant and yielding to the
Impreſſions of Pity, and by the Strength of Fancy re-
doubles the Horrors of any ſad Object ; yea, ſo remarkable is this Tenderneſs, that God, when he would moſt
magnify his own Compaſſion, illuſtrates it by that of Women, as the higheſt human Inſtances.   Indeed, ſuch a Pro-
penſion have Women to Commiſeration, that they are
uſually taxed with an Exceſs in it ; ſo that any imprudent
Lenity is proverbially called, A Womaniſh Pity ; and,
therefore, it may be thought an Impertinence to exhort
them to that, which, they can ſcarce avoid : But, to this

it

it may be anfwered, *Firft*, That in this degenerous Age, 'tis no News to fee People violate their Inftincts, as well as their Duties, and be worfe than their Nature inclines them; many Sins being committed, even, againft the Grain, and with Violence to Conftitution.

Yet, *Secondly*, 'Tis not a meer melting of the Eyes, or yearning of the Bowels we would recommend: Alafs, their Tears will not be Drink to a thirfty Soul, nor will fhivering at his Nakednefs cloath him; this is an infignificant Mercy: She who weeps over thofe Diftreffes fhe will not relieve, might have been fit to be entered in the Lift of the mourning Women among the *Jews* and *Heathens*, who were hired to make up the tragic Pomp of Funerals with their mercenary Sorrow, but had no real Concern in that Lofs they feem'd to bewail. 'Tis, therefore, a more active Sort of Compaffion to which we would invite them; and, yet, for Method's Sake, we fhall confider it under two diftinct Heads, Giving and Forgiving.

By Giving, in this Place, is meant, not a general Liberality, tho', that prudently bounded, is an Excellence well becoming Perfons of Fortune, but only fuch a Giving, as terminates upon the Needy, and is applyed to fuccour their Indigencies. To give to thofe from whom they may expect Returns, may be a Defign, but at the beft, can be but Generofity and Franknefs of Humour. 'Tis only then Mercy, (as Chrift himfelf has defined it) when it is to thofe from whom they can hope for nothing again.

And in this Virtue, Women have, in former Ages, eminently excelled; yea, fo effential was it, that we find *Solomon* thought not their Character compleat without it, but numbers it among the Properties of his virtuous Wo-

men,

men, *Prov.* xxxi. 20. *She ſtretcheth forth her Hand to the Poor, and reacheth her Hand to the Needy:* And it is a little obſervable, that after he has deſcribed her Induſtry and Diligence for the acquiring of Wealth, this is ſet in the Front of her Disburſements as the principal Uſe ſhe made of it; and precedes her providing Scarlet for her Houſhold, or fine Linnen and Purple for herſelf, v. 21, 22. The Application is very obvious, and admoniſhes all that own the ſame Title of virtuous Women, to prefer the Neceſſities of others before their own Superfluities and Delicacies: Nay, if they look further, and conſider who it is that is perſonated in the Poor, that begs in every needy diſtreſſed Suppliant, and that will finally own every Act of Mercy as done to himſelf; methinks they ſhould ſometimes think fit to ſacrifice, even, their moſt moderate Enjoyments to their Charity, be aſhamed to ſerve themſelves before their Saviour, or let him ſtand naked and hungry, whilſt they are ſolacing with that which would relieve him.

But how then ſhall they anſwer it, who ſuffer him to be ſupplanted, not by their Needs, but Exceſſes, who have ſo devoted their Hearts and Purſes to Vanity and Luxury, that they have neither Will nor Power to ſuccour the Wants of others? How unequal and diſproportionate is it, that thoſe, who ſtudy to fling away Money upon themſelves, cannot be tempted, by any Importunity and Diſtreſs, to drop an Alms to the Poor? What a prepoſterous Sight is it, to ſee a Lady, whoſe gay Attire gives her the glittering of the Sun, yet, have nothing of its other Properties, never to cheer any drooping languiſhing Creature by her Influence? 'Tis the Counſel of the Son of *Sirac, Not to give the Poor an Occaſion to curſe thee,* Eccluſ. iv. 5.

But

But, fure, fuch Perfons do it, if the Poor happen not to have more Charity than they exemplify to them : For when they fhall find fuch hard Hearts under fuch foft Raiment, fee them beftow fo much upon the decking their own Bodies, and nothing towards the neceffary Support of theirs, 'tis a fhrewd Trial of their Meeknefs, Poverty is apt of itfelf to imbitter the Spirit, and needs not fuch an additional Temptation.

Nay, farther, when a poor ftarving Wretch fhall look upon one of thefe gay Creatures, and fee that any one of the Baubles, the loofeft Appendage of her Drefs, a Fan, a Busk, perhaps a black Patch, bears a Price that would warm his empty Bowels; will he not have fharp Incitations not only to execrate her Pride and his own Poverty, but confequently to repine at the unequal Diftribution of Providence, and add Sin to his Mifery ? The Denial, therefore, of an Alms may be a double Cruelty to the Soul as well as to the Body. It is faid of *Xenocrates*, that a chafed Bird flying to his Bofom, he refcued it with much Satisfaction, faying, *He had not betrayed a Suppliant*; but this is in that Cafe reverfed and in a higher Inftance; for what can be more the betraying a Suppliant, than inftead of fupplying his Wants, to rob him of his Innocence, be his Snare in lieu of his Refuge ? This is a Confideration that it were to be wifhed, were more deeply imprefs'd upon the Women of this Age; and truly 'tis their Concern it fhould be fo, for fince at the laft Day the Inqueft fhall be fo particular upon this very thing, 'tis but neceffary they fhould examine how they are fitted to pafs that Teft.

Let them, therefore, keep a preparatory Audit within their own Breaft, reflect upon the Expences of their Vanity,

nity, what the Delicacy of their Food, what the Rich-
nefs and Variety of their Cloaths, nay, what the meer
Hypocrifes of their Drefs, in falfe Hair, and Complexion,
has coft them , to which they may alfo add the Charge of
their Recreations and Divertifements, thofe coftly Arts of
chafing away that Time, which, they will one Day wifh
to recall. Let them, we fay, compute all this, and then
confront to it the Account of their Charity, and much,
it is to be feared, the latter will, with many of them, be
comparatively as undifcernable as *Socrates* found *Alcibi-
ades*'s Land, in the Map of the whole World, and be fo
perfectly overwhelmed, that it will appear, little in their
own Sight, and nothing in God's.

For if the poor Widow's Mite acquired a Value, merely
from her Poverty, that fhe had no more; by the Rule of
Contraries we may conclude, how defpicable the fcanty
Oblations of the Rich are in God's Account. If even
their Liberality who gave much, was outvied by a Far-
thing, *Mark* xii. 41. to what Point of Dimunition muft
their niggardly Offerings, who give little, be reduced? efpecially when they fhall be compared with the numerous
and coftly Sacrifices they made to Pride and Luxury.
Nay, perhaps, fome have been guilty of more than the
Difproportion, even the total Omiffion of Charity, that
in a Multitude of Taylors Bills cannot produce the Account of one Garment for the Poor, that amidft the Delicacies of their own Diet; nay, perhaps, of their Dogs
too, never ordered fo much as the Crumbs of their Table
to any hungry *Lazarus:* But let all fuch remember, that
there will come a Time, when one of *Tabitha*'s Coats,
Acts ix. 39. will be of more Value than all their richeft
Ward-

Wardrobes, tho' they could number Gowns with *Lucullus*'s Cloaks, which the *Roman* Story reports to be 5000, and that when their luxurious Fare should only feast the Worms and render them passive in that Epicurism they acted before, they will wish they had made the Bellies of the Poor their Refectory, and by feeding them nourish'd themselves to Immortality.

Let this be seriously remembered now, least hereafter they fall under the same exprobating Remembrance with the rich Man in the Gospel, *Luke* xvi. 25. *Remember, that thou in thy Life Time receivedst thy good Things, and* Lazarus *that which was evil, but now he is comforted and thou art tormented.* A Text which St. *Gregory* professes, was ever sounding in his Ears, and made him look with Suspicion and Dread upon that Grandeur to which he was advanced, as fearing it might be design'd as his final Reward. With what Terror then may those look upon their present good Things, who, by engrossing them wholly to themselves, own them as their entire Portion, and implicitly disclaim their Share of the Future? For to that none must pretend, who receive their transitory Goods under any other Notion, than that of a Steward or Factor; as we may see in the Parable of the Talents, where those that had the Reward of the Five and Ten Cities were not such as had consumed their Talents upon their own Riot and Excesses, but such as had industriously employed them according to the Design of their Lord; and if it there fared so ill with the meer unprofitable Servant, who had hoarded up his Talent, what shall become of those who squander away theirs and can give no Account either of Use or Principal?

N° 3.   G   Were

Were thefe Confiderations duly laid to heart, we might hope to fee fome of the Primitive Charity revive, when Women of the higheft Rank converted their Ornaments and coftly Deckings into Cloathing for the Poor, and thought no Retinue fo defirable, fo honourable, as a Train of Alms-folks: But it is fpeaking improperly, to make the Poor their Attendants, for, indeed, they rather attended the Poor, did not only order the Supply of their Wants, but were themfelves their Minifters, waited about their fick Beds, drefs'd their moft loathfome Ulcers, and defcended to all the moft fervile Offices about them.

But thefe were fuch heights, fuch Tranfcendencies of Mercy, as required a deeper Foundation of Humility than will now be often met with; yet, let us take the Occafion to fay, that it may be a good Managery of a Charity to act (as far as they can) perfonally in it. For befides that, it prevents fome Abufes and Frauds, which deputed Agents may fometimes be tempted to, they pay God a double Tribute in it of their Perfons as well as their Fortunes. Next they bring themfelves into Acquaintance with the Poor, and by that means correct thofe Contempts and nice Difdains which their own Profperity is too apt to create. Farther yet, they excite their own Compaffion, which being a Motion of the fenfitive Part of the Mind, cannot be ftirr'd fo effectually by any thing, as by the Prefence of the Object; the moft pathetic tragical Defcription of a Diftrefs, being not able to affect us half fo much as one ocular Demonftration. *Laftly*, It is an apt Means to increafe their Thankfulnefs to Almighty God, whofe Bounty to themfelves muft needs make a deeper Impreffion, when 'tis compared with the neceffitous Condition of others.

For

For Things are beft illuftrated by their Contraries, and 'tis too obfervable in our depraved Nature, that we value not Things by their real pofitive Worth, but comparitively as they excel others, nor ever make a right Eftimate of what we enjoy, till our own, or others Wants inftruct us.

Upon all thefe Confiderations it may be a very becoming ufeful Circumftance in any charitable Miniftry to be themfelves the Actors, and to that End 'twill be a very commendable Induftry, to qualify themfelves to be helpful to the Poor in as many Inftances as they can, not only opening their Purfes, but Difpenfatories too, providing Medicines for fuch, as, either by Difeafe, or Cafualty, want that Sort of Relief.

Befides this Part of Mercy in Giving, there is another, that of Forgiving, which may happen to be of a larger Extent than the former; for whereas that was confin'd to the Poor, this has no fuch Limits, but as it is poffible to be injured by Perfons of all Ranks, fo this pardoning Mercy is to reach equally with that Poffibility. This is that Part of Charity which we peculiarly call Clemency, a Virtue which not only Chriftianity but Morality recommends. The Ancient *Romans* had it in fuch Veneration, that they number'd it not only among Virtues but Deities, and built it a Temple: And they were fomewhat towards the Right in it, for it was, tho' not God, yet fo eminent an Attribute of his, that nothing can more affimilate Man unto him.

There are many heroic Acts of this Kind to be met with among the virtuous Heathens. *Lycurgus* not only forgave *Alexander* who had ftruck out his Eye, but entertain'd him in his Houfe, and by his gentle Admonitions reclaim'd him from his former vicious Life. *Ariftides* being, after fignal

G 2

Services, and without Crime, unjuftly banifhed by his Ci-tizens, was fo far from acting, or imprecating againft them, that at his Departure from *Athens,* he folemnly prayed the Gods, that they might never, by any Trouble or Diftrefs, be forced to recall him: So *Phocion* being unjuftly con-demned, left it as a folemn Charge to his Son *Phocas,* that he fhould never revenge him. A multitude of the like Ex-amples might be produced, but we need not borrow Light from their faint Tapers, when we have the Sun-beams of Righteoufnefs, our bleffed Saviour, who, as he has recom-mended this Grace by his Precept, fo he has fignally exem-plified it to us in his Practice, the whole Defign of his Defcent to Earth being only to refcue his Enemies from Deftruction: And as every Part of his Life, fo the laft ·Scene of it was particularly adapted to this End, and his expiring Breath expended in mediating for his Crucifiers: And this Copy of his was tranfcribed by his firft Followers, the Primitive Chriftians, in their fevereft Martyrdoms, praying for their Perfecutors.

Thus are we, in the Apoftle's Phrafe, *compaffed about with a Cloud of Witneffes, Heb.* xii. 1. of eminent Ex-amples, which ought to have a forcible Influence upon all, but, methinks, fhould not fail to have it on that Sex, whofe native Tendernefs predifpofes them to the Virtue, and who need but fwim with the Stream of their own Inclinations. How can we think that their melting Eyes fhould ever fparkle Fire, or delight in Spectacles of Cruelty ? That their flexible tender Hearts fhould turn into Steel or Adamant, be uncapable of all Impreffions of Pity ? Yet, God knows, fuch Changes have too often been feen : Women have not only put off that Softnefs peculiar to them, but the com-

mon

mon Inftinƈt of Humanity, and have exceeded not only favage Men, but Beafts in Cruelty. There have been too frequent Inftances of the implacable Malice and infatiable Cruelties of Women. We need not call in the Aid of Poetic Fiƈtion, and tell them of *Clytemneftra, Medea,* or the *Belides,* with Hundreds of others, celebrated as Inftances of Heroic Wickednefs. There are Examples enough in more authentick Stories; the *Roman Tullia,* the *Perfian Paryfatis,* and that we may not pafs by the facred Annals, *Jezebel* and *Athalia.* We forbear to multiply Examples of this Kind, of which all Ages have produced fome fo eminent, as have render'd it a common Obfervation, That no Cruelty exceeds that of an exafperated Woman, and it is not much to be wonder'd at, fince nothing can be fo ill in its priftine State as that which degenerates from a better. No Enmity, we know, fo bitter as that of alienated Friends; no fuch Perfecution as that of Apoftates, and proportionably no fuch Ferocity as that of a perverted Mildnefs: So that the Poets were not much out, who as they reprefented the Graces under the Figures of Women, fo they did the Furies too: And fince 'tis in their Eleƈtion which Part they will aƈt, they ought to be very jealous over themfelves The Declinations to any Vice are gradual, fometimes at firft fcarce difcernable, and probably the greateft Monfters of Cruelty would, at the Beginning, have detefted thofe Inhumanities which afterwards they aƈted with Greedinefs.

It concerns them, therefore, to ward thofe Beginnings whofe End may be fo fatal. She that is quick in apprehending an Affront, perhaps, will not be fo quick in difmiffing that Apprehenfion; and if it be permitted to ftay,

'twill

'twill quickly improve, twenty little Circumſtances ſhall be ſuborn'd to foment it with new Suſpicions, till at laſt it grow to a Quarrel, from thence to Hatred, from that to Malice, and from that to Revenge: And when that black Paſſion has over-ſpread the Mind, like an *Egyptian* Darkneſs, it admits no Gleam of Reaſon or Religion, but hurries the Enraged blindfold to their own Ruin often, as well as others.

Every one ought to conſider at the firſt Incitement to Wrath, what is the real Ground of it: Perſons are ſometimes angry, perhaps, becauſe ſcandalous, or at leaſt ſuſpicious Behaviour, may have engaged a Friend to admoniſh them, an Office that has ſometimes proved very fatal; thoſe commonly that have moſt Guilt having leſs Patience to hear of it: And if this be the Caſe, it is the greateſt Injuſtice in the World to make that a Quarrel which is really an Obligation: And, therefore, inſtead of maligning their Monitor, they ought to thank and reverence him. Nay, tho' the Accuſation be not with that candid Deſign, but be meant as a Reproach, yet, if it be true, it ſhould not excite Anger at their Accuſers, but Remorſe and Reformation in themſelves.

It was the Saying of a Wiſe Man, *That he profited more by his Enemies, than his Friends; becauſe they would tell him roundly of his Faults.* And this is excellently improved by *Plutarch* in his Tract, *Of the Benefits to be reap'd from Enemies:* So that even a malicious Accuſation may be a Kindneſs, and conſequently ought not to be repaid with an Injury: But ſuppoſe, in the laſt Place, that the Aſperſion be not only unkind, but untrue, it will not even then be ſafe to let looſe to their Indignation. *Firſt,* in

refpect of Prudence, an angry Vindication ferving the Defign of the Enemy, and helping to fpread the Calumny;
whereas, a wife Neglect and Diffembling does often ftifle
and fupprefs it. *Secondly*, In refpect of Duty, for all that
own themfelves Chriftians muft confefs, they are under an
Obligation to forgive and not to revenge. Now if they
intend to pay a real Obedience to this Precept, 'twill be
the more eafy the fooner they fet to it. He that fees his
Houfe on fire, will not dally with the Flame, much lefs
blow, or extend it, refolving to quench it at laft: And
Anger is as little to be trufted, which if once throughly
kindled, will fcarce expire but with the Deftruction of
the Subject it works on

Let, therefore, the Difobliged not look back upon the
Injury, but forward to thofe Mifchiefs which too fharp a
Refentment may betray them too: Let them confider, that
the boiling of their Blood may finally caufe the Effufion
of another's, and Wrath may fwell into Murder. If they
would do thus, and inftead of thofe magnifying Optics
wherein they view the Wrong, make Ufe of the other
End of the Perfpective, to difcern this difmal Event at
Diftance, it would fure fright them from any nearer Approach, would keep them within thofe Bounds which their
Duty prefcribes them, and thereby acquaint them with a
much greater, and more ingenious Pleafure, than their
higheft Revenge can give them, *viz.* that of forgiving Injuries, and obliging the Injurious. This is a Pleafure fo
pure and refined, fo noble and heroic, that none but rational Natures are capable of it; whereas, that of Spight
and Revenge, if it can be called a Pleafure, is a meer be-
ftial one; every the moft contemptible Animal can be angry

gry when it is molested, and endeavours to return the Mischief.

It ought, therefore, to be an easy Determination, whether to embrace that Clemency and Compassion which we
see exemplified in the wisest and best of Men; nay, in
the omniscient immortal God, or that savage Fierceness
of the ignoblest Creatures. This is certain, that no Woman would be content to assume the outward Form of
any of those; why then should they subject their nobler
Part, the Mind, to such a Transformation? For as there
are no Monsters so deformed, as those which are compounded of Man and Beast; so among them all, nothing
can be more unnatural, more odious, than a Woman-Ty-
ger.

To conclude this Chapter. Let us observe the Advice
of *Solomon, Prov.* xvii. 14. *The Beginning of Strife is as*
when one letteth out Water: Therefore leave off Contention
before it be medled with. When once a Breach is made upon the Spirit by immoderate Anger, all the consequent
Mischiefs will flow in, like a rapid Stream when the Banks
are broken down; nor is there any Way to prevent it,
but by keeping the Mounds entire, preserving that Tenderness and Compassion which God and Nature do equally
enforce and recommend.

C H A P.

Chap. V.

Of Affability.

Affability and Courtefy, are, without doubt, amiable in all, but more efpecially in the Fair Sex, and more neceffary to them than to the other; for Men have often Charges and Employments which juftify, nay, perhaps, require fomewhat of Sternnefs and Aufterity, but Women ordinarily have few or no Occafions of it, and thofe who have well digefted the former Lectures of Meeknefs and Compaffion, will not be apt to put it on unneceffarily. Now Affability may be confidered either as a meer human Accomplifhment, or as a divine Virtue; in either Notion it is commendable, but it is the latter that gives it the higheft Excellence and Perfection.

To begin with the firft Notion of it, we may make an Eftimate of its Worth by its Caufe, and by its Effects. For its Caufe, it derives itfelf either from a native Candour and Generofity of Mind, or from a noble and ingenious Education, or fomething jointly from both; and thefe are as good Originals as any Thing meerly moral can flow from: And that thefe are, indeed, its Sources common Experience will atteft: Thofe of the greateft Minds, and beft Extractions, being ufually moft condefcending and obliging; whereas, thofe of moft abject Spirits and Birth, are the moft infulting and imperious. *Alexander* the Great, tho' terrible in the Field, yet, was of a gentle complaifant Converfation, familiarly treating thofe about him: Yet,

H *Crifpinus,*

Crifpinus, Narciffus, Nymphidius, and other enfranchifed Bond-men, we find infolently trampling on the *Roman* Senators and Confuls. 'Tis, therefore, a great Error for Perfons of Honour to think they acquire a Reverence by putting on a fupercilious Gravity, looking coily and difdainfully upon all about them; 'tis fo far from that, that it gives a Sufpicion that 'tis but a Pageantry of Greatnefs, fome Mufhroom newly fprung up that ftands fo ftiff, and fwells fo much: But inftead of teaching others to keep their Diftance, this faftidious Difdain invites them to a clofer Infpection, that if there be any Flaw, either in their Life or Birth, 'twill be fure to be difcovered, there being no fuch prying Inquifitor as Curiofity when 'tis egg'd on by a Senfe of Contempt.

On the other fide, if we confider the Effects of Courtefy, they are quite contrary, it endears to all, and often keeps up a Reputation in fpight of any Blemifhes; a kind Look or Word from a Superior is ftrangely charming, and infenfibly fteals away Men's Hearts from them. It is *Plutarch*'s Obfervation of *Cleomenes,* King of *Sparta,* that when the *Grecians* compared his Affability and Eafinefs of Accefs with the fullen State and Pride of other Princes, they were fo enamoured with it, that they judged him only worthy to be a King· And as there is no certainer, fo alfo no cheaper Way of gaining Love. A friendly Salutation is as eafy as a Frown or Reproach, and that Kindnefs may be preferved by them, which if once forfeited, will not at a far greater Price be recovered.

Befides, when human Viciffitudes are confidered, it may be a Point of Prudence too; the greateft Perfons may fometimes want Affiftance from the Meaneft; nay, fometimes

times the Face of Affairs is quite changed, and the Wheel of Fortune turns them loweſt that were uppermoſt, and proportionably elevates the Meaneſt. It is Wiſdom, therefore, ſo to treat all as to leave no Impreſſion of Unkindneſs, ſince none is ſo deſpicable but may poſſibly at one Time or other have an Opportunity to retaliate. It was, therefore, a prudent, as well as an equitable, Reſolution of the Emperor, who ſaid, *He would ſo entertain the Addreſſes of his Subjects, as, if he were a Subject, he would wiſh the Prince ſhould entertain him.* A Rule very worthy to ſway all Perſons of Honour in their Intercourſes with others; and ſince even among Perſons in Command there are Degrees, and ſhe which is ſuperior to one, is inferior to another; they have a ready way to compare the Civility they pay with that they expect. Let, therefore, one who meets with a cold neglect Treatment from any above her, examine her own Reſentments, and then reflect, that if ſhe give the like to thoſe below her, they will, doubtleſs, have the ſame Senſe, and, therefore, let her reſolve never to offer what ſhe ſo much diſlikes to bear; and ſhe that does thus, that makes ſuch Inferences, will convert an Injury into a Benefit; civilize herſelf by the Rudeneſs of others, and make that ill Nurture her own Diſcipline.

But hitherto we conſider Affability only in its ethnic Dreſs, as it is a human Ornament, 'twill appear yet more enamouring upon a ſecond View, when we look on it as bearing the Impreſs of the Sanctuary, as a divine Virtue: And that it is capable of being ſo, we have the Authority of St. *Paul,* who inſerts it in the Number of thoſe Chriſtian Graces which he recommends to his *Roman* Proſelytes,

felytes, *Condefcend to them of low Eflate*, Rom. xii. 16.
And that we may the better difcern its Value, 'tis obfervable, that he links it with the moft eminent Virtue of
Humility; for it immediately follows his Precept of *be not
high minded*. Indeed, 'tis not only joined with as a Friend
or Ally, but derived from it as its Stock and Principal:
And certainly a more divine Extraction it cannot have,
Humility being the *Alpha* and *Omega* of Virtues, that
which lays the Foundation, without which, the moft
towering Structure will but crufh itfelf with its own
Weight, and that which perfects and confummates the Building alfo, fecures and crowns all other Graces, which,
when they are moft verdant and flourifhing, are like *Jonas*'s Gourd, that may afford fome Shadow and Refrefhment for a while, but are apt to breed that Worm which
will deftroy them. When once they are fmitten with
Pride they inftantly fade and wither, fo neceffary is Humility both for acquiring and conferving all that is good in
us.

We may, therefore, conclude, that Courtefy and Obligingnefs of Behaviour which proceeds thence, is in refpect
of its Spring and Original, infinitely to be preferred to
that which defcends from no higher Stock than natural
or prudential Motives: And fince it is natural for every
Production to have fome Similitude to that which produces it, we fhall find it no lefs excellent in refpect of its
Properties than its Defcent. For inftance only in two,
Sincerity and Conftancy.

For the *Firft*, As far as Affability partakes of Humility
it muft of Sincerity alfo, that being a Virtue whofe very
Elements are Plainnefs and Simplicity: For as it has no
Defigns

Defigns which want a Cover, fo it needs none of thofe
Subtilties and Simulations, thofe Pretences and Artifices requifite to thofe who do. It is the Precept of the Apoftle,
*In Lowlinefs of Mind let each efteem others better than
himfelf:* Where we fee it is the Nature of a lowly Mind
to transfer that Efteem to others which he fubftracts from
himfelf: Now where fuch an Efteem is planted in the
Heart, it verifies all the Expreffions and our Significations
of Refpect, and renders the greateft Condefcentions (which
to an infolent Humour may feem extravagant and affected) real and unfeigned.

On the contrary, that Courtefy which derives no higher
than from meer human Principles, is not much to be con-
fided in. 'Tis the Pfalmift's Affirmation, *that all Men are
Lyars:* And, therefore, there is more than a Poffibility
of Deceit in their faireft Shews. Sometimes we know
fmooth and plaufible Addreffes have been defigned as the
Stale to vile and treacherous Practices. The extraordinary
Blandifhments and endearing Behaviour of *Abfolom* to the
People, was only to *fteal their Hearts,* and advance his
intended Rebellion, 2 *Sam.* xv. and *David* tells us of
fome, *Whofe Words are fofter than Butter, having War in
the Heart, whofe Words were fmoother than Oil, and, yet,
were very Swords, Pfal.* lv 21. and, God knows, this
Age has not fo much improved in Sincerity, that we fhould
think the fame Scenes are not daily acted over among us.

But befides all the blacker Projects of this Kind, which
nothing but the Event can detect, there is a lower Sort
of this Treachery, which is vifible, nay, fo avowed, that
it is one of the moft common Subjects of Mirth and Entertainment, and that is Scoffing and Derifion, a thing,
too

too frequent among all, but it is to be feared, more particularly among Women, those, at least, of the modish
Sort, their very Civilities and Caresses being often design'd
to gain Matter of Scorn and Laughter. Mutual Visits,
we know, are an Expression of Respect, and should flow
from a real Kindness, but if those now in Use be sifted,
how few will be found of that Make? They are at the
best but formal, a Tribute rather paid to Custom than
Friendship, and many go to see those, for whom they are
perfectly indifferent whether they find them alive or dead,
well or sick, nay, very often they are worse than thus, designed only to make Observations to bolt out something ridiculous wherewith to sport themselves as soon as they are
gone, and least the Inquest should return with a *Non in-*
ventus, they will accept of the slightest Discoveries, the
least misplacing of a Word, nay, of a Hair shall be Theme
enough for a Comedy.

But if a poor Country Gentlewoman fall within their
Circuit, what a Stock of Mirth does she afford them, how
curiously do they anatomize every Part of her Dress, her
Mein, her Dialect? nay, perhaps, to improve the Scene,
will recommend, yet, greater Absurdities to her, under the
Notion of the Mode, that so she may be the more ample
Subject of their Scorn. Such Visits as these, are but in-
sidious Instructions of a Spy rather than the good Office
of a Neighbour, and when it is remembred how great a
Portion of some Womens Time is spent in this Kind of
Diversion, we must conclude there have a Multitude of
Acts gone to make up the Habit. It were to be wished
they would seriously reflect on it, and unravel that inju-
rious Mirth by a penitential Sadness, and either spend their
Time

Time better than in vifiting, or elfe direct their Vifits to better Purpofes, and this they would certainly do if they would exchange their meer popular Civilities (that kind of Paint and Varnifh in Manners) for that true Chriftian Condefcenfion, which admits of no Deceit, but is as tranfparent as *Drufus* wifh'd his Houfe fhould be, that has no fecret Screws and Springs, to move the Eyes or Tongue a contrary Way from the Heart, but is in reality all that it pretends to be.

A Second Property of its Conftancy, for as it is true to others, fo it is to itfelf; 'tis founded on the folideft of Virtues, and is not fubject to thofe light and giddy Uncertainties, that the vulgar Civilities are: For he, that out of a Difefteem of his proper Worth, has placed himfelf in a State of Inferiority, will think it not an arbitrary Matter, but a juft Debt to pay a Refpect to thofe he thinks his Betters, and an humble Mind will in every body find fomething or other to prefer to himfelf. So, that he acts upon a fix'd Principle, and is not in Danger of thofe Contradictions in his Manners, which fhall render him one Day fweet and affable, and another fower and morofe: But fuch Changes are frequently incident to thofe who are fwayed by other Motives: Sometimes an Intereft changes, and then the moft fanning Sycophant can tranfplant his Flatteries and court a new Patron, yea, many Times to the Defpight and vilifying of the Old.

Sometimes, again, Fortune may change, a Man may fall from a profperous to an adverfe State, and, then, thofe who were prodigal of their Civilities whilft he needed nothing elfe, will withdraw even thofe from him, leaft they fhould encourage him to demand fomething more. An

Experiment

Experiment in this *Job* made in his Friends (or rather Flatterers) whom he fitly compares to winter Brooks running over when not needed, but quite dry when they are.

But the moſt frequent Change is that of Fancy and Humour, which has a more general Sway than Reaſon and Judgment. This is ſo obſervable in the vulgar Rabble, that often, in an Inſtant, they will ſhift Paſſions, and hate this Hour what they doated on the laſt. Of this all popular States have afforded many coſtly Experiments, but we need not go farther than the ſacred Story, where we find the Acclamations and *Hoſannatis* of the Multitude, quickly converted into *crucify him, crucify him.* This Levity of Mind has been obſerved ſo incident to Women, that 'tis become almoſt proverbial, for by how much their Paſſions are more violent, they are commonly the leſs laſting, and as they are reckon'd among thoſe colder Bodies that are particularly influenced by the Moon, ſo they ſeem to bear a great Reſemblance to her in her Viciſſitudes and Changes; yet, ſtill with a greater Degree of Uncertainty, for ſhe in all her Revolutions obſerves ſome conſtant Periods, and we can tell in her Wain when ſhe will be at full, ſo that ſhe has a kind of Certainty, even in her planetary Errors, but what Ephemerides can be framed for ſome Womens Humours? Who can tell how long the preſent will laſt? And what will be the next that will ſucceed?

We need not bring Inſtances of their Inconſtancy from that common Place of paſſionate Widows, who have let a new Love ſail even through thoſe Floods of Tears wherewith they bewailed the Old: For (beſides that that is a Caſe wherein poſſibly they may find Matter enough for Retortion) it is here a little wide from our Purpoſe, which de-

ſigns

figns no farther Inquisition than into their ordinary Conversation, wherein that Love of Variety, which is so remarkable in their Habit, their Diet, and their Diversions, often extends itself to their Company, their Friendships also, and Conversation. Those Intimacies which they cherished lately, quickly grow despicable, and at last nauseous, and consequently their Behaviour falls from kind and civil, to cold and disdainful. It is not to be doubted but this has often been proved by many of those humble Companions, which officiously attend them, who cannot always fix themselves, no, not by those Flatteries that first introduced them, some new Comer, perhaps, has better refined the Art, and does the same thing more acutely and ingeniously, and then the old one is to be turned off as too grofs a Sycophant; or if they have been so happy as to light upon some of a more generous Temper, who instead of a servile Compliance with their Humour, and high Characters of their Worth, entertain them with the true Images of themselves, and endeavours to make what others only speak them; this is that unpardonable Crime which forfeits all Degrees of Favour, and does not only avert but increase. A faithful Monitor is as unacceptable as a true Looking-glass to a deformed Person, which, at the best will be set aside, and escapes well if not broken; and while great Persons dispense their Favours or their Frowns, by such perverse Measures as these, they will be sure to do it unjustly, as well as unconstantly.

This is far from being an universal Charge, there are, certainly, Women of the highest Quality, who guide themselves by other Rules, that are deaf to all the Songs of Syrens, and have the Prudence to value a seasonable

I   Reproof

Reproof before the moſt extravagant Panegyrick; but this is owing to that Humility which we are now recommending, without which, 'tis as impoſſible for Greatneſs to be Proof againſt Flattery, as it is for a Pinnace with ſpreading Sails, and a violent Guſt of Wind, to ſail ſteadily without Ballaſt: And the frequent want of this is it which makes it no leſs frequent to ſee thoſe Unevenneſſes and Inequalities in Behaviour; thoſe Partialities in diſpenſing even the commoneſt Civilities which have been now repreſented.

And ſure 'tis none of the meaneſt Attributes, due to that excellent Virtue of Humility, that it can thus fix and poiſe the Mind, cure thoſe Vertigoes and giddy Humours incident to thoſe who are mounted aloft, and above all, that it is a ſure Antidote againſt the moſt inſinuating Poiſon of Flattery, a holy Spell or Amulet againſt the Venom of a Paraſite, which the Philoſopher juſtly calls, the worſt of tame Beaſts, as a Detractor is of wild, he being, indeed, a kind of Vulture, in the way of Seizure, no leſs than ravine, who firſt picks out the Eyes of that which he deſigns to prey upon, ſuffering not the Perſon concern'd to ſee any thing of that Deſtruction which he is to feel: And certainly none of the ominous Birds, no Night Raven or Screech Owl can bode half ſo diſmally as theſe domeſtick Birds of Prey, which are not only Preſages but Inſtruments of Ruin whereſoever they haunt.

'Tis, therefore, the univerſal Concern of thoſe that are Great and Proſperous, to chace them away, as *Abraham* did the Fowls from his Sacrifice, *Gen.* xv 11. but, yet, more peculiarly ſo of thoſe to whom Fortune has given a ſudden Riſe and unexpected Grandeur, they being, of all
others,

others, the moft obnoxious to this Sort of Harpies. The
Surprizes of Profperity do no lefs difturb the Judgment,
than thofe of Adverfity; and as one who is in an Inftant
fnacht up to fome high Tower, is fo amazed to fee himfelf there, that he has no juft Meafure of the Altitude, but
thinks every thing farther below him than it is, fo they
that afcend to Greatnefs by fwift and rapid Motions, have
their Heads fo turned that they are apt to over-value it, and
to look with Contempt on thofe, who before, perhaps,
they thought worth their Envy; and on a Mind thus prepared, Flattery may make an Impreffion, it fuborning even
Providence as a Witnefs on its Side, and inferring from the
Dignities obtained, the tranfcending Merit of the Obtain-
er, a Piece of Sophiftry which the flighteft Obferver may
eafily confute; all Ages giving Inftances of thofe whofe
Vices have preferred them, and by a ftrange Chymiftry
have extracted Honour out of infamous Acts Yet, to a
Mind poffefs'd with its own Admiration, this fhall pafs for
a Demonftration, fo treacherous a thing is Pride, that it
combines with all who defign to cheat us, and, indeed,
'tis not only an Acceffary but the Principal, none being in
danger by others Flatteries who are not firft feduced by
their own.

It will, therefore, be a Point of Wifdom for all Perfons
of Honour to increafe their Caution with their Fortune,
and as they multiply their Retinues without, fo efpecially
to inforce their Guard within, that they become not Slaves
to their own Greatnefs, fix not themfelves in fuch a Pofture
of State as to become immoveable to all the Offices of Humanity and Civility; nor think that their Admiffion to
Greatnefs is upon the fame Terms on which the *Jews*

were

were wont to receive their Proſelytes, that they muſt re-
nounce all their former Relations, but to remember, that
they differ no more from others than as a Counter ſet in
the Place of Thouſands or Hundreds, does from one ſet
in the Place of Tens or Units. A little Tranſpoſition may
quite alter the Caſe ; or, however, when they are all taken
off the Score, they are then indiſcriminately tumbled together, and one has no Precedence of another, either in
Place or Value : So undiſcernable will be the Difference
between the greateſt Queen and the meaneſt Servant, when
Death, that great Leveller, ſhall have mix'd them ; there
will be no Inquiſition in the Grave who came embalmed,
or perfumed thither : And, as a learned Man ſays, *The Ul-*
cers of Lazarus *will make as good Duſt as the Paint of* Jezebel.

✣ ✣

C H A P. VI.

The D U T Y *of* V I R G I N S.

HAVING given an Account of thoſe general Qualifications, which are at once the Duty and Ornament of the Female Sex, there are, notwithſtanding, ſpe-
cifick Differences ariſing from the ſeveral States and Circumſtances of Life, ſome, whereof, may exact greater
Degrees even of the former Virtues, and all may have
ſome diſtinct and peculiar Requiſites adapted to that particular State and Condition : And our propoſed Method engages

gages us to confider thefe in their proper Order; that is, Fuſt, *The Virgin State*; Secondly, *The Married*; and Laſtly, *That of Widowhood:* Which as they differ widely fiom each other, ſo for the difcharging theii refpective Duties, theie are paiticulai Cautions woithy to be adverted to.

Virginity, or the Viigin-State, is fiift in Ordei, the Infancy and Childhood of which we fhall paſs over, and addiefs to thofe who may be fuppofed to be ariived at Years of Difcretion, which may be properly reckoned about the Age of Sixteen, and ſo onwaid.

An old Maid is now thought fuch a Curfe as no Poetic Fury can exceed, look'd on as the moſt calamitous Creaitue in Nature; and we ſo far yield to the Opinion as to confefs it is ſo to thofe who are kept in that State againſt their Wills; but, fure, the Oiiginal of that Mifeiy is fiom the Defire, not the Reftiaint of Mairiage, let them but fuppiefs that once, and the other will never be their Infelicity · But we muſt not be ſo unkind to the Sex, as to think 'tis always fuch Defiie that gives them Averſion to Celibacy; we doubt not, many are fiighted only with the vulgar Contempt under which that State lies, for which if theie be no Cuie, yet, there is the fame Armour againſt this, which is againſt all other caufelefs Repioaches, *viz.* to contemn it Yet, we aie a little apt to believe, there may be a Prevention in the Cafe: If the fuperannuated Virgins would behave themfelves with Giavity and Refeivednefs, addict themfelves to the ftiicteſt Viitue and Piety, they would give the World fome Caufe to believe 'twas not their Neceffity, but their Choice, which kept them unmairie-l, that they weie pre-engag'd to a better Amoui,

espousec

efpoufed to the fpiritual Bridegroom: And this would give
them, among the foberer Sort, at leaft, the Reverence and
Efteem of Mations: Or if, after all Caution and Endeavour, they chance to fall under the Tongues of malicious
Slanderers, this is no more than happens in all other Inftances of Duty: And if Contempt be to be avoided,
Chriftianity itfelf muft be quitted as well as Virgin Chaftity: But if, on the other Side, they endeavour to difguife
their Age by all the Impoftures and Gaieties of a Youthful Drefs and Behaviour, if they ftill herd themfelves
among the youngeft and vaineft Company, betrays a young
Mind in an aged Body, this muft certainly expofe them
to Scorn and Cenfure. If no Play, no Ball or dancing
Meeting can efcape them, People will undoubtedly conclude, that they defire to put off themfelves, to meet with
Chapmen, who fo conftantly keep the Fairs　We wifh,
therefore, they would more univerfally try the former Ex-
pediments, which, we are confident, is the beft Amulet
againft the Reproach they fo much dread, and may alfo
deliver them from the Danger of a more coftly Remedy,
we mean, that of an unequal and imprudent Match, which
many have rufhed upon as they have ran frightened from
the other, and fo by an unhappy Contradiction, do both
ftay long and marry haftily, gall their Necks to fpare their
Ears, and run into the Yoke rather than hear fo flight and
unreafonable a Reproach. They need not be upbraided
with the Folly of fuch an Election, fince their own Experience is, to many of them, but too fevere a Monitor
We fhall not infift farther on this, but having given the
elder Virgins that Enfign of their Seniority as to ftand firft
in

in the Difcourfe, we fhall now addrefs more geneially to the ieft.

The two grand Elements, effential to the Virgin State, aie Modefty and Obedience, which tho' neceffaiy to all, arc, yet, in a more eminent Degiee requiied here: And therefore, tho' we have fpoken largely of the Viitue of Modefty in the former Pait of ihis Difcouife, yet, it will not be impeitinent to make fome faither Reflections on it, by Way of Application to Virgins, in whom Modefty fhould appear in its higheft Elevation, and fhould come up to Shamefacednefs. Hei Look, her Speech, her whole Behaviour fhould own an humble Diftruft of heifelf, fhe is to look on heifelf but as a Novice, a Probationei in the Woild, and muft take this Time rather to learn and obfeive, than to dictate and prefcribe. Indeed, there is fcarce any thing looks more indecent, than to fee a young Maid too forward and confident in her Talk. 'Tis the Opinion of the Wife-men, *Eccluf.* xxxii 8. *That a young Man fhould fcarce fpeak, tho' twice ask'd:* In Proportion to which, 'twill, fuie, not become a young Woman, whofe Sex puts her under gieatei Reftiaints, to be either importunate or magifteiial in hei Difcourfe: And tho' that which foimer Ages call Boldnefs, is now only Affuiance and good Breeding, yct, we have feen fuch bad Supeiftiuctuies upon that Foundation, as fuie, will not much recommend it to any confideiing Peifon.

But theie is another Bieach of Modefty, as it ielates to Chaftity, in which they are yet more efpecially concerned. The veiy Name of Virgin imports a moft ciitical Nicenefs in that Point. Every indecent Curiofity or impuie Fancy, is a deflowering of the Mind, and every the leaft Corruption

ruption of them gives some Degrees of Defilement to the
Body too. For between the State of pure immaculate Virginity and arrant Prostitution, there are many intermedial
Steps, and she that makes any of them, is so far departed
from her first Integrity. She that listens to any wanton
Discourse has violated her Ears, she that speaks any, her
Tongue; every immodest Glance vitiates her Eye, and
every the lightest Act of Dalliance leaves something of
Stain and Sulliage behind it. There is, therefore, a most
rigorous Caution requisite herein; for as nothing is more
clean and white than a perfect Virginity, so every the least
Spot or Soil is the more discernable: Besides, Youth is for
the most Part flexible, and easily wraps into a Crooked-
ness, and, therefore, can never set itself too far from a
Temptation. Our tender Blossoms we are fain to skreen
and shelter, because every unkindly Air nips and destroys
them; and nothing can be more nice and delicate than a
Maiden Virtue, which ought not to be exposed to any of
those malignant Airs which may blast and corrupt it, of
which, God knows, there are too many, some that blow
from within, and others from without.

Of the first Sort, there is none more mischievous than
Curiosity, a Temptation which foil'd human Nature even
in Paradise: And, therefore, sure a feeble Girl ought not
to trust herself with that which subdued her better for-
tified Parent. The Truth is, an affected Ignorance cannot be so blameable in other Cases as it is commendable in
this. Indeed, it is the surest and most invincible Guard,
for she who is curious to know indecent Things, 'tis Odds
but she will too soon and too dearly buy the Learning.
The suppressing and detesting all such Curiosities, is there-

fore,

fore, that eminent fundamental Piece of Continence we would recommend to them, as that which will protect and secure all the rest.

But when they have set this Guard upon themselves, they must provide against foreign Assaults too; the most dangerous whereof we take to be ill Company and Idleness. Against the First they must provide by a prudent Choice of Conversation, which should generally be of their own Sex; yet not all of that neither, but such who will at least entertain them innocently if not profitably. Against the Second they may secure themselves by a constant Series of Employments: We mean not such frivolous ones as are more idle than doing nothing, but such as are ingenuous, and some way worth their Time; wherein as the first Place is to be given to the Offices of Piety, so in the Intervals of those, there are divers others, by which they may not unusefully fill up the Vacancies of their Time, such are the acquiring of any of those ornamental Improvements which become their Quality, as Writing, Needle-works, Languages, Musick, or the like. If we should here insert the Art of Oeconomy and Houshold Managery, we should not think we affronted them in it; that being the most proper Feminine Business, from which neither Wealth nor Greatness can totally absolve them: And a little of the Theory in their Parents House, would much assist them towards the Practice when they came to their own. In a Word, there are many Parts of Knowledge useful for Civil as well as Divine Life; and the improving themselves in any of those, is a rational Employment.

But we know not how to reduce to that Head many of those Things which from Divertisements, are now stept up to be the folemn Bufinefs of many young Ladies, and, perhaps, of fome Old. Such is in the firft Place Gaming, a Recreation whofe Lawfulnefs we queftion not, whilft it keeps within the Bounds of a Recreation; but when it fets up for a Calling, we know not from whence it derives its Licence: And a Calling fure it feems to be with fome, a laborious one too, fuch as they toil Night and Day at, nay, do not allow themfelves that Remiffion which the Laws, both of God and Man, have provided for the meaneft Mechanic. The Sabbath is to them no Day of Reft, but this Trade goes on when all Shops are fhut. We know not how they fatisfy themfelves in fuch an habitual Wafte of their Time, (befides all the incidental Faults of Avarice and Anger,) but we much doubt that Plea, whatfoever it is which paffes with them, will fcarce hold Weight at his Tribunal, who has commanded us to *redeem*, not fling away *our Time*.

There is another thing to which fome devote a very confiderable Part of their Time, and that is, the reading Romances, which feems now to be thought the peculiar and only becoming Study of young Ladies It muft be confefs'd their Youth may a little adapt it to them when they were Children, and we wifh they were always in their Event as harmlefs, but it is to be feared they often leave ill Impreffions behind them. Thofe amorous Paffions, which it is their Defign to paint to the utmoft Life, are apt to infinuate themfelves into their unwary Readers, and by an unhappy Inverfion a Copy fhall produce an Original. When a poor young Creature fhall read there of fome triumphant Beauty, that has a number of captivated Knights proftrate at her Feet, fhe will probably be tempted to think

it

it a fine thing; and may reflect how much she loses time, that has not yet subdued one Heart: And then her Business will be to spread her Nets, lay her Toils to catch some body who will more fatally ensnare her: And when she has once wound herself into Amour, those Authors are subtil Casuists for all difficult Cares that may occur in it, will instruct in the necessary Artifices of deluding Parents and Friends, and put her Ruin perfectly in her own Power. And truly this seems to be so natural a Consequent of this Sort of Study, that of all the Divertisements that look so innocently, they can scarce fall upon any more hazardous. Indeed, 'tis very difficult to imagine what vast Mischief is done to the World, by the false Notions and Images of things, particularly of Love and Honour, those noblest Concerns of human Life represented in these Mirrors: But when we consider upon what Principles the Duellists and Hectors of the Age defend the Outrages, and how great a Devotion is paid to Lust, instead of virtuous Love, we cannot be to seek for the Gospel which makes these Doctrines appear orthodox.

As for the Entertainments which they find abroad, they may be innocent, or otherwise, according as they are managed. The common Intercourse of Civility is a Debt to Humanity, and, therefore, mutual Visits may often be necessary, and so (in some Degree) may be several harmless and healthful Recreations which may call them abroad, for we write not now to Nuns, and have no Purpose to confine them to a Cloister. Yet, on the other Side to be always wandring, is the Condition of a Vagabond; and of the two, 'tis better to be a Prisoner to one's Home than a Stranger. *Solomon* links it with some very unlaudable Qua-

K 2

lities

lities of a Woman, *Prov.* vii. 11. that *her Feet abide not in her House*; and 'tis an unhappy Impotence not to be able to stay at home when there is any thing to be seen abroad; that any Mask, or Revel, any Jollity of others muft be their Rack and Torment, if they cannot get to it. Alas, fuch Meetings are not fo fure to be fafe, that they had need be frequent, and they are of all others leaft like to be fafe to thofe, who much dote on them: And, therefore, thofe that find they do fo, had need to counterbiafs their Minds, and fet them to fomething better, and by more ferious Entertainments fupplant thofe Vanities, which at the beft are childifh, and may often prove worfe, it being too probable that thofe *Dinahs* which are ftill gadding, tho' on Pretence, only to fee the Daughters of the Land, may at laft meet with a Son of *Hamor*.

There is alfo another great Devourer of Time fubfervient to the Former, we mean Dreffing; for they that love to be feen much abroad, will be fure to be feen in the moft exact Form: And this is an Employment that does not fteal but challenge their Time , what they wafte here is *cum Privilegio*, it being, by the Verdict of this Age, the proper Bufinefs, the one Science wherein a young Lady is to be perfectly verfs'd · So that now all virtuous Emulation is to be converted into this fingle Ambition, who fhall excel in this Faculty : A Vanity which we confefs is more excufable in the Youngeft than in the elder Sort; they being fuppofable not yet to have outworn the Reliques of their Childhood, to which Toys and Gaiety were proportionable. Befides, 'tis, fure, allowable upon a fober Account, that they who defign Marriage fhould give themfelves the Advantage of decent Ornaments, and not by the negligent

Rudenefs

Rudenefs of their Drefs bely Nature, and ren'er themfelves lefs amiable than fhe has made them: But all this being gianted, 'twill by no Means juftify that exceffive Curiofity and Sollicitude, that Expence of Time, and Money too, which is now ufed. A very moderate Degree of all thofe will ferve for that oidinary Decency which they need provide for, will keep them fiom the Reproach of an affected Singularity, which is as much as a fober Perfon need take Care for: And we muft take Leave to fay, that in order to Marriage, fuch a Moderation is much likelier to fucceed than the contiary Extravagance. Among the prudenter Sort of Men it certainly is, if it be not among the Loofe and Vain, againft which 'twill be their Guard, and fo do them the greater Service. For certainly, he that choofes a Wife for thofe Qualities for which a wife Man would refufe her, underftands fo little what Marriage is, as poitends no gieat Felicity to her that fhall have him: But if they defire to marry Men of Sobriety and Difcietion, they are obliged in Juftice to bimg the fame Qualities they expect, which will be very ill evidenced by that Excefs and Vanity we now fpeak of.

For to fpeak a plain (tho' perhaps ungrateful) Truth, this (together with fome of the modifh Liberties now in Ufe) is it, which keeps fo many young Ladies about the Town unmarried 'till they lofe the Epithet of Young. Sober Men are afraid to venture upon a Humour fo difagreeing to their own, leaft whilft (according to the primitive Reafon of Marriage) they feek a Help they efpoufe a Ruin: But this is efpecially dreadful to a plain Country Gentleman, who looks upon one of thefe fine Women as a gaudy Idol, to whom, if he once become a Votary, he muft facrifice

a

a great Part of his Fortune and all his Content. How reasonable that Apprehension is, the many Wrecks of considerable Families do too evidently attest : But it is to be presumed some of the nicer Ladies have such a Contempt of any thing that they please to call Rustic, that they will not much regret the averting of those whom they so despise, they will not, perhaps, while they are in pursuit or hopes of others; but when those fail these will be look'd on as a welcome Reserve; and, therefore, 'twill be no Prudence to cut themselves off from that last Resort, least they, as many have done, betake themselves to much worse. For as in many Instances 'tis the Country which feeds and maintains the Grandeur of the Town, so of all Commerces there, Marriage would soonest fail if all rural Supplies were cut off.

But we have pursued this Speculation farther than, perhaps, our Virgin Readers will thank us for; we shall return to that which it was brought to inforce, and beseech them, that if not to Men, yet to approve themselves to God, they will confine themselves in the Matter of their Dress within the due Limits of Decency and Sobriety. We shall not direct them to those strict Rules which *Tertullian* and some other of the ancient Fathers have prescrib'd in this Matter, our Petition is, only, that our Virgins would at least so take care of their Bodies, as Persons that also have a Soul; which if they can be persuaded to, they may reserve much of their Time for more worthy Uses than those of the Comb, the Toilet and the Glass: And truly, 'tis not a little their Concern to do so, for this Spring of their Age is that critical Instant that must either confirm or blast the Hopes of all the succeeding Seasons.

The

The Minds of young People are ufually compared to a blank Sheet of Paper, equally capable of the beft or the worft Impreffions; 'tis pity they fhould be fill'd with childifh Scrawls and little infignificant Figures, but 'tis Shame and Horror they fhould be ftain'd with any vicious Characters, any Blots of Impurity or Difhonour. To prevent which, let the fevereft Notions of Modefty and Honour be early and deeply imprefs'd upon their Souls, graven as with the Point of a Diamond, that they may be as indelible as they are indifpenfibly neceffary to the Virgin State.

There is alfo another very requifite Quality, and that is Obedience. The younger Sort of Virgins are fuppofed to have Parents, or if any has been fo unhappy as to lofe them early, they commonly are left in the Charge of fome Friend or Guardian that is to fupply the Place; fo that they cannot be to feek to whom this Obedience is to be paid: And it is not more their Duty than their Intereft to pay it Youth is apt to be foolifh in its Defigns, and heady in the purfuit of them, and there can be nothing more deplorable than to have it left to itfelf: And, therefore, God, who permits not even the Brutes to deftitute their young ones till they attain to the Perfection of their Kind, has put Children under the Guidance and Protection of their Parents, till, by the maturing of their Judgments, they are qualified to be their own Conductors. Now this Obedience (as that which is due to all other Superiors) is to extend itfelf to all Things that are either good or indifferent, and has no Claufe of Exception, but only where the Command is unlawful, and in fo wide a Scene of Action there will occur fo many particular Occafions of Submiffion, that they had need have a great Reverence of their

Parents Judgments, and Diſtruſt of their own : And if it ſhould happen that ſome Parents are not qualified to give them the former, yet, the general Imbecility of their Age, will remain a conſtant Ground of the latter, ſo that they may ſafelier venture themſelves to their Parents Miſ-guidance, than their own, by how much the Errors of Humility and Obedience are leſs malignant than thoſe of Preſumption and Arrogance.

But this is a Doctrine which will ſcarce paſs for Orthodox with many of the young Women of our Days, with whom 'tis Prejudice enough againſt the prudenteſt Advice, that it comes from their Parents. It is the grand Ingenuity of theſe Times to turn every thing into Ridicule ; and if a Girl can but rally ſmartly upon the ſober Admonition of a Parent, ſhe concludes, ſhe is the abler Perſon, takes herſelf for a Wit, and the other for a Fop, (a bugbear Word, deviſed to fright all Seriouſneſs and Sobriety out of the World) and learns not only to diſobey but to contemn. Indeed, the great Confidence that Youth now ſeems to have of itſelf, as it is very indecent, ſo it is extremely pernicious. Children that will attempt to go alone before their Time, oft get dangerous Falls : And when thoſe who are but little removed from Children, ſhall caſt off the wiſer Conduct of others, they oft ſadly miſcarry by their own.

We know this Age has ſo great a Contempt of the former, that it is but Matter of Scorn to alledge any of their Cuſtoms, elſe we ſhould ſay, that the Liberties that are taken now, would then have been ſtartled at. They that ſhould then have ſeen a young Maid rambling abroad without her Mother, or ſome other prudent Perſon, would
have

have look'd on her as a Stray, and thought it but a neigh-
bourly Office to have brought her Home; whereas, now
'tis a Rarity to fee them in any Company graver than themfelves, and fhe that goes with her Parent, unlefs it be fuch
a Parent as is as wild as herfelf, thinks fhe does but walk
abroad with her Jailor: But, fure, there are no fmall Mifchiefs that attend this Liberty, for it leaves them perfectly
to the Choice of their Company, a thing of too weighty an
Importance for giddy Heads to determine, who will be
fure to elect fuch as are of their own Humour, with whom
they may keep up a Traffick of little Impertinencies and
trifling Entertainments, and fo by Confequence condemn
themfelves never to grow wifer, which they may do by an
ingenious Converfation. Nay, 'tis well if that negative Ill
be the worft, for it gives Opportunity to any that have ill
Defigns upon them. It will be eafy getting into their
Company who have no Guard to keep any body out, and
as eafy, by little Compliances and Flatteries, to infinuate
into their good Graces, who have not the Sagacity to difcern to what infidious Purpofes thofe Blandifhments are
directed; and when they once begin to nibble at the Bait,
to be pleafed with the Courtfhip, 'tis great Odds they do
not efcape the Hook.

Alas, how many poor innocent Creatures have been thus
indifcernibly enfnared; have at firft, perhaps, only liked
the Wit and Raillery, perhaps the Language and Addrefs,
then the Freedom and good Humour, till at laft they come
to like the Perfon. It is, therefore, a moft neceffary Caution for young Women not to truft too much to their own
Conduct, but to own their Dependance on thofe to whom
God and Nature has fubjected them, and to look on it not

as their Reſtraint and Burden, but as their Shelter and Protection. For where once the Authority of a Parent comes to be deſpis'd, tho' in the lighteſt Inſtance, it lays the Foundation of utmoſt Diſobedience. She that will not be preſcrib'd to in the Choice of her ordinary diverting Company, will leſs be ſo in chooſing the fix'd Companion of her Life; and we find it often eventually true, that thoſe who govern themſelves in the former, will not be govern'd by their Friends in the latter, but by Pre-engagements of their own prevent their Elections for them.

And this is one of the higheſt Injuries they can do their Parents, who have ſuch a native Right in them, that 'tis no leſs an Injuſtice than Diſobedience to diſpoſe of themſelves without them. This Right of the Parent is ſo undoubted, that we find God himſelf gives way to it, and will not ſuffer the moſt holy Pretence, no, not that of a Vow, to invade it, as we may ſee his own ſtating of the Caſe, *Numb.* xxx. How will he then reſent it to have this ſo indiſpenſible a Law violated upon the Impulſe of an impotent Paſſion, an amorous Inclination? Nor is the Folly leſs than the Sin. They injure and afflict their Parents, but they generally ruin and undo themſelves: And that upon a double Account, *Firſt*, As to the ſecular Part. Thoſe that are ſo raſh as to make ſuch Matches, cannot be imagin'd ſo provident as to examine how agreeable 'tis to their Intereſt; or to contrive for any thing beyond the Marriage. The Thoughts of their future temporal Conditions (like thoſe of the Eternal) can find no room amidſt their fooliſh Raptures, but as if Love were, indeed, that Deity which the Poets feigned they depend on it for all, and take no farther Care: And the Event does commonly

too foon inftruct them in the Deceitfulnefs of that Truft;
Love being fo unable to fuppoit them, that it cannot maintain itfelf, but quickly expires when it has brought the
Lovers into thofe Straits from whence it cannot refcue them.
So that, indeed, it does but play the Decoy with them,
brings them into the Noofe and then retires, for when fecular Wants begin to pinch them, all the Transports of
their Kindnefs do ufually convert into mutual Accufations,
for having made each other miferable.

And, indeed, there is no Reafon to expect any better
Event, becaufe in the fecond Place, they forfeit their Title
to the divine Blefling; nay, they put themfelves out of the
Capacity to ask it, it being a ridiculous Impudence to beg
of God to profper the Tranfgieffions of his Law. Such
Weddings feem to invoke fome of the Poetic Romantic
Deities, *Venus* and *Hymen,* from whence they derive a
Happinefs as fictitious as are the Gods that are to fend it

Let all Virgins, therefore, religioufly obferve this Part
of Obedience to their Parents, that they may not only have
their Benediction, but God's· And to that Puipofe let this
be laid as a fundamental Rule, that they never hearken to
any Propofal of Marriage made them from any other
Hand; but when any fuch Overture is made, divert the
Addrefs from herfelf, and direct it to her Parents, which
will be the beft Teft imaginable for any Pretender. For
if he know himfelf worthy of her, he will not fear to
avow his Defign to them; and, therefore, if he decline
that, 'tis a certain Symptom he is confcious of fomething
he knows will not give a valuable Confideration; fo that
this Courfe will repel no Suitor but fuch as it is their Intereft not to admit. Befides, 'tis moft agreeable to the Vir-

gin

gin Modefty, which fhould make Marriage an Act rather
of their Obedience than their Choice; and they that think
their Friends too flow paced in the Matter, and feek to
out-run them, give Caufe to fufpect they are fpurr'd on
by fomewhat too warm Defires.

But as a Daughter is neither to anticipate nor contradict
the Will of her Parents, fo (to hang the Ballance even) we
muft fay, fhe is not obliged to force her own, by marrying where fhe cannot love; for a negative Voice in the Cafe is
as much the Child's Right as the Parents. It is true fhe
ought well to examine the Grounds of her Averfion, and
if they prove only childifh and fanciful, fhould endeavour
to correct them by Reafon and fober Confideration, if after all fhe cannot leave to hate, we think fhe fhould not
not proceed to marry. Indeed, fhe cannot without a facri-
legious Hypocrify, vow fo folemnly to love where fhe at
the Inftant actually abhors: And where the married State
is begun with fuch a Perjury, 'tis no wonder to find it continued on at the fame Rate, that other Parts of the Vow
be alfo violated, and that fhe obferves the negative Part no
more than the pofitive, and as little forfake others, as fhe
does heartily cleave to her Husband. It is to be feared, that
this is a Confequence whereof there are too many fad Inftances now extant, for tho', doubtlefs, there are fome Virtues which will hold out againft all the Temptations their
Averfions can give, nay, which do at leaft even conquer
thofe Averfions, and render their Duty as eafy as they have
kept it fafe; yet, we find there are but fome that do fo,
that it is no infeparable Property of the Sex, and, therefore, it is fure too hazardous an Experiment for any of
them to venture on.

And

And if they may not upon the more generous Motive of Obedience, much lefs may they upon the worfe Inducements of Avarice and Ambition; for a Woman to make a Vow to the Man, and yet intend only to marry his Fortune, or his Title, is the bafeft Infincerity, and fuch as in any other Kind of civil Contracts, would not only have the Infamy but the Punifhment of a Cheat. Nor will it at all fecure them, that in this 'tis only liable to God's Tribunal: For that is not like to make the Doom lefs, but more heavy, it being as the Apoftle witneffes, *A fearful thing to fall in the Hands of the living God. Heb.* x. 31. In a Word, Marriage is God's Ordinance and fhould be confider'd as fuch, not made a Stale to any unworthy Defign: And it may well be prefum'd, one Caufe why fo few Matches are happy, that they are not built upon a right Foundation: Some are grounded upon Wealth, fome on Beauty, too fandy Bottoms, God knows, to raife any Felicity on, whilft in the Interim, Virtue and Piety, the only folid Bafis for that Superftructure, are fcarce ever confidered. Thus God is commonly left out of the Confultation: The Lawyers are reforted to to fecure the Settlements, all Sorts of Artificers to make up the Equipage, but he is neither advis'd with as to the Motives, nor fcarce fupplicated as to the Event of Wedding. Indeed, 'tis a deplorable Sight to fee with what Lightnefs and Unconcerndnefs young People go to that weightieft Action of their Lives; that a Marriage Day is but a kind of a Bacchanal, a more licenfed avowed Revel; when, if they duly confidered it, 'tis the Hinge upon which their future Life moves, which turns them over to a happy or miferable Being; and, therefore, ought to be entered
upon

upon with the greateſt Seriouſneſs and Devotion Our Church adviſes excellently in the Preface to Matrimony, and it were to be wiſhed that they would not only give it the hearing at the Time, but make it their Study a good while before ; yea, and the Marriage Vow too, which is ſo ſtrict and awful a Bond, that, methinks, they had need well weigh every Branch of it, ere they enter it ; and by the ferventeſt Prayers implore that God, who is the Witneſs, to be their Aſſiſtant too in its Performance.

C H A P. VII.

Of the Manner of BEHAVIOUR *towards* MEN.

THE Female Sex ought to maintain a Behaviour towards Men, which may be ſecure to themſelves without offending them. No ill-bred affected Shyneſs, nor a Roughneſs, unſuitable to their Sex, and unneceſſary to their Virtue, but a Way of living that may prevent all Cauſe of Railleries or unmannerly Freedoms ; Looks that forbid without Rudeneſs, and oblige without Invitation, or leaving Room for the ſaucy Inferences Men's Vanity ſuggeſts to them upon the leaſt Encouragements. This is ſo very nice, that it muſt engage them to have a perpetual Watch upon their Eyes, and to remember that one careleſs Glance gives more Advantage than a hundred Words not enough conſidered ; the Language of the Eyes being very much the moſt ſignificant and the moſt obſerved.

The

The Civility of Women, which is always to be preferved, muft not be carried to a *Compliance*, which may
betray them into irrecoverable Miftakes. This *French* ambiguous Word *Complaifance*, has led Women into more
Blame, than all other Things put together. It carries
them by Degrees into a certain Thing, called a *good kind*
of *Woman*, an eafy *idle Creature* that doth neither *Good*
nor *Ill* but by Chance, has no Choice, but leaves that to
the Company fhe keeps. *Time*, which by Degrees adds to
the Signification of Words, has made her, according to
the modern Stile, little better than one who thinks it a
Rudenefs to deny when civilly required, either her Service in Perfon, or her friendly Affiftance, to thofe who
would have a Meeting, or want a Confident. She is a
certain Thing always at Hand, an eafy Companion, who
has ever great Compaffion for diftreffed Lovers: She cenfures nothing but *Rigour*, and is never without a Plaifter
for a wounded Reputation, in which chiefly lies her Skill
in Surgery: She feldom has the Propriety of any particular
Gallant but lives upon Brokage, and waits for the Scraps
her Friends are content to leave her.

There is another Character not quite fo criminal, yet not
lefs ridiculous; which is, that of a good humour'd Woman, one who thinketh fhe muft always be in a Laugh,
or a broad Smile, becaufe Good-Humour is an obliging
Quality; thinks it lefs ill Manners to talk impertinently
than to be filent in Company. When fuch a prating En-
gine rides Admiral, and carries the Lanthorn in a Circle of
Fools, a chearful Coxcomb coming in for a Recruit, the
chattering of Monkeys is a better Noife than fuch a Con-
cert of fenfelefs Merriment. If fhe is applauded in it, fhe

13

is fo encouraged, that, like a Ballad Singer, who, if commended, breaks his Lungs, fhe lets herfelf loofe and over-
flows upon the Company. She conceives that Mirth is to
have no Intermiffion, and, therefore, fhe will carry it about
with her, tho' it be to a Funeral, and if a Man fhould
put a familiar Queftion, fhe does not know very well
how to be angry, for then fhe would be no more that
pretty Thing, called a good-humour'd Woman. This Neceffity of appearing at all Times to be fo infinitely pleafed,
is a grievous Miftake, fince in a handfome Woman that
Invitation is unneceffary ; and in one who is not fo ridiculous. It is not intended by this, that Women fhould forfwear Laughing, but let them remember, that Fools being
always painted in that Pofture, fhould frighten thofe who
are wife from doing it too frequently, and going too near a
Copy which is fo little inviting ; and much more from
doing it loud, which is an unnatural Sound, and looks fo
much like another Sex, that few Things are more offenfive.
That boifterous Kind of Jollity is as contrary to Wit and
good Manners, as it is to Modefty and Virtue. Befides, it
is a coarfe Kind of Quality, that throws a Woman into a
lower Form, and degrades her from the Rank of thofe
who are more refined. Some Ladies fpeak *loud* and make
a Noife to be the more minded, which looks as if they
beat their Drums for Voluntiers ; and if by Misfortune
none come into them, they may, not without Reafon, be
a good deal out of Countenance.

There is one Thing yet more to be avoided, which is,
the Example of thofe who intend nothing farther than the
Vanity of Conqueft, and think themfelves fecure of not
having their Honour tainted by it. Some are apt to believe

lieve their Virtue is too obfcure, and not enough known, except it is expofed to a broader Light, and fet out to its beft Advantage by fome publick Trials. Thefe are dangerous Experiments, and generally fail, being built upon fo weak a Foundation, as that of a too great Confidence in ourfelves. It is as fafe to play with Fire, as to dally with Gallantry. Love is a Paffion that has Friends in the Garrifon, and for that Reafon muft, by a Woman, be kept at fuch a Diftance, that fhe may not be within the Danger of doing the moft ufual Thing in the World, which is confpiring againft herfelf: Elfe the humble Gallant, who is only admitted as a Trophy, very often becomes the Conqueror; he puts on the Style of Victory, and from an Admirer grows into a Mafter, for fo he may be called from the Moment he is in Poffeffion. The firft Refolutions of ftopping at good Opinion and Efteem, grow weaker by Degrees againft the Charms of Courtfhip fkilfully apply'd. A Lady is apt to think a Man fpeaks fo much Reafon whilft he is commending her, that fhe has much ado to believe him in the Wrong when he is making Love to her: And when, befides the natural Inducements the Sex has to be merciful, fhe is bribed by well-chofen Flattery, the poor Creature is in Danger of being caught like a Bird liftening to the Whiftle of one who has a Snare for it. Conqueft is fo tempting a Thing, that it often makes Women miftake Mens Submiffions; which with all their fair Appearances, have generally lefs Refpect than Art in them. Women fhould remember, that Men who fay extreme fine Things, many Times fay them moft for their own Sakes; and that the vain Gallant is often as well pleafed with his own Compliments, as he could be with the kindeft Anfwer. Where

M

there is not that Oftentation, you are to fufpect there is a
Defign : And as ftrong Perfumes are feldom ufed but where
they are neceffary to fmother an unwelcome Scent, fo exceffive good Words leave room to believe they are ftrewed
to cover fomething, which is to gain Admittance under a
a Difguife Women muft, therefore, be upon their Guard,
and confider, that of the two, Refpect is more dangerous
than Anger. It puts even the beft Underftandings out of
their Place for the Time, till fecond Thoughts reftore
them ; it fteals upon us infenfibly, and throws down our
Defences, and makes it too late to refift, after we have given it that Advantage Whereas Railing goes away in Sound,
it has fo much Noife in it, that by giving Warning it be-
fpeaks Caution Refpect is a flow and fure Poifon, and,
like Poifon, fwells us within ourfelves. Where it prevails
too much it grows to be a kind of Apoplexy in the Mind,
turns quite round, and after it has once feized the Underftanding, becomes mortal to it. For thefe Reafons, the
fafeft way is to treat it like a fly Enemy, and to be perpe-
tually upon the Watch againft it.

One Advice may be added to conclude this Head, which
is, that Women fhould let every feven Years make fome
Alteration in them towards the graver fide, and not be like
the Girls of fifty, who refolved to be always young, whatever Time with his Iron Teeth determined to the contrary.
Unnatural Things carry a Deformity in them never to be
difguifed ; the Livelinefs of Youth in a riper Age, looks
like a new Patch upon an old Gown ; fo that a gay Ma-
tron, a chearful old Fool, may be reafonably put into the
Lift of the tamer Kind of Monfters. There is a certain
Creature called, a grave Hobby-Horfe, a kind of a She
                                                    Numps,

Numps, that pre'ends to be pulled to a Play, and muft needs go to *Bartholomew* Fair, to look after the young Folks, whom fhe only feems to make her Care; in reality fhe takes them for her Excufe. Such an old Butterfly is, of all Creatures, the moft ridiculous, and fooneft found out It is good to be early in your Caution, to avoid any thing that comes within Diftance of fuch defpicable Patterns, and not like fome Ladies, who defer their Converfion till they have been fo long in Poffeffion of being laughed at, that the World doth not know how to change their Style, even when they are reclaimed from that which gave the firft Occafion for it.

The Advantages of being *referved* are too many to be fet down ; we will only fay, that it is a Guard to a good Woman, and a Difguife to an ill One It is of fo much Ufe to both, that thofe ought to ufe it as an *Artifice* who refufe to practice it as a *Virtue*.

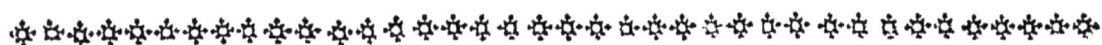

Chap. VIII.

Of *Female* Friendships *and* Censure.

WE would recommend to the Fair Sex, in a particular Manner, a ftrict Care in the Choice of their Friendfhips. Perhaps the beft are not without their Objections; but however, they ought to be fure that they do not ftray from the Rules that the wifer Part of the World has fet them. The Leagues offenfive and defenfive feldom

M 2

hold

hold in Politicks, and much lefs in Friendfhips. The violent Intimacies, when once broken, of which they fcarce ever fail, make fuch a Noife; the Bag of Secrets untied, they fly about like Birds let loofe from a Cage, and become the Entertainment of the Town. Befides, thefe great Dearneffes, by Degrees, grow injurious to the reft of their Acquaintance, and throw them off There is fuch an offenfive Diftinction when the dear Friend comes into the Room, that it is flinging Stones at the Company, who are not apt to forgive it.

It is wrong to lay out Friendfhip too lavifhly at firft, fince it will, like other Things, be fo much the fooner fpent, neither fhould it be fuffered to be of too fudden a Growth; for as the Plants which fhoot up too faft are not of that Continuance as thofe which take more Time for it, fo too fwift a Progrefs in pouring out Kindnefs, is a certain Sign that by the Courfe of Nature it will not be long lived. Ladies who pitch upon Friends under the Weight of any criminal Objection, muft be refponfible to the World for it. In that Cafe they bring themfelves under the Difadvantages of their Character, and muft bear their Part of it. Choofing implies approving, and if a Friend be chofe againft whom the World has given Judgment, it is not fo well-natured as to believe that Perfon averfe to her way of living, fince fhe is not difcouraged by it from admitting her into her Kindnefs: And Refemblance of Inclinations being thought none of the leaft Inducements to Friendfhip, fhe will be look'd upon at leaft as a Well-wifher, if not a Partner, with her in her Faults. Thofe who can forgive them in another will not be lefs gentle to themfelves.

If

If a Friend happens to fall from the State of Innocence after Kindness is engaged to her, a Woman should be slow in her Belief in the Beginning of the Discovery: But as soon as she is convinced by a rational Evidence, she ought, without breaking too roughly, to make a fair and quick Retreat from such a mistaken Acquaintance: Else by moving too slowly from one that is so tainted, the Contagion may reach so far, as to give Part of the Scandal, tho' not of the Guilt. This Matter is so nice, that as a Person must not be too hasty to join in the Censure upon a Friend when she is accused, so, on the other Side, she should not defend her with too much Warmth; for if she should happen to deserve the Report of common Fame, besides the Vexation belonging to such a Mistake, her Advocate will draw an ill Appearance upon herself, and it will be thought she pleaded for her not without some Consideration of herself. The Anger which must be put on to vindicate the Reputation of an injur'd Friend, may incline the Company to suspect she would not be so zealous, if there was not a Possibility that the Case might be her own. For this Reason, Women are not to carry their Dearness so far as absolutely to lose their Sight where their Friend is concerned. Because Malice is too quick-sighted, it does not follow that Friendship must be blind. There is to be a Mean between these two Extreams, else the Excess of Good-Nature may betray one into a very ridiculous Figure, and by Degrees may bring a Lady to such Offices as she should not be proud of. Ignorance may lessen the Guilt, but will improve the Jest upon those, who shall be kindly solicitous to procure a Meeting, and innocently contribute to the Ills they would avoid: Whilst the contriving Lovers, when

they

they are alone, shall make her the Subject of their Mirth, and, perhaps, with Respect to the Goddess of Love be it spoken, it is not the worst Part of their Entertainment, at least it is the most lasting, to laugh at the believing Friend, who was so easily deluded

Good Sense ought to be a chief Ingredient in the Choice of Friends, else let a Woman's Reputation be never so clear, it may be clouded by the Impertinence of her Confident. It is like our Houses being in the Power of a drunken or a careless Neighbour, only so much worse, as that there will be no Insurance here to make Amends, as there is in the Case of Fire.

To conclude on this Head. If Formality is to be allowed in any Instance, it is to be put on to resist the Invasion of such forward Women as shall press themselves into the Friendship of others, where, if admitted, they will either be a Snare or an Incumbrance.

We will come next to the Consideration, how Women are to manage their *Censure*, in which both Care and Skill will be a good deal requisite. To distinguish is not only natural but necessary; and the Effect of it is, that we cannot avoid giving Judgment in our Minds, either to absolve or condemn, as the Case requires. The Difficulty is, to know when and where it is fit to proclaim the Sentence. An Aversion to what is criminal, a Contempt of what is ridiculous, are the inseparable Companions of Understanding and Virtue; but the letting them go farther than our own Thoughts, hath so much Danger in it, that though it is neither possible nor fit to suppress them intirely, yet it is necessary they should be kept under very great Restraints. An unlimited Liberty of this Kind is little less than send-

ing

ing a Herald and proclaiming War to the World, which is an angry Beaft, when fo provoked. The Conteft will be unequal, tho' we are never fo much in the Right: And if a Woman begins againft fuch an Adverfary, it will tear her in Pieces with this Juftification, that it is done in its own Defence. They muft, therefore, take Heed of laughing except in Company that is very fure It is throwing Snow-Balls againft Bullets, and it is the Difadvantage of a Woman, that the Malice of the World will help the Brutality of thofe who will throw a flovenly Untruth upon her. They are for this Reafon to fupprefs their Impatience for Fools; who, befides they are too ftrong a Party to be unneceffarily provoked, are of all others, the moft dangerous in this Cafe. A Blockhead in his Rage will return a dull Jeft that will lie heavy, though there is not a Grain of Wit in it. Others will do it with more Art, and a Perfon muft not think herfelf fecure becaufe her Reputation may, perhaps, be out of the Reach of *Ill-will*, for if it finds that Part guarded, it will feek one which is more expofed. It flies, like a corrupt Humour in the Body, to the weakeft Part. If a Woman has a tender Side, the World will be fure to find it, and to put the worft Colour upon all fhe fays or does, it will give an Aggravation to every thing that may leffen her, and a fpiteful Turn to every thing that might recommend her. Anger lays open thofe Defects which Friendfhip would not fee, and Civility might be willing to forget, Malice needs no fuch Invitation to encourage it, neither are any Pains more fuperfluous than thofe we take to be ill fpoken of. If Envy, which never dies, and feldom fleeps,

I

is content fometimes to be in a Slumber, it is very unskilful to make a Noife to awake it.

Befides, a Lady's Wit will be mifapply'd if it is wholly
directed to difcern the Faults of others, when it is fo neceffary to be often ufed to mend and prevent her own. The
fending our Thoughts too much abroad has the fame Effect as when a Family never ftays at home; Neglect and
Diforder naturally follows; as it muft do within ourfelves,
if we do not frequently turn our Eyes inwards, to fee
what is amifs with us, where it is a Sign we have an unwelcome Profpect, when we do not care to look upon it,
but rather feek our Confolations in the Faults of thofe we
converfe with

Avoid being the firft in fixing a hard Cenfure; let it be
confirmed by the general Voice before you give into it;
neither fhould any one then give Sentence like a Magiftrate,
or as if fhe had a fpecial Authority to beftow a good or ill
Name at Difcretion. She fhould not dwell too long upon
a weak Side, a Touch and away, but take a Pleafure to
ftay longer where fhe can commend; like Bees that fix
only upon thofe Herbs out of which they may extract the
Juice of which their Honey is compofed. A Virtue ftuck
with Briftles is too rough for this Age, it muft be adorned
with fome Flowers, or elfe it will be unwillingly entertain-
ed; fo that even where it may be fit to ftrike, it fhould be
done like a Lady, gently; and then fhe may affure herfelf,
that where fhe cares to do it, fhe will wound others more,
and hurt herfelf lefs, by foft Strokes, than by being harfh
or violent.

The Triumph of Wit is to make *Good-Nature* fubdue
Cenfure; to be quick in feeing Faults and flow in expofing
them.

them. It is to be confidered, that the invifible Thing
called, a good Name, is made up of the Breath of Numbers that fpeak well of a Perfon, fo that if by a difobliging Word the Meaneft is filenced, the Gale will be lefs
ftrong which is to bear up her Efteem, and tho' nothing is
fo vain as the eager Purfuit of empty Applaufe, yet, to be
well thought of, and to be kindly ufed by the World, is
like a Glory about a Woman's Head, it is a Perfume fhe
carries about her, and leaves wherever fhe goes, it is a
Charm againft Ill-will. Malice may empty her Quiver,
but cannot wound, the Dirt will not ftick, the Jefts will
not take: Without the Confent of the World a Scandal
does not go deep, it is only a flight Stroke upon the injured
Party, and turns with the greater Force upon thofe who
gave it.

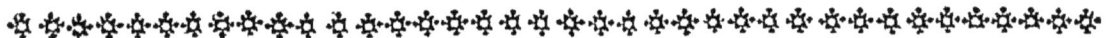

CHAP. IX.

Of VANITY *and* AFFECTATION.

WE muft with more than ordinary Earneftnefs give
Caution againft Vanity, it being the Crime to
which the Female Sex feems to be moft inclined; and fince
Affectation for the moft Part attends it, they are not well
to be divided. They cannot properly be called *Twins*, becaufe more properly Vanity is the Mother, and Affectation
the darling Daughter; Vanity is the Sin, and Affectation is
the Punifhment; the Firft may be called the Root of Self-

Love, the other the Fruit. Vanity is never at its full
Growth 'till it fpreads into Affectation and then it is complete.

Not to dwell any longer upon the Definition of them,
we will pafs to the Means and Motives to avoid them. In
order to which, it muft be confidered, that the World
challenges the Right of diftributing Efteem and Applaufe;
fo that where any affume by their fingle Authority to be
their own Carvers, it grows angry, and never fails to feek
Revenge: And if we may meafure a Fault by the Greatnefs of the Penalty, there are few of a higher Size than
Vanity, as there is fcarce a Punifhment which can be
heavier than that of being laughed at.

Vanity makes a Woman, tainted with it, fo top-full of
herfelf, that fhe fpilleth it upon the Company: And becaufe her own Thoughts are intirely employed in Self-Con-
templation, fhe endeavours, by a cruel Miftake, to confine
her Acquaintance to the fame narrow Circle of that which
only concerns her Ladyfhip, forgetting that fhe is not of
half that Importance to the World that fhe is to herfelf,
fo miftaken fhe is in her Value by being her own Ap-
praifer: She will fetch fuch a Compafs in Difcourfe to bring
in her beloved Self, and, rather than fail, her fine Petticoat, that there can hardly be a better Scene than fuch a
Trial of ridiculous Ingenuity. It is a Pleafure to fee her
angle for Commendations, and rife fo diffatisfied with the
ill-bred Company if they will not bite. To obferve her
throwing her Eyes about to fetch in Prifoners, and go a-
bout cruizing like a Privateer, and fo out of Countenance
if fhe return without Booty, is no ill Piece of Comedy.
She is fo eager to draw Refpect that fhe always miffes it,

yet

yet thinks it fo much her Due, that when fhe fails, fhe grows wafpifh, not confidering, that it is impoffible to commit a Rape upon the Will, that it muft be fairly gained, and will not be taken by Storm; and that in this Cafe the Tax ever raifes higheft by a Benevolence. If the World, inftead of admiring her imaginary Excellencies, takes the Liberty to laugh at them, fhe appeals from it to herfelf, for whom fhe gives Sentence, and proclaims it in all Companies On the other Side, if encouraged by a civil Word, fhe is fo obliging, that fhe will give Thanks for being laughed at in good Language. She takes a Compliment for a Demonftration, and fets it up as an Evidence, even againft her Looking-Glafs: But the good Lady being all this while in a moft profound Ignorance of herfelf, forgets that Men would not let her talk upon them, and throw fo many fenfelefs Words at their Heads, if they did not intend to put her Perfon to Fine and Ranfom, for her Impertinence. Good Words of any other Woman, are fo many Stones thrown at her, fhe can by no Means bear them, they make her fo uneafy, that fhe cannot keep her Seat, but up fhe rifes and goes Home half burft with Anger and ftrait-lacing: If by great Chance fhe fays any thing that has Senfe in it fhe expects fuch an exceffive Rate of Commendations, that to her thinking, the Company ever rifes in her Debt. She looks upon Rules as Things made for the common People, and not for Perfons of her Rank; and this Opinion fometimes tempts her to extend her Prerogative to the difpenfe-ing with the Commandments. If by great Fortune fhe happens, in Spite of her Vanity, to be honeft, fhe is fo troublefome with it, that as far as in her lies, fhe makes a fcurvy thing of it. Her bragging of her Virtue, looks as

N 2

if

if it coft her fo much Pains to get the better of herfelf, that the Inferences are very ridiculous. Her good Humour is generally applied to the laughing at good Senfe. It would do one good to fee how heartily fhe defpifes any thing that is fit for her to do. The greateft Part of her Fancy is laid out in choofing her Gown, as her Difcretion is chiefly employed in not paying for it. She is faithful to the Fafhion, to which not only her Opinion, but her Senfes are wholly refigned: So obfequious fhe is to it, that fhe would be ready to be reconciled even to Virtue with all its Faults, if fhe had her dancing Mafter's Word that it was practiced at Court.

To a Woman fo compofed, when Affectation comes in to improve her Character, it is then raifed to the higheft Perfection. She firft fets up for a fine Thing, and for that Reafon will diftinguifh herfelf right or wrong, in every thing fhe does. She would have it thought that fhe is made of fo much finer Clay, and fo much more fifted than ordinary, that fhe has no common Earth about her. To this End fhe muft neither move nor fpeak like other Women, becaufe it would be vulgar, and, therefore, muft have a Language of her own, fince ordinary *Englifh* is too coarfe for her. The Looking-Glafs in the Morning dictates to her all the Motions of the Day, which by how much the more ftudied, are fo much the more miftaken. She comes into a Room as if her Limbs were fet on with ill made Screws, which makes the Company fear the pretty Thing fhould leave fome of its artificial Perfon upon the Floor. She does not like herfelf as God Almighty made her, but will have fome of her own Workmanfhip, which is fo far from making her a better Thing than a Woman,

that

that it turns her into a worse Creature than a Monkey. She falls out with Nature, against which she makes War without admitting a Truce, those Moments excepted in which her Gallant may reconcile her to it. When she hath a Mind to be soft and languishing, there is something so unnatural in that affected Easiness, that her Frowns could not be by many Degrees so forbidden When she would appear unreasonably humble, one may see she is so excessively proud, that there is no enduring it. There is such an impertinent Smile, such a satisfied Simper, when she faintly disowns some fulsome Commendation a Man happens to bestow upon her against his Conscience, that her Thanks for it are more visible under such a thin Disguise, than they could be if she should print them If a handsomer Woman taketh any Liberty of dressing out of the ordinary Rules, the mistaken Lady followeth without distinguishing the unequal Pattern, and makes herself uglier by an Example misplaced, either forgetting the Privilege of good Looks in another, or presuming, without sufficient Reason, upon her own. Her Discourse is a senseless Chime of empty Words, a Heap of Compliments so equally applied to differing Persons, that they are neither valued nor believed. Her Eyes keep Pace with her Tongue, and are, therefore, always in Motion. One may discern that they generally incline to the compassionate Side, and that, notwithstanding her Pretence to Virtue, she is gentle to distressed Lovers, and Ladies that are merciful. She will repeat the tender Part of a Play so feelingly, that the Company may guess, without Injustice, she was not altogether a disinterested Spectator. She thinks that Paint and Sin are concealed by railing at them: Upon the latter she

is

is lefs haid, and being divided between the two oppofite
Piides of hei Beauty and her Virtue, fhe is often tempted
to give broad Hints that fomebody is dying for her, and
of the two, fhe is lefs unwilling to let the World think fhe
may be fometimes profan'd, than that fhe is never worfhip-
ped.

Very great Beauty may, perhaps, fo dazzle for a Time,
that Men may not fo clearly fee the Deformity of thefe
Affectaions; but when the Brightnefs goeth off, and that
the Lover's Eyes are by that Means fet at Liberty to fee
things as they are, he will naturally return to his Senfes
and recover the Miftake into which the Lady's good Looks
had at fiift engaged him; and being once undeceived;
ceafes to worfhip that, as a Goddefs, which he fees only
an artificial Shrine moved by Wheels and Springs to delude
him.   Such Women pleafe only like the firft opening of
a Scene, that has nothing to recommend it but being new:
They may be compared to Flies, that have pretty fhining
Wings for two or three hot Months, but the firft cold Weather makes an End of them; fo the latter Seafon of thefe
fluttering Creatures is difmal; from their neareft Friends
they receive a very faint Refpect; fiom the reft of the
World, the utmoft Degree of Contempt.

This Picture may fupply the Place of any other Rules
which might be given to prevent a Woman's refembling
it; the Deformity of it, well confidered, is Inftruction
enough; from the fame Reafon, that the Sight of a
Diunkard is a better Sermon againft that Vice, than the
beft that was ever preached upon that Subject.

C H A P.

CHAP. X.

Of PRIDE *and* DIVERSIONS.

AFTER having faid this againft Vanity, we do not intend to apply the fame Cenfure to Pride, well placed and rightly defined. It is an ambiguous Word, one kind of it is as much a Virtue, as the other is a Vice. But we are naturally fo apt to choofe the worft, that it is become dangerous to commend the beft Side of it.

A Woman is not to be proud of her fine Gown; nor when fhe has lefs Wit than her Neighbours, to comfort herfelf that fhe has more Lace. Some Ladies put fo much Weight upon Ornaments, that if one could fee into their Hearts, it would be found, that even the Thoughts of Death made lefs heavy to them by the Contemplation of their being laid out in State, and honourably attended to the Grave. One may come a good deal fhort of fuch an Extream, and yet ftill be fufficiently impertinent, by fetting a wrong Value upon things which ought to be ufed with more Indifference. A Lady muft not appear follicitous to ingrofs Refpect to herfelf, but be content with a reafonable Diftribution, and allow it to others, that fhe may have it returned to her. She is not to be troublefomely nice, nor diftinguifh herfelf by being too delicate, as if ordinary Things were too coarfe for her; this is an unmannerly and an offenfive Pride, and where it is practiced deferves to be mortified, of which it feldom fails. She is not to lean too much upon her Quality, much lefs, to defpife

fpife thofe who are below it. Some make *Quality* an *Idol*, and then their Reafon muft fall down and worfhip it. They would have the World think, that no Amends can ever be made for the want of a *great Title*, or an ancient *Coat of Arms*, they imagine, that with thefe Advantages they ftand upon the higher Ground, which makes them look down upon Merit and Virtue, as Things inferior to them. This Miftake is not only *fenfelefs*, but *criminal* too, in putting a greater Price upon that which is a Piece of *good Luck*, than upon things that are valuable in themfelves. *Laughing* is not enough for fuch a Folly; it muft be feverely whipped, as it juftly deferves. It will be confeffed, there are frequent Temptations given by pert Upftarts to be angry, and by that to have our Judgments corrupted in thefe Cafes: But they are to be refifted; and the utmoft that is to be allowed, is when thofe of a new Edition will forget themfelves, fo as either to brag of their weak Side, or to endeavour to hide their Meannefs by their Infolence, to cure them by a little feafonable Raillery, a little Sharpnefs well placed, without dwelling too long upon it.

Thefe and many other Kinds of *Pride* are to be avoided. That which is to be recommended, is an Emulation in a Woman to rife to a Character, by which fhe may be diftinguifhed; an Eagernefs for Precedence in Virtue, and all fuch other Things as may gain a greater Share in the good Opinion of the World. *Efteem* to *Virtue* is like a *cherifhing Air* to *Plants* and *Flowers*, which makes them blow and profper; and for that Reafon it may be allowed to be in fome Degree the Caufe as well as the Reward of it. That *Pride* which leads to a *good End*, cannot be a *Vice*,

fince

fince it is the Beginning of a Virtue, and to be pleafed with juft Applaufe, is fo far from a Fault, that it would be an ill Symptom in a Woman, who fhould not place the greateft Part of her Satisfaction on it. Humility is, no Doubt, a great Virtue, but it ceafes to be fo, when it is afraid to fcorn an ill Thing Againft Vice and Folly it is becoming the Female Sex to be haughty, but they muft not carry the Contempt of things to Arrogance towards Perfons, and it muft be done with fitting Diftinctions, elfe it may be inconvenient by being unfeafonable: A Pride that raifeth a little Anger, to be outdone in any thing that is good, will have fo good an Effect, that it is very hard to allow it to be a Fault.

It is no eafy Matter to carry even between thefe differing Kinds defcrib'd, but remember, that it is fafer for a Woman to be thought too proud, than too familiar.

The laft Thing we have to recommend to young Women *particularly*, tho' it likewife affects thofe of every Age and Station of Life, is, a wife and fafe Method of ufing Diverfions. To be too eager in the Purfuit of Pleafure whilft they are young, is dangerous, to catch at it in riper Years, is grafping a Shadow; it will not be held: Befides, that by being lefs natural it grows to be indecent. Diverfions are moft properly applied to eafe and relieve thofe who are opprefled, by being too much employed. Thofe that are idle have no need of them, and yet they, above all others, give themfelves up to them. To unbend our Thoughts, when they are too much ftretched by our Cares, is not more natural than it is neceffary, but to turn our whole Lives into a Holiday, is not only ridiculous, but deftroys Pleafure inftead of promoting it. The Mind,

O   like

like the Body, is tired by being always in one Pofture, too ferious breaks, and too diverting loofens it: It is Variety that gives the Relifh; fo that Diverfions too frequently repeated, grow firft to be indifferent, and at laft tedious: Whilft they are well-chofen and well-timed, they are never to be blamed; but when they are ufed to an Excefs, tho' very innocent at firft, they often grow to be criminal, and never fail to be impertinent.

Some Ladies are befpoken for merry Meetings, as *Beffus*, in the Play, was for Duels　They are engaged in a Circle of *Idlenefs*, where they turn round for the whole Year, without the Interruption of a ferious Hour.　They know all the Players Names, and are intimately acquainted with every Booth in *Bartholomew-Fair*.　No Soldier is more obedient to the Sound of his Captain's Trumpet, than they are to that which fummoneth them to a *Puppet-Play* or a Monfter.

The Spring, that brings out Flies and Fools, makes them Inhabitants in the Parks; in the Winter they are an Incumbrance to the Play-Houfe, and the Ballaft of the Drawing-Room.　The Streets all this while are fo weary of thefe daily Faces, that Men's Eyes are overlaid with them.　The Sight is glutted with fine Things, as the Stomach with fweet ones; and when a Fair Lady will give too much of herfelf to the World fhe grows lufcious, and opprefles inftead of pleafing.　Thefe jolly Ladies do fo continually feek Diverfion, that in a little Time they grow into a Jeft, yet are unwilling to remember, that if they were feldomer feen, they would not be fo often laugh'd at. Befides, they make themfelves cheap, than which there cannot be an unkinder Word beftowed upon the Female Sex.

To

To play fometimes to entertain Company, or for Women to divert themfelves, is not to be difallow'd; but to do it fo often as to be called, Gamefters, is to be avoided, next to Things that are moft criminal. It has Confequences of feveral Kinds not to be endured, it will engage them into a Habit of Idlenefs and ill Hours, draw them into mixed Company, make them neglect their Civilties abroad, and their Bufinefs at home, and impofe into their Acquaintance fuch as will do them no Credit.

To deep Play there will be yet greater Objections: It will give Occafion to the World to ask fpiteful Queftions: How they dare venture to lofe, and what Means they have to pay fuch great Sums? If they pay exactly, it will be enquired from whence the Money comes? If they owe, and efpecially to a Man, they muft be fo very civil to him for his Forbearance, that it lays a Ground for having it farther improved, if the Gentleman is fo difpofed, who will be thought no unfair Creditor, if, where the Eftate fails, he feizes upon the Perfon. Befides, if a Lady could fee her own Face upon an ill Game, at a deep Stake, fhe would certainly forfwear any thing that could put her Looks under fuch a Difadvantage: And as a certain ingenious Poet fays, fpeaking of Ladies playing at Hazard,

If the Fair Ones their Charms did fufficiently prize,
Their Elbows *they'd fpare for the Sake of their Eyes.*

To dance fometimes will not be imputed to a Lady as a Fault; but then fhe is to remember, that the End of her learning it was, that fhe might the better know how to move gracefully. It is only an Advantage fo far, when it

goes

goes beyond it, one may call it excelling in a Miſtake, which is no very great Commendation. It is better for a Woman never to dance, becauſe ſhe has no Skill in it, than to do it too often, becauſe ſhe does it well. The eaſieſt, as well as the ſafeſt, Method of doing it, is in private Company, among particular Friends, and then careleſly like a Diverſion, rather than with Solemnity, as if it was a Buſineſs, or had any thing in it to deſerve a Month's Preparation, by ſerious Conference with a Dancing Maſter.

C H A P. XI.

Of W I V E S.

H AV I N G now conducted the Virgin to the Entrance of another State, we muſt ſhift the Scene and attend her thither alſo: And here ſhe is launched into a wide Sea, that one Relation of a Wife drawing after it many others; for as ſhe eſpouſes the Man, ſo ſhe does his Obligations alſo, and wherever he, by Ties of Nature, or Alliance, owes a Reverence or Kindneſs, ſhe is no leſs a Debtor. Her Marriage is an Adoption into his Family, and therefore ſhe is, to every Branch of it, to pay what their Stations there do reſpectively require. To define which more particularly, would be a Work of more length than profit, we ſhall, therefore, confine the preſent Conſideration to the Relation ſhe ſtands in to her Huſband, (and what is uſually concomitant with that) her Children, and

and her Servants, and fo fhall confider her in the three Capacities of a Wife, a Mother, and a Miftrefs.

In that of a Wife her Duty has feveral Refpects, as it relates, *Firft*, To his Perfon, *Secondly*, To his Reputation; *Thirdly*, To his Fortune. The firft Debt to his Perfon is Love, which we find fet as the prime Article in the Marriage Vow. And, indeed, that is the moft effential Requifite, without this it is only a Bargain and Compact, a Tyranny, perhaps, on the Man's Part, and a Slavery on the Woman's. It is Love only that cements the Hearts, and where that Union is wanting, it is but a Shadow, a Carcafs of Marriage Therefore, as it is very neceffary to bring fome Degree of this to this State, fo it is no lefs to maintain and improve it in it. This is it which facilitates all other Duties of Marriage; makes the Yoke fit fo lightly, that it rather pleafes than galls. It fhould, therefore, be the Study of Wives to preferve his Flame, that, like the Veftal Fire, it may never go out: And to that End carefully to guard it from all thofe things which are naturally apt to extinguifh it, of which Kind are all Frowardnefs and little Perverfenefs of Humour; all fullen and morofe Behaviour, which by taking of from the Delight and Complacency of Converfation, wll, by degrees, wear off the Kindnefs.

But of all we know nothing more dangerous than that unhappy Paffion of Jealoufy, which tho' it is faid to be the Chld of Love, yet, like the Viper, its Birth is the certain Deftruction of the Parent. As, therefore, they muft be nicely careful to give their Hufbands no Colour, no leaft Umbrage for it; fo fhould they be as refolute to refift all that occurs to themfelves, be fo far from that bufy Curiofity,

Curiofity, that Induftry to find Caufes of Sufpicion, that even where they prefented themfelves they fhould avert the Confideration, put the moft candid Conftruction upon any doubtful Action. And, indeed, Charity in this Inftance has not more of the Dove than of the Serpent. It is infinitely the wifeft Courfe, both in relation to her prefent Quiet, and her future Innocence. The entertaining a jealous Fancy, is the admitting the moft treacher--ous, the moft difturbing Inmate in the World, and fhe opens her Breaft to a Fury that lets it in. 'Tis certainly one of the moft enchanting Frenzies imaginable, keeps her always in a moft reftlefs importunate Search after that which fhe dreads and abhors to find, and makes her equally miferable when fhe is injured and when fhe is not.

And as fhe totally lofes her Eafe, fo 'tis odds but fhe will part alfo with fome Degrees of her Innocence. Jealoufy is commonly attended with a black Train; it mufters all the Forces of our irafcible Part to abet its Quarrel, Wrath and Anger, Malice and Revenge; and by how much the Female Impotence to govern thofe Paffions is the greater, fo much the more dangerous is it to admit that which will fo furely fet them in an Uproar. For if *Jealoufly* be, as the wife Man, fays, *the Rage of a Man*, Prov. vi. 34. we may well think it may be the Fury, the Madnefs of a Woman. And, indeed, all Ages have given tragical Inftances of it, not only in the moft indecent Fiercenefs and Clamour, but in the folemn Mifchiefs of actual Revenges. Nay, it is to be doubted there have been fome whofe Malice has rebounded; who have ruined themfelves in Spight, have been adulterous by way of Retaliation, and taken more fcandalous Liberties than thofe they complained of in their
Hufbands:

Husbands: And when such enormous Effects as these are the Issues of Jealousy, it ought to keep a Woman on the strictest Guard against it.

But, perhaps, it may be said, that some are not left to their Jealousy and Conjectures, but have more demonstrative Proofs. In this Age it is, indeed, no strange thing for Men to publish their Sin, and the Offender does sometimes not discover but boast his Crime. In this Case it will, it must be confessed, be scarce possible to disbelieve him; but even here a Wife has this Advantage, that she is out of the Pain of Suspense She knows the utmost, and, therefore, is at Leisure to convert all that Industry which she would have used for the Discovery, to fortify herself against a known Calamity; which sure she may as well do in this as in any other, a patient Submission being the one Catholicon in all Distresses, and as the Slightest can overwhelm us if we add our own Impatience towards our sinking, so the Greatest cannot if we deny it that Aid. They are, therefore, far in the Wrong, who in case of this Injury, pursue their Husbands with Virulencies and Reproaches This is, as *Solomon* says, *Prov.* xxv. 20. *The pouring Vinegar upon Nitre,* applying Corrosives when Balsams are most needed; whereby they not only increase their own Smart, but render the Wound incurable. They are not Thunders and Earthquakes, but soft gentle Rains that close the Scissures of the Ground; and the Breaches of Wedlock will never be cemented by Storms and loud Outcries. Many Men have been made worse but scarce any better by it; for Guilt covets nothing more than an Opportunity of recriminating; and where the Husband can accuse the Wife's

Bitterness,

Bitterneſs, he thinks he needs no other Apology for his own Luſt.

A wiſe Diſſimulation, or very calm Notice, is ſure the likelieſt Means of reclaiming, for where Men have not wholly put off Humanity, there is a native Compaſſion to a meek Sufferer. We have naturally ſome Regret to ſee a Lamb under the Knife, whereas, the impatient Roaring of a Swine diverts our Pity; ſo that Patience in this Caſe is as much the Intereſt, as Duty, of a Wife.

But there is another Inſtance wherein that Virtue has a ſeverer Trial, and that is, when a Wife lies under the cauſeleſs Jealouſies of the Husband. This is, ſure, one of the greateſt Calamities that can befal a virtuous Woman, who as ſhe accounts nothing ſo dear as her Loyalty and Honour, ſo ſhe thinks no Infelicity can equal the aſperſing of thoſe, eſpecially when it is from him, to whom ſhe has been the moſt ſollicitous to approve herſelf.

That we may the better preſcribe a Cure for this Evil, we ſhall enter into an Enquiry into the Springs and Cauſes of it.

JEALOUSY *is that Pain which a Man feels from the Apprehenſion, that he is not equally beloved by the Perſon whom he entirely loves.* Now, becauſe our inward Paſſions and Inclinations can never make themſelves viſible, it is impoſſible for a jealous Man to be thoroughly cured of his Suſpicions. His Thoughts hang at beſt in a State of Doubtfulneſs and Uncertainty; and are never capable of receiving any Satisfaction on the advantageous Side, ſo that his Inquiries are moſt ſucceſsful when they diſcover nothing: His Pleaſure ariſes from his Diſappointments,

and

and his Life is fpent in Purfuit of a Secret that deftroys his Happinefs if he chance to find it

An ardent Love is always a ftrong Ingredient in this Paffion, for the fame Affection which ftirs up the jealous Man's Defires, and gives the Party beloved fo beautiful a Figure in his Imagination, makes him believe fhe kindles the fame Paffion in others, and appears as amiable to all Beholders: And as Jealoufy thus arifes from an extraordinary Love, it is of fo delicate a Nature, that it fcorns to take up with any thing lefs than an equal Return of Love Not the warmeft Expreffions of Affection, the fofteft and moft tender Hypocrify, are able to give any Satisfaction, where we are not perfuaded that the Affection is real and the Satisfaction mutual. For the jealous Man wifhes himfelf a kind of Deity to the Perfon he loves: He would be the only Pleafure of her Senfes, the Employment of her Thoughts, and is angry at every Thing fhe admires or takes Delight in, befides himfelf.

The jealous Man's Difeafe is of fo malignant a Nature, that it converts all he takes into its own Nourifhment. A cool Behaviour fets him on the Rack, and is interpreted as an Inftance of Averfion or Indifference; a fond one raifes his Sufpicions, and looks too much like Diffimulation and Artifice. If the Perfon he loves be cheerful, her Thoughts muft be employed on another; and if fad, fhe is certainly thinking on himfelf. In fhort, there is no Word or Gefture fo infignificant, but it gives him new Hints, feed his Sufpicions, and furnifhes him with frefh Matters of Difcovery: So that if we confider the Effects of this Paffion, one would rather think it proceeded from an inveterate Hatred than an exceffive Love; for certainly none can meet with

P

more

more Difquietude and Uneafinefs than a fufpected Wife, if
we except the jealous Husband

But the great Unhappinefs of this Paffion is, that it naturally tends to alienate the Affection which it is fo follicitous to engrofs; and that for thefe two Reafons, becaufe it
lays too great a Conftraint on the Words and Actions of
the fufpected Perfon, and at the fame Time fhews you have
no honourable Opinion of her, both of which are ftrong
Motives to Averfion.

Nor is this the worft Effect of Jealoufy, for it often
draws after it a more fatal Train of Confequences, and
makes the Perfon you fufpect guilty of the very Crimes
you are fo much afraid of. It is very natural for fuch who
are treated ill and upbraided falfely, to find out an intimate
Friend that will hear their Complaints, condole their Suffer-
ings, and endeavour to footh and affwage their fecret Re-
fentments Befides, Jealoufy puts a Woman often in Mind
of an ill Thing, that fhe would not otherwife, perhaps,
have thought of, and fills her Imagination with fuch an
unlucky Idea, as in Time grows familiar, excites Defire,
and lofes all the Shame and Horror which might at firft attend it. Nor is it a Wonder, if fhe, who fuffers wrongfully in a Man's Opinion of her, and has, therefore, nothing to forfeit in his Efteem, refolves to give him Reafon
for his Sufpicions, and to enjoy the Pleafure of the Crime
fince fhe muft undergo the Ignominy. Such probably were
the Confiderations that directed the wife Man in his Advice to Husbands; *Be not jealous over the Wife of thy Bofom, and teach her not an evil Leffon againft thyfelf.* Eccluf.

And here, among other Torments, which this Paffion
produces, we may ufually obferve, that none are greater
Mourners

Mourners than jealous Men, when the Person who provoked their Jealousy is taken from them. Then it is that their Love breaks out furiously and throws off all the Mixtures of Suspicion which choaked and smothered it before. The beautiful Parts of the Character rise uppermost in the jealous Husband's Memory, and upbraid him with the ill Usage of so divine a Creature as was once in his Possession; whilst all the little Imperfections that were before so uneasy to him, wear off from his Remembrance, and shew themselves no more.

We may see by what has been said, that Jealousy takes deepest Root in Men of amorous Dispositions, and of these we find three Kinds who are most over-run with it.

The First, are those who are conscious to themselves of any Infirmity, whether it be Weakness, old Age, Deformity, Ignorance, or the like. These Men are so well acquainted with the unamiable Part of themselves, that they have not the Confidence to think they are really beloved, and are so distrustful of their own Merits, that all Fondness towards them puts them out of Countenance, and looks like a Jest upon their Persons. They grow suspicious on their first looking in a Glass, and are stung with Jealousy at the Sight of a Wrinkle. A handsome Fellow immediately alarms them, and every thing that looks young or gay turns their Thoughts upon their Wives.

A second sort of Men, who are most liable to this Passion, are those of cunning, wary, and distrustful Tempers. It is a Fault very justly found in Histories composed by Politicians, that they leave nothing to Chance or Humour, but are still for deriving every Action from some Plot or Contrivance, for drawing up a perpetual Scheme of Causes

and

and Events, and preferving a conftant Correfpondence between the Camp and the Council-Table.   And thus it happens in the Affairs of Love with Men of too refined a
Thought.   They put a Conftruction on a Look, and find
out a Defign in a Smile, they give new Senfes and Significations to Words and Actions, and are ever tormenting
themfelves with Fancies of their own raifing: They generally act in a Difguife themfelves, and, therefore, miftake all outward Shews and Appearances for Hypocrify in
others, fo that we believe no Men fee lefs of the Truth
and Reality of Things, than thefe great Refiners upon In-
cidents, who are fo wonderfully fubtle and over-wife in
their Conceptions

Now what thefe Men fancy they know of Women by
Reflection, lewd and vicious Men believe they have learned by Experience.   They have feen the poor Husband fo
mifled by Tricks and Artifices, and in the midft of his Inquiries fo loft and bewildered in a crooked Intrigue, that
they ftill fufpect an under-plot in every Female Action,
and efpecially where they fee any Refemblance in the Behaviour of two Perfons, are apt to fancy it proceeds from
the fame Defign in both.   Thefe Men, therefore, bare
hard upon the fufpected Party, purfue her clofe through all
her Turnings and Windings, and are too well acquainted
with the Chace, to be flung off by any falfe Steps or
Doubles: Befides, their Acquaintance and Converfation
has lain wholly among the vicious Part of Womenkind,
and, therefore, it is no Wonder they cenfure all alike, and
look upon the whole Sex as a Species of Impoftors: But if,
notwithftanding their private Experience, they can get
over thefe Prejudices, and entertain a favourable Opinion
of

of some Women, yet, their own loose Desires will stir up new Suspicions from another Side, and make them believe all Men subject to the same Inclinations with themselves.

Whether these or other Motives are most predominant, we learn from the modern Histories of *America*, as well as from our own Experience in this Part of the World, that Jealousy is no Northern Passion, but rages most in those Nations that lie nearest the Influence of the Sun. It is a Misfortune for a Woman to be born between the Tropicks, for there lie the hottest Regions of Jealousy, which as you come Northward cools all along with the Climate, 'till you scarce meet any thing like it in the Polar Circle. Our own Nation is very temperately situated in this Respect, and if we meet with some few disordered, with the Violence of this Passion, they are not the proper Growth of our Country, but are many Degrees nearer the Sun in their Constitution than in their Climate.

After this frightful Account of Jealousy, and the Persons who are most subject to it, it will be but fair to shew by what Means the Passion may be best allay'd and those who are possessed with it set at Ease. Other Faults, indeed, are not under a Wife's Jurisdiction, and should, if possible, escape her Observation; but Jealousy calls upon her particularly for its Cure, and deserves all her Art and Application in the Attempt: Besides, she has this for her Encouragement, that her Endeavours will be always, pleasing, and that she will still find the Affection of her Husband rising towards her in Proportion as his Doubts and Suspicions vanish; for, as we have seen all along, there is so great a Mixture of Love in Jealousy as is well worth the separating.

The

The firſt Rule we ſhall propoſe to be obſerved is, that you never ſeem to diſlike in another what the jealous Man is himſelf guilty of, or to admire any thing in which he himſelf does not excel. A jealous Man is very quick in his Applications, he knows how to find a double Edge in an Invective, and to draw a Satyr on himſelf out of a Panegyric on another. He does not trouble himſelf to conſider the Perſon, but to direct the Character; and is ſecretly pleaſed or confounded as he finds more or leſs of himſelf in it The Commendation of any Thing in another, ſtirs up Jealouſy, as it ſhews you have a Value for others, beſides himſelf, but the Commendation of that which he himſelf wants, inflames him more, as it ſhews, that in ſome Reſpects, you prefer others before him. Jealouſy is admirably deſcribed, in this View, by *Horace*, in his Ode to *Lydia*.

When Telephus *his youthful Charms,*
His roſy Neck and winding Arms,
With endleſs Rapture you recite,
And in that pleaſing Name delight;
My Heart inflam'd by jealous Heats,
With numberleſs Reſentments beats;
From my pale Cheek the Colour flies,
And all the Man within me dies:
By Turns my hidden Grief appears
In riſing Sighs and fallen Tears,
That ſhew, too well, the warm Deſires,
The ſilent, ſlow, conſuming Fires,
Which on my inmoſt Vitals prey,
And melt my very Soul away.

The

The jealous Man is not, indeed, angry if you diflike another, but if you find thofe Faults which are to be found in his own Character, you difcover not only your Diflike of another, but of himfelf. In fhort, he is fo defirous of engroffing all your Love, that he is grieved at the want of any Charm, which he believes has Power to raife it; and if he finds, by your Cenfures on others, that he is not fo agreeable in your Opinion as he might be, he naturally concludes you could love him better if he had other Qualifications, and that by Confequence your Affection does not rife fo high as he thinks it ought   If, therefore, his Temper be grave or fullen, you muft not be too much pleafed with a Jeft, or tranfported with any thing that is gay and diverting. If his Beauty be none of the beft, you muft be a profeffed Admirer of Prudence, or any other Quality he is Mafter of, or at leaft vain enough to think he is.

In the next Place, you muft be fure to be free and open in your Converfation with him, and to let in Light upon your Actions, to unravel all your Defigns, and difcover every Secret however trifling or indifferent. A jealous Husband has a particular Averfion to Winks and Whifpers, and if he does not fee to the Bottom of every thing, will be fure to go beyond it in his Fears and Sufpicions. He will always expect to be your chief Confident, and where he finds himfelf kept out of a Secret, will believe there is more in it than there fhould be: And here it is of great Concern, that you preferve the Character of your Sincerity uniform and of a-piece, for if he once finds a falfe Glofs put upon any fingle Action, he quickly fufpects all the reft, his working Imagination immediately takes a falfe Hint,

and

and runs off with it into feveral remote Confequences, till
he has proved very ingenious in working out his own Mifery

If both thefe Methods fail, the beft way will be to let
him fee you are much caft down and afflicted for the ill
Opinion he entertains of you, and the Difquietudes he him-
felf fuffers for your Sake.   There are many who take a kind
of barbarous Pleafure in the Jealoufy of thofe who love
them, that infult over an aching Heart, and triumph in
their Charms which are able to excite fo much Uneafinefs :
But thefe often carry the Humour fo far, till their affected
Coldnefs and Indifference quite kills all the Fondnefs of a
Lover, and are then fure to meet in their Turn with all the
Contempt and Scorn that is due to fo infolent a Behaviour.
On the contrary, it is very probable a melancholy, dejected
Carriage, the ufual Effects of injured Innocence, may foft-
en the jealous Husband into Pity, make him fenfible of the
Wrong he does you, and work out of his Mind all thofe
Fears and Sufpicions that make both Man and Wife unhappy.   At leaft it will have this good Effect, that he will
keep his Jealoufy to himfelf, and repine in private, either
becaufe he is fenfible it is a Weaknefs, and will, therefore,
hide it from your Knowledge, or becaufe he will be apt to
fear fome ill Effect it may produce, in cooling your Love
towards him, or diverting it to another.

There is ftill another Secret that can never fail, if you
can once get it believed, and which is often practiced by
Women of great Cunning than Virtue : This is to change
Sides for a while with the jealous Man, and to turn his
own Paffion upon himfelf ; to take fome Occafion of growing jealous of him, and to follow the Example he himfelf
hath

hath fet you. This counterfeited Jealoufy will bring him
a great deal of Pleafure, if he thinks it real ; for he knows,
experimentally, how much Love goes along with this Paffion, and will, befides, feel fomething like the Satisfaction of
a Revenge, in feeing you undergo all his own Tortures.
But this, indeed, is an Artifice fo difficult, and at the fame
Time fo difingenuous, that it ought never to be put in
Practice but by fuch as have Skill enough to cover the Deceit, and Innocence to render it excufable.

The late Marquifs of *Hallifax*, in his curious Treatife,
called, *Advice to a Daughter*, has made no mention how
a Wife is to behave herfelf to the jealous Husband, but
has given prudent Inftructions with regard to other Sort of
Men.

Women, faith that noble Writer, are to confider they
live in a Time that hath rendered fome kind of Frailties fo
habitual, that they lay claim to large Grains of Allowance.
The World in this is fomewhat unequal, and the mafculine
Sex feems to play the Tyrant in diftinguifhing partially for
themfelves, by making that in the utmoft Degree criminal
in the Woman, which in a Man paffes under a much
gentler Cenfure. The Root and the Excufe of this Injuftice, is the Prefervation of Families from any Mixture
which may bring a Blemifh to them : And whilft the Point
of Honour continues to be fo placed, it feems unavoidable
to give the Female Sex the greater Share of the Penalty :
But if in this it lies under any Difadvantage, it is more than
recompens'd, by having the Honour of Families in their
Keeping. The Confideration fo great a Truft muft give
the Woman, makes full Amends; and this Power the
World has lodged in them, can hardly fail to reftrain the

N° 6 Q Severity

Severity of an ill Husband, and to improve the Kindnefs and Efteem of a good one This being fo, they fhould remember, that next to the Danger of committing the Fault themfelves, the greateft is that of feeing it in their Husbands. They fhould not feem to look or hear that Way: If he is a Man of Senfe, he will reclaim himfelf, the Folly of it, is of itfelf fufficient to cure him: If he is not fo, he will be provoked, but not reformed. To expoftulate in thefe Cafes, looks like declaring War, and preparing Reprifals, which to a thinking Husband would be a dangerous Reflection · Befides, it is fo coarfe a Reafon, which will be affign'd for a Lady's too great Warmth upon fuch an Occafion, that Modefty, no lefs than Prudence, ought to reftrain her: Since fuch an indecent Complaint makes a Wife much more ridiculous, than the Injury that provoked her to it: But it is yet worfe, and more unskilful, to blaze it in the World, expecting it fhould rife up in Arms to take her Part · Whereas, fhe will find, it can have no other Effect, than that fhe will be ferved up in all Companies, as the reigning Jeft at that Time, and will continue to be the common Entertainment, 'till fhe is refcued by fome newer Folly that comes upon the Stage, and drives her away from it The Impertinence of fuch Methods is fo plain, that it does not deferve the Pains of being laid open. In Cafes of this Kind, the Fair Sex fhould be affured, that Difcretion and Silence will be the moft prevailing Reproof. An affected Ignorance, which is feldom a Virtue, is a great one here: And when a Husband fees how unwilling a Woman is to be uneafy, there is no ftronger Argument to perfuade him not to be unjuft to her: Befides, it will naturally make him more yielding in other Things:

Things: And whether it be to cover or redeem his Offence, she will have the good Effects of it while it lasts, and all that while have the most reasonable Ground that can be of presuming such a Behaviour will at last entirely convert him. There is nothing so glorious to a Wife, as a Victory so gained: A Man so reclaimed is for ever after subjected to her Virtue; and her bearing for a Time is more than rewarded by a Triumph that will continue as long as her Life.

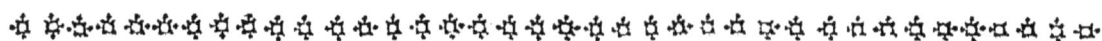

CHAP. XII.

Of a WIFE's BEHAVIOUR *to a* DRUNKARD.

THE next Thing we will suppose, is, that the Husband loves Wine more than is convenient. It will be granted, that though there are Vices of a deeper Dye, there are none that have a greater Deformity than this, when it is not restrained: But with all this, the same Custom, which is the more to be lamented for its being so general, should make it less uneasy to every one in particular, who is to suffer by the Effects of it, so that in the first Place, it will be no new thing for a Woman to have a Drunkard for her Husband, and there is, by too frequent Examples, Evidence enough that such a thing may happen, and yet a Wife may live too without being miserable. Self-Love dictates aggravating Words to every thing we feel, Ruin and Misery are the Terms we apply to whatsoever we

do

do not like, forgetting the Mixture allotted to us by the Condition of human Life, by which it is not intended we should be quite exempt from Trouble. It is fair, if we can escape such a Degree of it as would oppress us, and enjoy so much of the pleasant Part as may lessen the ill Taste of such Things as are unwelcome to us. Every thing has two Sides, and for our own Ease we ought to direct our Thoughts to that which may be least liable to Exception. To fall upon the worst Side of a Drunkard, gives so unpleasant a Prospect, that it is not possible to dwell upon it Let us pass then to the more favourable Part, as far as a Wife is concerned in it

If the Irregularities of the Expression could, in Strictness, be justified, we might say, That a Wife is to thank God her Husband has Faults. Mark the seeming Paradox, for your own Instruction, it being intended no farther. A Husband without Faults is a dangerous Observer, he hath an Eye so piercing, and sees every thing so plain, that it is exposed to his full Censure. And tho' a Woman's Virtue may disappoint the sharpest Enquiries, yet few can bear to have all they say or do represented in the clear Glass of an Understanding without Faults. Nothing softens the Arrogance of our Nature, like a Mixture of some Frailties. It is by them we are best told, that we must not strike too hard upon others, because we ourselves do so often deserve Blows: They pull our Rage by the Sleeve, and whisper Gentleness to us in our Censure, even when they are rightly applied. The Faults and Passions of Husbands bring them down to their Wives, and make them content to live upon less unequal Terms, than faultless Men would be willing to stoop to, so haughty is Mankind till humbled

by

by common Weakneſs and Defeẟs, which in our corrupt State contribute more towards reconciling us to one another, than all the Precepts of the Philoſophers and Divines. So that where the Errors of our Nature make Amends for the Diſadvantages of the Women's, it is more their Part to make Uſe of the Benefit, than to quarrel at the Fault.

Thus in Caſe a Drunken Husband falls to a Woman's Lot, if ſhe will be wiſe and patient, his Wine ſhall be of her Side; it will throw a Veil over her Miſtakes, and will ſet out and improve every thing ſhe does, that he is pleaſed with. Others will like him leſs, and by that Means he may, perhaps, like his Wife the more. When after having dined too well, he is received at home without a Storm, or ſo much as a reproachful Look, the Wine will naturally work out all in Kindneſs, which a Wife muſt encourage, let it be wrapped up in never ſo much Impertinence. On the other Side, it would boil up into Rage, if the miſtaken Wife ſhould treat him roughly, like a certain Thing called, a kind Shrew, than which the World, with all its Plenty, cannot ſhew a more ſenſeleſs, ill-bred, forbidding Creature. A Woman ſhould conſider, that where the Man will give ſuch frequent Intermiſſions of the Uſe of his Reaſon, the Wife inſenſibly gets a Right of governing in the Vacancy, and that raiſes her Charaẟer and Credit in the Family, to a higher Pitch, than, perhaps, could be done under a ſober Husband, who never puts himſelf into an Incapacity of holding the Reins. If theſe are not entire Conſolations, at leaſt they are Remedies to ſome Degree. They cannot make Drunkenneſs a Virtue, nor a Husband given to it a Felicity; but Ladies will do themſelves no ill Office in the endeavouring, by

theſe

thefe Means, to make the beft of fuch a Lot, and by the help of a wife Obfervation, to make that very fupportable which would otherwife be a Load that would opprefs them

The next Cafe is, the Misfortune of a Cholerick or ill-humour'd Husband. To this may be faid, That paffionate Men generally make Amends at the Foot of the Account. Such a Man, if he is angry one Day without any Caufe, will the next Day be as kind without any Reafon · So that by marking how the Wheels of fuch a Man's Head are ufed to move, a Woman may eafily bring over all his Paffions to her Party. Inftead of being ftruck down by his Thunder, fhe may direct it where and upon whom fhe fhall think it beft applied Thus are the ftrongeft Poifons turn'd to the beft Remedies, but then there muft be Art in it, and a skilful Hand, elfe the leaft bungling makes it mortal. There is a great deal of nice Care requifite to deal with a Man of this Complexion. Choler proceeds from Pride, and makes a Man fo partial to himfelf, that he fwells againft Contradiction, and thinks he is leffened if he is oppofed. Women, in this Cafe, muft take heed of increafing the Storm, by an unwary Word, or kindling the Fire whilft the Wind is in a Corner which may blow it in their Faces: They are dexteroufly to yield every thing till he begins to cool, and then by flow Degrees they may rife, and gain upon the Man: Gentlenefs, well-timed, will, like a Charm, difpel his Anger ill placed, a kind Smile will reclaim, when a fhrill pettifh Anfwer would provoke him ; rather than fail, upon fuch Occafions, when other Remedies are too weak, a little Flattery may be ad-mitted, which by being neceffary, will ceafe to be crimi-nal.

If

If ill Humours and Sullennefs, and not open and fudden Heat, is his Difeafe, there is a Way of treating that too, fo as to make it a Grievance to be endured. In order to it, a Woman, in the firft Place, ought to know, that naturally good Senfe has a Mixture of Surly in it: And there being fo much Folly in the World, and for the moft Part fo triumphant, it gives frequent Temptations to raife the Spleen of Men who think right. Therefore, that which may be generally called, ill Humour, is not always a Fault; it becomes one, when either it is wrong applied, or that it is continued too long, when it is not fo: For this Reafon, a Wife muft not too haftily fix an ill Name upon that which may, perhaps, not deferve it, and though the Cafe fhould be, that the Husband might too fourly refent any thing he difliked, it may fo happen, that more Blame fhall belong to her Miftake, than to his ill-Humour. If a Husband behaves himfelf fometimes with an Indifference that a Wife may think offenfive, fhe is in the wrong to put the worft Senfe upon it, if by any Means it will admit a better. Some Wives will call it ill-Humour, if their Husbands change their Style from that which they ufed whilft they made their firft Addrefs to them: Others will allow no Intermiffion or Abatement in the Expreffions of Kindnefs to them, not enough diftinguifhing Times, and forgetting that it is impoffible for Men to keep themfelves up all their Lives to the Height of fome extravagant Moments. A Man may, at fome Times, be lefs careful in little Things without any cold or difobliging Reafon for it: As a Wife may be too expecting in fmaller Matters without drawing upon herfelf the Inference of being unkind. And if a Husband fhould be really fullen, and have fuch frequent Fits,

as

as might take away the Excufe of it, it concerns a Wife to have an Eye prepared to difcern the firft Appearances of cloudy Weather, and to watch when the Fit goes off, which feldom lafts long if it is let alone: But whilft the Mind is fore every thing galls it; and that makes it neceffary to let the Black-Humour begin to fpend itfelf before fhe comes in, and ventures to undertake it

If in the Lottery of the World a Woman fhould draw a Covetous Husband, it muft be confefs'd fhe has no great Reafon to be proud of her good Luck; yet even fuch a one may be endured too, though there are few Paffions more untractable than that of Avarice. She muft firft take Care that her Definition of Avarice may not be a Miftake: She is to examine every Circumftance of her Husband's Fortune, and weigh the Reafon of every Thing fhe expects from him, before fhe has Right to pronounce the Sentence. The Complaint is now fo general againft all Hufbands, that it gives great Sufpicion of its being often ill-grounded; it is impoffible they fhould all deferve that Cenfure, and, therefore, it is certain that it is many Times mifapplied. He that fpares in every thing is an inexcufable Niggard: He that fpares in nothing is an inexcufable Madman. The Meaning is, to fpare in what is leaft neceffary, to lay out more liberally in what is more required in our feveral Circumftances. Yet, this will not always fatisfy. There are Wives who are impatient of the Rules of Oeconomy, and are apt to call their Husband's Kindnefs into queftion, if any other Meafure is put to their Expence than that of their own Fancy. A Woman fhould be fure to avoid this dangerous Error, fuch a Partiality to herfelf, which is fo offenfive to an underftanding Man, that he will very ill

bear

bear a Wife's giving herself such an injurious Preference to all the Family, and whatever belongs to it.

But to admit the worst, and that the Husband is really a close handed Wretch, she must in this, as in other Cases, endeavour to make it less afflicting to her; and, first, she must observe seasonable Hours of speaking, when she offers any thing in Opposition to this reigning Humour, a third Hand and a wise Friend, may often prevail more than she will be allowed to do in her own Cause. Sometimes she is dextrously to go along with him in Things where she sees that the niggardly Part of his Mind is most predominant, by which she will have the better Opportunity of persuadeing him in Things where he may be more indifferent. Our Passions are very unequal, and are apt to be raised or lessened, according as they work upon different Objects; they are not to be stopped or restrained in those things where the Mind is more particularly engaged. In other Matters they are more tractable, and will sometimes reason a Hearing, and admit a fair Dispute. More than that, there are few Men, even in this Instance of Avarice, so entirely abandoned to it, that at some Hours, and upon some Occasions, will not forget their Natures, and for that Time turn Prodigal. The same Man who will grudge himself what is necessary, let his Pride be raised and he shall be profuse; at another Time his Anger shall have the same Effect; a Fit of Vanity, Ambition, and sometimes Kindness, shall open and enlarge his narrow Mind; a Dose of Wine will work upon this tough Humour, and for the Time dissolve it. The Wife's Business must be, if this Case happens, to watch these critical Moments, and not let one of them slip, without making her Advantage of it:

R

And

And a Wife may be said to want Skill, if by these Means
she is not able to secure herself, in a good Measure, against
the Inconveniences this scurvy Quality in her Husband
might bring upon her, except he should be such an incurable Monster, as it is to hope there are not many of

The last Supposition, is of a Woman's meeting with a
Husband, weak and incompetent to make use of the Privileges that belong to him.   It will be yielded, that such a
one leaves room for a great many Objections · But God
Almighty seldom sends a Grievance without a Remedy, or
at least, such a Mitigation as takes away a great Part of the
Sting and Smart of it.   To make such a Misfortune less
heavy, a Wife is to bring first to her Observation, that she
very often makes a better Figure, for her Husband's making no great one : And there seems to be little Reason, why
the same Lady that chooses a Waiting Woman with worse
Looks, may not be content with a Husband with less Wit;
the Argument being equal from the Advantage of the Comparison.   If she may be more ashamed in some Cases, of
such a Husband, she will be less afraid than, perhaps, she
would be of a wise one.   His unseasonable Weakness may,
no doubt, sometimes grieve her, but then set against this,
that it gives her the Dominion, if she will make the right
Use of it: It is next to his being dead, in which Case the
Wife has a Right to administer, therefore, if she has such
an Ideot, she should be sure, that none, except herself,
may have the Benefit of the Forfeiture : Such a Fool is a
dangerous Beast, if others have the keeping of him; and
she must be very undexterous, if when her Husband shall
resolve to be an Ass, she does not take care he may be her
Ass : But she must go skillfully about it, and above all things

take

take Heed of diftinguifhing in Publick what kind of Husband he is: Her inward Thoughts muft not hinder the outward Payment of the Confideration that is due to him : Her flighting him in Company, befides that it would, to a difcerning By-Stander, give too great Encouragement for the making nearer Applications to herfelf, is in itfelf fuch an indecent Way of affuming, that it may provoke the tame Creature to break loofe, and fhew his Dominion for his Credit, which he was content to forget for Eafe. In fhort, the fureft and moft approved Method will be, to do like a wife Minifter to an eafy Prince, firft give him the Orders which are afterwards to be received from him.

With all this, that which fhe is to pray for, is a wife Husband ; one that by knowing how to be a Mafter, for that very Reafon will not let her feel the Weight of it ; one whofe Authority is fo foftened by his Kindnefs, that it gives her Eafe without abridging her Liberty ; one that will return fo much Tendernefs for her juft Efteem of him, that fhe will never want Power, tho' fhe will feldom care to ufe it. Such a Husband is as much above all the other Kinds of them, as a rational Subjection to a Prince, great in himfelf, is to be preferred before the Difquiet and Uneafinefs of unlimited Liberty.

A little muft be added to this Head, concerning a Wife's Behaviour to her Husband's Friends, which requires the moft refined Part of her Underftanding to acquit herfelf well of it. She is to ftudy how to live with them, with more Care than how to apply to any other Part of Life ; efpecially at firft, that fhe may not ftumble at the firft feting out. The Family into which fhe is grafted will generally be apt to expect, that like a Stranger in a Foreign

Country,

Country, fhe fhould conform to their Methods, and not
bring in a new Model by her own Authority. The Friends,
in fuch a Cafe, are tempted to rife up in Arms as againft an
unlawful Invafion, fo that fhe is with the utmoft Caution
to avoid the leaft Appearances of any thing of this kind.
And that fhe may, with lefs Difficulty, afterwards give her
Directions, fhe muft be fure, at firft, to receive them from
her Husband's Friends. Let her gain them to her by early
applying to them, and they will be fo fatisfy'd, that as nothing is more thankful than Pride, when it is complied
with, they will ftrive which of them fhall moft recommend her: And when they have helped her to take root
in her Husband's good Opinion, fhe will have lefs Dependance upon them, tho' fhe ought not to neglect any reafonable Means of preferving it. She is to confider, that a
Man governed by his Friends, is very eafily inflamed by
them; and that one who is not fo, will, yet, for his own
Sake, expect to have them confidered. It is eafily improved to a Point of Honour in a Husband, not to have his
Relations neglected, and nothing is more dangerous, than
to raife an Objection, which is grounded upon Pride: It is
the moft ftubborn and lafting Paffion we are fubject to,
and where it is the firft Caufe of the War, it is very hard
to make a fecure Peace. A Wife's Caution in this is of
the laft Importance to her

And that fhe may the better fucceed in it, fhe fhould
carry a ftrict Eye upon the Impertinence of her Servants;
and take heed that their ill Humour may not engage her
to take Exceptions, and their too much affuming in fmall
Matters, raife Confequences which may bring her under
great Difadvantages. She fhould remember that in the
Cafe

Cafe of a Royal Bride, thofe about her are generally fo far fufpected to bring in a Foreign Intereft, that in moft Countries they are infenfibly reduced to a very fmall Number, and thofe of fo low a Figure, that it does not admit the being jealous of them. In little and in the Proportion, this may be the Cafe of every new-married Woman, and, therefore, it may be more advifeable for her, to gain the Servants fhe finds in a Family, than to tie herfelf too faft to thofe fhe carries into it.

A Woman is not to over-look thefe fmall Reflexions, becaufe they may appear low and inconfiderable, for it may be faid, that as the greateft Streams are made up of the fmall Drops at the Head of the Springs from whence they are derived, fo the greater Circumftances of her Life will be in fome degree directed by thefe feeming Trifles, which having the Advantage of being the firft Acts of it, have a greater Effect than fingly in their own Nature they could pretend to.

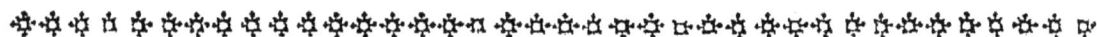

CHAP. XIII.

Of *the* HOUSE, FAMILY *and* CHILDREN.

A Woman is to lay this before her, that there are Degrees of Care to recommend her to the World in the feveral Parts of her Life. In many things, tho' the doing them well may raife her Credit and Efteem, yet, the Omiffion of them would draw no immediate Reproach up-

on

on her. In others, where her Duty is more particularly applied, the Neglect of them is amongst those Faults which are not forgiven, and will bring her under a Censure, which will be much a heavier thing than the Trouble she would avoid. Of this Kind, is the Government of her House, Family, and Children; which since it is the Province allotted to the Female Sex, and that the discharging it well, will, for that Reason, be expected from the Woman; if she either desert it out of Laziness, or manage it ill for want of Skill, instead of a Help she will be an Incumbrance to the Family where she is placed.

No Respect is lasting but that which is produced by our being in some Degree useful to those that pay it. Where that fails, the Homage and the Reverence go along with it, and fly to others where something may be expected in exchange for them: And upon this Principle the Respects even of the Children and the Servants will not stay with one that does not think them worth their Care; and the old House-Keeper shall make a better Figure in the Family, than the Lady with all her fine Cloaths, if she wilfully relinquishes her Title to the Government. Therefore, let her take Heed of carrying her good Breeding to such a Height, as to be good for nothing, and to be proud of it. Some think it has a greater Air to be above troubleing their Thoughts with such ordinary things as their House and Family, others dare not admit Cares for fear they should hasten Wrinkles; mistaken Pride makes some think they must keep themselves up, and not descend to these Duties which do not seem enough refined for great Ladies to be employ'd in; forgetting all this while, that it is more than

the

the greateſt Princes can do, at once to preſerve Reſpect, and to neglect their Buſineſs. No Age ever erected Altars to inſignificant Gods: They had all ſome Quality applied to them to draw worſhip from Mankind; this makes it the more unreaſonable for a Lady to expect to be conſidered, and at the ſame Time reſolve not to deſerve it. Good Looks alone will not do, they are not ſuch a laſting Tenure as to be relied upon, and if they ſhould ſtay longer than they uſually do, it will by no Means be ſafe to depend upon them: For when Time has abated the Violence of the firſt liking, and that the Napp is a little worn off, tho' ſtill a good Degree of Kindneſs may remain, Men recover their Sight which before might be dazzled, and allow themſelves to object as well as to admire.

In ſuch a Caſe, when a Huſband ſees an empty airy thing ſail up and down the Houſe to no kind of Purpoſe, and look as if ſhe came thither only to make a Viſit: When he finds that after her Emptineſs has been extreme buſy about ſome very ſenſeleſs Thing, ſhe eats her Breakfaſt half an Hour before Dinner, to be at greater Liberty to afflict the Company with her Diſcourſe; then calls for her Coach, that ſhe may trouble her Acquaintance, who are already cloy'd with her; and having ſome proper Dialogues ready to diſplay her fooliſh Eloquence at the Top of the Stairs, ſhe ſets out like a Ship out of the Harbour, laden with Trifles, and comes back with them: At her Return ſhe repeats to her faithful Waiting-Woman, the Triumphs of that Day's Impertinence; then wrapped up in Flattery and clean Linnen, goes to Bed ſo ſatisfy'd, that it throws her into pleaſant Dreams of her own Felicity. Such a one is ſeldom ſerious but with her Taylor, her

Children

Children and Family may now and then have a Random Thought, but she never takes Aim but at something very impertinent. When a Husband, whose Province is without Doors, and to whom the Oeconomy of the House would be in some Degree indecent, finds no Order nor Quiet in his Family, meets with Complaints of all kinds springing from this Root, the mistaken Lady, who thinks to make Amends for all this by having a well-chosen Petticoat, will at last be convinced of her Error, and, with Grief, be forced to undergo the Penalties that belong to those who are willfully insignificant. When this scurvy Hour comes upon her, she first grows angry, then when the Time of it is past, would, perhaps, grow wiser, not remembring that we can no more have Wisdom than Grace, whenever we think fit to call for it. There are Times and Periods fixed for both, and when they are too long neglected, the Punishment is, that they are irrecoverable, and nothing remaining but an useless Grief for the Folly of having thrown them out of our Power. A Woman ought to think what a mean Figure she makes, when she is so degraded by her own Fault, whereas there is nothing in those Duties which are expected from her, that can be a lessening to her, except her want of Conduct makes it so. She may love her Children without living in the Nursery, and may have a competent and discreet Care of them, without letting it break out upon the Company, or exposing herself by turning her Discourse that way, which is a kind of laying Children to the Parish, and it can hardly be done any where, that those who hear it will be so forgiving, as not to think they are overcharged with them. A Woman's Tenderness to her Children, is one of

the

the leaft deceitful Evidences of her Virtue, but yet the Way of expreffing it, muft be fubject to the Rules of good Breeding. And though a Woman of Quality ought not to be lefs kind to them, than Mothers of the meaneft Rank are to theirs, yet fhe may diftinguifh herfelf in the Manner, and avoid the coarfe Methods which in Women of a lower Size might be more excufable She muft begin early to make them love her, that they may obey her This Mixture is no where more neceffary than in Children, and a Mother is not to expect Returns of Kindnefs from them, without Grains of Allowance, and yet, it is not fo much a Defect in their Good Nature, as a fhortnefs of Thought in them. Their firft Infufficiency makes them lean fo entirely upon their Parents for what is neceffary, that the Habit of it makes them continue the fame Expectations for what is unreafonable, and as often as they are deny'd, fo often they think they are injured: And whilft their Reafon's yet in the Cradle, their Anger looks no farther than the Thing they long for and cannot have, and to be difpleafed for their own Good, is a Maxim they are very flow to underftand: So that it may be concluded, the firft Thoughts of Children will have no fmall Mixture of Mutiny; which being fo natural, a Parent fhould not be angry unlefs fhe would increafe it. She fhould deny them as feldom as fhe can, and when there is no avoiding it, fhe muft do it gently, fhe muft flatter away their ill-Humour, and take the next Opportunity of pleafing them in fome other thing, before they either afk or look for it: This will ftrengthen her Authority, by making it foft to them, and confirm their Obedience, by making it their Intereft. A Woman ought to have as ftrict a Guard upon herfelf a-

mongft

mongft her Children as if fhe was amongft her Enemies. They are apt to make wrong Inferences, to take Encouragement from half Words, and mifapply what fhe may fay or do, fo as either to leffen their Duty, or to extend their Liberty farther than is convenient. She fhould keep them more in Awe of her Kindnefs than of her Power: And above all, take Heed of fupporting a favourite Child in its Impertinence, which will give Right to the reft of claiming the fame Privilege. If fhe has a divided Number, let her leave the Boys to the Father's more peculiar Care, that fhe may, with greater Juftice, pretend to a more immediate Jurifdiction over thofe of her own Sex. She is to live fo with them that they may never choofe to avoid her, except when they have offended, and then let them tremble, that they may diftinguifh: But their Penance muft not continue fo long as to grow too four upon their Stomachs, that it may not harden inftead of correcting them: The kind and fevere Part muft have their feveral Turns feafonably applied, but your Indulgence is to have the broader Mixture, that Love, rather than Fear, may be the Root of their Obedience

Servants are in the next Place to be confidered; and a Woman muft remember not to fall into the Miftake of thinking, that becaufe they receive Wages, and are fo much inferior to her, therefore, they are below her Care to know how to manage them. It would be as good Reafon for a Mafter Workman to defpife the Wheels of his Engines, becaufe they are made of Wood Thefe are the Wheels of a Family, and let her Directions be never fo faultlefs, yet if thefe Engines ftop or move wrong, the whole Order of her Houfe is either at a Stand, or difcompofed:

pofed : Befides, the Inequality which is between her and them, muft not make her forget, that Nature makes no fuch Diftinction, but that Servants may be looked upon as humble Friends, and that Returns of Kindnefs and good Ufage, are as much due to fuch of them as deferve it, as their Service is due to us when we require it. A foolifh Haughtinefs in the Style of fpeaking, or in the Manner of commanding them, is in itfelf very indecent; befides that it begetteth an Averfion in them, of which the leaft ill Effect to be expected is, that they will be flow and carelefs in all that is enjoined them: And fhe will find it true by her Experience, that fhe will be fo much the more obey'd as fhe is lefs imperious. She fhould not be too hafty in giveing her Orders, nor too angry when they are not altogether obferved, much lefs is fhe to be loud, and too much difturbed: An Evennefs in diftinguifhing when they do well or ill, is that which will make her Family move by a Rule, and without Noife, and will the better fet out her Skill in conducting it with Eafe and Silence, that it may be like a well-difciplined Army, which knows how to anticipate the Orders that are fit to be given them. A Woman is never to neglect the Duty of the prefent Hour, to do another thing, which though it may be better in itfelf, is not to be unfeafonably preferred. She muft allot well-chofen Hours for the Infpection of her Family, which may be fo diftinguifhed from the reft of her Time, that the neceffary Cares may come in their proper Place, without any Influence upon her good Humour, or Interruption to other things. By thefe Methods fhe will put herfelf in Poffeffion of being valued by her Servants, and then their Obedience will naturally follow.

S 2

We

We muſt not forget one of the greateſt Articles belonging to a Family, which is, the Expence It muſt not be ſuch, as by failing either in the Time or Meaſure of it, may rather draw Cenſure than gain Applauſe If it was well examined, there is more Money given to be laugh'd at, than for any one thing in the World, tho' the Purchaſers do not think ſo. A well ſtated Rule is like the Line, when it is once paſſed, we are under another Pole ; ſo the firſt ſtraying from a Rule, is a Step towards making that which was before a Virtue, to change its Nature, and to grow either into a Vice, or at leaſt an Impertinence. The Art of laying out Money wiſely, is not attained to without a great deal of Thought, and it is yet more difficult in the Caſe of a Wife, who is accountable to her Husband for her Miſtakes in it It is not only his Money, his Credit too is at Stake, if what lies under the Wife's Care is managed, either with indecent Thrift, or too looſe Profuſion The Woman is, therefore, to keep the Mean between theſe two Extremes, and it being hardly poſſible to hold the Balance exactly even, let it rather incline toward the liberal Side, as more ſuitable to her Quality, and leſs liable to Reproach. Of the two a little Money miſpent is ſooner recovered, than the Credit which is loſt by having it unhandſomely ſaved, and a wiſe Husband will leſs forgive a ſhameful Piece of Parſimony, than a little Extravagance, if it be not too often repeated. His Mind in this muſt be her chief Direction, and his Temper, when once known, will in a great Meaſure juſtify her Part in the Management, if he is pleaſed with it.

A Wife in her Cloaths ſhould avoid being too gaudy, and not value herſelf upon an embroidered Gown ; ſhe

ought

ought to remember, that a reasonable Word, or an obliging Look will gain her more Respect than all her fine Trappings. This is not said to restrain Women from a decent Compliance with the World, provided they take the wiser and not the foolisher Part of their Sex for their Pattern. Some Distinctions are to be allowed, whilst they are well suited to their Quality and Fortune, and in the Distribution of the Expence, it seems that a full Attendance, and well-chosen Ornaments for her House, will make a Lady a better Figure, than too much glittering in what she wears, which may with more Ease be imitated by those that are below her. Yet this must not tempt her to starve every thing but her own Apartment, or in order to more Abundance there, give just Cause to the least Servant she has, to complain of the Want of what is necessary. Above all, let her fix it in her Mind an unchangeable Maxim, That nothing is truly fine, but what is fit, and that just so much as is proper for her Circumstances of their several Kinds, is much finer than all she can add to it. When she once breaks through these Bounds, she launches into a wide Sea of Extravagance; every thing will become necessary, because she has a mind to it, not because it is fit for her but because some-body else has it. This Lady's *Logic* sets Reason upon its Head, by carrying the Rule from Things to Persons, and appealing from what is right to every Fool that is in the wrong. The Word *necessary* is miserably applied, it disorders Families and overturns Government, by being so abused. Let her remember, that Children and Fools want every thing, because they want Wit to distinguish; and, therefore, there is no stronger Evidence of a crazy Understanding, than the making too large a Catalogue

logue of Things neceffary, when in Truth there are fo very few Things that have a Right to be placed in it. Try every thing firft in your Judgment before you allow it a Place in your Defire, or a Husband may think it as neceffary for him to deny, as it is for his Wife to have whatever is unreafonable, and if fhe fhall too often give him that Advantage, the Habit of refufing may, perhaps, reach to Things that are not unfit for her.

There are unthinking Ladies, who do not enough confider, how little their own Figure agrees with the fine Things they are fo proud of. Others when they have them, will hardly allow them to be vifible; they cannot be feen without Light, and that is many times fo faucy and fo prying, that like a too forward Gallant, it is to be forbid the Chamber. Some, when one is ufhered into their dark *Ruelle*, it is with fuch Solemnity, that a Man would fwear there was fomething in it, till the unskillful Lady breaks Silence, and begins a Chat, which difcovers it is a Puppet-Play, with magnificent Scenes. Many efteem Things rather as they are hard to be gotten, than that they are worth getting: This looks as if they had an Intereft to purfue that Maxim, becaufe a great Part of their own Value depends upon it. Truth in thefe Cafes would be often unmannerly, and might derogate from the Prerogative great Ladies would affume to themfelves, of being diftinct Creatures from thofe of their Sex, which are inferior, and of lefs difficult Accefs.

In other Things too, the Condition of a Woman muft give Rule to her, and, therefore, it is not a Wife's Part to aim at more than a bounded Liberality; the farther Extent of that Quality, otherwife to be commended, belongs

to

to the Hufband, who has better Means for it   Genei ofity wrong placed becomes a Vice · It is no moie a Viitue when it giows into an Inconvenience · Viitues muft be enlaiged or reftiained according to diffeiing Cucumftances   A Piincely Mind will undo a piivate Family . Therefore, Things muft be fuited, oi elfe they will not defeive to be commended, let them in themfelves be never fo valuable : And the Expectations of the Woild aie beft anfwered, when we acquit ouifelves in that Mannei which feems to be piefciib'd to our feveral Conditions, without ufuiping upon thofe Duties, which do not fo paiticulaily belong to us.

We will clofe the Confideiation of this Article of Expence, with this fhort Woid, Do not fetter yourfelf with fuch a Reftraint in it as may make you iemaikable, but remember, that Viitue is the gieateft Oinament, and good Senfe the beft Equipage.

Never iecede from the Principles of Virtute, nor iegard them only as eftablifhed by Cuftom ; there are two Tribunals before which you muft expect to appear, your Confcience and the Woild : You may efcape the World, but never your own Confcience   You owe to youifelf the Teftimony of youi Merit, however, you fhould not abandon publick Appiobation, becaufe from a Contempt of Reputation, rifes a Contempt of Virtue.

A Woman, if fhe thought iight, would know, that it is not neceffary to be deterr'd by Laws, to oblige hei to contain herfelf within the Bounds of her Duty : The Examples of thofe who deviate from it, and the Misfortunes which immediately fucceed, are foicible enough to put a Stop to the moft violent Inclination :   And, perhaps, there is no Woman of Gallantry whatever, but were fhe fincere,

would

would confefs, that the greateft of her Misfortunes was to have forgotten her Duty

From a Senfe of Shame, if well managed, many Advantages may be reaped. We fpeak not of that Shame that troubles our Repofe, without contributing to the Improvement of our Manners, but of that which prevents our doing ill, for fear of Difhonour. This Shame is fometimes the moft faithful Guardian of Female Virtue: Few alafs! are virtuous now-a-Days, for Virtue's Sake!

Great Virtues atone for a great many Defects: Supreme Valour in Men, and extreme Modefty in Women. Every thing was pardoned in *Agrippina*, Wife of *Germanicus*, in favour of her Chaftity: This Princefs was ambitious and proud; but, fays *Tacitus, All her Paffions were confecrated by her Chaftity.*

If a Woman is fenfible and delicate on the Score of Reputation; if fhe fears to be attacked on the effential Virtues, there is a fure Means to calm her Fears, and content her Delicacy: It is to be virtuous. Let her think of purifying her Sentiments, while they are reafonable and full of Honour, fhe may refolve to be contented in herfelf; it is a certain Revenue of Pleafures; if fhe be truly virtuous, fhe will not fail of being applauded.

CHAP.

C H A P. XIV.

Of W I D O W S.

THE next State that can fucceed to that of Marriage, is Widowhood, which, tho' it fuperfedes thofe Duties which we terminated merely in the Perfon of the Hufband, yet, it endears thofe which may be paid to his Afhes. *Love is ftrong, as Death.* Cant. viii. 6. and therefore, when it is pure and genuine, cannot be extinguifhed by it, but burns like the Funeral-Lamps of old, even in Vaults and Charnel-Houfes. The conjugal Love tranfplanted into the Grave, as into a finer Mould, improves into Piety, and lays a kind of facred Obligation upon the Widow, to perform all Offices of Refpect and Kindnefs which his Remains are capable of.

Now thofe Remains are of three Sorts, his Body, his Memory, and his Children. The moft proper Expreffion of her Love to the Firft, is in giving it an honourable Interment; we mean not fuch as may vie with the *Poland* Extravagance, of which it is obferved, that two or three near fucceeding Funerals ruin the Family, but prudently proportioned to his Quality and Fortune, fo that her Zeal to his Corpfe may not injure a nobler Relict of him, his Children : And this Decency is a much better Inftance of her Kindnefs, than all thofe tragical Furies wherewith fome Women feem tranfported towards their dead Hufbands, thofe frantic Embraces and Careffes of a Carcafs, which betray a little too much the Senfuality of their Love:

N° 7   T   And

And it is fomething obfervable, that thofe vehement Paffions quickly exhauft themfelves, and by a kind of fympathetic Efficacy, as the Body (on which their Affection was fix'd) mouldeis, fo doth that alfo; nay, often it attends not thofe leifurely Degrees of Diffolution, but by a more piecipitate Motion, feems iathei to vanifh than confume.

The more valuable Kindnefs therefoie, is, that to his Memory, endeavouring to embalm that, keep it fiom perifhing; and by this innocent Magic (as the *Egyptians* weie wont by a moie guilty) fhe may converfe with the Dead, reprefent him fo to her own Thoughts, that his Life may ftill be repeated to her· And as in a bioken Miirour, the Refraction multiplies the Images, fo by his Diffolution eveiy Hour prefents diftinct Ideas of him, fo that fhe fees him the oftner for his being hid from her Eyes: But as they ufe not to embalm without Odois, fo fhe is not only to preferve, but peifume his Memoiy, iender it as fragrant as fhe can, not only to herfelf, but others, by ieviving the Remembrance of whatevei was Praife-woithy in him, vindicating him fiom all Calumnies and falfe Accufations, and ftifling, or allaying, even the tiue ones as much as fhe can: And indeed, a Widow can no Way better provide for her own Honour, than by this Tendernefs of her Husband's.

Yet there is another Expreffion of it, inferior to none of the former, and that is, the fetting fuch a Value upon her Relation to him, as to do nothing unworthy of it. 'Twas the dying Charge of *Auguftus* to his Wife *Livia, Behave thyfelf well, and remember our Marriage:* And fhe who has been Wife to a Peifon of Honour, muft fo remember it, as not to do any thing below herfelf, or which he

(could

(could he have forefeen it) fhould juftly have been afhamed of.

The laft Tribute fhe can pay him, is in his Children. Thefe he leaves as his Proxies to receive the Kindnefs of which himfelf is uncapable ; fo that the Children of a Widow may claim a double Portion of the Mother's Love; one upon their native Right as her's; the other, as a Bequeft in Right of their dead Father: And, indeed, fince fhe is to fupply the Place of both Parents, it is but necef-fary fhe fhould put on the Affections of both, and to the Tendernefs of a Mother, add the Care and Conduct of a Father. *Firft*, In a fedulous Care of their Education ; and next, in a prudent Managery of their Fortunes; an Order that is fometimes unhappily inverted, and Mothers are fo concern'd to have the Eftate profper in their Tuition, that the Children cannot; whilft (by an unfeafonable Frugality) to fave a little Expence, they deny them the Advantages of an ingenious and genteel Breeding: Swell their Eftates, perhaps, to a vaft Bulk, but fo contract and narrow their Minds, that they know not how to difpofe them to any real Benefit of themfelves or others: And this is one of the moft pernicious Parfimonies imaginable. A Mother, by this, feems to adopt the Fortune, and abdicate the Child, who is only made the Beaft to bear thofe Loads of Wealth fhe will lay on, and which fhe evidently owns as the greateft Treafure, fince in Tendernefs to that fhe neglects him.

Yet fometimes the fame Effect fprings from another Caufe, and Children are ill bred, not becaufe the Mother grudges the Charge, but out of a Feminine Fondnefs, which permits her not to part with them to the proper

T 2 Places

Places for their Education: Like *Jacob* to *Benjamin*, her Soul is so bound up in them, that she cannot lend them a while, even, to their own most necessary Concerns: And this, tho' not so ignoble a Motive as the other, is of no less Mischief, at least, to her Sons, who being by it confined to Home, are consequently condemned to be poisoned, if with nothing else, yet, with the Flatteries of Servants and Tenants, who think those the best Expedient to secure their own Station. And with these the young Master or Landlord is so blown up, that as if his Manors were the Confines of the World, he can look at nothing beyond them, so that when at last he breaks loose from his Mother's Arms, and comes Abroad, he expects scarce to find his Equals, much less his Betters; thinks he is still to receive the same fawning Adorations which he was used to at Home: And being possess'd with this insolent Expectation, he will scarce be undeceived, but at the Price of many Affronts: Nay, perhaps, he may buy his Experience with the Loss of his Life; by his ill Manners draw on a Quarrel, wherein he finally perishes. That this is no impossible Supposition, some unhappy Mothers have found to their unspeakable Affliction.

It is not to be denied, but there are also Dangers consequent to the breeding Children Abroad, Vice having insinuated itself, even, into the Places of Erudition, and having not only as many but the very same Academies with Virtue and Learning; so that the extreme Depravation of the Times new states the Question; and we are not to consider which is best, but which is the least ill-disposure of Children: And in that Competition, sure the home Education will be cast, for there they may suck in all the Venom

and

and nothing of the Anditote, they will not only be taught
bafe things, but, as is before obferved, by the bafeft Tutors,
fuch as will add all the moft fordid Circumftances to the
improving of a Crime Whereas, Abroad they are, firft,
not like to meet with any whofe Intereft it is fo much to
make them vicious : And, Secondly, they may (as ill as
the World is) meet with many who may give them both
Precepts and Examples of a better Kind, befides, the Difcipline ufed in thofe Communities makes them know themfelves; and the various Sorts of Learning they may acquire,
will not only prove ufeful Divertifement (the want of which
is the great Spring of Mifchief) but will, if rightly applied, furnifh them with ingenious and virtuous Principles,
fuch as may fet them above all vile and ignoble Practices.
So that there feems a Confpiration of Motives to wreft the
Child from the relucting Mother, and to perfuade her for
a while to deny herfelf that Defire of her Eyes, that fo he
may at laft anfwer the more rational Defire of her Heart.

As to the other Part of her Obligation, the managing
of their Fortune, there is the fame Rule for her as for all
other Perfons that have a Truft, *viz.* to do as for themfelves; that is, with the fame Care and Diligence, if not a
greater, as in her own peculiar Concern. We do not fay,
that fhe fhall confound the Property, and make it, indeed, her own, by applying it to her peculiar Ufe : A Thing
which it is to be feared, is often done, efpecially by the
gayer Sort of Widows, who, to keep up their own Equipage, do fometimes incroach upon their Son's Peculiar :
And we wifh even that (tho' bad enough) were the only
Cafe wherein it were done ; but 'tis fometimes to make her
a better Prize to a fecond Hufband. She goes into another
Family,

Family, and as if she were a Colony sent out by her Son, he must pay for the planting her there. Indeed, the oft repeating this Injury, has advanc'd it now into a Custom, and the Management of the Minor's Estate is reckon'd on as Part of the Widow's Fortune: But it is not easy to see what there is in the Title of a Mother, that can legitimate her defrauding her Child, it rather envenoms the Crime, and adds Unnaturalness to Deceit Besides, 'tis a preposterous Sort of Guilt. Orphans and Widows are in Scripture link'd together as Objects of God's and good Men's Piety and of ill Men's Oppression, and how ill, alas, does civil War look among Fellow Sufferers? The Widow to injure the Orphan, is like the uncooth Oppression *Solomon* speaks of, *Prov.* xxviii. 3. *A poor Man that oppresseth the Poor is like a sweeping Rain which leaveth no Food.* Such kind of Rapines are as excessive in their Degree, as prodigious in their Kind: And we believe there are many Instances of Sons, who have suffered more by the Guardianship of their Mothers than they could probably have done by the Outrage of Strangers.

How well such Mothers answer their Obligations to other dead Husbands, must be left to their own Consciences to discuss, we shall only offer them these Steps of Gradation by which to proceed. *First*, That Injustice of any Sort is a great Sin. *Secondly*, That when 'tis in a Matter of Trust 'tis complicated with Treachery also. *Thirdly*, That of all Trusts, those to the Dead have always been esteem'd the most sacred. If they can find any Allay to these by the two remaining Circumstances, that 'tis the Trust of a Husband, and the Interest of a Child, we shall confess them very subtil Casuists.

We

We have hitherto fpoke of what the Widow owes to her dead Husband; but there is also fomewhat of peculiar Obligation in relation to herfelf. God, who has placed us in this World to purfue the Interefts of a better, directs all the fignal Acts of his Providence to that End, and intends we fhould fo interpret them: So that every great Change that occurs, is defign'd either to recall us from a wrong Way, or to quicken our Pace in the Right; and a Widow may more than conjecture, that when God takes away the Mate of her Bofom, reduces her to a Solitude, he does by it found a Retreat from the lighter Jollities and Gayeties of the World, and as in Compliance with civil Cuftom fhe immures herfelf, fit in Darknefs for a while; fo fhe fhould put on a more retired Temper of Mind, a more ftrict and fevere Behaviour; and that not to be caft off with her Veil, but to be the conftant Drefs of her Widowhood. Indeed, that State as it requires a great Sobriety and Piety, fo it affords many Advantages towards it. The Apoftle tells us, *That fhe who is married careth for the Things of the World, how fhe may pleafe her Husband.* 1 *Cor.* vii. 34. There are many things which are but the due Compliances of a Wife, which, yet, are great Avocations, and Interrupters of a ftrict Devotion; when fhe is manumitted from that Subjection, when fhe has lefs of *Martha's Care of ferving*, fhe is then at Liberty to choofe *Mary's* Part, *Luke* x. 42. She has her Time and her Fortune at her own Command, and confequently may much more abound in the Works both of Piety and Charity. We find God himfelf retrench'd the Wife's Power of binding her own Soul, *Num.* xxx. Her Vows were totally infignificant without her Husband's Confirmation; but the Widow might de-

vote

vote herself to what Degree she pleas'd: Her Piety has no Restraint from any other inconsistent Obligation, but may swell as high as it can. Those Hours which were before her Husband's Right, seem now to devolve on God, the grand Proprietor of our Time; that Discourse and free Converse wherewith she entertain'd him, she may now convert into Colloquies and spiritual Intercourse with her Maker; and that Love which was only human before, by the Change of its Object acquires a Sublimity, is exalted into Divine; from loyal Duty and conjugal Affection becomes the eternal Work and Happiness of Angels, the Ardour of a Cherubim. Thus may she in a higher Sense verify *Sampson*'s Riddle, *Judges* xiv. 14. *fetch Honey out of a Carcass*, make her Husband's Ashes (like those of the Heifer under the Law, *Heb.* ix. 13.) *her Purification*; his Corruption may help to put on Incorruption, and her Loss of a temporary Comfort may instate her in an Eternal.

And as herself, so her Fortune may also be consecrated; and, indeed, if she be, that will also: If she have made an Escape out of *Egypt* there shall not a Hoof be left behind her, *Exod.* x. 26. no Part of her Possessions will be assign'd to Vanity and Excess. She who hath really devoted herself to Piety, *fasted and prayed* with *Anna*, Luke ii. 37. will also be *full of good Works and Alms-deeds* with *Tabitha*, Acts ix. 36. Thus she may be a Mother when she ceases to bear; and tho' she no more increase one Family, she may support many: And certainly, the Fertility of the Womb is not so valuable as this of the Bowels: Fruitfulness can be but a Happiness, Compassion is a Virtue: Nay, indeed, it is a greater and more certain Happiness. A Child is not brought forth but with Pangs and

Anguish

Anguifh, but a Work of Mercy is produced not only with Eafe but Delight. Befides, fhe that bears a Child, knows not whether it may prove a Blefling or a Curfe, but Charity gives certain Title to a Blefling, and engages the moft folvent Paymafter, even God himfelf, who owns all fuch Disburfements as a Loan to him. *He that hath Pity upon the Poor, lendeth unto the Lord: And that which he hath given will he pay him again.* PROV. xix. 17.

There was, in the Primitive Times, an Ecclefiaftical Order of Widows, which St. *Paul* mentions, 1 *Tim.* v. whofe whole Miniftry was devoted to Charity. They were indeed, of the poorer Sort, fit rather to receive than give Alms, yet, the lefs they could do with their Purfes, the more was required of their Perfons, the humbler Offices of wafhing the Saints Feet, the careful Task of bringing up Children, and a diligent Attendance on every good Work: And fure there is parity of Reafon, that thofe who upon the Score of their Wealth, exempt themfelves from thofe laborious Services, fhould commute for it by more liberal Alms. In the Warmth and Zeal of Chriftianity, Women of the higheft Quality performed both Sorts of Charity, forgot their Greatnefs in their Condefcenfions, yet affum'd it again in their Bounty; founded Hofpitals, and yet with a *Labour of Love,* as the Apoftle ftiles it, *Heb.* vi. 10. difdain'd not fometimes to ferve in them: But thefe are Examples not like to be tranfcrib'd in our Days, Greatnefs is now grown to fuch an Unweildinefs that it cannot ftoop, tho' to the moft Chriftian Offices, and yet, can as little foar up in any Munificent Charities; it ftands like *Nebuchadnezzar's* Golden Image, a vaft Bulk only to be ador'd.

U

Now

Now certainly, if any Women be qualified to avert this Reproach, it muſt be the Dowagers of great Families and Fortunes: They have none to controul their Viſits to the Sick and Afflicted, or to reſent a Diſparagement from their Humility, neither have they an Account to give of their Poſſeſſions to any but God and themſelves; to him ſure they can bring none ſo like to procure them the Eulogy of *well done thou good and faithful Servant*, Math. xxv. 2 1. as a Catalogue of their Alms. Nor, indeed, can they any other way diſpoſe their Fortune ſo much to their own Contentment, they may poſſibly cloy and ſatiate their Senſes, make Proviſion for the Fleſh; but that no way ſatisfies their Reaſon, much leſs their Conſcience. The Soul, which is the ſuperior Part, is quite left out in that Diſtribution; nothing is communicated to it but the Guilt of thoſe dear bought Exceſſes. The only way it has to be a Sharer in their Wealth, is by a charitable diſpenſing. The Poor are its Proxies as well as God's, and tho' in all other Reſpects we may ſay to the Soul, as the Pſalmiſt does to God, *My Goods extend not to thee:* Yet, by this way, it becomes not only a Partaker, but the chief Proprietor, and all is laid out for its Uſe. The harbouring an Out-caſt, builds it *an everlaſting Habitation.* The Cloathing the Naked, arrays in *pure white Linen*; and the Feeding the Hungry, makes it a Gueſt at the *Supper of the Lamb.* Nay, it gains not only an indefeaſible Title to theſe happy Reverſions, but it has a great deal in preſent Poſſeſſion, a huge rational Complacence in the right applying of Wealth, and doing that with it for which it was deſigned. Yet more, it gives a ſenſitive Delight, nothing being more agreeable to human Nature, than doing Good to its own Kind.

Kind. A feafonable Alms leaves a greater Exultation and Tranfport in the Giver, than it can ordinarily raife in the Receiver; fo exemplifying the Maxim of our Bleffed Lord, that it is *a more bleffed thing, than to receive,* Acts xx 35. This, indeed, is a way to elude the fevere Denunciation of the Apoftle. 1 *Tim.* v. 6. *A Widow that liveth in this Pleafure, is* not *dead whilft fhe liveth*, but on the contrary, fhall live when fhe dies, when fhe refigns her Breath, fhall improve her Being; the Prayers of the Poor, like a Benign Gale, fhall affift her Flight to the Region of Blifs; and fhe who has here cherifh'd the afflicted Members, fhall there be indiffolubly united to their glorious Head.

And now, methinks, Widowhood, under this Afpect, is quite transform'd, is not fo forlorn, fo defolate an Eftate as 'tis ufually efteem'd: And would all Widows ufe but this Expedient, thus devote themfelves to Piety and Charity, it would, like the healing Tree, *Exod.* xv. 25. fweeten thefe Waters of *Marah*, render the Condition, not only fupportable, but pleafant; and they would not need to make fuch affrighted, fuch difadvantageous Efcapes as many do, from it. 'Tis true, the Apoftles Affirmation is unqueftionable, that *the Wife, when her Hufband is dead, is at Liberty to be married to whom fhe will*, 1 *Cor.* vii. 39. But the Advice he fubjoins is authentic too, *fhe is happier if fhe fo abide.* She that may folace herfelf in the Society, in the Love of her God, makes an ignoble defcent to human Embraces; fhe that may purchafe Heaven with her Wealth, buys a very dear Bargain of the beft Hufband on Earth; nay, indeed, upon a meer fecular Account, it feems not very prudent to relinquifh both Liberty and Property, to efpoufe, at the beft, a Subjection, but, perhaps,

a Slaa Slavery: It a little refembles the mad Frolicks of freed Gally-Slaves, who play away their Liberty as foon as they regain it.

Marriage is fo gıeat an Adventure, once feems enough for the whole Life; for whether they have been profperous or adverfe in the fiıft, it does almoft difcourage a fecond Attempt. She that has had a good Hufband, may be fuppofed to have his Idea fo fix'd in her Heart, that it will be hard to introduce any new Form: Nay, farther, fhe may very reafonably doubt, that in this common Dearth of Virtue, two good Hufbands will fcarce fall to one Woman's Share, and one will become more intolerable to her, by the Reflections fhe will be apt to make on the Better. On the other Side, ıf fhe have had a bad, the Smart, fure, cannot but remain after the Rod is taken off; the Memory of what fhe has fuffered fhould, one would think, be a competent Caution againft new Adventures; yet, Experience fhews us, that Women, tho' the weaker Sex, have commonly Fortitude enough to encounter and baffle all thefe Confiderations. It ıs not, therefore, to be expected that many will, by any thing that hath or can be faid, be diverted from remarrying: And, ındeed, fhe that does not preferve her Widowhood upon the Accounts afore-mentıoned, may, peıhaps, better ıelinquifh it. St. *Paul*, we fee, advıfes, that thofe Wıdows who found no better Employment *than going from Houfe to Houfe*, that gıew, by their Vacancy, to *be Tatlers and Bufy-bodıes,* 1 *Tım.* v. 13. fhould maıı y again, ıt being the beft way to fix thefe wandeıing Planets, to find them Bufinefs of their own at Home, that fo they may not ramble Abroad to intermeddle with that of otheıs: And the Tıuth ıs, they that cannot brook the Retırednefs and
Gravity,

Gravity, which becomes a Widow, had better put themfelves in a State that lefs requires it, and if they refolve not
to conform their Minds to their Condition, to bring their
Condition to their Minds: But in the doing that, there will
be fome Cautions very neceffary to be obferved. We fhall
reduce them to two, the one relating to the Time, the
other to the Equality of the Match.

First in refpect of Time, common Decency requires
that there be a confiderable Interval between the parting
with one Husband and the choofing another This has
been fo much obferved by Nations, that were at all civiliz'd,
that we find *Numa* made it a Law, that no Widow fhould
marry under 10 Months, and if any did, fhe was to facrifice as for the Expiation of a Crime: And this continued
in force many Ages after, infomuch, that when upon Reafons of State *Auguftus* found it ufeful to marry his Sifter
Octavia to *Antonius*, nothing lefs than a Decree of the
Senate could licence the anticipating the Time; fo jealous
Obfervers were they of this Point of Civility, that they
thought the whole State was concerned in the Violation.
It is true we have no Law in the Cafe, but we have fomewhat of Cuftom, tho' it is uncertain how long it may laft,
fince the frequent Breaches of it threaten quite to cancel it:
Yet, a Woman that is tender of her Honour will fcarce
give her Example towards the refcinding it. The Wounds
of Grief are feldom healed by any Hand but that of Time,
and, therefore, too fudden a Cure fhews the Hurt pierced
not deep; and fhe that can make her Mourning Veil an
Optic to draw a new Lover nearer to her Sight, gives Caufe
to fufpect the Sables were all without.

The

The next Thing confiderable, is, the Equality of the Match   Marriage is fo clofe a Link, that to have it eafy it is good to have the Parties as even propoitioned as may be. And, Firft, In refpect of Quality and Fortune, it is to be wifhed there fhould be no eminent Difproportion.   Thofe that meet moft upon a Level, are leaft fubject to thofe Up-braidings that often attend a great Defcent of either Party. It is, therefore, no prudent Motive, by which fome Widows are fway'd who marry only for a great Title, who often do not meet with fo much of Obeifance from Strangers, as they do with Contempt from their Husband and his Relations.   There have been Examples of Lords, who have ufed rich, but inferior Widows like Spunges, fqueez'd them to fill themfelves with their Wealth, and them only with the Air of a big Name.   On the other Side, for a Woman to marry very meanly too mnch below herfelf, is rather worfe, thofe kind of Matches are ordinarily made in a tranfport of Paffion, and when that abates and leaves her to fober Reflections, fhe will probably be fo angry with herfelf, that fhe will fcarce be well pleafed with her Husband.   A State of Subjection is a little fweetned by the Worth and Dignity of the Ruler; for as it is more honourable, fo 'tis alfo more eafy, the ferviler Spirits being, of all others, the moft imperious in Command: And, fure, 'twill not a little grate a Woman of Honour, to think fhe has made fuch a one her Mafter, who, perhaps, would before have thought it a Preferment to have been her Servant: Nay, farther, fuch Marriages have commonly an ill Reflection on the Modefty of the Woman, it being ufually prefum'd that where the Diftance was fo great, as to difcourage fuch an Attempt on his Part, there was fome Invitation

vitation on her's· So that upon all Accounts she is very
forlorn who thus difpofes of herfelf. Yet it is too well
known fuch Matches have oft been made, and the fame
Levity and Inconfideration may betray others to it, and,
therefore, it is their Concern well to ballaft their Minds,
and to provide that their Paffion never get the Afcendant
over their Reafon.

Another very neceffary Equality is, that of their Judge-
ment as to Religion. We do not mean that they are to
catechize each other, as to every minute fpeculative Point;
but that they be of the fame Profeffion, fo as to join together in the Worfhip of God. It is fure very uncomfortable
that thofe who have fo clofely conbined all their other Interefts, fhould be difunited in the greateft, that one Church
cannot hold them, whom one Houfe, one Bed does; and
that Religion which is in itfelf the moft uniting thing,
fhould be the only Difagreement between them. It is very
true, it is often made a Compact in fuch Matches, that
neither fhall impofe their Opinion upon the other: Yet, it
is to be doubted, that this is but feldom kept, unlefs it be
by thofe whofe Carelefsnefs of all Religion abates their
Zeal to any one: But where they have any Earneftnefs in
their Way, efpecially where one Party thinks the other in
a damnable Error, it will fcarce be poffible to refrain endeavouring to reduce them, and that Endeavour begets
Difputes, thofe Difputes Heats, thofe Heats Difgufts, and
thofe Difgufts, perhaps, end in Averfion; fo that at laft
their Affections grow as unreconcileable as their Opinions,
and their religious Jars draw on domeftic. Befides, if
none of thefe perfonal Debates happen, yet the Education
of the Children will be Matter of Difpute, the one Parent

rent will ftill be countermining the other, each feeking to recover the other's Profelytes: Nay, it introduces Faction into the inferior Parts of the Family too: The Servants, according to their different Perfuafions, bandy into Leagues and Parties, fo that it endangers, if not utterly deftroys all Concord in Families, and all this Train of Mifchiefs fhould, methinks, be a competent Prejudice againft fuch Matches.

There is yet a third Particular wherein any great Difproportion is much to be avoided, and that is in Years. The Humours of Youth and Age differ fo widely, that there had need be a great deal of Skill to compofe the Difcord into a Harmony. When a young Woman marries an old Man, there are commonly Jealoufies on the one Part, and Loathings on the other, and if there be not an eminent Degree of Difcretion in one or both, there will be perpetual Difagreements. But this is a Cafe that does not often happen among thofe we now fpeak to; for tho' the Avarice of Parents fometimes forces Maids upon fuch Matches, yet, Widows, who are their own Choofers, feldom make fuch Elections. The Inequality among them commonly falls on the other Side, and old Women marry young Men. Indeed, any Marriage is in fuch, a Folly and Dotage. They who muft fuddenly make their Beds in the Duft, what fhould they think of a Nuptial Couch? And to fuch the Anfwer of the Philofopher is appofite, who being demanded what was the fitteft Time for marrying; replied, *For the Young not yet, for the Old not at all.*

But this Dotage becomes perfect Frenzy and Madnefs when they choofe young Husbands: This is an Accumulation of Abfurdities and Contradictions. The Husband and

and the Wife are but one Perfon; and yet at once young and old, frefh and withered. It is reverfing the Decrees of Nature: And, therefore, it was no ill Anfwer which *Dionyfius* the Tyrant gave his Mother, who in her Age defigned fuch a Match, *That tho' by his regal Power he could difpenfe with pofitive Laws, yet, he could not abrogate thofe of Nature, or make it fit for her, an old Woman, to marry a young Man.* It is, indeed, an Inverfion of Seafons, a confounding the Kalendar, making a mongrel Month of *May* in *December* And the Conjunction proves as fatal as it is prodigious, it being fcarce ever feen that fuch a Match proves tolerably happy: And, indeed, it is not imaginable how it fhould; for, firft, it is to be prefumed, that fhe who marries fo muft marry meanly. No young Man who does not need her Fortune will take her Perfon. For tho' fome have the Humour to give great Rates for inanimate Antiquities, yet, none will take the Living gratis. Next, fhe never miffes to be hated by him fhe marries: He looks on her as his Rack and Torment, thinks himfelf under the lingering Torture devifed by *Mezentius*, a living Body tied to a Dead. Nor muft fhe think to cure this by any the little Adulteries of Art: She may buy Beauty, and, yet, can never make it her own; may paint, yet, never be fair. 'Tis like enameling a mud Wall, the Coarfenefs of the Ground will fpoil the Varnifh; and the greateft Exquifitnefs of Drefs, ferves but to illuftrate her native Blemifhes. So that all fhe gains by this, is, to make him fcorn as well as abhor her.

Indeed, there is nothing can be more ridiculous, than an old Woman gaily fet out, and it was not unaptly faid of *Diogenes* to fuch a one, *If this Decking be for the Living,*

you

you are deceived; if for the Dead, make Haste to them ·
And, without Doubt, many young Husbands will be ready
to say as much : Nay, because Death comes not quick
enough to part them, there are few have Patience to attend
its loitering Pace: The Man bids adieu to the Wife tho'
not to her Fortune, takes that to maintain his Luxuries
elsewhere, allows her some little Annuity, and makes her
a Pensioner to her own Estate : So that he has his Design,
but she none of her's: He married her Fortune, and he
has it ; she for his Person, and has it not: And which is
worse, buys her Defeat with the Loss of all, he commonly leaving her as empty of Money as he found her of Wit.

And truly this is a Condition deplorable enough, and,
yet, usually fails, even, of that Comfort which is the last
Reserve of the Miserable, *viz* Pity.   It is the wise Man's
Question, *Eccluf* xii. 13. *Who will pity a Charmer that is
bitten with a Serpent?* He might have presumed less on
his Skill, and kept himself at a safer Distance : And, sure,
the like may be said of her. Alass! what are her feeble
Charms, that she should expect by them to fix the giddy
Appetites of Youth? and since she could so presume without Sense, none will regret that she should be convinced by
Smart · Besides, this is a Case wherein there have been a
Multitude of unhappy Precedents which might have cau-
tioned her.   He that accidentally falls down an undiscover-
ed Precipice is compassionated for his Disaster, but he that
stands a great while on the Brink of it, looks down and sees
the Bottom strewed with the mangled Carcasses of many
that have thence fallen, if he shall deliberately cast himself
into their Company, the Blame quite extinguishes the
· Pity, he may astonish, but not melt the Beholders: And,
truly,

truly, fhe who cafts herfelf away in fuch a Match, betrays
not lefs, but more Wilfulnefs. How many Ruins of unhappy Women prefent themfelves to her, like the Wrecks
of old Veffels, all fplit upon this Rock? And if fhe will
needs fteer her Courfe purpofely to do the fame, none
ought to grudge her the Shipwreck fhe fo courts.

Nor has fhe only this negative Difcomfort to be depriv'd
of Pity, but fhe is loaded with Cenfures and Reproach.
The World is apt enough to malicious Errors, to fix Blame
where there is none, but 'tis feldom guilty of the Chari-
tative, does not overlook the fmalleft Appearance of
Evil, but generally puts the worft Conftruction on any
Act that it will, with any Probability, bear, and according
to that Meafure Women in this Condition can expect no
very mild Defcants on them. Indeed, fuch Matches are
fo deftitute of any rational Plea, that 'tis hard to derive
them from any other Motive than the Senfitive. What
the common Conjectures are in that Cafe, is as needlefs as
it is unhandfome to declare: We will not fay how true they
are, but if they be, it adds another Reafon to the former,
why fuch Marriages are fo improfperous. All Diftortions
in Nature are ufually ominous; and, fure, fuch preternatural Heats in Age, may very well be reckon'd as difmal
Prefages, and very certain ones too, fince they create the
Ruin they foretel. And truly, 'tis not only juft, but convenient, that fuch Motives fhould be attended with fuch
Confequences; that the Bitternefs of the one may occafion
fome Reflection on the Sordidnefs of the other. It is but
kindly, that fuch an Alhallontide Spring fhould meet with
Frofts, and the Unpleafantnefs of the Event chaftife the
Uglinefs of the Defign; and, therefore, we think thofe

X 2   who

who are confcious of the one, fhould be very thankful for the other, think it God's Difcipline to bring them again to their Wits, and not repine at that Smart which themfelves have made neceffary.

And now we wifh all the ancienter Widows, would ferioufly weigh how much it is their Intereft not to fever thofe two Epithets, that of Ancient they cannot put off, it daily grows upon them; and that of Widow is, fure, a more proportionaable Adjunct to it, than that of Wife; efpecially when it is to one to whom her Age might have made her Mother. There is a Veneration due to Age, if it be fuch as difowns not itfelf: *The hoary Head,* fays *Solomon, is a Crown of Glory, if it be found in the Way of Righteoufnefs, Prov.* xvi 31. but when it will mix itfelf with Youth, it is difclaimed by both, becomes the Shame of the Old, and the Scorn of the Young. What a ftrange Fury is it then which poffeffes fuch Women, that when they may difpofe their Fortunes to thofe advantageous Defigns before-mentioned, they fhould only buy with them, fo indecent, fo ridiculous a Slavery? that when they may keep up the Reputation of Modefty and Prudence, they fhould expofe themfelves to an univerfal Contempt for the want of both; and that they who might have had a Reverence, put themfelves, even, out of the Capacity of bare Compaffion.

This is fo high a Frenzy, as, fure, cannot happen in an Inftant; it muft have fome preparatory Degrees, fome rooting in the Conftitution and Habit of the Mind. Such Widows have, fure, fome lightnefs of Humour, before they can be fo giddy in their Brains, and, therefore, thofe that will fecure themfelves from the Effect, muft fubftract

the

the Caufe ; if they will ftill be wifhing themfelves young, 'tis Odds, but within a while they will perfuade themfelves they are fo. Let them, therefore, content themfelves to be old, and as Fafhions are varied with Times, fo let them put on the Ornaments proper to their Seafon, which are, Piety, Gravity, and Prudence. Thefe will not only be their Ornament, but their Armour too, this will gain them fuch a Reverence, that will make it as improbable they fhould be affaulted, as impoffible they fhould affault. For, we think, one may fafely fay, It is the want of one, or all of thofe, which betrays Women to fuch Marriages.

And, indeed, it may be a Matter of Caution, even to the younger Widows, not to let themfelves too much loofe to a light frolick Humour, which, perhaps, they will not be able to put off when it is moft neceffary they fhould. It will not much invite a fober Man to marry them while they are young ; and if it continue with them 'till they are old, it may, as natural Motions ufe, grow more violent towards its End : And precipitate them into that ruinous Folly we have before confidered. Yet, fhould they happen to efcape that, fhould it not force them from their Widowhood, it will, fure, very ill agree with it ; for how prepofterous is it for an old Woman to delight in Gauds and Trifles, fuch as were fitter to entertain her Grand-Children ? to read Romances with Spectacles, and be at Mafks and Dancings, when fhe is fit only to act the Antics ? Thefe are Contradictions to Nature, the tearing off her Marks, and where fhe has writ fifty or fixty, to leffen, beyond the Proportion of the unjuft Steward, and write fixteen : And thofe who thus manage their Widowhood, have more Rea-

fon

son to bewail it at last than at first, as having more experimentally found the Mischief of being left to their own
Guidance It will, therefore, concern them all to put
themselves under a safer Conduct, by an assiduous Devotion
to render themselves up to the leading of the one infallible
Guide, who, if he be not *a Covering of the Eyes,* Gen.
xx. 16. to preclude all second Choices, may, yet, be *a
Light to them* for discerning who are fit to be chosen ; that
if they see fit to use their Liberty and marry, they may,
yet, take the Apostle's Restriction with it, 1 *Cor.* vii. 39.
that *it be only in the Lord* , upon such sober Motives, and
with such due Circumstances as may approve it to him,
and render it capable of his Benediction.

We have now gone thro' the several Parts of the Method proposed The First has presented those Qualifications which are equally necessary to every Woman.   These
as a Root, send Sap and Vigour to the distinct Branches,
animate and impregnate the several successive States thro'
which she is to pass.   He that hath pure Ore or Bullion,
may cast it into what Form best fits his Use ; nay, may
translate it from one to another ; and she who has that
Mine of Virtues, may furnish out any Condition ; her being good in an absolute Consideration, will certainly make
her so in a Relative.   On the other Side, she who has not
such a Stock, cannot keep up the Honour of any State ;
like corrupted Liquor, empty it from one Vessel to another,
it still infects and contaminates all.   And this is the Cause
that Women are alike complained of under all Forms, because so many want this fundamental Virtue : Were there
more

more good Women, there would be more modeſt Virgins, loyal and obedient Wives, and ſober Widows.

We muſt, therefore, intreat thoſe who will look on this Book, not only to ſingle out that Part which bears their own Inſcription, but that they think themſelves no leſs concerned in that which relates indefinitely to their Sex; endeavour to poſſeſs themſelves of thoſe Excellencies, which ſhould be as univerſal as their Kind : And when they are ſo ſtor'd with Matter, they may leave Providence to diverſify the Shape, and to aſſign them their Scene of Action.

And now, would to God it were as eaſy to perſuade, as it is to propoſe, and that this Diſcourſe may not be taken only as a Gazette for its Newneſs, and diſcarded as ſoon as read ; but that it may at leaſt advance to the Honour of an Almanack, be allowed one Year ere it be out of Date, and in that Time, if frequently and ſeriouſly conſulted, it may, perhaps awaken ſome Ladies from their ſtupid Dreams, convince them, that they were ſent into the World for nobler Purpoſes, than only to make a little glittering in it, like a Comet, to give a Blaze, and then diſappear : And, truly, if it may operate but ſo far as to give them an effective Senſe of that, we ſhall think it has done them a conſiderable Service. They may, for certain, from that Principle, deduce all neceſſary Conſequences, and we wiſh they would but take the Pains to draw the Corollaries, for thoſe Inductions they make to themſelves, would be much more efficacious than thoſe which are drawn to their Hands. Propriety is a great Endearment: We love to be Proſelytes to ourſelves; and People oft reſiſt others Reaſons, who would, upon mere Partiality, pay Reverence to their own.

But

But besides this, there would be another Advantage, if they could be but got to a Custom of considering, by it they might insensibly undermine the grand Instrument of their Ruin. That careless Incogitancy, so remarkably frequent among all, and not least among Persons of Quality, is the Source of innumerable Mischiefs; 'tis the *Delilah*, that at once lulls and betrays them; it keeps them in a perpetual Sleep, binds up their Faculties, so that, tho' they are not extinct, yet they become useless. *Plato* used to say, *That a Man asleep was good for nothing*; and 'tis certainly no less true of this Moral Drowsiness than the Natural: And as in Sleep the Fancy only is in motion, so these inconsiderate Persons do rather dream than discourse, entertain little trifling Images of Things which are presented by their Senses, but know not how to converse with their Reason. So that in this drowsy State, all Temptations come on them with the same Advantage, with that of a *Thief in the Night*; a Phrase by which the Scripture expresses the most inevitable unforeseen Danger, 1 *Thess.* v. 2. We read in *Judges*, how easily *Laish* became a Prey to a handful of Men, merely because of this supine negligent Humour of the Inhabitants, which had cut them off from all Intercourse with any whom might have succour'd them: And certainly it gives no less Opportunity to our spiritual Assailants, leaves us naked and unguarded to receive all their Impressions. How prodigious a thing is it then, that this State of Dulness and Danger should be effectedly chosen? yet we see it too often is, even by those whose Qualities and Education fit them for more ingenious Elections, nay, which is yet more Riddle, that very Aptness disenables, and sets them above what it prepares them for.

for. Labour is looked on as utterly incompatible with Greatnefs, and Confideration is look'd on as Labour of the Mind, and there are fome Ladies who feem to reckon it as a Prerogative to be exempted from both; will no more apply their Underftandings to any ferious Difcufion, than their Hands to the Spindle and Diftaff, the one they think pedantick, as the other is mean. In the mean time, by what ftrange Meafures do they proceed? they look on Ideots as the moft deplorable of Creatures, becaufe they want Reafon; and, yet, make it their own Excellence and Preheminence to want the Ufe of it; which is, indeed, fo much worfe than to want the thing, as Sloth is worfe than Poverty, a moral Defect than a natural: But we may fee by this, how much civil and facred Eftimates differ; for we find the *Bereans* commended, not only as more diligent, but as more noble too, *Acts* xvii. 11. becaufe they attentively *confidered* and ftrictly examin'd the *Doctrine preach'd to them:* By which they may difcern, that in God's Court of Honour, a ftupid Ofcitancy is no ennobling Quality, however it comes to be thought fo in theirs.

And if this one Point might be gain'd, if they would but fo far actuate their Reafon, as deliberately and duly to weigh their Intereft, they would find that fo ftrictly engaging them to all that is virtuous, that they muft have a very invincible Refolution for Ruin if that cannot perfuade them: And, we hope, all Women are not *Medeas*, whom the Poet brings in avowing the Horridnefs of that Fact, which, yet, fhe refolv'd to execute. They are generally rather timorous and apt to ftart at the Apprehenfion of Danger; let them but fee a Serpent, tho' at a great Diftance, they will need no Homilies or Lectures to be per-

N° 8   Y   fuaded

suaded to fly it: And, sure, did they but clearly discern what a Sting there is in those vicious Follies they embrace, their Fear would make them quit their Hold, put them in such a trembling, as would, like that of *Belshazzar*'s, flacken their Joints, and make those things drop from them, which before they most tenaciously grasped. For, indeed, in Sin there is a Conspiration of all that can be dreadful to a rational Being, so that one may give its Compendium by the very Reverse of that which the Apostle gives of Godliness, 1 *Tim.* iv. 8. for as the one *has the Promises,* so the other has the Curses *of this Life, and of that to come.*

In this Life, every depraved Act, much more Habit, has a black Shadow attending it: It casts one inwards upon the Conscience in uncomfortable Upbraidings and Regrets. It is true, indeed, some have the Art to disguise that to themselves by casting a yet darker over it, suppressing all those Reluctings by an industrious Stupefaction, making their Souls so perfect Night, that they cannot see those black Images their Consciences represent: But as this renders their Condition but the more wretched, so neither can they blind others tho' they do themselves. Vice casts a dark Shadow outwards too, not such as may conceal, but betray itself: And as the Evening Shadows increase in Dimension, grow to a Monstrosity and Disproportion, so the longer any ill Habit is continued, the more visible, the more deform'd it appears, draws more Observation and more Censure.

'Twere, indeed, endless to reckon up the temporal Evils to which it exposes its Votaries. Immodesty destroys their Fame, a vain Prodigality their Fortune, Anger makes
them

them mad, Pride hateful, Levity renders them despis'd, Obstinacy desperate, and Irreligion is a Complication of all these, fills up their Measure both of Guilt and Wretchedness. So that had Virtue no other Advocate, her very Antagonist would plead for her; the miserable Consequences of Vice, would, like the Flames of *Sodom*, send all considering Persons to that little Zoar, which how despicable soever it may have appeared before, cannot but look invitingly when Safety is inscrib'd on its Gates.

But it must infinitely more do so if they please to open a Visto into the other World, make use of divine Perspectives to discern those distant Objects which their grosser Senses do here intercept. There they may see the dismal Catastrophe of their Comedies, the miserable Inversion of all unlawful or unbounded Pleasures: There that prophetic Menace concerning *Babylon*, which we find *Rev.* xviii. 7. will be literally verified upon every unhappy Soul, *according as she exalted herself and lived delicately, so much the more Tribulation give her :* The Torment of that Life will bear Proportion to the Pride and Luxuries of this. It will, therefore, be necessary for those who here wallow in Pleasures, to confront to them the Remembrance of those Rivers of Brimstone, and ask themselves the Prophet's Question, *Who can dwell with everlasting Burnings ?* We find *Isaiah*, when he denounces but temporal Judgments against the Daughters of *Zion*, exactly pursues the Antithesis, and to every Part of their effeminate Delicacy he opposes the direct contrary Hardship, instead of *sweet Smells there shall be a Stink ; instead of a Girdle a Rent ; instead of a well set Hair Baldness, instead of a Stomacher a Girding with Sackcloth, and Burning instead of Beauty.* Isaiah iii. 24.

It

It were well the Daughters of our *Zion* would copy out this Lecture, and prudently foresee how every particular Sin or Vanity of theirs will have its adapted Punishment in another World: And, sure, this Consideration well digested, must needs be a forcible Expedient to cleanse them from all *Filthiness of Flesh and Spirit*, as the Apostle speaks 2 *Cor.* vii 1. For is it possible for her to cherish and blow up her libidinous Flames here, who considers them but as the first Kindlings of those inextinguishable ones hereafter? Can she make it her Study to please her Appetite, that remembers that *Dives*'s unintermitted Feasts ends in as unallayable a Thirst? Or can she deny the Crumbs of her Table to that *Lazarus*, to whom she foresees she shall then supplicate for a Drop of Water? In fine, can she lay out her whole Industry, her Fortune, nay, her Ingenuity too, in making Provision for the Flesh, who considers, that that Flesh will more corrupt by pampering, and breed the Worm that never dies? Certainly no Woman can be so desperately daring, as thus to attack Damnation, resist her Reason and her Sense, only that she may ruin her Soul; and unless she can do all this, her Foresight will prove her Escape, and her viewing the bottomless Pit in Landskip and Picture, will secure her from a real Descent into it.

But now that this Tract may not make its Exit in the Shape of a Fury, bring the Meditations to Hell and there leave them, it must now at last shift the Scene, and as it has shew'd the Blackness of Vice by that outer Darkness to which it leads, we also will let in a Beam of the celestial Light to discover the Beauty of Virtue; remind the Reader that there is a Region of Joy as well as a Place of Torment, and Piety and Virtue is that milky Way that leads

to

to it, a State, compared to which the Elyſium of the Heathen is as inconſiderable as it is fictitious, the Mahometan Paradiſe as flat and as inſipid as it is groſs and brutiſh; where the Undertaking of the Pſalmiſt ſhall be completely anſwered, *thoſe that fear the Lord ſhall want no Manner of thing that is good*, Pſalm. xxxiv. 10. And this happy State is as acceſſible as excellent. God is not unſincere in his Propoſals, offers not theſe Glories only to tantalize and abuſe us, but to animate and encourage Mankind. He ſets up an inviting Prize, and not only marks out, but levels the Way to it, makes that our Duty which is alſo our Pleaſure, yea, and our Honour too. So has he contrived for our Eaſe, that knowing how hardly we can diveſt our Voluptuouſneſs and Ambition, he puts us not to it: All he demands is but that he may chooſe the Objects, and in that he is yet more obliging, for by that at once he refines and ſatisfies the Deſires: He takes us off, indeed, from the fulſome Pleaſures of Senſe, which, by their Groſſneſs, may cloy, yet, by Reaſon of their Emptineſs, can never fill us, and brings us to taſte the more pure ſpiritual Delights which are the true Elixir of Pleaſures, in Compariſon whereof all the Senſual are but as Dregs or Fæces in an Extraction, after the Spirits are drawn off. In like Manner he calls us from an aſpiring to thoſe Pinnacles of Honour, where we always ſit tottering and often fall down, but, yet, invites us to ſoar higher, where we ſhall have the *Moon* with all her Viciſſitudes and Changes *under our Feet. Rev.* xii. 1. and enjoy a Grandeur as irreverſible as ſplendid.

Thus does he ſhew us a Way to hallow our moſt unſanctified Affections, thus, according to the Prophecy of *Zechariah, May Holineſs be writ, even, upon the Bells of the Horſes.*

Horses, Zec. xiv. 20. upon our moſt brutal Inclinations, and thus may all thoſe Feminine Paſſions which now ſeduce Women from Virtue, advance them in it   Let her that is amorous, place her Love upon him who is (as the Spouſe tells us, *Cant.* v 10) *the chiefeſt among ten thouſand*, ſhe that is angry, turn her Edge againſt her Sins; ſhe that is haughty, diſdain the Devil's Drudgery, ſhe that is fearful, dread him who *can deſtroy both Body and Soul in Hell, Matt.* v. 29 and ſhe that is ſad, reſerve her Tears for her penitential Offices.   Thus may they conſecrate even their Infirmities; and tho' they cannot deify, or erect Temples to them, as the *Romans* did to their Paſſions, nay, their Diſeaſes; yet, after they are thus cleanſed, they may ſacrifice them as the *Jews* did the clean Beaſts in the Tabernacle.   Only Irreligion and Profaneneſs is exempt from this Privilege, no Water of Purification can cleanſe it, or make it ſerviceable in the Temple, that like the Spoils of *Jericho*, is ſo execrable, that it muſt be devoted to Deſtruction, as *an accurſed thing, Joſ* vi. 17. For tho' God does not deſpiſe the Work of his own Hands, hath ſo much Kindneſs to his Creatures, that he endeavours to reduce all our native Inclinations to their primitive Rectitude, and, therefore, does not aboliſh, but purify them; yet, Atheiſm is none of thoſe, it is a Counterblaſt from Hell, in Oppoſition to that mighty Wind in which the holy Spirit deſcended.   Tho' the Subject in which it ſubſiſts may be reformed, the Perſon may turn Chriſtian, and the Wit that maintained its blaſphemous Paradoxes may be converted to holier Uſes, yet the Quality itſelf is capable of no ſuch happy Metamorphoſis, that muſt be extirpated, for it cannot be made tributary: Which ſhews how tranſcendent an

Ill

Ill that is which cannot be converted to Good, even that Omnipotence which can, out of the very Stones, raife Children to *Abraham*, attempts not any Tranfmutation of this, which ought, therefore, to poffefs all Hearts with a Deteftation of it, and advance them in an earneft Purfuit of all the Parts of Piety.

And that is it which we would now once more, as a farewel Exhortation, commend to our Female Readers, as that which virtually contains all other Accomplifhments; it is that Pearl in the Gofpel for which they may part with all and make a good Bargain too. *The Fear of the Lord is the Beginning of Wifdom*, fays the Wifeft of Men, *Prov.* i 7. and by his Experience he fhews, that it is the completing End of it too, for he no fooner declin'd from that, but he grew to Dotage and Difhonour. Let all thofe, therefore, to whom God has difpenfed an outward Affluence, and given them a vifible Splendour in the Eyes of the World, be careful to fecure themfelves *that Honour which comes from God only*, John v. 44 unite their Souls to that Supreme Majefty who is the Fountain of true Honour; who, in his beftowing the Crown of Righteoufnefs, proceeds by the fame Meafures by which he difpos'd the Crown of *Ifrael*, when he avow'd to *Samuel*, that he *look'd not on the outward Appearance, but beheld the Heart*, 1 Sam. xvi. 7. If God fee not his own Image there, all the Beauty and Gaiety of the outward Form is defpicable in his Eyes, like the Apples of *Sodom*, only a kind of painted Duft: But if Piety be firmly rooted there, they then become, like the King's Daughter, all glorious within too; a much more valuable Bravery than the *Garment of Needle Work and Vefture of Gold*, Pfalm xlv. 14. And this is it that muft

enter

enter them into the King's Palace, into that *new Jerusalem,* where they shall not wear, but inhabit *Pearls* and *Gems, Rev.* xxi. 19. be beautiful without the Help of Art or Nature, by the meer Reflexion of the divine Brightness, be all that their then enlarg'd Comprehensions can wish, and infinitely more than they can here imagine.

Having now said all that we think sufficient for the Instruction of our Fair Readers, for their Religious and Moral Behaviour, we shall proceed, according to Promise, to give them Directions in all Parts of GOOD HOUSEWIFRY, and begin with Rules to be observed in the Art of COOKERY and a Collection of Receipts, which we propose to make the fulleft and moft complete of any ever yet published.

C H A P.

CHAP. XV.

COOKERY.

Of GRAVIES, SOOPS, BROTHS *and* POTTAGES.

To make a strong BROTH *for* Soops *and* Sauces.

TAKE a Leg of Beef, or any other Piece, a pretty good Quantity, and boil it in four Gallons of Water; scum it clean, season it with Salt, some whole Pepper, six or eight Onions, some whole Cloves and Mace, a good Bundle of Thyme and Parsley, some whole *Jamaica* Pepper, and boil it four Hours 'till it has boiled half away, then strain it off, and keep it for Use.

To make a Brown Gravy *for* Soops *and* Sauces

TAKE three or four Pounds of coarse lean Beef, and put it into a Frying-pan with some fat Bits of Bacon at the Bottom, and cut five or six Onions in Slices, and a Carrot cut in Pieces, some Crusts of brown Bread, and a Bundle of Thyme, cover it close and set it over a gentle Fire, and let it fry very brown on both Sides, but not burn, then put into it two or three Quarts of the above strong Broth; season it with Pepper, and let it stew one Hour, and then strain it through a Hair-Sieve; scum off

Z   the

the Fat, and keep it for Ufe: And if you make for Soops, you make a bigger Quantity.

Giavy *for Brown* Sauces.

TAKE fome Neck of Beef cut in thick Slices, then flour it well, and put it in a Sauce-Pan with a Slice of fat Bacon, an Onion fliced, fome Powder of Sweet Marjoram, fome Pepper and Salt, cover it clofe and put it over a flow Fire, and ftir it three or four Times, and when the Gravy is brown put fome Water to it, and ftir altogether, and let it boil about half an Hour, then ftrain it off and take the Fat off the Top, adding a little Lemon-juice.

Gravy *for White* Sauces.

TAKE Part of a Knuckle of Veal, or the worft Part of a Neck of Veal, boil about a Pound of this in a Quart of Water, an Onion, fome whole Pepper, fix Cloves, a little Salt, a Bunch of Sweet Herbs, half a Nutmeg fliced, let it boil an Hour, then ftrain it off and keep it for Ufe.

A cheap Giavy.

TAKE a Glafs of Small Beer, a Glafs of Water, an Onion cut fmall, fome Pepper and Salt, a little Lemon-Peel grated, a Clove or two, a Spoonful of Mufhroom Liquor, or pickled Walnut Liquor; put this in a Bafon, then take a Piece of Butter, and put it in a Saucepan, then put it on the Fire and let it melt; then druge in fome Flour, and ftir it well 'till the Froth finks and it will be brown, put in fome fliced Onion, then put your Mixture to the Brown Butter, and give it a Boil up.

A Fifh

A *Fish* Gravy *for* Soop.

TAKE Tench, or Eels, well fcoured from Mud, and fcour their Outfides well with Salt, then having pulled out their Gills, put them into a Kettle with Water, Salt, a Bunch of Sweet Herbs, and an Onion ftuck with Cloves, let all thefe boil an Hour and a half, and then ftrain off the Liquor through a Cloth, add to this the Peelings of Mufhrooms well wafhed, or Mufhrooms themfelves cut fmall; boil thefe together, and ftrain the Liquor through a Sieve into a Stew-pan, upon fome burnt or fryed Flour, and a little Lemon which will foon render it of a good Colour and of a fine Flavour fit for Soops, which may be varied according to the Palate, by putting Pot Herbs and Spices, according to every one's Palate, into this Soop, a little before you ferve it.

A *good* Stock *for* Fifh-Soops.

PREPARE Scate, Flounders, Eels and Whitings, lay them in a broad Gravy-pan, put in a Faggot of Thyme, Parfley, and Onions; feafon them with Pepper, Salt, Cloves and Mace; then pour in as much Water as will cover your Fifh; put in a Head of Sellery, and fome Parfley Roots: Boil it very tender about an Hour, then ftrain it off, for any Ufe, for Fifh or meagre Pottages. This Stock will not keep above a Day; if you would make a brown Stock, you muft pafs your Fifh off in browned Butter, and ftove it, then put in your Liquor and Seafoning.

A Stock

A Stock *for an* Herb Soop.

YOU muſt take Chervil, Beets, Chards, Spinage, Sellery, Leeks, and ſuch like Herbs, with two or three large Cruſts of Bread, ſome Butter, a Bunch of Sweet Herbs, and a little Salt; put theſe with a moderate Quantity of Water into a Kettle, and boil them for an Hour and an half, and ſtrain out the Liquor, through a Sieve, and it will be a good Stock for Soops, either of Aſparagus Buds, Lettuce, or any other Kind, fit for *Lent* or Faſt Days.

Broth *of* Roots.

BOIL about two Quarts of Seed Peaſe; when they are very tender, bruiſe them to a Maſh; put them into a Boiler, that holds a Buſhel of Water, and hang it over the Fire for an Hour and a half, then take it off, and let it ſettle. Take next a middle-ſiz'd Kettle, and ſtrain into it, thro' a Sieve the clear Puree, into which put a Bunch of Carrots, a Bunch of Parſnips, and a Bunch of Parſley Roots; a Dozen Onions: Seaſon it with Salt, a Bunch of Pot Herbs, and an Onion ſtuck with Cloves. Boil all of it together, and put in a Bunch of Sorrel and another of Chervil, and two or three Spoonfuls of Juice of Onions, ſee that the Broth be well taſted, and make Uſe of it to ſimmer all Sorts of Soops made of *Legumes.*

A Green Peaſe Soop *without Meat.*

WHILE you are ſhelling the Peaſe, ſeparate the Young from the Old, and boil the old ones till they are ſo ſoft that you can paſs them through a Colander, then put the Liquor and the pulped Peaſe together into this;

put

put in the young Peafe whole, adding fome Pepper, two or three Blades of Mace and fome Cloves.

When the young Peafe are boiled enough put a Faggot of Thyme and Sweet Marjoram, a little Mint, Spinage, and a green Onion fhred, but not too fmall, with half, or three Quarters of a Pound, or more, of Butter, into a Sauce-pan, and as thefe boil up fhake in fome Flour, to boil with it, to the Quantity of a good Handful, or more; put alfo a Loaf of *French* Bread into the Broth to boil; then mingle the Broth and Herbs, &c. together; feafon it with Salt to your Palate; and garnifh with fome fmall white Toafts neatly cut, and fome of the young Peafe.

A young Green Peafe Soop.

PUT fome young Peafe into a Stew-pan, with a Piece of good frefh Butter, and a Faggot of Sweet Herbs, feafon them with Pepper and Salt, and, after you have toffed them three or four times on the Stove, put fome Veal Gravy to them, and let them boil gently: Then take two round Loaves of *French* Bread, of about a Pound Weight each, cut them in Halves, and take out all the Crumb, if the four Crufts will go into your Difh ufe them all, or as many as it will contain. Put your Crufts into a Stew-pan, with a Pinch of half-beaten Pepper, and a little Salt dafhed over them; then take a Spoonful of good Broth, and ftrain it over your Crufts, let them take a Boil or two, till they be tender, and immediately put them into your Soop-difh, and put them over the Stove, and let them juft ftick to the Difh, but not burn, your Peafe being well tafted, put them upon your Crufts, and ferve them hot.

A dry'd

A dry'd Peafe Soop.

YOU may make this of Beef; but a Leg of Pork is much better, or the Bones of Pork, or of the Shin and Hock of a Leg of Pork Strain the Broth through a Sieve, and to every Quart of Liquor, put half a Pint of fplit Peafe, or to three Quarts of Liquor a Quart of whole Peafe.

The whole Peafe muft be paffed through a Colander; but the fplit Peafe do not need it, put in Sellery accordingly as you like it, cut fmall; dryed Mint and Sweet Marjoram in Powder, feafon alfo with Salt and Pepper, boil all till the Sellery is tender.

If you boil a Leg of Pork, this is to be done when the Meat is taken out of the Pot, but if you make Soop from the Bones boil thefe Ingredients afterwards in the Liquor.

When you ferve it up, lay a *French* Roll in the Middle of the Difh, and garnifh the Border of the Difh with rafped Bread fifted.

Some put in All-Spice powdered, which is agreeable enough: Others ferving it up put in toafted Bread cut into Dice; and others, in the Boiling, add the Leaves of white Beets.

A very good Peafe Soop.

BOIL three or four Pounds of lean coarfe Beef in two Gallons of Water, with three Pints of Peafe, till the Meat is all in Rags, and ftrain it from the Meat and Husks, but, half an Hour before you ftrain it, put in two or three Anchovies Then put into a Sauce-pan as much as you would have for that Meal, with an Onion ftuck with

Cloves,

Cloves, a Race of Ginger bruifed, a Faggot of Thyme, Savoury and Parfley, and a little Pepper; boil it for near half an Hour, then ftir in a Piece of Butter, and having fryed fome Forc'd-Meat-Balls, Bacon, and *French* Bread, cut into Dice, with Spinage boil'd green, put thefe to the Soop in the Difh.

A Peafe Soop *for* Lent *or any Fafting Days.*

BOIL a Quart of good Peafe in fix Quarts of Water, 'till they are very foft, then take out fome of the clear Liquor, and ftrain the Peafe from the Husks, as clean as may be, then boil fome Butter, and when it breaks in the Middle put in an Onion and fome Mint, cut very fmall, Spinage, Soriel, and a little Sellery, cut grofly; let thefe boil for a Quarter of an Hour, ftirring them often, then with one Hand fhake in fome Flour, while, with the other Hand, you pour in the thin Liquor, then put in the ftrained Liquor, fome Pepper, Mace, and Salt, and boil it for an Hour longer; then put a Pint of fweet thick Cream to as much of it as will make a large Difh, laying a *French* Roll crifped and dipped in Milk in the Middle of the Difh.

A good Spring Soop.

GET twelve Cabbage-Lettuces, fix green Cucumbers, pare them and cut out the Cores; then cut them in little Bits, and fcald them in boiling Water, and put them into ftrong Broth, let them boil 'till very tender, with a Handful of Green Peafe, and fome *French* Roll.

A Soop

A Soop de Santé *the French Way.*

PUT over twelve Pounds of Beef feafoned moderately
with Spices, and Salt, boil it 'till your Broth is ftrong,
ftrain it to a good Knuckle of Veal blanched, then boil it
up a fecond Time, putting your Pullet to it that you defign to ferve in the Middle of your Soop; let it boil 'till it
comes to the Strength of a Jelly, put to it, in the Boiling,
a Bit of Bacon that is not rufty, ftuck with fix Cloves:
Your Broth being thus ready, at the fame Time make a
Pan of good Gravy thus: Take a Stew-pan, or brafs Difh,
place in the bottom of it a Quarter of a Pound of Bacon,
cut in Slices clean from Ruft, likewife the Bignefs of half an
Egg of Butter, take five or fix Pounds of a Fillet of Veal,
and cut it in Slices twice as thick as you do for *Scotch* Collops, and place it on your Bacon in your Stew-pan, covering all the Bottom over. If you have no Veal ufe Buttock
of Beef, fet it over a clear Fire not very hot, and let it
colour: When it begins to crack put a little of the Fat of
your boiling Broth to it, ftir it as little as poffible, becaufe
it makes it thick, and throw in three or four fliced Onions,
one Carrot, two Turnips, a little Parfley, a Sprig of
Thyme, a little whole Pepper and Cloves: All thefe Ingredients being fryed together, 'till you think it comes to a
good Colour, if in Summer, a few Mufhrooms will give it
a good Tafte. When it is of a good Colour, add to it
your boiling Broth, from your Knuckle of Veal, leaving
fome to keep your Veal and Pullet white, to foak your
Bread with for the Soop, and other Ufes in the Kitchen.
Your Broth and Gravy being in Readinefs, take fuch Herbs
as the Country where you are will afford, fuch as Sellery,

Endive,

Endive, Sorrel, a little Chervil, or Cabbage-Lettuce, well picked and washed, mince them down with your mincing Knife, and squeeze the Water from them, place them in a little Pot or deep Sauce-pan, put to them so much of your Broth and Gravy as will just cover them, let them boil tender; then take the Crusts of two *French* Rolls and boil them up with three Pints of Gravy, and strain it through a Strainer, or Sieve, and put it to your Herbs, if you have no *French* Bread to thicken it with, take the Bigness of an Egg of Butter, a small Handful of Flour, and brown it over the Fire, and a little minced Onion, if the Eaters be Lovers of it, if not, let the Onion that was in the Gravy serve. Add to your brown some Gravy, and boil it and strain it through a Sieve to your Herbs, instead of *French* Bread; let your Herbs be pretty tender before you put your Thickening in, boil all together half an Hour, and skim off the Fat, place in the Bottom of your Dish, that you intend to serve your Soop in, some *French* Bread, in Slices, or the Crust dryed before the Fire, or in an Oven, boil it up with some of your Broth, so put your Fowl and Herbs on the Top of it: Let your Garnishing be a Rim, on the Outside of it Sellery, or Endive, tender boiled in good Broth, and cut in Pieces about three Inches long; if you cannot spare Herbs, take a Bit of Forced-Meat, and boil'd Carrot, to garnish it; serve it hot, and take Care there is no Fat on it.

A Soop de Santé *the* English *Way.*

YOUR Gravy and Broth being ready, as in the above Receipt, instead of Herbs take Carrots, and Turnips, and cut them in square Slices an Inch long, and the

Bigness

Bigneſs of a Quill, blanch them off in boiling Water, but blanch the Carrots more than the Turnips, and ſtrain them out in a Colander, from the Water, where they are blanched in, then take two Quarts of Gravy, the Cruſt of two *French* Rolls, and boil them as before directed, ſtrain it through a Strainer or Sieve, and put it to the Carrots and Turnips, let them boil gently in it over the Fire, 'till they are tender; your Bread being ſoaked in your Diſh, put in the Middle of it a Knuckle of Veal, or a Pullet, or Chicken. Let your Garniſhing be Carrot, or Turnip, cut in ſmall Dice, and boiled tender, ſkim off the Fat; ſo ſerve it.

Soop *Lorraine.*

HAving very good Broth, made of Veal and Fowl, and ſtrained clean, take a Pound of Almonds, and blanch them, pound them in a Mortar, very fine, putting to them a little Water, to keep them from oiling, as you pound them, and the Yolks of four Eggs tender boiled, and the Lean of the Legs and Breaſt of a roaſted Pullet or two, pound all together very fine, then take three Quarts of very good Veal Broth, and the Cruſt of *French* Rolls cut in Slices, let them boil up together over a clear Fire, then put to it your beaten Almonds; let them juſt boil up together, ſtrain it through a fine Strainer to the Thickneſs of a Cream, as much as will ſerve the Bigneſs of your Diſh; mince the Breaſts of two roaſted Pullets, and put them into a Loaf as big as two *French* Rolls, the Top cut off, and the Crumb cut out, ſeaſon your Haſh with a little Pepper and Salt, a ſcraped Nutmeg, and the Bigneſs of an Egg of Butter, together with five or ſix Spoonfuls of your ſtrained Almonds; let the Bread that you put in the Bottom of

your

your Soop, be *French* Bread dryed before the Fire, or in
an Oven, so soak it with clean Broth, and a little of your
strained Soop, place your Loaf in the Middle, put in
your Hash warm; you may put four Sweetbreads, tender
boiled, about your Loaf if you please. Let your Garnishing be a Rim and sliced Lemon, so serve it up.

A Vermicelli Soop.

TAKE two Quarts of good Broth made of Veal
and Fowl, put to it about half a Quarter of a
Pound of Vermicelli, a Bit of Bacon stuck with Cloves;
take the Bigness of half an Egg of Butter, and rub it
together, with half a Spoonful of Flour, and dissolve it
in a little Broth, to thicken your Soop: Boil a Pullet or
Chickens for the Middle of your Soop. Let your Garnishing be a Rim, on the Outside of it cut Lemon, soak
your Bread in the Dish with some of the same Broth; take
the Fat off and put your Vermicelli in your Dish; so serve
it.

You may make a Rice Soop the same way, only your
Rice being first boiled tender in Water, and it must boil an
Hour in strong Broth, but half an Hour will boil the Ver-
micelli.

Soop au Bourgeois.

HAVING good Broth and Gravy in Readiness,
take four Bunches of Sellery, and ten Heads of Endive, wash them clean, and take off the Outside; cut
them in Pieces an Inch long, and swing them well from
the Water. This Soop may be made brown or white:
If you intend it brown, put the Herbs into two Quarts

of boiling Gravy, having firſt blanched them in boiling
Water five or ſix Minutes; then take the Cruſt of two
French Rolls, boil it up in three Pints of Gravy, ſtrain it
through a Strainer or Sieve, and put it to the Herbs, when
they are almoſt ready; for that is to be minded in all Soops,
that your Thickening is not to be put in till your Herbs are
almoſt tender. You may put in the Middle of your Soop
a Pullet or Chickens. Let your Garniſhing be a Rim,
and on the Outſide ſome of your Sellery cut in Pieces three
Inches long, your Bread being ſoaked in ſome good Broth
or Gravy, and your Herbs boiling hot; ſo ſerve it.

A Savoy Soop.

L E T your Savoys be cut in four Pieces, and three
Parts boiled in fair Water; then ſqueeze them when
cold, with your Hand, clean from the Water; place in a
large Sauce-pan, or little Braſs Diſh, ſuch a Quantity as
your Diſh will hold: There muſt be room betwixt each
Piece of Savoy to take up Soop with a large Spoon. Put
them a boiling with as much Broth or Gravy as will cover
them. Set them a ſtewing over the Fire two Hours before
Dinner, at the ſame time take a Sauce-pan with a Quarter
of a Pound of Butter, put it over the Fire with a Handful
of Flour, keep it ſtirring 'till it is brown; put to it two
minced Onions, and ſtir it a little afterwards, then put to
it a Quart of Veal Gravy, boil it a little, and pour it all
over your Savoys. You force Pigeons betwixt the Skin and
the Body with good Forc'd-Meat, made of Veal, or you
take a Duck or Ducklings, being truſſed up for boiling,
then fry them off, and put them a ſtewing with your Savoys; let a little Bacon, ſtuck with Cloves, be put in with
them

them to ſtew. Let your Garniſhing be a Rim, and on the Outſide of it Slices of Bacon, a little Savoy betwixt each Slice, taking the Fat clean off, ſoak your Bread in your Diſh, with ſome good Broth or Gravy, place your Savoys at a due Diſtance, and your Fowl in the Middle; ſo ſerve it.

A Kervel Maes Pottage.

GET a Knuckle of Veal, chop it all in little Pieces, except the Marrow-bone, ſeaſon the Fleſh with a little Salt, Nutmeg, pounded Biſcuit, and Yolks of Eggs, and make little Force - Meat - Balls of the Bigneſs of a Pigeon's Egg; which being boiled in a Broth-Pot for the Space of a full Hour, then take three or four Handfuls of Chervil picked clean, two or three Leeks, and a good Handful of Beet Leaves, mince them together, and add two or three Spoonfuls of Flour well mixed, with two or three Spoonfuls of Broth, that it may not be lumpy, and do it over the Stove as you would do Milk-Pottage. This Pottage muſt appear green. On *Fiſh* Days cut ſome Eels in Pieces, with which make the Broth, and you may put in a Handful of Sorrel among the other Herbs.

A Sorrel Soop *with Eggs.*

BOIL a Neck of Mutton, and a Knuckle of Veal, skim them clean, and put in a Faggot of Herbs, ſeaſon with Pepper, Salt, Cloves and Mace, and when it is boiled enough ſtrain it off, let it ſettle and skim the Fat off, then take your Sorrel and chop it, but not ſmall; paſs it in brown Butter, put in your Broth, and ſome Slices of *French* Bread, and ſtove in the Middle a Fowl, or a Piece of a Neck of Mutton; then garniſh your Diſh with Slices

of

of fryed Bread, and stewed Sorrel, with six poached Eggs, laid round the Dish, or in the Soop.

Crawfish Soop.

BOIL Crawfish, pick the Shells from the Tails of them, and leave the Bodies, Tails and Legs together, prepare two Dozen thus to garnish your Dish; for which, if it be large you ought to have a hundred Crawfish   Pick the Tails out of the rest from the Shells; put them in a Sauce-pan, then you will find a little Bag at the End next the Claws, which is bitter like Gall, that you must take Care to throw away, likewise any thing that is white and woolly in the Belly; then put the Shells in a Marble or Wooden Mortar, and pound them to a Paste.   While your Shells are thus pounding, put in a large Sauce-pan or Stew-pan, three Quarters of a Pound of Butter, the Crust of two *French* Rolls, three or four Onions sliced, two Dozen Corns of whole Pepper, one Dozen of Cloves, a Sprig of Thyme, and a Handful of Parsley; fry these Ingredients softly over the Fire half a Quarter of an Hour, 'till your Bread is crisp, but take Care you do not burn your Herbs: At the same Time, take Care to prepare your Fish for your Stock, which is to be two Carps, two Eels, and a Thornback, if you cannot have Carp, you must use Whitings or Flounders, in the Place of Carp, with your Eels and Thornback, skin the Carps and Eels, and cut the thick Fish from the Back of your Carp, and save it to make a Forced-Meat of: And, likewise save the Head and Bones of your Carp as you can, in order to be forced in the Middle of your Soop.   Then chop your Eels to Pieces, and skinned Thornback, or what other fresh

Fish

Fiſh you have, to the Quantity of four or five Pounds Weight, and put them to your above-mentioned Ingredients, ſet them a ſtewing over the Fire, and let them ſtew half an Hour together, ſtirring them now and then, that they burn not to the Bottom. When the Rawneſs is fryed off the Fiſh, then pour in four or five Quarts of boiling Water or Broth, and ſeaſon it moderately with Salt; let it boil half an Hour, then ſkim all the Fat off, and take up with a Skimmer, all the Cruſt of Bread that was fryed, from the Fiſh, and two Quarts of your Fiſh Broth, and put to your pounded Crawfiſh, boil it over your Fire with the Fiſh-broth, and ſtrain it thro' a fine Strainer, to the Thick-neſs of a Cream: If your Strainer is not fine, your Soop will prove gritty with the Shells; to prevent that, let it ſtand a little in the Diſh you ſtrain it in, and pour it ſoftly into a Sauce-pan; ſo the Grit will ſtay behind. Put the Remainder of your Shells that is in your Strainer, to your fryed Fiſh, and the Remainder of your Stock, ſtirring it together, ſtrain it into another Sauce-pan, and ſave it to ſoak your Bread with: For it will be thinner, and not of ſo high Colour as the former Your Stock being thus getting in Readineſs, cauſe the Fiſh that you cut off the Back of your Carp, to be minced fine, and add to it, three or four buttered Eggs, the Crumb of a *French* Roll, boiled in Milk or Cream, a boiled Onion, and a little Parſley minced fine, the Bigneſs of an Egg of Butter, a little Pepper and Salt, ſcrape in a Nutmeg, and ſqueeze in half a Lemon: Mince all theſe together to a Paſte, then force the Bodies of your Carps, where you cut your Fiſh off, into the ſame Shape as they were, ſmooth-ing them over with your Hand and a beaten Egg; pour
over

over a little melted Butter, ftrew over it a little Handful
of grated Bread ; then bake it three Quarters of an Hour
before you have Occafion for it, buttering the Bottom of
the Pan, or Mazarine you bake it in. Let your Bread
be cut in thin Slices, and dryed before the Fire, or in an
Oven, and foaked in fome of your thin Stock : Then take
your Carp up from the Fat and place it in the Middle of
your Difh; then put the Tails of your pickled Crawfifh
into your beft Stock, boil it up only over the Fire, before
you fend it away fqueeze in half a Lemon, then pour it
round your baked Carp in your Pottage-Difh. Let your
Garnifhing be a Rim of the fame Forc'd-Meat, or if it is
fcarce, take clean Pafte, and lay on the Outfide of it the
two Dozen of Crawfifh, mentioned in the Beginning of
the Receipt, having firft heated them in a little of your
Stock ; fo ferve it.

A Lobfter Soop.

MAKE a Forced-Meat of Fifh, as in the laft Receipt, only inftead of Carps, you may take Tenches, Pikes, Trouts, or Whitings and Flounders ; or what
other frefh Fifh the Country where you are can afford, to
the Value of four or five Pounds Weight; make your
Stock of it as you are directed in the preceding Receipt :
Keep your Forced-Meat as clean from Bones as poffibly
you can, and make it up in the Bignefs of a double *French*
Roll, being hollow in the Middle, and open on the Top ;
bake it half an Hour before you ufe it, place it in the
Middle of your Soop. At the fame time pound the Spawn
of your Lobfters, (being two or four of them, according
to the Bignefs of your Difh,) and ftrain it with your Cullis,

lis, as you did your Crawfiſh Soop; and take the Meat of your Lobſters, and cut in large Dice, warm it up in a Sauce-pan with a little of the Cullis, a little Pepper and Salt, ſqueeze in a Lemon, and add a little Butter, put in your Forced Loaf in the Middle of your Soop. Your Bread ſoaked and your Cullis hot, ſqueeze in a little Lemon, and diſh it up. Let your Garniſhing be a Rim of Paſte, and on the Outſide of it lay ſome cut Lemon, ſo ſerve it.

A Muſcle Soop.

TAKE a Quantity of Muſcles, make them clean, boil them and pick them out of the Shells; then waſh them again and put them into a Sauce-pan: Take three or four Pounds of freſh Fiſh, and a Cullis, as for the Crawfiſh Soop, and ſtrain it through a Sieve to the Thickneſs of a Cream; put a little of it to your Muſcles; cut off the Top of a *French* Roll, take out the Crumb and fry it in a little Butter; place it in the Middle of your Soop, your Bread being ſoaked with ſome of your Cullis. Let your Garniſhing be a Rim of Paſte; lay the Muſcle-Shells round the Outſide of it; thicken up your Muſcles with the Yolk of an Egg, as you do a Fricaſey, and put one or two in each Shell, round your Soop, likewiſe fill up the Loaf in the Middle; the Cullis being boiling hot, ſqueeze into that, and on the Muſcles, a little Lemon; ſo ſerve it.

You may make a Cockle Soop the ſame Way.

A Scate *or* Thornback Soop.

MAKE your Stock or Cullis as you did for your Crawfiſh Soop, only you have no Shells to put in it for colouring: Your Scate or Thornback being skinned take half a Pound of the beſt of the Fiſh fiom the Bones, cut it to Pieces, and throw it into your Cullis, with ſome other freſh Fiſh, ſuch as the Country affords Your Cullis being ſtrained off ready, as for your Crawfiſh Soop, to the Thickneſs of a Cream, mince the lean Part of the Fiſh you cut from the Bones, and put it over the Fire in a little Sauce-pan with a little Butter, Pepper and Salt, ſtir-iing it 'till the Raw is off of it; then mince it with your Knife on a clean Table the ſecond Time, and put it in your Sauce-pan again: If it is good Fiſh, it will eat as tender as a Chicken haſhed; put a little Lemon to it, and place it in a *French* Roll in the Middle of your Soop; your Cullis being hot, and your Bread ſoaked in the Bottom of your Diſh, ſqueeze in ſome Lemon. Let your Garniſhing be a Rim on the Outſide; ſo ſerve it.

An Oyſter Soop.

YOUR Stock muſt be of Fiſh; then take two Quarts of Oyſters, ſet them and beard them; take the hard Part of the Oyſters from the other, and beat them in a Mortar with ten hard Yolks of Eggs; put in ſome good Stock, ſeaſon it with Pepper, Salt and Nutmeg; then thicken up your Soop as Cream; put in the reſt of your Oyſters, and garniſh with Oyſters.

A good Gravy Soop.

GET a Leg of Beef, and boil it down with ſome Salt, a Bundle of Sweet-Herbs, an Onion, a few Cloves, a Bit of Nutmeg, boil three Gallons of Water to one; then take two or three Pounds of lean Beef cut in thin

Slices;

Slices; then put in your Pan a Piece of Butter, as big as an Egg, and flour it, and let the Stew-pan be hot, and shake it 'till the Butter be brown; then lay your Beef in your Pan over a pretty quick Fire, cover it close, give it a Turn now and then, and strain in your strong Broth, with an Anchovy or two, a Handful of Spinach and Endive boiled green, and drained and shred gross; then have some Pallates ready boiled and cut in Pieces, and toasted and fryed: Take out the fryed Beef, and put all the rest together with a little Pepper, and let it boil a Quarter of an Hour, and serve it up with a Knuckle of Veal, or a Fowl boiled in the Middle.

Another Gravy Soop.

GET a Leg of Beef, and a Piece of the Neck, and boil it 'till you have all the Goodness out of it; then strain it from the Meat; then take half a Pound of fresh Butter, and put it in a Stew-pan and brown it, then put in an Onion stuck with Cloves, some Endive, Sellery and Spinach, and your strong Broth, and season it to your Palate with Salt, Pepper and Spices, and let it boil together; and put in Chips of *French* Bread dried by the Fire; and serve it up with a *French* Roll toasted in the Middle.

An Almond Soop.

YOUR Stock must be Veal and Fowl, then beat a Pound of *Jordan* Almonds very fine in a Mortar, with the Yolks of six hard Eggs, putting in a little cool Broth sometimes; then put in as much Broth as you think will do; strain it off, and put in two small Chickens, and some Slices of *French* Bread; season it gently, so serve away; garnish with Whites of Eggs beat up.

Rice

Rice Soop.

YOUR Stock muſt be of Veal and Fowl; put in half a Pound of Rice, and a Pint of good Gravy, and a Knuckle of Veal, ſtove it tender, ſeaſon with Mace and Salt, then make a Rim round your Diſh, and garniſh with Heaps of Rice, ſome coloured with Saffron, placing one Heap of White, and one of Yellow all round.

An Italian Pottage.

IT is a Sort of Olio, diſhed in ſeparate Compartments, in the Middle of your Diſh, for which Purpoſe make a Croſs of Paſte, then bake it in the Oven; in the firſt Angle make a Biſque; in the Second a Pottage of ſmall Chickens; in the Third a Pottage *à la Reine (en Profitrolle* ;) and in the Fourth a Pottage of forced Partridges. Obſerve, that each Soop is to have its different Broth belonging to it, with different Garniture.

A Soop *of* Forced Green Geeſe.

MAKE a Force-Meat of Gooſe Liver, a Piece of Bacon, a Calf's Udder or Beef-Sewet, ſome Crumbs of Bread ſoaked or boiled in Milk, and three or four Eggs; chop altogether, and ſeaſon with Pepper, Salt, Sweet-Herbs and Spices; when this is done, put your Force-Meat into your Gooſe's Belly, then put it into a Pot with ſome good Broth, and ſet it a doing gradually over the Fire; then take the Cruſts of *French* Rolls as uſual, and put them in a Stew-pan, with ſome of the ſame Broth your Gooſe is boiled in, and ſet your Cruſts a ſimmering and ſoaking gently over a Stove; when they are tender, put them in

your

your Soop-Diſh, and the Gooſe upon them ; then put over your Gooſe a Cullis of Green Peaſe (if in Seaſon) or elſe Aſparagus Tops. Garniſh the Rim of your Diſh with middling Bacon, and ſerve it hot.

A Turnip Soop.

HAving good Veal Gravy in Readineſs, take ſome good Turnips, pare them and cut them in Dice, one or two Dozen, according to their Size, and the Bigneſs of your Diſh ; fry them of a brown Colour in clarified Butter or Hog's Lard. Take two Quarts of good Gravy, and the Cruſts of two *French* Rolls, boiled up together and ſtrained through a fine Strainer. Your Turnips being ſtrained from the Fat they were fryed in, put them together, boil them 'till tender. You may roaſt two Ducks to put in the Middle. Let your Garniſh be a Rim, on the Outſide of it ſome ſmall diced Turnips, boiled white in Broth, and betwixt every Parcel of them a Piece of fryed Turnip, in Shape of a Cock's Comb. Soak your Bread in ſome good Fat and Gravy, and then ſerve it.

A Pottage à la Jacobine.

PRepare a Brace of Partridges with a Chicken, and roaſt them, take off all the Fleſh, and chop it very ſmall, then put it in a Stew-pan with a little Cullis, then take all the Crumb out of a *French* Roll, and fill it with this minced Meat ; but obſerve to keep ſome to put upon your Pottage. Pound all your Partridge Bones, and put them in a Stew-pan, with a Spoonful or two of Broth, let them have only two Boils, and let them be well reliſhed ; then ſtrain them through a Strainer, and put the Liquor

quor into a little Pot, with the reft of your minced Meat;
cut a *French* Roll into very thin Slices at the Bottom of
your Difh, and a Layer of glazed *Parmefan* Cheefe, and
put a Row of Bread, continuing them alternately, till you
have enough for the Pottage; then put your Difh on a
Stove, and put to it fome Broth, let it fimmer gently;
being ready to ferve up, put in your *French* Rolls, ftuffed
with the minced Meat, and fill it up very gently with good
Broth: Garnifh the Rim of your Difh with Pieces of Puff-
pafte, cut in Triangles, throwing your Cullis over all;
ferve it hot.

A Pottage *of* Forced Pigeons *with brown Onions.*

GET fome large Pigeons, pick, draw, and trufs
them well, loofen the Skin of the Breaft with your
Finger, and force them with a Force-Meat thus: Get
fome white Flefh of Fowls, or elfe a Piece of Veal with a
little Bacon and Calf's Udder, blanched and feafoned with
Pepper, Salt, Sweet Herbs and Spices; a few Mufhrooms,
Truffles, Parfley, and young Onions, three or four Yolks
of raw Eggs, and a few Crumbs of Bread boiled in Cream;
mince all well together, and pound them in a Mortar;
force your Pigeons with this Forced-Meat, ftop the Vent
of your Pigeons with a Skewer, and blanch them, leaving
them but a Moment in the boiling Water, pick them clean
over again, and fet them a boiling in a Pot of good Broth.
Take fome fmall round Onions, cut off the Ends and
blanch them in Water; then peel them, and put them into
a Pot with good Broth, and Veal Gravy, and fet them a
boiling; when boil'd, take them out very carefully for fear
of breaking them, and put them into a Sieve to drain:
Take

Take a *French* Roll, cut off the Cruft, and put it into a Stew-pan, and put to your Cruft the Broth your Onions were boiled in, and fet them to foak and fimmer; when tender put them in your Soop-Difh with your forced Pigeons upon them, and garnifh your Difh with the Onions; fill up your Soop Difh with Veal Gravy, and fee that it be well tafted, ferve it hot. If you would have a Binding, inftead of Veal Gravy, bind it with clear Cullis of Veal and Ham.

Pottage of Turkies with Onions is made the fame way.

Pottage *of* Partridges

YOUR Partridges being picked, drawn, truffed and fcalded, lard them with middling Lards of Bacon well feafoned, and half roaft them, then take them off, and put them into a Pot with a Bundle of Roots, fome Onions, and fome good Broth; fet them a boiling. Make a Cullis after this Manner; take a Pound or two of a Fillet of Veal, and a Piece of Ham, cut them in Slices to garnifh the Bottom of a Stew-pan, flice an Onion, Carrot, and Parfnip, and put the whole covered up, over a flow Fire; when the Liquor fticks to the Pan without burning, put in a little Piece of Butter, and a Duft of Flour; tofs that feven or eight Times over the Stove, then wet it with half Gravy, half Broth, and put in fome Crufts of Bread, a little Parfley, a Chibbol, Mufhrooms, Truffles, and a very little Sweet Bafil, and let all fimmer together; pound a roafted Partridge; the Cullis being enough, take out the Slices of Veal and put in the Partridge; ftrain it through a Strainer, and put it into a Pot, and keep it hot; boil fome Crufts of *French* Rolls in the Soop-Difh you intend to

ferve

ferve it in, or in a Stew-pan, with the Liquor that your Partridges were boiled in , when tender, lay them in your Soop-Difh, and lay your Partridges handfomely upon them ; fee that your Cullis be well tafted, pour it upon your Pottage, and ferve it hot.

A Bain-Marie.

GE T three Pounds of Buttock of Beef, three Pounds of Fillet of Veal, and a Pound of Leg of Mutton, the whole without its Fat, with a Capon and a Partridge ; take an Earthen Pot big enough to hold all this Meat ; fcald the Pot before you ufe it, then put into it the Meat aforefaid, and feafon it with an Onion ftuck with two Cloves, and a little Salt, pour into it three Pints of Water, cover the Pot and ftop it clofe all round with Pafte and Paper, to keep in the Steam. Put on the Fire a large Kettle of Water, and fet it a boiling, then put your earthen Pot into this Kettle, and keep fo much Water always boiling ready to put into the Kettle, as the other waftes, keep always filling fo, for the Space of five Hours : After which take it off and open it, and ftrain the Broth through a Sieve or a Napkin, let it fettle. This is ufed for fick People, or to foak Crufts in for Pottages ; and when you have a Mind to do it with Rice, you need only to fill the Belly of the Capon with Rice, picked very clean, and do it the fame Way as above-mentioned.

A Pottage *of* Partridge *á la Reine.*

HAving drawn, picked and truffed your Partridges, lard them with large Lardoons of Bacon, and half roaft them, then take them off the Spit, and put them into

a Pot

a Pot with fome good Broth of a Piece of Beef and Veal, fet them a boiling over a flow Fire, then take a Pound or two of a Fillet of Veal, and a Piece of Ham, cut both into Pieces or Slices, and garnifh the Bottom of a Stew-pan, and add an Onion or two, a few Carrots and Parfnips, fet them a fweating on a Stove flowly; and when they begin to ftick to the Pan, and appear brown, pour in fome good Broth, and feafon the whole with two or three Cloves, fome Mufhrooms cut in Slices, Parfley, Cives, and Crumbs of Bread; let them all ftew together very flowly, and when they are well foaked, and the Veal and Ham enough, take them out of the Pan, and mix one of your Partridges, being pounded, in it. Then ftrain your Cullis over it, and put to it the Cruft of a *French* Roll or two, foaked in fome of the Broth the Partridges were boiled in, put a Brace of roafted Partridges in the Middle, and ferve away hot.

A Pottage *of* Chefnuts.

TAKE fome large Chefnuts and peel them, then put them into a Pafty-pan with Fire, under and over, put them in the Oven, peel off the under Skin, then fet them a boiling in good Broth; put in a Stew-pan about half a Pound of Veal, a few Slices of Ham, fome fliced Carrot and Onion, fet them in a Stove to fweat 'till they ftick to the Pan without burning; moiften them with good Broth; you muft have fome Carcaffes of Partridges or Pheafants ready pounded; take the Meat out of your Stew-pan with a Skimmer, and put in your pounded Carcaffes; obferve that your Broth be well tafted, put in a little of your Cullis, and ftrain it through a Strainer, afterwards put it into a little Pot or Sauce-pan and keep it hot. Pare

C c

off

off the Crusts of a *French* Roll, and put them in a Stew-pan; put some good Broth to your Crusts, and let them simmer a while over the Stove, but take Care there be no Fat: When enough, put them in your Soop Dish, garnish the Rim with Chesnuts; put in your Pottage two large Pigeons, or two Partridges with your Cullis over them, and serve it hot.

A Pottage *à la Houzarde.*

TAKE two Chickens, pick them very clean, truss them, and put them in the Broth Pot for half an Hour, then take them out, and cut them in Pieces as for a Fricasey, and put them into a Stew-pan with some melted Butter, seasoned with Pepper, Salt, Sweet Herbs, and fine Spices, and rasped Bread and *Parmesan* Cheese, upon them, one after another, as you do Smelts or fryed Gudge-ons, then put them handsomely in a Pasty-pan, and let them take a fine Colour in the Oven. Take a *French* Roll, cut it in Slices, make a Layer of Bread in your Soop-Dish, and another of *Parmesan* Cheese, another of Cabbage, and one of Bread over all, that the Cabbage may not appear; put your Dish on the Stove, with some good Broth in it; let it simmer 'till the Bread be almost dry, then druge it with *Parmesan* Cheese, and brown it with the Cover of a Pasty-pan; then shove a thin Skimmer under your Bread in the Dish, and put in some Broth 'till your Bread swims in it. When it is ready to serve, lay your Chickens on hand-somely, and serve it hot.

Lentil

Lentil Soop.

GET one Quart of Lentils, put to them a Gallon of foft Water, two Pounds of good Ham or Pickle Pork, two Pounds of Mutton, two Pounds of Pork; feafon with All-fpice and Salt; put in a Faggot of Herbs, and ftove all very tender; fave a few whole to put in a *French* Roll for the Middle; the reft pulp off as thick as Cream, fo ferve away. Garnifh with Bacon and Lentils.

Melot Soop.

GET one Pound of Melot, and fteep it one Hour in good ftrong Broth; then fet it on a gentle Fire to fimmer; feafon with Salt, and Mace, then put in two Pigeons and a Quart of good Gravy; ftove it two Hours, make a Rim of Pafte round the Edges, and lay fome Melot ftoved, round, with fome Slices of *French* Bread.

A Veal Soop.

TAKE a Knuckle of Veal and cut it to Pieces, boil it with a Pullet and half a Pound of *Jordan* Almonds, beat fmall; ftove it well, and very tender: You may boil a Chicken to lay in the Middle; then skim it clean, and feafon it with Salt and a Blade of Mace; then take the Yolks of four Eggs, and beat them in a little good Broth; fo draw it up thickifh as Cream, and ferve it away hot.

A Veal Soop *with Barley.*

YOUR Stock muft be with a Fowl, a Knuckle of Veal, and fome Mutton, feafoned only with Mace; then ftrain all off; put in half a Pound of *French* or Pearl

Barley

Barley; boil it one Hour, ſeaſon it well, and boil in the Middle a Fowl, or two Chickens; and juſt as you ſerve it put in chopped Parſley.

Scotch Barley-Broth.

GET a Neck, a Loin, or a Breaſt of Mutton, cut it to Pieces, waſh it, put as much Water as will cover it, then when it boils skim it clean, and ſeaſon it with Pepper and Salt, ſome diced Carrots, Turnips, ſome Onions, a Faggot of Thyme and Parſley, and ſome Barley, ſtove all this well together; then skim it well : You may put in a Knuckle of Veal, or a Sheep's Head ſinged, with the Wooll on, ſoaked and ſcraped, and it will be white; ſo ſerve away with the Meat in your Broth.

To make a Pottage with Ducks and Turnips.

TAKE a Duck, draw and truſs it very neatly; blanch it, and put a Piece of Beef in a Stew-pan, with a Piece of Mutton, and your Duck; ſet all a doing ſlowly over the Stove. When your Pottage begins to ſtick to the Stew-pan, put ſome good Broth into it, then take out your Meat, ſtrain your Broth, and put it in a Pot with ſome Turnips, Carrots, and Onions, then put your Pot on the Fire, and make it boil gently; in the mean time cut ſome Turnips in the Form of Dice, or in any other Form you pleaſe, to be thrown upon your Pottage, then blanch them, and put them in a ſmall Pot of very good Broth, let them boil 'till they be enough: As ſoon as you are ready to ſerve, take off the Cruſts of a *French* Roll, and put them in a Stew-pan, ſtrain ſome good Broth upon them, without Fat, then let them ſimmer over the Stove 'till they be

tender:

tender· When they are enough, put them in your Soop-Dish; garnish the Rim of it with Turnips ready for that Purpose, then put in your Duck and the remaining Turnips cut into small Dice, fill up your Soop-Dish and serve it hot, but be sure it be well tasted.

Young Geese, Teals, Knuckles of Roe-Bucks and Wild Boars, may be served in the like Pottages of Turnips, as likewise Wood-Pigeons, and other Pigeons.

A Cow-Heel Pottage.

PUT in your Pot seven or eight Pounds of Buttock of Beef, a Leg of Mutton cut in two, three or four Pounds of a Leg of Veal, and the Knuckle of a Ham; put your Pot over the Stove 'till the Meat sticks a little to it, then pour out some Broth without Fat, put in also a Fowl, and an old Partridge, some Carrots, Parsnips, Turnips, and a Bunch of Sellery, and let it boil very slowly: Then boil your Cow-Heel, and finish the doing of it in a little Braize, that is, in a good Seasoning; when all is ready take the Crusts of *French* Rolls, and put them in a Stew-pan, strain some clear Broth upon them, taking off all the Fat, and let them soak and simmer a while over the Stove; then put it into the Soop-Dish, with your Cow-Heel upon it. Lastly, fill it up with Broth, and serve it very hot. Let it be well tasted.

Pottage *of* Rice, *the* Polish *Way, called,* Roussole.

PICK and wash your Rice very clean, put it in a Pot with a Knuckle of Veal, and a Fowl cut in Quarters; moisten them with hot Water and let them boil very slowly; put in a Handful of Parsley Roots, and a Handful of

Parsley

Parfley Leaves, a good Pinch of Mace pounded, a Pinch of Pepper, and a Piece of Butter; boil it gently, and keep it from thickening; give it a good Tafte; and juft before you ferve, put in a Handful of Parfley, and difh up your Pottage in the Difh you ferve it up in, put your quarter'd Fowl upon it, and ferve it up hot.

A Rice Olio, *with a* Cullis *of* Crawfifh.

WASH fome Rice very clean, and put it in a Pot of good Broth; make it boil very flowly, and add half a Dozen live Crawfifh: When your Rice is done enough and well tafted, pour upon it a good Cullis of Crawfifh, with the Tails; take the Crawfifh out of your Pottage, and ferve it hot.

A Rice Olio, *with a Cullis* à la Reine.

BOIL a Fowl with your Rice in a Pot of good Broth, and make a white Cullis thus: Take a Piece of Veal and Ham, and cut them like fmall Dice, add an Onion, with fome good Broth; take the White of a roafted Fowl, and pound it in a Mortar, when pounded, take the Meat out of your Cullis, and put in the White of your pounded Fowl, ftrain it all through a Strainer, and put it to your Rice, and put your Fowl in the Difh that you ferve your Pottage in: Let it be well tafted, and ferve it hot.

An Olio.

PUT a Leg of Beef over the Fire at Six o'Clock in the Morning, with fix Pounds of a Brifcuit of Beef, cut in five or fix Pieces, feafoned moderately with Spices and Salt, skim it, let it boil 'till your Broth is very ftrong;
take

take a Neck of Veal, a Neck of Mutton, a Piece of a Loin of Pork, if no Pork, then take half a Pig, or, if you have neither of them, take half a Gang of Hogs Feet, boil them tender with good Seasoning, cut your Mutton, Pork, and Veal in square Pieces, two Ribs to a Piece, skin your Pork, give it all two or three Boils in boiling Water, then let it drain in a Colander, when it is drained, either roast it or fry it, of a good Colour, if you roast it, you must do it quick that it loose not its Gravy: Then take your Biscuit Beef out of your Broth, before it be quite tender, because it must boil along with the other Meat, place it in a large Brass Dish or Stew-pan; at the same time get ready the Herbs and Roots following, *viz.* three Savoys cut in four Pieces each, six Carrots cut in long Slices, two Bunches of Sellery, six Leek Heads, a Hand long, twelve Parsley Roots, six Heads of Endive, or Cabbage Lettuce; put over five or six Dozen of Carots, Turnips, and Onions, as big as the Yolks of Eggs; blanch all these off in boiling Water, and drain them through a Colander; then tie each Sort of the Herbs up by itself, with a piece of Packthread twice round, place them in your Stew-pan with your Meat above-mentioned, and strain your Broth from your Leg of Beef, through a Sieve on the Top of your Meat and Herbs, as much as will barely cover it, and set it a boiling softly three Hours before you use it: Then fry off your Turnips, Carrots, and Onions that were cut round, in Hog's Lard, or clarifyed Butter, place them in a Sauce-pan, then get the Fowls following, or what the Country can afford, *viz.* two Chickens, two Pigeons, two Woodcocks, four Snipes, two Teals or Widgeons, two Dozen of Larks; let them be singed and
trussed

truffed up for boiling, blanch them in boiling Water, then throw them out on a Colander; when they are cold, lard half of them with fmall Lardoons, and either roaft or fry them brown, as you did your Meat aforefaid, as quick as you can, becaufe they may not lofe their Goodnefs. When your faid Meat and Herbs are half dreffed put your Fowls on the Top of it, with the Breafts down, with as little Broth as barely covers all; then put fome good Broth and Gravy to your fryed Roots, and fplit your Hogs Feet, and put in them a little Bit of Bacon ftuck with Cloves; fet all a ftewing together; put likewife a Quarter of a Pound of middling Bacon, ftuck with two Dozen of Cloves, in the Middle of your Meat that is ftewing, and two or three Cloves of Garlick, tyed up in a Rag, with a Pennyworth of Saffron, you muft take Care in the Boiling that it take not too muft Tafte of either: Cover all up, and let it ftew foftly, then make your Thickening ready as follows: If in Summer, boil up two Quarts of Green Peafe, and put to them three Pints of good ftrong Broth, and ftrain them through a Strainer as thick as you can, and thicken your Olio with this; but it muft not be fo thick as a Cullis for any other Soop; likewife, put a little into your fryed Roots; or if in Winter, you may ufe Blue Peafe; but if you have neither of thefe, put a Quarter of a Pound of Butter in a Saucepan, a fmall Handful of Flour, brown it foftly over a clear Fire, rubbing it with a Ladle; when brown, put to it Gravy, let it boil up, and ftrain it through a fine Sieve; about an Hour before you ferve it, pour half of it over your Olio, and half over your fryed Roots; put into it fix whole Onions; let all ftew foftly together, giving a Shake now and then that it fet not to, and take Care that it be

tender

tender boiled, but come not to a Mash; set it off before you intend to dish it up, and skim the Fat off clean, then prepare some dryed Bread in the Bottom of your Dish, a good stout Rim of clean Paste, an Inch high, set on with the Yolk of an Egg, and dryed in an Oven; then put some of the same Broth from your Olio to soak your Bread with. It will take half an Hour's Time to dish it in order; when you dish it up, take up all your Meat, Fowls, and Herbs, and put them into another Dish, and begin with your coarsest Meat first, in the Bottom of your Dish; such as Beef, Pork, mixed with some of your Roots; lay your first Row out, touching your Rim, and so by Degrees draw it into the Top in the Manner of a Sugar Loaf, the finest of your Fowl next to the Top, with the Hogs Feet and Ears: Then take the fryed Roots, the Fat being clean taken off, lay them handsomely, with your Spoon, in all the Vacancies and hollow Places round and over your Olio; take care you do not hide your Fowl too much, and that you put not too much Broth in your Dish when you dish it up, because you must leave Room for some of your boiling Cullis to be poured over it when you serve it away; then strain the Remainder of your Broth that you stewed your Roots in, and likewise some of that in your Stew-pan, be sure there is no Fat on it; put into it the Crust of half a *French* Roll, when it is tender soaked, put it into a Silver Cup, or *China* Bason, with about a Quart of your Broth. So serve it up on a Plate with your Olio, as it goes away: Take Care you make it not too salt, because there come Salt from your larded Fowls, and from your Bacon that is stuck with Cloves; be sure that none of your Liquor run over the Rim of your Dish. According to your Company, and Big-

D d

nefs

nefs of your Difh, you may put in half the Quantity of Meat above-mentioned, fo ferve it.

Another Spanifh Olio.

GET fome Griftle of Beef from the lower Part of the Brifcuit, cut in Pieces, the Bignefs of two Fingers, and put them in Water; take alfo fome Griftle of a Breaft of Mutton, and fome Griftle of a Breaft of Veal, and Sheep's Rumps, and cut them into handfome Pieces; then garnifh a Broth Pot all round with Slices of Beef an Inch thick, and put in your Griftle of Beef, with a good Quantity of Roots, a Bunch of Sellery very neat, becaufe it muft be ufed in ferving up, a Bunch of Leeks, moiften the Whole with Broth, and when the Beef is fomewhat forward, put in your Griftle of Veal and Mutton, and Sheep's Rumps, two Hog's Feet and Ears, two Partridges, two Pigeons, the Knuckle of a Ham, a good Cervelas, half a White Cabbage, being well blanched, drained, and tied up with Packthread, feafon the Whole with Onions, and put in a Mignonette, and then cover it with Slices of Beef; take two Pounds of Veal, cut them in Slices, and fet them to fweat gently over the Stove, 'till they ftick to the Stewpan; but don't let them burn: Put fome good Broth into it, and put it in your Olio. You muft put to fteep over Night fome Giavance, that is, *Spanifh* Peafe, in lukewarm Water, in the Morning pick them clean one after another, then wafh them in hot Water, and boil them in a Saucepan with good Broth. Your Olio, being done, give it the beft Tafte you can; then take out all your Meat and Roots, and put them in a large Difh; range handfomely in the Difh or Olio-Pot you ferve up in, your Griftles of Beef, Veal,

Veal, and Mutton, and Roots, which muft be well cleaned When every thing is in good Order in your Difh, then
put in your Hog's Feet and Ears, Cabbage, Sellery and
Leeks, in the fame Form; add, laftly, your Giavance with
a little Olio Broth, and ferve it hot. You muft ferve it in
covered *China* Cups, with Slices of toafted Bread, as big as
your two Fingers; fill each Cup with Broth, and put a
Toaft at their Sides. Take Care your Broth be well relifhed; and ferve it as hot as you can.

A Pottage *of* Wood-Pigeons, *by Way of an* Olio.

AFTER your Wood Pigeons are truffed; blanch
them in Water, and put them in the Pot with fome
good Gravy, a Bunch of Roots, fuch as Carrots, Turnips,
Parfnips, *&c.* fome young Onions, a Faggot of Sellery,
and a Bunch of Sweet Herbs; when all are boiled, pre-
pare the Crufts of Rolls as ufual, in the fame Broth your
Wood-Pigeons are done in, then put the Bread in your
Soop-Difh, and over it your Wood-Pigeons. Garnifh the
Rim of your Difh with the Roots, pouring in good Veal
Gravy over all; then ferve it hot: The Garniture fhould
only juft cover the Rim of the Difh, in order to have
Room for the Soop.

You may make Ufe of Quails, or any other Fowl, and
Wood-Pigeons may ferve for Cabbage Soop, as you think
fit.

A Pottage *of* Teals *or other Birds with* Mufhrooms

GET fome Teals, or fuch like Birds, draw and trufs
them; lard them with large Lardoons of Bacon well
feafoned, then half roaft them, and take them off, and fet
D d 2

them

them a doing in a Pot with some good Broth, Pepper and Salt, and a Bunch of Sweet-Herbs, when they are half done, have some picked Mushrooms in Readiness, cut them in small Dice, and toss them in melted Bacon, putting two good Pinches of Flour to them, your Mushrooms being enough, put them into the Pot where your Teals are boiling, let them all boil well together; when the Broth is enough order the Crusts of *French* Rolls as usual, and put them in your Soop-Dish, and put your Teals on the Crusts, and before you serve up, put some good Gravy to them, with the Juice of a Lemon. Garnish the Rim of your Dish with Mushrooms prepared in the following Manner. Take as many small Mushrooms as will serve to garnish your Dish, pick and wash them, and put them in a Stew-pan, with the Juice of a Lemon, a little Salt, and some Broth, when they are done, garnish the Rim of your Dish with them, but let them be very white; another time you may force them for the same Garniture.

A Pottage *of* Spanish Cardoons.

TAKE a *French* Roll or two, and having cut off the Crusts, put them into a Stew-pan, with some good Broth, let it take a Boil or two; when your Crusts are tender, put them in your Soop-Dish, and garnish your Dish with Cardoons, then lay on your Crusts two Partridges, or two Pigeons, which you must have ready, or else a little Loaf of *(Profitrolle)* and some Hearts of Cardoons in thin Slices over it: Pour over it some good Veal Gravy half thickened, let it be well tasted, and serve it hot. When the Veal Gravy is thus prepared, then take a Pound and a half of a Fillet of Veal, and a little Piece of Ham,

cut

cut both in Slices, and garnish the Bottom of a large Stew-pan with it, and an Onion, a Carrot, and a Parsnip; cover it, and let it stew gently on a Stove: When the Liquor sticks to the Pan, and has taken a fine Colour, put in a Piece of Butter, and drudge it lightly over with Flour, then toss it round about seven or eight times over the Stove, and put to it half good Broth and half Gravy, season it with a white Chibbol, a little Parsley, a little Sweet Basil, a few Mushrooms, and Truffles, if you have any, and with two or three Cloves; let it all boil gently, then take out the Slices of Veal, and strain the rest through a Strainer; let it be of a good Colour, and use it to throw on your Pottage.

A Terrine á la Bavoroise.

TAKE half a Dozen Quails all ready truffed, four middling Pigeons, two young Rabbits; cut off the hind Legs, and laid them with Bacon, and the Backs with small Bacon, cut off the Heads and Flanks, and laid them likewise. Take an Eel cut in Pieces the Length of your Rabbits, put in your Stew-pan some Slices of Veal and Ham, then put in your Quails and Legs of Rabbits, together with Champignons and Truffles; season it with Pepper, Salt, Sweet Basil, Onions, some Slices of Lemons, and a Couple of Glasses of White Wine; cover them Top and Bottom alike, cover the Stew-pan, set it a stewing with Fire under and over; it being half done, put in it your Pigeons, with Veal Sweatbreads, and let it stew 'till done: Your Eels and Rabbits being larded, put a Stew-pan over the Fire, with half a Bottle of White Wine, seasoned with Salt, Cloves, Sweet Basil and Onions cut into

Slices;

Slices, as soon as your Wine boils, put in your Eels, let them boil a little, after that take them out, and put in your Rabbits in a Stew-pan, with some Slices of Ham and Veal; moisten them with Broth, adding to it a Couple of Onions and so let them stew. When they are stewed, take them out, strain the Broth through a Silk Strainer, and put them again into your Stew-pan, then put them over the Fire, and let them stew, 'till they turn to Caramel This done, put in your Rabbits and your Eels, cover your Stew-pan, and put it upon hot Ashes, that they may glaze, and your Eels may be quite done: Take out your Quails, Pigeons, and Rabbits Legs, place them neatly in a Stew-pan, put the Stew-pan wherein they have been doing over the Fire and moisten it with a Ladle full of Gravy, and as much Cullis; skim it well, then strain off this Cullis, let it have a good Taste; place your Quails and Pigeons, *&c,* in your Terrine, and pour your Cullis over them with the Juice of a Lemon, and then your Rabbits and Eels glazed, cross-ways, laid upon them, and serve them up hot.

A Hodge Podge.

GET of the Sticking-Piece of Beef, or Brisuit, about six Pounds, a Knuckle of Veal, a Cow-Heel, and a Pig's Ear; let them be a little more than covered with Water, put them on the Fire, keep skimming them, and let them boil about an Hour; then season them with Pepper and Salt; put in Carrots and Turnips, cut in handsome Pieces, not sliced, some Onions, Beet Leaves, Sellery, Thyme, and Winter Savory in a Faggot, to be taken out again, then let them all stew over a moderate Fire above two Hours more.

Another

Another way to make a Hodge Podge.

GET fome of the lower End of a Bifcuit of Beef, cut it into Pieces two Inches long and broad, put them into cold Water, then blanch them; when blanch'd, put into a Pot Slices of Beef, and the Bifcuit Piece, with a great many Carrots and Parfnips, then feafon it with Pepper, Salt, a Bunch of Sweet Herbs, half a Dozen Onions, a piece of Ham, and if you think proper, a piece of Cervelas, then cover it with Slices of Beef, moiften it with Broth, cover the Pot, and put Fire under and over it; when done, take out the Meat and the Carrots; then put the Bifcuit Piece, with other Meat, into a Stew-pan, and drefs your Carrots as neatly as you can, put them to your Meat, then ftrain off the Broth the Brifcuit Pieces were boiled in, with the reft of the Meat, skim it well, and let it be well feafoned, if there is too much Liquor boil it to a fmaller Quantity, put fome Butter in a Stew-pan, with a Handful of Flour, ftir it with a Wooden Ladle 'till it is pretty brown, then moiften it with the Broth of the Hodge Podge; skim it well, let it be well tafted, put to it Parfley cut fmall, and put over your Griftles of Beef and Carrots; keep it hot: Being ready to ferve up, place it in a Terrine, and ferve it for Entry. You may ferve it up in a Difh as well as a Terrine; you may alfo add to it Mutton Griftles.

Plumb-Pottage *for* Chriftmas.

TO ten Gallons of Water, take a Leg and Shin of Beef, boil it very tender, and when the Broth is ftrong enough, ftrain it out, wipe your Pot, and put the
Broth

Broth in again ; flice fix *French* Rolls, the Crumb only, and mittony it, that is, foak it in fome of the Fat of the Broth over a Stove a Quarter of an Hour, then put in five Pounds of Currants well wafhed, five Pounds of Raifins, and two Pounds of Prunes ; let them boil 'till they fwell ; then put in three Quarters of an Ounce of Mace, half an Ounce of Cloes, two Nutmegs, all of them beat fine, and mix it with a little Liquor cold, and put them in a very little while. Take off the Pot, and put in three Pounds of Sugar, a little Salt, a Quart of Sack, and a Quart of Claret, the Juice of two or three Lemons. You may put in a little Sagoe if you like it. Pour this into earthen Pans to keep it for Ufe.

Another Plumb-Pottage.

GET two Gallons of ftrong Broth ; put to it two Pounds of Currants, two Pounds of Raifins of the Sun, half an Ounce of Sweet Spice, a Pound of Sugar, a Quart of Claret, a Pint of Sack, the Juice of three Oranges and three Lemons ; thicken it with grated Biskets, or Rice Flour, with a Pound of Prunes.

A White Soop.

BOIL a Pound of Rice tender in Water and Milk, then put it in 2 Quarts of ftrong Broth, Herbs, Balls, a *French* Roll cut in Dice and all fryed ; feafon it, and put a forced Chicken in the Middle.

To

To make a Veal Glue, *or* Cake Soop, *to be carried in the Pocket.*

TAKE a Leg of Veal, ftrip it of the Skin and the Fat, then take all the mufcular or flefhy Parts from the Bones, boil this Flefh gently in fuch a Quantity of Water, and fo long a Time, 'till the Liquor will make a ftrong Jelly when it is cold: This you may try by taking out a fmall Spoonful now and then, and letting it cool. Here it is to be fuppofed, that tho' it will jelly prefently in fmall Quantities, yet all the Juice of the Meat may not be extracted; however, when you find it very ftrong, ftrain the Liquor through a Sieve, and let it fettle; then provide a large Stew-pan, with Water, and fome *China* Cups, or glazed Earthen Ware; fill thefe Cups with Jelly taken clear from the Settling, and fet them in a Stew-pan of Water, and let the Water boil gently 'till the Jelly becomes thick as Glue: After which, let them ftand to cool, and then turn out the Glue upon a Piece of new Flannel, which will draw out the Moifture, turn them once in fix or eight Hours, and put them upon a frefh Flannel, and fo continue to do 'till they are quite dry, and keep it in a dry warm Place: This will harden fo much, that it will be ftiff and hard as Glue in a little Time, and may be carried in the Pocket without Inconvenience. You are to ufe this by boiling about a Pint of Water, and pouring it upon a Piece of the Glue or Cake, of the Bignefs of a fmall Walnut, and ftirring it with a Spoon 'till the Cake diffolves, which will make very ftrong good Broth. As for the feafoning Part, every one may add Pepper and Salt as they pleafe, for there muft be nothing of that Kind put among the Veal when you make the Glue, for any Thing of that Sort will make it mouldy.   As we have obſerved above, that there is nothing of Seaſoning in this Soop, ſo there may be always added what you deſire, either of Spices or Herbs, to make it favoury to the Palate ; but it muſt be noted, that all the Herbs that are uſed on this Occaſion, muſt be boiled tender in plain Water, and that Water muſt be uſed to pour upon the Cake Gravy inſtead of ſimple Water : So may a Diſh of good Soop be made without Trouble, only allowing the Proportion of Cake Gravy anſwering to the a-boveſaid Direction.   Or if Gravy be wanted for Sauce, double the Quantity may be uſed that is preſcribed for Broth or Soop.   There has been made a Cake Gravy of Beef, which for high Sauces and ſtrong Stomachs, is ſtill of good Uſe; and, therefore, we ſhall here give the Method of it.

To make Cake Soop *of* Beef, *&c.*

GET a Leg, or what they call, in ſome Places, a Shin of Beef, prepare it as preſcribed above for the Leg of Veal, and uſe the muſcular Parts only, as di-rected in the foregoing Receipt; doing every thing as above-mentioned, and you will have a Beef Glue, which, for Sauces, may be more deſirable in a Country Houſe, as Beef is of the ſtrongeſt Nature of any Fleſh : Some preſcribe to add to the Fleſh of the Leg of Beef, the Fleſh of two old Hares, and of old Cocks to ſtrengthen it the more; this may be done at Pleaſure, but the Stock of all theſe Cakes Gravies or Glues is the Firſt   Theſe, indeed, are good for Soops and Sauces, and may be enriched by Sellery, Cher-vil, Beat, Chards, Leeks, or other Soop Herbs.   A little of this is alſo good to put into Sauces, either of Fleſh, Fiſh

or

or Fowl, and will make a fine Mixture with the travelling Sauce.

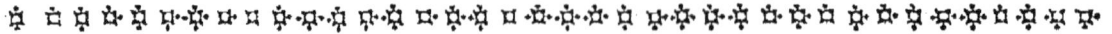

CHAP. XVI.

Of FISH.

The Times when Fish are in Season.

SEVERN Salmon, in Season from *Alhollandtide* 'till *June*.

Thames Salmon, in Season from *April*, and allowed to be caught to *Holy-Rood*, the 13th of *September*.

Sturgeon, catch'd in the Eastern Parts, in *April*, *May*, and *June*, (excellent Fish roasted fresh) but chiefly eaten pickled, most caught at *Hamborough*, and at a Place belonging to the King of *Prussia*, called, *Pillow*: Sometimes catch'd in the River *Severn*, and now and then in the *Thames*.

Turbut, in Season all the Year, but scarce in the Months of *December*, *January*, and *February*.

Carp Spawn in *May*, in Season all the Year, at some Place or other: *Thames* Carp reckoned the best.

Whitings and Cod, in Season here chiefly in *November*, but in the Northern Countries longer.

Lampreys, in Season from *Christmas* to *June*, to be potted; catch'd in the River *Severn*.

Mackarels

Mackarels, in Seafon the latter End of *April,* and continue *May* and *June*

Lobfters and Crabs, come in in *Auguft,* and hold 'till *Chriftmas,* which is called the firft Seafon; and from *Chriftmas* to *June,* is called the fecond Seafon.

Oyfters, in Seafon from the Beginning of *September* to *April.*

Herrings, in Seafon in *June,* but the biggeft Seafon when in full Roe is in *September, October,* and *November.*

Trouts, in Seafon in *April, May,* and the Beginning of *June . Hampfhire* the chief Country for them.

Soles, Thornback, Crawfifh, and Eels, always in Seafon.

S A L M O N S.

To drefs Salmon au Court-bouillon.

AFTER having drawn and cleaned your Salmon, fcore the Sides pretty deep, that it may take the Relifh of your *Court-bouillon* the better: Lay it on a Napkin, and feafon it with Salt, Pepper, Cloves, Nutmeg, Onions, Cives, Parfley, fliced Lemon, Bay-Leaf and Bafil. Work up the Quantity of about a Pound of Butter with a little Flour, and put it into the Belly of the Salmon; then wrap the Salmon in the Napkin, bind it about with a Packthread and lay it in a Fifh-Kettle, of a Size proportionable to the Largenefs of your Fifh; put to it a Quantity fufficient to boil it in, of Wine, Water and Vinegar, and fet it over a quick Fire: When it is done enough take it off, and keep

it

it fimmering over a Stove, 'till you are ready to ferve; then take up the Salmon, unfold the Napkin it is in, and lay another in the Difh in which you intend to ferve it, place the Salmon upon it. Garnifh with green Parfley, and ferve it for the firft Courfe.

To drefs a whole Salmon, *or Pieces of it* à la Braife.

LARD it with large Lardoons, well feafoned, and bind it about with Packthread: Take two or three Pounds of a Fillet of Veal, cut it in Slices, and lay it with fome Bards of Bacon, on the Bottom of a Stew-pan; cover the Pan, and fet it over a flack Fire; when the Meat begins to ftick powder it with a Handful of Flour, and give it feven or eight Turns over the Stove, keeping it always moving; then moiften it with good Broth and a few Spoonfuls of Gravy. Lay the Salmon in an oval Stew-pan; pour the Liquor of your Braife upon it, and lay it over your Slices of Veal, put in a Bottle of *Champaign* or White Wine. See that there be Liquor enough, ftrew in a Seafoning of Pepper, Salt, Spices, and favoury Herbs, Cives, Parfley, and fome Slices of Onion and Lemon, add a Lump of Butter, and lay fome Slices of fat Bacon over all of it; fo fet it to ftew over a gentle Fire, when it is enough done take it off the Fire, and let it ftand a Couple of Hours, in the Liquor, to give it a Relifh; but let the Pan be always covered to keep it warm. When you are ready to ferve, take it up, drain it, untie the Packthread, lay it in the Difh you intend to ferve it in, pour upon it a Ragoo of Crawfifh made with Gravy, or elfe a Ragoo of Veal Sweetbreads, Cocks-Combs, &c. and ferve it hot.

The

The same dressed Maigre *for* Fish Days.

LARD it with Anchovies and the Flesh of Eels, bind it about with Packthread, and put it in an oval Stew-pan, or Fish-Kettle, of the Size of your Fish. Put a Lump of Butter as big as your Fist, into a Sauce-pan; set it over a Stove, and when it is melted, throw in a Handful of Flour and brown it, keeping it always moving, then put to it some Fish Broth, and pour the whole into the Stew-pan to your Salmon; to which put likewise a Bottle of *Champaign* Wine, or White Wine, so that there may be Liquor enough to stew it in. Season it with Salt, Pepper, savoury Herbs and Spices, Onions, Cives, Parsley, and Slices of Lemon; so get it ready over a slack Fire. When it is enough done, let it stand a Couple of Hours in its Liquor, that it may have the Relish of it, then take it up, unbind and drain it, lay it in the Dish you intend to serve in, and pour upon it either a Ragoo of Melts, Mushrooms, and Truffles, or one of Crawfish Tails, and its Garnishings; so serve it.

Salmon *in Cases*.

GET a piece of Salmon; take off the Skin, cut it in thin Slices; mince some Parsley, green Onions and Mushrooms, put your Parsley and green Onions into a Stew-pan, with some Butter, seasoned with Pepper and Salt, then put in your Salmon without putting it over the Fire again, and toss it up to give it a Taste; place your Slices of Salmon in a Paper Case, put your Seasoning upon it, and strew Crumbs of Bread over all, let it bake to a

fine

fine Colour. Your Salmon being done, serve it up with Lemon Juice for a small Entry or *Hors d'Oeuvre*.

To dress a Jole of Salmon the Dutch Way.

GET a Jole of Salmon, scale and wash it very clean, and put some Water upon the Fire, take your Salmon, and put it upon a Fish-plate, which you must put into your Kettle. Put a Stew-pan with a little Vinegar over the Fire, season your Salmon with Salt, some Onions sliced, Thyme, Sweet Basil, and Parsley in Branches; then put your Vinegar hot over it, moisten it with boiling Water, and let the Liquor be of a good Taste; when done, make a Sauce with a piece of good Butter, a little Flour and Water, a Dash of Vinegar, a few Anchovies, a little Nutmeg, and some Shrimps picked, and thicken it, when ready to serve, dish up your Salmon. Let your Sauce be well tasted, put it upon your Salmon and serve it up hot for your Entry.

Broiled Salmon.

BROIL some pieces of Salmon, seasoned with Pepper, Salt, and rubbed with Butter. Make a Sauce in this Manner; take some Butter, put it into a Stew-pan, with a Dust of Flour, a green Onion, and an Anchovy Season the same with Salt, Pepper, and Nutmeg, moisten it with Water, and a little Vinegar, and toss it over the Stove, put half a Ladleful of Crawfish Cullis into it, put it again over the Stove to heat: Let your Sauce be relishing, dish it up, put your pieces of Salmon over it, and serve it up hot for Entry.

Another

Another way

HAVING cut your Salmon into pieces, melt fome good Butter in a Stew-pan, feafon it with Salt, Pepper, and Bay-Leaves, then put in your pieces of Salmon, to take a Tafte, then broil them gently. Make a white Sauce in this Manner   Put good frefh Butter into a Stewpan, with a Duft of Flour, a Couple of Anchovies minceed, take out their great Bones and wafh them, add fome Capers, Salt, Pepper, Nutmeg, whole green Onions, with a little Water and Vinegar : Your Salmon being broiled, tofs it up, and let it be well tafted, then take out your Onions, put your Sauce over your pieces of Salmon, and ferve it up hot for Entry.

T U R B U T S.

A Turbut au Court-bouillon.

HAVING gutted, wafhed and dryed your Turbut, fold it up in a Napkin, and lay it in a large round Sauce-pan ; put as much Salt and Water into another Sauce-pan as will be fufficient to boil it, ftir it about from Time to Time, 'till the Salt is melted ; then let it ftand awhile, and ftrain it through a Linnen Cloth into the Sauce-pan to the Turbut.   When it is enough take a Sauce-pan, and fet over live Embers ; put in two Quarts of Milk, and let it ftand till you are ready to ferve ; then take up the Turbut, lay it on a Napkin folded, in a Difh.   Let your Garnifhing be green Parfley, fo ferve it for the firft Courfe.

A Turbut

A Turbut *with Veal Gravy*

HAVING prepared your Turbut, lay it in a large round Sauce-pan, with a Seasoning of Salt, Pepper, two Bunches of Sweet Herbs, two Onions stuck with Cloves, and one Bay-Leaf: Lay into another Sauce-pan, two or three Pounds of a Fillet of Veal cut in Slices, and some Bards of Bacon; cover the Sauce-pan, and set it over a Stove with a slack Fire. When the Meat begins to stick, put in a piece of Butter, and a small Handful of Flour; stir it about over the Stove with a wooden Spoon, and when it is brown, moisten it with good Broth, and scrape off with the Spoon all that sticks to the Sauce-pan, cover the Turbut with Slices of Bacon; make a Bottle of *Champaign* or White Wine boiling hot, pour it on the Turbut with the Veal Gravy, and lay the Slices upon it, so set it a stewing, and when it is enough done, let it stand in the Liquor a Couple of Hours over live Embers, that it may have the Relish of it: Then serve it for the first Course, with a a Ragoo of Sweetbreads, Cocks-combs, Truffles and Mush-rooms, or with a Ragoo of Crawfish.

We likewise dress a Turbut for Fish Days in the same Manner, only that instead of the above Ingredients of Flesh, we use Butter and Fish Broth, and serve it with a Ragoo of the Melts of Carps, or with any other meagre Ragoo.

To bake a Turbut.

LAY some Butter in a silver Dish, of the Size of your Turbut, and spread it all over it; let your Sea-soning be Salt, Pepper, a little scraped Nutmeg, some

minced

minced Parſley, ſome whole Cives, near a Pint of *Champaign* or White Wine: Cut off the Head and Tail of the Turbut, and having laid it in the Diſh, ſeaſon it above as under, rub it over with melted Butter, drudge it well with Bread crumbed very ſmall, and bake it in an Oven, take care it be very brown, and ſerve it with a Crawfiſh Cullis, or with a Sauce of Anchovies, we ſometimes ſerve it dry.

Turbuts *the* Italian *Way*

TAKE a middling Turbut, gut, waſh, and drain it, take a baking Pan, and put in it ſome Slices of Bacon, Sweet Baſil, and Lemon cut in Slices; now put in your Turbut, ſeaſon it with Salt, Pepper, fine Spice, Cloves, Lemon Juice, and Lemons cut in Slices; cover it with ſome Slices of Bacon, and put it to bake in the Oven: Mince a Dozen Shalots, put them into a Stew-pan with a Glaſs of *Champaign*, put in ſome Beef Gravy, a little Gravy of Ham, put it over the Fire, and put in it two Spoonfuls of good Oil, the Juice of two Lemons, ſome Salt and pounded Pepper; your Turbut being done, diſh it up, put your Sauce over it, ſerve it up hot for a firſt Courſe or Remove.

C O D.

To crimp Cod *the* Dutch *Way.*

TAKE a Gallon of Pump Water, put in one Pound of Salt, and boil it half an Hour; ſkim it well, you may put in a Stick of Horſe-Radiſh, a Faggot of Sweet Herbs, and one Onion, but Water and Salt are beſt; put

in

in your Slices of Cod when it boils, and three Minutes will boil them: Take them out and lay them on a Sieve or Pye-plate, and send away with raw Parsley about it, and oily Butter in a Cup

To roast a Cod's Head.

TAKE the Head, wash and scour it very clean, then scotch it with a Knife, and strew a little Salt on it, and lay it on a Stew-pan before the Fire with something behind it; throw away the Water that runs from it the first half Hour; then strew on it some Nutmeg, Cloves, Mace and Salt, and baste it often with Butter, turning it 'till it is enough. If it be a large Head it will take four or five Hours roasting, then take all the Gravy of the Fish, as much White Wine, and more Meat Gravy, some Horse-Radish, one or two Shalots, a little sliced Ginger, some whole Pepper, Cloves, Mace, and Nutmeg, a Bay-Leaf or two, beat this Liquor up with Butter, and the Liver of the Fish boiled, and broke, and strained in it, and the Yolks of two or three Eggs, some Oysters and Shrimps, with Balls made of Fish, and fried Fish round it. Garnish with Lemon and Horse-Radish.

To boil a Cod's Head.

SET a Kettle on the Fire with Water, Vinegar and Salt, a Faggot of Sweet Herbs or an Onion or two: When the Liquor boils put in the Head on a Fish Bottom, and in the boiling put in cold Water or Vinegar; when it is boiled, take it up, or put it in a Dish that fits your Fish Bottom: For the Sauce, take Gravy or Claret boiled up with a Faggot of Sweet Herbs, or an Onion, two or three

Anchovies

Anchovies drawn up with two Pounds of Butter, a Pint of Shrimps, Oyſters, the Meat of a Lobſter ſhred fine, then put the Sauce in Silver or *China* Baſons, ſtick ſmall Toaſts on the Head, lay on, and about it, the Spawn, Melt, or Liver. Garniſh it with fried Parſley, ſliced Lemon, Barberries, or Horſe-Radiſh, and fried Fiſh.

A ſtewed Cod.

TAKE your Cod and lay it in thin Slices in the Bottom of a Diſh, with a Pint of Gravy, and half a Pint of White Wine, ſome Oyſters and their Liquor, ſome Salt, and Pepper, a little Nutmeg, and let it ſtew 'till it is almoſt enough, then thicken it with a Piece of Butter rolled in Flour, let it ſtew a little longer, ſerve it hot. Garniſh with Lemon ſliced.

Fricaſey *of* Cod.

GET the Sounds, Roes, &c of ſeveral Cods, ſplit them and ſcrape them well, then blanch them: Being blanched, put them in freſh Water, waſh them very clean, and cut them into ſquare Pieces, the Bigneſs of the End of a Thumb. Then put a Lump of Butter in a Stewpan, toſs it up with an Onion cut ſmall, after that put in your Pieces, and give them two or three Toſſes, this done, put a little Flour over them, moiſten them with a little Fiſh Broth, ſeaſoned with Salt, Pepper, Sweet Herbs, fine Spice, and let them ſtew gently: Being done, thicken it with Yolks of Eggs, Parſley cut ſmall, with a Daſh of Vinegar or Verjuice, and ſerve them hot for Entry.

Fricaſey

Fricafey *of* Cod *the* Italian *Way.*

GET the Sounds of Cods according to the Bignefs of the Difh you will make; cut them into Fillets, and tofs them up in Oil with an Onion cut fmall, moiften them with a Glafs of White Wine, and a little Fifh Broth, feafoned with Salt, Pepper, and beaten Spice, and let them ftew foftly; let them be of a good Tafte; thicken them with Yolks of Eggs, much Lemon Juice, and Parfley cut fmall You may add Champignons and Truffles, being thickened, difh them up, and ferve them hot for Entry.--- You may alfo make them in Hotch-Potch, called, *Menu du Roi,* or like Beef Palates, and Hog's Ears: And you may likewife fill up thefe Sounds with Forced-Meat made with the Flefh of *Cabillau,* or other Flefh cut into Slices mixed with Force-Meat done in a Seafoning, ferve them up with a White Sauce, or an *Italian* Sauce. You garnifh your Difh with foft Roes of Cods fried.

C A R P S.

To ftew Carps white.

FIRST fcale them, gut them and cleanfe them; fave the Roes and Melts, then ftove them in fome good white Broth, and feafon them with Cloves and Mace, Salt, and a Faggot of Herbs; put in a little White Wine, and when ftewed enough, thicken your Sauce with the Yolks of five Eggs, and pafs off the Roes, and dip them in the Yolks of Eggs, and Flour, and fry them with fome Sippets of *French* Bread; then fry fome Parfley, and when

you

you difh them, gainifh with the Roes, Paifley and Sippets.

To ſtew Carps *brown.*

SCALE and cleanſe them, then paſs them off in brown Butter on both Sides, or lay them in your Pan raw; ſtrew all over ſome grated Bread, Pepper and Salt, Thyme and Paifley minced, put into them one Quart of Claret, and one Pint of Gravy, according to the Largeneſs of your Fiſh; they muſt not be quite covered; put in alſo four Anchovies, ſome grated Horſe-Radiſh, one Shalot chopped ſmall, two Slices of Lemon and a Piece of Butter, Gold Colour, with a Spoonful of Flour, and put to your Carp, which will thicken it as Cream; fry ſome Sippets with the Roe and Melt, and ſome Parſley to ſerve up hot.

To fry Carp.

AFTER having ſcaled and drawn them, ſlit them in two, ſtrew them over with Salt; drudge them well with Flour, and fry them in clarified Butter. When they are fried, you may either ſerve them dry, and eat them only with Juice of Orange, or elſe you may prepare a Ragoo of Muſhrooms, the Melts of Carps and other Fiſh, and Artichoke Bottoms: Fry ſome thin Slices of Bread, and put them into the Sauce, together with ſome ſliced Onion and ſome Capers, let them boil in it. Diſh up your Carp, throw your Ragoo upon it, and let your Garniture be fried Cruſts of Bread and ſliced Lemon.

To

To dress Carp á la daube

GET a Couple of Soals and a Pike, and bone them : Of the Flesh of them make a Farce, hashing it very small, together with a few Cives, some Spice, Salt, Pepper, Nutmeg, fresh Butter, and some Crumb of Bread soak'd in Cream : Thicken your Farce with Yolks of Eggs. Then take a large Carp, fill the Body of it with this Farce, and put it a stewing in an oval Stew-pan, over a little Fire, in White Wine, seasoned with Salt, Pepper, Cloves, some Slices of Lemon, a Bunch of Sweet Herbs, and good fresh Butter : While it is a stewing get ready a Ragoo of Mushrooms, Truffles, Morels, Artichoke Bottoms, Melts of Carp, and Tails of Crawfish : Lay your Carp on an oval Dish, pour your Ragoo upon it, and serve it up very warm.

Another Way to stew Carps

CUT them in Pieces according to their Size, set them a stewing in a Kettle or Sauce-pan, with White Wine or Claret, and season them well with Salt, Pepper, Onion shred small, Capers and some Crusts of Bread : Let all this stew together, and when it is enough, and the Sauce grown thick, serve it up.

A Carp à la Chambor

YOU must take a large Carp, scale and wash it, lard it with thick Bacon and Ham ; being larded, take half a Dozen of Pigeons with fat Livers, Sweetbreads, Mushrooms and Truffles, if you have any ; put altogether for a Moment, in a Stew-pan, season it with Pepper, Salt,

Sweet

Sweet Herbs, a little Cullis, and Lemon Juice; then put this into your Carp, and few it up. Lay a Napkin over your Dreffer, take fome Slices of Bacon, fpread them over your Napkin the Length of your Carp, put more Slices over it; then fold it up in the fame Napkin, and tie it on both Ends; then take a Leg of Veal, cut it into thin Slices, put them in a Stew-pan with fmall Slices of Ham, Onions and Carrots cut alfo into Slices. Put the Stew-pan over the Fire, let them fweat like Gravy of Veal; and when they begin to ftick, moiften them with Broth; then put them in an oval Stew-pan, together with the Meat and Gravy. Now put in your Carps feafon'd with Pepper, Salt, Sweet Herbs, Cloves, Mace, three Bottles of White Wine, and a Lemon cut into Slices: Cover your Carp with the Liquor, let it boil very gently. Make a Ragoût with Sweetbreads of Veal, Mufhrooms, Truffles, Cocks-Combs, fat Livers and foft Roes of Carps. Take half a Dozen of young Pigeons, which you drefs *au Soleil,* or with Sweet Bafil, or inftead of Pigeons, a Couple of Chickens cut in four and marinated, or elfe larded with thin Bacon, and glazed like Fricandos. Take half a Dozen of Sweetbreads of Veal, larded with fine Bacon; let them ftew and glaze like Fricandos. Take alfo a Dozen of large fine Crawfifh; boil them, then pick their Tails, cut off the fmall Claws; if you have Crawfifh enough to make a Cullis, you may ufe it inftead of other Cullis. Your Carp being done and ready to be ferved up, take it out, let it drain, keep in Readinefs your Ragoût of Pigeons, Sweetbreads of Veal and Crawfifh, unfold the Napkin take off the Fat; then difh up your Carp with the Ragoût over it. Garnifh your Difh
with

with one Crawfifh, one Pigeon, and one Sweatbread, placed
by turns 'till it is full; ferve it up hot.

Thefe Sorts of Entries generally ferve to remove Soops.

Entry of Carps à l'Eftoufade.

SCALE and wafh your Carps, gut and wafh the Infide with Wine; take an oval Stew-pan, the Bignefs of
the Carp, put in fome Onions cut in Slices, and then your
Carp; feafon it with Pepper, Salt, Cloves, a Dafh of
Vinegar and a Bottle of Wine, moiften it with hot Water,
put it over a Stove, let it ftew, when ftewed, take it off,
put Wine with which you have wafhed your Carp into a
Stew-pan, with fome Anchovies cut fmall, let it have a
boil or two, then ftrain it off, put it again into the Stew-
pan with a good Lump of Butter, and a Duft of Flour to
thicken the Sauce, add Lemon Juice: Put your Stew-pan
over the Fire, thicken your Sauce, let it be relifhing, being
well done, put in fome good Buttter rolled in Flour,
take out the Bunch: Being ready to ferve difh it, and ferve
it up hot.

Other Entry of Carps *ftewed.*

TAKE a Carp, fcale, wafh and gut it, fplit it in two,
cut each half in three Pieces, put them in a Stew-pan,
with a Dozen of fmall Onions blanched, feafon them with
Pepper and Salt, a Bunch made with Parfley and Sweet
Herbs, moiften them with half a Bottle of good Wine,
put them a ftewing, take fome Butter, put it in a Stew-
pan with fome Flour, put it over the Fire, ftir it 'till it
begins to have a Colour; moiften it with a little Fifh Gravy, or with Water; this being well mixed and ftirred to-

gether

gether, put it into the Stew-pan with your Carp: Let it be relifhing, difh it, and ferve it up hot.

Entry of a broiled Carp.

SCALE and gut your Carp, flice it upon the Back, rub it with melted Butter, pepper and falt it, then broil it; put to it a Ragoût made with Mufhrooms, foft Roes, Artichoke Bottoms, with Onions and Capers: Being ready to ferve, difh it, with this Ragoût over it; ferve it up hot.

A forced Carp.

GET a Couple of Soals with a Pike, bone them, mince the Flefh with a few Onions, fine Spice, Pepper, Salt, Nutmeg, frefh Butter, and fome Crumbs of Bread boiled in Cream or Milk; thicken your minced Flefh with Yolks of Eggs, with the Whites whipped up to Snow. Take a large Carp, fill it with this minced Flefh, ftew it with White Wine in an oval Stew-pan, over a flow Fire, feafoned with Pepper, Salt, Cloves, a Bunch of Sweet Herbs and frefh Butter. Keep in Readinefs a large Ragoût made with Morels, Truffles, Mufhrooms, Bottoms of Artichokes, foft Roes of Carps, and Crawfifh Tails; let it be palatable: Make your Ragoût pretty thin; put to it a good Cullis of Crawfifh, or any other Cullis, then difh your Carp with the Ragoût over it; ferve it up hot.

L A M P R E Y S.

The beft of this Sort of Fifh are taken in the River *Severn,* and when they are in Seafon, the Fifhmongers and others in *London,* have them generally potted from
Gloucefter ;

Gloucefter ; but if you are wheie they may be had fiefh, they are to be diefs'd different Ways.

To fry Lampieys.

BLEED them and keep the Blood ; then wafh them in hot Water to take off their Slime, and cut them in Pieces. Fry them in claiified Butter with a little fiied Flour, White Wine, Salt, Pepper, Nutmeg, a Bunch of fine Herbs and a Bay-Leaf ; fry all this together veiy well, then put in the Blood, with a few Capers, and ferve it hot.

To drefs Lampreys *with fweet Sauce.*

HAving fliced and cut them in Pieces, take out the String that runs along their Backs : Tofs them up in Butter and a little fiied Flour, 'till they are biown ; then add fome Red Wine, a little Sugar, Cinamon, Salt, Peppei, and two or three Slices of Lemon ; when they are enough done, put in the Blood, give them a Tuin or two more ; fo difh up youi Ragoo and ferve it hot.

To make a Lamprey-Pye.

CLEANSE them well from the Slime, fet by the Blood, and let your Seafoning be Salt, Pepper, Currants, Dates, beaten Cinamon, candid Lemon-Peel and Sugar ; then put them into a Pye ; when it is baked, pour in the Blood and a little White Wine, and when you ferve it fqueeze in the Juice of a fmall Lemon.

To broil Lampreys.

HAving taken off the Slime, cut them in Pieces, as
you do Eels, that you intend to broil, melt a Lump
of Butter, and put to it some shred Cives, Parsley, and
savoury Herbs, with Pepper and Salt, put your Pieces of
Lamprey into the Sauce-pan, and stir it all well together,
then take them out, and drudge them with very fine
Crumbs of Bread, and broil them over a gentle Fire Serve
them with a brown Sauce made as follows: Take a little
Lump of Butter, put it into the Sauce-pan, with a Pinch
of Flour, and brown it; add some Cives, Parsley and
Mushrooms, all shred very small, a few Capers and an Anchovy, and season the Whole with Pepper and Salt, moist-
en it with a little Fish Broth, and thicken it with a Crawfish or other Cullis Pour this Sauce into the Bottom of
your Dish, lay your Lampreys all round it, and serve them
hot.

We serve it likewise with a sweet Sauce made with Wine
or Vinegar, a Lump of Sugar, a small Stick of Cinamon,
and a Bay-Leaf, all boiled together. Then we take out
the Cinamon and Bay-Leaf, pour the Sauce into a Dish,
and lay the broil'd Lamprey round it; so serve it warm.

Sometimes we serve a broil'd Lamprey with Oil, in this
Manner: We take some Oil and Vinegar, Pepper, Salt, a
little Mustard, one Anchovy, a few Capers, and a little
Parsley, shred very small, we beat all this together in a
Porringer, then pour it into a Saucer, which we place in
the Middle of the Dish, and garnish it all round with
Lampreys, so serve it.

At

At other Times we ſerve our broil'd Lamprey dry, in Plates or little Diſhes.

E E L S.

The Eels that are taken in Rivers or Running Waters are better than Pond Eels, and of them too the Silver ones are moſt eſteemed.

Several Ways to dreſs Eels, *according to Mr.* LAMB.

To farce Eels.

YOU may farce them on the Bone in the Nature of a white Pudding, you make your Farce of the Fleſh of your Eels, which you muſt pound in a Mortar, and to it put ſome Cream, ſome Crumbs of Bread, with Parſley, Cives, Truffles and Muſhrooms, ſeaſoned as uſual. Lay this Farce very handſomely on the Bones of your Eels, drudge them well with very ſmall Crumbs of Bread, and bake them in an Oven in a Tart-pan, 'till they are of a fine brown Colour.

To dreſs Eels *with white Sauce.*

SKIN them, and cut them in Pieces, and blanch them in boiling Water, then dry them with a Napkin, toſs them up in Butter, with Salt, Pepper, Cloves, and Lemon Peel, together with a Glaſs of White Wine. Toſs up likewiſe ſome Artichoke Bottoms, Muſhrooms and Aſparagus Tops, with Butter, and ſavoury Herbs; then make a white Sauce with the Yolks of Eggs and Verjuice; ſo ſerve them.   *To*

To dreſs Eels *with brown Sauce.*

WHEN you have cut them in Pieces, toſs them up in clarified Butter, a little Flour, a little Fiſh Broth, or thin Puree, Muſhrooms, Cives and Parſley ſhred very ſmall, and a Faggot of Herbs; to which add Salt, Pepper, Cloves, and Capers, make all this boil together, and when your Ragoo is almoſt ready, put to it a little Ver-juice and White Wine, and let it boil a little longer; then thicken it with an Egg to take off the Fat, and ſerve it warm.

To fry Eels.

STRIP them, take out the Bones, cut them in Pieces, and lay them to marinate for two Hours in Vinegar, Salt, Pepper, Bay-Leaves, ſliced Onion and Juice of Lemon; then drudge them well with Flour, and fry them in clarifyed Butter; ſerve them dry with fried Parſ-ley.

To broil Eels.

AFTER having ſtripped and cut them in Pieces, make Gaſhes in them, and lay them awhile in melted Butter, a few ſavoury Herbs, Parſley, Onion, Pepper, and Salt, then warm this a little, and ſhake it all well together, this done, take out the Eels Bit by Bit, drudge them with the Crumbs of Bread, and broil them over a gentle Fire 'till they are of a fine brown Colour; when they are broiled make a brown Sauce with Cives, Parſley and Capers, then put your Sauce in the Diſh, and lay the Eels round it.

We

We likewife ferve broiled Eels with green Sauce, which we make as follows Pound fome Sorrel and fqueeze out the Juice : Then cut an Onion very fmall, and tofs it up with Butter and minced Capers: Mix with it your Juice of Sorrel, fqueeze in an Orange, and add fome Pepper and Salt; fo ferve it for the firft Courfe. We alfo fometimes ferve it with *Sauce Robart.*

To drefs Eels à la daube.

MINCE the Flefh of Eels and Tench, feafon it with Salt, Pepper, Cloves, and Nutmeg; cut the Flefh of another Eel into Lardoons, of which lay one Layer on the Skins, and then another of the minced Flefh, continuing to do fo, 'till you have made it into the Shape of a Brick of Bread; wrap it up in a Linnen Cloth, and ftew it in half Water, half Red Wine, feafoned with Cloves, Bay-Leaf and Pepper. Let it cool in its own Liquor, cut it in Slices, and ferve it in Plates or little Difhes.

To drefs Eels *the* Englifh *Way.*

RUB an Eel with Salt, then with a Towel, to take off the Slime, skin it and cut it in three or four Pieces, according to its Length; lay them in a Difh, and pour on them fome good White Wine, when they have lain a little while in it, take them out, and cut Notches from Space to Space on the Back and Sides, fill up thefe Incifions with a fort of Farce, which make as follows: Take the Crumb of White Bread, and crumb it very fmall; take likewife all Sorts of favoury Herbs, Parfley and Cives and fhred them very fmall; fome Pepper, Cloves, Nutmeg and

Salt;

Salt; add to this the Yolks of some hard Eggs, a convenient Quantity of fresh Butter, and having mixed all this together, fill up with this Farce the Incisions you made in
the Eel; which you then slip again into its Skin, and tie it
at both Ends, prick it in several Places with a Fork, and
then either roast it on the Spit, or broil it on the Gridiron,
when it is done enough, take off the Skin, and serve it dry
with Juice of Lemons, or else make a White Sauce of good
Butter, Vinegar, Salt and White Pepper, together with
Anchovies and Capers.

Note, That only the large Eels are dressed in this Manner.

To spitchcock an Eel.

YOU must split a large Eel down the Back, and joint
the Bones, but do not strip off the Skin; cut the
Fish in three or four Pieces, and while they are boiling
over a gentle Fire, baste them with Butter, Vinegar and
Salt.   Use no other Sauce but Butter and Juice of Lemon.

For Collar'd Eel, *see among the Receipts for* Collaring.

T E N C H.

To stew Tench.

CUT them in Pieces, and fry them in browned Butter; then set them to stew in the same Butter with
White Wine, Verjuice, Salt, Pepper, Nutmeg, a Bunch of
Sweet Herbs, a Bay-Leaf or two, and a little Flour. When
the Fish is stewed enough, put in some Capers, and Oysters,
                                                    with

with the Juice of Mufhrooms, and Lemon. Garnifh the Difh with fried Bread.

A Fricafey *of* Tench *with a White Sauce.*

HAving taking off the Slime, gut them, and cut off their Heads; flit them in two, and cut each Half in three Pieces. Melt fome Butter in a Sauce-pan, and put in your Tench, together with a few Mufhrooms. Let your Seafoning be Salt, Pepper, a Bunch of Sweet Herbs, and an Onion ftuck with Cloves: Tofs up all this together, and then add to it a little boiling Water, and a Pinch of Flour; make a Pint of White Wine boiling hot, and put it into the Fricafey, when it is wafted away as it ought to be, prepare a Thickening with the Yolks of three or four Eggs, beat up in a little Verjuice or boiled White Wine, and bind your Fricafey with it, as you do one of Pullets; put in a little minced Parfley, and a little fcraped Nutmeg, fo ferve it.

A Fricafey *of* Tench *with a Brown Sauce.*

HAving prepared your Tenches, as in the laft Receipt, put fome Flour and Butter into a Sauce-pan, and brown it; then put in your Tench with Mufhrooms, and the Seafoning laft above-mentioned, when you have toffed them up, moiften them with a little Fifh Broth, or Juice of Onion, and having boiled a Pint of White Wine, put it into your Fricafey, when it is enough, bind it with a brown Cullis, and ferve it. When Afparagus and Artichoke Bottoms are in Seafon we ufe them in this Fricafey, having firft blanched them.

To farce Tench.

YOU muſt take off the Slime, and ſlit the Skin along the Back of your Tenches, and with the Point of your Knife raiſe it up from the Bone; then cut the Skin croſs-ways at the Tail and Head, and ſtrip it off; then take out the Bone. This done, bone a Tench or a Carp; put to the Fleſh of it, ſome Muſhrooms, a little Parſley and ſome Cives; ſeaſon it with Salt, Pepper, ſweet Spices, and a very little Sweet Herbs, then having minced it all well together, pound it in a Mortar, put to it a Piece of Butter, the Yolks of three or four raw Eggs, the Bigneſs of a couple of Eggs of the Crumb of Bread ſoaked in Cream, and pound it all well together; then farce your Tenches with it, and ſew them up. Set a Pan over the Stove with ſome clarified Butter, and when it is hot fry the Tenches in it, one by one, 'till they are brown, and then take them up. Melt the Bigneſs of two Eggs of Butter in a Sauce-pan, then put to it a little Flour, and keep moving it 'till it is brown, moiſten it with a little Fiſh Broth, and a little White Wine boiling hot, lay your Tenches into this brown, adding a Seaſoning of Salt, Pepper, a Bunch of Sweet Herbs, an Onion ſtuck with Cloves: So keep them ſimmering in it over a gentle Fire, when they are enough, lay them in a Diſh, pour on them a Ragoo of Melts, and ſerve them.

At other Times they may be ſerved with a Ragoo of Crawfiſh or Oyſters.

You may likewiſe broil theſe farced Tenches, rubbing them firſt over with melted Butter or Salt; and when they

are

are broiled of a fine brown Colour, ferve them with a Ragoo of Truffles or Mufhrooms.

Boiled Tench.

T A K E Tench, frefh from the Pond, gut them, and clear them from their Scales, then put them into a Stew-pan, with as much Water as will cover them, fome Salt, fome whole Pepper, fome Lemon-Peel, a Stick of Horfe-Radifh, a Bunch of Sweet Herbs, and a few Cloves; then boil them 'till they are tender, and when they are enough, take fome of the Liquor, and put to it a Glafs of White Wine, and a little Lemon Juice, or Verjuice, and an Anchovy fhred: Then boil it a few Minutes, and thicken it with Butter rubbed in Flour, tofsing up a Pint of Shrimps with the Sauce, and pour it over the Fifh. Serve it with Garnifh of fried Bread, cut the Length of one's Finger, fome Slices of Lemon and Horfe-Radifh fcraped, with fome pickled Mufhrooms, if you will, or you may tofs fome of them in the Sauce.

To bake Tench.

T A K E your Tench frefh from the Pond, gut them and clean them from the Scales, then kill them, by giving them a hard Stroke on the Back of the Head, or elfe they will live many Hours, and even jump out of the Pan in the Oven, when they are half enough. Then lay them in a Pan, with fome Mufhrooms, Katchup, fome ftrong Gravy, half a Pint of pickled Mufhrooms, as much White Wine as Gravy, three or four large Shalots, an Anchovy or two, two or three Slices of fat Bacon, fome Pepper, Cloves, and Nutmeg, at Pleafure, a little Salt, fome

Lemon

Lemon Peel, and a Bunch of Sweet Herbs; then break some Bits of Butter, and lay them on your Fifh, then cover all as clofe as you can, and give them an Hour's bakeing.

When they are enough, lay them in a hot Difh, and pour off the Liquor, and ftrain it, only preferving the Mufhrooms; then add to it a Spoonful of Lemon Juice, and thicken your Sauce with the Yolks of four Eggs, beaten with Cream, and mixed by degrees with the Sauce. Pour this over your Fifh, and ferve it hot with a Garnifh of Beat Roots fliced, fome Slices of Lemon Peel, and fome Horfe-Radifh fcraped.

Another way to bake Tenches.

PRepare and farce your Tenches as above; rub a filver Difh or a Pafty-pan with Butter; over which lay a Seafoning of Salt, Pepper, Sweet Herbs and Spices, an Onion cut in Slices, fome whole Cives, and a little minced Parfley; then lay in your Tenches: Lay fome of the fame Seafoning over them, fprinkle them with melted Butter, drudge them with very fine Crumbs of Bread, and bake them in an Oven, we ferve them with Ragoos of all Sorts, *Legumes*, which muft be laid under them; or with a Cullis of Crawfifh, or with Anchovy Sauce, and fometimes dry.

B A R B E L S.

B A R B E L S.

To stew Barbels.

HAVING scaled and drawn your Barbels, put them into a Stew-pan, with Wine, fresh Butter, Salt, Pepper, and a Bunch of Sweet Herbs; when they are ready, knead a Bit of Butter with a little Flour, and put it in to thicken the Sauce, so serve them.

Others dress them as above, excepting the Butter, of which they use none: But when the Barbels are stewed, then serve them up with a Ragoo made of Mushrooms, Truffles, Morels, Artichoke Bottoms, Salt, Pepper, fresh Butter, Broth made of Fish, or Juice of Onions.

To dress Barbels au Court-Bouillon.

IT is generally the largest Fish that is dressed in this Manner: Take, therefore, a large Barbel, and draw it, but do not scale it. Lay it on a Dish, and throw on it Vinegar and Salt scalding hot: Then set your Fish over the Fire with White Wine, Verjuice, Salt, Pepper, Cloves, Nutmeg, Bay Leaves, Onions, Lemon, or Orange Peel; when it boils very fast put in your Barbel, and when it is boiled, take it up and serve it dry upon a clean Napkin, instead of a Dish of Roast Meat. Let your Garniture be Parsley or Garden Cresses.

To broil Barbels.

HAving scaled and drawn them, cut small Notches in their Sides, then rub them over with melted Butter, and strew pounded Salt upon them, so broil them on a

Gridiron. Let the Sauce be frefh Butter, with Salt, Pepper, Nutmeg, Capers, Anchovies, and Cives fhred fmall; ufe a little Flour to thicken it, and put in a little Water with two or three Drops of Vinegar, and keep it continually fhaking 'till it is come to a due Thicknefs, then pour it on the Fifh. Let your Garniture be fried Mufhrooms, with Roes of Carps and Slices of Lemon.

To hafh Barbels.

BONE them, and hafh the Flefh ; put it into a Saucepan, and dry it over the Fire 'till it is grown white; then mix it with Mufhrooms, Truffles, Cives, and Parfley cut very fmall: Brown fome frefh Butter in a Saucepan with a little Flour, and put in the Hafh; let it have two or three Turns, feafon it with Salt, Pepper, and a Slice or two of Lemon; moiften it with fome Fifh Broth, and three or four Spoonfuls of Crawfifh Cullis, or of other Fifh to thicken it, and ferve it hot for a firft Courfe.

To boil Barbels.

AFTER they are fcaled and drawn, make fmall Incifions in the Sides of them ; then rub them with melted Butter, and ftrew them over with pounded Salt: This done, lay them on the Gridiron, and when they are broiled, make your Sauce with frefh Butter, Salt, Pepper, Nutmeg, Anchovies, Capers, Cives fhred fmall, with a little Flour to thicken it, put to it likewife a Drop of Water, and as much Vinegar, fhaking it continually 'till it be thickened, and then pour it on your Fifh : Otherwife you may ufe the fame Sauce as for a roafted Pike.

M U L L E T S.

MULLETS.

There are two Sorts of Mullets, the Sea-Mullet and River-Mullet, both equally good.

To boil Mullets.

BOIL the Fish, but lay by the Roes and Livers, when the Fish is boiled, pour away most Part of the Water, and put into the rest a Pint of Claret, some Salt and Vinegar, and two sliced Onions, with a Bundle of Winter Savoury, Marjoram and Thyme, sliced Nutmeg, broken Mace and the Juice of a Lemon. Boil all these well together, then put in the Fish, and when you judge that it tastes strong of the Ingredients, put in three or four Anchovies, and serve it up with stewed Oysters.

To broil Mullets.

AFTER having scaled and gutted them, we cut Gashes in the Sides of them, dip them in melted Butter, and then broil them. We make a Sauce with clarified Butter, fried Flour, Capers, Slices of Lemons, Faggot of Herbs, Pepper, Salt, Nutmeg, and Verjuice, or Juice of Orange.

To fry Mullets.

HAving prepared them as above, fry them in clarified Butter: Let your Sauce be some of the same Butter in which they were fried, with Anchovies, Capers, Juice of Orange, and Nutmeg. Rub the Dish with a Shalot, or a Clove of Garlick.

You may likewise put them in a Pie, as you do several other Fish.

To

To *marinate a* Mullet.

YOU muſt, to a Quart of Water, take a Gallon of Vinegar, a good Handful of Bay-Leaves, as much Roſemary, a Quarter of a Pound of Pepper beaten, put all theſe together, and let them ſeeth ſoftly, and ſeaſon it with a little Salt, then fry your Fiſh with frying Oil, 'till it is enough, and afterwards put it into an earthen Veſſel, and lay the Bay Leaves and Roſemary between and about the Fiſh, and pour the Broth upon it, and when it is cold, cover it up to keep 'till you want it.

P I K E.

To roaſt a Pike.

GET a large Pike, gut it, and clean it, and lard it with Eel and Bacon, as you lard a Fowl; then take Thyme and Savoury, Salt, Mace and Nutmeg, ſome Crumbs of Bread, Beef Sewet and Parſley; ſhred all very fine, and mix it up with raw Eggs; make it in a long Pudding, and put it in the Belly of your Pike, ſkewer up the Belly, and diſſolve Anchovies in Butter, and baſte with it; put two Splints on each Side the Pike, and tie it to the Spit; melt Butter thick for the Sauce, or, if you pleaſe, Oyſter Sauce, and bruiſe the Pudding in it. Garniſh with Lemon.

Pike au Swimmier.

SCALE and gut it, then waſh and dry it, make a good deal of Force-Fiſh with Eel, Whiting, Anchovy, Sewet, Pepper, Salt, and crumbed Bread, alſo Yolks
of

of Eggs, Thyme, and Parsley, and a Bit of Shalot; then fill the Belly full of this Forcing, and draw with a Pack-Needle some Packthread through the Eyes, the Middle and Tail, in the Shape of an S; then wash it over with Butter and Egg, and crumb it over with Bread. You may bake it, or roast it with a Caul over it, and sauce it with Capers and Butter the *French* way.

Another way to dress a Pike

YOU may roast it with a good Forcing in the Belly, with Oysters, Liver, Sewet, Crumbs of Bread, Thyme, Parsley, and Eggs, Anchovies, and a Shalot; fill the Belly, and either bake or roast it, sauce it with Oyster Sauce, the *French* way is with Caper Sauce, and you may boil it with Anchovy Sauce, or fry it in Slices, and serve it with plain Butter or fried Parsley.

To souce a Pike.

PUT your Pike into as much Water as will cover it, with a Handful of Bay-Leaves, some Cloves and Mace. Let it boil 'till it is so tender that a Straw may be run thro' it; then take it up, and put in Liquor, White Wine and Vinegar, with an Anchovy: When your Pike is cold, slip it into the Pickle, which will turn to a Jelly, and keep for a considerable time.

To dress a Pike *with Oysters.*

FIRST scale and gut it, and wash it clean, cut it in Pieces, and put them into a Stew-pan, with White Wine, Parsley, Cives, Mushrooms, and Truffles; all of them hashed together, with Salt, Pepper, and Butter, and

I i　　　　　　　　　　　　set

set it over a Stove to stew, blanch some Oysters in Water,
and a little Verjuice; then throw them, with their own
Liquor, into the Stew-pan, but not 'till the Pike is near
enough, when done, serve it, garnishing your Dish with
sliced Lemon.

S C A T E and T H O R N B A C K.

To crimp Scate.

IT must be cut into long Slips cross-ways, the Flesh into
ten Pieces, Inch broad, and ten long, more or less, according to the Breadth of your Fish; then boil it off quick in
Water and Salt, and send it dry on a Dish turned upside
down in another, and serve Butter and Mustard in one
Cup, and Butter and Anchovy in another.

Scate *or* Thornback, *the* Dutch *or* English *way.*

HAVING skinned them on both Sides, cut the two
Sides from the Body, and each Side down through
the Middle; then lay each Half cross-ways, and cut it in
Slices cross-ways, half an Inch thick   When you come
up toward the thick Part, cut it thinner; throw it in cold
Water with the Liver, an Hour or two before you boil it.
If your Fish is fresh, it will make it curdle and turn crimp.
Then boil it in a brass Dish, with fresh Water, Salt, and
Vinegar; skim it well in the boiling; put your Liver a
boiling two or three Minutes before you put in your cut
Fish, which will be boiled in a Quarter of an Hour; take
up your Slices carefully, that you break them not, for they
will be turned round like a Hoop, and very tender, drain
                                                    them

them well, and flip them into your Dish, with some Sippets under them. Let your Sauce be a Pound of Butter, a Spoonful of Vinegar, two Spoonfuls of Water, a little Duft of Flour, the Yolks of two Eggs, some scraped Nutmeg, a little beaten Pepper, and minced Anchovy, draw this up together to the Thicknefs of a Cream; then put in a good Spoonful of Muftard, and half a Lemon, pour it hot over your Fifh, and lay the Liver upon it. Let your Garnifhing be a little picked Parfley, clean wafhed, fo ferve it up

This Sauce is proper for boiled Smelts or Sparlings, or for boiled frefh Herrings.

Scate *or* Thornback, au Court-bouillon.

GUT it and wafh it well with Water, then boil it in Water with Vinegar, Salt, Pepper, Cloves and favoury Herbs, when it is almoft boiled throw in the Liver to boil in a Moment, then take the Fifh off the Fire, and let it ftand in its own Liquor. When it is almoft cold take it up, skin it, and pick out the Thorns, having cleaned it well, lay it in a Difh, and ferve it with a brown Sauce, made of oiled Butter and Parfley toffed up in it, with a Drop of Vinegar.

Scate, *with Anchovy Sauce.*

THE Scate being boiled, as in the foregoing Receipt, let it ftand to cool, then skin it and take out the Thorns in like Manner; lay it handfomely in the Difh you intend to ferve it in, and fet it over a Chafing-Difh of Coals, mean while prepare the following Sauce: Put into a Sauce-pan fome frefh Butter and a Pinch of Flour;

feafon

feafon it with Salt, Pepper, and Nutmeg, moiften it with a little Vinegar and Water; wafh a couple of Anchovies, mince them, and put them into the Sauce, and turn it over the Stove; when the Sauce is thickened, pour it on your Scate, and ferve it hot for the firft Courfe.

At another time you may ferve it with Capers in a White Sauce, or with a Crawfifh Cullis in White Sauce likewife, and pour it on your Fifh.

To fry Scate *with a Brown Sauce.*

GUT your Scate, cut it in two in the Middle, and blanch it in fcalding Water, take off the Skin and the Thorns, and fet it a cooling; then drudge it with Flour, and fry it in clarified Butter, when it is fried, take it up, drain it, and put it into a Sauce-pan. Make a brown Sauce as follows · Mince fome Cives and Parfley, fet a Sauce-pan over a Stove with a Lump of frefh Butter, and melt it; then put in a little Flour and brown it; when it is browned put in the Cives and Parfley, together with Fifh-broth, or Juice of Onions, feafon it with Salt and Pepper; let it fimmer a while, then put it into the Sauce-pan to your Scate, with fome minced Capers, and let it all fim-mer together, take up your Scate, and having laid it in a Difh, bind your Sauce with a Crawfifh or other good Cul-lis, pour it on your Scate and ferve it.

At another Time the Scate being fried, and having fim-mered in the brown Sauce, as above, it may be ferved with pouring on a Ragoo of Crawfifh, or of Melts, or Mufcles.

F L O U N-

F L O U N D E R S and *P L A I C E.*

Flounders *with Sorrel.*

GUT them and cleanse them well, then flash them cross-ways three Cuts only on one Side, and lay them in your Sauce-pan, put in as much Water as will just cover them, with a little Vinegar, Salt, and one Onion, boil them quick, then boil four Handfuls of Sorrel, pick off the Stalks and chop it very small, and put about half a Pound of melted Butter, or more, according to the Quantity of your Fish, so put it over your Flounders, and serve away quick.

To dress Flounders *or* Plaice *with Garlick and Muftard.*

GET Flounders very new, and cut all the Fins and Tails, then take out the Guts and wipe them very clean, they muft not be at all washed, then with your Knife scotch them on both Sides very grofly, then take the Tops of Thyme, and cut them very small, and take a little Salt, Mace, and Nutmeg, and mingle the Thyme and them together, and season the Flounders, lay them on the Gridiron and bafte them with Oil or Butter, let not the Fire be too hot, when that Side next the Fire is brown, turn it, bafte it on both Sides 'till you have broiled them brown, when they are enough, make your Sauce with Muftard, two or three Spoonfuls according to Difcretion, fix Anchovies diffolved very well, about half a Pound of Butter drawn up with Garlick, Vinegar, or bruifed Garlick in other Vinegar, rub the Bottom of your Difh with

Garlick,

Garlick, fo put your Sauce to them and ferve them : You may fry them if you pleafe.

A Fricafey *of great* Plaice *or* Flounders.

RUN your Knife all along upon the Bone, on the Back-Sides from Head to the Tail, and take the Bone clear out; then cut your Plaice in fix Collops, dry them very well from the Water, fprinkle them with Salt, and flour them well, and fry them in a very hot Pan of Beef-Dripping, fo that they may be crifp, take them out of the Pan and keep them very warm before the Fire, then make clean the Pan, and put into it Oyfters and their Liquor, fome White Wine, the Meat out of the Shell of a Crab or two: Mince half the Oyfters, fome grated Nutmeg, three Anchovies, let all thefe ftew up together, then put in half a Pound of Butter, and put in your Plaice or Flounders, and tofs them well together, and difh them on Sippets, and pour the Sauce over them. Garnifh the Difh with Yolks of hard Eggs, minced and fliced Lemon. After this Manner do Salmon, or any firm Fifh.

Another Way to drefs Flounders.

FLEA off the black Skin, and fcore the Fifh over on that Side with a Knife, lay them on a Difh, and pour on them fome Vinegar, and ftrew good Store of Salt, let them lie for half an Hour; in the mean Time fet on the Fire fome Water and a little White Wine, Garlick and Sweet Herbs, as you pleafe, putting into it the Vinegar and Salt wherein they lay, when it boils put in the biggeft Fifh, then the next 'till all be in, when they are boiled take them out, and drain them very well, then draw fome fweet But-

ter

ter thick, and mix with it some Anchovies shred small, which being dissolved in the Butter, pour it on the Fish, strewing a little sliced Nutmeg, and minced Oranges and Barberries.

To stew Flounders.

G E T small Flounders, and put them in a Stew-pan, with as much Water as will cover them, put into the Liquor a Blade of Mace, some Salt, a Bit of Lemon Peel, and a Spoonful of Lemon Juice, when just done, pour off the Liquor into a Sauce-pan, and melt your Butter with it, put in a Piece of Anchovy, a Bit of Shalot, Mushrooms, and Katchup, draw it thick: Dish your Fish with Sippets of Bread, and pour your Sauce over it.

S O A L S.

Soals *with a Ragoo of Crawfish.*

Y O U must take some Soals, and having gutted, scraped, washed and dryed them, cut off the Heads and the Tails; slit them along the Back, and take out the Bones Take a small Soal and bone it, lay the Flesh on a Table, with a little Parsley and Cives, some Mushrooms, the Yolks of three or four raw Eggs, the Bigness of an Egg of Bread soaked in Cream, and fresh Butter in Proportion, season this with Salt, Pepper, Sweet Herbs, and a little Spice, mince it all well together, and pound it in a Mortar, then farce your Soals with it. Rub the Bottom of a Dish, or Pasty-pan, over with Butter; season it with Salt, Pepper, a very little Sweet Herbs, and minced Parsley, together

ther with a couple of whole Leeks, then turn in the Soals, the farced Side downmoft, and feafon the uppermoft Side with Salt, Pepper, and Nutmeg, fprinkle them over with melted Butter, drudge them flightly with Bread crumbed very fine, and fet them to bake in the Oven, or under a baking Cover, when they are done enough, and of a fine Colour, lay them in a Difh, and pour a Ragoo of Crawfifh upon them   We likewife ferve them with a Ragoo of Oyfters, or of Mufhrooms or Truffles

To drefs Soals *in* Champaign *Wine.*

GET fome middle-fiz'd Soals, and having gutted and fcaled them, cut off the Head and Tail, and the Fins all round them ; lay them in a Stew-pan, feafon them with Salt, Pepper, an Onion ftuck with Cloves, a Bunch of Sweet Herbs, fome whole Cives, minced Parfley, and Slices of Lemon: Pour on them a Pint of *Champaign* Wine, and a little Fifh Broth, to which add a Lump of Butter, and fome Crumbs of Bread grated very fine; fet all this over a Stove with a quick Fire.   When the Soals are enough ftewed, and the Liquor is wafted away as it ought, thicken it with a brown Cullis, or with one of Crawfifh : Lay the Soals handfomely on a Difh, pour the Sauce upon them, and ferve them warm for firft Courfe.

To marinate Soals.

LET large Soals be well wafhed, fkinn'd and dry'd; that done, beat them with a Rolling-Pin, and dip them on both Sides in the Yolks of Eggs temper'd with Flour : Then putting your Fifh into a Frying-pan, with as much *Florence* Oil as will cover them, fry them 'till they

are

are brown, and come to a bright yellow Colour. At that Inftant, take them up, drain them on a Plate, and fet them by to cool. For the Pickle, take White Wine Vinegar well boiled with Salt, Pepper, Nutmeg, Cloves and Mace: It is requifite to turn the Liquor into a broad earthen Pan, that the Fifh may lye at full Length, and the Difh is to be garnifhed with Flowers, Fennel and Lemon Peel.

A Surtout *of* Soals.

MAKE a Farce of the Flefh of a Carp and an Eel as follows: Mince it on a Table with fome Mufh-rooms, Parfley and Cives, feafon the whole with Salt, Pep-per, a little Sweet Herbs and Spice, and put it into a Mor-tar, take the Bignefs of two Eggs of the Crumb of Bread, put it into a Sauce-pan, with fome Cream or Milk, and boil it over a Stove, when it comes to be half thickened, put in the Yolks of two Eggs, ftir them well about in it, and when it is boiled very thick, take it off and fet it a cooling: Mean while, the Farce being well pounded, add to it as much Butter as your Difcretion thinks fit, three or four Yolks of raw Eggs, and the Bread Cream, pound the whole again together, then take it out of the Mortar: Fry two or three Soals, and when they are fried, raife up the Flefh in long Flakes or Slices, fet a Sauce-pan over a Stove with a Lump of Butter, a Handful of fmall Mufh-rooms, and fome Truffles cut in Slices, tofs them up, moift-en them with a little Broth, feafon the whole with Salt, Pepper, and a Bunch of Sweet Herbs, and boil it; when it is enough boiled, take the Fat clean off, and having bound the Sauce with a brown Cullis, or one of Crawfifh, put in the Slices or Flakes of your Soals, and let them fim-

K k

mer

mer over a gentle Fire, then take them off and set them a cooling: Take a Silver Dish, spread the Bottom of it with some of the Farce round it, when your Ragoo of Soals is cold, pour it into the Dish, and cover it with some of the same Farce, dip a broad Knife in beaten Eggs, and rub it gently over the Farce to make it lie smooth, lay all round it some thin Slices of thin Bread, sprinkle it over with melted Butter, drudge it with very fine Crumbs of Bread, and set it to bake in an Oven, when it is baked and of a fine Colour, take it out of the Oven, clear it well of the Fat, wipe the Brims of the Dish very clean, and serve it hot for the first Course.

Note, We make all Sorts of Surtouts of Fish, in the same Manner, that is to say, always with the same Farce, it is only the Ragoo you put in, that makes the Difference and gives the Name to it.

L O B S T E R S.

To roast Lobsters.

RUN a small Bird-Spit thro' the Lobsters Belly, then tie them fast to the Spit with Packthread, and when they are enough they will crackle, lay a whole one, the largest of all, in the Middle of the Dish, butter the rest in Shells, as in the following Receipt, with Pepper, Lemon and an Anchovy dissolved in White Wine; mix the whole together, and serve them up with Lemon and Oysters.

To

To roaſt Lobſters *alive*

HAving tied them faſt on the Spit, baſte them with Salt and Water 'till they look red, and then with Butter and Salt ; let the Sauce be Anchovies diſſolved in White Wine, a little Pepper and the Juice of a Lemon.

To Butter Lobſters.

TAKE out the Meat, pick it ſmall, and ſet it to ſtew gently in a Sauce-pan over a Stove, with White Wine, Salt, and a Blade of Mace, when it is very hot, put to it ſome Butter, and Crumbs of Bread ; warm the Shells before the Fire, fill them with Meat, and ſo ſerve them up.

To broil Lobſters.

FIRST boil them, then lay them on the Gridiron ; baſte them either with Butter alone or mixed with Vinegar ; let them broil leiſurely, and when you think they are enough, ſerve them up with Butter and Vinegar beat thick, to which put ſome grated Nutmeg and ſliced Lemon.

To pot Lobſters.

TAKE a Dozen of large Lobſters, take out all the Meat of their Tails and Claws after they are boiled ; then ſeaſon them with beaten Pepper, Salt, Cloves, Mace, and Nutmeg, all finely beaten and mixed together, then take a Pot, put therein a Layer of freſh Butter, upon which put a Layer of Lobſter, and then ſtrew over ſome Seaſoning, and repeat the ſame 'till your Pot is full, and your Lobſter all in, bake it about an Hour and half, then ſet it

K k 2　　　　　　　　　　　　by

by two or three Days, and it will be fit to eat: It will keep
a Month or more, if you pour from it the Liquor when it
comes out of the Oven, and fill it up with clarified Butter:
Eat it with Vinegar.

To *dress* Crabs.

HAVING taken out the Meat and cleanfed the
Skins, put it into a Stew-pan, with a Quarter of a
Pint of White Wine, or Canary, fome Crumbs of White
Bread, an Anchovy and a little Nutmeg: Then fetting
them over a gentle Fire, flip in the Yolk of an Egg with
a little beaten Pepper, and ftir all well together, in order
to be ferved up for a fide Difh.

To *butter* Prawns, Shrimps, *or* Crawfifh.

TAKE out all the Tails, and leave the Body Shells,
clean them, make a Stuffing with fome of the Infides, Eggs, Crumbs of Bread, Anchovies, Pepper, Salt,
Nutmeg, and a Piece of Butter, or Sewet, chopped very
fine. Mix all this well, put in a little Thyme and Parfley
minced, and fill the Body Shells therewith; the other Part
you muft butter as you do Lobfters, which lay round your
Body Shells, and bake them in a gentle Oven: You may
put fome Oyfters and Marrow in your forced Fifh, if you
pleafe, fo ferve away hot.

To *make an artificial* Crab *or* Lobfter.

IT is to be fuppofed that you have by you the large Shells
of Sea Crabs clean'd; then take Part of a Calf's Liver,
boil it and mince it very fmall, and a little Anchovy Liquor, and but very little, to give it the Fifh Tafte. Mix

it well with a little Lemon Juice, some Pepper, and some Salt, with a little Oil, if you like it, and fill the Shells with it; and then the Outside Part of the Liver, being a little hard, will feel to the Mouth like the Claws of the Crab broken and picked, and the inner Parts will be soft and tender, like the Body of a Crab One may serve this cold, and it will deceive a good Judge, if you do not put too much of the Anchovy Liquor in it It is very good cold, but if you would have it hot, take the following Receipt

To make artificial hot buttered Sea-Crabs.

MAKE the great Shells of Crabs clean, and prepare some Liver, as before, or if you cannot get Calf's Liver, get a Lamb's Liver, or a young Sheep's Liver will do tolerably well Boil these, and shred them as directed before, and put a little Anchovy Liquor to them, then add a little White Wine, some Pepper and Salt at pleasure, and some other Spice at Discretion, with Butter necessary to make it mellow, over a gentle Fire, or a little Sallet Oil, if you like Oil. Then add a little Lemon Juice in the Shells, stirring the Mixture together, then serve them up hot with Lemon sliced.

To make artificial Crabs.

TAKE some of the White of a roasted or boiled Chicken's Breast, and shred it very small; then add some Roots of Potatoes boiled and beat into Pulp, mix these together, and grate a little Lemon Peel upon it, and add a little Anchovy Liquor to it with some Oil; and put a little Lemon Juice to it, or Vinegar, with some Pepper
and

and Salt, ferve it upon Sippets, garnifhed with fliced Lemon. Thefe may be butter'd in Shells as the former, but the firft is rather the beft.

To make artificial Lobfters.

PRactice the fame Method with either of the former, and to imitate the Tail of the Lobfter, put in the Tails of Shrimps, Buntings, Prawns, or Crawfifh; the laft cut in Pieces, and ferve them either upon Sippets in a Plate, or in the large Shell of the Lobfter

This is a fort of Salmy, or Salmy-Gundy, as they call it in *England*; but is very much like the thing we want: and we think if the Shrimps, or others, were put into the firft, it would make it better than putting in the Anchovy Liquor; but if they are to imitate a Crab, they muft chop the Shrimps or Prawns very fmall.

P E R C H E S.

Perches *with Anchovy Sauce.*

GUT your Perches, and ftew them in a *Court-bouillon,* as follows: Lay them into a Stew-pan with fome fliced Onion and Lemon, fome Parfley, Cives, Bay Leaves, Bafil, Cloves, Pepper and Salt, two Glaffes of White Wine, a little Vinegar, and as much Water as will cover them; fo ftew them over a Stove; then take them off, and fet them to cool a little in the *Court-bouillon:* When they have ftood a while take them out, skin them without breaking the Flefh, lay them in a Difh, and cover them that they may not grow cold. Put fome frefh But-

ter

ter into a Sauce-pan, with a little Flour, a couple of minced Anchovies, some Capers, and a whole Leek, a Slice or two of Lemon, the whole being seasoned with Salt, Pepper, and a little Nutmeg, add to it a little Water and Vinegar Keep turning the Sauce over a Stove with a Spoon, and when the Butter is melted and thickened, take out the Leek and sliced Lemon, pour it on the Perches, and serve them for the first Course.

Perches *with a Cullis of Crawfish.*

YOUR Perches being stewed in a *Court-bouillon,* skin them and lay them in a Dish, as in the foregoing Receipt, make a Sauce as follows: Put the Quantity of two Eggs of fresh Butter into a Sauce-pan with one minced Anchovy, some Pepper, Salt, a little grated Nutmeg, a Pinch of Flour, a Drop or two of Water, and as much Vinegar, turn it over a Stove with a Spoon, when the Butter is melted and a little thickened, put in some Crawfish Cullis, pour this Sauce on your Perches, and serve them for the first Course. They may be served likewise with all Sorts of Cullises as well as this.

Perch *dressed in* Fillets.

LET Mushrooms be well cleansed and boiled in a little Cream: Then your Fillets or Slices of Perch being ready cut, mix them together, and let all boil, with a thickening Sauce made of three Yolks of Eggs, Parsley shred, grated Nutmeg, and the Juice of a Lemon; stir them very gently, for fear of breaking your Fillets, and when they are enough, dress them. Garnish with Lemon Slices, &c.

TROUTS.

T R O U T S.

To fry Trouts

FIRST with a Knife, gently fcrape off all the Slime from your Fifh, wafh them in Salt and Water, gut them and wipe them very clean with a Linnen-Cloth, that done, ftrew Wheat-Flour over them, and fry them in fweet Butter, 'till they are brown and crifp: Then take them out of the Frying-Pan, and lay them on a Pewter-Difh well heated before the Fire, pour off the Butter they were fried in, into the Greafe Pot, and not over the Trouts: Afterwards, good Store of Parfley and young Sage being fry'd crifp in other fweet Butter, take out the Herbs and lay them on your Fifh. In the mean while, fome Butter being beaten up with three or four Spoonfuls of fcalding-hot Spring-Water, in which an Anchovy has been diffolved, pour it on the Trouts, and let them be ferv'd up. Garnifh with the Leaves of Strawberries, Parfley, &c.

After this Manner Grailings, Perches, fmall Pikes or Jacks, Roaches and Gudgeons may be fry'd; their Scales being firft fcrap'd off: And you may thus fry fmall Eels, when they are flead, gutted, wiped clean, and cut into Pieces of four or five Inches long, feveral Pieces of Salmon, or a Chine of it, may likewife be drefs'd in the fame Manner.

The beft way of boiling Trouts.

LET the Trouts be wafh'd, and dry'd with a clean Napkin; then open them, and having taking out the Guts, with all the Blood, wipe them very clean on the Infide,

fide, without wafhing, and give each three Scotches with a Knife to the Bone, only on one Side: After that, pour into a Kettle or Stew-pan as much hard ftale Beer, with Vinegar, and a little White Wine and Water, as will cover the Fifh: Then throw into the Liquor a good Quantity of Salt, a Handful of fliced Horfe-Radifh-Root, with a fmall Faggot of Parfley, Rofemary, Thyme and Winter Savoury. That done, fet the Pan over a quick Wood-Fire, and let the Liquor boil up to the Height before you put in your Fifh; then flip them in one by one, that they may not fo cool the Liquor, as to make it fall While the Fifh are boiling, beat up Butter for the Sauce with a little of the Liquor, and as foon as it is enough, drain off the Liqour, lay your Trouts in a Difh, and pour melted Butter upon them, ftrewing them plentifully over, with fhav'd Horfe-Radifh, and a little powder'd Ginger Garnifh the Sides of the Difh with fliced Lemon, and fend it to the Table.

In the fame Manner you may drefs Grayling, Carp, Bream, Roach and Salmon; only they are to be fcal'd, which muft be done very lightly and carefully with a Knife. A Pike may alfo be thus drefs'd, the Slime being firft well fcour'd off with Water and Salt: And a Perch may be ordered after the fame Manner, but the Skin muft be taken off, before you pour on the Sauce.

To pot Trouts.

SCALE and clean your Trouts very well, wafh them in Vinegar, and flit them down the Back, after which put Pepper and Salt into the Incifion, and on their Outfides, and let them lie upon a Difh three Hours; then lay them in an earthen glaz'd Pan, with Pieces of Butter upon

N° 12.   L l   them,

them, and put them in an Oven two Hours, if they are
Fish of fourteen Inches long, or lefs in Proportion, taking
Care to tie fome Paper clofe over the Pan. When this is
done, take away from them all the Liquor, and put them
in a Pot, and as foon as they are quite cold, pour fome
clarify'd Butter upon them, fo cover them, and they
will eat as well as potted Chars.

To fouce Trouts.

TAKE a Quart of Water, a Pint of White Wine,
and two Quarts of White Wine Vinegar, with Pepper, Salt, Nutmeg, Cinamon and Mace, an Onion ftuck
with Cloves, a little Lemon Peel, and a Faggot of Sweet
Herbs, let thefe boil together a little while, and put in
your Trouts, and boil them according to their Bignefs,
then take them out of the Liquor to be cold, and put your
Souce Liquor into a Stone Jar to cool: If 'tis not fharp add
more Vinegar, and a little Salt, and keep your Fifh therein,
if you would have them hot, you may take them out of
the above Souce, when enough; and take for Sauce, a little of the Liquor, *French* White Wine, an Anchovy wafhed clean, and fome Mace, with Oyfters and Shrimps, and
Butter kneaded in Flour. Garnifh with fried Smelts, and
fliced Lemon, and ferve it

You may do Salmon, Pike, Mullet, and moft other
Fifh the fame Way, only if you drefs them to eat hot immediately, you may alter the Sauce if you pleafe.

To make Virginia-Trouts.

TAKE pickled Herrings, cut off their Heads, and
lay the Bodies two Days and Nights in Water; then
wafhing them well, feafon them with Pepper, Cinamon,

Cloves,

Cloves, Mace, and a little red Saunders: Afterwards
them clofe in a Pot with a little chopp'd Onion, ftic
over them, and caft between every Layer. When you
have done thus, put in a Pint of Claret, cover them with
a double Paper ty'd on the Pot, and fet them in the Oven
with Houfhold Bread. They are to be eaten cold.

To drefs Haddocks *the* Dutch Way.

BEING fcaled and gutted, gafh them, with a fharp
Knife, into the Back-Bone on both Sides, and throw
them into cold Water for an Hour; then boil them in Salt,
Water, and Vinegar. They will boil in lefs than half an
Hour, but that muft be according to the Bignefs, only
boil them 'till they will come from the Bone. Then for your
Sauce, take Turnips, cut them as fmall as Yolks of Eggs,
and boil them tender in Water and Salt: In *Holland* they
boil them with the Fifh, and they take very little more
boiling than they, becaufe they are better than ours, but if
you boil *Englifh* Turnips, you muft boil them a little before
you put in your Fifh, but you muft not boil your Turnips
fo tender as if they were to eat with Beef and Mutton;
then drain them from the Liquor, and put two or three
Dozen of Turnips, according to the Bignefs of your Difh,
into a Pound of drawn Butter, and a little fine minced
Parfley, fo put your Haddocks into the Difh, and Sippets
under them, and pour your Turnips and Sauce over them,
throw a little minced Parfley about your Difh, fo ferve it.
You may do Whitings or Soals the fame Way.

L l 2 *CHUBS.*

C H U B S.

To roaſt a Chub.

SCALE your Chub, waſh it well, and take out the
Guts; to that End, make a little Hole as near the
Gills as you can, and cleanſe the Throat, afterwards, having put ſome Sweet Herbs into the Belly, tie the whole
Fiſh with two or three Splinſters to the Spit, and roaſt it,
baſting the ſame often, with Vinegar, or Verjuice and Butter, mix'd with good Store of Salt: By this Means, the
watery Humour, with which all Chubs abound, is effectually dryed up. A Tench may be dreſſed after the ſame
Manner.

To broil a Chub.

WHEN you have ſcaled the Chub, cut off its Tail
and Fins, waſh it clean, and ſlit it thro' the Middle, then give it three or four Cuts or Scotches on the Back,
with a Knife, and broil it on Wood-Coals; all the Time
it is broiling, baſte it with Sweet Butter, mingled with a
good deal of Salt, and a little Thyme ſhred very ſmall.

To boil a Chub.

SET a Kettle over the Fire, with Beer-Vinegar and
Water, ſo much as will cover the Fiſh, and put Fennel therein, with good Store of Salt: As ſoon as the Water
boils, ſlip in your Chub, being firſt ſcalded, gutted and
cleanſed, about the Throat: When 'tis enough, take it out,
lay it on a Board to drain, and after an Hour's lying thus,

pick

pick all the Fiſh from the Bones. Then turn it into a Pewter-Diſh ſet over a Chafing Diſh of Coals, with melted Butter, and ſend it very hot to the Table.

S T U R G E O N.

Of a Sturgeon, *how it ought to be cured, for cold Meat, or dreſſed hot for the Table.*

The Sturgeon is a Fiſh commonly found in the Northern Seas, but now and then we find them in our great Rivers, the *Thames*, the *Severn*, and the *Tyne*, this Fiſh is of a very large Size, even ſometimes to meaſure eighteen Feet in Length: They are in great Eſteem when they are freſh taken, to be cut in Pieces, of eight or ten Pounds, and roaſted or baked; beſides, to be pickled and preſerved for cold Treats: And moreover, the Cavier, which is eſteemed a Dainty, is the Spawn of this Fiſh.

To cure, or pickle Sturgeons *from* Hamborough.

TAKE a Sturgeon, gut it and clean it very well within Side, with Salt and Water, and in the ſame Manner clean the Outſide, wiping both very dry with coarſe Cloaths, without taking any of the great Scales from it: Then take off the Head, the Fins and Tail, and if there is any Spawn in it, ſave it to be cured for Cavier: When this is done, cut your Fiſh into ſmall Pieces, of about four Pounds each, and take out the Bones, as clean as poſſible, and lay them in Salt and Water for twenty four Hours; then dry them well with coarſe Cloaths, and ſuch

Pie

Pieces as want to be rolled up, tie them clofe with Bafs Strings, that is, the Strings of Bark which compofe the Bafs Mats, fuch as the Gardeners ufe; for that being flat, like Tape, will keep the Fifh clofe in the boiling, which would otherwife break, if it was tied with Packthread, ftrew fome Salt over the Pieces, and let them lie three Days, then provide a Piece of Wicker, made flat, and wide as the Copper or Cauldron you will boil your Fifh in, with two or three Strings, faftened to the Edges, the Ends of which fhould hang over the Edges of the Copper. The Pans we generally boil our Fifh in, are fhallow and very broad, then make the following Pickle, *viz* One Gallon of Vinegar to four Gallons of Water, and to that Quantity put four Pounds of Salt When this boils, put in your Fifh, and when it is boiled enough, take it out, and lay it in fingle Pieces, upon Hurdles, to drain, or upon fuch Boards as will not give any extraordinary Tafte to the Fifh. Some will boil in this Pickle a Quarter of a Pound of whole Black Pepper.

When your Fifh is quite cold, lay it in clean Tubs, which are called Kits, and cover it with the Liquor it was boiled in, and clofe it up, to be kept for Ufe.

If at any Time you perceive the Liquor to grow mouldy or begin to mother, pafs it thro' a Sieve, add fome frefh Vinegar to it, and boil it; and when it is quite cold, wafh your Fifh in fome of it, and lay your Pieces a frefh in the Tub, covering them with Liquor as before, and it will keep good feveral Months. This is generally eaten with Oil and Vinegar.

To

To prepare the Cavier *or Spawn of the* Sturgeon.

WASH it well in Vinegar and Water, and then lay it in Salt and Water two or three Days; then boil it in fresh Water and Salt, and when it is cold, put it up for Use. This is eaten upon Toasts of White Bread with a little Oil.

To roast a Piece of fresh Sturgeon.

GET a Piece of fresh Sturgeon, of about eight or ten Pounds, let it lie in Water and Salt, six or eight Hours, with its Scales on, then fasten it on the Spit, and baste it well with Butter for a Quarter of an Hour, and after that, drudge it with grated Bread, Flour, some Nutmeg, a little Mace powdered, Pepper and Salt, and some Sweet Herbs dryed and powdered, continuing basting and drudging of it 'till it is enough, then serve it up with the following Sauce, *viz.* One Pint of thin Gravy and Oyster Liquor, with some Horse-Radish, Lemon Peel, a Bunch of Sweet Herbs, some whole Pepper, and a few Blades of Mace, with a whole Onion, an Anchovy, a Spoonful or two of Liquid Katchup, or some Liquor of pickled Walnuts, with half a Pint of White Wine, strain it off, and put in as much Butter as will thicken it. To this put Oysters parboiled, Shrimps or Prawns pick'd, or the Inside of a Crab, which will make the same Sauce very rich, then garnish with fried Oysters, Lemon sliced, buttered Crabs and fried Bread, cut in handsome Figures, and pickled Mushrooms N. B. If you have no Katchup, you may use Mushroom Gravy, or some of the travelling Sauce mentioned in this Book, or else a small Tea Spoonful of the dry Pocket-Sauce.

To

To roaft a Collar, or Fillet of Sturgeon.

GET a Piece of frefh Sturgeon; take out the Bones, and cut the flefhy Part into Lengths, about feven or eight Inches, then provide fome Shrimps, chopp'd fmall with Oyfters, fome Crumbs of Bread, and fuch Seafoning of Spice as you like, with a little Lemon Peel grated; When this is done, butter one Side of your Fifh, and ftrew fome of your Mixture upon it; then begin to roll it up, as clofe as poffible, and when the firft Piece is rolled up, then roll upon that another, prepared as before, and bind it round with a narrow Fillet, leaving as much of the Fifh apparent as may be, but you muft remark, that the Roll fhould not be above four Inches and a half thick, for, elfe one Part would be done enough before the Infide was hardly warmed; therefore, we have fometimes parboiled the infide Roll before we begin to roll it.

When it is at the Fire bafte it well with Butter, and drudge it with fifted Rafpings of Bread. Serve it with the fame Sauce as directed for the Former.

A Piece of frefh Sturgeon *boiled*.

WHEN your Sturgeon is clean, prepare as much Liquor to boil it in, as will cover it; that is, take a Pint of Vinegar to about two Quarts of Water, a Stick of Horfe-Radifh, two or three Bits of Lemon Peel, fome whole Pepper, a Bay Leaf or two, and a fmall Handful of Salt, boil your Fifh in this, 'till it is enough, and ferve it with the following Sauce:

Melt a Pound of Butter, then add fome Anchovy Liquor, Oyfter Liquor, fome White Wine, fome Katchup

boiled

boiled together with whole Pepper and Mace ſtrained , put to this the Body of a Crab, and ſerve it with a little Lemon Juice.   You may likewiſe put in ſome Shrimps, the Tails of Lobſters, cut to Pieces, ſtewed Oyſters, or Crawfiſh cut into ſmall Bits.   Garniſh with pickled Muſhrooms and roaſted or fried Oyſters, Lemon ſliced, and Horſe-Radiſh ſcraped.

A Ragoo of Sturgeon.

YOUR Sturgeon being cut into Pieces and thoſe Pieces larded, flour them a little, in order to fry them brown with Lard : As ſoon as they are come to a Colour, ſlip them into a Stew-pan, with good Gravy, Sweet Herbs, ſome Slices of Lemon, Truffles, Muſhrooms, Veal Sweetbreads and a good Cullis : Afterwards, the whole Meſs being well cleared from the Fat, put in a Drop of Verjuice, and ſerve it hot.

R O A C H E S.

Roaches *ragoo'd.*

BROIL the Roaches on a Gridiron after they have been ſoak'd in Butter : Fry the Livers in a Pan with a little Butter, in order to be beaten in a Mortar, and paſs'd thro' the Strainer : Then put this Cullis to your Fiſh, ſeaſoned with Salt, White Pepper, and Orange or Lemon Juice ; before they are dreſs'd, rub the Diſh with a Shalot or a Clove of Garlick.

To marinate Roaches.

SET them to steep in Oil, with Wine, Lemon Juice, and other usual Seasonings; then bread them well, and bake them in a gentle Oven, so as they may take a fine Colour: Afterwards they are to be neatly dressed in a Dish, and garnished with fried Bread, and green Parsley.

S H A D S.

To broil Shads.

THESE Fish are to be well scaled and cut: Afterwards, having rubbed them with Butter and Salt, broil them on a Gridiron, 'till they come to a fine Colour: They are to be dished with Sorrel and Cream, adding Parsley, Chervil, Chibbol, Salt, Pepper, Nutmeg, and Sweet Butter · They may also be served up with a Ragoo of Mushrooms, or a brown Sauce with Capers.

To boil Shads.

HAving scaled and cut your Shads, let them boil in White Wine, with Vinegar, Salt, Pepper, Cloves, a Bay Leaf, Onions and green Lemon, and send them to the Table on a Napkin.

To dress a Shad au Court-bouillon.

SCALE and score your Shad, then boil it in White Wine with a little Vinegar, Salt, Pepper, Bay Leaf, Onions stuck with Cloves, Slices of Lemon, and a Lump of Butter; when it is boiled, serve it dry on a Napkin for a Dish of the first Course.

S M E L T S.

S M E L T S.
To fry Smelts.

LAY them to marinate in Vinegar, Salt, Pepper, Bay Leaves and Cives, then dry them well with a Linnen-Cloth, drudge them well with Flour, and dry them; so serve them up hot with fried Parsley.

To dress Smelts *in Ragoo.*

PUT them into a Sauce-pan with a little White Wine, scraped Nutmeg, sliced Lemon, and fried Flour; when they are almost enough, add some minced Capers and serve them.

To dress Smelts au Court-bouillon.

PUT them into a Stew-pan with White Wine, sliced Lemon, Pepper, Salt and Bay Leaf; when they are enough, serve them on a Napkin with green Parsley, or else with a Ramolade.

D A B S.
To marinate a Dab *or* Sandling.

CUT your Fish along the Back, to the End that the Pickle may penetrate the same: When it is marinated bread it well with Chippings seasoned, and bake it in an Oven. Garnish your Dish with Petty Patties.

Dab *in a* Sallet.

LET the Dab be boiled in a Pickle after the usual Manner, and when cold, cut it into Fillets, with which you are to garnish a Plate, and a small Sallet;

seasoning

feafoning the whole with Salt, Pepper, Vinegar, and Oil.

O Y S T E R S.

To ftew Oyfters.

TAKE a Pint of Oyfters, fet them over the Fire in their Liquor, with half a Pint of White Wine, a Lump of fweet Butter, fome Salt, a little White Pepper, and three Blades of Mace, let them ftew foftly about half an Hour, then put in another Piece of Butter, and tofs altogether: As foon as it is melted, turn your Oyfters, &c. upon Sippets made ready and laid in Order in a Difh.

To roaft Oyfters.

YOU muft take the largeft Oyfters you can get, and as they are opened, throw them into a Difh with their own Liquor, then take them out, put them into another Difh, and pour the Liquor over them, but take Care that no Gravel get in ; that done, fet them covered on the Fire, and fcald them a little in their Liquor: As foon as they are cold, draw feveral Lards through every Oyfter, the Lardoons being firft feafoned with Pepper, Cloves, and Nutmeg, beaten very fine. Afterwards, having fpitted your Oyfters on two wooden Lark-Spits, tie them to another Spit and roaft them: In the mean while, bafte them with Anchovy Sauce, made with fome of the Oyfter Liquor, and let them drip into the fame Difh, wherein the Sauce is, when they are enough, bread them with the Cruft of a Roll grated; and when they are brown, draw them off. At laft blow off the Fat from the Sauce with

which

which the Oyſters were baſted, and put the ſame thereto; ſqueeze in the Juice of a Lemon, and ſo let all be ſerved up.

Oyſters *grilled in Shells.*

LET them be firſt bearded, and lightly ſeaſoned with Salt, Pepper and ſhred Parſley: Afterwards, the ſcollop Shells being well buttered, lay your Oyſters in neatly, adding their Liquor and grated Bread · Let them ſtew thus half an Hour, and then brown them with a red hot Fire-ſhovel or a broad Iron heated for that Purpoſe. Shrimps may be grilled after the ſame Manner, and they will prove very good.

Another particular Way of dreſſing Oyſters.

HAving open'd your Oyſters, ſave the Liquor, and put thereto ſome White Wine, with which you are to waſh the Oyſters one by one, and lay them in another Diſh: Then ſtrain to them that mingled Liquor and Wine wherein they were waſh'd, adding a little more Wine, with an Onion chopp'd, ſome Salt and Pepper: Cover the Diſh, and ſtew them 'till they are more than half enough; that done, turn them, with the Liquor, into a Frying-pan, and fry them a pretty while; then ſlip in a good Piece of Butter, and let them fry ſo much longer. In the mean Time, having prepared Yolks of Eggs, (four or five to a Quart of Oyſters) beaten up with Vinegar, ſhred Parſley and grated Nutmeg, mix them with the Oyſters in the Pan, which muſt ſtill be kept ſtirring, left the Liquor make the Eggs curdle: Laſtly, let all have a thorough Walm over the Fire, and ſend them to the Table.

To pickle Oyſters.

GET the largeſt Oyſters, waſh them clean, and let them ſettle in their own Liquor : Then ſtrain it, and add a little White Wine Vinegar, with Salt, whole long Pepper, a Race of Ginger, three Bay Leaves and an Onion. Theſe being well boiled together, ſlip in your Oyſters, and let them boil leiſurely 'till they are tender ; be ſure to clear them from the Scum as it riſes : When they are enough take them out, and ſet them by 'till the Pickle is cold : Afterwards, they may be put into a long Pot, or into a Caper-Barrel, and they'll keep very well ſix Weeks.

To make Oyſter-Loaves.

HAving prepared what Number of *French* Rolls you think fit, cut a Hole on the Top of every one, about the Compaſs of half a Crown, and ſcoop out the Crumb, ſo as not to break the Cruſt: Then let ſome Oyſters ſtew in their own Liquor, with a little White Wine, Salt, whole Pepper, Nutmeg, and a Blade of Mace; take off the Scum carefully, and thicken the Liquor with a Piece of Butter roll'd up in Flour. Afterwards fill up your Rolls with the Oyſters and Sauce, and lay on the Piece again that was cut off. At laſt, having put the Rolls into a Diſh, pour melted Butter over them, and ſet them in an Oven to to be made criſp.

Oyſters au Parmeſan.

RUB over the Bottom of a Silver Diſh with good Butter, and having opened your Oyſters, lay them in it, and ſtrew over them a little Pepper and minced Parſley.
Then

Then put to them half a Glass of *Champaign* Wine, cover them with Slices of fresh Butter cut very thin, strew over them some fine grated Cheese; lay a Tart-pan over the Dish, and set them a stewing with Fire over and under them 'till they are of a fine brown Colour; then take off all the Fat, clean the Brims of your Dish, and serve them very hot.

N B. Instead of grated Cheese, you may put only Crumbs of Bread, and then they are called stewed Oysters.

Oysters à la Daube.

OPEN your Oysters and season them with Parsley, Basil and Cives, shred very small, putting a little of it to each Oyster with Pepper and a little White Wine: Then cover them with the upper Shell, and broil them on a Gridiron; lay from Time to Time, a red hot Shovel over them. When they are enough, take off the upper Shell, and serve them in the under one.

Petty Patties of Oysters.

GET as many Oysters in the Shells as you would make Patties, then mince the Melts and Flesh of Carps, Tenches, Pikes, and the Flesh of Eels, season all this with Pepper, Salt, pounded Cloves and White Wine; wrap up your Oysters in it, of which only one is to be put in each Patty, with a little fresh Butter. Bake them, and serve them hot, either as *Hors d'Oeuvres*, or for Garnishing.

To

To make an Oyster Pye.

FOR a Plate or little Dish, blanch off a Quart of Oy-
sters or more, take them from the Tails and Shells,
and drain them from the Liquor; then take a Quarter of a
Pound of Butter, a minced Anchovy, two Spoonfuls of
grated Bread, a Spoonful of minced Parsley, a little beaten
Pepper, a scraped Nutmeg, a little or no Salt, because your
Oysters and the Anchovy have a Seasoning in themselves;
Then make a Paste as follows: Take about a Quarter of a
Pound of Butter, work it with a good Handful of Flour;
put to it a Spoonful or two of cold Water, then part it in
two, and roll out each half, as if it were for a Tart: It is
proper you should bake your Oyster Pye on the Mazarine
you serve it in, or a little Patty Pan; then place on the Bottom Paste half of your mixed Butter, Anchovy and Parsley aforesaid. Lay on your Oysters, two or three thick at
most, put the rest of your Butter and Parsley on the Top,
and a Slice of Lemon, then wet it about with some of
your Oysters Liquor, strewing a little beaten Pepper and
Nutmeg over your Oysters, and two Spoonfuls of your Liquor: Then cover it up as you do a Tart, only turn and
cut it handsomely round, and turn the Edge of your Paste,
all round, an Inch high. Bake it three Quarters of an
Hour before you have Occasion for it; then cut up its
Cover, and squeeze in a Lemon. Shake it gently together,
and cut your Cover in Bits, and lay handsomely round it:
So serve it for the first Course. *Note,* you may bake it
without a Cover.

Scollop-

Scollop-Shells of Oyſters.

SET and beard them, feaſon them lightly with Pepper, Salt and minced Parſley: Butter the Scollop-Shells very well; then, when your Fiſh or Oyſters are neatly laid in, pour their Liquor, thickened with grated Bread, over them, let them grill half an Hour and brown them with a red hot Salamander, or Fire-ſhovel: You may garniſh a Diſh of Fiſh with them, or ſerve them by themſelves for the ſecond Courſe.

A Matelotte *of* Fiſh.

GET a Carp, an Eel, ſome Tench, Pike, Barbel, in ſhort, what Fiſh you can get, and judge proper for your Purpoſe; after having gutted and ſcaled them, cut them in Pieces, and lay them in a Stew-pan, with ſome Truffles and Muſhrooms, an Onion ſtuck with Cloves, ſome Cives and Parſley, Bay Leaves, and a little Baſil: Seaſon this with Salt and Pepper, put to it ſome White Wine, a little Fiſh Broth, or Juice of Onion, but juſt enough to cover the Fiſh, then ſet it over a quick Fire, and when the *Court-bouillon* is half waſted away, put ſome Butter, more or leſs, according to the Quantity of your Fiſh, into a Sauce-pan, and brown in it a little Flour, then empty the Liquor of your Matelotte into that Sauce-pan, mix your brown and that well together, and pour the whole back again into your Matelotte, and keep it ſtewing 'till it is enough done; then put to it ſome Crawfiſh, or other meagre Cullis, lay it handſomely in a Diſh, and ſerve it warm for the firſt Courſe.

N n

To

To make an Olive *of all Sorts of* Fiſh.

YOU muſt take of all Sorts of Fiſh that are not flat, as Carps, Pikes, Mullets, Trouts, &c. being cleanſed and waſhed, take the firmeſt and biggeſt for boiling, and the other for frying and farcing: Your Fiſh being boiled off quick, as likewiſe your other Fiſh being all ready, diſh on your Sippets ſome large Fiſh turned round in the Middle of your Diſh, or a Collar of Salmon baked in the Oven, with the Heads of Fiſhes on the Top of it, and your fried Fiſh betwixt them, your Smelts and Gudgeons round the Brims of your Diſh, and have a Force-Meat made of Fiſh in little Balls, place them between the Boiled and the Fried; then having your Oyſters, Cockles, Prawns, Periwinkles, Crawfiſh, or ſliced Lobſters, or any of theſe ready in your Sauce of thick Butter, as likewiſe your Anchovies, pour it all over your Fiſh, having Nutmeg grated therein: Garniſh it with Lemon, and ſend it ſmoaking hot.

A Biſque *of* Fiſh

YOU may take what freſh Fiſh you pleaſe and clean it very well, then ſteep it in White Wine Vinegar, whole Spice, ſome whole Onions, Sweet Herbs ty'd up, one Lemon ſhred, a Handful of Salt, cover the Fiſh almoſt with Ingredients; let it ſteep an Hour, then have ready boiling, a Thing of fair Water, then put in your Fiſh with the Ingredients on the Fire, and when it is about half enough, put in the boiling Water to it, and this way will make the Fiſh much firmer than the old Way, then fry ſome of the other in hot Liquor, then a rich Sauce made with Oyſters, Shrimps, Muſhrooms, two Anchovies, Capers,

Capers, a Bundle of Sweet Herbs, two whole Onions, one ftuck with Cloves, Horfe-Radifh fcrap'd, Nutmeg, the Juice of a Lemon, the Yolks of two Eggs, mix all thefe together with two Pounds of Butter, and draw it up very thick, then difh your Fifh on Sippets, and run over your Sauces. Garnifh your fried Fifh with Parfley, Horfe-Radifh, and cut Lemon, and ferve it up hot. Thus you may do all frefh Fifh.

Fifh Sauce.

TAKE fome good Gravy, and make it pretty ftrong of Anchovies, and a little Horfe-Radifh, then work a Piece of Butter in fome Flour, and put to it, with fome more Butter, and draw it up thick: Then with ftewed Oyfters and Shrimps put it to your Fifh. Garnifh with fried Parfley, Lemon, and Sippets.

Another

GET two Anchovies, and boil them in a little White Wine a Quarter of an Hour, with a little Shalot cut thin; then melt your Butter very thick, and put in fome picked Shrimps, and pour it over your Fifh. You may add Oyfter Liquor.

Fifh Sauce *to keep the whole Year.*

GET twenty four Anchovies, chop them Bones and all; put to ten Shalots, a Handful of fcraped Horfe-Radifh, four Blades of Mace, one Quart of *Rhenifh* Wine, or White Wine, one Pint of Water, one Lemon cut in Slices, half a Pint of Anchovy Liquor, one Pint of Claret, twelve Cloves, twelve Pepper Corns; boil them together,

'till

'till it comes to a Quart; then ſtrain it off in a Bottle, and two Spoonfuls will be ſufficient to a Pound of melted Butter.

Another Sauce *for Fiſh.*

A Little Thyme, Horſe-Radiſh, Lemon Peel, and whole Pepper, being boiled in fair Water, add four Spoonfuls of White Wine, with two Anchovies, and let all boil together for a while, then ſtrain them out, and turn the Liquor into the ſame Pan, with a Pound of freſh Butter; as ſoon as it is melted, remove the Pan, and ſlip in the Yolks of two Eggs, well beaten with three Spoonfuls of White Wine. Laſtly, ſet your Sauce over the Fire again, and ſtir it continually, 'till it is as thick as Cream; then pour it on your Fiſh very hot, and ſend to the Table.

A particular Sauce *called,* Ramolade.

THIS Sauce, being proper for ſeveral Sorts of Fiſh cut into Fillets or thin Slices, is made of Parſley, Chibbols, Anchovies and Capers all chopp'd ſmall, and put into a Diſh with Oil, Vinegar, a little Salt, Pepper, and Nutmeg well tempered together. After the Fillets are dreſs'd, this Ramolade is uſually turned over them, and ſometimes Juice of Lemon is added, when they are to be ſerved up cold.

CHAP.

CHAP. XVII.

BUTCHER's MEAT.

B E E F.

To dress Beef à la Braise.

GET two or more Ribs of Beef, only the fleshy Part
of them that is next the Chine, cutting off the long
Bones, and taking away all the Fat; lard it with large
Pieces of Bacon, seasoned with Spices, Sweet Herbs, Parsley, young Onions, a little Quantity of Mushrooms and
Truffles shred very small. When your Beef is thus larded,
bind it about with Packthread for fear it should break to
Pieces when you come to take it out of the Stew-pan,
which must be bigger or less according to the Size of your
Beef. Cover the Bottom of it with Slices of fat Bacon,
and over that lay Slices of lean Beef an Inch thick well
beaten, and seasoned with Spice, Herbs, Onions, Lemon
Peel, Bay Leaves, Pepper, and Salt; then put in the Beef,
observing to lay the fleshly Side downmost, that it may the
better take the Taste of the Seasoning. You must season
the upper Part of it as you did the lower, and lay over it
in like Manner Slices of fat Beef, and over them Slices of
Bacon : This done, cover your Stew-pan, and close it well
with Paste all round the Edge of the Cover, then put some
Fire as well over as under it : While your Beef is thus
getting ready, make a Ragoo of Veal Sweetbreads, Capons Livers, Mushrooms, Truffles, Asparagus Tops, and
Artichoke

Artichoke Bottoms, which you muft tofs up with a little melted Bacon, moiften with good Gravy, and thicken with a Cullis made of Veal and Gammon of Bacon. When you are ready to ferve take up your Beef, and let it drain a little; then lay it in the Difh in which you intend to ferve it, and pour your Ragoo upon it

This Beef *à la Braife* is fometimes ferved with a hafhed Sauce, made in the following Manner. We take a little of the Lean of a Gammon of Bacon, fome young Onions, a little Parfley, fome Mufhrooms, and Truffles, and fhred all of them very fmall together: Then we tofs it up with a little Lard, moiften it with good Gravy, and thicken it with the Cullis laft mentioned, and when we ferve up the Beef, we pour this Sauce upon it.

At other Times, it may be ferved up with a Ragoo of Cardoons, or Succory, or Sellery, or of roafted Onions, or Cucumbers, which loft is made as follows:

Take fome Cucumbers and pair them, cut them in two in the Middle, take out the Seeds; then cut them in fmall Slices, and marinate them for two Hours, with two or three fliced Onions, Vinegar, and a little Pepper and Salt; after this, fqueeze your Cucumbers in a Linnen-Cloth, and then tofs them up, in a little melted Bacon, when they begin to grow brown, put to them fome good Gravy, and fet them to fimmer over a Stove. When you are ready to ferve, take off the Fat from your Cucumbers, thicken them with a good Cullis made of Veal and Gammon of Bacon, and pour them on your Beef.

This Ragoo of Cucumbers ferves likewife for all Sorts of Butcher's Meat, that is, either roafted or ftewed in whole Joints in its own Gravy.

Beef

Beef *à la Braise*, is made of all the Pieces that grow next the Chine from the Neck to the Rump, as well as of the Ribs.

Beef *farced*.

THE same Pieces of Beef only are farced that are dressed *à la Braise*; that is to say, those that are commonly called Roasting Pieces, and those may be farced with a Salpicon, the Receipt, for making of which, see hereafter. Or else when your Beef is almost roasted, raise up the Skin or Outside of it, and take the Flesh of the Middle, which you must shred very small, with the Fat of Bacon and Beef, fine Herbs, Spices, and good Garnishings. With this you farce or stuff Beef between the Skin and the Bone, and sew it up very carefully to prevent the Flesh from dropping into the Dripping-pan, when you make an end of roasting it.

Biscuit *of Beef* à la Chalonnoise.

YOU must take a Biscuit of Beef, and set it a boiling, when it is half boiled, take it up and lard it with large Lardoons of Bacon, then put it on a Spit, and to make it stick fast, take two Sticks and tie them at both Ends of it. Have in your Dripping-pan a Marinade made of Vinegar, Pepper, Salt, Spice, Onion, the Rine of Lemon and Orange, Rosemary, and Sage, and keep basting with it all the while it is roasting: When it is enough, set it a simmering in the Sauce, which you may thicken with Chippings of Bread, or Flour stirred in a little strong Broth. Let your Garnishings be Mushrooms, Palates, and Asparagus.

A Rump

A Rump *of* Beef *roll'd*

HAving taken out the Bones, make a Slit the whole Length of it, and fpread it as much as you can: Lard it with large Lardoons of Bacon well feafoned · Make a Farce of the Flefh of the Breafts of Fowls, Beef-Sewet, Mufhrooms, and boiled Ham: Seafon your Farce with Pepper, Salt, Sweet Herbs, Spices, Parfley, and fmall Onions, a few Crumbs of Bread, moiftened with Cream, and three or four Yolks of raw Eggs, hafh all thefe together and pound it in a Mortar. Having fpread this Farce on the Piece of Beef, roll it up at the two Ends, and tie it faft with Packthread: Take a Pot or Kettle of the Size of your Piece of Beef, and garnifh the Bottom of it firft with Bards of Bacon, and then with Slices of Beef well feafoned with Salt, Pepper, Herbs, Spices, Onions, Carrots, and Parfnips, put the Piece of Beef into the Pot, and cover it with Beef and Bacon, as under it; cover your Pot very clofe, put Fire under and over it, keep it ftewing for ten or twelve Hours: Make hafhed Sauce with fome Ham of Bacon cut in Dice, with hafhed Mufhrooms and Truffles, fmall Onions, and Parfley. Tofs up all this in a Sauce-pan with a little melted Bacon, and moiften it with good Gravy, when it is enough, take off all the Fat, and thicken the Sauce with a Cullis of Veal and Bacon. When you are going to ferve, mix among it a hafhed Anchovy and a few Capers: Take up your Beef and drain it very well, then lay it in your Difh, pour your Sauce upon it; fo ferve it very warm.

At

At another Time you may ferve it with a Ragoo of Calves Sweetbreads, and Cocks Combs, or with a Ragoo of Cucumbers and Succory.

Beef *Fillets.*

FILLETS or Slices of Beef larded, and marinated with Vinegar, Salt, Pepper, Cloves, Thyme, and Onions, muft be roafted leifurely on a Spit, and then put into good Gravy with Truffles; and garnifhed with marinated Pigeons or Chickens.

To ragoo Beef, *fee the Chapter of* Ragoos.

Beef *efcarlot.*

TAKE a Brifcuit of Beef and rub all over half a Pound of Bay Salt, and a little White Salt mix'd with it; then lay it in an Earthen Pan or Pot; turn it every Day, and in four Days it will be red, then boil it four Hours very tender, and ferve it with Savoys, or any Kind of Greens, or without, with pick'd raw Parfley all round.

Beef à la Daub.

GET a Rump or Buttock of Beef, lard it and force it, then pafs it off brown; put in fome Liquor or Broth, and a Faggot of Herbs; feafon with Pepper, Salt, Cloves and Mace; ftove it four Hours very tender, and make a Ragoo of Morels, Truffles, Mufhrooms, Sweetbreads and Pallates, and lay all over. Garnifh with Petty Patties and ftick Atlets over.

N° 13.   O o   Beef

Beef á la Mode *in Pieces.*

YOU muſt take a Buttock, and cut it in two Pound Lumps, laid them with groſs Lards ſeaſoned, paſs them off brown, and then ſtove them in good Liquor or Broth of Sweet Herbs as will juſt cover the Meat; put in a Faggot and ſeaſon with Cloves, Mace, Nutmeg and Salt ; and when tender, ſkim all well, and ſo ſerve away hot or cold.

Beef *Olives.*

CUT a Rump of Beef into long Streaks, cut them ſquare, and waſh them with an Egg and ſeaſon them; lay on ſome Force-Meat, and roll them and tie them up faſt, and either roaſt them or ſtove them tender. Sauce them with Shalots, Gravy and Vinegar.

A Haſh *of raw* Beef.

CUT ſome thin Slices of tender Beef and put them in a Stew-pan, with a little Water, a Bunch of Sweet Herbs, ſome Lemon Peel, and Onion, with ſome Pepper, Salt, and ſome Nutmeg, cover theſe cloſe, and let them ſtew 'till they are tender, then pour in a Glaſs or two of Claret, and when it is warm, clear your Sauce of the Onion, Herbs, *&c.* and thicken it with burnt Butter. It is an excellent Diſh. Serve it hot, and garniſh with Lemon ſliced, and red Beet-Roots, Capers, and ſuch like.

Thin Beef-Collops *ſtewed.*

CUT raw Beef in thin Slices, as you would do Veal for *Scots* Collops, lay them in a Diſh, with a little Water, a Glaſs of Wine, a Shalot, ſome Pepper and Salt,

and

and a little Sweet Marjoram powdered ; then clap another Dish over that, having first put a thin Slice or two of fat Bacon among your Collops ; then set your Mess, so as to rest on the Back of two Chairs, and take six Sheets of whited-brown Paper, and tear it in long Pieces, and then lighting one of them, hold it under the Dish, 'till it burns out, then light another, and so another 'till all your Paper is burnt, and then your Stew will be enough, and full of Gravy. Some will put in a little Mushroom Gravy, with the Water and the other Ingredients, which is a very good Way.

Stewed Beef-Steaks.

GET good Rump-Beef-Steaks, and season them with Pepper and Salt, then lay them in the Pan, and pour in a little Water, then add a Bunch of Sweet Herbs, a few Cloves, an Anchovy, a little Verjuice, an Onion, and a little Lemon Peel, with a little Bit of Butter, or fat Bacon, and a Glass of White Wine Cover these close, and stew them gently, and when they are tender, pour away the Sauce, and strain it, then take out the Steaks, and flour them, and fry them, and when you put them in the Dish, thicken the Sauce, and pour it over them.

An admirable Way of boiling a Rump *of* Beef.

HAving common Salt, all Sorts of pot Herbs, and a little Salt Petre, rub your Beef all over with them, and let it lie three or four Days, put it in a large Pot, with Water, over a good Fire, and put in Onions, Carrots, Garden Herbs, Cloves, Pepper, and Salt, boil your Beef, and when ready, lay it in a Dish, garnished with green Parsley, and serve it.

　　　　　　　　　To

To stew a Rump *of* Beef.

TAKE an oval Stew-pan, with a close Cover, lay in a Rump of Beef, but cut off the Bone, cover the Beef with Water, put in a Spoonful of whole Pepper, two Onions, a Bunch of Sweet Marjoram, Savoury, Thyme, and Parsley, half a Pint of Vinegar, a Pint of Claret, and season it with Salt, set it on the Stove, close covered, to stew four Hours, shaking it sometimes, and turning it four or five times, if it be too dry, pour in warm Water; make Gravy as for Soop, and put in three Quarts of it, keep it stewing 'till Dinner is near ready, then stew twelve Turnips, cut the broad Way in four Slices, and flour them well, and fry them at twice in boiling Beef-Sewet, and drain them When the Beef is tender, put it dry in a Dish, and put the Turnips into the Gravy; shake them together, and let them heat over the Fire, and pour it over the Beef; melt two Ounces of Butter in the Sauce-pan, where you shook up your Turnips, and a little Gravy, and pour all over the Beef, and serve it.

Portugal Beef.

BROWN the Thin of a Rump of Beef in a Pan of brown Butter, and force the Lean of it with Sewet, Bacon, boiled Chesnuts, Anchovies, an Onion, and season it, stew it in a Pan of strong Broth, and make for it a Ragoo of Gravy, pickled Gerkins, and boiled Chesnuts; thicken it with brown Butter, and garnish it with sliced Lemon.

To

To dry Beef *after the* Dutch *Way.*

HAving the beſt Part of the Buttock of a fat Ox, cut it in what Shapes you pleaſe, then take a Quart of Petre Salt, and as much good Bay Salt, as will ſalt it very well, and let it ſtand in a cold Cellar ten Days in Salt, in which Time you muſt turn and rub in the Salt, then take it out of the Brine, and hang it in a Chimney, where a Wood-Fire is kept, for a Month; in which Time it will be dry, and will keep a Twelve-month When you eat it, boil it tender, and when cold, cut it in thin Shivers, and eat it with Vinegar, and Bread and Butter

Palates *of* Beef, *en gratin.*

LET ſome raſped Parmeſan be put in the Bottom of your Diſh, with a little Cullis, put in your Palates, pour ſome Cullis, and ſtrew ſome Parmeſan over them, then ſend your Diſh to the Oven to get a Colour, and when that is done, add ſome Eſſence of Ham, and Juice of Lemon.

Fillets *of* Beef *after the* Indian *Way.*

TAKE a Fillet of Beef, lard it with middling Bacon, and ſlice it on the Side it is not larded. Then marinate your Fillet during two Hours, with Salt, Pepper, Sweet Herbs, Garlick cut ſmall, the Juice of two Lemons, and a Glaſs of good Oil. Put your marinated Fillet, wrapt up in Paper, upon a Skewer, tie this to the Spit, and baſte it with your Marinade, which muſt be mixed with a Glaſs of White Wine. Your Fillet being done, take off the Papper, diſh it up with an *Italian* Sauce, and ſerve it up hot for a firſt Courſe,

A Dutch

A Dutch *Way of dressing* Beef *callled,* Patei-Stuck-Ghe-roockt.

THIS is a Biiscuit of Beef, soaked eight Days in biine, and then hung up for three Months. It is then to be washed in several Waters to get the Salt out, and boiled with Cauliflowers, Cabbage, Spinage, and thickened Butter served with it. It may be likewise stewed with Carrots.

A Salpicon.

A Salpicon is a Sort of Ragoo, so called, and is used in great Dishes of roast Meat, in the first Course, such as Chines of Beef or Mutton, Barons of Beef, and Quarters of Mutton or Veal, &c. It is made as follows:

GET some Cucumbeis, cut them in Dice, and lay them in a Dish to marinate in Vinegai, Peppei and Salt, and an Onion or two, cut in Slices, cut some of the Lean of a Ham of Bacon in Dice, take some Mushrooms and Truffles, the Breasts of Pullets, fat Livers and Veal Sweetbreads. Squeeze the Cucumbeis, toss them up in a Sauce-pan over a Stove with a little melted Bacon; moisten them with Gravy, and let them simmer in it over a gentle Fire; then take the Fat clean off· Set over a Stove another Sauce-pan with a little melted Bacon, into which put the Ham you had cut in Dice, a few Cives and a little Parsley. Mince the Mushrooms, Truffles, and Sweetbreads, and toss up all the Ingredients together, and then moisten them with some Gravy, season them with Pepper, Salt, and a Bunch
of

of Herbs; and when they have fimmered a while in it, take off all the Fat; when they are almoft enough, put to them the fat Livers, and the Breafts of your Pullets cut in Dice; then bind your Salpicon with fome Cullis of Veal and Ham, and fome Effence of Ham. When the Cucumbers are ready, bind them likewife with the fame Cullis, and put the whole into the fame Sauce-pan, that is to fay, put the Ragoo of Cucumbers into the Salpicon.

Make a Hole in your Piece of roaft Meat, in the Part you think moft convenient, for Example, if it be a Quarter of Veal or Mutton, make it in the Leg, and having taken out the Flefh, that may ferve for fome other Ufe, put the Salpicon in the Room of it.

A Salpicon may be ferved in a Difh by itfelf.

To roaft a Tongue *and* Udder

BOIL the Tongue a little, blanch it, and lard it with Bacon, the Length of an Inch, being firft feafoned with Nutmeg, Pepper, and Cinamon, and ftuff the Udder full of Cloves, then fpit and roaft them; bafte them with Sweet Butter, and ferve them up with Claret Sauce Garnifh with fliced Lemon.

Tongues *with forced* Udders *roafted.*

YOU muft firft boil off your Ox Tongues, and your Udders, then make a good Forced-Meat with Veal; and as for your Tongues, you muft lard them, and your Udders you muft raife the Infide, and fit them with Forced-Meat, wafhing the Infide with the Yolk of an Egg, then tie the Ends clofe, and fpit them, and roaft them: Make a Sauce with Syrup of Claret or Gravy. You may draw the Udders on the Top with Lemon Peel and Thyme.

Ox

Ox Tongues *à la Mode.*

HAving large Ox Tongues, boil them tender, then blanch them and take the Skin off, and laid them on both Sides, leaving the Middle, then brown them off, and ftove them one Hour in good Gravy and Broth, feafon with Spice and a Faggot of Herbs, and put in fome Morels, Truffles, Mufhrooms, Sweetbreads, and Artichoke Bottoms, then fkim off the Fat and ferve either hot or cold.

Neats Tongues *à la Braife.*

CUT away the Roots of the Tongues, and then put them into boiling Water, that you may take off the Skin as clear as poffible, laid them with large Bits of a raw Gammon of Bacon well feafoned: Then take a Boiler, and cover the Bottom of it with Bards of Bacon, and Slices of Beef well beaten: Lay in your Tongues with fliced Onions, and all Sorts of Sweet Herbs, and Spices, and feafon them befides, with Pepper and Salt; cover them befides with Slices of Beef and Bacon, in the fame Manner as under them, fo that they may be entirely wrapped up in them; put them to ftew *à la Braife*, with Fire over and under: You muft keep them fo eight or ten Hours, that they may be thoroughly done. After which, you muft have in Readinefs a good Cullis of Mufhrooms, or fome other good Ragoo with all Sorts of Ingredients, as Mufhrooms, Morels, Truffles, Sweetbreads, *&c.* Having takeing up your Tongues, you drain them and take off the Fat; then lay them in a Difh, and your Ragoo over them; if you would garnifh the Difh, you may cut one of the

Tongues

Tongues in Slices, or elfe garnifh it with Fricandos, all ferved very warm.

Calves Tongues are fometimes dreffed in the fame Manner, and if one will, they may be farced without larding and ferved up with the fame Ragoo

Another Way to drefs a Neat's Tongue

BOIL it in Water with a little Salt, and a Faggot of Sweet Herbs · When it is almoft enough, cut off the Root, take off the Skin, and lard it with long Bits of Bacon; then lay it down to the Fire, and while it is roaft-ing, bafte it with Butter, Salt, Pepper and Vinegar When it is roafted, cut it in large Slices, and tofs it up a Moment in a Stew-pan, with a Ramolade made of Anchovies, Ca-pers, Parfley and Onions fhred very fmall: Then tofs all up in good Beef Gravy, with Salt, Pepper, a few Rocamboles, and a Drop of Vinegar, and ferve it for the firft Courfe

We ferve it likewife after having cut it in Slices, with a Ragoo of Mufhrooms, Sweetbreads, Artichoke Bottoms, Salt, Pepper, Butter, or melted Bacon: We fet it a fim-mering in this Ragoo, and fo ferve it, but obferve, that when we ferve it this Way, we ufe no Vinegar in bafting it but only Butter.

Calves Tongues are dreffed in the fame Manner, and may be ferved whole, either with a *Poivrade*, or a fweet Sauce.

To make a Sauce Poivrade.

PUT fouce Vinegar into a Sauce-pan with a little Veal Gravy, one whole Leek, an Onion cut in Slices, and two or three Slices of Lemon; feafon it with Pepper and Salt, and when it is boiled ftrain it thro' a Sieve, pour it into a Porringer, and ferve it hot.

P p

MUTTON.

M U T T O N.

To dress a Leg *of* Mutton à la Royale.

HAving taking off the Fat, and the Flesh and Skin that is about the Shank Bone, laid the Leg with large Laidoons well seasoned, laid likewise, at the same Time, a round Piece of a Buttock of Beef, or of a Leg of Veal, then season all this very well, drudge it with Flour, and put it into boiling Hog's Lard to give it a Colour: Then put it into a Pot with all Sorts of savoury Herbs, an Onion or two stuck with Cloves, and put in some Broth or Water, cover the Pot very close, and let it boil two Hours, mean while, get ready a Ragoo of Mushrooms, Truffles, Asparagus Tops, Artichoke Bottoms and Veal Sweetbreads, to which put a good Cullis. Take up your Leg of Mutton, lay it in a Dish, and cut your Piece of Beef or Veal into Slices, to make a Rim round your Mutton, pour the Ragoo hot upon it, and so serve away.

Shoulder *of* Mutton *in Epigram.*

GET a Shoulder of Mutton and roast it, take off the Skin as neatly as you can, about the Thickness of a Crown, leaving the Shank Bone to it; then take the Meat and cut it in small thin Slices, the Bigness of a Shilling; then put it in a Cullis that is well seasoned, and take Care not to let it boil; then take the Skin of your Shoulder of Mutton, and put some Crumbs of Bread, with sweet Herbs, over it, and put it on the Gridiron, and when it has taken Colour, see that your Hash be well seasoned; dish it up, putting on the broiled Skin

'This some call a Shoulder of Mutton in *Gallimaufry.*

Mutton

Mutton Collops

YOU muft take fome Mutton that is well mortified, that is, ftale, but fweet, take out the Skin and Si- news, and cut them fmall and thin, about the Bignefs of a Crown Piece, fuch a Quantity as you think will be enough for your Difh; take a Stew-pan with fome Butter, and lay your Collops in, one after another; take Care they are very thin, and put a little Salt, Pepper, Spices, Parfley, and green Onions, chopped very fine, over them, with fome Truffles, or Mufhrooms, and put your Stew-pan over a Fire that is very quick, and ftir them with a Spoon, and when you think they are done, drefs them in the Difh you are to ferve them in. Then put in the Pan a little Cullis and Gravy, with a Rocambole, and when it is boiled up, and a little thick, put in the Juice of a Lemon, and put it over your Collops, and ferve them up hot.

A Harrico *of* Mutton.

HAving a Neck or Loin of Mutton, cut it into fix Pieces, feafon it with Pepper and Salt, then pafs them off on both Sides in a Frying-pan or Stew-pan; put to them fome good Broth, a Faggot of Herbs, fome diced Carrots or Turnips fried off, and two Dozen of Chefnuts blanched, and three or four fmall Lettuces; ftew all this well together: You may put in half a Dozen fmall, round, whole Onions, and when very tender, skim off the Fat well, and ferve away: Garnifh with forced Lettuce, and Turnips, and Carrots fliced.

Hind

Hind Saddle *of* Mutton.

HAving the two hind Quarters of a Sheep, cut off the two Knuckles, that it may set even on the Dish; then take off the Skin as neatly and as far as you can towards the Rump, without taking it quite off, or breaking it: Then take some lean Ham, Truffles, green Onions, Parsley, Thyme, Sweet Herbs, Pepper, Salt, and Spices well chopped together, and strew it over your Mutton, where the Skin is taken off; then put the Skin over neatly and wrap it over with Paper well buttered, and tie it and put it to roast, and being roasted, take off the Paper, and strew over some Crumbs of Bread, and when it is well coloured, take it off the Spit, dish it up, and put under it an Essence of Ham, or a Shalot Sauce, and serve it up hot for the first Course.

Hind Saddle *of* Mutton *done* à la *St.* Menehout.

CUT your Mutton as above-mentioned, and laid it with large Lardoons of Bacon seasoned with Pepper, Salt, Sweet Herbs, small Onions and Parsley; then garnishing an oval or large Gravy-pan that will hold it, put at the Bottom some Bards of Bacon and Slices of Beef, put in also some small Onions, Parsley, Sweet Herbs, and then put in your Mutton, seasoned with Pepper, Salt and Spice, a Bottle of Wine and strong Broth, and put the same over it as under, Bards of Bacon, Slices of Beef, with a little Garlick and Bay Leaves, and put it a stewing with Fire over and under; and when done, take it out, and put it in the Dish, pare it neatly, and put some Crumbs of Bread over it, mixed with *Parmesan* Cheese, and put it in an Oven to

take

take a good Colour, then ferve it up hot, with Effence of Ham under it, for the firft Courfe.

Leg *of* Mutton *Ham Fafhion.*

YOU muft take a hind Quarter very large, and cut like a Jigget, that is, with a Piece of the Loin; then rub it all over with Bay Salt, and let it lie one Day; then put it into the following Pickle: Take a Gallon of Pump Water, put into it two Pounds of Bay Salt, two of White Salt, fix Ounces of Salt Petre, and four of Peter Salt, one Pound of common brown Four-penny Sugar, fix Bay Leaves, one Ounce of Lapis Prunella. Mix all this in your Liquor, then put in your Mutton, and in feven Days it will be red thorough, then hang it up by the Handle and fmoak dry it with Deal-Duft, and Shavings, making a great Smother under it, and in five Days it will be ready. You may boil it with Greens, and it will cut as red as a Cherry, fo ferve it as you would a Ham.

Amphilias *of* Mutton.

HAving two Necks or two Loins, bone them, leaveing the upper top Bones on about an Inch; then lard one with Bacon, the other with Parfley, skewer them, and you may either ftove or roaft them, you may fry fome Cucumbers, and ftew them after, and lay under, or make a Sauce Robart with Onions, Muftard, Vinegar, Gravy, and lay under either ftewed Sellery or Endive, which you choofe.

To force a Leg *of* Mutton *or* Lamb.

LET all the Meat be taken out, leave the Skin whole; then take the Lean of it, and make it into Force-Meat thus: To two Pounds of your lean Meat,

three

three Pounds of Beef Sewet; take away all Skins from the Meat and Sewet, then shred both very fine, and beat it with a Rolling Pin, 'till you know not the Meat from the Sewet, then mix with it four Spoonfuls of grated Bread, half an Ounce of Cloves and Mace beaten, as much Pepper, some Salt, a few Sweet Herbs, shred small, mix all these together with six raw Eggs, and put it into the Skin again, and sew it up. If you roast it, serve it with Anchovy Sauce; if you boil it, lay Cauliflowers, or *French* Beans under it. Garnish with Pickles, or stewed Oysters, and put under it, with Forced-Meat Balls, or Sausages fried in Butter.

To boil a Leg *of* Mutton.

LARD your Mutton with Lemon Peel and Beet Root, and boil it as usual: For Sauce, take strong Broth and White Wine, Gravy, Oysters, Anchovies, an Onion, a Faggot of Herbs, Pepper, Salt and Mace, and a Piece of Butter rolled up in Flour.

Mutton Cutlets *the* French *Way.*

SEASON your Cutlets with Pepper, Salt, Nutmeg and Sweet Herbs; then dip two *Scotch* Collops in the Batter of Eggs, and clap on each Side of each Cutlet, and then a Rasher of Bacon each Side again: Broil them, or bake them in a flow Oven; when they are done, take off the Bacon, and send your Collops and Cutlets in a Ragoo, and garnish them with sliced Orange and Lemon.

Cutlets

Cutlets à la Mointenon.

HAving cut your Cutlets handfomely, beat them thin with your Cleaver, and feafon them well with a little Pepper and Salt , then cover them all over, except within two Inches of the Rib-Bone, as thick as a Crown Piece, with fome Forced-Meat, and fmooth it over with a Knife. This done, take as many half Sheets of White Paper as you have Cutlets, and butter them, on one Side, with melted Butter : Dip your Cutlets likewife in melted Butter, and throw a little grated Bread on the Top of your Forced-Meat all round : Lay each Cutlet on a half Sheet of Paper crofs the Middle of it, leaving the Bone about an Inch out , then clofe the two Ends of your Paper on the Sides, as you do a Turnover-Tart, cut off the Paper that is too much, broil your Mutton Cutlets half an Hour, your Veal three Quarters of an Hour : Then take off the Paper, and lay them round in the Difh, with the Bones outmoft : Let your Sauce be Butter, Gravy, and Lemon.

To hafh a Shoulder *of* Mutton.

LET your Shoulder be half roafted, and cut it in very thin Slices , then take a Glafs of Claret, a Blade of Mace, two Anchovies, a few Capers, a Shalot, Salt, a Sprig of Thyme, Savoury and Lemon Peel, and let it ftand covered for half an Hour ; and when enough, fhake it up with fome Capers, and ferve it.

A Mutton Hafh.

TAKE a roafted Leg of Mutton, take off all the Skin, and cut the Meat from the Bone in thin Slices, and ftrew upon it fome Parfley and Cives, with fome Truffles,

and

and Mushrooms cut pretty small, then put it all together, into a Sauce-pan, with some Pepper and Salt, and a Slice or two of Lemon, with the Rind taken off. Put some good Gravy, and give it two or three Turns over the Stove, thicken it with a Cullis, and serve it.

A Hash *of cold* Mutton.

TAKE Gravy, Oyster Liquor, Anchovies and Nutmeg, according to the Quantity of Meat, and boil it up; then strew in your Meat, and give it a heat or two; put in half a Pound of Sweet Butter, and half a Pint of White Wine, and send it to the Table. Garnish the Dish with Raspins of *French* Bread and Lemon.

Carbonaded Mutton.

YOU must cut a Joint of Mutton into thin Slices, as if for broiling, and fry them in melted Lard, before they are stewed in Broth, with Salt, Pepper, and Cloves, a Bunch of Herbs and Mushrooms, then flour it a little to thicken it. Garnish your Dish with Mushrooms and fried Bread, and serve it with Capers, and a little Lemon Juice.

To roll a Breast *of* Mutton.

BONE the Mutton and make a savoury Forced-Meat, wash it over with the Batter of Eggs; then spread the Forced-Meat on it, and roll it into a Collar, and bind it with Packthread; roast it 'till enough, and put under it a Regalia of Cucumbers.

A

A Shoulder *of* Mutton *in Blood.*

WHEN you kill your Mutton, fave the Blood, take out all the Knots and Strings; take a little grated Bread, Sweet Marjoram, Thyme, and other Sweet Herbs; wafh them and dry them in a Cloth, fhred them very fmall with a little grated Nutmeg; mix all thefe in a little warm Blood of the Sheep, and ftuff the Shoulder with it very much; lay it in fteep five Hours, with the reft of the Blood; then lay the Shoulder in the Caul, fprinkle it with Blood, and roaft it, let it be well roafted, and ferve it with Venifon Sauce.

Shoulder *of* Mutton *with a Ragoo of* Turnips.

GET a Shoulder of Mutton, take out the Blade Bone as neatly as you can, and put in the Place, a Ragoo of Sweetbreads, with Mufhrooms, Truffles, Cocks Combs well feafoned; when done, let it be cold before you put it in, and take Care to few it tight, that it may keep its natural Form, and put it in a Stew-pan, with fome Bards of Bacon, Slices of Veal and Ham, Onions, Parfley, Thyme, Sweet Herbs, Salt, Pepper, Spices, with a Ladle full of Broth, and put it a doing with Fire under and over, then you muft have fome Turnips cut in what Shape you think proper, and blanch them in boiling Water, then ftrain them off, and let them be well drained; then put them in a good Cullis, and let them be done enough; then take your Shoulder of Mutton out of the Braife, and fee it be well drained from all the Fat, difh it up, and put over it your Ragoo of Turnips, and ferve it up hot for the firft Courfe.

Q q   Shoulder

Shoulder *of* Mutton á la Rouchi.

TAKE a Fore Quarter of Mutton, take out the Bones as neatly as you can from the Neck and Breaft, and laid the Fillet, not parting them from the Shoulder, and put it on a Spit to roaft, and when it is done, put under it fome ftewed Endive, and ferve it up hot with the laided Part uppermoft for the firft Courfe.

Leg *of* Mutton *larded* á la Braife, *with a Ragoo of Chefnuts.*

GET a Leg of Mutton, take off the Skin, and lard it with Bacon and Ham through and through, but feafon your Ham and Bacon well, tie it and put it in a Braife; then take fome Chefnuts, roaft them, and take off both Skins very clean, and put them in fome good Cullis of Veal and Ham, and put them over a flow Fire, and when you find they begin to be very foft, fee they be well relifhed, and put them over your Mutton, and ferve it hot for the firft Courfe.

Sheeps Rumps *with Rice.*

YOU muft take fome Sheeps Rumps well cleaned and blanched, and put them a ftewing in a good Braife; and when they are enough, take them out to cool, then take fome Rice well wafhed and picked, put it in a Pot with fome good Fat Broth, with an Onion ftuck with Cloves, a little Pepper and Salt, and fee it be well feafoned and very thick, and when it is done, put it to cool, then take your Sheeps Rumps, and put them round the Rice as neatly as you can; do them round in Eggs, and Crumbs of
Bread

Bread over them : And when you have done them all, take
a Frying-pan with fome Hog's Lard, put it over a Stove,
and when your Fat is hot, put your Sheeps Rumps in it,
and fee they be of a good Colour, and difh them up with
fried Parfley round.

Sheeps Rumps *with* Parmefan *Cheefe.*

PUT your Sheeps Rumps in a good Braife, as before,
and when done, put them to cool, then take fome
Crumbs of Bread very fine, and as much *Parmefan* Cheefe
mixed together, then take your Rumps and dip them in
Eggs, and put the Crumbs of Bread and *Parmefan* Cheefe
over ; and if you find that once doing over is not enough,
do them twice, and fry them in good Hog's Lard of a
good Colour, and ferve them with fried Parfley.

L A M B.

To roaft a Quarter *of* Lamb,

ONE half being larded, drudge the other with fmall
Crumbs of Bread, wrap it up in Paper before you
lay it down, for fear it fhould burn ; when it is almoft roafted, drudge, as before, the Part of it that is not larded,
with Crumbs of Bread, adding to them fome Salt and Parfley fhred fmall , make a brifk Fire to brown it well, and
ferve it with Juice of Lemon and Orange.

Lamb *with* Rice.

GET a Fore Quarter, and roaft it about three Parts ;
take a Pound of Rice, and put in two Quarts of
good Broth, and two Blades of Mace, and fome Salt and
Nutmeg ;

Nutmeg; ftove it an Hour, and take it off; put in the
Yolks of fix Eggs, and a Pound of Butter, then put your
Lamb in Joints in the Difh and the Rice all over it, wafh
it over with Eggs and fo bake it.

A Leg *of* Lamb forced.

YOU muft take the Meat out of the Leg clofe to the
Skin and bone and mince it with Beef Sewet,
Thyme, Parfley and Onions, beat it in a Mortar with favoury Spice and two Anchovies; then wafh the Infide of
the Skin with the Batter of Eggs and fill it, bafte Flour
and bake it · The Sauce may be feafoned with Gravy or
put to it a Regalia of Cucumbers, Cauliflowers or *French*
Beans.

For Lamb Pie, *fee the Chapter of* Paftry.

V E A L.

Loin *of* Veal à la Braife.

PArboil your Loin of Veal, and lard it with large Lardoons, feafoned with Pepper, Salt and Nutmeg.
Garnifh the Bottom of an oval Stew-pan with Slices of
Bacon and Veal, feafoned with Salt, Pepper, Sweet Herbs
and Spices, minced Parfley, Slices of Onions, Carrots,
Parfnips and Lemon: Then lay in your Loin of Veal, the
Kidney Side uppermoft, feafon it over as under, cover it
in like Manner with Slices of Veal and Bacon; fo having
covered your Stew-pan, very clofe, ftew it with Fire over
and under it; when it is enough, drain it well, then lay it
in a Difh, pour upon it a Ragoo of Veal Sweetbreads,
Cocks Combs, Mufhrooms, Morels and Truffles, or of
Cucumbers, or of Lettuce; fo ferve it for the firft Courfe.

Loin

Loin *of* Veal *marinated.*

PArboil and lard it with large Lardoons, lay it in a great deep Dish, put to it a sufficient Quantity of Vinegar, together with Salt, Pepper, some Slices of Lemon and Onion, Bay Leaves, and whole Cives, and let it marinate in it three or four Hours, then put it on a Spit, lard it with Slices of Ham and Bards of Bacon, wrap it round with Paper, and lay it down to the Fire; put into the Dripping-pan a Pound of Butter, together with the Pickle in which you marinated the Veal, and baste it with it from Time to Time as it is roasting; when it is enough, take off the Paper and Slices of Bacon, brown it well with a brisk Fire, so serve it with some Essence of Ham under it, and garnish with fried Veal Cutlets.

A Pillaw *of* Veal.

GET a Neck or Breast of Veal half roasted, and cut it in six Pieces, season it with Pepper, Salt and Nutmeg, and butter the Inside of your Dish, then stove a Pound of Rice tender, with some good white Broth, Mace, and Salt, you must stove it very thick, put in the Yolks of six Eggs; stir it about very well, and cool it, and put some at the Bottom of your Dish, and lay your Veal on a round Heap, and cover it all over with Rice; wash it all over with the Yolks of Eggs, and bake it one Hour and half; then open the Top and pour in some good thick Gravy, and squeeze in an Orange, and so serve away hot. Garnish with sliced Orange and Veal Cutlets.

Bombarded

Bombarded Veal.

GET a Fillet of Veal, cut out of it five lean Pieces, as thick as your Hand, round them up a little, then lard them very thick on the round Side, lard five Sheeps Tongues, being boiled, blanched and larded with Lemon Peel and Beet Root, then make a well feafoned Forced-Meat, with Veal, lean Bacon, Beef Sewet, and an Anchovy, roll it up into a Ball, being well beat, then make another tender Forced-Meat with Veal, fat Bacon, Beef Sewet, Mufhrooms, Spinage, Parfley, Thyme, Sweet Marjoram, Winter Savoury, and green Onions, feafon and beat it. Then put your Forced Ball into Part of this Forced-Meat, put it into a Veal Caul, and bake it in a little Pot: Then roll up that which is left in another Veal Caul, wet with the Batter of Eggs, roll it up like a *Bolonia* Saufage, tie it at both Ends flightly round and boil it, your Forced Ball being baked, put it in the Middle of the Difh, your larded Veal being ftewed in ftrong Broth, lay round it, and the Tongues, fried brown, between each, then pour on them a Ragoo, lay about it the other Forced-Meat, cut as thin as a half Crown, and fried in the Batter of Eggs; then fqueeze on it an Orange, and garnifh it with fliced Lemon.

Veal alamode, à la Daub.

HAving a good Fillet of Veal interlarded as the Beef, add to the ftewing of it a little White Wine; then make for it a Ragoo, and garnifh it with fliced Lemon.

To

To *stew* Veal.

YOU muſt cut your Veal into ſmall Pieces, ſeaſon it with Salt, whole Pepper, Mace, an Onion and Lemon-Peel, in order to be ſtewed in Water, with a little Butter: When your Meat is enough, ſtir in the Yolks of Eggs beaten, and let all have a Walm or two, before they are taken off from the Fire.

To *make* Balls *of* Veal.

GET the Lean of a Leg of Veal, and cut out the Sinews, mince it very ſmall, and with it ſome Fat of Beef Sewet, if the Leg be of a Cow-Calf, the Udder will be good inſtead of Sewet, when it is very well tempered together with the Chopping Knife, have ſome Cloves, Mace, and Pepper beaten, and with Salt ſeaſon your Meat, putting in ſome Vinegar; then make up the Meat into little Balls, and ſet them to boil in good ſtrong Mutton-Broth, as ſoon as they are boiled enough, take the Yolks of five or ſix Eggs well beaten, with as much Vinegar as you pleaſe, and ſome of the Broth mingled together; ſtir it into all your Balls and Broth, give it a Walm on the Fire; then diſh up the Balls upon Sippets, and pour the Sauce on it.

Olives *of* Veal.

YOU muſt take ten or twelve *Scotch* Collops, and waſh them over with Batter of Eggs, and ſeaſon them, and lay over them a little Forced-Meat, and roll them up, and roaſt them, make for them a Ragoo, and garniſh the Diſh with ſliced Orange.

Olives

Olives *of* Veal *another Way.*

WE take the Flesh of a Fillet of Veal, with some Marrow, two Anchovies, the Yolks of two hard Eggs, a few Mushrooms and Oysters, a little Thyme, Marjoram, Parsley and Spinage, Lemon Peel, Salt, Pepper, Nutmeg and Mace finely beaten, then take your Veal Caul, and lay several Lays of middling Bacon, and of the Ingredients above, one upon another, and roll all up in the Caul to be roasted or baked, and when it is enough, cut it in thin Slices, and serve it in a Dish of strong Gravy.

To make Olives *of* Veal.

CUT the Flesh of a Leg of Veal into thin Slices; take Thyme, Marjoram, Parsley, Marrow, Cloves, Mace, Nutmeg and Salt; chop all these together, and roll them up in some of the long Pieces, then spit them on a Bird-Spit, and tie them on, and when they are roasted, make Sauce for them of Butter, and the Juice of two or three Oranges.

An admirable Way of dressing Collops.

CUT a Leg of Veal into thin Slices, and hack them with the Back of a Knife; then lard them thin with Bacon; then take a few Sweet Herbs, and some Nutmeg, cut small, strew over the Meat, and flour them, and a little Salt; then take them and fry them brown in sweet Butter. For the Sauce, take half a Pint of Gravy, a Quarter of a Pint of Claret, one Anchovy, one Shalot; shred them and boil them together; then put in a Quarter of a Pound of sweet Butter, the Yolks of two Eggs well beaten;

then

then pour out the Butter you fried them in, if any is left, and put in your Sauce, and fhake it together; difh them up very hot, with Lamb's Stones, and Sweetbreads, fried brown. Garnifh your Difh with Lemons, or Truffles and Morels.

Scotch Collops *another Way.*

CUT a Fillet of Veal into thin Slices; cut off the Skin and Fat, lard them with Bacon, make three Pints of Gravy, as for Soop, flour your Collops, and fry them brown, and lay them by; then take a Quarter of a Pound of Butter, and put it into a deep Stew-pan; let it melt, and ftrew in a Handful of Flour, fhaking and ftirring it 'till it is brown; then put in the Gravy, and one whole fmall Onion, a Bunch of Herbs, which muft be foon taken out; let it boil a little, and put in the Collops to ftew half a Quarter of an Hour: Put in Balls of Forced-Meat ready fried; beat the Yolks of two Eggs, break into them fix Ounces of Butter, a little Vinegar, take up a little Liquor out of the Stew-pot and mix with it, then pour it all in, and fhake them well together; take out the Collops, lay them on the Difh, and let the Sauce thicken a little more, and pour it over the Meat: You may add fried Bacon, Mufhrooms and Palates; put in the Juice of a Lemon.

White Scotch Collops.

CUT your Veal in thin Slices, lard it with Bacon, feafon it with Cloves, Mace, Sweet Herbs, and grated Bread; ftew the Knuckle with as little Broth as you can, a Bunch of Sweet Herbs, a little Cloves and Mace; then take a Pint of it, and put in two Anchovies, a Quarter of

N° 14.   R r   a Pint

a Pint of White Wine, and some Mushrooms ; thicken it up with the Yolks of three Eggs, and a Piece of Butter.

Another Way to dress Scotch Collops.

WE take the Flesh Part of a Leg of Veal, and lard it with Bacon, as much as you think fit, sliced very thin, then take half a Pint of Ale, and do the Veal in it, 'till the Blood be out, then pour out the Ale into a Porringer, and take a little Thyme, Savoury and Sweet Marjoram chopp'd small, strew it over the Veal, and fry it in Butter, and flour it a little, 'till enough, then put it into a Dish ; put the Butter away, and fry thin Bits of Bacon and lay in the Middle of the Dish. For the Sauce, put into the Ale four Anchovies, and a little White Wine, the Yolks of two Eggs, a little Nutmeg, or Pepper : Melt the Anchovies before you put in the Eggs, and when it begins to thicken, put in a Piece of Butter, and shake it about 'till it is melted ; then pour it over your Meat. You may do it in Gravy instead of Ale ; melt your Anchovies in White Wine.

To make Savoury Balls.

WE take the Flesh of Fowl, Beef Sewet, and Marrow, of each the like Quantity ; seven Oysters, a little lean Bacon, with Sweet Herbs, Pepper, Salt, Nutmeg, and Mace ; pound them, and make it up into Balls.

To make Force-Meat-Balls.

TAKE a Pound of Veal, and the same Weight of Beef Sewet, and a Bit of Bacon, shred altogether, beat it in a Mortar very fine; then season it with

Sweet

Sweet Herbs, Pepper, Salt, Cloves, Mace and Nutmegs,
and when you roll it up to fry, add the Yolks of two or
three Eggs to bind it: You may add Oysters, or Marrow
at an Entertainment.

Breast *of* Veal *in* Galantine.

BONE a Breast of Veal, stretch it, and beat it as flat
as you can; season it with Parsley, Thyme, Marjoram, Winter Savoury, Marygolds, all well minced, Pepper, Salt, Nutmeg; roll it up well, and tie it very close,
then tie it up in a Cloth, and boil it in good seasoned Broth,
Wine, and a little Thyme. When it is boiled, let it cool
in the same Liquor; send it up either whole or in Slices,
upon a Napkin. Garnish it as you like.

Jigget *of* Veal à la Daub.

AFTER having taken off the Skin, blanch it, lard
it with small Lardoons, and lay it to soak in Verjuice, White Wine, Salt, a Faggot of Sweet Herbs, Pepper, Bay Leaves and Cloves: Then roast it, basting it with
the same Wine, mixed with Verjuice, and a little Broth:
When it is roasted, if you intend to eat it hot, make your
Sauce of the Dripping, a little fried Flour, Capers, Slices
of Lemon, Juice of Mushrooms, and Anchovies. Let
your Jigget simmer in it for some Time, and serve it away.
A Leg of Mutton may be done the same Way.

A Loaf *of* Veal.

BEAT some thin Slices of Veal flat with your Cleaver;
take Meat enough to make your Loaf with; then
take another Lump of your Slices of Veal, and cut into

Bits, together with some Beef Sewet, some Bacon and a Calf's Udder blanched, put all together in a Stew-pan over the Fire, season it with Pepper, Salt, Sweet Herbs, fine Spice, Chibbols, Parsley, Garlick, Mushrooms and Truffles, if you have any, toss it up and stir it together, and put into it Crumbs of Bread boiled in Milk, and four or five Yolks of Eggs: All this being well minced, garnish the whole Bottom of a Stew-pan, with some thin broad Slices of Bacon, and over them some Slices of Veal, and then your Forced-Meat all round it the Thickness of two Fingers: At last, put in a small Ragoo made of Gristles of Veal, and some green Pease; let all be well done, and of a good Taste, and put this Ragoo into your Loaf of Veal, putting, at the same Time, more of your Forced-Meat, and small Slices of Veal over the same; bring your Slices of Bacon to lay about it, and let them stew: It being done, take out the said Slices of Bacon, pour out the Fat, turn it upside down in the Dish, skim it well, and put your Ragoo of green Pease over it, or instead of Pease a Cullis.

At another Time you may serve up your Loaf with a Ragoo of Sweetbreads of Veal, Cocks Combs, Mushrooms, Truffles, or an Essence of Ham.

At another Time, you may make use of a Calf's Caul, instead of Slices of Veal, and serve it up.

At another Time, instead of taking Gristles of Veal to put into your Loaves, take Fillets of all Sorts of Fowls; and put over your Loaf an Essence, or a Ragoo of *Spanish* Cardoons, or such other Sauce or Ragoo as you think fit.

At

At another Time, inftead of fuch Fillets, you may make ufe of a Ragoo of Sweetbreads.

Veal *Blanquets*

HAving a Piece of roaft Veal, cut off all the Skin and nervous Parts, into little thin Slices; put fome Butter in a Stew-pan over the Fire, with fome chopp'd Onion; fry it a little, then add a little Duft of Flour to it, and wet it with good clear Broth : Put to it a Faggot of Sweet Herbs and young Onions, feafon it with Spice; make it of a good Tafte, then put in your Veal, bind it with Eggs and Cream like a Fricafey, a little Shalot, Rocambole, and Parfley chopp'd fmall, and a little grated Nutmeg and grated Lemon Peel, with fome Lemon Juice, make it favoury, and laft of all, put in a Spoonful of Oil; ferve it hot.

A Shoulder *of* Veal, à la Piemontoife.

HAving a Shoulder of Veal, take off the Skin, that it may hang at one End, cut Lardoons of Bacon and Ham, feafoned with Pepper, Salt, fine Spice, fine Herbs, and lard the Shoulder of Veal with it; cover it again with the Skin, and braife it; then take Sorrel and Lettuce picked and wafhed clean, chop it very well, put it over the Fire in a Stew-pan with a little Butter, chopp'd Parfley, Onions and Mufhrooms. The Herbs being ftewed tender, put to it fome good Cullis, Bits of Ham and Sweetbreads, cut in Dice. When the Shoulder of Veal is ready, take it out and drain it, put it in the Difh you intend it for, take off the Skin, put fome of the Sweet Herbs under and over, put the Skin over it again, wet it with melted Butter, and

ftrew

ftrew over it fome *Parmefan*; give it a Colour in the Oven; ferve it hot.

A Neck *of* Veal *in Farced-Meat Cutlets.*

BOIL the Neck of Veal in your Soop; when it is boiled, take it out, and cut all the Flefh from off the Bones, and make it into a good Farced-Meat, then form the Farced-Meat like Cutlets, with the Ribs fticking out, put them into a Baking-pan, do them over with Yolks of Eggs and Crumbs of Bread, put them in the Oven, give them a good Colour, then put them in your Difh with Gravy under them; ferve them hot.

For ragooing a Breaft *of* Veal, *fee the Chapter of* Ragoos.

To hafh a Calf's Head.

YOUR Calf's Head being flit and cleaned, and half boiled, and cold, cut one Side into thin Slices, fry it in a Pan of Butter; then having a Sauce-pan on the Stove, with a Pint of Gravy, a Pint of ftrong Broth, a quarter of a Pint of Claret, and as much White Wine, a few Savoury Balls, and a Pint of Oyfters, with Lamb's Stones and Sweetbreads, boiled and blanched, and fliced, with Mufhrooms and Truffles, two or three Anchovies, with two Shalots, and a Faggot of Sweet Herbs, toffed up and ftewed together; feafon it with Nutmeg, Mace, Pepper and Salt; then fcotch the other Side, a-crofs, and a-crofs; flour, bafte, and broil it: The Hafh being thickened with brown Butter, put it in the Difh; lay about it fried Balls, and the Tongue fliced and larded with Bacon, and Lemon Peel; then fry, in the Batter of Eggs, fliced Sweetbreads,

carved

carved Sippets and Oysters, lay in the Head, and place these about the Dish, and garnish it with sliced Orange.

To hash a Calf's Head *another Way*

BOIL your Calf's Head 'till the Meat is near enough for eating, take it up, and cut it into thin Slices; then put to it half a Pint of White Wine, and three Quarters of a Pint of Gravy; put to this Liquor two Anchovies, half a Nutmeg, a little Mace, and a small Onion stuck with Cloves, boil this up in the Liquor, a Quarter of an Hour; then strain it, and let it boil gently again, then put in your Meat, with a little Salt, and some Lemon Peel shred fine, and let it stew a little, mix the Brains with the Yolks of Eggs, and fry them for garnish; when your Head is ready, shake in a Bit of Butter, and serve it up.

An admirable Way to roast a Calf's Head.

GET a Calf's Head with the Skin on, and scald it, and boil it an Hour and half, when cold, lard it with Lemon Peel, and then spit it; when it is enough, make good savoury Sauce, as you do for a hashed Head, and put into it Forced-Meat-Balls, fried Sweetbreads, Eggs, and Clary, a little Bacon, some Truffles and Morels, Mushrooms and Oysters, and a little Lemon Juice, and mix it all well together, with the Sauce, and pour over the Head. It may be done as well with the Skin off, as it comes from the Butcher's.

Calf's Head *Surprise.*

YOU must bone it and not split it, cleanse it well, and fill up the vacant Place with Meat, and make it in the same Form as before; you may put in the Middle a
Ragoo

Ragoo, and cover it with Force-Meat; then wafh it with Egg, and crumb it, and bake it; fo ferve it.

To roaft Veal Sweetbreads

LARD them with fmall Lardoons, run a Skewer thro' them, fasten them to the Spit, and roaft them 'till they are very brown; then lay them in a Difh, in which you have put fome Effence of Ham, or good Gravy, fo ferve them.

To fry Veal Sweetbreads.

AFTER having blanched and cut each Sweetbread in three or four Pieces, lay them in a Difh with an Onion cut in Slices, fome whole Cives, and a Bay Leaf, Salt, Pepper, two or three Cloves, and Juice of Lemon; let them marinate in this for two Hours, mean while, make a Batter as follows: Put into a Pan one Handful of Flour, and a little Salt, beat it into Batter with fair Water, and one Egg, melt as big as a Walnut of Butter, and add to it: Take Care it be not too thick, nor too thin: Take the Sweetbreads out of the Marinade, and having dried them well between two Napkins, put them into the Batter; heat fome Hog's Lard in a Frying-pan, and put in your Sweetbreads one by one, draining them well from the Batter, when they are fried brown, take them up and drain them; then fry fome Parfley; lay a Napkin in a Difh, place your Sweetbreads upon it, and the fried Parfley in the Middle; fo ferve them for Plates, or little Difhes.

Sweetbreads

Sweetbreads *of* Veal á la Dauphine.

TAKE the largeſt Sweetbreads you can get, order them as for a Ragoo, open them and ſlit them round, then fill them with Stuffing made of Chickens · Put Slices of Veal and Bacon in a Stew-pan, ſeaſon them with Salt, Pepper, Sweet Herbs, fine Spices, whole Chibbols and an Onion cut in Slices. Then put in the Sweetbreads, ſeaſon and cover them with Slices of Veal and Bacon; cover the Stew-pan, ſtew them with Fire under and over: The Sweetbreads being done, take them out, take out the Slices of Bacon, put in a Ladle full of good Broth, let it ſtew, ſtrain the Broth through a Silk Strainer, take off the Fat, then put the Broth in a clean Stew-pan 'till it turns to a Jelly, put in the Sweetbreads to glaze; being glazed, put an Eſſence in your Diſh, with your Sweetbreads laid upon it.

Fricando's *of* Veal.

HAving a Leg of Veal, cut off ſome Slices, beat them well with the Handle of a Knife, lard them, lay them on a Table, the larded Side downwards, cover them the Thickneſs of a Crown Piece, with a Farce made of Veal, Beef Marrow, a little Bacon, and ſome Eggs, ſeaſoned with Salt, Pepper, and ſavoury Herbs. Having thus farced them, dip your Hand in beaten Eggs, and ſmooth the Edges of them: Lay them in a Stew-pan with a little Bacon under them, cover the Pan, and ſet it over the Stove; put likewiſe, a little Fire upon it. You muſt keep them thus, 'till they are brown on both Sides, then take them up, let the Fat drain from them, and then put them

S ſ again

again into a Stew-pan, with fome Beef Gravy; let them fimmer a while in it; take off all the Fat, put in a Drop of Verjuice, then lay them in a Difh; pour on them a Ragoo of Mufhrooms, Truffles and Sweetbreads, and ferve them warm.

When Fricando's are ufed for garnifhing, they are dreffed the fame Way, but not larded.

P O R K and P I G.

To do a Leg *of* Pork *Ham Fafhion.*

YOUR Pork muft be cut like a Ham, then take a Quart of ordinary Salt, and a Quart of Bay Salt, and heat it very hot, then mix it with a Pound of coarfe Sugar, and an Ounce of Salt Petre beaten fine, and rub the Ham very well with it, and cover it all over with what is left, for it muft go all on, fo let it lie three Days; then turn it every Day for a Fortnight, then take it out, and fmoke it as you do Bacon or Tongues: The Salt muft be put on as hot as you can.

To falt Hams *to tafte like* Weftphalia *ones*

GET Salt Petre, falt your Ham with it very well, let it lie therein for a Week, take clean Afhes of Afh-Wood, boil them in fair Water, to a ftrong Lee, let it ftand and fettle, then take off the clean Water, and boil it again, making it a ftrong Broth with ordinary Salt, when it is cold, put in the Ham, let it lie a Month in Brine; then dry it well, without fmoaking, and they will have the right Tafte of *Weftphalia* Hams.

To

To salt Hams.

YOU muſt take the Ham when it is hot, being juſt killed, with two Ounces of Bay Salt, and two Ounces of Salt Petre, then cover it, and let it ſtand nine Days, then ſalt it with theſe two Salts, and hang it up in a Chimney of Wood Smoak for three Days, then hang it in the Kitchen, where it may have a little Warmth of the Fire.

To pickle ſix Hams *of* Pork.

HAving one Peck of Bay Salt, half a Pound of Salt Petre, and five Pounds of brown Sugar, put to it as much hot Water as will heat the Hams Blood warm, and mix it well together, if your Hams are large, they muſt lie three Weeks in Pickle, or more, but if ſmall, two will do: Keep them under the Pickle, and ſtir your Pickle twice a Week well to them. If you love the right *Weſt-phalia* Taſte, let them hang in the Smoak three Weeks or a Month.

The ſame Time will do for a Tongue in the Pickle and Smoke; and is the right Way for a Piece of Beef of the ſame Subſtance.

To pickle Pork.

HAving taken out the Bones, cut them into Pieces, of a Size to lie handſomely in the Tub or Pan you intend to pickle it in; then rub every Piece well with Salt Petre; then take common Salt and Bay Salt, of the laſt, half the Quantity of the other, and rub the Pieces well again with theſe; put Salt at the Bottom of the Veſſel, and lay in the Pieces one upon another as close as you can, cover every Piece with Salt, and fill the hollow Places on the Sides with Salt likewise, and as the Salt melts on the Top, strew on more, thus ordered, it will keep a great while.

To make Royal-Sausages.

WE take some Flesh of Partridges, Quails, Snipes and Pigeons, some of a Chicken, with a little Veal, and fat of Ham; all must be raw, and mix these with Cives, Parsley, Mushrooms and Truffles, five Eggs, the Whites of but two, and two Spoonfuls of Cream, season all this with Pepper, Salt, Mace, Nutmeg, and Cinamon, and a little Onion, and roll it up in large Rolls; and cut Slices of Veal, and roll round each Sausage, being about six Inches in Length, and three in Thickness, and stew them in your Pan upon Slices of Bacon, and cover them with thin Slices of Beef over a clear Fire, not too fierce, and cover your Pan very close, they will take up some Time in doing, and when done, set them by to be cold, and take them from the Fat, and the Veal, and cut them in what Size you will, and serve them. Garnish with Lemon Peel.

To make common Sausages.

TAKE a Pound of the Flesh of a Leg of Pork and shred it fine; then take a Pound of Hog's Fat, and cut it small with a Knife; and to every Pound of Fat, take half an Ounce of White Pepper, one large grated Nutmeg, a Penny worth of beaten Cloves and Mace, a Spoonful of shred Sage, and two or three Tops of Rosemary cut very

fine,

fine, and falt it to your Palate; then mix all thefe well together, with a little cold Water, and fo fill your Guts prepared for the Purpofe.

To make Saufages *another Way.*

TAKE Pork, more Lean than Fat, and fhred it; then take off the Fleak of Pork, and mince it, feafon each Part with minced Sage, and pretty high with Pepper, Salt, Mace and Nutmeg; then clear your fmall Guts, and fill them, mixing fome Bits of fat Bacon between the minced Meat; fprinkle a little Wine with it, and it will fill the better, then lay them in Links.

Bolognia Saufages.

GET four Pounds of lean Buttock of Beef, cut it in thin Pieces; put into it one Pound of diced Sewet, one Pound of diced Bacon; feafon with All-fpice and Pepper juft bruifed, and with Bay Salt, and Salt Petre mixed up with your Seafoning, then tie them up in Skins as big as your Wrift. You muft mix in a little Powder of Bay Leaves, then dry them as you do Tongues, and eat them without boiling.

Black Puddings.

PUT in a Stew-pan fome Hog's Blood, a little Milk, and a Ladle full of fat Broth; then cut a fufficient Quantity of thin Slices of Hog's Fat, with fome Parfley, Cives, and Sweet Herbs cut fmall; put the whole into your Stew-pan, feafon it with Salt, Pepper, Spice, and Onions done in hot Afhes, and cut fmall, mix this with your Blood, then make your Puddings as big as you pleafe:

Your

Your Guts being well cleanfed, fcraped and fcalded, blanch them in hot Water, and prick them with a Pin, and if you fee the Fat come out, they are blanched enough, then take them out of the Water, broil them, and ferve them up hot.

Another Way to make Black Puddings.

WHEN you catch the Blood from the Hog, fprinkle a Handful of Salt into it, to prevent the Blood from cloding : To two Quarts of Blood, put a Quarter of a Peck of Oatmeal once cut, then boil a Quart of Milk and put in the Crumb of a fine Penny Loaf : And after it is cold, put it to the Blood and ftir it all together, then put in half an Ounce of *Jamaica* Spice, and a whole Nutmeg beat together, ftir in a large Handful of Pennyroyal, and Sweet Marjoram cut fmall. When you fill your Gut, have by you Hog's Lard, cut in Dice, and mix it with the other Ingredients as you fill the Gut : After you have made as many Links as you defign, tie them in Bunches, then put them into a Kettle of boiling Water, and let them boil half an Hour ; obferve that you prick the Links with a Pin, and take Care you breathe not in the Kettle, for if you do they will burft. After which, hang 'em in a Chimney and they will keep good a Fortnight.

Hog's Chitterlings, *or* Andouilles.

HAving the large Gut of a Hog, cleanfe it well, and put it to foak a Day or two in Water, and then blanch it in hot Water, with a little Salt, Slices of Onions and fome Slices of Lemon ; then put it in frefh Water, take it out again a little while, cut it on a Table, into Pieces,

according

according to the Length you would have your Puddings, then dip them in White Wine for a little while, to take off the ill Scent, cut some Fat off the Hog's Belly into Slices, the Length you will make your Puddings, and some Lean into the same Slices, and season them well, then put them on a limber Skewer, and slide them through your Gut, and when your Skewer is quite in it, tie up both Ends with Packthread: Your *Andouilles*, or Puddings being thus formed, put them in a Kettle with Water, Onion shred, Cloves and two Bay Leaves, let them boil slowly, skim them well, and put in a Quart of Milk, let these Puddings grow cold in the same Liquor they are boiled in, then take them out, and take Care not to break them; they may be broiled on Paper, and served up immediately.

Calf's Chitterlings, *or* Andouilles.

HAving some of the biggest Calves Guts, cleanse them, cut them in Pieces proportionable to the Length of the Puddings you design to make, and tie one End of these Pieces, then take some Bacon, with a Calf's Udder, and Chaldron blanched, and cut in Dice or Slices; then put them in a Stew-pan, and season them with fine Spice pounded, a Bay Leaf, some Salt, Pepper, Shalot, cut small, and about half a Pint of Cream, toss it up, then take off the Pan, and thicken your Mixture with four or five Yolks of Eggs, and some Crumbs of Bread, then fill up your Chitterlings with the Stuffing, keep it warm, then tie the other Ends with Packthread, blanch and boil them like Hog's Chitterlings, let them grow cold in their own Liquor. Before you serve them up, boil them over a moderate Fire, and serve them up pretty hot. This Sort of *Andouilles* or

Puddings may be made in Summer, when Hogs are feldom killed.

Calf's Chitterlings *another Way.*

CUT a Calf's Nut in Slices of its Length, and the Thicknefs of a Finger, together with fome Ham, Bacon, and the White of Chickens cut after the fame Manner; put the whole into a Stew-pan, feafon it with Salt, Pepper, Sweet Herbs and Spice, take Guts cleanfed, cut and divide them in Parcels, fill them with your Slices; then lay in the Bottom of a Kettle fome Slices of Bacon and Veal, place them over your little Chitterlings, feafon them with Sweet Bafil, Bay Leaves, Salt, Pepper, Slices of Onion, and Cloves of Garlick, and make another Laying with Slices of Bacon and Veal over them, pour in it a Pint of White Wine, and let it ftew with Fire under and over; being done, broil your Puddings on a Sheet of Paper, and ferve them up hot.

Pork *ftuffed and roafted.*

MAKE a Stuffing in your Leg of Pork with Sage, Onion, Parfley, Pepper and Salt, Crumbs of Bread, a little Fat, and two Eggs; then ftuff your Pork with it, after which lay a Caul all over it, and roaft it, when half roafted take it off and fcotch it with a Knife and crifp it.

Pork *Cutlets.*

YOU muft take a Loin or Neck of Pork, cut off the Skin and cut it into Cutlets, feafon them with Sage, Parfley and Thyme cut fmall, Pepper and Salt, and Crumbs of of Bread; mince altogether and broil them, fauce them with Muftard, Butter, Shalot, Vinegar, and Gravy; fo ferve them away hot.

A Hog's Head *Cheefe Fafhion.*

BONE it and lay it to cleanfe twenty four Hours in Water and Salt, and fcrape it well and white, lay Salt on the Infide, to the Thicknefs of a Crown Piece and boil it very tender, then lay it in a Cheefe Prefs, cover it with a Cloth, and when cold it will be like a Cheefe: You may fauce it.

Chine *or* Leg *of* Pork *roafted and ftuffed.*

YOU muft take a Leg or Chine and make a Stuffing with Sage, Parfley, Thyme, and the Fat Leaf of the Pork, Eggs and Crumbs of Bread, feafon with Pepper, Salt, Nutmeg and Shalot, and ftuff it thick, then roaft it gently, and when a Quarter is roafted, cut the Skin in Slips; make your Sauce with Lemon Peel, Apples, Sugar, Butter and Muftard.

A Pig *roafted.*

PUT in the Belly, a Piece of Bread, fome Sage and Parfley chopped fmall, and fome Salt; few up the Belly and fpit it and roaft it, when warm thorough rub it all over with a Feather dip'd in Oil to prevent its bliftering, then fplit it and cut off the Ears and the Under-Jaws, and lay round, and make a Sauce with the Brains, thick Butter, Gravy and Vinegar, and lay under: Make Currant Sauce in a Cup.

T t

A Pig

A Pig *three Ways.*

FIRST skin your Pig up to the Ears, and then cut it in Quarters and draw it with Thyme and Lemon as you do Lamb, or roast it plain as Lamb, send it to Table with Mint Sauce, and garnish with Water-Cresses; then take the Skin and make a good thick Plumb-pudding Batter with good Sewet, Fruit and Eggs; fill up the Skin to the Ears, which sew up, and put it in your Oven and bake it, and it will appear as a roast Pig. Another Way is, when you go to kill your Pig, whip him about the Yard 'till he lies down; then stick him, scald him and roast him, and he will eat well; or you may bone him and stuff him with good Savoury Force-Meat, or roast him plain with Sage, Salt and Bread in his Belly, and serve with Currant Sauce, and savoury Sauce under.

A Pig *Lamb Fashion.*

SKIN it and leave the Skin whole with the Head on, then chine it down as Mutton, and lard it with Lemon Peel and Thyme, and roast them in Quarters as Lamb; the other Part fill full with a good Country thick Plumb-Pudding; sew up the Belly and bake it; the Pig will look as if roasted.

A Pig Rolliard.

YOU must bone it, leaving the Head whole, and wash it over with Eggs; season it with Pepper, Salt and Nutmeg, and lay over some Force-Meat, then roll it up, and either roast it or bake it, or stove it: You may cut it in six Pieces and send the Head in the Middle; make

Sauce

Sauce with the Brains and Sage, Butter, Gravy, and Vinegar ; fo ferve away hot.

A Pig *in Jelly.*

CUT it in Quarters and lay it in your Stew-pan: To one Calf's Foot and the Pig's Feet, put in a Pint of Rhenifh Wine, the Juice of four Lemons, and one Quart of Water; feafon with Nutmeg and Salt, ftove it gently two Hours, let it ftand 'till cold, and fend it up in its Jelly.

To drefs a Pig *the* French *Way.*

SPIT your Pig, lay it down to the Fire, and let it roaft 'till it is thoroughly warm, then cut it off the Spit, and divide it into about twenty Pieces, fet them to ftew in White Wine and ftrong Broth, feafoned with grated Nutmeg, Pepper, two Onions cut fmall, fome ftripped Thyme, Gravy, Butter, Elder Vinegar, and two or three Anchovies; when it is enough, difh it in the Liquor it was ftewed in, with fliced Orange and Lemon upon it.

To drefs a Pig au Pere-douillet.

HAving cut off the Head, cut the Pig in Quarters; lard them with large Lardoons well feafoned: Lay a Napkin in the Bottom of a Kettle, and put fome Bards of Bacon upon it; upon them place the Fore Quarters of the Pig, and the Head in the Middle of them; feafon it with Cloves, Nutmeg, Mace and Cinamon, with Bafil, Bay Leaf, Salt, Pepper, two Rocamboles, a fliced Onion and Lemon, Carrots, Parfnips, Parfley and Cives, then cover it with Bards of Bacon; and having laid them in a Stew-pan, cover it, and set it over a Stove; when it begins to stick, as when you make Veal Gravy, moisten it with good Broth, but take Care to keep it from browning, pour it into the Kettle, with a Bottle of White Wine, and stew your Pig in it: When it is enough, take it off the Fire, and if you would serve it cold, in Plates or little Dishes, let it stand 'till it is cold in its own Liquor, then take it out and drain it well, wipe it with a Linnen-Cloth to make it as white as you can, and serve it on a Napkin laid in a Dish, the Head in the Middle, the four Quarters round it, and garnished with Parsley. You may likewise serve it hot for a Dish of the first Course, as follows: When your Pig is almost ready, take some Veal Sweetbreads, Mushrooms, and Truffles, toss them up in a Sauce-pan, with a little melted Bacon, moisten them with good Gravy, and when they have simmered, 'till they are ready, take off the Fat, and thicken them with a Cullis of Veal and Ham; having thus prepared your Ragoo, and the Pig being ready, take it up, drain it well, lay the Head in the Middle of the Dish, the four Quarters round it, so pour the Ragoo upon it, and serve it hot.

To dress a Pig *the* German *Way.*

GET a Pig, cut it in Quarters and toss them up in melted Bacon, then boil them in good Broth, seasoned with an Onion stuck with Cloves, a Faggot of Herbs, Salt, Pepper, and Nutmeg; when it is almost boiled, put in half a Pint of White Wine: Then toss up in the same melted Bacon in which you toss'd up your Pig, some Oysters, and a little Flour, a Slice or two of Lemon, some Capers and ston'd Olives; when you are ready to serve away,

squeeze

fqueeze in the Juice of a Lemon, and garnifh the Brims of your Difh with the Brains of your Pig fried, and fome fried Parfley.

A Pig Matelote.

SCALD and gut your Pig, and cut off the Head and the Petty-Toes, then cut your Pig in four Quarters, put them with the Head and Toes in cold Water. Cover the Bottom of a Stew-pan, with Slices of Bacon, and place over them the faid Quarters with the Petty-Toes, and the Head cut in two. Seafon the whole with Salt, Pepper, Sweet Bafil, Thyme, Bay Leaves, Onions cut in Slices, and Garlick, with a Bottle of White Wine; lay over more Slices of Bacon, put over it a little Water, let it boil. Then take two large Eels, fkin, gut, and wafh them; cut them into Pieces of five or fix Inches long, and when your Pig is half boiled, put in it your Eels; then boil a Dozen of large Crawfifh, cut off the Claws and take off the Shells of the Tails. When your Pig and Eels, are enough, lay firft your Pig with the Petty-Toes, and the Head into the Difh, you defign to ferve them up in, then place over them your Eels and your Crawfifh with fome Ham Gravy and fome Cullis of Crawfifh if you have any, and then ferve it up for a firft Courfe or Remove,

To fouce a Pig.

CUT off the Head of a fair large Pig, then flit him through the Midft, then take out his Bones, then lay him in warm Water one Night, then collar him up like Brawn, then boil him tender in fair Water, and when he is boiled, put him in an Earthen Pot or Pan, in Water and
Salt,

Salt, for that will make him white, and feason the Flefh, for you muft not put Salt in the boiling, for that will make it black, then take a Quart of the fame Broth, and a Quart of White Wine, boil them together to make fome Souce for it, put into it two or three Bay Leaves, when it is cold uncloath the Pig, and put it into the fame Souce, and it will continue a Quarter of a Year. It is a neceffary Difh in any Gentleman's Houfe; when you ferve it in, ferve it with green Fennel, as you do Sturgeon with Vinegar in Saucers.

To make a fat Lamb *of a* Pig.

SCALD a fat Pig, and cut off his Head, flit him and trufs him up like a Lamb, then being flit through the Middle, and fkinned, parboil him a little, then draw him with Parfley, as you do a Lamb, then roaft it and drudge and ferve it up with Butter, Pepper, and Sugar.

V E N I S O N.

To roaft a Haunch *of* Venifon.

MAKE up a fubftantial Fire before you lay it down, then bafte it and flour it, and with very fine Skewers faften a Piece of Veal Caul over the Fat Part; if that cannot be had, the White of an Egg, or Paper well buttered will ferve. A Haunch of twelve Pounds Weight will take up three full Hours to be well foaked. Your Sauce muft be Gravy, with a great deal of Claret in it; the fafhionable fweet Sauce is Jelly of Currants made hot: What was formerly ufed was, Pap-fauce made of White Bread boiled in Claret, with a large Stick of Cinamon, and when boiled

'till

'till fmooth, take out the Cinamon and add Sugar. It is difficult to give general Rules about roafting and boiling, becaufe Cooks are apt to neglect a Fire, and not mind the Diftance, that it may neither fcorch nor pawl; but as to Time, allowing a Quarter of an Hour to every Pound of Meat, at a fteady Fire, your Expectations will hardly ever fail, from a Fowl to a Sirloin of the largeft Ox: And the fame Method may be allowed in boiling

A Civet *of* Venifon.

HAving boiled your Venifon, a Breaft or Neck, cut it in Cutlets; when it is almoft boiled, take a Saucepan, and brown in it half a Pound of Butter, and as it browns add a Quarter of a Pound of Flour, little and little, 'till the Brown be of a good Colour, be fure not to burn it: Then add half a Pound of Sugar, and as much Claret as will make it of the Thicknefs of a Ragoo. When you are going to ferve it up, put in the Venifon, and tofs it three or four Times, and fo ferve it with the Juice of Lemon.

To keep Venifon *all the Year.*

GET a Haunch and parboil it a while, then feafon it with two Nutmegs, a Spoonful of Pepper, and a good Quantity of Salt, mingle them all together, then put two Spoonfuls of White Wine Vinegar, and having made the Venifon full of Holes, as you do when you laid it, when it is larded, put in at the Holes, the Spice and Vinegar, and feafon it therewith, then put Part into the Pot with the Fat Side downwards, cover it with two Pounds of Butter, then clofe it up clofe with coarfe

Pafte;

Paſte; when you take it out of the Oven take away the Paſte, and lay a round Trencher with a Weight on the Top of it to keep it down, 'till it be cold, then take off the Trencher, and lay the Butter flat upon the Veniſon, then cover it cloſe with ſtrong White Paper; if your Pot be narrow at the Bottom it is better, for it muſt be turned upon a Plate, and ſtuck with Bay Leaves when you pleaſe to eat it.

Another Way to dreſs Veniſon.

IT muſt be blanched on a Gridiron, then larded and ma-rinated according to the Seaſon. Spit it with Slices of Bacon and Paper round; beſprinkle it with your Marinade. When roaſted enough, it muſt be ſerved up hot, either with a Pepper Sauce, or Sweet Sauce.

To make artificial Veniſon *for a* Paſty.

GET a Sirloin of of Beef, or a Loin of Mutton, bone it, beat it with a Rolling-Pin, and ſeaſon it with Pepper and Salt, then lay it twenty four Hours in Sheep's Blood, then dry it with a Cloth and ſeaſon it a little more, and it is fit to fill your Paſty.

Boiled Veniſon.

HAving a Haunch of Veniſon, ſalt it well, and let it remain a Week, then boil it, and ſerve it with a Furniture of Cauliflowers, *Ruſſia* Cabbages, ſome of the *Hertfordſhire* Turnips cut in Dice, and boiled in a Net, and toſſed up with Butter and Cream, or elſe have ſome of the yellow *French* Turnips, cut in Dice, and boiled like the former; or we might add ſome red Beet Roots boiled in
Dice,

Dice, and buttered in the fame Manner. Place thefe regularly, and they will afford a pleafant Variety both to the Eye and the Tafte.

Venifon *in Ragoo.*

LARD your Venifon with thick Bacon and feafon with Salt and Pepper, ftew it in Broth or hot Water, put in it two Glaffes of White Wine, and feafon the whole with Salt, a Bunch of Sweet Herbs, three or four Bay Leaves, and a Slice of green Lemon: Being done enough, thicken your Sauce with good Cullis. Serve it up with Capers and Lemon Juice over it.

Venifon *in Blood.*

YOUR Shoulder, Neck or Breaft, muft be boned, and laid in Blood, feafoned with Winter Savoury, Sweet Marjoram and Thyme, having a little Sewet in it chopp'd fmall, and ftirr'd on the Fire to be thick; then roll up your Neck or Breaft with fome of the fet Blood and Sweet Herbs, and roaft or ftove it gently in good Broth and Gravy, with Shalots and Claret, fo ferve away hot.

Venifon *in Avet.*

CUT your Venifon into Pieces the Bignefs of a Shoulder of a Hare, lard them with thick Bacon, feafoned with Salt and Pepper; then put them in a Pot with Broth, White Wine, a Bunch of Sweet Herbs, Salt, Pepper, Nutmeg, Bay Leaves, and green Lemon Slices; the whole being well ftewed, thicken your Sauce with Cullis, and put in a Dafh of Vinegar, and ferve it up for firft Courfe. All Sorts of Venifon muft be dreffed with a Sauce high feafoned.

CHAP. XVIII.

Of CULLISES *and* SAUCES *for* BUTCH-ER'S MEAT.

The most usual Cullis.

THIS Cullis is made several Ways, which are here explained, but this first is reputed the best, and the most in Vogue among all those that have Skill in COOKERY. They take Meat according to the Quantity of Cullis they have a Mind to make: As for Example, if you treat about ten or twelve Persons, you can take no less than a Leg of Veal to make your Cullis with, and the Nut of a Ham to make it good. Cut your Leg of Veal in Pieces the Bigness of your Fist, place them in your Stew-pan; then put in your Slices of Ham, a couple of Carrots and Onions cut in two, and put over your Cullis covered; let it stew softly at first, and as it begins to be brown, take off the Cover, and turn it, to colour it on all Sides the same, but take Care not to burn the Meat: When it has a pretty brown Colour, moisten your Cullis with Broth made of Beef or other Meat; season your Cullis with a little Sweet Basil, some Cloves, with some Garlick; pare a Lemon, cut it into Slices, and put it into your Cullis with some Mushrooms. Put into a Stew-pan a good Lump of Butter, and set it over a slow Fire, put in it two or three Handfuls of Flour, stir it with a Wooden Ladle, and let it take a Colour: If your Cullis be pretty brown, you must put in some Flour: Your Flour being brown with your Cullis, then

pour

pour it very softly into your Cullis, keeping your Cullis stirring with a Wooden Ladle, then let your Cullis stew softly,
and skim off the Fat, put in a couple of Glasses of *Champaign*, or other White Wines; but take Care to keep your
Cullis very thin, so that you may take the Fat well off and
clarify it: To clarify it, you must put it upon a Stove that
draws well, and cover it close, and let it boil without un-
covering, 'till it boils over, then uncover it, and take off
the Fat that is round the Stew-pan, then wipe it off the
Cover also, and cover it again, and by that Means you will
have the finest Cullis in the World, provided you follow these
Rules close. If by Chance your Cullis is too pale, and
that you would give it a good Colour, you need but put a
Bit of Sugar in a Silver Dish or a Stew-pan, with a Drop
of Water, and set it over a Stove, and let it turn to a Caramel, moistening the same with a little Broth, and then put
it into your Cullis, and with a Spoon take off the Fat, 'till
you see your Cullis be of a good Colour, and if it is of a
good Colour, Caramel needs not be put in it. When your
Cullis is done, take out the Meat and strain off your Cullis
in a Sieve, or a Silk Strainer, which is much better. This
Cullis is proper for all Sorts of Ragoos, and to be over Fowls
put in Pies and Terrines.

Cullis *another Way.*

HAving some Veal cut it in Pieces, place them in your
Stew-pan with Slices of Ham, a couple of Carrots
cut in two, and a couple of Onions; cover your Stew-pan
over a gentle Fire; when the Meat begins to stick to the
Bottom of your Pan, uncover it, and cover it all over, but
let it not be burnt, if it is done as it should be, moisten it

with

with Broth, and feafon it with Sweet Herbs, Slices of Lemon, fome Cloves of Garlick, and Cloves, take as much
Flour as you think fit, according to the Quantity of Cullis
you are to make, and mix it thin with cold Broth, or Water, then ftrain off your Flour into your Cullis and put, by
degrees, more to it, let it ftew foftly and be well done; if
the Colour is not deep enough, put Gravy in it; then the
Fat being well taken off, and it having a good Tafte, take
out the Meat, ftrain off your Cullis, and you may make
Ufe of it on all Occafions.

Cullis *another Way.*

Y O U R Veal being cut in Pieces, put them into your
Stew-pan with fome Slices of Ham, a couple of
Carrots cut in two, a couple of Onions cut in Slices; cover
your Stew-pan, and let it ftew foftly, your Meat being of
a good Colour, take it out, put a good Lump of Butter into
your Stew-pan, put it over the Fire, take a Wooden Ladle,
and fcrape the Brown off well that fticks to your Stew-pan;
put in it as much Flour as you think fit, according to the
Quantity of Cullis you will make, let it ftew 'till it be of
a good Colour, then moiften it with Broth, and put the
Meat in again, and feafon it with a few Sweet Herbs, Cloves
of Garlick, Lemon Slices, with fome Glaffes of *Champaign,* or other White Wine, let it ftew well, and take the
Fat well off, and being well done, and of a good Relifh,
ftrain it off in a Sieve, or elfe in a Silk Strainer, and you
may ufe it with all Sorts of Entries.

Cullis

Cullis *of* Ham

IS made divers Ways; we begin with that which, according to the Judgment of the best Cooks, is best, which is ordered as followeth, *viz.* Take a Stew-pan, put in it three Pounds of Veal cut like Dice, take a Ham, take off the Sward and the Fat, and cut it into Slices well shaped, and put them in a Stew-pan, with your Veal, and a couple of Carrots cut in two, and a couple of Onions: Cover your Stew-pan, and do it very gently over a flow Fire at first, and when you see your Meat begin to stick to your Pan, uncover it, and turn your Slices of Ham, that they may take a Colour, then take out your Slices of Ham and the Veal; put in your Stew-pan a Lump of Butter, and a little Flour, and stir it well with a Wooden Ladle, moisten it with good Broth, not salt, and put in again your Meat and your Ham, and season it with Lemon Slices, some Cloves of Garlick, and some Glasses of *Champaign*, or other White Wines; go on a thickening your Cullis with the most usual Cullis: Skim off the Fat; when done, take out all your Meat with the Ham; strain off your Essence in a Silk Strainer, and use the same with all Sorts of Meat, and hot Pastry made with Meat, or Fish dressed with Gravy; put again your Slices of Ham into your Essence, to make Use of them on several Occasions, *viz.* being cut into Dice when for a Piece of Beef, or Artichoke Bottoms, and when cut in Slices for Chickens, for young Fowls, or what you think fit.

Cullis

Cullis *the* Italian *Way.*

PUT in a Stew-pan half a Ladle full of Cullis, as much Effence of Ham, half a Ladle full of Gravy, and as much of Broth, three or four Onions cut in Slices, four or five Cloves of Garlick, a little beaten Coriander Seed, with a Lemon pared and cut in Slices, a little Sweet Bafil, Mufhrooms, and good Oil; put all over the Fire; let it ftew a good Quarter of an Hour, take the Fat well off, let it be of a good Tafte, and you may ufe it with all Sorts of Meat and Fifh, particularly with glazed Fifh, with Chickens, Fowls, Pigeons, Quails, Ducklings, and in fhort, with all Sorts of tame and wild Fowl.

Cullis *of* Crawfifh.

HAving the middling Sort of Crawfifh, put them over the Fire, feafoned with Salt, Pepper, Sweet Herbs, and Onions cut in Slices; being done, take them out, pick them, and keep the Tails after they are fcaled; pound the reft together with the Shells in a Mortar; the more they are pounded the finer your Cullis will be: Take a Bit of Veal the Bignefs of a Fift, with a fmall Bit of Ham, an Onion cut in four, put it to fweat very gently, if it fticks but a very little to the Pan, powder it a little, moiften it with Broth, put in it fome Cloves, Sweet Bafil in Branches, fome Mufhrooms, with a Lemon pared and cut in Slices; being done, fkim the Fat well, let it be of a good Tafte, then take out your Meat with a Skimmer, and go on a thickening it a little, with Effence of Ham, then put in your Crawfifh, and ftrain it off; being ftrained, keep it to make ufe of it with all Sorts of firft Courfe, with Crawfifh.

Cullis

Cullis *of* Crawfish *another Way*.

BOIL your Crawfish for Soops, being boiled, pick them, pound your Shells to make your Cullis, take a Piece of Veal cut into Slices, put them in a Stew-pan with fome Slices of Ham, two or three Onions with fome Bits of Carrots, and put it over the Fire, let it be a doing gently, being a little fticking, moiften it with good Broth; put in it fome Crumbs of Bread ufed for Soops, your Craw-fish being pounded, take your Meat and Roots out of your Cullis; take off the Fat, and let be of a good Tafte, put in your pounded Crawfish, ftrain it off, and put this into a fmall Kettle, pick the Crawfish Tails, and put them in your Cullis, keeping it hot: This Cullis may ferve for all Sorts of Soops with Cullis of Crawfish Tails, with thofe of Rice, and with foaked Crufts, &c.

White Cullis à la Reine.

WE take a Piece of Veal and cut it in fmall Bits, with fome thin Slices of Ham, and two Onions cut in four Pieces, moiften it with Broth feafoned with Mufhrooms, a Bunch of Parfley, green Onions, three Cloves, and fo let it ftew; being ftewed, take out all your Meat and Roots with a Skimmer, put in a few Crumbs of Bread and let it ftew foftly; take the white of a Fowl, or of a couple of Chickens, and pound it in a Mortar, being well pounded, mix it in your White Cullis, but it muft not boil, and your Cullis muft be very white, but if it is not white enough, you muft pound one or two Dozen of Sweet Almonds pared and put into your Cullis; then boil a Glafs full of Milk and put it in your Cullis, let it be of a
good

good Tafte, and ftrain it off, then put it in a fmall Kettle, and keep it warm; and you may ufe it for all Sorts of white Soops, and for white Crufts of Biead and Bifques.

Gieen Cullis *with Green Peafe.*

GET Green Peafe, let them be heated without Liquor, take a Handful of Parfley, as much Spinage, with a a Handful of green Onion Tops; blanch all thefe in boiling Water, then put them into frefh Water; take them out and fqueeze them well and pound them, put into a Stew-pan a Piece of Veal cut in Dice, fome Slices of Ham, alfo an Onion cut fmall, put it over the Stove to ftew gently, being a little clammy, moiften it with your foaking Broth, and let it ftew foftly; put in it a Handful of green Parfley, green Onions, Cloves, a Bunch of Savoury; being ftewed and of a good Tafte, take out your Meat and Greens; then pound your Peafe, and mix them with your Cullis, and the Tops of green Onions, and ftrain it off with a Ladle full of Cullis. This Cullis may be ufed with all Sorts of Terrines with Green Peafe, Ducklings with Green Peafe Purey, and with all Sorts of Difhes that are made with a green Sauce; when you ftew your green Peafe, or Cucumbers cut in Dice in their Seafon, put fome of this Cullis over them.

Green Cullis *for Soops.*

GET Peafe, boil them in a fmall Kettle, with good Broth; take a Piece of Veal, a Bit of Ham, an Onion, cut all together into fmall Dice, and put them a fweating very gently over a Fire; being a little clammy, moiften them with your foaking Broth; feafon it, and let it ftew foftly; take Parfley, the Tops of green Onions and Spinage,

of

of each a Handful, and after they are picked, wafhed and blanched in boiling Water, fqueeze them well, and pound them, then take them out of the Mortar, and pound your Peafe, your Meat being ftewed, take it out of the Cullis with a Skimmer, take off the Fat from your Cullis, let it be of a good Tafte, and mix your Peafe and the Tops of green Onions with it, and fo ftrain it off: This Cullis may be ufed with all Sorts of green Soops, and Soop Crufts.

Sauce *in* Ravigotte

YOU muft take Terragon, Pimpernel, Mint, Parfley, green Onions, a little of each, blanch the whole in boiling Water, then put it into cold Water, take it out again and fqueeze it, and cut it very fmall, then put it in a Stew-pan with a Rocambole bruifed, a little Gravy, a little Cullis, and the Juice of a Lemon, Salt, beaten Pepper, an Anchovy cut fmall, and a little Oil, put all this a Moment over the Fire, and let it be well relifhed. This kind of Sauce may be ufed with all Sorts of roafted Meat, putting it in a Saucer.

Sauce *in* Ravigotte *another Way*

WE take the fame Sort of Herbs, prefcribed in the Ravigotte above, wafh them well, cut them fmall, and pound them, putting into the Mortar a little Gravy, a couple of Rocamboles, a little Pepper, a little Cullis; put all together into a Stew-pan, heat it, and ftrain it off; being ftrained off, add to it a Spoonful of Oil, keep it warm and ferve it up in a Saucer with roaft Meat; you may alfo ufe it with Chicken.

X x

A Sauce

A Sauce *with Fennel and Goofeberries.*

HAving young Fennel, cut it very fmall, put it in a Stew-pan with a little Butter and a Duft of Flour, feafon it with Pepper, Salt and Nutmeg, moiften it with a little Gravy or Water, your Sauce being thickened, throw in it your Goofeberries blanched; let it be of a good Tafte, and ufe it with what you think fit. This Sauce is commonly ufed with Mackarel.

Minced Sauce.

CUT Onions, Mufhrooms and Truffles, if you have any, very fmall, with Capers and Anchovies, put into a Stew-pan a little Butter with your Onions, put your Sauce-pan over a brifk Fire, give it two or three Toffes; now put in it your Mufhrooms and Truffles, ftrowing over them a Duft of Flour, and moiften them with good Gravy, then put in it your Capers and Anchovies, with a Glafs of White Wine; thicken your Sauce with a Spoonful of Cullis. Let it be of a good Tafte, and you may ufe it with all Difhes with a minced Sauce

Hot Sauce *in Ramolade.*

PUT into a Stew-pan fome Onions cut into Slices, with one or two Spoonfuls of Oil; fet this a Moment over the Fire, and put into it fome Gravy and Cullis, a Glafs of Wine, two or three Cloves of Garlick, half a Lemon cut into Slices, a little Sweet Herbs, Cloves, Capers cut fmall, and Parfley Let it be of a good Tafte; put into it a fmall Spoonful of Muftard, and ftrain it off; make ufe of this Sauce with all Difhes with hot Ramolade.

Sauce

Sauce *in* Ramolade *another Way*.

C U T some green Onions, Capers, Anchovies, and Parsley, small, each by itself upon a Plate, with a Clove of Garlick, and a Crumb of Shalot, put all this into a Stew-pan together, with a few Sweet Herbs, two Spoonfuls of Oil, as much of good Mustard, the Juice of a Lemon, with a little Cullis: Stir all well together, and you may use it with all Sorts of Fowls and broiled Meat, and with roasted Meat in a Saucer.

A thick Sauce *with Pepper*.

W E put into a Stew-pan Slices of Onion, Thyme, Sweet Basil, a Bay Leaf, two or three Cloves of Garlick, a Ladle full of Gravy, and as much Cullis, some Slices of Lemon with a Glass of Vinegar; put it over a Stove, let it be of a good Taste, and take off the Fat, strain it off, and serve it up in a Saucer with roasted Meat; the same Sauce may be used with all Sorts of Meat, that requires a thick Pepper-sauce; and may also be made without Cullis.

Caper Sauce.

Y O U must put in a Stew-pan some Cullis of Ham, with Capers, to which you give three or four Chops with a Knife; season it with Pepper and Salt: Let it be relishing and serve it up hot.

Sauce *with Truffles*.

G E T Truffles, pare, wash them in Water, and cut them small, this done, put them in a Stew-pan with thin Cullis of Veal and Ham, season it with Salt and Pepper, let it ftew foftly, let it be of a good Tafte, and ferve it up hot

The Sauce with Mufhrooms is made after the fame Manner.

Onion Sauce.

HAving put into a Stew-pan fome Veal Gravy, with a couple of Onions, cut in Slices, feafon it with Pepper and Salt, let it ftew fofily, then ftrain it off, put it in a Saucer, and ferve it up hot

Green Onion Sauce.

YOU muft put into your Stew-pan Green Onions pared and cut fmall, with a little of melted Bacon, feafoned with a little Pepper and Salt; moiften it with Gravy, and let it ftew a Moment, thicken your Sauce with Cullis of Veal and Ham, let your Sauce be of a fharp Tafte and good Relifh, and ferve it up hot

Sauce *with frefh Mufhrooms.*

GET Mufhrooms, pare and mince them with a little green Onion and Parfley, put in a Stew-pan a little melted Bacon, and having given it four or five Toffes, moiften it with Gravy, let it ftew foftly over a flow Fire, fkim the Fat well off, and thicken your Sauce with Cullis of Veal and Ham, let it be relifhing, and ferve up hot

Carriers Sauce.

GET green Onions, pare and cut them very fmall, put them in a Sauce-boat with Pepper, Salt and Water, ferve it up cold   This is Sauce for roaft Mutton.

The

The same with Oil

WE take a few green Onions and Parsley, put them in a Saucer with Oil, Pepper and Salt, you may add to it a little Vinegar, and serve it up cold.

Sauce *with Pepper*

PUT Vinegar in a Stew-pan, with a little Veal Gravy, green Onions whole, an Onion cut in Slices, with a Slice of Lemon, seasoned with Pepper and Salt, after a Boil or two, taste it, strain it off, pour it into a Saucer, and serve it up hot.

Sauce-Robart

TAKE Onions, cut them into Dice, put them into a Stew-pan with a little Butter, and keep them stirring, being half brown, drain off the Fat, strewing some Flour over them; moisten it with Gravy, and let it stew softly over a slow Fire, season it with Pepper and Salt, then thicken it with Veal and Ham Cullis, putting in a little Mustard; make it relishing, and use it upon Occasion.

Ham Sauce

CUT three or four Slices of Ham, beat them flat, put them a sweating over a Stove, being clammy, strew over them a little Flour, and keep them stirring; moisten them with Gravy, and season them with Pepper, and a Bunch of Sweet Herbs, let it stew gently, if it is not thick enough, add to it a little Cullis of Veal and Ham, let it be of a high Relish; strain it off, and use it for all Sorts of white Meat roasted.

Green

Green Sauce

TAKE the Grafs of Wheat or of other Grains, pound it in a Mortar with a Cruft of Bread, take out the Grafs thus pounded, put it in a Sieve, and feafon it with Pepper and Salt, moiften it a little with Veal Gravy and Vinegar, then ftrain it and ferve it up cold with Lamb or Fowl.

Sauce *with Mutton Gravy and Shalots.*

YOU muft pare your Shalots, cut them very fmall, put them in a Difh with Pepper and Salt, and Mutton Gravy or Veal Gravy; you may ufe this Sauce for Legs of Mutton, or with Fowls.

Anchovy Sauce.

WASH well two or three Anchovies, take out the Bones, cut them fmall, and put them in a Stew-pan, with a thin Cullis of Veal and Ham, feafoned with Pepper and Salt; let it be hot and relifhing; you may ufe this Sauce with roafted Meat.

To make Muftard.

HAving made choice of good Seed, pick and wafh it in cold Water; it muft alfo be drained and rubbed dry in a clean Cloth; then pound it fine in a Mortar with ftrong Wine Vinegar; ftrain it and keep it clofe covered: Otherwife, your Seed may be ground in a Muftard-quern, or in a Bowl with a Cannon-Bullet.

A general

A general Sauce.

MINCE a little Lemon Peel very fmall, a little Nut-meg, beaten Mace, and Shalot, ftew them in a lit-tle White Wine and Gravy, fo melt your Butter therein; if it be for Hafhes of Mutton or Fifh, add Anchovies, a little of the Liquor of ftewed Oyfters, and Lemon Peel.

The beft Way to beat up Butter *for* Spinage, Green Peafe, *or* Sauce *for* Fifh.

TAKE two or three Spoonfuls of fair Water, and put it into a Pipkin or Sauce-pan, there muft be no more than what will juft cover the Bottom of the Veffel: Let this boil by itfelf, as foon as it does fo, flip in half a Pound of Butter, when it is melted, remove your Pipkin from the Fire, and holding it up by the Handle, fhake it round ftrongly, for a good while, and the Butter will come to be fo thick, that you may almoft cut it with a Knife, Then fqueeze fome Lemon or Orange into it, or elfe put in Verjuice or Vinegar, and heat it again, as long as you pleafe, over the Fire. It will ever after be thick, and never grow oily, tho' it be cold and heated again 20 Times: If you would have Spinage, Peafe, or Fifh boiled the ordinary Way, you may take fome of their Liquor inftead of Water.

Having put this Butter to boiled Peafe in a Difh, cover it with another; then fhake them very ftrongly, and a good while together: This is by far the beft Method that can be ufed to butter Peafe, without putting in (as is commonly done) Butter, to melt in the Middle of them, for that will turn to Oil, if you heat them again, whereas, this Sort

will

will never change   Therefore it is moft expedient to make ufe of fuch thickened Butter upon all Occafions.

To burn Butter *for any* Sauce.

SET the Butter over the Fire in the Sauce-pan, and let it boil 'till it is as brown as you like it; then fhake in Flour, ftir it all the while; fo ufe it for any Sauce that is too thin.

C H A P. XIX.

Of P O U L T R Y.

Fowls *and* Rabbits, *&c. when in Seafon.*

IN *January, February,* and *March,* Turkey-Poults, Green-Geefe, Ducklings, fmall fat Chickens, fome Pigeons, tame fucking Rabbits, Pheafant and Partridge with Eggs, are in Seafon. And in *March,* Leverets, Wild Pigeons, Wild Rabbits. In *April, May, June,* the Chickens come to be large Fowls, fo that Turkies, Geefe, Ducks and Fowls are in Seafon all the Year

In *July* and *Auguft,* Wild Ducks that fhed their Feathers, which are called, Flappers, or Moulters, come very fat, and at the latter End of the Year moft Sort of Fowls, both Wild and Tame, are good and in Seafon, as Swans, Buftards, Wild-Geefe, Brand-Gees, Wild Ducks, Teal, Widgins, Shufflers, Penteals, Eafterlings, Heathcocks, Woodcocks,

Woodcocks, Snipes, Plovers, Larks, Quails, Black-Birds, Thrushes, Felfars, Pheasants, Partridges, Bittern, Geese, Tame-Ducks, Cock-Turkies, and Hen-Turkies, Capons, Virgin-Pullets, and Hens with Egg, and Chickens, likewise Hares and Rabbits.

Note, That the Cock-Turky is out of Season after *Christmas*, but the Hen continues in Season 'till *Easter*, and is with Egg all the Spring.

T U R K I E S.

A young Turky *with* Oysters.

PICK your Turky, draw it and singe it neatly, cut the Liver of it into Bits, and put it in a Stew-pan, together with a Dozen of Oysters and a Bit of Butter, seasoned with Salt, Pepper, Sweet Herbs, All-spice, Mushrooms, Parsley, and Chibbol, let it be a Moment over the Fire, then stuff your Turky with these Ingredients, and let it be blanched a little as before, then spit it, then tie over it Bards of Bacon and Paper, mean while, have a Ragoo ready for your Turky, make it thus: Take three Dozen of Oysters, and blanch them in boiling Water, drain them, take off your Bards, then put in a Stew-pan some Essence of Ham, and set it a boiling; skim off the Fat, taste it, and put this with your Oysters into another Pan: When your Turky is roasted, dish it up, and put your Ragoo over it, with the Juice of a Lemon, let it be relishing, and serve it up hot for a first Course.

Y y

A young

A young Turky *with Oysters, and Crawfish Cullis.*

GET a young Turky, and order it as that before, but inſtead of uſing Eſſence of Ham, you may put a Crawfiſh Cullis over it, with the Juice of a Lemon; let it be reliſhing and ſerve it up hot for the firſt Courſe.

A young Turky *with Oysters after the* Dutch *Fashion.*

YOU muſt take a young Turky ordered as that above, put it to roaſt, make a Ragoo with Oyſters as followeth · Blanch as many Oyſters as you pleaſe, take out the Beards; then put Butter in a Stew-pan, with about half a Spoonful of fine Flour, and a Drop of Gravy; ſeaſon the whole with Salt, Pepper, Nutmeg, with a little Vinegar, as ſoon as your Sauce is thickened, put in your Oyſters, and let it be reliſhing When your Turky is roaſted, diſh it up with your Ragoo over it, ſerve it up hot.

Young Turky *roaſted with Shalots.*

ORDER your Turky as thoſe before; the Shalot only makes the Difference: Your Turky being roaſted, make a Sauce thus: Warm ſome Shalots cut ſmall in a Stew-pan with Gravy and Cullis, ſome Juice of Lemon and pounded Pepper, and ſerve up your Turky hot, pouring this Sauce over it.

A young Turky *roaſted with Mango's.*

ORDER your Turky as that before, the Ragoo only makes the Difference. Take ſome Mango's, the ſofteſt you can get, take off the Fleſh by thin and ſmall Slices, take out the Inſide, and blanch them in boiling

Water

Water; then put them in fresh Water, put them in a Stew-pan with some Essence and Gravy, and let them have a Boil. When your Turky is ready, dish it up with your Mango's over it, and serve it up for a first Course.

Young Turkies *with Chesnuts and Sausages.*

ORDER a Turky-Poult in the same Manner above-mentioned; but besides the Stuffing, put in the Body of this Turky a good many Chesnuts, after they have been in hot Embers peel them, with small Sausages, then blanch it with Slices of Bacon and Paper round it; put it on the Spit, and take more of the same Chesnuts, and put them in a Baking-pan, with Fire under and over, then put them in a Stew-pan with some Broth, let them stew 'till they are done; then take out the Broth, and put in a Ladle full of Essence, some Cullis and Gravy. Your Turky being roasted, dish it up, put your Chesnuts over it, and serve it up hot for the first Course.

Young Turkies *with Saffron after the* Polish *Way.*

GET a young Turky, draw it, truss it, and spit it with Slices of Bacon and Paper round it; then put in a Stew-pan Slices of Onions, and boil them with some Broth; being done, strain them off, and if they are too thick, put some more Broth to them; and these Onions must be as thick as an Essence of Ham; then put a very little pounded and dryed Saffron in a Cup, mix it with a little pot Broth, and pour it by Degrees into your Cullis 'till it begins to have a fine Colour, but not too deep: Your Turkies being taken off, cut off the Wings and the Legs, and put them in your Cullis: Serve them up for the first Course.

At

At another Time, you may take fome Parfley Roots cut in Slices, boil and mix them with Cullis and the Saffron as before; and inftead of roafting your Turky, you may boil it in a Kettle, ferve it up hot for a firft Courfe, with the Cullis of Parfley Roots over it.

Young Turkies *ftuffed with Crawfifh*

PICK and draw young Turkies clean, and finge them; then put your Fingers between the Skin and the Flefh, and having taken out the Breaft, make your Forced-Meat as follows: Take fome Beef Sewet, blanched Bacon, Calf's Udder blanched, the Flefh of a Chicken, fome Mufhrooms, Truffles, Salt, Pepper, Sweet Herbs, All-fpice, Crumbs of Bread boiled in Cream, and a couple of Eggs. The whole being well minced and palatable, put Part of it in the Belly of your Turkies, with a fmall Ragoo of Crawfifh Tails, and a little of their Cullis, tie both Ends of your Turkies to keep in your Stuffing; put the Remainder over it, and blanch it again with Butter, Salt, Pepper, Parfley, and Chibbol, taking particular Care it be done very white; thruft a Skewer through the Thighs, fpit it, and wrap it up in Bards of Bacon, and Paper tied with Packthread, and roaft them with a moderate Fire: When done, unfpit them, take off the Bacon, difh them handfomely up, putting over them a Ragoo of Crawfifh; fo ferve up for the firft Courfe.

Another Way of dreffing young Turkies *with Crawfifh.*

GET a young Turky, pick it, draw it well, put the Liver upon your Dreffer, with a little fcraped Bacon, fome Parfley, Chibbols, Salt, Pepper, Sweet Herbs, All-fpice,

All-fpice, Mufhrooms, Truffles, and fome Butter, mince all this well and put it in your Turky : Let it fry a little in a Stew-pan, with Butter, Sprigs of Parfley, Cives, Salt, Pepper, and Sweet Herbs, let your Turky be well blanched, and when you have fpit it, cover it with Bards of Bacon and Paper, and when roafted, difh it up, and put a Ragoo into it, or fome Cullis of Crawfifh

Another Time, inftead of mincing the Liver of your Turky, cut it in four or fix Bits, with fome other Livers, Crawfifh Tails, fome fcraped Bacon, fhred Parfley, Cives, Salt, Pepper, All-fpice and Sweet Herbs, the whole being well mixed together, ftuff therewith your Turky, blanched as before, when done, difh it up, putting over it a Crawfifh Cullis, and ferve it up for the firft Courfe

Entry of Turky Wings.

HAving the Wings of Turkies, fcald them, being well picked and fcalded, blanch them, when blanched, cut off the fmall End, and break the Bone with a Knife in the Middle of the Wing : Put them in a Stew-pan, put in it fome Champignons, a Bit of Butter, a Bunch made of Parfley, green Onions, and a Branch of Sweet Bafil, with three Cloves; the Bunch being tied together, put it, with your Wings, over the Fire, and tofs them up now and then, ftrew a Duft of Flour over them, and moiften them with Broth; being moiftened, feafon them with a little Salt and Pepper, and let them boil very foftly, being boiled, make a thick Sauce with five Yolks of Eggs, and beat them up with Cream or Milk; put in it a little Nutmeg, a couple of Shalots cut very fmall: Let your Fricafey be of a good Tafte, and thicken it; being thickened, put in
a little

a little Parſley cut ſmall, with a little Lemon Juice : It being diſhed, ſerve it up for Entry, or *Hors d'Oeuvres.*

You may make your Fricaſey with a brown Sauce, in moiſtening it with Gravy, and being done, thicken it with Cullis.

Roaſted young Turkies *with* Spaniſh *Cardoons.*

HAving picked and drawn your Turkies, lay the Liver on the Dreſſer with ſcraped Bacon, ſome Parſley, Chibbol, Muſhrooms, Salt, Pepper, Sweet Herbs, and fine Spice; and being minced, put it in the Bellies of your Turkies, then blanch them with a Bit of Butter, ſome Parſley and Chibbols, when blanched, put them on the Spit, with Slices of Bacon and Paper round it, keep your Cardoons ready, let them be very white, and cut half a Finger's Length, and put them in a Stew-pan, with half a Ladle full of Veal Gravy, and half a Ladle full of Ham Cullis; let them have a Boil, and having taken off the Fat, add to them the Juice of an Orange. Your Turkies being done, and the Bacon and Paper taken away; diſh them up with your Cardoons over them, and ſerve them up hot for the firſt Courſe.

Young Turkies *with Cream.*

HAving a young Turky or two, according to the Bigneſs of your Diſh, and being ordered and roaſted as before, let them be cold; then take a Bit of a Nut of Veal, take off the Skin and cut it into Bits, with ſome Bacon well blanched, ſome Beef Sewet, a Calf's Udder, ſome Muſhrooms, Parſley, Chibbol, Sweet Herbs, fine Spice, Salt, and Pepper; put the whole on the Fire in a Stew-pan;

pan; and when done, take it out and mince it upon a Dreſſer, then take the White of your Turky, put it in a Mortar, with a Piece of Bread boiled in Milk, together with ſix Yolks of Eggs, and half of the Whites beat up to Snow, pound it all together, then take a Silver Diſh, or Baking-pan, and put in the Bottom of it ſome of this minced Meat, and lay your Turky over it, and fill up your Diſh with the reſt of your Meat, leave a hollow Place in the Middle of your Diſh, put in it a Ragoo of Sweetbreads, Cocks Combs and Muſhrooms, lay alſo ſome minced over the ſame, let your Turky be round and plump; rub your Turky over with beaten Eggs, and having ſtrewed ſome Crumbs of Bread over it, put it in the Oven, or let it be done under the Cover of a Baking-pan, Fire under and over. Your Turky being enough, and of a good Colour, take it out, and clean well the Border of your Diſh, put a little Eſſence or Cullis round your Turky, and ſerve it up hot for a firſt Courſe. If you have no Silver Diſh, let it be done in a Baking-pan, and afterwards ſlide the whole into your Diſh.

The Manner of truſſing TURKIES, *and all other* FOWLS, *ſee at the End of this Chapter*

FOWLS and PULLETS

Fowls *farced with Crawfiſh.*

YOU muſt take ſome Fowls, pick them very clean, gut and ſinge them, thruſt your Finger between the Skin and the Fleſh; take out the Craw, then make Forced-Meat with the Fleſh of the Breaſt as follows: Take Beef Sewet,

Sewet, blanched Bacon, a Calf's Udder alſo blanched, Chick-en's Fleſh, ſome Champignons, Truffles, or Muſhrooms, (when in the Way) Pepper, Salt, Sweet Herbs, fine Spice, Crumbs of Bread ſoaked in Milk or Cream, and a couple of raw Eggs, all which muſt be cut ſmall, mixed together, and well reliſhed; put Part of this Forced-Meat into your Fowls Belly, and a Ragoo of Crawfiſh Tails and Muſh-rooms, with a little Crawfiſh Cullis, then put the Remain-der of the Forced-Meat over it, and ſew up both Ends cloſe; do them again in the Stew-pan with Butter, Salt, Pepper, Parſley, and green Onions, and above all let them be very white, then ſtick a Skewer through the Legs of your Fowls, and put them on the Spit wrapping them up in ſome Slices of Bacon, with Paper round them; tie them well and roaſt them at a ſlow Fire; and when they are roaſted take them off the Spit, and diſh them handſomely, then pour over them a Ragoo of Crawfiſh Tails, and ſerve them up hot for an Entry.

Another Time, you may ſerve up your Fowls in pour-ing a Cullis over them inſtead of Crawfiſh Tails.

Fowls *with Crawfiſh another Way.*

TAKE ſome fine Pullets, pick them clean, gut and ſinge them, put the Livers upon the Dreſſer, with a little ſcraped Bacon, Parſley, green Onions, Pepper, Salt, Sweet Herbs, fine Spice, with Champignons and Truffles, if you have any, a Bit of Butter; mince all together, and put it into the Belly of your Fowls; then put them into a Stew-pan with a Lump of Butter, Branches of Parſley, green Onions, Pepper, Salt, and Sweet Herbs; let your Fowls be well blanched before you put them to the Spit;

wrap

wrap them up in Slices of Bacon, with a Paper round
them; when they are done, dish them, and serve them
with a Ragoo as above, or else in a Cullis of Crawfish.

Another time, instead of mincing the Livers of your
Fowls, cut them in four or six Pieces, with some other
Livers and Crawfish Tails, scraped Bacon, Parsley cut
small, green Onions, Pepper, Salt, Sweet Herbs, and fine
Spice; all being well minced together, put it into the Bellies of your Fowls, and let them be blanched the same way
as those above; after they are done, dish them, add to
them Crawfish Cullis, and serve them up hot.

Fowls *with* Oysters.

PICK and singe well your Fowls, and gut them; cut
the Liver into Bits, with a Dozen of Oysters, and
a Bit of Butter, seasoned with Pepper and Salt, Sweet
Herbs, fine Spice, Champignons, Parsley and green Onions; put all into a Stew-pan for a Moment over the Fire;
then put all together into the Bellies of your Fowls, and do
them again as above; and in spitting them, cover them
with Slices of Bacon and a Sheet of Paper; keep a Ragoo
of Oysters in Readiness for the time your Fowls be dressed,
and make your Ragoo thus: Take three Dozen of Oysters,
blanch them in boiling Water, put them into a Colander
to drain, and take out the Hard in the Middle; put in a
Stew-pan a Ladle full of Ham Cullis, or as much as you
think fit: If you have but one Fowl, there need not be so
much of it; put it over the Fire, skim off the Fat, and
taste it, then put your Oysters in, changing your Stew-
pan: When your Fowls are done put your Ragoo over

N° 16.   Z z   them,

them, with the Juice of a Lemon, and let it be relishing, and serve your Fowls up for an Entry.

Fowls *with* Oysters *the* Dutch *way*.

DRESS your Fowls as before, roast them, and make your Oyster-Ragoo in this Manner : Blanch what Quantity of Oysters you think fit, being blanched, singe them, and take off the Beards and Hard in the Middle ; put in a Stew-pan good Butter, a Dust of Flour with a little Gravy ; season the whole with Pepper and Salt, Nutmeg, and a Dash of Vinegar, put your Stew-pan upon the Stove, your Sauce being thicken'd, put in your Oysters, let it be of a good Taste ; when your Fowls are ready, dish them up, put your Oyster-Ragoo over them, and serve them up hot.

Chickens *with* Oysters *the* Flemish *way*.

DRESS your Chickens as before, and make your Ragoo as follows: Blanch your Oysters in their Liquor, which lay by, and pick them as before, put Part of their Liquor in a Stew-pan, with four Yolks of Eggs, some Butter, Parsley, Terragon, all together, well blanched and cut small, Lemons cut in Slices or small Squares, an Anchovy cut small, Pepper, Salt, and Nutmeg ; then put your Oysters over the Fire, and take care the Sauce don't turn ; when your Fowls are roasted, take them off the Spit, and take the Wings and Legs from the Body, slice them upon the Breast, and crush them between two Dishes, then put your Ragoo of Oysters over them ; let it be of a good Taste and serve it up hot for an Entry.

Roasted

Roasted Fowls *with* Anchovies.

DRESS your Fowls the same way as before, and put them on the Spit, take some Anchovies, wash them, cut a Couple of them small, and the other in Slices, put those that are cut small in a Stew-pan, with good Cullis and Gravy, a Bit of Butter, and the Juice of a Lemon; your Fowls being roasted, take them off the Spit, and dish them up, put your Anchovy-Cullis over them, and your Anchovies in Slices, and serve them up hot for an Eatry.

A roasted Fowl *with Shalots.*

YOUR Fowl must be order'd as before, except only, that you put a few Shalots into the Forced-Meat; your Fowl being done, take it off, then order your Shalots as follows, *viz.* take some Shalots cut very small, put them in a Stew-pan with Gravy and Cullis, the Juice of a Lemon and a little beaten Pepper, and place in it your Fowl and Sauce, and serve them up hot for an Entry.

A Fowl *with* Cream.

GET one or two Fowls, according to the Bigness of your Dish, clean, order and spit them; they being roasted, take them off, and let them grow cold: Take a Bit of a Nut of Veal, take the Skin well off, and cut it into Slices, together with a Piece of Bacon blanched, some Beef-Sewet, a Calf's Udder, some Champignons, Parsley, green Onions, Sweet Herbs, fine Spice, Pepper and Salt, put all together in a Stew-pan over the Fire; when it is enough, take it off, put it upon a Dresser, and mince it well; take the Breasts of your Fowls and mix them with

this

this Forced-Meat, being cut fmall, put them in a Mortar,
with fome Crumbs of Bread boiled in Milk; which being
cold, put it to your Forced-Meat, together with fix Yolks
of Eggs, and the Half of the Whites whipped up to
Snow: Pound all well together, and put this Forced-Meat
in the Bottom of a filver Difh, or other Difh, and your
Fowls upon it, and fill it up with what was left of the
Forced-Meat, with a Hole in the Middle, to put in a fmall
Ragoo of Sweetbreads of Veal, Cocks Combs, and Champignons, then cover your Ragoo, and make your Fowls
as round and as plump as you can: Beat up an Egg, and
cover your Fowls therewith, fee you make them very
fmooth, ftrew them with fine Crumbs of Bread, and bake
them in the Oven, or under the Cover of a Baking-pan:
They being bak'd, and of a good Colour, fkim off the
Fat; wipe the Border of your Difh clean, and fet a Cullis
on the Side of your Fowls, and ferve them up hot for an
Entry. If you cannot get a filver Difh, you may take a
Baking-pan, with an Abbefs on the Bottom, after that
your Fowls are put into the Difh.

A Fowl à la Braife.

GET a Fowl, pick and gut it, trufs the Legs infide
the Belly, and lard it with thick Bacon, the Bignefs
of the Half of a fmall Finger, feafon it with Pepper and
Salt, Sweet Herbs and fine Spices, then lard your Fowl,
and bind it with Packthread; take a long deep Stewing-
pan, and put in it fome Slices of Bacon and Veal, then put
your Fowls into it, feafoned with Pepper and Salt, Sweet
Bafil, Thyme, Bay Leaves, Onions, and a Crumb of Garlick; continue to cover it with Slices of Bacon and Veal,

and moiften it with a Glafs of Wine, and one or two Ladles full of Broth ; ftew it, Fire under and over , being done, difh it up, putting a minced Sauce over it, or a Ragoo of Sweetbreads of Veal, Cocks Combs and Champignons, or a Cullis of Ham, or a Ragoo of Oyfters: All which depends on the Fancy of the Cook, if only it hath a good Tafte , then ferve it up hot for an Entry.

A Fowl *with large* Onions.

GET a Fowl, clean and order it like that above, lard it, fpit it, and bafte it with good Butter , cut large Onions into Slices, and put them in a Stew-pan with a Lump of Butter, then put it over the Fire , it being of a good Colour, ftrew it with a Duft of Flour, moiften it with Gravy, feafon it and skim it well, if it is not thick enough, put in a little of your Cullis: Your Fowl being done, take it off and difh it up , fee your Ragoo be relifhing, and put your Onions over it, with the Juice of a Lemon, and ferve it up hot for an Entry.

Roafted Fowl *with* Chefnuts.

GUT your Fowl, cut the Liver fmall, together with Parfley, green Onions, fcraped Bacon, Butter, Pepper, Salt, Sweet Herbs and fine Spice , take Chefnuts, peel them, and put them into a Braife, to take off the fmall Skin , then mix them with Force Meat, put all together into the Belly of your Fowl, and blanch it in a Stew-pan with a Bit of Butter. Spit your Fowl, wraped up in Bards of Bacon, with Paper tied round it. Take your peeled Chefnuts, put them in a Baking-pan, with Fire under and over, and take off the fmall Skin, then put them

in a Stew-pan with Broth, and let them be done thoroughly; pour out the Broth, and put in half a Ladleful of Effence of Ham, a little Cullis, and a little Gravy; your
Fowl being done, draw it off the Spit, and take off the
Bards of Bacon; difh it up, put your Chefnuts over it,
with the Juice of a Lemon, and ferve it up hot for an
Entry.

Pullets *à la Sainte-Menehout.*

HAving trufs'd the Legs in the Body, flit them along
the Back, fpread them open on a Table, beat them,
take out the Thigh Bones. Take a Pound and a half of
Veal, cut it in Slices, lay it in a Stew-pan of a convenient
Size to hold your Pullets; cover it, and fet it over a Stove;
when it begins to cleave to the Stew-pan, put in a little
Flour, and keep moving your Pan over the Fire to brown
it, moiften it with as much Broth as is neceffary to ftew
the Pullets. Seafon it with Salt, Pepper, favoury Herbs
and Spices, fome fhred Parfley, a Bunch of Herbs, and
fome Onions; lard your Pullets with large Lardoons well
feafoned, place them in the Stew-pan, lay fome Bards of
Bacon on the Pullets, cover the Stew-pan, and fet them
over a flack Fire. When they are about half done, uncover the Stew-pan, put in half a Pint of Milk, and a little Cream; then cover your Pan again, and continue to
ftew them. When they are done enough, take off the
Stew-pan, and let the Pullets cool in their Liquor; when
they are cool, take them out, rub them over with the Fat
of the Liquor in which they were ftewed, drudge them
well with Bread crumbed very fine, place them in a Pafty-
pan, or a Silver Difh, and brown them in an Oven, or
under

under a Baking Cover, when they are come to a fine Colour lay them in a Dish, pour on them some Essence of Ham, and serve them up for a first Course.

You may broil them on a Gridiron over a little Fire, instead of putting them into the Oven, or else

You may fry them, but in this Case, before you drudge, you must dip them in beaten Eggs, then drudge them with Bread, as above, and fry them in Hog's Lard 'till they are brown; then take them up, and set them a draining. Fold a Napkin in the Dish in which you intend to serve them, lay them handsomely upon it with fryed Parsley, and serve them for the first Course.

Pullet *or* Chicken Surprize.

ROAST them off; if a small Dish, two Chickens, or one Pullet will be sufficient. Take the Lean of your Pullet or Chickens from the Bone, cut it in thin Slices an Inch long, and toss it up in six or seven Spoonfuls of Milk or Cream, with the Bigness of half an Egg of Butter, grated Nutmeg, Pepper and Salt; thicken it with a little Dust of Flour, to the Thickness of a good Cream, then boil it up, and set it to cool; then cut six or seven thin round Slices of Bacon, place them in a Patty-pan, and put on each Slice some Forced-Meat, then work them up in Form of a *French* Roll, with raw Egg in your Hand, leaving a hollow place in the Middle; then put in your Fowl, and cover them with some of the same Forced-Meat, rubbing it smooth over with your Hand, and an Egg, make them of the Height and Bigness of a *French* Roll; throw a little fine grated Bread over them, bake them three Quarters of an Hour in a gentle Oven, or under a baking Cover,

Cover, 'till they come to a yellow brown, place them on
your Mazarine, that they may not touch one another, but
so that they may not fall flat in the baking: But you may
form them on your Kitchen-Table, with your Slices of
Bacon under them; then lift them up with your broad
Kitchen-Knife, and place them on that which you intend
to bake them on.   Let your Sauce be Butter and Gravy,
and squeezed Lemon, and your Garnishing fried Parsley
and cut Orange.   You may put the Legs of one of your
Chickens into the Sides of one of your Loaves that you intend to put in the Middle of your Dish.   This is proper
for a Side-Dish, for first Course, either in Summer or Winter, where you can have the Ingredients above-mentioned.

To dress Pullets à la Tartare.

YOU must truss a Couple of Pullets as for boiling;
slit them along the Back, spread them open upon a
Dresser, and beat them.   Put in a Stew-pan of the Size
of the Pullets, some Parsley, Cives, and Savoury Herbs
shred very small, and seasoned with Salt, and Pepper: Lay
the Pullets into the Stew-pan with the Breasts downwards;
put some of the above Seasoning upon them, then pour in
some melted Bacon, stir them about, and let them lie in this
Mixture two Hours, to give them the Taste of it.   Then
set the Stew-pan over the Fire, to melt the Bacon again,
and keep the Pullets moving in it for half a Quarter of an
Hour; after which take them out, drudge them well with
Bread crumbed very fine, and lay them to broil on a Gridiron over a slack Fire, 'till they are grown brown: Prepare
a hashed Sauce, lay it in the Bottom of a Dish, and the
Pullets upon it.

A Fowl

A Fowl *in Fillets with* Piſtaches.

SPIT your Fowls, and let them roaſt; they being
done, take them off, and cut off the Wings, and the
White off the Breaſt; keep a ſmall Sauce ready in a Stew-
pan, made with Sweet Herbs, a little good Butter, ſmall
Champignons cut into Slices; put it over the Fire with a
Duſt of Flour in it, ſtir and moiſten it with a Ladle full
of good Broth; ſee it be of a good Taſte, the Piſtaches
being ſcalded and cut into Slices, put them in, and make
a thick Sauce with four or five Yolks of Eggs, beat the
ſame up with Cream; then put in the White and Legs
of your Fowls, with the Juice of a Lemon, you muſt
cut your Wings only in two, then place the Slices of your
Fowls in the Bottom of the Diſh, with your Sauce over it,
and let there be no Sauce remaining, make it as reliſhing as
poſſibly can be, and ſerve it up hot for an Entry.

A Fowl, Chicken, *or* Capon à la Bourgeoiſe.

GET a Fowl, ſinge, pick, draw and truſs it; take a
Kettle or earthen Pot, put Water in it, enough to
ſoak your Fowl; put your Pot over the Fire with a handful of Salt; and when the Water boils, put in your Fowl,
but let it not boil too much: Put a Lump of Butter in a
Stew-pan, or earthen Pot, with a Duſt of Flour, Nutmeg,
Pepper, Salt and Oyſters, if any are to be had; put your
Stew-pan over the Fire, and thicken your Sauce; which
being thickened and pretty reliſhing, take out your Fowl
and diſh it up with your Oyſter Sauce over it.

At another time you take a little Parſley, ſome green O-
nions, a little Mint, and a little Terragon, if you have

any; but you may make your Sauce with Parfley only;
but if you can get Anchovies, cut a Couple fmall, and
put them into it; cut half a Lemon, after having taken
off the Rind, into fmall fquare Pieces, and fqueeze in the
other half, then put in a little Butter, with a Duft of Flour,
and a little Water, Pepper, and Salt, and fet your Sauce a
ftewing. Your Fowl being done, difh it up with your
Sauce over it.

At another time put fome Endive with your Fowl; and
when it is done, give it three or four Cuts with a Knife,
and put it into a Stew-pan with a little Butter, and a Duft
of Flour, and fet it over the Fire, then moiften it with a
little of the fame Broth your Fowl hath been boiled in; if
it be not thick enough, thicken it with Eggs.

At another time you may drefs your Fowl with Onions,
in boiling them with your Fowl, you may put them in a
Stew-pan or earthen Difh, with a Lump of Butter rolled
in Flour, Pepper and Salt; put it over the Fire with fome
of the fame Broth your Fowl was boiled in; thicken your
Sauce, and ferve it up hot for an Entry.

A Fowl *in Hafh.*

YOU muft take fome Fowls ready dreffed, then take
the Flefh and cut it very fmall; take the Carcaffes,
put them in a Stew-pan with good Broth, an Onion cut in
Slices, Parfley, and Sweet Herbs, when it is boiled enough,
ftrain it off, then put in it a Bit of Butter rolled in Flour,
and let it ftew a Moment again, then put in it your Hafh
of Fowls; let your Hafh be relifhing, thicken it with three
Yolks of Eggs, or more, according to the Quantity of
Hafh

Hash you make, it being thick, put in it the Juice of a Lemon, and serve them up hot for *Hors d'Oeuvre.*

A Hash of Fowls *the* English *way.*

LET your Fowls be ready dressed, take off the White, cut the same into small square Pieces, and put it in a Stew-pan; boil the Carcasses in a little Broth, then strain it through a silk Strainer, take this Broth, and put in it your Pieces of Fowl, cut into small Squares, and put it over the Fire; add to it a Bit of Butter rolled in Flour, a little Pepper and Salt, and if there is Occasion for it, the Juice of a Lemon; dish it up, garnish it with small Pieces of Bread fried, and serve it up hot for *Hors d'Oeuvre.*

Fowls à la Mommorency.

HAving a Fowl, singe, gut, truss, and blanch it over a Charcoal Fire; then lard it with thin Bacon; being larded, split it in the Back, put into the Belly a small Ragoo with Sweetbreads of Veal, Champignons, Truffles, and some Bottoms of Artichokes; put it a stewing in a Stew-pan with Slices of Bacon, Ham, and Veal, being stewed, take it off and put in it a little Broth; let it have a Boil, then strain it off in a Silk Strainer, and skim the Fat well off; then set it on again and let it stew 'till it turns to Caramel, then put it in your Fowls, and put your Bacon Side into the Caramel, put it upon hot Cinders, that it may glaze as it should: Being ready to serve up, put a Cullis of Ham, or a Sauce made the *Italian* Way into your Dish, then your Chickens over it, and serve it up hot for an Entry.

To

To dress Pullets *with Slices of* Ham.

FIRST truss your Pullets, cut some Slices of Ham, for each Pullet one, beat them a little, and season them with shred Cives and Parsley; loosen the Skin of your Pullets Breasts with your Finger, and slide in a Slice of Ham, between the Skin and the Flesh; then blanch your Pullets, by laying them before the Fire; wrap them up in Bards of Bacon, and roast them; when roasted, and the Bards taken off, put them in a Dish, and pour on them some Essence of Ham.

C H I C K E N S.

Chickens *with* Mushrooms *and* Sweet Herbs *roasted.*

TAKE Chickens, clean them well, and draw them; rasp some Bacon and put a few Mushrooms, Parsley, and young Onions and a little Sweet Basil, with the Livers of your Chickens, seasoned with Pepper and Salt. Hash all and mix it together, put it in the Bodies of your Chickens, then put them in a Sauce-pan, with a Piece of Butter, Parsley, young Onions, Salt, and Sweet Basil. Being done, Packthread them and spit them, and put them to the Spit wrapped with Bards of Bacon, and let them roast slowly. Make a Ragoo of Mushrooms, after this Manner: If they are dryed Mushrooms, steep them in luke-warm Water for one Hour or two, then take them out, and put them in a Stew-pan with some Gravy, and let them stew on a slow Fire. Having stewed a Quarter of an Hour, thicken them with some Cullis When your Chickens are done, take them from the Spit, unbard them, and dress

them

them handſomely in their Diſh: See that your Ragoo of Muſhrooms be of a good Taſte, and ſharp, put it upon your Chickens, and ſerve it hot for a firſt Courſe.

Chickens *with* Sweet Herbs *roaſted.*

DRESS your Chickens neatly, raſp ſome Bacon, a little Ham, haſh them well with Parſley, young Onions, and the Livers of Chickens haſhed, ſeaſoned with Pepper and Salt; mix it all together, and put it in the Bodies of your Chickens. You muſt obſerve to faſten them always at both Ends: Let them do in a Stew-pan, with a Bit of Butter, whole Parſley, young Onions whole; ſpit them and wrap them with Bards of Bacon, and covered with Sheets of Paper, and put them to roaſt ſlowly. When they are done, take them off and unbard them, and dreſs them neatly in their Diſh, throw an Eſſence of Ham on them, and ſerve them hot for a firſt Courſe.

Chickens *with* Farce-Meat *and* Cucumbers *roaſted.*

DRESS your Chickens neatly, take off the Breaſts and bone them, put the Fleſh upon the Table, with ſome Ham and blanched Bacon, and a Calf's Udder blanched, ſome Champignons, a little Parſley, and young Onions, a few Sweet Herbs, fine Spices, three or four Yolks of Eggs, ſome Crumbs of Bread, ſoaked in Cream or Milk, and boil the Bread, then leave it to cool, being cool, put it with the Farce, and Haſh all well together, and ſtuff your Chickens with it. Cloſe them at both Ends, keep a little of the Farce, let them ſtew as before, run a a Skewer thorough their Legs, and ſpit them wrapped with Bards of Bacon, and covered with Sheets of Paper, and

let

let them do flowly   Take four middling Cucumbers, pale them, and empty their Infides, being well emptied, blanch them in fome Broth; being blanched, put them into cold Water, then ftuff them with the Farce, and flour them at each End.   Take a Stew-pan and put fome Bards of Bacon in it, and lay your Cucumbers over, feafon them and wet them with a Ladle full of Broth, and let it boil, take half a Spoonful of your Cullis, and put it in a Stew-pan; let your Cullis be of a good Tafte.   When your Chickens are done, take them out, drefs them in their Difh, and put your Cucumbers to drain, then put them round your Chickens, and put your Cullis over them, with the Juice of a Lemon, and ferve it hot.

You may drefs Capons the fame Way.

Chickens à la Braife.

HAving the fatteft Chickens you can get, parboil them; lard them with large Lardoons of Bacon, and of Ham, both very well feafoned; when they are larded, tie them about with a Packthread; then garnifh the Bottom of a fmall Kettle with Bards of Bacon and Slices of Beef well beaten, and feafoned in the fame Manner as for the other Braifes already mentioned : Put the Chickens into the Kettle, the Breafts downwards, feafon them above as underneath ; lay over them Slices of Beef and Bards of Bacon, cover the Kettle, and fet them to ftew, with Fire over the Kettle as well as under it.   Then make a Ragoo as follows : Take fome Veal Sweetbreads and cut them in Morfels, add to them fome Cocks Combs, fome Mufh-rooms and Truffles cut in Slices; feafon all this with Pep-per, Salt, and a Bunch of Savoury Herbs ; put it into a

Sauce-

Sauce-pan, and tofs it up over a Stove with fome melted
Bacon. Then put fome Gravy amongft it, and fet it to fimmer over a gentle Fire; when it is half done, put to it
fome Afparagus-Tops, and Artichoke-Bottoms cut in Quarters and blanched, then continue to prepare your Ragoo,
and when it is enough, be careful to take off all the Fat,
and thicken it with a Cullis of Veal and Ham, take up
your Chickens, let them drain, and then put them into the
Stew-pan amongft your Ragoo; and when you are ready to
ferve, take them out, unbind the Packthread, and lay
them handfomely in the Difh you intend to ferve them in:
Take Care your Ragoo be well relifhed and the Fat be well
taken off, then pour it on the Chickens, and ferve them
warm for the firft Courfe.

We ferve Chickens *à la Braife* fometimes with a Ragoo
of Crawfifh, or of Oyfters, as likewife with all Sorts of
Ragoo's of Legumes.

Farced Chickens *with* Anchovies.

HAving fome grated fat Bacon, feafon it with Salt,
Pepper, fome Parfley, Cives, and two Anchovies,
fhred very fmall; mix all together, and having loofened
the Skin of the Breafts of your Fowls, put it between the
Skin and the Flefh: Tie them with Packthread, fold them
up in Bards of Bacon and Sheets of Paper; then Spit your
Chickens, and while they are roafting at a gentle Fire, take
two Anchovies, wafh them very clean, bone them and fhred
them very fmall, then put them in a Stew-pan, and melt
them in a clear Cullis of Veal, Ham, and Bacon. Keep
the Cullis over hot Embers, and when the Chickens are
roafted, take off the Bards and difh them up, pouring the

Cullis

Cullis of Anchovies upon them, and ferve them for the firſt Courſe.

We dreſs likewiſe Capons, Pullets, Quails, Partridges, Fillets of Veal and Mutton with Anchovies, in the ſame Manner as Chickens, and ſerve them alſo for firſt Courſe.

To boil Chickens *and* Aſparagus.

FORCE the Chickens with good Forced-Meat, and boil them white, cut the Aſparagus an Inch long, ſo parboil it with Water, a little Butter and Flour, and drain it, then take a Sauce-pan with a little Butter and Salt, and diſſolve it ſlowly, taking Care that it do not become brown. Add to the Aſparagus a little minced Parſley and Cream, a Faggot of Fennel, ſome Nutmeg, Pepper and Salt, ſtew it over a ſlow Fire; ſo ſerve it over your Chickens; ſqueeze in a little Lemon.

To marinate Fowls.

YOU muſt take Pullets, Chickens, or Veal Sweet-breads, Muſhrooms, Oyſters, Anchovies, Marrow, and a little Lemon-peel, a little Pepper, Salt, Nutmeg, and a little Thyme, Marjoram and Savoury, a few Chives; mingle all theſe together with the Yolk of an Egg, then raiſe up the Skin of the Breaſts of your Fowls, and ſtuff it; and ſtick it up again, and lard them, fill their Bellies with Oyſters, and roaſt them; make good ſtrong Gravy Sauce: So you may do Pheaſants, Turkies, or what Fowls you pleaſe.

A par-

A particular Manner of stewing Chickens *or* Rabbits.

GET two, three, or four Chickens, about the Bignefs of a Partridge, and boil them 'till they are half
done: Then take them off, and cut them into little Pieces,
feparating the Joint-Bones one from another; let not the
Meat be minced, but cut into great Slices, not fo exactly,
but more or lefs; the Breaft Bones are not fo proper to be
put in: However, put the Meat, together with the other
Bones (upon which there muft alfo be fome Meat remaining) into a good Quantity of that Water or Broth wherein
the Chickens were boiled, and fet it over a Chafing Difh of
Coals, between two Difhes, that fo it may ftew on 'till it
be fully enough, but firft feafon it with Salt, and grofs
Pepper, and afterwards, add Oil to it, more or lefs according to the Goodnefs thereof. A little before you take the
Meat from the Fire, put in fuch a Quantity of Juice of
Lemons as may beft agree with your Tafte. This makes
an excellent Difh of Meat, which is to be ferved up in the
Liquor; and though for a Need, it may be made with
Butter inftead of Oil, and with Vinegar inftead of Lemon Juice, yet, is the other incomparably better for fuch
as have not an Averfion for Oil. The fame Difh may be
alfo made of Veal, or Partridge, or Rabbits; and indeed,
the beft of them all is Rabbits, if they be fo drefs'd before
Michaelmas; for afterwards they grow rank; fince though
they are fatter, yet the Flefh is more hard and dry.

Chickens *Chiringrate.*

CUT off their Feet and lard them, brown them off,
make a Ragoo Sauce and ftew them in it; when
you are going to ferve, put to your Chickens cold Ham

B b b   fliced sliced. Let it stew a little with your Chickens; so serve them with your sliced Ham about them.

For Fricasey *of* Chickens, *see the Chapter of* Fricaseys.

Chickens *with* Sellery.

BOIL them off white with a Piece of Ham, then boil off two Bunches of Sellery; cut them two Inches along the white End, and lay them in a Sauce-pan; put in some Cream, Butter, and Salt; stove them a little and thickish, then lay your Chickens in your Dish, with your Sellery between. Garnish with sliced Ham and Lemon.

Chickens *with* Tongues, Cauliflowers *and* Greens.

TAKE six Hogs Tongues, boil them and skin them, six Chickens boiled off white, one Cauliflower boiled, and some Spinach , put your Cauliflower in the Middle of your Dish, your Chickens about, and between, a Tongue with Heaps of Spinach round, and Slices of Bacon.

Chickens *Royal.*

LARD them and force the Bellies and pass them off, then stove them in good Gravy and Broth Gold Colour: Make a Ragoo of Mushrooms, Morels, Truffles and Cocks Combs, and when your Chickens are enough, dish them up, lay your Ragoo over, and garnish with Petty Patties and fried Sweetbreads.

Scotch Chickens.

CUT your Chickens in Quarters; singe them and wash them well, and then put as much Water as will just cover them; put them on a gentle Fire, and when
they

they boil ſkim thom well, and put in ſome Salt, Mace and Nutmeg, a Faggot of Thyme, Paiſley, and a little Pepper; and when your Chickens are tender, chop half a Handful of Parſley and put it in your Chickens, then beat up ſix Eggs, Yolks and Whites together; and as your Chickens boil up, put in your Eggs a Top; and ſo ſerve them all together; the Broth will be very clear.

D U C K S.

Ducklings á la Mode

CUT them in Quarters, lard one half and brown them off, ſtove them in half a Pint of Claret, a Pint of Gravy and two Shalots, one Anchovy and a Faggot of Herbs; ſtove them tender, ſkim off the Fat, take out the Faggot and ſqueeze in a Lemon; ſhake it together; the Sauce muſt be thick as Cream, ſo ſerve away to Table hot.

Stoved Ducks *the* Dutch *Way*

YOU muſt truſs two Ducks cloſe without the Legs, and lard one; ſeaſon with Pepper and Salt, and fill the Bellies with ſmall Onions; then lay at the Bottom of your Stew-pan half a Pound of Butter, and put in your Ducks, and cover them with ſliced Onions; then another half Pound of Butter; ſtove this two Hours gently, keeping it covered all the while; when you find all diſcoloured, and your Ducks tender, diſh them, ſhaking a little Vinegar amongſt them.

B b b 2

Duck

Duck *or* Teal *with* Horfe-Radifh.

TRUSS them to boil, if two, lard one, and pafs them off in brown Butter, then put to them a Pint of clear Broth and two Plates of Horfe-Radifh, feafon with Salt, and ftove thefe together 'till tender; then ftrain off your Horfe-Radifh from your Ducks, and put in a good Piece of Butter; you may fcrape your Horfe-Radifh very fine, which is the beft Way; then lay your Ducks in your Difh, and your Horfe-Radifh all over, and garnifh with fcraped Horfe-Radifh and fliced Lemon, and ferve away hot.

To drefs a Wild Duck *with* Lemon Juice.

HALF roaft your Duck, then take it off the Spit, and lay it in a Difh, carve it, but leave the Joints hanging together: In the Incifion put Salt, and beaten Pepper, and fqueeze the Juice of Lemons; turn it on the Breaft, and prefs it hard with a Plate, and fet it a little to ftew on your Stove, turn it again, and ferve it hot in its own Gravy

To ftew a Duck *wild or tame.*

HAving a Stew-pan, put at the Bottom of it Slices of Bacon and Beef, add fome Parfnips, Carrots and Onions fliced, and fome Slices of Lemon, a few Savoury Herbs, with Pepper, Salt and Cloves; then put in your Duck, cover it when it is ftewed enough, take up the Duck, and make a Ragoo of Lambs Sweetbreads, with Cocks Combs, Truffles, Mufhrooms, and Artichoke Bottoms, tofs up all this in melted Butter, and pour on the Duck.

Tc

To boil Ducks *after the* French *Fashion*

LET the Ducks be larded, fpitted and half roafted: Then draw them and put them into a Pipkin, as alfo a Quart of Claret Wine, fome Chefnuts, a Pint of great Oyfters, that have the Beards taken from them, three Onions minced very fmall, fome Mace, a little beaten Ginger, and a little Thyme ftripped: Then put in the Cruft of a *French* Roll grated, to thicken it, and fo difh it upon Sippets: This may be diverfified: If there be ftrong Broth, there need not be fo much Wine put in it, and if there be no Oyfters, or Chefnuts, you may put in Artichoke Bottoms, Turnips, Cauliflowers, Bacon in thin Slices, Sweetbreads, &c.

Ducks à la Braife *with* Turnips.

LARD a Duck with large Lardoons, well feafoned, take a Stew-pan of a convenient Size, and garnifh the Bottom of it with Bards of Bacon and Slices of Beef, to which add fome Onions, Carrots, and Parfnips fliced, fome Slices of Lemon, fome favoury Herbs, Pepper, Salt, and Cloves, then put in your Duck, cover it in the fame Manner as under it, and put Fire, likewife, under and over it. This is a Difh for the firft Courfe, which is ferved in feveral Manners. When it is with Turnips, they are to be cut in Dice, or round them in the Shape of Olives, they muft be tofs'd up in Hog's Lard, to give them a brown Colour, then fet them to drain; and, after that, put them to fimmer in good Gravy, and thicken them with a good Cullis When the Duck is ready to be ferved up, drain it well, then lay it in the Difh, pour upon it the Ragoo of Turnips, and ferve it hot. If you will be at the Charge of ſtewing it *à la Braiſe*, when you have larded your Duck, drudge it well with Flour, and toſs it up in melted Bacon to brown it; then put it into a Pot and make a Brown, either with melted Bacon, or Butter and Flour, to which put ſome good Broth and near a Pint of White Wine, ſeaſoning the whole with Salt, Pepper, Cloves, Onions, Slices of Lemon, Par-ſley, and ſavoury Herbs, ſo ſet the Duck to ſtew, and when it is done, ſerve it with the following Ragoo :

Ragoo *for a* Duck *à la Braiſe.*

IT is made either with Veal or Lambs Sweetbreads, with fat Livers, Cocks Combs, Muſhrooms, Truffles, Aſparagus Tops, and Artichocke Bottoms: Toſs up all this in melted Bacon, moiſten it with good Gravy, bind it with a Cullis of Veal and Ham, and when you have diſh-ed up your Duck, pour the Ragoo upon it.

Ducks Tongues.

GET as many Ducks, or Geeſe Tongues as you can; fifty Tongues will fill up a ſmall Diſh. Blanch them, put them in a Stew-pan over ſome Slices of Bacon, with Onions cut in Slices, and ſome Sprigs of Sweet Baſil; ſea-ſon it with Salt, Pepper, and ſome Slices of Bacon, moiſten it with a Spoonful of Broth, let it ſtew together. The Tongues being done, drain them, and put them, in ſome Eſſence of Ham, or an *Italian* Sauce, put them, for a Minute, over the Fire to take a Reliſh. Being ready to ſerve, let your Tongues be reliſhing, add the Juice of a Lemon; ſerve them up hot for a dainty Diſh.

At

At another Time, you may garniſh them with Muſhrooms, Truffles, Cocks Kidneys and Cocks Combs.

G E E S E.

To dreſs a Green Gooſe.

YOU muſt take a Stew-pan of a convenient Size, and
cut your Gooſe in two; put at the Bottom of your
Pan, Bards of Bacon and Beef, with Onions, Savoury,
Thyme, and Marjoram, with Carrots, Slices of Lem-
mon, Pepper, Cloves, and Salt; put in the Gooſe over a
good Charcoal Fire, 'till enough, often ſtir and turn it;
then make a Ragoo of Green-Peaſe, toſſed up with a little
freſh Butter, and Flour, a Bunch of Herbs, Salt and Pepper; moiſten it with Gravy; and when you ſerve it, thick-
ne it with the Yolks of two Eggs, beat in Cream: Diſh up
your Gooſe, and pour the Ragoo upon it.

This Ragoo ſerves for a Breaſt of Veal, or Pigeons ſtewed.

Geeſe *larded and ſtoved.*

YOU muſt truſs your Geeſe cloſe and lard one Side,
put in ſome Sage and Onion chopped ſmall, rolled
up with Eggs, Crumbs of Bread, Pepper, Salt, and Butter; then paſs them and ſtove them gently in good Broth
and Gravy 'till tender: Make a clean thick Lear, ſqueeze
in an Orange and ſerve away hot.

Green Geeſe à la Daube.

LARD your Green Geeſe with large Lardoons, ſeaſon
with Salt, Pepper, Cloves, Nutmeg, Bay Leaf,
Cives, Lemon Peel, and wrap them up in a Napkin; boil
them

them in Broth, and White Wine; when the Broth is pretty well wasted away, and you judge them to be enough, take them off, and set them to cool in the Liquor in which they are boiled; then take them out, and serve them dry on a clean Napkin, and garnish with green Parsley: We sometimes boil with them some Slices of Veal and Bards of Bacon, to strengthen them and keep them white

We dress Turkies, Capons, Partridges, and other Fowls in the same Manner.

To boil a Goose *with* Cabbage *or* Sausages.

SALT your Goose, two or three Days, then truss it to boil; cut Lardoons as big as the Top of your Finger, as much as will lard the Flesh of the Breast; and season your Lardoons with Pepper, Mace, and Salt. Afterwards, set all a boiling in Beef Broth, if you have any, or Water, seasoning your Liquor with a little Salt, Pepper grosly beaten, an Ounce or two, a Bundle of Bay Leaves, Rosemary and Thyme, tied all together: In the mean while, having prepared your Cabbage or Sausages boiled very tender, squeeze all the Water from them, put them into a Pipkin, with a little strong Broth or Claret Wine, and an Onion or two; season it with Pepper, Salt, and Mace to your Taste; add six Anchovies dissolved, and let all stew a good while on the Fire: Put in a Ladle full of thick Butter, with a little Vinegar, when your Goose is boiled enough, and lay your Cabbage on Sippets of Bread, the Goose on the Top of your Cabbage, and some of the Cabbage on the Top of your Goose.

Geese

Geefe à la mode.

TAKE two Geefe, and raife their Skins on the Breafts, and making a Stuffing of Pullet, Chicken, or Veal Sweetbreads, Mufhrooms, Anchovies, Oyfters, Marrow, and a little Lemon Peel, a little Pepper, Salt, Nutmeg, Thyme, Marjoram, and a Clove of Garlick, mingle all thefe with the Yolk of an Egg; put a little under the Skin on the Breafts, and fome in their Bellies. Lard your Geefe with Lemon and Thyme, then put in as much Butter in your Stew-pan as will brown them on both Sides; then put them in the Butter with ftrong Gravy, feafoned very high, and when they are ftewed enough, take them out; thicken the Sauce with Butter rolled up in Flour, and the Yolks of Eggs, with half a Pint of Claret, and let them boil to be thick; then fry Oyfters and Forced-Meat Balls, and crifped Sippets to lay round your Difh, and ferve it. Garnifh with grated Bread, and Flowers, round your Difh.

P I G E O N S.

To boil Pigeons.

STUFF your Pigeons with Parfley and Butter, put them into an earthen Pot, with fome fweet Butter, and let them boil: Afterwards, add thereto fome Parfley, Thyme, Rofemary and Spinage fhred; with a little grofs Pepper, and Salt: Then ftrain in the Yolk of an Egg, with fome Verjuice, lay Sippets in the Difh, and let it be ferved up.

N° 17.   C c c   Pigeons

Pigeons au Poir.

MAKE a good Forced-Meat of Veal, take fmall Squails and ftove them off in Gravy, fill the Bellies with Forced-Meat in the Shape of a Pear, ftick a Leg a Top, and it will be the Bignefs of a *Windfor* Pear, wafh them over with an Egg, and crumb them and bake them gently.

Pigeons *forced and ftoved*.

CUT the Legs off, trufs them clofe and lard them with grofs Lard; pafs them off and ftove them with half a Pint of Rhenifh Wine, fome clear Broth, and Cabbage Lettuce; force your Lettuce, feafon with Pepper, Salt and Mace, Squeeze in a Lemon and ferve away; let your Sauce be thick as Cream, and garnifh with your Forced Lettuce and Lemon.

Pigeons Surtout.

HAving cleanfed your Pigeons, make for them Forcing, then tie a large *Scotch* Collop on the Breaft of each, fpit and cover them with Paper, and roaft them, then make for them a Ragoo, and garnifh the Difh with fliced Orange.

Pigeons à la Crepeaudine.

WHEN you have picked and gutted your Pigeons, trufs them with their Legs within their Bodies; then cut up the Breaft and throw the fame over their Heads, and beat them flat; put them in a Stew-pan with melted Bacon, or Butter, fome Parfley, green Onions, Pepper,

Salt,

Salt, and Sweet Herbs, put all over the Fire to make it have a Taste, then strew them with fine Crumbs of Bread, and let them be broiled, and serve them up with Gravy, a Shalot cut small, or green Onions and the Juice of a Lemon over them, and serve them up hot for an Entry.

Pigeons en Compôte.

PULL and draw your Pigeons, truss them handsomely, the Legs in the Bodies, and parboil them, then lard them with large Lardoons, seasoned with Salt, Herbs, Pepper, Spices, minced Cives and Parsley, and stew them *à la Braise.* While they are a stewing, make a Ragoo of Cocks Combs, Fowls Livers, Truffles, and Mushrooms, tossing them up in a little melted Bacon, then moisten your Ragoo with Gravy, set it to simmer over a gentle Fire, take off the Fat, and thicken it with a Cullis of Veal and Ham. Take up your Pigeons and drain them, then put them into the Ragoo, and let them simmer in it to give them the Taste of it: Lay them in a Dish, pour the Ragoo upon them, and serve them for the first Course.

Pigeons en Compôte *with* White Sauce.

YOUR Pigeons being scalded, drawn, trussed, and blanched, put them into a Stew-pan, with a little melted Bacon, a Bunch of Herbs, an Onion stuck with Cloves, Veal Sweetbreads, Cocks Combs, Mushrooms and Truffles, the whole seasoned with Salt and Pepper; toss them up over a Stove, put in a little Flour, and give them three or four Turns: Put to them some good Broth, and make them simmer in it over a gentle Fire: When they are enough done, take off the Fat, and thicken them with

Ccc 2

a white

a White Cullis, but if you have no Cullis, make ufe of, inftead of it, the Yolk of two or three Eggs beaten up in Cream, with a little fhred Parfley. So difh them up and ferve them for the firft Courfe.

Pigeons au Gratin.

HAving young Pigeons picked dry, blanch them again over a Charcoal Fire, then pick them very clean, and when they are well picked, fplit them in the Back; then take the Livers, which you mince with fcraped Bacon, Parfley, green Onions, Champignons and Truffles, feafoned with Pepper, Salt, fine Spice and Sweet Herbs; but all moderately: Then put in a filver Difh Slices of Bacon, of Veal, and of Ham; after that place in it your Pigeons and put your Forced-Meat, mentioned before, in their Bellies; and lay over each Pigeon a fmall Slice of Ham and Veal: There is no need to put Seafoning, by reafon of the Ham: Cover them with another Difh, half as fmall again as the other, and take a white Napkin moiften'd, which put all round the Difh, to hinder it from takeing Vent, then put it a ftewing over a fmall Stove; it being done, difh it up with Effence of Ham in another Difh, and ferve it up hot for a fmall Entry, or *Hors d'Oeuvre.*

Another way of dreffing Pigeons au Gratin.

GET fome Pigeons as above, pick and order them very clean; put fome Slices of Bacon and Veal in a Stew-pan; alfo fome Slices of Ham and Onions, then place in your Pigeons: Make a fmall Seafoning with Parfley, fcraped Bacon, green Onions, Salt, Sweet Herbs, fome fat Liver, Champignons and Truffles, the whole being

ing

ing well minced together, put it in the Bellies of your Pigeons, and let the Seasoning be as it should, but take care not to make it too salt, then cover it with a Layer of Veal and Slices of Bacon, and when they are done, make a little Cullis of Partridges, which you must put into your Dish about the Breadth of two Fingers deep, then put your Pigeons into it, and so put your Dish upon a Stove, to make them stick to the Bottom of it, keep the Border of your Dish clean, then put in it a little Essence of Ham, or else an *Italian* Sauce and serve up hot.

A Pupton of Pigeons.

YOU must take savoury Forc'd-Meat and roll it out as Paste, and put it in a tossing Pan, then lay in thin Slices of Bacon, Squab Pigeons, sliced Sweetbreads, Tops of Asparagus, Mushrooms, Yolks of hard Eggs, the tender Ends of shiver'd Palates, and Cocks Combs boil'd, blanch'd and sliced: Then cover it over with another Forc'd-Meat as a Pye, when bak'd, turn it into a Dish and pour Gravy in it.

To stew Pigeons

MELT a good Quantity of Butter, mingle it with Parsley, Sorrel and Spinage, which you must stew in some Butter, and when it is cold put it into some of their Craws with a Bay-Leaf, save some of it for Sauce: Then stew the Pigeons in as much strong Gravy as will cover them, with some Cloves, Mace, Salt, Pepper, and Winter Savoury, a little Lemon Peel, a Shalot or two, then brown some Butter and put in, and when they are stewed enough, put in a little Bit of Butter rolled up in Flour,

and

and the Yolk of an Egg, with some of the Herbs you left out, shake it up all together, and serve away hot.

Another *Way of dressing* Pigeons.

GET young Pigeons and parboil them, then chop some raw Bacon very small, with a little Parsley, a little Sweet Marjoram, or Sweet Basil and a small Onion; season this with Salt and Pepper, and fill the Bodies of the Pigeons with it. When this is done, stew the Pigeons in Gravy, or strong Broth, with an Onion stuck with Cloves, a little Verjuice and Salt, when they are enough, take them out of the Liquor, and dip them in Eggs that have been well beaten, and after that, roll them in grated Bread, that they may be covered with it. Then make some Lard very hot, and fry them in it 'till they are brown, and serve them up with some of the Liquor they were stew'd in, and fried Parsley.

Pigeons *in* Paste.

FILL the Belly of your Pigeon with Butter, a little Water, some Pepper and Salt, and cover it with a thin light Paste, and then put it in a Linnen-Cloth, and boil it for a Time, in Proportion to its Bigness, and serve it up. When this is cut open, it will yield Sauce enough of a very agreeable Relish.

Pigeons à la Braise.

PICK, gut and truss large Pigeons, lard them with thick Bacon well seasoned; then take a Stew-pan, and garnish it with Slices of Bacon, Veal and Onions; place in it your Pigeons, and season them with Pepper, Salt, fine

Spices,

Spices, and Sweet Herbs, and cover them under and over, and let them ſtew; being ſtewed, let them drain, keep a Ragoo ready made with Sweetbreads of Veal, Truffles and Champignons, your Sweetbreads of Veal being blanched, put them into the Stew-pan, together with your Truffles and Champignons, adding to them a Ladle full of Gravy, and a little Cullis, and let it ſtew: All being done, and of a good Taſte, diſh up your Pigeons, pour a Ragoo over them, and ſerve them up hot for an Entry.

For Pigeon-Pie, *ſee the Chapter of* Paſtry.

PARTRIDGES.

Young Partridges *in* Gallimaufry.

AFTER you have picked, ſinged and drawn your Partridges, put them on the Spit with a Bit of Butter in the Inſide of each, wraping them up with Bards of Bacon in Paper, when they are done enough, cut them as you would your Chickens for a Fricaſey, then put them in a Stew-pan, with a little Broth, a little ſhred Cives, and a Shalot, a little Parſley, Salt, and Pepper, a Rocambole well minced, a ſmall Handful of Crumbs of Bread, ſome Zeſt, with the Juice of an Orange; heat them a little on the Fire, and give them two or three Toſſes without boiling them in their Diſh, and ſerve them up hot for a firſt Courſe Diſh.

Partridges *the* Spaniſh *Way*

WHEN you have ſinged, picked and drawn your Partridges, you muſt mince ſome of their Livers with a Bit of Butter, ſome ſcraped Bacon, Muſhrooms,

green

green Truffles, if they are to be had, Parſley, Chibbol, Salt, Pepper, Sweet Herbs, and All-ſpice. The whole being minced together, put it in the Inſide of your Partridges, and then ſtop both Ends of them; after which, give them a fry in a Stew-pan; and being done, ſpit them, and wrap them up in Slices of Bacon and Paper, then take a Stew-pan, and having put in an Onion cut in Slices, a Carrot cut in little Bits, with a little Oil; give them a few Toſſes over the Fire, then moiſten them with Gravy, Cullis, a little Eſſence of Ham, putting therein half a Lemon cut in Slices, four Cloves of Garlick, a little Sweet Baſil, Thyme, a Bay Leaf, a little Parſley, Chibbol, a Couple of Glaſſes of White Wine, and if you have any of the Carcaſſes of Partridges, let them be pounded, and put them in this Sauce; but if you have none, you may put in their Stead ſome of the pounded Livers of your Partridges, having firſt taken away their Galls; when the Fat of your Cullis is taken away, be careful to make it reliſhing, and after your pounded Livers are put in your Cullis, you muſt ſtrain them through a Sieve. Your Partridges being done, take them off, as alſo take off the Bacon and Paper, and lay them in their Diſh, with your *Spaniſh* Sauce over them.

Young Partridges *with* Olives.

GET of Partridges the Number you think proper, according to the Bigneſs of your Diſh, pick them well, draw them clean, but do not cut their Hole in the Back-Side, take away their Gall, and mince them with ſome Parſley, Chibbol, Muſhrooms, Sweet Herbs, All-ſpice, Salt, Pepper, ſcraped Bacon, with a Bit of Butter; put
the

the whole in the Infide of your Partridge, put in the Rump in the Hole of their Backfide, do not take off their Feet, and let them take a fry in the Stew-pan, with a Bit of Butter, fome Sprigs of Parfley, a little Chibbol, and fome Salt, after which, fplit them, wrapped up in Slices of Bacon, and fome Sheets of Paper, then get fome Olives, and having taken their Stones away, blanch them in boiling Water, then put them in a Stew-pan with a Cullis, fome Effence of Ham, and fome Gravy, let them boil and take off the Fat, let the whole be pretty relifhing; your young Partridges being done, take them off, and the Slices of Bacon, with the Paper, being taken off, lay them in their Difh with your Olives over them, and ferve them hot for the firft Courfe.

Young Partridges *with* Oyfters.

PICK fome young Partridges, draw them, but do not cut the Back-fide Hole of them, mince their Livers, and having got fome Oyfters, blanch them, and take out the Hard, after which, put them in a Stew-pan, with a Bit of Butter, the minced Livers, fome Parfley, Chibbol, Salt, Pepper, Sweet Herbs, and All-fpice, then give it two or three Toffes, and ftuff your young Partridges with it, after which, put each Rump into its Hole, and let your Partridges fry a little, and put them on the Spit, wrapped up in Slices of Bacon and Paper, then get fome more Onions, blanched as the others, put them in a Stew-pan, with half a Spoonful of good Effence of Ham, and a little of your Cullis, which having boiled as much as is neceffary, to fhorten it at Pleafure, put the Juice of a Lemon therein. Your young Partridges being done, draw them off, taking

off

off the Bacon and Paper, after which, lay them in their
Dish with your Ragoo of Oysters over them, and serve them
up hot for a first Course.

A Hash *of* Partridges.

HAving roasted your Partridges, cut the Wings and
Legs off, and take all the Meat, which you must
mince well, then take and pound their Carcasses, which
being well pounded, must be put in a Stew-pan, with a little Essence of Ham, let them warm a little, and strain
them through a Sieve. Then take your minced Partridges,
and put them in a Cullis just strained, the Quantity you
think fit: Being ready to serve, keep your Hash hot, but take
Care it doth not boil; put in it squeezed Rocamboles, and
the Juice of an Orange; after which, serve it up for a first
Course.

At another Time, put therein the White of a Fowl, and
your Hash will be so much the nicer.

P H E A S A N T S.

To roast Pheasants.

PICK and draw your Pheasants, blanch and lard them
with fine Bacon, spit them with Paper round them,
to be done before a slow Fire. When almost done, take
the Paper off to let them get a Colour, and dish them up
handsomely.

To dress Pheasants *with* Carp Sauce

BARD your Pheasants, roast them, and take Care
they do not dry. To make the Sauce, lay in the
Bottom of a Stew-pan, some Veal Slices, as you do when
you

you make Gravy, add to this Veal, fome Slices of a Gammon of Bacon, fome fliced Onion, fome Parfley Roots,
and a Bunch of Sweet Herbs Then gut a Carp, wafh it
in one Water only, without fcaling it, cut it in Pieces, as if
you were to ftew it, and lay them in the fame Stew-pan;
brown this a little over the Stove, as if you would make
Gravy of it; then wet it with good Gravy, pour in a Bottle of Champaign Wine, and add a Clove of Garlick,
fome minced Truffles and Mufhrooms, and fome fmall
Crufts of Bread: Boil all this well together, and take Care
it be not too falt. When it is well boiled, ftrain it in a
Sieve, forcing it through, that the Sauce may be pretty
thick; if it be not, put to it fome Partridge Cullis, and
pour it into a Sauce-pan: Before you ferve, bind your Pheafants with Packthread, put them into this Sauce, and keep
them warm: When you would ferve, unbind them, lay
them in a Difh and pour the Sauce upon them.

Pheafants *with* Oyfters *the* Italian *Way with a* White
Sauce.

GET fome Pheafants pick them clean and draw them,
cut their Livers fmall, take fome Oyfters, *viz.* to
each Pheafant half a Dozen will be enough; blanch them,
and put them in a Stew-pan with their Livers, and a
Lump of Butter, fome Parfley, green Onions, Pepper, and
Salt, Sweet Herbs, fine Spice, put all together a Moment
over the Fire, and put it afterwards, into your Pheafants.
Blanch them in a Stew-pan with Oil, green Onions, Parfley, Sweet Bafil, and Lemon Juice: Then put them on
the Spit, covered with Slices of Bacon, and Paper tied
round; take fome Oyfters, and blanch them in their own

Liquor,

Liquor, then prick them, take a Stew-pan, put in it four
Yolks of Eggs, the half of a Lemon cut into small Dice,
a little beaten Pepper, a little scraped Nutmeg, a little Parsley cut small, a Rocambole, an Anchovy cut small, a little Oil, a small Glass of Champaign, or other White Wine,
a Lump of Butter with a little Ham Cullis, then put your
Sauce over the Fire and thicken it · Take Care the Sauce
does not turn, put in it your Oysters, see that your Sauce
be relishing. Your Pheasants being done, draw them off,
take off the Bacon, and dish them up with the Oyster Ragoo over them, and serve them up hot for an Entry.

Pheafants *with* Olives.

GET as many Pheafants as you think will make up
your Dish, pick, singe, and draw them clean, but
don't cut the lower Part of the Belly, or Vent. Take off
the Galls from your Livers, and cut these small, with some
Parsley, green Onions, Champignons, Sweet Herbs, fine
Spice, Pepper, Salt, scraped Bacon, and a Bit of Butter,
and put all this into the Belly of your Pheafant, and thrust
the Rump into the lower Part of the Belly, or Vent, to prevent your Forced-Meat from coming out; blanch them in
a Stew-pan, with Butter, Parsley, green Onions, Salt, Basilic,
all in Branches, put your Pheafants on the Spit, wrapp'd
up in Slices of Bacon, and Paper tied round. Take some
Olives, take out their Stones, blanch them in hot Water;
they being blanched, put them in a Stew-pan, with Cullis,
Essence of Ham and Gravy; put them a boiling, skim-
ing the Fat well off, see that all together be relishing:
Your Pheafants being roasted, draw them off, and take off
the

the Slices of Bacon ; dish them up, put your Olives over them, and serve them hot for an Entry or second Course.

S N I P E S.

To roast Snipes.

DR A W them or not, as you like them , but if they are drawn, then put small Onions into the Bellies of your Snipes , and while they are roasting put Claret, Vinegar, Salt, Pepper, and Anchovy into the Dripping-pan , to which, when they are roasted, add a little grated Bread and some Butter, shaking the whole well together, and so serve them up.   If you do not draw them, then only take out the Guts, mince them very small, and put them into Claret, with a little Salt, Gravy and Butter.   Or you may make the Sauce thus . Having boiled some Onions, butter them, and season them with Pepper and Salt, and put to them the Gravy of any fresh Meat.

Snipes *in* Surtout.

HA V E a minced Meat ready done, of which you must make a Border in a Dish your Surtout is to be served in. Your Snipes being roasted, make a Salmi, which put to cool before you put it into the Dish, after which, cover them with the Remainder of your Stuffing, which you colour with Eggs, and strew over them Crumbs of Bread , put them into the Oven to get a good Colour, and serve it up hot.

Snipes *in* Ragoo.

SLIT them in two, but take out nothing from their Bellies, tofs them up with melted Bacon, feafon them with Salt and Pepper, the Juice of Mufhrooms, and when they are enough fqueeze in fome Lemon, and ferve them.

Ortelans *roafted.*

BARD them or let them be plain, putting a Vine-Leaf betwixt them ; when they are fpitted, fome Crumbs of Bread may be ufed as for Larks ; when you roaft them, let them be fpitted Side-ways, which is the beft.

Ruffs *and* Reifs.

THEY are a *Lincolnfhire* Bird, and you may fatten them as you do Chickens, with white Bread and Milk, and Sugar, they feed faft, and will die in their Fat if not killed in Time, trufs them crofs legged as you do a Snipe, and fpit them the fame Way, but you muft gut them ; put Gravy and Butter and Toaft under them, and ferve them quick.

Curlews *potted.*

HAving trufs'd them crofs legg'd, cut off the Heads, or thruft them through like a Woodcock ; feafon them with Pepper, Salt, and Nutmeg ; gut them firft, then put them in a Pot with two Pounds of Butter ; cover them and bake them one Hour, then take them out, and when cool, fqueeze out all the Liquor and lay them in your Pot, and cover them with clarified Butter.

Potted

Potted Wheat-Ears

T H E Y are a *Tunbridge* Bird : Pick them very clean, season them with Pepper and Salt, put them in a Pot, cover them with Butter, and bake them one Hour, take them and put them in a Colander to drain the Liquor away, then cover them over with clarified Butter, and they will keep.

Q U A I L S.

To roaſt Quails.

G E T Quails, truſs them, ſtuff their Bellies with Beef Sewet and Sweet Herbs chopped well together ; ſpit them on a ſmall Spit, and when they grow warm, baſte firſt with Water and Salt, but afterwards with Butter, and drudge them with Flour. For Sauce, diſſolve an Anchovy in Gravy, into which put two or three Shalots ſliced and boiled, add the Juice of two or three *Seville* Oranges and one Lemon ; diſh them in this Sauce, and garniſh with Lemon Peel and grated Manchet : Be ſure to ſerve them up hot.

A Fricaſey *of* Quails.

W E toſs them up in a Sauce-pan with a little melted Bacon, ſome Muſhrooms, Truffles, and Morels, with a Slice of Ham well beaten ; let your Seaſoning be Salt, Pepper, Cloves, and a Bunch of ſavoury Herbs. If you have no Cullis, you may put in a little Flour, give it two or three Turns over the Stove, moiſten it with good Gravy, and add a Glaſs of Champaign ; then ſet it to ſimmer over a ſlack Fire : When they are almoſt done, thicken

en

en the Ragoo with a good Cullis, but if you have none, let your Thickening be two or three Eggs well beaten up in a little Gravy or Verjuice.

Another Way to dress Quails.

SLIT your Quails along the Back, make a Farce with scraped Bacon, a little of the Lean of a Ham, one Truffle, some Fowls Livers, and the Yolk of a raw Egg, the whole minced and pounded together, and seasoned with Salt, Pepper, Nutmeg, and savoury Herbs; farce your Quails with it, then garnish the Bottom of a Stew-pan with Slices of Bacon and some of Veal over them; then lay in your Quails the Breasts downwards; cover them with Slices of Veal and Ham, both seasoned, as well those under them, as those upon them, with Salt, Pepper, savoury Herbs, and Spices. Lay a Plate over the Meat, so as that it may touch it, and a Napkin all round the Plate, then cover the Stew-pan with its own Cover; set it over a gentle Fire, and stew it very softly two Hours: The Moment before you serve, open the Stew-pan, take out the Slices of Veal and Bacon, and set your Quails over the Stove to brown them; when they are fine and brown, and the Liquor sticks to the Stew-pan, take them up, and lay them in the Dish in which you intend to serve them, take out all the Fat that remains in the Stew-pan, moisten that which sticks to it with half Broth, half Gravy to loosen it, strew in a little pounded Pepper, squeeze in the Juice of a Lemon, strain the whole through a Sieve upon the Quails, so serve them.

A Pupton

A Pupton *of* Quails.

YOU muſt take, accordıng to the Quantity you would make, ſome Veal, Beef Sewet, and Bacon, wıth a little Paıſley and Lıver, a little of the Lean of a Ham, and a few Muſhıooms, ſeaſon thıs wıth Salt, Peppeı, Cloves, Nutmeg, ſavoury Heıbs, and a Dozen Corıander Seeds pounded, add to thıs the Crumb of a *French* Roll ſoaked in Cream, and the Yolks of four or five raw Eggs, haſh the whole togetheı and pound ıt in a Moıtaı. Garnıſh the Bottom and Sides of a large Sauce-pan wıth Slices of Bacon, and then farce, rubbıng your Hand with beaten Egg to make the Farce lıe the ſmootheı. Then havıng made a Ragoo of Quails, lay them into the Sauce-pan, coveı them wıth the ſame Farce, for fear the Sauce of the Ragoo ſhould get out, and rub the Farce oveı with beaten Egg, lay oveı ſome Bards of Bacon, then ſet it to bake with Fire under and over it. When it ıs enough done, turn ıt upſide down into the Dıſh, in which you intend to ſeıve it, make a Hole in the Top of it, of the Size of a Crown Pıece, pour in ſome Cullis or other, ſo ſerve it up for the firſt Courſe, either with Garnıſhing or without.

To dreſs Quails à la Braıſe.

FARCE the Bellies of your Quails with a good Farce made of the Breaſt of a Capon, Beef Marrow, and the Yolks of raw Eggs, ſeaſoned with Salt, Pepper and a little Nutmeg. Stew them in a Stew-pan, havıng firſt garnıſhed the Bottom of it with Slices of Bacon and Beef, both beaten ; place your Quaıls upon them, and put in a Pıece of raw Ham, mınced and ſeaſoned with Salt,

Pepper,

Pepper, and a Bunch of Savoury Herbs : Lay over them, in like Manner, some beaten Slices of Beef and Bacon : Cover your Stew-pan very close, and put Fire over and under. While this is thus stewing, make a Ragoo of Veal or Lamb Sweetbreads tossed up in Butter with Mushrooms, Truffles, and Cocks Combs ; put in the Quails a little before you serve, and bind your Ragoo with a good white Cullis, or with the Yolks of Eggs beaten up in Cream : When you would serve them brown, moisten the Ragoo with Gravy, and thicken with a Cullis of a good Ham and Veal, if you have not any Cullis of Partridges. Take the Quails out of the Ragoo, lay them in a Dish, pour your Ragoo upon them, and serve them.

A Bisque of Quails *and other Fowls.*

T R U S S your Quails, and toss them up in your Stew-pan 'till they are of a fine brown Colour. Then put them in a little Pot with good Broth, Bards of Bacon, a Bunch of Sweet Herbs, some Cloves, and other Spices, with a good Slice of Beef well beaten, another of lean Bacon, and two or three of Lemon, and boil all together over a gentle Fire. Garnish your Bisque with Veal Sweetbreads, Artichoke Bottoms, Mushrooms, Truffles, Fricando's, and Cocks Combs, with the Finish of which last make a Rim round your Bisque, and pour a little Veal Cullis upon it.

W O O D-

W O O D C O C K S.

To dress Woodcocks.

CUT your Woodcocks in four Quarters, and put them in a Sauce-pan, but remember to save the Entrails, if they be new, to thicken the Sauce: Put to your Meat, when in the Sauce-pan, some Truffles, and Sweetbreads, and toss it up all together, with some melted Bacon, and put to it some good Gravy, and season it all together with Pepper and a little Onion; pour in a little White Wine, and stew it all together, and when you think it is enough, put in the Entrails you saved, to thicken the Sauce, if you think them good enough, if not, you may make Use of any good Cullis you have by you. Before you put in your Thickening, skim off all the Fat, very clean; lay your Woodcocks in the Dish; squeeze in the Juice of an Orange, and serve them for the first Course.

To dress Woodcocks *another way.*

FIRST half roast them, then cut them in Pieces, and put them into a Sauce-pan, and put to them some Wine, according to what Quantity of Woodcocks you have, with some Truffles, Mushrooms, and Capers, and let them all be minced with a little Anchovy, and stew it all together; but be careful you do not let it boil; and when it is done, take off all the Fat, and thicken it with a good Cullis, and wring in the Juice of an Orange, and serve it up.

Larks

Larks *Pear Fashion.*

YOU muft trufs your Larks clofe, and cut off the Legs and feafon them with Pepper, Salt, Cloves, and Mace; then make a good Force-Meat with Sweetbreads, Morels, Mufhrooms, Crumbs, Egg, Parfley, Thyme, Pepper and Salt, after which, put in fome Sewet and make it up ftiff, then wrap up every Lark in Force-Meat, and make it pointed like a Pear, and ftick one of the Legs a Top, they muft be wafhed with the Yolk of an Egg and Crumbs of Bread, bake them gently, and ferve them without Sauce, or they will ferve for a Garnifh.

Larks *in Shells.*

BOIL twelve Hen, or Duck Eggs foft; take out all the Infide, making a handfome Round at the Top; then fill half the Shells with paffed Crumbs and roaft your Larks; put one in every Shell, and fill your Plate with paffed Crumbs brown, fo ferve as Eggs in Shells.

Plovers *Capucine, or* Larks.

GET four Hogs Ears, boil them tender, put a Piece of Force-Meat in the Ears, and likewife your Birds with their Heads outwards, fet them upright, the Tips of the Ears falling backwards, wafh them with Eggs and crumb them, and bake them gently; hafh four others with Sauce Robart, fo ferve them.

E G G S.

E G G S.

To make Eggs eat like Mushrooms.

GET six Eggs, and boil them hard, peel them, and cut them in thin Slices, put a quarter of a Pound of Butter into the Frying-pan, and make it hot; then put in your Eggs, and fry them quick half a quarter of an Hour, throw over them a little Salt, Pepper, and Nutmeg. For Sauce, take half a Pint of White Wine, the Juice of a Lemon, a Shalot shred small, a quarter of a Pound of Butter, and stir it all together, and lay it on Sippets, and serve it.

Eggs en Crepine.

HAving some raw Ham, Veal Sweetbreads, fat Livers, Truffles and Mushrooms, cut all into Dice, tofs them up in melted Bacon, moisten the whole with Gravy, set it a simmering for half an Hour, and then bind it with a Cullis of Veal and Ham. See that your Ragoo be well relished and set a cooling. Take ten new laid Eggs, and divide the Whites from the Yolks; whip up the Whites to a Froth, and beat up the Yolks, either in a little Cullis or Cream, strain them through a Sieve, and pour them into your Ragoo, together with the Whites, and mix the whole well together. Then take a flat bottomed Sauce-pan, lay a Veal Caul in the Bottom of it, pour in your Ragoo, fold the Caul down upon it, and bake it in an Oven When it is enough, turn it upside down into a Dish, and serve it hot.

Another

Another time, inftead of ferving it dry, you may throw
on it a Cullis of Veal and Ham, or a Rogoo of Mufhrooms

Eggs à la Tripe.

BOIL them hard, take off the Shells, and cut them in
Slices long-ways. Take a Bit of frefh Butter, put it
in a Stew-pan, let it melt over a Stove, put in your Eggs,
and tofs them up with fhred Parfley, feafoned with Salt
and Pepper : When they are enough, pour in a little Cream,
and ferve them warm in Plates or little Difhes.

If you would not ferve them with Cream, you may,
while you are toffing them up in the Sauce-pan, add a little fhred Onion, and inftead of the Cream, beat up two
Yolks of Eggs, in a little Verjuice or Vinegar and Water,
thicken your Eggs with it, and ferve them as you do the
others with Cream.

Fricafey *of* Eggs.

YOU muft take eight Eggs, boil them hard, cut
them into Quarters into a Pint of ftrong Gravy, and
half a Pint of White Wine; feafon with Cloves and a
Blade of Mace, a little whole Pepper and a little Salt;
fcald a little Spinage to make them look green, with a Pint
of large Oyfters to lay round your Difh; then put the
Eggs in the Stew-pan, with a few Mufhrooms and Oyfters,
and roll up a Piece of Butter in the Yolk of an Egg and
Flour, and fhake it up thick for Sauce, and you may make
Gravy Sauce if you pleafe. Garnifh with crifp'd Sippets,
Lemon and Parfley. A Side-Difh.

Amulet

Amulet *of* Eggs.

HAving what Quantity of Eggs you want, beat them well, feafon them with Salt and whole Pepper if you like it, then have your Fiying-pan ready with a good deal of fiefh Butter, let it be thoroughly hot, then put in your Eggs with four Spoonfuls of ftrong Giavy, then have ready cut Parfley and Cives, and thiow over them, and when it is enough turn it on the other Side, and fqueeze the Juice of a Lemon, or an Orange over it. Serve it for a Side-Difh.

Stuffed Eggs.

BOIL a Dozen Eggs hard, peel them, fplit them in two, and take the Yolks out of them, put them in a Moitai with a Bit of Butter, young Onions, fhied Parfley, Mufhrooms, and a Piece of Ciumb of Bread boiled in Milk, if you have any Flefh of Fifh put fome in it, and feafon it with Salt, Pepper, Sweet Herbs and fine Spices. Pound them all well together, and fill the Whites of your Eggs with it, and fmooth them by dipping your Knife in Egg. Then take the Difh you defign to ferve them in, put fome Faice at the Bottom of it, then put your ftuff'd Whites of Eggs in Ordei upon it; then biead them, and bake them in an Oven, to give them a Colour When they aie done, put a little Sauce of any thing you think proper, without coveiing them, and feive them hot for a fecond Courfe.

H A R E S.

H A R E S.

To roaſt a Hare.

LARD one Side of it and not the other, then ſpit it; whilſt it is roaſting, baſte it with Milk and Cream, ſerve it with thick Claret Sauce.

Another Way to roaſt a Hare.

HAVING got ſome Liver of Hare, ſome fat Bacon, grated Bread, an Anchovy, Shalot, a little Winter Savoury, and a little Nutmeg, beat theſe into a Pſte, and put them into the Belly of the Hare; baſte the Hare with ſtale Beer; put a little Bit of Bacon in the Pan, when it is half roaſted baſte it with Butter. For Sauce, take melted Butter, and a little Bit of Winter Savoury.

Another.

LARD him with Bacon, and make a Pudding of grated Bread, the Heart and Liver parboiled, and chopp'd ſmall, with Beef Sewet and Sweet Herbs, mixed with Marrow, Cream, Nutmeg, Salt, Pepper and Eggs; ſow up his Belly, and roaſt him. When it is done, for Sauce, draw up your Butter with Cream, or Gravy and Claret.

Another Way of dreſſing a Hare.

BASTE it with ſtale Beer, 'till the Blood is waſhed off, then empty the Pan; put into it ſome Cream, a Bit of Anchovy, a Bit of fat Bacon, a little Bit of Onion, and baſte it with this till it is enough: Then take a little

Butter,

Butter, fome of the Liquor out of the Pan, and mix it for Sauce. You may put the Pudding as above, in the Belly of it.

Hares *jugged.*

CUT it into Pieces, half lard them, and feafon them; then have a Jug of Earth with a large Mouth, put in your Hare with a Faggot of Herbs, and two Onions ftuck with Cloves, cover it down clofe, that nothing gets in, and boil it in Water three Hours, then turn it out and ferve away.

Hare *Civet.*

YOU muft bone it and take out all the Sinews, then cut one half in thin Slices, the other half in Pieces an Inch thick; fry them off quick Collop Fafhion, and put in fome thick Gravy and Muftard, and Elder Vinegar; ftove it tender, and thick as Cream, fo ferve away with the Head whole in the Middle.

R A B B I T S.

Rabbits *Portuguefe.*

YOU muft trufs them Chicken Fafhion, and lard them; the Head muft be cut off, and the Rabbit turned with the Back upward, and two of the Legs ftripp'd to the Claw End, and fo truffed with two Skewers, then lard them, or roaft or boil them with Spinach, Cauliflowers and Bacon, as Chickens.

N° 18   F f f   *A* Rabbit

A Rabbit *with* Onions.

YOU muſt trufs your Rabbits clofe and waſh them very well, then boil them off white ; boil your Onions by themſelves, changing the Water two or three Times; then let them be thoroughly ſtrained, and chop them and butter them very well; put in a Gill of Cream, ferve your Rabbits, and cover them over with Onions.

Young Rabbits a la Saingara.

LARD your Rabbits, and ſpit them, which being done, fry a little Bacon, put in fome Flour, mixed together, Slices of Ham, beaten flat, adding a Bunch of Sweet Herbs, and good Gravy, not falt. Let it ſtew, and when ready, thicken your Sauce with Culas, putting in it a little Vinegar. Your Rabbits being roaſted, cut them in four, put over them your aforefaid Ragoo of Ham, take off the Fat, and ferve it up hot for a firſt Courfe.

Rabbits *Surprize.*

ROAST off two or three half grown Rabbits, according to the Bignefs of your Diſh; cut off th Heads clofe by the Shoulders, and the firſt Joints of the Hind Legs, then take out all the lean Meat from the Back Bones, and cut it and tofs it up in fix or feven Spoonfuls of Milk or Cream, with the Bignefs of half an Egg of Butter, grated Nutmeg, Pepper and Salt; thicken it with a little Duſt of Flour, to the Thicknefs of a good Cream, then boil it and fet it to cool, then take the like Quantity of Forced-Meat, and tofs it up likewife, and place it all round each of the Rabbits, leaving a long Trough in the

Back

Back open, that you think will hold the Meat you cut out with the Sauce; then cover it with the fame Forced-Meat, fmoothed, as well as you can, with your Hand and a raw Egg, fquare at both Ends, throw on them a little grated Bread; then butter a Mazarine, or Patty-pan, and take them from your Dreffer, where you formed them, and place them on it. Bake them three Quarters of an Hour, before you ferve them, 'till they are of a brown Colour: Let your Sauce be Butter, Gravy and Lemon, and your Garnifhing, fliced Orange and fried Parfley; fo ferve it for the firft Courfe.

To boil Rabbits.

HAving trufs'd them for boiling, lard them with Bacon, then boil them quick and white. For the Sauce, take the boiled Liver, fhred it with fat Bacon, and tofs thefe up together in ftrong Broth, with White Wine and Vinegar, Mace, Salt, Nutmeg and Parfley minced, Barberries and drawn Butter; lay your Rabbits in a Difh, and pour it all over them, and garnifh with fliced Lemon and Barberries.

An Efclope *of* Rabbits.

CUT your Rabbits in Quarters, and ftew them *à la Braife*, as you do feveral other Things. Then make a Ragoo of Veal Sweetbreads, Fowls Livers, Cocks Combs, Morels, Mufhrooms, and Truffles: Tofs them up all together, in a Sauce-pan, with melted Bacon, moiften it with Gravy and let it fimmer half an Hour, then take the Fat clean off and bind it with a Cullis of Veal and Ham: Take up your ftewed Rabbits, and put them into

F f f 2 your

your Ragoo, where let them lie 'till they are cold : Raife a Pie of thin Pafte, and put your cold Ragoo and Rabbits in it, cover it with a Lid of the fame Pafte, and turn down the Edges that the Top may be as plain as the Bottom ; fo fet it into the Oven : When it is baked turn it upfide down into the Difh, make a Hole in it to fee if it be dry, and if it be, pour in fome good Cullis, and ferve it hot for the firft Courfe.

We make Efclopes of all Sorts of Fowls tame and wild, firft ftewed *à la Braife* with Ragoos, in the fame Manner as this of Rabbits.

S A U C E S for P O U L T R Y.

Sauce *for a* Hare.

GET half a Pint of Claret, and a little Oyfter Liquor, and put to it fome good Gravy, and a large Onion ftuck with Cloves, and fome whole Cinnamon and Nutmeg cut in Slices ; then let it boil 'till the Onion is boiled tender ; then take out the Onion and whole Spice, and put to it three Anchovies, and a Piece of Butter, fhake it well together and fend it to the Table.

To make Sauce for Green Geefe *or young* Ducks.

GET almoft half a Pint of the Juice of Sorrel, and a little White Wine, a little grated Nutmeg, and a little grated Bread, let it boil a Quarter of an Hour, and put to it as much Sugar as will fweeten it ; if you pleafe you may put in a few fcalded Goofeberries or Grapes, and a Piece of Butter, fhake it up thick, and put it to the Geefe, being roafted. This Sauce is proper for Chickens.

Sauce

Sauce *for* Wild Ducks.

TAKE a little Handful of Sage, one large Onion shred small, season it with a little Salt, and roll them up with Butter into Balls, then put them in the Ducks, and roast them, then take half a Pint of Claret, in it dissolve two Anchovies, then take half as much Butter as Wine, then thicken them with the Yolks of two Eggs, then put your Ducks in your Dish, and pour your Sauce through them, and pull out your Balls, so serve them.

A good Sauce *for* Teal, Mallards, Ducks, *&c.*

WE take a Quantity of Veal Gravy, according to the Bigness of your Dish of Wild Fowl, seasoned with Pepper and Salt, squeeze in the Juice of two Oranges and a little Claret: This will serve all Sorts of Wild Fowl.

To make a Sauce *for* Turkies *or* Capons

GET half a Pint of White Wine, and a little Gravy, and Oyster Liquor, and a little grated Nutmeg, and put to it three or four large Onions boiled tender and mashed small, with a little small Pepper, and two or three Anchovies, minced small, boil it a Quarter of an Hour, with a little grated White Bread, and put to it a Piece of Butter, and then put in the Fowls, being roasted.

Sauces *for roast* Pigeons *or* Doves

1. GRAVY and Juice of Orange.
   2. Boiled Parsley minced and put amongst some Butter and Vinegar beaten up thick.

3 Gravy.

3. Gravy, Claret, and an Onion ftewed together with a little Salt.

4. Vine Leaves roafted with the Pigeons, minced and put in Claret and Salt, boiled together, fome Butter and Gravy.

5. Sweet Butter and Juice of Orange, beat together and made thick.

6. Minced Onions boiled in Claret almoft dry, then put to it Nutmeg, Sugar, Gravy of the Fowl, and a little Pepper.

7. Or Gravy of the Pigeons only.

Sauces *for all Manner of roaft* Land Fowl, *as,* Turky, Buftard, Peacock, Pheafant, Partridge, *&c.*

1. SLICED Onions being boiled, ftew them in fome Water, Salt, Pepper, fome grated Bread, and the Gravy of the Fowl.

2. Take Slices of White Bread, and boil them in fair Water with two whole Onions, fome Gravy, half a grated Nutmeg, and a little Salt; ftrain them together through a Strainer, and boil it up as thick as Water-Gruel, then add to it the Yolks of two Eggs, diffolved with the Juice of two Oranges.

3. Take thin Slices of Manchet, Gravy of the Fowl, fome Sweet Butter, grated Nutmeg, Pepper, and Salt, ftew all together, and being ftewed, put in a Lemon fliced with the Peel.

4. Onions fliced and boiled in fair Water, and a little Salt, a few Bread Crumbs, beaten Pepper, Nutmeg, three Spoonfuls of White Wine, and fome Lemon Peel finely minced and boiled all together; being almoft boiled, put

in

in the Juice of an Orange, beaten Butter, and the Gravy of the Fowl.

5 Stamp Small Nuts to a Paste, with Bread, Pepper, Saffron, Cloves, Juice of an Orange, and strong Broth, strain and boil them together very thick.

6. Quince, Prunes, Currants, and Raisins boiled, muskified Bisket stamped and strained with White Wine, Rose Vinegar, Nutmeg, Cinnamon, Cloves, Juice of Oranges and Sugar; boil it not too thick.

7. Take a Manchet, pare off the Crust and slice it, then boil it in fair Water, and being boiled somewhat thick, put in some White Wine, Wine Vinegar, Rose or Elder Vinegar, Sugar and Butter.

8. Almond Paste, and Crumbs of Manchet, stamp them together with some Sugar, Ginger and Salt, strain them with Grape, Verjuice, and Juice of Oranges, boil it pretty thick.

The Manner of truſſing a Rabbit *for Boiling.*

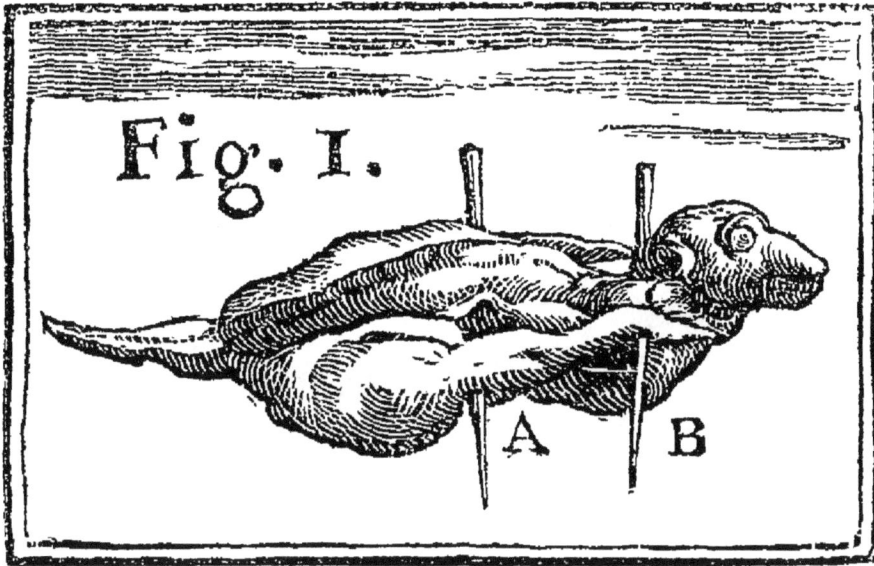

CUT the two Haunches of the Rabbit cloſe to the Back Bone, two Inches, and turn up the Haunches, by the Side of the Rabbit, skewer the Haunches through the Middle Part of the Back as at A, then put a Skewer through the utmoſt Joints of the Legs, the Shoulder Blades and Neck, as at B, truſſing the Shoulders high and bending the Neck backwards that the Skewer may paſs through the whole.

The Manner of trussing a Rabbit *for Roasting.*

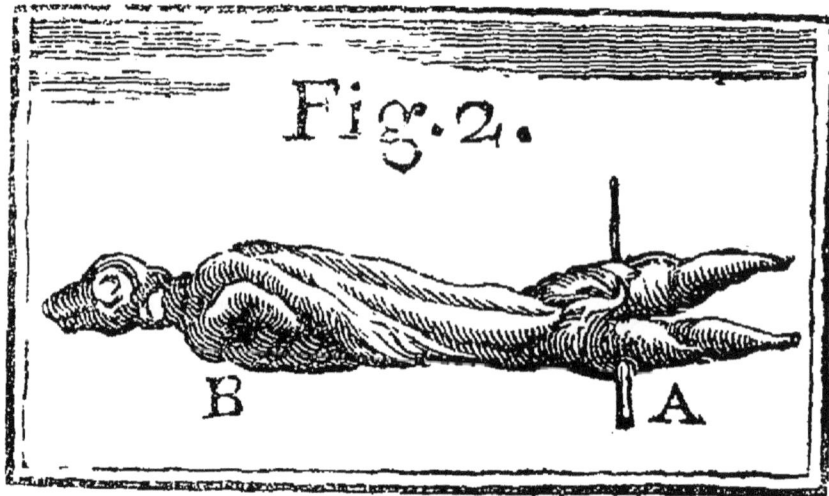

YOU cafe the Rabbit all, excepting the lower Joints of the fore Legs, and thofe you chop off, then pafs a Skewer through the Middle of the Haunches after you have laid them flat, as at A and the fore Legs which are called the Wings muft be turned as at B fo that the fmaller Joint may be pufh'd into the Body, through the Ribs. This, as a fingle Rabbit, has the Spit pafs'd through the Body and Head, but the Skewer takes hold of the Spit to preferve the Haunches. But to trufs a Couple of Rabbits, there are feven Skewers, and then the Spit paffes only between the Skewers, without touching the Rabbits.

G g g

Of truſſing a Pigeon.

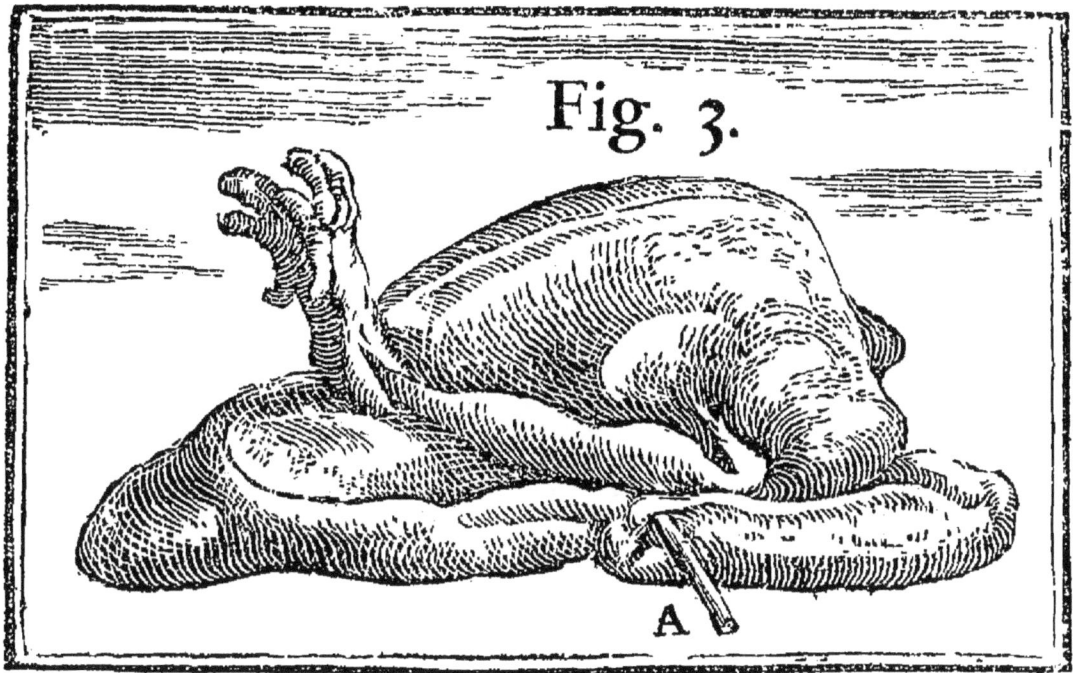

Fig. 3.

A

DRAW it, but leave in the Liver, for that has no
Gall; then puſh up the Breaſt from the Vent, and
holding up the Legs, put a Skewer juſt between the Bent
of the Thigh and the Brown of the Leg, firſt having turned the Pinions under the Back; and ſee the lower Joint of
the biggeſt Pinions, are ſo paſs'd with the Skewer, that
the Legs are between them and the Body, as at A.

A Gooſe

A Goose *to truss.*

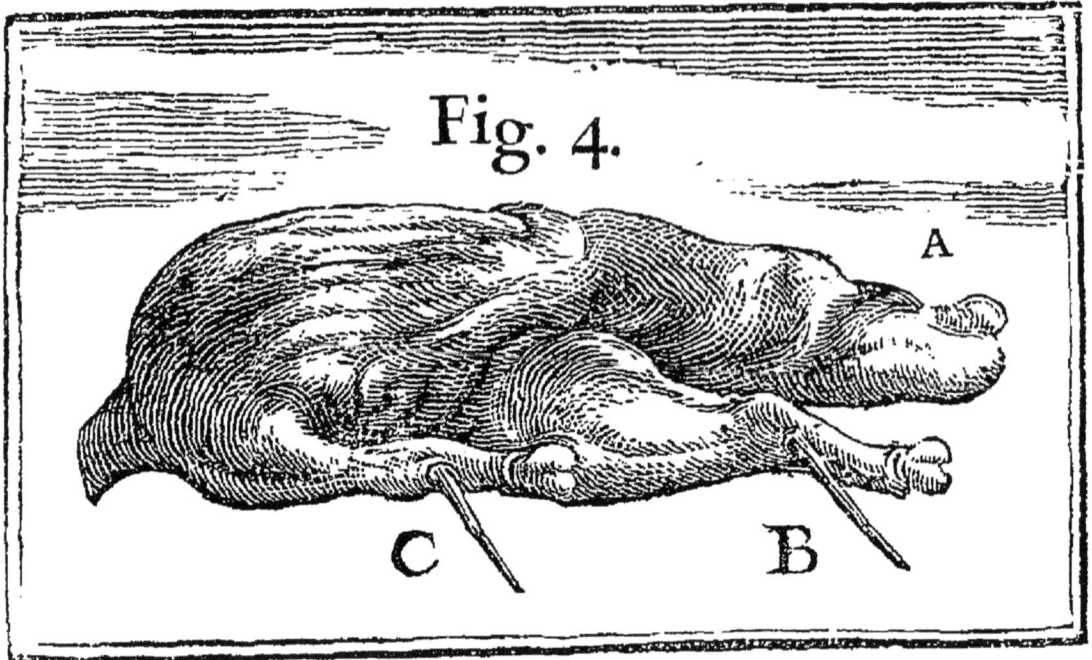

Fig. 4.

A Goose has no more than the thick Joints of the Legs
and Wings left to the Body, the Feet and the Pinions being cut off, to accompany the other Gibblets,
which consist of the Head and Neck, with the Liver and
Gizzard. Then at the Bottom of the Apron of the Goose
A, cut an Hole, and draw the Rump through it; then pass
a Skewer through the small Part of the Leg, through the
Body, near the Back, as at B, and another Skewer through
the thinnest Part of the Wings, and through the Body,
near the Back, as at C, and it will be right.

The

The truffing of an Eafterling.

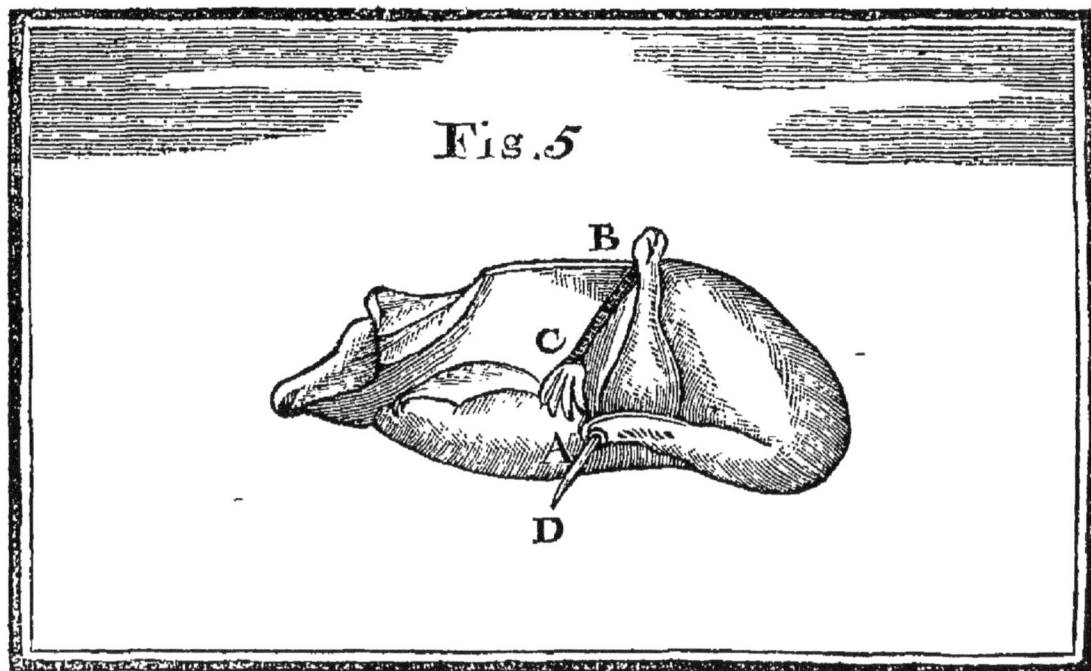

Fig. 5

A Duck, an Eafterling, a Teal, and a Widgeon, are all truffed in the fame Manner. Draw it, and lay afide the Liver and Gizzard, and take out the Neck, leaveing the Skin of the Neck full enough to fpread over the Place where the Neck was cut off. Then cut off the Pinions at A, and raife up the whole Legs, 'till they are upright in the Middle of the Fowl B, and prefs them between the Stump of the Wings and the Body of the Fowl; twift the Feet towards the Body, and bring them forwards, with the Bottom of the Feet towards the Body of the Fowl, as at C. Then take a Skewer, and pafs it through the Fowl, between the lower Joint, next the Foot and the

Thigh

Thigh, taking hold, at the fame Time, of the Ends of the Stumps of the Wings A: Then will the Legs, as we have placed them, ftand upright. D is the Point of the Skewer.

The Manner of truffing a Chicken *like a* Turkey Poult, *or of truffing a* Turkey Poult.

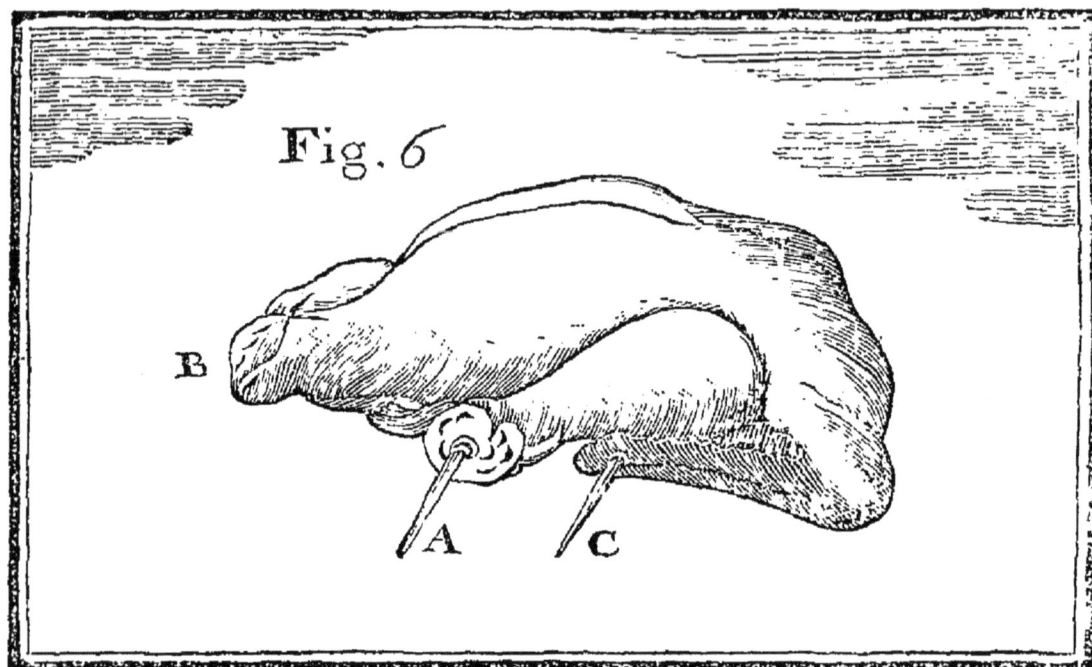

Fig. 6

HAving a Chicken, cut a long Slit down the Neck, on the Fore Part; then take out the Crop and the Merry-Thought, as it is called, then twift the Neck and bring it down under the Back, 'till the Head is placed on the Side of the the left Leg; bind the Legs in, with their Claws on, and turn them upon the Back. Then between the bending of the Leg and the Thigh, on the right Side, pafs a Skewer through the Body of the Fowl; and when it

is through, run the Point through the Head, by the same
Place of the Leg, as you did before, as at A : You muſt
likewiſe pull the Rump B through the Apron of the Fowl.
Note, The Neck is twiſted like a Cord, and the bony Part
of it muſt be quite taken out, and the Under-Jaw of the Fowl
taken away , neither ſhould the Liver and Gizzard be ſerved
with it, though the Pinions are left on.   Then turn the
Pinions behind the Back, and paſs a Skewer through the
extreme Joint, between the Pinion and the lower Joint of
the Wing, through the Body near the Back, as at C, and
it will be fit to roaſt in the faſhionable Manner.

  N. B. Always mind to beat down the Breaſt Bone, and
pick the Head and Neck clean from the Feathers before you
begin to truſs your Fowl.

  A Turkey Poult has no Merry-Thought, as it is called ;
and therefore, to imitate a Turkey the better, we take it out
of a Chicken through the Neck.

T H E

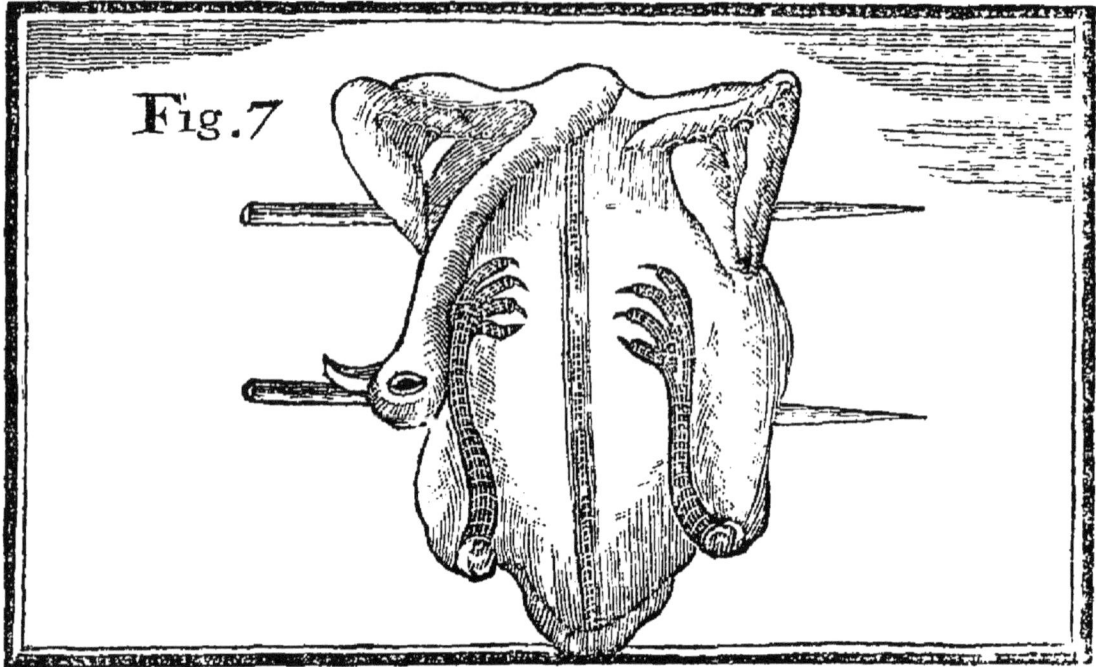

Fig. 7

T H E above F I G U R E fhews the Manner how the Legs and Pinions will appear when they are turned to the Back; as alfo, the Pofition of the Head and Neck of the Chicken or Turkey Poult.

To truſs *a* Pheaſant *or* Partridge.

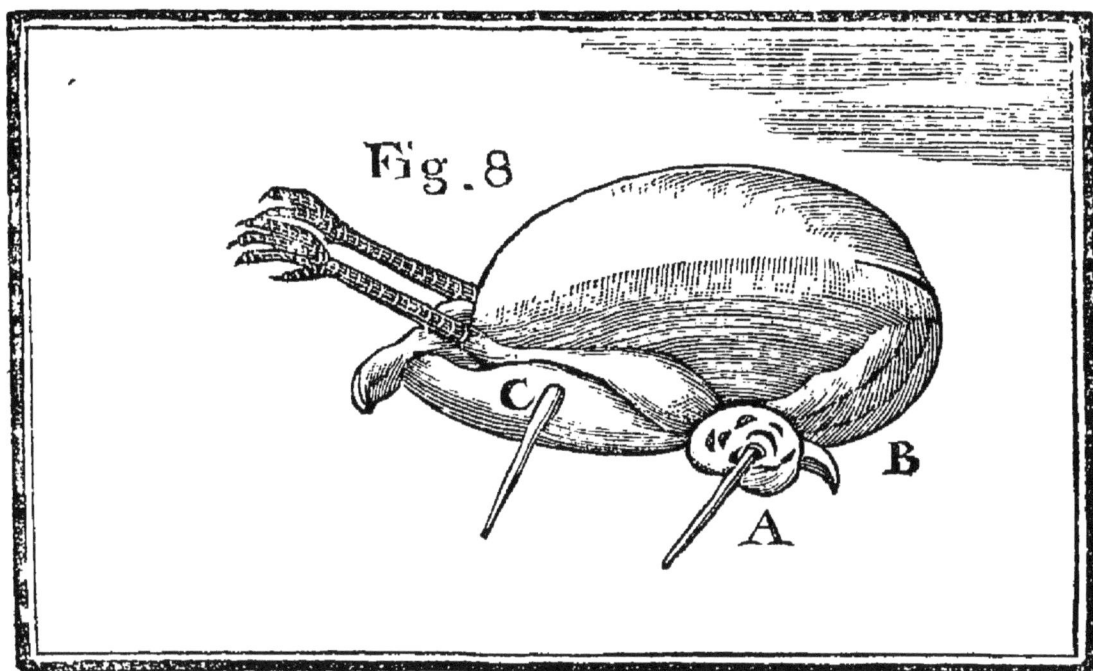

BOTH the Pheaſant and the Partridge are truſſed the
ſame Way, only the Neck of the Partidge s cut off,
and the Head of the Pheaſant is left on: The Plate above
ſhews the Pheaſant truſſed   When it is drawn, cut off the
Pinnions, leaving only the Stump Bone next the Breaſt,
and paſs a Skewer through its Point, and through the Body near the Back, and then give the Neck a Turn; and
paſſing it by the Back, bring the Head on the Outſide of
the other Wing Bone, as at A, and run the Skewer thro'
both, with the Head ſtanding towards the Neck, or the
Rump, which you pleaſe: B is where the Neck runs.
Then take the Legs, with their Claws on, and preſs them

by the Joints together, fo as to prefs the lower Part of the
Breaft, then prefs them down between the Sidefmen, and
pafs a Skewer through all, as at C. Remember a Partridge muſt have its Neck cut off, or elſe in every thing is
truſſed like a Pheaſant.

The Manner of truſſing an Hare in the moſt faſhionable
Way.

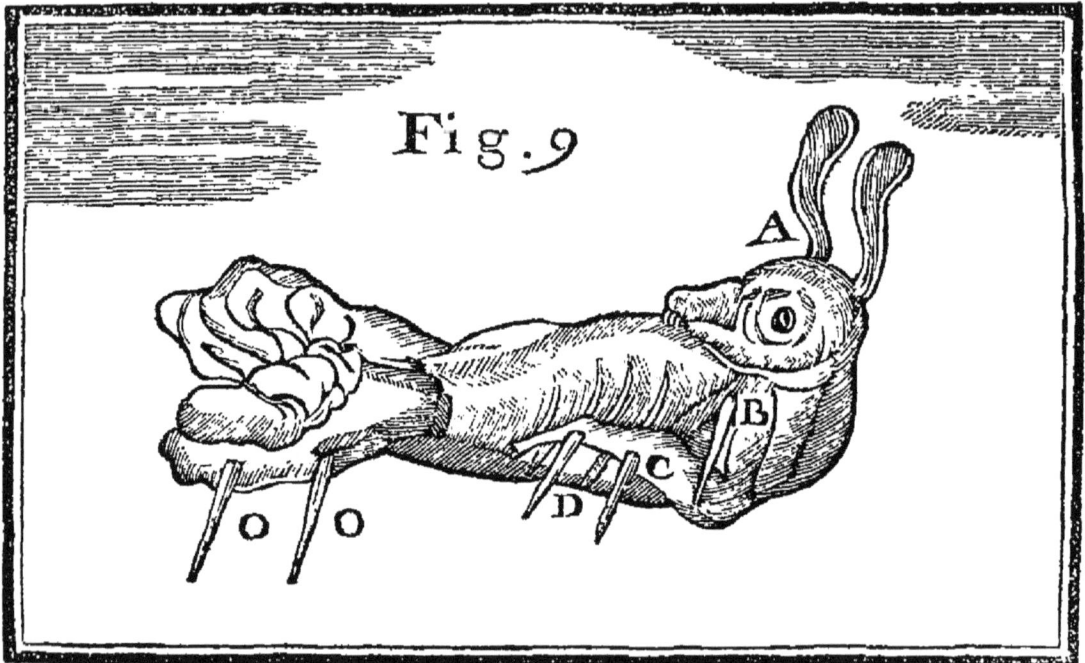

C A S E an Hare, and in caſing it, juſt when you come
to the Ears, paſs a Skewer juſt between the Skin and
the Head, and by Degrees raiſe it up 'till the Skin leaves
both the Ears ſtripp'd, and then take off the reſt as uſual.
Then give the Head a Tiwſt over the Back, that it may
ſtand, as at A, putting two Skewers in the Ears, partly
H h h   to

to make them ſtand upright, and to ſecure the Head in a right Diſpoſition, then puſh the Joint of the Shoulder Blade, up as high as may be, towards the Back, and paſs a Skewer between the Joints, as at B, through the Bottom Jaw of the Hare, which will keep it ſteady, then paſs an-other Skewer through the lower Branch of the Leg at C, through the Ribs, paſſing cloſe by the Blade Bone, to keep that up tight, and another through the Point of the ſame Branch, as at D, which finiſhes the upper Part. Then bend in both Legs between the Haunches, ſo that their Points meet under the Scut, and skewer them faſt, with two Skewers, as at O O.

A Fowl

A Fowl *truſſed for boiling.*

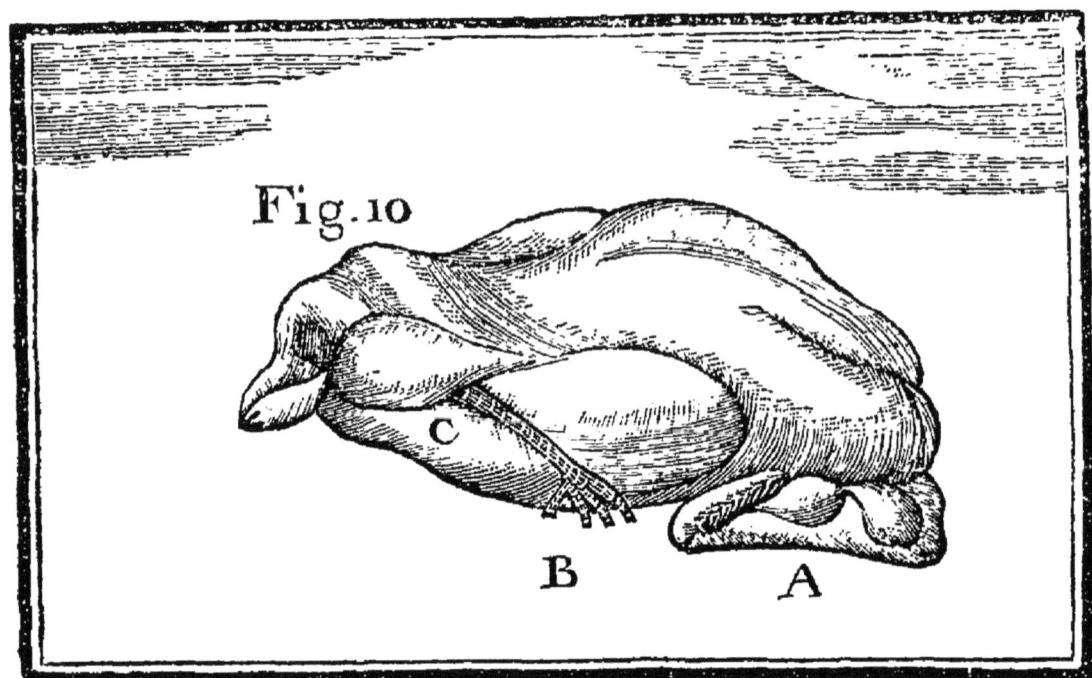

Fig.10

YOU muſt, when it is drawn, twiſt the Wings 'till you bring the Pinion under the Back; and you may, if you will, encloſe the Liver and Gizzard, one in each Wing, as at A, but they are commonly left out. Then beat down the Breaſt Bone, that it does not riſe above the fleſhy Part; then cut off the Claws of the Feet, and twiſt the Legs, and bring them on the Outſide of the Thigh, towards the Wing, as at B, and cut an Hole on each Side the Apron, juſt above the Sideſman, and put the Joints of the Legs into the Body of the Fowl, as at C: So this is truſſed without a Skewer.

H h h 2 CHAP.

CHAP. XX.

Of *R A G O O S.*

To *ragoo a* Breast *of* Veal.

HALF roast it, then put it into the Stew-pan, over a a Stove with Gravy, 'till it is enough, tofs it up with Balls, Mufhrooms, Truffles, Morels, Oyfters, &c. firft ftuffing it all up the Brifcuit with Forced-Meat.

Another *Way to ragoo a* Breaft *of* Veal.

BONE it, and cut out a handfome fquare Piece, then cut the other Parts into fmall Pieces, brown it in Butter; then ftew and tofs them up in a Pint of Gravy, ftrong Broth, a little Claret and White Wine, an Onion, and two or three Anchovies, Cocks Combs, Lamb's Stones, and Sweetbreads, blanched and fliced with Balls, Oyfters, Truffles, Morels, and Mufhrooms, a little Pepper, Salt, Mace, Nutmeg, and Lemon Juice; thicken it with Butter; put the Ragoo in the Difh, and lay on the fquare Piece, diced Lemon, Sweetbreads, Sippets, and Bacon fried in the Batter of Eggs, garnifh with fliced Orange, and ferve it.

Another *Way.*

YOU muft take a Breaft of Veal, cut off all the Neck and Flap, then ftuff it with Forced-Meat, and lay it to roaft half an Hour, then take fome ftrong Gravy, and
a Stew-

a Stew-pan big enough for the Veal, and burn fome Butter in it 'till it is brown, then fhake in Flour to thicken
your Butter, and put in the Gravy, and let it boil, put in
fome Anchovies, ftuff a large Onion with Cloves, and put
it in; feafon it to your Tafte with Pepper, Salt, and Nutmeg, and put in your Veal, let it ftew 'till enough; make
your Forced-Meat of Veal, Bacon, Beef Sewet, feafoned
with Pepper, Salt Anchovy, Thyme and Parfley; put in
two or three Eggs, and thicken it with White Bread
Crumbs: Make your Forced-Meat before you roaft your
Veal, and ftuff all the Way up the Brifcuit. Fry Balls for
your Sauce, and take out the Onion and add Lemon.

A Ragoo *of* Lamb's Stones *and* Sweetbreads.

WASH your Lamb's Stones and Sweetbreads well,
and blanch them in boiling Water, then put them
in cold Water, when you take them out, lay them on a
Linnen-Cloth, dry them well, put them in a Sauce-pan
with a little melted Bacon, and a Bunch of Herbs, feafon
them with Salt and Pepper; add to them fome fmall
Mufhrooms, and fliced Truffles. Having toffed up all thefe
over a Stove, moiften it with Gravy, and make it fimmer
over a gentle Fire: When they are done enough, take off
all the Fat, and bind the Ragoo with a Cullis of Veal
and Ham.

A mix'd Ragoo *of* Cocks Combs, Cocks Kidneys, *and* fat
Livers.

PUT in a Stew-pan a Bit of Butter, a Bunch of Sweet
Herbs, fome Mufhrooms and Truffles; put it, for a
Minute, over the Fire, flour it a little, moiften it with

half

half a Spoonful of Broth, feafon it with Salt and Pepper; let it boil a little, then put fome Cocks Combs, Cocks Kidnies, fat Livers and Sweetbreads; let your Ragoo be palatable, thicken it with Eggs; ferve it up hot for a dainty Diſh.

A Ragoo *of* Melts *of* Fiſh en graſs.

BLANCH the Melts of your Fiſh in boiling Water, then take them out, and throw them into cold: Toſs up in a Sauce-pan, with a little melted Bacon, fome fmall Muſhrooms, fome Truffles cut in Slices, and a Bunch of Herbs; feafon the whole with Pepper and Salt, moiſten it with Veal Gravy, and fet it to fimmer as uſual. When they are done enough, take the Fat clean off, bind your Ragoo with a Cullis of Veal and Ham; then put in your Melts and Carps, and make them fimmer over a gentle Fire. See that it be well taſted.

A Ragoo *of* Melts *and* Fiſh en Maigre.

WHEN they are blanched and thrown into cold Water, as in the Receipt above, put fome Butter into a Sauce-pan with a very little Flour and brown it; put into your Brown fome fmall Muſhrooms and fliced Truffles, and toſs them up over a Stove; then moiſten them with good Fiſh Broth, feafoned with Pepper, Salt, a Faggot of Herbs, and let them fimmer over a gentle Fire. This done, take off the Fat, and put in the Melts to fimmer as above; when they are enough, bind your Ragoo with a Crawfiſh, or other maigre Cullis.

A Ragoo

A Ragoo *of* Muscles.

WASH your Muscles, then scrape them, blanch them in fresh Butter, season them with Salt, Pepper, Parsley, Chibbol, Raspings of Bread, and a Dash of Vinegar. When your Muscles are done enough, serve them up hot.

A Ragoo *of* Muscles *with a white Sauce.*

GET your Muscles out of their Shells, blanch them in fresh Butter, with Parsley and Sweet Herbs cut small; then season them with Salt, Pepper, and Nutmeg; and when their Liquor is boiled short, thicken it with Eggs and Lemon Juice, and serve up this Ragoo with Scate, or for a dainty Dish.

A Ragoo of Muscles with a brown Sauce is made after the same Manner, your Muscles being blanched and moistened with Gravy.

A Ragoo *with* Palates *of* Beef.

BOIL your Beef Palates, then take the Skin off, and clean them well; cut them in fine Slices, and put them into a Stew-pan with melted Bacon, a Bunch of Sweet Herbs, and some Mushrooms, season them with Salt and Pepper, moisten them with Gravy, and let them stew over a slow Fire, being done enough, thicken this Ragoo with a Cullis of Veal and Ham, or a Cullis of Partridges, which should be palatable and high relished.

A Ragoo

A Ragoo *with* Beef Palates *the* Italian Way.

LET your Palates be ordered and cleaned as before; then cut them in small Slices like Dice, and put them in the Stew-pan with half a Glass of Oil, as much of White Wine, a Spoonful of Cullis, and a Bunch of Sweet Herbs. Let it stew flowly, and when ready tafte it, let it be relifhing, take off the Fat, and difh and ferve up for a fecond Courfe.

A Ragoo *of* Oyfters.

OPEN your Oyfters, put them in a Stew-pan with their Liquor, blanch them, then take them out one after another, cleanfe them well and put them in a Difh. Blanch fome Mufhrooms and Truffles in Butter, moiften them with Gravy, thicken the Sauce with a Cullis of Veal and Ham; then put in your Oyfters, warm them without boiling, let your Ragoo be palatable, and ferve it up hot.

Another Ragoo *of* Oyfters.

OPEN your Oyfters and blanch them in their own Liquor, without boiling them; then take them out, cleanfe them, and put them in a Difh. Blanch fome Mufhrooms, with frefh Butter, moiften them with Cullis, and warm your Oyfters in it. The Ragoo being relifhing difh it up.

Another

Another Ragoo *of* Oysters.

YOUR Oysters being opened, drain them over a Sieve, put a Dish under to receive their Liquor. Melt some fresh Butter in a Stew-pan, put in it a Dust of Flour, keep it stirring 'till it is brown; moisten it with a little Gravy, put in some small Crusts of Bread; toss it up, season it with Pepper, Parsley and Cives. Your Ragoo being high relished, serve it up for a dainty Dish.

To ragoo a Piece of Beef.

GET the hinder Part of a Buttock of Beef, and lard it with thick Lardoons: Afterwards having put it into a Pot, with two Pounds of good Lard, some broad thin Slices of Bacon, and the necessary Seasoning, let it soak gently between two Fires, about twelve Hours. At last, you may put in a little Brandy, and garnish with Pickles.

A Loin *of* Veal *ragoo'd.*

FIRST lard your Loin of Veal, season it with Salt, Pepper, and Nutmeg, and when it is almost roasted enough, put it into a Stew-pan, covered, with the Dripping, some Broth, a Glass of White Wine, a Faggot of fine Herbs, fried Flour, and a Piece of green Lemon: Let it be served up with short Sauce, after having taking off the Fat; and garnish with larded Veal Sweetbreads, Cutlets, or what else you think fit.

A Ragoo *of* Cocks Combs.

PICK and clean them well, put them into a Sauce-pan with a little melted Bacon, some Mushrooms and Truffles cut in Slices, and a Bunch of Herbs: Season all

N° 19. I i i this

this with Salt and Pepper, and having toffed it up over a Stove moiften it with good Gravy, and fet it to fimmer over a flack Fire; when it is enough, take off all the Fat, thicken it with a Cullis of Veal and Ham; fo ferve it in Plates or little Difhes.

This Ragoo ferves likewife to garnifh all Difhes of the firft Courfe that are ftewed *à la Braife*

A Ragoo *with the Heads of* Afparagus.

CUT the Heads of fome Afparagus and whiten them. When they are blanched enough, put them in a Stew-pan with fome Cullis and a little Effence of Ham; and let the whole ftew over a flow Fire. When it is ftewed enough, throw therein a Bit of Butter no bigger than a Nut, dipped in fome fine Flour, and ftir your Ragoo now and then. Take Care that it be relifhing, pour in a little Vinegar, and ferve it hot. You may make ufe of this Ragoo for all Sorts of Fowls or other Meat.

A White Ragoo *of* Afparagus.

CUT and blanch fome Afparagus as before, put them in a Stew-pan, with a Bit of Butter, fry them a little, powder them with a Spoonful of fine Flour, moiften them with Broth, feafon them with Salt and Pepper, and let them be ftewed Make a Thickening with feveral Yolks of Eggs, diluted with fome Broth, and put therein a little Nutmeg. Your Afparagus being relifhing, thicken them with the faid Yolks, and make ufe of this Ragoo to put under fome larded Collops, or other Sorts of Meat.

A Ragoo

A Ragoo *of* Endive.

TAKE some of the best white Endive, pick them, and blanch them in boiling Water. After which, put them in cold Water, then squeeze them well, and put them on a Table to be minced a little. This being done, put your Endive in a Stew-pan, moisten them with a clear Cullis of Veal and Ham; and let the whole be stewed on a slow Fire. When this is stewed and grown relishing, make use of it for every Sort of Dish with Endive; but if this Ragoo is not thought thick enough, put in a little Essence of Ham, or a little Cullis therein, before you serve it.

Another Ragoo *of* Endive.

THE Endive must be prepared as that before, with the following Difference only, that is to say, When it is minced you must fry it, with a good Bit of Butter, then moisten it with Broth instead of Cullis, and when it is relishing, thicken it with a Thickening of Yolks of Eggs and Cream. You may make use of this Endive with all Sorts of larded Collops, Veal Cutlets, and Fillets of any Meat.

I i i 2　　　　　CHAP.

CHAP. XXI.

OF *F R I C A S E Y S.*

Fricasey *of* Chickens.

AFTER you have drawn and washed your Chickens, half boil them, then take them up and cut them in Pieces, and put them in a Frying-pan, and fry them in Butter, then take them out of the Pan and clean it, and put in some strong Broth, some White Wine, some grated Nutmeg, a little Pepper and Salt, and a Bunch of Sweet Herbs, and a Shalot or two, let these, with two or three Anchovies, stew on a slow Fire and boil up; then beat it up with Butter and Eggs, 'till it is thick; and put your Chickens in, and toss them well together, lay Sippets in the Dish, and serve it up with sliced Lemon and fried Parsley.

Another Fricasey *of* Chickens *or* Rabbits.

GET Rabbits or Chickens; but if Chickens, you must skin them, cut them into small Pieces, and beat them flat, and lard them with Bacon; season it with Salt, Pepper, and Mace; drudge it with Flour, and fry it in sweet Butter, to a good Colour, then get the Quantity of good Gravy as your Fricasey requires, with Oysters and Mushrooms, two or three Anchovies, and some Shalot, a Bunch of Sweet Herbs, and if you like it, a Glass of Claret, season it high, and before you put in your Meat, simmer it well together, 'till the Goodness of the Herbs is out, then take out the Herbs, and Anchovy Bones, and cut a Lemon in Dice, and put in with your Chickens or Rabbits, and let it stew gently 'till it be tender, but be sure to keep it stirring all the while it is over the Fire, and make it as thick as Cream, and serve it up with Force-Meat Balls, crisp'd Bacon, and fried Oysters, and garnish it as you like.

A White Fricasey.

HALF roast or parboil your Chickens, then skin them, and cut them in Pieces, and stew them in strong Broth, with some Pepper, and a Blade of Mace, with a little Salt, two Anchovies and a small Onion, let it stew 'till it is tender, then take out your Onion, and put in a Quarter of a Pint of Cream, a Piece of Butter, work'd up in Flour, and the Yolks of two Eggs well beaten, and stir it over the Fire 'till it is as thick as Cream, and wring in the Juice of a Lemon, and be careful it don't curdle, serve it up on Sippets, and put over it some Mushrooms and Oysters.

To make a Fricasey *of* Ox Palates.

HAving Ox Palates, after they are boiled very tender, blanch and pare them clean, season them with fine beaten Cloves, Nutmeg, Pepper, Salt, and grated Bread: Then fry your Palates in Butter 'till they are brown on both Sides, take them out, and put them into a Dish, adding thereto some Mutton Gravy, in which two or three Anchovies are dissolved, grate in your Sauce a little Nutmeg, squeeze in the Juice of a Lemon, and send them to the Table.

Another Fricasey *of* Chickens.

HAving three Chickens, about six Months old, flea them, and cut them in Pieces, put them into your Stew-pan, with as much Gravy and Water, as just to cover them, put in two Anchovies, well washed, some whole Pepper, Salt, and a Blade of Mace, a small Onion, and a few Cloves, set them to stew gently over a slow clear Fire, and when they are near enough, take them from the Liquor, and fry them in Vinegar, but a very little, strain the Liquor, and take as much of it as you will want for Sauce, put to it a little Parsley, Thyme and Sorrel boiled green, and shred fine; half a Pint of sweet Cream, two Yolks of Eggs well beaten, some grated Nutmeg; shake them all over the Fire, 'till it is thick, add to it half a Pound of Butter, and shake it 'till it is melted, and then serve it up.

A Fricasey *made for an* Instalment Dinner *at* Windsor.

HAving six squab Pigeons, and six small Chickens, scald them, and truss them and set them by, and then have some Lamb's Stones, blanched, parboiled, and sliced, and fry some Sweetbreads floured; have also some Asparagus Tops, the Yolks of two Eggs; some *Pistacho* Nut Shells, the Marrow of six Marrow Bones; let half the Marrow be fried in white Butter; let it be kept warm 'till Dinner Time; then take your Stew-pan and fry the Fowls and Pigeons with sweet Butter, when fried, pour out the Butter, and put to them some Gravy, large fried Oysters, and a little Salt, and put in the hard Yolks of Eggs, the rest of the Sweetbreads not fried, the *Pistacho* Nuts,

Nuts, Afparagus and Marrow; then ftew them well, and put in a little grated Nutmeg, a little Pepper, and a little Shalot, and three or four Spoonfuls of White Wine, then have the Yolks of ten Eggs diffolved in a Difh, with fome White Wine Vinegar, and a little beaten Mace, and put it to the Fricafey, and cut fome White Bread in Sippets, and lay at the Bottom of the Difh, fet on Charcoal, with fome Gravy; then give the Fricafey two or three Toffes up, and pour it on the Sippets. Garnifh your Difh with fried Sweetbreads, Marrow, Oyfters, and fliced Almonds, and ferve it up.

Fricafey *of* Pigeons.

YOU muft take eight Pigeons new killed, cut them into fmall Pieces, and put them into a Frying-pan with a Pint of Claret, and a Pint of Water, feafon your Pigeons with Salt, and Pepper, then take a little Sweet Marjoram, Thyme, a few Cives, or an Onion; fhred the Herbs very fmall, and put them into the Frying-pan with the Pigeons, with a good Piece of Butter, fo let them boil gently, 'till there be no more Liquor left than will ferve for the Sauce; then beat four Yolks of Eggs, with a Spoonful and half of Vinegar, and half a Nutmeg grated, when it is enough, put the Meat on the one Side of the Pan, and the Liquor on the other. Then put the Eggs into the Liquor on the Fire, and ftir it 'till it is the Thicknefs of Cream, then put the Meat into the Difh, and pour over the Sauce, lay crifp'd Bacon and Oyfters over it, and garnifh with rafp'd Lemon; fo ferve it.

Fricafey

Fricafey *of* Muſhrooms.

GET the largeſt and biggeſt Muſhrooms you can
get, and ſome ſmall ones amongſt them; cut the
largeſt into four Pieces, peel them and throw them into
Salt and Water, let them lie in the Water and Salt half an
Hour, then take them out and put them into a Bell-Metal
or ſilver Skillet, and ſtew them in their own Liquor, with
a little Cream to make them look white, and cut hard;
leſs than half an Hour will ſtew them; then ſtrain them
out into a Sieve, and take a Quarter of a Pint of that Liquor they were ſtewed in, with as much White Wine and
ſtrong Gravy, boil all theſe together with a little whole
white Pepper, Mace and Nutmeg, two Anchovies, one
Sprig of Thyme, a Shalot or two; ſeaſon it very high to
your Taſte, with theſe Things: When it has boiled well
together, ſtrain out the Spice, Anchovy Bones and Shalot,
and put it into your Stew-pan again with the Muſhrooms
to it, and have ready the Yolks of three Eggs, with the
Quantity of as much Butter as an Egg rolled up in Flour,
and beat it well with a Spoonful of Cream, and ſo ſhake
it up together, the Muſhrooms and all very thick, ſo that
it may hang about the Fricaſey, and ſcald a little Spinage
and ſhake over it; ſo ſerve it.

Fricafey *of* Tripe.

GET a double Tripe, cut ſome of the fat Part in
Slices, and dip them in Eggs or a Batter, and fry
them to lay round your Diſh; and the other Part cut,
ſome in long Slips, and ſome in Dice, and toſs them up
with Mint, Onion, chopp'd Parſley, melted Butter, Yolks

of

of Eggs and a little Vinegar, feafon with Pepper and Salt, and fo ferve away.

Another Way You may broil fome, and fome you may boil with Salt, Onion and Rofemary, and fend it up in the Liquor in which it is boiled.

To fricafey Quails.

TOSS them up in a Sauce-pan, with a little melted Butter, fome Mufhrooms and Truffles, with a Slice of Ham well beaten; feafon them with Salt, Pepper, Cloves and a Faggot of favoury Herbs, put in a little Flour; give it two or three Turns over the Stove, and moiften it with Gravy; add a Glafs of Champaign Wine, and let it fimmer over a gentle clear Fire; when almoft done, thicken the Ragoo with two or three Eggs, beat up in Gravy or Verjuice, and ferve them.

A Fricafey *of* Pigeons *in* Blood.

YOU muft take very fmall Pigeons, bleed them, and keep the Blood, put into it the Juice of a Lemon, to hinder it from turning, thefe Pigeons muft be fcalded and gutted; cut them in halves, and put them in a Stew-pan with a little melted Bacon; feafon them with Pepper, Salt, a Bunch of Sweet Herbs, Champignons, Truffles, Cocks Combs, and Sweetbreads of Veal or Lamb, put all together over the Fire; ftrew it with a Duft of Flour, moiften it with Gravy, and let it ftew foftly with a flow Fire, it being done, fkim off the Fat, and thicken it with Veal Cullis; ftrain off your Blood in a Sieve, beat it up with Yolks of Eggs, and a little Parfley cut fmall; and when you are ready to ferve up, put the Blood in your Fricafey,

K k k

and

and put it over the Fire, keeping it always stirring; take Care to keep it from boiling, and let your Fricasey have a good Taste: Dish it up handsomely, and serve it up hot for an Entry, or *Hors d'Oeuvre:* You may serve them up whole or in halves, that depends on the Fancy of the Cook.

To make a Fricasey of Sheeps Trotters.

SLIT the Bones of your Trotters, and pick them very clean, then put them in a Frying-pan with a Ladle full of strong Broth, a Piece of Butter, and a little Salt; after they have fried a while, add a little Parsley, green Chibbols, a little young Spear Mint and Thyme, all shred very small, and a little beaten Pepper· When you think they are fried almost enough, have a Lear made for them with the Yolks of two or three Eggs, some Mutton Gravy, a little Nutmeg, and the Juice of a Lemon squeezed therein, and put this Lear to the Trotters as they fry in the Pan, then toss them once or twice, and put them forth into the Dish you intend to serve them in.

To make a Fricasey of Calf's Chaldron.

YOU must take a Calf's Chaldron, after it is a little more than half boiled, and when it is cold, cut it into little Bits as big as Walnuts; season the whole with beaten Cloves, Salt, Nutmeg, Mace, a little Pepper, an Onion, Parsley, and a little Terragon, all shred very small; then put it into a Frying-pan with a Ladle full of strong Broth, and a little Sweet Butter; when it is fried enough, have a little Lear made with Mutton Gravy, the Juice of a Lemon and Orange, the Yolks of three or four Eggs,

and

and a little grated Nutmeg; put all to the Chaldron in the Pan, tofs your Fricafey two or three Times, then difh it, and fo ferve it up.

Calf's Head Fricafey.

HAving Slices of the Head, clean and boiled tender, as big as Walnuts, then tofs them up with Mufh-rooms, Sweetbreads, and Artichoke Bottoms, Cream, and the Yolks of Eggs; feafon it with Mace and Nutmeg, and fqueeze in a Lemon, fo ferve away hot.

For a Fricafey *of* Tench, *fee the Article of* Tench, p. 241.

For a Fricafey *of* Flounders, *fee the Article of* Flounders, p. 254.

To fricafey Sturgeon.

CUT it into thin Slices, and feafon it with Pepper, Salt, and Nutmeg, ftrew over a little Flour, and fry it brownifh; then take a Bit of Butter, pafs it brown with Flour, put in fome good Gravy, one Anchovy, and the Juice of an Orange; fo ferve away.

K k k 2

CHAP.

CHAP. XXII.

Of KITCHEN-GARDEN STUFF.

BEANS.

An Amulet *of* Green Beans

LET the Beans be blanched, and fried in Sweet Butter, with a little Parsley and Chibbol: That done, pour in some Cream, season them well, and let them boil over a gentle Fire. In the mean while, an Amulet is to be made with new laid Eggs and Cream, and salted at Discretion. When it is enough, dress it on a Dish, thicken the Beans with one or two Yolks, and turn them on your Amulet, so as all may be served up hot.

Amulets of the like Nature, may be made of Mushrooms, Truffles, Green Pease, Asparagus, Artichoke Bottoms, Spinage, Sorrel, &c. all being first cut into small Pieces, or shred fine.

Beans *blanched.*

BOIL your Beans so that the Skin comes off, then fry some thin Slices of Ham or Bacon, and some Parsley to lay round your Beans; toss up your Beans with melted Butter, and so serve hot.

A Bean Tansey.

BLANCH them and beat them in a Mortar very fine; season them with Pepper, Salt, Cloves, and Mace, you may do it savoury or sweet; the savoury Way

is

is as above, then put in the Yolks only of fix Eggs, and a Quartein of Butter, you muſt butter your Pan, and bake it as you do a Tanſey, and ſtick Slices of fried Bacon a Top: The ſweet Way is, with Beans, Bisket, Sugar, Sack and Cream, and eight Yolks of Eggs, ſo bake it, and ſtick on the Top ſome Orange and Lemon Peel candy'd.

Peaſe Francoiſe.

SHELL your Peaſe, and paſs a Quarter of a Pound of Butter, Gold Colour, with a Spoonful of Flour; then put in a Quart of Peaſe, four Onions cut ſmall, and two good Cabbages, or Sileſia Lettuces, you muſt cut them as ſmall as Onions, then put in half a Pint of Gravy ſeaſoned with Pepper, Salt and Cloves, ſtove this well an Hour very tender; you put in half a Spoonful of double refin'd Sugar, and fry ſome Artichokes and lay round the Side of the Diſh, ſerve with a forced Lettuce in the Middle.

Peaſe *the* Portugeze *Way*

WASH your Peaſe, cut into them ſome Lettuce, in Proportion to the Peaſe you have, put into them a Bit of Sugar as big as the End of your Thumb, ſome fine Oil, four or five Mint Leaves, cut ſmall, with Parſley, Onions, Shalots, a Crumb of Garlick, a little Winter Savoury, Nutmeg, Salt, a little Pepper, and a little Broth: Put them over the Fire, and let theſe have but little Broth. When you will ſerve them up, you poach ſome freſh Eggs in it, making a Hole for the Place each Egg is to have, then cover your Stew-pan again, boil your Eggs with a little

tle Fire upon the Cover, then flide them into your Difh and ferve them up hot.

Fine Beans are dreffed in the fame Manner; but we muft take Care not to blanch thefe Beans, and to put them in juft as they are, the fame as the Peafe, without putting them in Butter.

Green Peafe *with* Cream.

WASH your fine green Peafe in hot Water; then put them in a Colander to drain, put them in a Stew-pan, with a Lump of Butter, and a Bunch of Sweet Herbs, put them upon the Fire, and tofs them up, put a Duft of Flour to them, and moiften them with boiling Water, feafoned with Salt, and a Bit of Sugar; let them ftew; being ftew'd, or boiled fhort, and ready to be ferved up, put in a little Cream; let them have a good Tafte; difh them up, and ferve them up hot for Entremets.

Another Way to do Green Peafe.

TAKE fine Green Peafe, wafh them in hot Water, then put them in a Colander to drain, put them in a Stew-pan with a Lump of Butter, fet them over the Fire and tofs them up, ftrew a Duft of Flour over them, and moiften them with hot boiling Water, feafoned with Salt, and a Bit of Sugar; make up a Bunch of Lettuces bound with Packthread, a Bunch of Green Onions, and put thefe in your Peafe: They being done, take out the Lettuces and Onions. Let them have a good Tafte, and ferve up hot.

Another

Another Way.

HAving your Peafe wafhed in hot Water, drain them, put them in a Stew-pan with a Lump of Butter, and a Bunch of Sweet Herbs, then fet them over the Fire, tofs them up, ftrew them with a Duft of Flour, and moiften them with a little boiling Water, and let them ftew fofily; being ftewed, thicken them with Effence of Ham, let them have a good Tafte, being ready to be ferved up, put in a Dozen of fried Crufts of Bread, difh them up, and ferve them hot for an Entremet

A good Way to preferve Green Peafe.

HAving Green Peafe the Quantity you like, which you muft blanch, put Salt in the Water, and when they have had two Boils, take them out and fpread them upon a clean Table-Cloth, and leave them fo 'till they are cold. Let them dry in the Sun, if you have Convenience for it, otherwife in the Oven not too hot, being dry'd, put them into a dry Place; and when you would ufe them, put them in luke-warm Water, to make them turn green again, and if you have large dry Peafe, put a Handful to them, and that will thicken them, and let them ftew; being ftew'd, put a Lump of Butter in a Stew-pan, a Bunch of green Onions, and a Bunch of Lettuces, if you have any, and then your green Peafe, fee that the large ones be taken out, tofs them up, ftrow a Duft of Flour over them, moiften them with good Broth, and feafon them with Salt and a little Sugar, and let them go on ftewing, Let them have a good Tafte, and being ready to be ferv'd up, thicken them with Eggs, if you think fit, or

else

elſe with Cream　If you have not a Mind to ſerve them this Way, thicken them with a little Eſſence of Ham, put in your Diſh ſome Bits of Cruſts of Bread fried, with your Peaſe over them, and ſerve them up hot for Entremets.

Cabbage *forced whole.*

PArboil a large white Cabbage, then take it out and cool it; when it is cold, cut out the Heart of it as big as your Fiſt, and fill it up with good Force-Meat made of Sweetbreads, Marrow, Eggs, Crumbs of Bread, Pepper, Salt, and Nutmeg, Thyme and Parſley, make it up all together and force your Cabbage; ſtove it well in Gravy one Hour, and ſend it whole to Table; thicken your Sauce and pour all over, and garniſh with Slices of Ham, or Bacon broiled.

Stewed Red Cabbage.

CUT your Cabbage very ſmall and fine, and ſtove it with Gravy and Sauſages, and a Piece of Ham, ſeaſon it with Pepper, and Salt; before you ſend it away, put in a little Elder Vinegar, and mix it well together, which will turn it of a rediſh Colour, ſo ſerve away hot.

Savoys *forced and ſtoved whole.*

SET two green Savoys off; then take out the Inſide and fill the Vacancy with good Forced-Meat; tie the Savoys up, force one, the other plain; then ſtove them in good Broth and Gravy; ſeaſon with Pepper, Salt, and Nutmeg; and when you have ſtoved them enough, thicken ſome Gravy and put in a little Vinegar; ſo ſerve it away.

Lettuce

Lettuce *forced.*

SET off twelve, and then cool them; when cold, take out the Heart, fill them full with Sweetbreads, and Force-Meat; set them in your Pan, Stalk upwards, and stove them half an Hour, season them as before, and serve away.

To force Cucumbers.

PARE them and core out the Seed, then force them with light Force-Meat and stove them in good Broth or Gravy, and when tender, cut two in Slices, and the other send whole; squeeze in a Lemon, and serve away hot.

To stew Cucumbers.

YOU must core them and cut them into large Dice, or round, as you please, and then fry them brown with an Onion, put in some Gravy and Elder Vinegar, and season with Pepper and Salt; so serve it under Mutton or roast Beef.

To farce Cucumbers.

PARE large Cucumbers, then scoop out all the Seeds, first cutting off one End. Then prepare the following Farce for them: Take the Hearts of some Cabbage Lettuce stew'd tender in Salt and Water; drain them well, and chop them small, and cut some Onion very fine, shred a little Parsley that has been boil'd tender, and a Mushroom pickled; and add a little All-spice, finely powdered, and some Pepper, a little Salt, and some Fat of Bacon chopp'd

small.

fmall.   Mix thefe well together, with the Yolk of an Egg
or two, according to your Quantity, and ftuff the Cucumbers full of it.   Then tie the Ends, that were cut off clofe,
with Packthread, and ftew them in Water and Salt 'till
they are tender ; then drain them and flour them, and fry
them brown in Hog's Lard very hot, and let them drain ;
then take off the Threads that hold them together, and
lay them in your Difh, and pour the following Sauce over
them, *viz* Take Gravy well feafoned, and as much Claret,
boil thefe together, with fome Lemon Peel, and All-fpice ;
and thicken this Sauce with burnt Butter.   Thefe are good
to be ferved with Mutton Cutlets, as well as alone.

To drefs Skirrets.

THE Skirret, tho' it is none of the largeft Roots,
yet is certainly one of the beft Products of the Garden, if it be rightly drefs'd ; the Way of doing which, is,
to wafh the Roots very well, and boil them 'till they are
tender, which need not be very long.   Then the Skin of
the Roots muft be taken off, and a Sauce of melted Butter
and Sack poured over them : In this Manner they are ferved
at the Table, and eaten with the Juice of Orange, and
fome likewife ufe Sugar with them, but the Root is very
fweet of itfelf.

Some, after the Root is boil'd, and the Skin is taken off,
fry them, and ufe the Sauce as above: So likewife the
Roots of Salfify and Scorzonera are to be prepared for the
Table.

Scorzoneras

Scorzoneras *butter'd.*

SCRAPE them and boil them very tender, and cut them into Pieces two Inches long, then fqueeze in a Lemon; put in half a Pint of Cream and four Ounces of Butter, with a little Salt and Nutmeg: You may fry them alfo.

Alexander *butter'd or fry'd.*

FIRST parboil them and get the Skin off, then boil them in their Lengths very tender, and make a Batter with Rhenifh Wine, Eggs and Flour, and then dip them in, and fauce them with melted Butter, Sack and Sugar; you may do them favoury.

Chardoons *buttered.*

BLANCH them and cut out all the Strings and leave them two Inches long; then boil them in Water and Salt, and a little Bit of fat Bacon, or Butter, and when they are tender, ftrain them off, and tofs them up in thick melted Butter, Pepper and Salt.

Chardoons *fry'd and butter'd.*

THEY are a wild Thiftle that grow in every Ditch or Hedge, you muft cut them about ten Inches and ftring them, tie them up, twenty in a Bundle, and boil them as Afparagus, or cut them in fmall Dice and boil them as Peafe, and tofs them up with Pepper, Salt and melted Butter.

Chardoons à la Fromage.

WE ſtring them and cut them an Inch long; ſtove them in good Gravy 'till tender; ſeaſon with Pepper and Salt, and ſqueeze in one Orange , then thicken it with Butter browned with Flour, put it in your Diſh and cover it all over with grated *Parmeſan* or *Cheſhire* Cheeſe, and then brown it over with a hot Cheeſe Iron; ſo ſerve away quick and hot

Fry'd Sellery.

BOIL it half an Hour, then let it cool, and make a a Batter with a little Rheniſh Wine, the Yolks of Eggs, with a little Flour and Salt; dip every Head in, and fry them with clarified Butter, and ſauce them with melted Butter.

Sellery *with* Cream.

YOU muſt tie up your Bunches and boil them tender, cut them three Inches long the beſt and Heart of it, then take half a Pint of Cream and four Yolks of Eggs; ſeaſon with Salt, and put in a ſmall Piece of Butter, and ſhake it together thick, and ſerve away hot.

For Endive *ragoo'd ſee* p. 435.

Spinach *with* Eggs.

BOIL your Spinach well and green, and ſqueeze it dry and chop it fine; then put in ſome good Gravy and melted Butter, with a little Cream, Pepper, Salt and Nutmeg; then poach ſix Eggs and lay over your Spinach,

fry

fry fome Sippets in Butter, and ftick all round the Sides, fqueeze one Orange, fo ferve it hot.

Sorrel *with* Eggs.

YOUR Sorrel muft be quick boil'd and well ftrained; then poach three Eggs foft and three hard, butter your Sorrel well, fry fome Sippets, and lay three poach'd Eggs and three whole hard Eggs betwixt, and ftick Sippets all over the Top, and garnifh with fliced Orange and curl'd Bacon or Ham fried.

Clary *fry'd with* Eggs.

WASH, pick, and dry your Clary with a Cloth; then beat up the Yolks of fix Eggs with a little Flour and Salt, make the Batter light, and dip in every Leaf and fry them fingly, and fend them up quick and dry.

Clary *Amulet.*

SCALD your Clary and chop it fmall, and beat it up with eight Eggs, feafon with a Shalot chopp'd, Pepper, and Salt, then fry it off quick as you do a Pancake, fqueeze over an Orange.

Afparagus *with* Cream.

HAving cut the green Part of your Afparagus in Pieces, an Inch long, and blanch them a little in boiling Water, then tofs them up in a Stew-pan with good Butter or Lard, but take Care they be not too fatty: Put to them fome Cream, a Bunch of Pot Herbs, and feafon them moderately: Before you ferve them, beat one or two Yolks

of

of Eggs in Cream, to thicken the Sauce, into which put a little Sugar, and then serve them.

Afparagus *with* Gravy.

WE cut them in Pieces as before, and tofs them up with melted Lard, Parfley, Chaivil, cut very fmall, and a whole Leek, which you muft remember to take away; feafon them with Salt, Pepper, and a little Nutmeg, and fet them a fimmering in a Stew-pan over a gentle Fire, with a little good Broth; when they are enough done, take from them all the Fat, pour over them fome Mutton Gravy, and fqueeze upon them the Juice of a Lemon, fo ferve them.

Afparagus *with* Butter.

BOIL them in Water and a little Salt; take Care they be not over done, when they are boiled enough, fet them a draining; then lay them in a Difh, and let your Sauce be Butter, Salt, Vinegar, and Nutmeg, or white Pepper, and the Yolk of an Egg to thicken it, keep it continually moving, and pour it on your Afparagus; then ferve them.

To make an Amulet *of* Afparagus.

BLANCH and cut the Afparagus in fmall Pieces, fry them in frefh Butter, with a little Parfley and Chibbols, then pour fome Cream upon them, and having feafoned them well, boil them on a gentle Fire: Mean while, make an Amulet with new laid Eggs, Cream and Salt: When it is enough, drefs it on a Difh, and having thickened the Afparagus with one or two Yolks of Eggs, pour it on the Amulet, and ferve it up hot.

A Way

A Way to preserve Afparagus.

HAving cut off the hard Part of the Stalk that is not eatable; give the reft one Boil in Butter and Salt, then put them into fair Water: When they have laid 'till they are cold, take them out and drain them dry, then put them into a Veffel, where they may be at their full Length without breaking, put to them fome Salt, whole Cloves, fliced Lemon, and as much Water as Vinegar: Lay a Napkin in the Veffel over them, and cover the Napkin with melted Butter, keep them in a Place neither hot nor cold; and when you would ufe them, drefs them in the fame Manner you do thofe that are newly gathered

A R T I C H O K E S.

Artichoke Bottoms *with* Cream.

GET Artichoke Bottoms, boil them in Water, and when they are boiled tofs them up with Butter in a Stew-pan, then put to them fome Cream, with a Bunch of Cives and Parfley; thicken your Sauce with the Yolk of an Egg, and put in it a little Salt and Nutmeg. Serve them in Plates or little Difhes.

Artichokes *in* Puree

AFTER you have well wafhed and clean'd the Bottoms of your Artichokes, boil them in blanched Water, putting in it a good large Lump of Butter, kneaded up with a little Flour and Salt: When they are boiled, take them out of the Water, and having made them into Puree, ftrain them through a Sieve in the fame Manner as you do

Peafe,

Peafe. Then fet them to fimmer in a Stew-pan over a gentle Fire, with frefh Butter, Salt, Pepper and Nutmeg, and Cloves pounded in a Mortar; add to this a Bunch of Parfley, young Onions and Thyme, with a Leaf of Bays.

When you are almoft ready to ferve, pound in a Mortar fome blanch'd fweet Almonds, fome candy'd Lemon Peel, Biskets, Bitter Almonds, Yolks of hard Eggs, and a convenient Quantity of Sugar: Mix all thefe Ingredients together with a little Orange-Flower-Water; and having incorporated this Compofition with your Puree of Artichokes, fet it a Moment over the Fire, and then ferve it up.

Artichokes being of great Ufe in C O O K E R Y, throughout the whole Year, for almoft all Sorts of Ragoos, Soops, &c. it is neceffary to lay in a good Provifion of them by obferving the following Direction.

To keep Artichokes *all the Year.*

G E T a Quantity of Water proportionable to your Number of Artichokes, fo that they may keep in it, and boil it with as much Salt as you judge neceffary: Then take it off the Fire, and let it ftand 'till the Foulnefs of the Salt be fettled at the Bottom; then pour it into the Veffel in which you intend to keep your Artichokes: Blanch them in boiling Water, only fo long, that you may take out the Choaks; wafh them in two or three feveral Waters, 'till you are fure they are very clean, then put them into the Pickle you have already made for them, pouring on the Top of it fome Oil or good Butter, that no Air may enter: And, if you will, you may put a little Vinegar to your Pickle. Cover your Veffel very carefully with Paper, and lay a Board over it, that the leaft Breath of Air

may

may not get in. When you would ufe your Artichokes you muft fteep them in frefh Water to take away the Salt. They will keep in this Manner a Year or more.

Artichokes may likewife be kept dry: To this End, when you have blanched them and taken out the Chokes, as above directed, lay them a diaining on Grates or Hurdles of Ofier; then put them into an Oven moderately hot, 'till they become as dry as Wood: Before you ufe them, you muft fteep them for two Days in luke-warm Water; by which Means they will come to themfelves, and be as frefh as when they were firft gathered. In blanching them off, put in the Water a little Verjuice, Salt and Butter, or good Beef Sewet.

There is likewife another Way of keeping them: Choofe the beft Artichokes you can get; and with a fharp Knife cut off the Leaves and Chokes, and throw each Bottom immediately into fair Water, otherwife they will turn black. When you take them out of the Water, throw them into Flour, and cover them all over with it; then range them one by one on a Hurdle, and dry them in the Oven. When you would make ufe of them, lay them firft a foaking for twenty four Hours, and then boil them as you do other Artichokes. You will find that by this Means they will never have loft their Tafte.

Artichokes *with* White Sauce.

TAKE very young Artichokes and boil them in Water and a little Salt: When they are boiled, tofs up the Bottoms with Butter and Parfley, feafoned with Salt and white Pepper. Let your Sauce be Yolks of Eggs, a Drop or two of Vinegar and a little Gravy.

N° 20. M m m Mufhrooms

Mushrooms *with* Cream.

CUT your Mushrooms in Pieces, and tofs them up over a brisk Fire in Butter, feafoned with Salt, Nutmeg and a Bunch of Herbs. When they are done enough, and moft of the Butter wafted away, put to them fome Cream, and ferve them.

A Loaf *with* Mushrooms.

MAKE a Hole in the Bottom of a Loaf, keep the Bit taken off, take out all its Crumb, fill it up with a Harfh of Partridges, ftop the Hole with the referved Bit of Cruft, and tie the Loaf round with Packthread, dip it in Milk and fry it in Hog's Lard 'till it has a good Colour. Take a Handful of Mushrooms, ftew them in a Stew-pan with fome Effence of Ham: Being done, thicken the Sauce with Effence of Ham. Then put your Loaf in, foak it about a Minute; then put it in the Difh, and the Ragoo being made relifhing, muft be put over it, and fo ferve it hot.

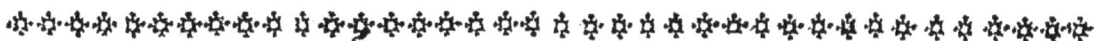

C H A P XXIII.

Of P U D D I N G S, *&c.*

Baked Potatoe Pudding.

WE take two Pounds of white Potatoes, boil and peel them, and beat them in a Mortar fo fine as not to difcover what they are; then take half a Pound of Butter,

ter, and mix it with the Yolks of eight Eggs, and the Whites of three, beat them well, and mix a Pint of Cream and half a Pint of Sack, a Pound of refin'd Sugar, with a little Salt and Spice, and bake it.

Orange Pudding.

YOU muſt take two right *Seville* Oranges; take off a little of the Outſide Rind, and ſqueeze out the Juice and Seeds, lay them in Water three Days, ſhifting the Water every Day: Then ſet on a Pot of Water, make it boil, and put them in a Mortar, and beat them into a Paſte; then put in double their Weight of double refin'd Sugar, eight Eggs, leave out half the Whites; then boil a Pint of Cream, ſet it to be cold, and put them in with three or four Spoonfuls of Sack; grate the Quantity of a Half-penny Roll, and put in, with half a Pound of ſweet Butter melted: Sweeten it to your Taſte, and put it into a Diſh with Puff-paſte round it, and it will require no more baking than a Cuſtard.

Another Orange Pudding.

HAving the Peel of a large *China* Orange, mince it ex-ceeding ſmall, and pound it in a Mortar; then take the Yolks of ſixteen Eggs well beaten, with a little Roſe Water, and put to it a little more than half a Pound of Sugar, and as much Butter being melted, and ſeaſon it with a little Nutmeg, and put it in a Diſh, being covered with Puff-paſte, and lay Puff-paſte, over it, and garniſh it in what Form you pleaſe.

A Lemon

A Lemon Pudding.

HAving two clear Lemons, grate off the Outfide Rinds; then grate two Naples Biskets, and mix with your grated Peel, and add to it three Quarters of a Pound of fine Sugar, 12 Yolks and fix Whites of Eggs well beat, and three Quarters of a Pound of Butter melted, and half a Pint of thick Cream, mix thefe well together, put a Sheet of Pafte at the Bottom of the Difh; and juft as the Oven is ready, put your Stuff in the Difh; fift a little double refined Sugar over it before you put it in the Oven. An Hour will bake it.

An Almond Pudding.

BLANCH and pound half a Pound of Almonds with four grated Biskets, and three Quarters of a Pound of Butter, Sack, and Orange-Flower-Water, then mix it with a Quart of Cream boiled and mix'd with eight Eggs, Sweet Spice and Sugar, cover the Difh with Puff-pafte, pour in the Batter and bake it.

Another Almond Pudding *to bake or boil.*

BEAT a Pound of Almonds as fmall as poffible; put to them fome Rofe Water and Cream as often as you beat them; then take one Pound of Beef Sewet, finely minced, with five Yolks of Eggs, and but two Whites; make it as thin as Batter for Fritters, mixing it with fweet thick Cream; feafon it with beaten Mace, Sugar, and Salt; then fet it into the Oven in a Pewter Difh, and when you draw it forth, ftrew fome Sugar on the Top. Garnifh your Difh with Sugar.

A Carrot

A Carrot Pudding.

SCRAPE raw Carrots very clean, then grate them with a Grater, without a Back. To half a Pound of Carrots, take a Pound of grated Bread, a Nutmeg, a little Cinnamon, a very little Salt, half a Pound of Sugar, and half a Pint of Sack, eight Eggs, a Pound of Butter melted, and as much Cream as will mix it well together, stir it and beat it up well, then sheet a Dish with Puff-paste and send it to the Oven.

Another Carrot Pudding.

BOIL a large Carrot tender, then set it to be cold, and pass it thro' a Sieve very fine; then put in half a Pound of melted Butter, beaten together with eight Eggs, leave out half the Whites, with three Spoonfuls of Sack, and one Spoonful of Orange-Flower-Water, half a Pint of good Cream, a Nutmeg, Bread grated, a little Salt, and make it of a moderate Thickness, and give it the same baking as a Custard.

A Marrow Pudding.

TAKE a Quart of Cream or Milk, put in four Ounces of Bisket, eight Yolks of Eggs, some Nutmeg, Salt, and the Marrow of two Bones; save some Bits to lay about the Top; season with a little Sugar; put in two Ounces of Currants plump'd; set it gently on the Fire, then cool it, and bake it in Puff-paste.

A French

A French Barley Pudding.

PUT to a Quart of Cream fix Eggs, well beaten, but three of the Whites; then feafon it with Sugar, Nutmeg, a little Salt, Orange-Flower-Water, and a Pound of melted Butter, then put to it fix Handfuls of *French* Barley that has been boiled tender in Milk: Butter a Difh and put it in, and bake it. It muft ftand as long as a Venifon Pafty.

A Pith Pudding.

TAKE a Quantity of the Pith of an Ox, and let it lie all Night in Water to foak out the Blood, the next Morning ftrip it out of the Skins, and beat it with the Back of a Spoon in Orange-Flower-Water, 'till it is as fine as Pap; then take three Pints of thick Cream, and boil in it two or three Blades of Mace, a Nutmeg quartered, a Stick of Cinnamon; then take half a Pound of the beft Jordan Almonds, blanched in cold Water, then beat them with a little Cream, and as they dry put in more Cream, and when they are full beaten ftrain the Cream from them to the Pith; then take the Yolks of ten Eggs, the Whites of but two; beat them very well, and put them to the Ingredients, then take a Spoonful of grated Bread, or Naples Bisket; mingle all thefe together with half a Pound of fine Sugar, the Marrow of four large Bones, and a little Salt, and bake it in Puff-pafte.

Pippin Pudding.

BOIL twelve Pippins tender, and fcrape them clean from the Core, and put in a Pint of Cream feafoned with Orange-Flower, or Rofe Water and Sugar to your
Tafte,

Taſte, and put good Puff-paſte in your Diſh , bake it in a ſlack Oven, and grate Loaf Sugar over it befoie it is quite done.

Another Pippin Pudding.

T A K E as much Pulp of boiled Pippins as you think will make your Pudding, and ſix Eggs well beaten, the Whites of but three, two large Spoonfuls of Naples Biſket finely grated , ſugar it to your Palate ; take the Rind of an Orange or Lemon boiled tendei, and beaten in a Mortar , then mix all well together in the Mortar, with a Quarter of a Pound of freſh Butter, and put it in your Diſh, with Paſte Top and Bottom. Let it not be done too much.

Italian Pudding.

H Aving a Pint of Cream, ſome white Manchet Bread, ten Eggs, a beaten Nutmeg ; butter the Bottom of your Diſh, and iound the Sides: Then cut twelve Pippins in round Slices, and lay in the Bottom ; throw a little Orange Peel over them, and ſome fine Sugar ; poui half a Pint of Claret over them, and then the Pudding , make Puff-paſte over it, and it will be baked in half an Hour ; lay the Paſte round the Sides of your Diſh.

A baked Rice Pudding.

Y O U muſt blanch the Rice in Water, then boil it in Milk, with Sugar, Cinnamon, and Salt 'till it is very thick ; let it ſtand 'till it is cold, and add to it Eggs according to the Rice, half the Whites only. Put in ſome Currants and Raiſins, and a little melted Butter, with ſome Sewet and diced Marrow.

Another

Another richer Rice Pudding.

GET a Quart of Milk, six Ounces of Rice finely powdered, six Eggs, half the Whites only, and half a Pound of Butter ; put in the Rice when the Milk boils, let it boil some Time, and then put in the Sugar and Butter, and stir it well, and when cold, put in the Eggs, then bake it in a Dish. It must be well baked. Put at the Bottom of the Dish some Orange Marmalade and Marrow.

Oat-Meal Pudding.

GET a Pint of fine Oat-Meal, boil it in new Milk and Cream, a little Cinnamon and Nutmeg, and beaten Mace, and when it is about the Thickness of a Hasty-Pudding, take it off, and stir in half a Pound of Sweet Butter, and eight Eggs, (leave out half the Whites) very well beaten, and put in two or three Spoonfuls of Sack, and make Puff-paste, and lay round your Dish, and butter it very well, and bake it, but not too much.

A baked Bread Pudding.

GET a Quart of Cream, boil it with two Manchets, and grate in one Nutmeg, six Yolks and four Whites of Eggs well beaten, with your Bread and Cream, at least half an Hour together ; then put into it a Pound of Beef Sewet finely minced, half a Pound of Sugar, a little Salt, bake it three Quarters of an Hour in a quick Oven, the same Way boiling without Sewet is as good.

Another

Another Sort.

PARE off all the Cruft of a Penny white Loaf, and flice it thin into a Difh with a Quart of Cream, fet it over a Chafing-Difh of Coals, 'till the Bread be almoft dry, then put in a Piece of Sweet Butter, and take it off and let it ftand to be cold ; then take the Yolks of three Eggs, the White of one with a little Rofe Water, Sugar and Nutmeg ; ftir them very well together ; then put it in another Difh, butter it, and when it comes out of the Oven, grate over it fome fine Sugar.

Another Sort.

TAKE grated Bread, and as much Flour ; then take four Eggs, two Whites, a good Quantity of Sugar, wet it with Cream to the Thicknefs of Pancake Batter ; then put in fome Raifins of the Sun, and butter your Difh very well, and bake it half an Hour ; ftrew over it grated Sugar.

Another Sort.

PUT to a Quart of Cream, a Pound of Beef Sewet cut fmall, feafon it with Nutmeg, Rofe Water and Sugar : Then grate two Manchets, and beat feven Eggs, put in half a Pound of Currants ; mingle all thefe well together, butter the Difh, and bake it not too much, grate Sugar over it when it comes out of the Oven.

The Spread-Eagle Pudding.

CUT off the Cruft of three Half-penny Rolls, then flice them into your Pan ; then fet three Pints of Milk over the Fire, make it fcalding hot, but do not let it

boil

boil, fo pour it over your Bread and cover it clofe, and let it ftand an Hour, then put in a good Spoonful of Sugar, a very little Salt, a Nutmeg grated, a Pound of Sewet after it is fhred, half a Pound of Currants, wafhed and picked, four Spoonfuls of cold Milk, ten Eggs, but five of the Whites; and when all is in, ftir it, and mix it well, butter a Difh. Lefs than an Hour will bake it.

A Green Pudding.

HAving fome boiled Mutton minced, with Beef Sewet fhreded, a little Thyme, Marjoram and Parfley, and a Handful of Spinach, then mix all thefe together with a little grated Bread, and three Yolks of Eggs, fome Cream, Sugar and Nutmeg, Currants, and a little Flour; then roll it up in a Sheep's Caul, and bake it.

A Ratifia Pudding.

YOU muft take a Quart of Cream, boil it with four or five Laurel Leaves, then take them out and break in half a Pound of Naples Bisket, half a Pound of Butter, fome Sack, Nutmeg, and Salt, take it off the Fire, cover it up, when it is almoft cold, put in two Ounces of Almonds blanched and beaten fine, and the Yolks of five Eggs, mix all well together, and bake it in a moderate Oven, half an Hour, fcrape Sugar on it as it goes into the Oven.

A Bacon Pudding.

BOIL a Quart of Cream with a Handful of Sugar, and a little Butter, the Yolks of eight Eggs, and three Whites, beat together, with three Spoonfuls of Flour, and

and two Spoonfuls of Cream; when the Cream boils, put in the Eggs, stirring it 'till it comes to be thick, and put it in a Dish and let it cool, then beat a Piece of fat Bacon in a Stone Mortar, 'till it comes to be like Lard, take out all the Strings from it, and put your Cream to it by little and little 'till it is well mixed; then put some Puff-paste round the Brim of your Dish, and a thin Leaf at Bottom, and pour it into the Dish. Do the Top Chequerwise with Puff-paste, and let it bake half an Hour.

Petit Puddings.

WE take a Handful of grated Bread, a Spoonful of Flour, the Yolks of two Eggs, a Spoonful of Orange-Flower-Water, a Handful of Beef Sewet, shred all very small, a little Nutmeg, and Salt, a Spoonful of Cheese Curds; work it well together, and wet it as little as you can, and make it up with Cream, or new Milk, lay it in round Balls in the Bottom of your Dish, which must be well buttered: Bake them not too much: When they are baked put them in another Dish, with a Spoonful of Sack or White Wine, melted Butter and Sugar together poured on them.

Chesnut Pudding.

PUT a Dozen and half of Chesnuts in a Skillet of Water, and set them on the Fire, blanch and peel them, and when cold, put them in cold Water; then stamp them in a Mortar, with Orange-Flower-Water and Sack, 'till they are very small, mix them in two Quarts of Cream, and eighteen Yolks of Eggs, the Whites of three or four; beat the Eggs with Sack, Rose Water and Sugar;

put

put it in a Dish with Puff-paste, ftick in fome Lumps of Marrow or frefh Butter, and bake it.

A Sweetmeat Pudding.

YOU muft put a thin Puff-pafte at the Bottom of your Dish, then have of candy'd Orange, and Lemon Peel, and Citron, of each an Ounce, flice them thin and put them in the Bottom on your Pafte, then beat eight Yolks of Eggs, and two Whites, near half a Pound of Sugar, and half a Pound of Butter melted, mix and beat all well together, and when the Oven is ready, pour it on your Sweetmeats in the Dish An Hour or lefs will bake it.

A fine plain baked Pudding.

YOU muft take a Quart of Milk, and put in fix Laurel Leaves into it; when it has boiled a little take out your Leaves, and with fine Flour make that Milk into Hafty-Pudding, pretty thick; then ftir in half a Pound of Butter more, then a Quarter of a Pound of Sugar, a fmall Nutmeg grated, twelve Yolks, fix Whites of Eggs well beaten; mix and ftir all well together, butter a Dish, and put in your Stuff: A little more than half an Hour will bake it.

A Dripping Pudding.

MAKE a good Batter as for Pancakes, put it in a hot Tofs-pan over the Fire with a Bit of Butter to fry the Bottom a little, then put the Pan and Batter under a Shoulder of Mutton inftead of a Dripping-pan, keeping frequently fhaking it by the Handle and it will be light and favoury,

favoury, and fit to take up when your Mutton is enough; then turn it in a Difh, and ferve it hot.

A Bread *and* Butter Pudding.

WE take a Two-penny Loaf, and a Pound of frefh Butter; fpread it in very thin Slices, as to eat, cut them off as you fpread them, and ftone half a Pound of Raifins, and wafh a Pound of Currants, then put Puff-pafte at the Bottom of a Difh, and lay a Row of your Bread and Butter, and ftrew a Handful of Currants, and a few Raifins, and fome little Bits of Butter, and fo do 'till your Difh is full; then boil three Pints of Cream, and thicken it, when cold, with the Yolks of ten Eggs, a grated Nutmeg, a little Salt, near half a Pound of Sugar, fome Orange-Flower-Water, and pour this in, juft as the Pudding is going into the Oven.

Boiled P U D D I N G S.

A fine boiled Rice Pudding.

YOU muft take a Quarter of a Pound of Flour of Rice, put it over the Fire in a Pint of Milk, keep ftirring it conftantly, that it may not clod or burn to, then take it off and put it in an earthen Pan, and put to it half a Pound of Butter, when it is hot enough to melt, but not oil it, put to it half a Pint of Cream, the Yolks of eight Eggs, the Whites of but two, put Sugar to your Palate, put into it the Peel of a whole Lemon fhred as fine as pof-fible: Then put it in *China* Cups, and boil it. Sauce it with melted Butter and a Spoonful of Sack.

Oxford

Oxford Puddings.

GET grated Bread, picked Currants, fine fhred Sewet and Sugar, a Quarter of a Pound of each, mix them together, grate in a good deal of Nutmeg and Lemon Peel, then break in two Eggs, and ftir all together, tie them in five Cloths, and boil them half an Hour or more.

Neat's Foot Pudding.

GET Neats Feet; being tender boiled, take them from the Bones, and mince them very fmall, with half as much Sewet as Feet; mix them together, with Sugar, Cinnamon and Salt, and a Quarter of a Pound of Cition and Orange-Peel minced very fine, then break fix or eight Eggs, Yolks and Whites; take two Handfuls of grated Bread, and as many Currants as you think convenient, mix all thefe together, butter the Bag, tie it up and boil it two Hours. Then ferve it with a Sweet Sauce.

A Cabbage Pudding.

HAving two Pounds of the lean Part of a Leg of Veal, take of Beef Sewet the like Quantity; chop them together, then beat them together in a Stone Mortar, adding to it half a little Cabbage fcalded, and beat that with your Meat; then feafon it with Mace and Nutmeg, a little Pepper and Salt, fome green Goofeberries, Grapes, or Barberries, in the Time of Year. In the Winter, put in a little Verjuice, then mix all well together, with the Yolks of four or five Eggs, well beaten; then wrap it up in green Cabbage Leaves; tie a Cloth over it, boil it an Hour; melt Butter for Sauce.

A Spinach

A Spinach Pudding.

SCALD your Spinach, and chop it very fine, or the Juice will do, mix with Cream, the Yolks of eight Eggs, four Ounces of Bisket, and four of melted Butter, season with Sugar, Nutmeg, and Salt; then set it on the Fire 'till it is stiff, but do not boil it, then cool it and bake it in Puff-paste or boil it.

A Quaking Pudding

WE take a Pint and somewhat more of thick Cream, ten Eggs, put in the Whites of three only, beat them very well with two Spoonfuls of Rose Water Mingle, with your Cream, three Spoonfuls of fine Flour, mix it so well that there be no Lumps in it, put it all together, and season it according to your Taste. Butter a Cloth very well, and let it be thick that it may not run out, and let it boil for half an Hour, as fast as you can, then take it up and make Sauce with Butter, Rose Water and Sugar, and serve it.

You may stick some blanched Almonds upon it, if you please.

Another Quaking Pudding.

GET a Quart of Cream, and beat three or four Spoonfuls, with two or three Spoonfuls of Flour of Rice, a Penny Loaf grated, and seven Eggs; then put to it a little Orange-Flower-Water, Sugar, Nutmeg, Mace and Cinnamon, butter the Cloth, and tie it up, but not too close, put it in when the Pot boils, and boil it an Hour, then turn it out into the Dish; stick on it sliced Citron,

and

and pour over it Butter with Sack, Orange-Flower-Water, with Lemon Juice and Sugar.

A Bread Pudding.

SET a Quart of Cream over the Fire to boil; put into it a Blade or two of Mace, eight Cloves, a Bit of Cinnamon, with a little Nutmeg, Salt and Sugar, when it has boiled, have ready the Crufts of two *French* Rolls cut in Slices, and put into it, and let it ftand 'till it is cold, then drain all the Cream that the Bread has not foaked, and rub it through the Colander, put in fix Eggs, take out the Whites, then ftir it all together well, butter your Difh, and put it in, tying it over with a Cloth and Packthread.   Little more than an Hour will boil it.

A Brown-Bread Pudding.

GET half a Pound of Brown-Bread, and double the Weight of it in Beef Sewet, a Quarter of a Pint of Cream, the Blood of a Fowl, a whole Nutmeg, fome Cinnamon, a Spoonful of Sugar, fix Yolks of Eggs, three Whites, mix it all well together, and boil it in a Wooden Difh two Hours.   Serve it with Sack and Sugar, and Butter melted.

A Curd Pudding.

FIRST take the Curd off a Gallon of Milk and whey it well, and rub it through a Sieve, then take fix Eggs, three Whites, a little thick Cream, three Spoonfuls of Orange-Flower-Water, one Nutmeg grated, grated Bread, and Flour, of each three Spoonfuls, a Pound of Currants and ftoned Raifins, mix all thefe together; butter a thick
Cloth

Cloth, and tie it up in it: Boil it an Hour, for Sauce, melt Butter and Orange-Flower-Water and Sugar.

New-College Puddings.

HAving grated a Penny stale Loaf, and put to it a like Quantity of Beef Sewet finely shred, and a Nutmeg grated, a little Salt, some Currants, and then beat some Eggs in a little Sack, and some Sugar, and mix all together and knead it as stiff as for Manchet, and make it up in the Form and Size of a Turky Egg, but a little flatter; then take a Pound of Butter, and put it in a Dish, and set the Dish over a clear Fire in a Chafing-Dish, and rub your Butter about the Dish, 'till it is melted, put your Puddings in and cover the Dish, but often turn your Puddings, until they are all brown alike, and when they are enough, scrape Sugar over them, and serve them hot for a Side-Dish.

A Hasty-Pudding.

BREAK an Egg into fine Flour, and with your Hand work up as much as you can into as stiff a Paste as is possible; then mince it as small as Herbs to the Pot, as small as if it were to be sifted, then set a Quart of Milk a boiling, and put in your Paste so cut as before mentioned; put in a little Salt, some beaten Cinnamon and Sugar, a Piece of Butter as big as a Walnut, and keep it stirring all one Way, 'till it is as thick you would have it, and then stir in such another Piece of Butter; and when it is in the Dish, stick it all over with little Bits of Butter.

A stewed

A stewed Pudding.

YOU must grate a Two-penny Loaf, and mix it with half a Pound of Beef Sewet, finely shred, and three Quarters of a Pound of Currants, and a Quarter of a Pound of Sugar, a little Cloves, Mace and Nutmeg, then beat five or six Eggs, with three or four Spoonfuls of Rose Water, and beat all together, and make them up in little round Balls the Bigness of an Egg, some round, and some long, in the Fashion of an Egg, then put a Pound of Butter in a Pewter Dish, and when it is melted and thorough hot, put in your Puddings, and let them stew 'till they are brown, turn them, and when they are enough, serve them up with Sack, Butter and Sugar for Sauce.

A good Plumb Pudding.

WE take a Pound and a Quarter of Beef Sewet, after 'tis skinned and shred very fine, then stone three Quarters of a Pound of Raisins, and mix with it, and a grated Nutmeg, a Quarter of a Pound of Sugar, a little Salt, and a little Sack, four Eggs, four Spoonfuls of Cream, and about half a Pound of fine Flour; mix these well together, pretty stiff, tie it in a Cloth, and let it boil four Hours. Melt Butter thick for Sauce.

A Cow-Heel Pudding.

CUT off all the Meat of a large Cow-Heel, but the black Toes, put them away, but mince the rest very small, and shred it over again, with three Quarters of a Pound of Beef Sewet, put to it a Penny Loaf grated,
Cloves,

Cloves, Mace, Nutmeg, Sugar, and a little Salt, some
Sack and Rose Water· Mix these well together with six
raw Eggs, well beaten, butter a Cloth, and put it in, and
boil it two Hours. For Sauce, melt Butter, Sack and Sugar.

A Rye-bread Pudding.

TAKE half a Pound of sour Rye-bread grated,
half a Pound of Beef Sewet, finely shred, half a
Pound of Currants clean washed, half a Pound of Sugar,
a whole Nutmeg grated; mix all well together, with five
or six Eggs: Butter a Dish: Boil it an Hour and a Quarter,
and serve it up with melted Butter.

A Custard Pudding.

HAving a Pint of Cream, mix with it six Eggs well
beat, two Spoonfuls of Flour, half a Nutmeg grated,
a little Salt and Sugar to your Taste; butter a Cloth, put
it in when the Pot boils, boil it just half an Hour, melt
Butter for Sauce.

A Shaking Pudding *with* Almonds.

BOIL a Pint of Cream, boil it with a Blade of
Mace; strow it over with some beaten Almonds, a
little Orange-Flower-Water, or Rose Water; then take
four Eggs, leave out two Whites, strain the Cream, Eggs
and Almonds together; then take some Sugar and sweeten
it, and thicken it with grated Bread or Bisket, then take
a Cloth and rub it with Flour, and tie it up and dip it into
Rose Water, then boil it, and when it is boiled eat it with
Butter, Sugar and White Wine, stick it with blanched
Almonds; so serve it.

A cheap

A *cheap* Rice Pudding

YOU muſt take a Quarter of a Pound of Rice, and half a Pound of Raiſins, tie them in a Cloth allowing a great deal of Room for the ſwelling of your Pudding. Boil it two Hours. For Sauce, pour over it Butter melted with Sugar and Nutmeg

Turkey *or* Capons *in* Guts.

HAving a roaſted Turkey or Capon, or both, according to the Quantity of Puddings you would make, cut out the Breaſts and mince them very ſmall, then cut ſome Hog's Fat very thin, and put all this into a Sauce-pan with two Onions roaſted, and then pounded in a Mortar, a little ſavoury Herbs, and ſome ſhred Parſley; ſeaſon all this with the uſual Spices, add to it the Whites of two or three Eggs beaten : Next take a Quart of Milk, and having beaten up in it the Yolks of a Dozen Eggs, ſet it over a Stove and boil it to a Cream, taking Care that it does not curdle; then mix the whole together, and warm it over the Fire, ſo put it into Guts: Then blanch them off in Water and Milk, with ſome ſliced Onion. When you would ſerve them up, lay a Sheet of Paper rubbed over with Hog's Lard, or other Greaſe, upon a Gridiron, and the Puddings upon the Paper, ſo broil them over a ſlack Fire, for fear they ſhould break.

Puddings *of* Fowls Livers.

MINCE a Quarter of a Pound of Hog's Fat very ſmall, with one Pound of Fowls Livers, and one Pound of the Fleſh of Capon, ſeaſon all this with ſavoury

Herbs,

Herbs, Cives, Salt, Pepper, grated Nutmeg, pounded Cloves and Cinnamon, add to it the Yolks of six raw Eggs and a Quart of Cream, or rather more, as you fee Occasion, put it into Guts, then boil thefe Puddings in Milk, with fome Salt and fliced Lemon. Broil them as in the laft Receipt, and ferve them with the Juice of Orange.

Calf's Liver Pudding

MINCE a Calf's Liver, and pound it in a Mortar, together with a third Part as much of Hog's Fat as Liver, fome of which cut alfo in fmall Dice Seafon thefe Ingredients as in the laft Receipt, and put them into Guts in the Manner above directed. Then boil your Puddings in White Wine, with Salt and Bay Leaves, over a flack Fire; let them cool in the Liquor in which they are boiled, and when you would ufe them, broil and ferve them as in the laft Receipt.

Note, That inftead of Hog's Guts, we often ufe thofe of Sheep, Calves, or Lambs.

Marrow Puddings *in* Skins.

GET the Crumbs of four *French* Rolls, and half a Pound of coarfe Bisket; cut the *French* Rolls in Slices, and put them in an earthen Pan or Sauce-pan; fet over the Fire two Quarts of Milk, make it Blood-warm, pour it over your Bread, and cover it clofe up 'till it is cold, then rub your Bread and Milk through a Colander with a Wooden Ladle. Take a Pound of Marrow and mince it, put to it five Eggs, beaten up very fine, and ftrained thro' a Strainer or Cloth, to keep out the Treads, then mix the Marrow, beaten Eggs and Bread all together. Seafon the
whole

whole with Sugar according to your liking, as you do another Pudding, scrape in half an Nutmeg, add two or three Spoonfuls of Rose Water, a Quarter of a Pound of Almonds, beaten as fine as a Paste, in a Marble Mortar with a little Salt, mix all these Ingredients very fine together, then have small Ox Guts, very well cleaned, and the Insides turned out. Make a small Funnel that will hold a Quarter of a Pint, with a Tail about five Inches long, all of a Wideness, so that it can easily go into the Guts; the Mouth of the Funnel must not be above two Inches deep, because you must thrust your Meat through with your Thumb into the Guts. Cut the Guts a Yard long, and fill them with your Ingredients; tie them in Span long, the two Ends of that Span long tied together: Then tie in the Middle of the Spans to the Ends, so that you will have two Puddings in each Piece; take Care to keep them lank not filling them too full; put them over the Fire in a large brass Dish of Water, and boil them gently a Quarter of an Hour, turning them with your Skimmer that the Marrow rife not to one Side; then take them out, lay them on a Colander 'till cold, but turn them in the cooling. In the Winter they will keep a Week or more, but in the Summer not above three Days or four; therefore, take Care to make your Quantity according to your Occasion. About an Hour before you want them, place them in a Sauce-pan with a little Butter, put them over the Fire 'till they fry as yellow as gold; when one Side is yellow, turn the other down, or you may put them in the Mouth of an Oven. When you serve, cut them asunder. They are proper for a little Dish, or Plate, for a second Course.

They

They will be proper likewife for garnifhing a boiled Pudding or Fricafey of Chickens for the firft Courfe

Almond Puddings *in* Skins.

TAKE two Pounds of Beef Sewet, or Marrow, fhred very fmall, and a Pound and half of Almonds blanched, and beaten very fmall with Rofe Water, one Pound of grated Bread, a Pound and a Quarter of fine Sugar, a little Salt, one Ounce of Mace, Natmeg, and Cinnamon, twelve Yolks of Eggs, four Whites, a Pint of Sack, a Pint and half of thick Cream, fome Rofe or Orange-Flower-Water, boil the Cream, and tie a little Saffron in a Rag, and dip it in the Cream to colour it. Firft beat your Eggs very well, then ftir in your Almonds, then the Spice and Salt, and Sewet, and then mix all your Ingredients together, fill your Guts but half full, put fome Bits of Citron in the Guts as you fill them Tie them up, and boil them about a Quarter of an Hour.

White Puddings *with* Currants

WE take three Pounds of grated Bread to four Pounds of Beef Sewet finely fhred, two Pounds of Currants, Cloves, Mace and Cinnamon, of each half an Ounce beaten fine, a little Salt, a Pound and half of Sugar, a Pint of Sack, a Quart of Cream, a little Rofe Water, twenty Eggs well beaten, but half the Whites; mix all thefe well together, and fill the Guts half full. Boil them a little, and prick them as they boil, to keep them from breaking the Guts. Take them up on clean Cloths.

Black

Black Puddings.

BOIL all the Hog's Harflet in about four or five Gallons of Water 'till 'tis very tender, then take out all the Meat, and in that Liquor fteep near a Peck of Grotts, put in the Grotts as it boils, and let them boil a Quarter of an Hour; then take the Pot off the Fire, and cover it up very clofe, and let it ftand five or fix Hours, chop two or three Handfuls of Thyme, a liltle Savoury, fome Paifley, and Penny-Royal, fome Cloves, and Mace beaten, a Handful of Salt; then mix all thefe with half the Grotts, and two Quarts of Blood; put in moft of the Leaf of the Hog; cut it in fquare Bits like Dice, and fome in long Bits, fill your Guts, and put in the Fat as you like it; fill the Guts three Quarters full, put your Puddings into a Ketttle of boiling Water; let them boil an Hour, and prick them with a Pin to keep them from breaking. Lay them on clean Straw when you take them up.

The other half of the Grotts you may make into white Puddings for the Family; chop all the Meat fmall, and fhred two Handfuls of Sage very fine, an Ounce of Cloves and Mace finely beaten, and fome Salt; work all together very well with a little Flour, and put it into the large Guts, Boil them about an Hour, and keep them and the Black Puddings near the Fire 'till ufed.

Black Puddings *another Way*.

PUT to half a Pint of Oatmeal, eight Pints of new Milk, fteep it all Night, or boil it to the Thicknefs of Pudding; then put to it eight Pints of grated Bread and four Eggs, a little Salt, Cloves and Mace, fome Sage and

Penny-

Penny-Royal, fome Sweet Herbs, mix them together; then take a Pint and a half of Blood, and ftrain it into it, and if it be not foft enough, put in fome more Milk, with half a Pound of Beef Sewet finely fhreded, one Pound and a half of Lard cut into long Pieces; fill them, and give them one Boil, then take them up and prick them with a Pin and put them in again, boiling them enough. You may put Cream inftead of Milk.

For two other Ways of making Black Puddings, *fee* p. 325, 326.

A Florendine.

TAKE two Pounds of Cheefe Curds, a Pound of blanch'd Almonds finely pounded, half a Pound of Currants, a little Rofe Water and Sugar to you Palate; mingle thefe well together, with fome Spinach ftew'd and cut fmall. Lay Puff-pafte on the Top and Bottom of the Difh, and bake it in an Oven moderately heated.

A Florendine *of* Oranges *or* Apples.

CUT half a Dozen of *Seville* Oranges in two, fave the Juice, take out the Pulp and lay them in Water for twenty four Hours, fhift them three or four Times, then boil them in three or four Waters, in the fourth put to them a Pound of fine Sugar and their Juice: Boil them to a Syrup, and let them ftand in this Syrup in an earthen Pot. When you ufe them cut them in thin Slices. To ten Pippins pared, quartered and boiled up in Water and Sugar, put two of thefe Oranges, lay them on your Puff-pafte in a Difh as before.

N° 21.   P p p   *A* Flo-

A Florendine *of* Rice.

BOIL half a Pound of Rice in fair Water 'till it is very tender, then put to it a Quart of Milk or Cream, boil it 'till it is thick, and season it with Sweet Spice and Sugar, beat eight Eggs very well and mix with it   Add to it half a Pound of Currants, half a Pound of Butter, and the Marrow of two Bones, three grated Biskets, Sack and Orange-Flower-Water, having covered your Dish with Puff-paste, put in your Mixture and bake it.

A Florendine Magistral.

CUT thin Slices of a Leg of Veal, like *Scotch* Collops, beat them with a Knife on both Sides, season them with Salt, Pepper, Cloves and Mace. Cut as many thin Slices of fat Bacon, roll them up and put them into your Pye-Dish.   Add two or three Shalots and two or three Anchovies, some Oysters, and forty or fifty Forc'd-Meat Balls, and Lemon par'd and sliced, put in a Quarter of a Pint of Gravy, half a Pint of strong Broth, and half a Pint of White Wine, cover it with Puff-paste and bake it.

A Florendine *of a* Kidney *of* Veal.

YOU must shred the Kidney, Fat and all, with a little Spinach, Parsley, and Lettuce, three Pippins, and some Orange Peel, season with Spice and Sugar, put in a good Handful of Currants, two or three grated Biskets, Canary or Orange-Flower-Water, and two or three Eggs, mix them well together, put them into a Dish covered with Puff-paste, lay on the Lid and garnish the Rim.

A Tanzey.

A Tanzey.

TAKE a Peck of Spinach, and a little Tanzey, and about three Quarters of a Pint of Cream, fifteen Eggs, and take out five of the Whites, and take a small Nutmeg grated, and a Penny Loaf grated, or something more if it be small, and near a Quarter of a Pound of Sugar; strain your Eggs, and sift your Bread, and when you have mix'd all together, butter a Skillet, and set it over a soft Fire, and stir it 'till you think it is pretty thick, then have ready your Frying-pan, over a flow Fire, for fear of burning, with a Bit of Butter melted, and pour in your Tanzey, and stir it all one Way, 'till you think it will be stiff enough, then flat it down close with your Spoon, and let it stand still a little while to grow together, only shake it a little softly, to keep it from scorching, and turn it with a Pie-plate and it will soon be enough.

Another Tanzey.

BEAT ten Eggs very well and put them to a Pint of Cream, season'd with Nutmeg, Sugar and Salt, then green it with Spinach and a Bit of Tanzey, as soon as you put the Juice of the Herbs to it, with which you must make it very green, set it over the Fire, the Skillet being first butter'd, and when it is thickened enough, have a Dish ready to put it in, and bake it.

Another Tanzey.

GRATE half a Pound of Naples Biskets, then take eighteen Eggs, half the Whites, one Nutmeg grated, put the Sugar to the Eggs, and strain it to your Bisket;

with

with four or five Spoonfuls of Sack, and half a Pint of
Cream, then colour it with the Juice of Spinach, or green
Wheat, and a little Tanzey, then take a Sauce-pan and
butter it well, and put your Tanzey in it and keep it ftirring over Charcoal or Wood-Coal, 'till it be very thick,
then have a Difh juft big enough for it, and that muft be
butter'd every where, or it will ftick and melt the Difh,
then put your Stuff in the Difh over the Coals, with a gentle Fire, not to bubble, but to harden; cover it with a But-
ter-pan, and when it is enough turn it on the Plate, and
fet that on the Coals.   When it is enough, ferve it up with
Orange quarter'd, and ftrew'd Sugar.

Another Tanzey.

TAKE nine Eggs, but half the Whites, and beat
them well together, put refin'd Sugar to them, and
ftrain it, then add half a Pint of Cream, and as much
Juice of Spinach, or Wheat, as will colour it; with a little Tanzey, two Naples Biskets grated, a Nutmeg, and
fix Spoonfuls of Sack, let the Biskets foak fome time; then
take your Sauce-pan, and put in fome Butter, and warm it
over the Fire, and do it round the Sauce-pan, then put in
the Stuff and ftir it over a Charcoal Fire, when it is thick
enough, put it into a Difh that will juft hold it, and cover
it with a Plate, and put it over your Stoves, not to boil, but
harden.   When you think it is ftiff enough, turn it on the
Plate and ferve it.

White

White Pot.

TAKE three Pints of new Milk, or Cream, the Yolks of five Eggs, two Whites, beat your Eggs with a little Rose Water, Nutmeg, two or three Spoonfuls of white Sugar, slice half a white Loaf very thin in the Milk, and when 'tis a little steeped, break it with your Hands, then put in your beaten Eggs and break it a little more; then put in a little Bit of Sweet Butter on the Top, or Marrow if you please, scatter a few Raisins on the Top, you may put Puff-paste round the Dish. Bake it half an Hour in a slow Oven.

A Rice White Pot.

BOIL a Pound of Rice in two Quarts of Milk, 'till it is tender and thick, then beat it well in a Mortar with a Quarter of a Pound of blanch'd Almonds, then boil two Quarts of Cream with Crumb of white Bread and Blades of Mace, mix all together with the Yolks of eight Eggs, some Rose Water, and sweeten it with Sugar to your Palate, cut some candy'd Orange and Citron Peels thin and lay it in when it is in the Oven. Let not the Oven be too hot, for if it be it will soon spoil.

Pancakes

GET two Quarts of fine Flour, and half a dozen Eggs, leaving out half the Whites, season it with Cinnamon, Cloves, Mace, Nutmeg, and a little Salt, make it into a Batter with Milk, beat and mix it all together, and put in half a Pint of Sack, put your Pan on the Fire with some Butter, and when it is hot, put in your Batter, and run it

thin

thin over the Bottom of your Pan, supplying it with little Bits of Butter; tofs it very often, and bake it crifp and brown.

Pancakes Royal.

HAving half a Pint of Cream, half a Pint of Sack, the Yolks of eighteen Eggs, and half a Pound of fine Sugar, feaſon it with beaten Cinnamon, Nutmeg and Mace, beat and mix all thefe; then put in as much Flour as will make it ftiff enough to run thin over your Pan, let your Pan be hot, and fry them in clarify'd Butter. This Sort of Pancakes will not be crifp, but are very good.

Another Sort of Pancakes.

TAKE a Pint of Cream, and eight Eggs, Whites and all, a whole Nutmeg grated, and a little Salt, then melt a Pound of rare Difh Butter, and a little Sack: Before you fry them, ftir it in, it muft be made as thick with three Spoonfuls of Flour, as ordinary Batter, and fried with Butter in the Pan, the firft Pancake but no more: Strew Sugar; garnifh with Orange, turn it on the Back-fide of a Plate.

Rice Pancakes.

HAving a Quart of Cream, and three Spoonfuls of Flour of Rice, boil it 'till it is as thick as Pap, and as it boils, ftir in half a Pound of Butter, a Nutmeg grated, then pour it out into an earthen Pan, and when it is cold, put in three or four Spoonfuls of Flour, a little Salt, fome Sugar, nine Eggs well beaten, mix all well together, and fry them in a little Pan, with a fmall Piece of Butter. Serve them up four or five in a Difh.

To make fine Pancakes *fried without Butter or Lard.*

TAKE a Pint of Cream, and fix new laid Eggs; beat them very well together, put in a Quarter of a Pound of Sugar, one Nutmeg, or a little beaten Mace, and fo much Flour as will thicken all as much as ordinary Pancake-Batter: Your Pan muft be heated reafonably hot, and wiped with a clean Cloth, that done, put in your Batter as thick or thin as you pleafe.

Fritters.

WE take of the fineft Flour well dried before the Fire, mix it with a Quart of new Milk, not too thick, fix or eight Eggs, a little Nutmeg and Mace, a little Salt, Sack or Ale, beat them well together, make it pretty thick with Pippins, fo fry them dry.

Another Sort

PUT to half a Pint of thick fweet Cream, four Eggs well beaten, a little Brandy, fome Nutmeg and Ginger, make this into a thick Batter with Flour Your Apples muft be Golden-Pippins, pared and cut in thin Slices, dip them in the Batter, and fry them in Lard: It will take up two Pounds of Lard to fry this Quantity.

Apple Fritters.

BEAT the Yolks of eight Eggs, the Whites of four, well together, and ftrain them into a Pan, then take a Quart of Cream, warm it as hot as you can indure your Finger in it; then put to it a Quarter of a Pint of Sack, three Quarters of a Pint of Ale, and make a Poffet of it, when your Poffet is cool, put to it your Eggs, beating them well

well together, then put in Nutmeg, Ginger, Salt, and Flour to your liking: Your Batter should be pretty thick; then put in Pippins sliced or scraped; fry them in good Store of hot Lard with a quick Fire.

Curd Fritters.

HAving a Handful of Curds, and a Handful of Flour, and ten Eggs well beaten and strained, some Sugar, and some Cloves, Mace, and Nutmeg, a little Saffron, stir all well together, and fry them in very hot Beef Dripping, drop them in the Pan by Spoonfuls, stir them about 'till they are of a fine Yellow-brown; drain hem from the Sewet, and scrape Sugar on them, when you serve them up.

Fritters Royal.

YOU must take a Pint of Sack, make a Posset with new Milk, then take the Curd from the Posset, and put it into a Bason, with half a Dozen Eggs, season it with a little Nutmeg, beat it with a Wisk very well together, adding Flour to make it as thick as Batter usually is for that Purpose; put in some fine Sugar, and fry it in clarify'd Beef Sewet; make it hot in the Pan before you put it in: Serve it for a Side-Dish, or a second Course Dish.

Skirret Fritters.

WE take a Pint of the Pulp of Skirrets, and a Spoonful of Flour, the Yolks of Eggs, Sugar and Spice; make it into a thick Batter, then fry them out in Fritters, and serve them for a Side-Dish.

White

White Fritters.

HAving some Rice, wash it in five or six several Waters, then dry it very well before the Fire: After this pound it well in a Mortar, and sift it through a Lawn Sieve, that it may be very fine, you must have at least an Ounce of it. Then put it into a Sauce-pan, and wet it with Milk, and when it is well incorporated with it, add to it another Pint of Milk, set the whole over a Stove, and take Care to keep it always moving: We likewise put to it the Breast of a roasted Pullet, minced very small, a little Sugar, some candied Lemon Peel grated, and keep it over the Fire 'till it is almost come to the Thickness of a fine Paste. Flour a Peel very well, pour it out upon it, and spread it abroad with your Rolling-pin: When it is quite cold, cut it in little Morsels, taking Care that they stick not to one another; flour your Hands, roll up your Fritters very handsomely, and fry them in Hog's Lard. When you are going to serve, put to them a little Orange-Flower-Water; and strew some Sugar upon them; so serve in Plates or little Dishes: They may sometimes be used for garnishing.

Water Fritters.

PUT into a Sauce-pan some Water, a Bit of Butter as big as a Walnut, a little Salt, and some candied Lemon-Peel, minced very small. Make this boil over a Stove, then put in two good Handfuls of Flour, and turn it about by main Strength, 'till the Water and Flour be well mixed together, and none of the last stick to the Sauce-pan; then take it off the Stove, put into it the Yolks of two Eggs,

Q q q   mix

mix them well with it, continuing to put in more Eggs by two and two at a Time, 'till you have put in ten or twelve, and your Paste be very fine. Then drudge a Peel thick with Flour and dipping your Hand into Flour, take out your Paste Bit by Bit, and lay it on the Peel; when it has lain a little while, roll it, and cut it into Little Pieces, taking Care that they stick not to one another, a little before you are going to serve, fry them in Hog's Lard, and when you have laid them in the Dish, throw some Sugar and Orange-Flower-Water upon them and serve them in Plates or little Dishes.

We make Broth Fritters the same Way, only make use of Broth instead of Water.

Syringed Fritters.

TAKE about a Pint of Water, and a Bit of Butter, the Bigness of an Egg, with some green Lemon Peel rasp'd, preserved Lemon Peel, and crisp'd Orange-Flowers, put all together in a Stew-pan, over the Fire, and when boiling, throw in some fine Flour, keep it stirring, put in it by Degrees more Flour 'till your Batter be thick enough. Then put it in a Mortar with Almonds pounded, or Bitter Almonds, Biskets, two Eggs, Yolk and White: Temper it with Eggs farther, 'till your Batter be thin enough to be syringed. Fill your Syringe, and your Hog's Lard being hot, syringe your Fritters in it, to make of it a true Lover's Knot; and being well coloured, strew them with Sugar, serve them up hot for a dainty Dish.

At another Time you may rub a Sheet of Paper with Butter, over which you syringe your Fritters, and make them in what Shape you please, and your Hog's Lard
being

being hot, turn the Paper upside down over it, and your Fritters will eafily drop off. When fried ftrew them with Sugar and glaze them.

Vine Leaf Fritters.

TA K E the fmalleft Vine Leaves you can get, and having cut off the great Stalk, put them in a Difh with fome *French* Brandy, green Lemon rafped and fome Sugar. Put in a Stew-pan a good Handful of fine Flour, mixed with fome White Wine or Beer : Then put in your Vine Leaves, and fry them immediately, place one after another in the Hog's Lard, fee they do not ftick together. Let them be pretty well coloured when fried and ftrewed with Sugar and glazed with a red hot Fire-fhovel.

A Fraze *with* Pippins.

CU T eight Pippins in pretty thick Slices, and fry them in Hog's Lard, or clarify'd Butter; when they are tender, lay them on a Sieve to drain the Fat from them, then take four Eggs, keeping out two Whites, beat them up with fome Flour, half a Pint of Cream, a little Salt and fome Sugar; then put into your Batter a little Butter; fry half of it at a Time, and when it is fried a little, put your fried Pippins thick all over it. When enough, fry the other alfo, fo ferve them on fmall Difhes, ftrew'd over with fome good Sugar.

Another Pippin Fraze.

YO U muft pare a Dozen Pippins, cut them in thick Slices, and fry them in clarified Butter; when they are tender, lay them to drain, keep them as whole as you

can;

can; then make a Batter as follows: Take five Eggs, leaving out two Whites, beat them up with Cream and Flour, a little Salt, some Sack and Sugar; make it the Thickness of Pancake-Batter, and put in melted Butter; pour half your Batter into your Pan, and place your Apples all over it, then pour in the other half of your Batter; bake it thoroughly, and of a fine Colour; strew over it some double refined Sugar, and serve it.

An Almond Fraze.

GET a Pound of Jordan Almonds, blanch them, and steep them in a Pint of sweet Cream, ten Yolks of Eggs and four Whites, having beat your Almonds in a Stone Mortar, put in Sugar and grated White Bread, stir them well together; fry them with good Butter, keeping them stirring in the Pan 'till they are of a good Thickness, and when it is done enough, strew over it good fine Sugar, and serve it.

Black Caps.

HAving twelve good Apples, cut them in two, and take out the Cores; place them on a Tin Patty-pan, with their Skins on, put to them four Spoonfuls of Water, and scrape double refin'd Sugar over them: Set them in a hot Oven 'till the Skins are black a little in the Middle, and the Apples tender, which will be in about three Quarters of an Hour, and dish them up: Scrape a little fine Sugar over them again.

Pain-

Pain-Perdu, *or* Cream Toasts.

HAving two *French* Rolls, cut them in Slices, as thick as your Finger, Crumb and Cruft together, lay them on a Difh, put to them a Pint of Cream, and half a Pint of Milk, ftrew them over with beaten Cinnamon and Sugar, turn them frequently 'till they are tender; but take Care not to break them, then take them from the Cream, with a Slice, break four or five Eggs, turn your Slices of Bread in the Eggs, and fry them in clarified Butter, make them of a good brown Colour, not black; fcrape a little Sugar on them.

They may be ferved as a fecond Courfe Difh, but fitteft for Supper.

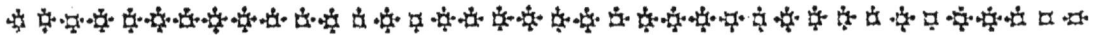

❖ ❖❖❖ ❖❖❖❖❖❖❖ ❖❖❖ ❖❖ ❖ ❖❖❖ ❖❖❖ ❖❖❖ ❖ ❖❖❖❖❖❖❖ ❖ ❖ ❖❖ ❖ ❖❖ ❖❖❖❖❖ ❑ ❑

C H A P XXIV.

Of P A S T R Y.

Puff-pafte.

LAY down a Pound of Flour, break into it two Ounces of Butter and two Eggs; then make it into Pafte with cold Water, then work the other Part of the Pound of Butter to the Stiffnefs of your Pafte; then roll out your Pafte into a fquare Sheet: Stick it all over with Bits of Butter, flour it, and roll it up like a Collar; double it up at both Ends that they meet in the Middle, roll it out again as aforefaid, 'till all the Pound of Butter is in.

Pafte

Paſte *for a* Paſty.

LAY down a Peck of Flour, work it up with ſix Pounds of Butter and four Eggs, with cold Water.

Paſte *for a high* Pye.

LAY down a Peck of Flour, and work it up with three Pounds of Butter melted in a Sauce-pan or boiling Liquor, and make it into a ſtiff Paſte.

Paſte Royal *for* Patty-pans.

LAY down a Pound of Flour and work it up with half a Pound of Butter, two Ounces of fine Sugar and four Eggs.

Paſte *for a* Cuſtard.

LAY down Flour and make it into a ſtiff Paſte, with boiling Water, ſprinkle it with cold Water to keep it from craking.

P I E S.

A ſavoury Lamb Pie.

SEASON your Lamb with Pepper, Salt, Cloves, Mace and Nutmeg; ſo put it into your Coffin with a few Lamb's Stones and Sweetbreads, ſeaſoned as your Lamb, alſo ſome large Oyſters, and ſavoury Forc'd-Meat-Balls, hard Yolks of Eggs, and the Tops of Aſparagus two Inches long, firſt boiled green; then put Butter all over the Pie, and lid it, and ſet it in a quick Oven an Hour and an half, then make the Liquor with Oyſter Liquor, as much Gravy,

Gravy, a little Claret, with one Anchovy in it, a grated Nutmeg. Let thefe have a Boil, thicken it with the Yolks of two or three Eggs, and when the Pie is drawn pour it in.

Another Sort.

AFTER you have cut your Hind-Quarter of Lamb into thin Slices, feafon it with favoury Spice and lay them into the Pie, alfo lay in an hard Lettuce, Artichoke Bottoms, and the Tops of an hundred of Afparagus, lay Butter over them. Clofe up the Pie, bake it, and when it comes out of the Oven pour in a Lear.

A sweet Lamb Pie.

AFTER cutting your Lamb into fmall Pieces, feafon it with a little Salt, Cloves, Mace and Nutmeg: Your Pie being made, put in your Lamb or Veal, ftrew on it fome ftoned Raifins, Currants, and fome Sugar, then lay on it fome Forced-Meat-Balls made fweet, and in the Summer fome Artichoke Bottoms boiled, and fcalded Grapes in the Winter Boil *Spanifh* Potatoes cut in Pieces, candy'd Citron, candy'd Orange and Lemon Peel, and three or four large Blades of Mace; put Butter on the Top; clofe up your Pie and bake it. Make the Caudle of White Wine, Juice of Lemon and Sugar, thicken it up with the Yolks of two or three Eggs, and a Bit of Butter, and when your Pie is baked, pour in the Caudle as hot as you can, and fhake it well in the Pie and ferve it up.

A Mutton

A Mutton Pie.

GET a Loin of Mutton, *&c.* cut it into Steaks, feason them with favoury Spice, lay them in the Pie,
and put on fome Butter clofe it, bake it, and when it
comes out of the Oven, chop a Handful of Capers, Cucumbers and Oyfters, in Gravy, an Anchovy and drawn
Butter, and put it in.

A Veal Pie.

AFTER cutting the beft Part of a Leg of Veal into thin Slices, beat it with a Rolling-pin, feafon them
with Salt, Pepper, Cloves, and Mace, then cut a Pound
of Bacon into thin Slices, roll them up one by one, with a
Slice of Veal in the Middle; then put them in a Difh,
with two or three Anchovies, two Shalots, a few Oyfters,
fome Forced-Meat-Balls, and a fliced Lemon with the
Peel off, add half a Pint of White Wine, half a Pint of
good Broth, fome Gravy and Butter; cover it with Puff-
pafte, and bake it in a gentle Oven.

Another Sort.

AFTER cutting a Fillet of Veal into three Pieces,
feafon it with Pepper, Salt, Spice and Herbs; raife
your Pie, and cover the Bottom of it with Forced-Meat;
then lay in your Veal, and Sweetbreads round it, with
fome Afparagus Tops, Mufhrooms, Truffles, and pounded Bacon; then lid your Pie, and bake it; cut it open juft
before you ferve it, skim off all the Fat, and pour in a good
Cullis of Veal.

A Lamb

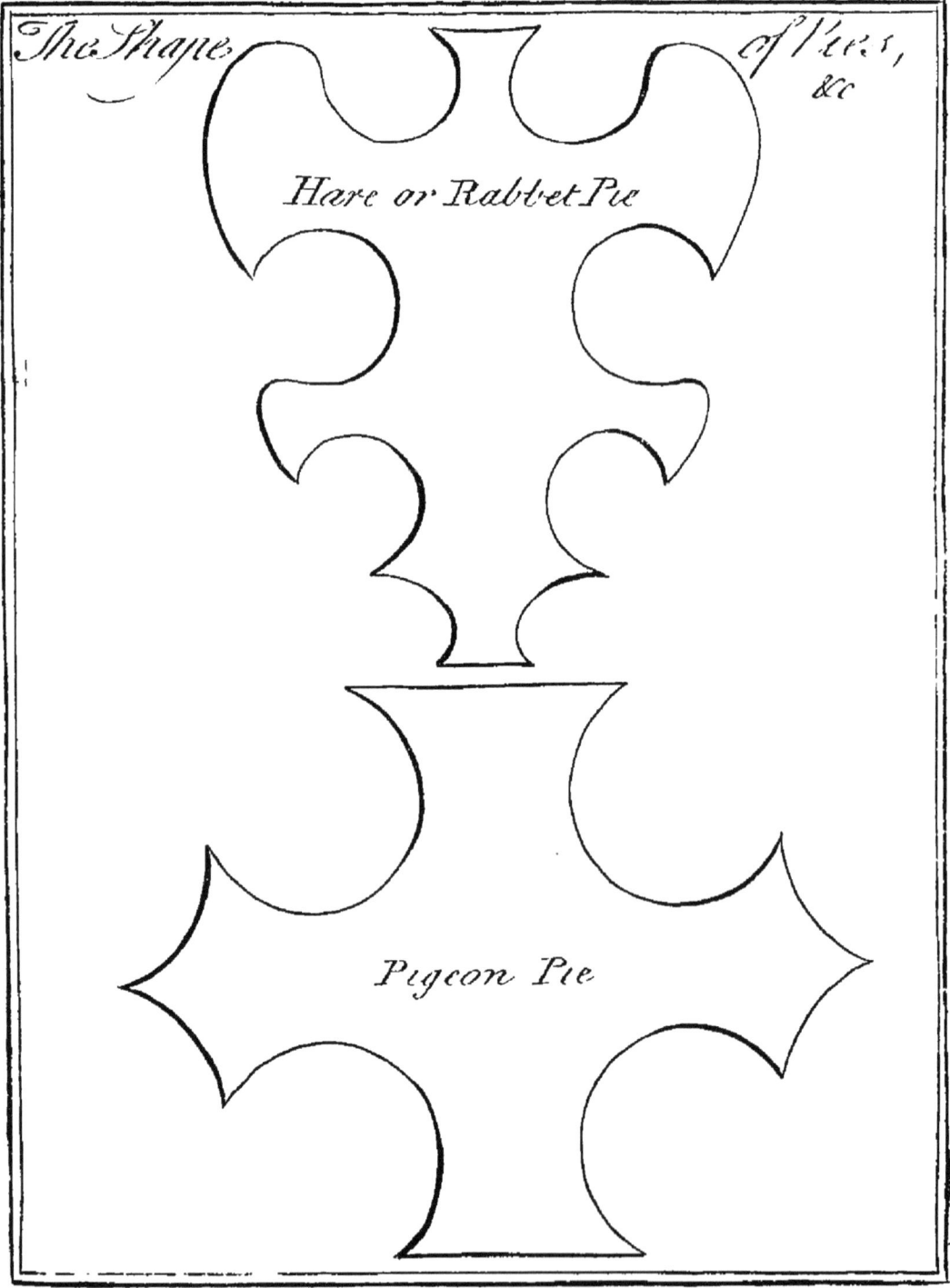

Hare or Rabbet Pie

Pigeon Pie

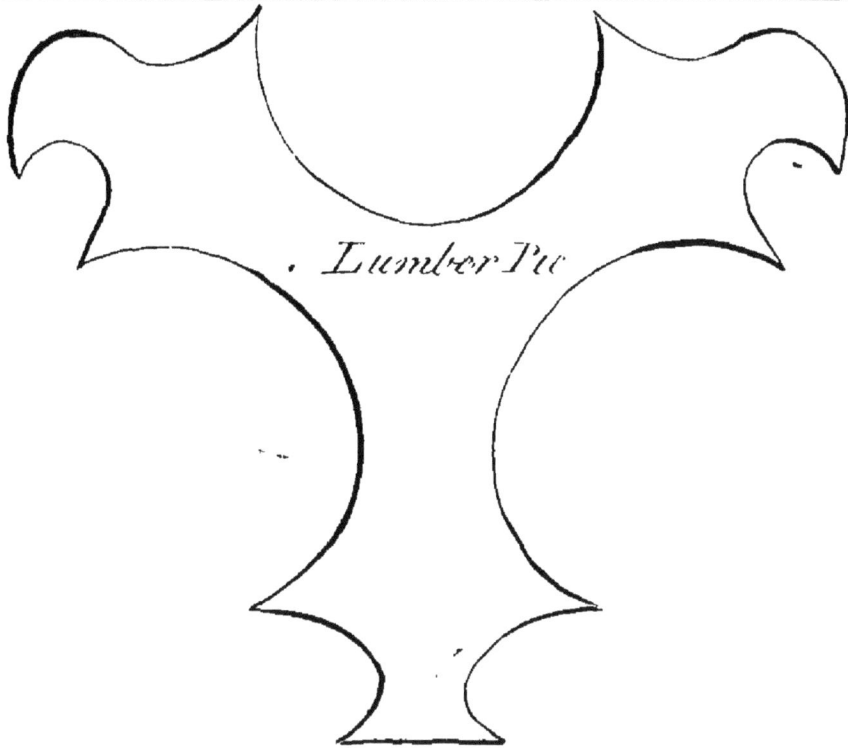

Lumber Pie

Giblet Hen or Mutton Pie

Calves Head Pie

Chicken Pie

Wild Foul Pie

Swan Turky or Goose Pie

Set   Custards

Mincd Pies

Pear Pie high
Apple Pie low

Minc'd Pies

Lamb or Veal Pie

Neats Tongue Pie

Egg   Pies

Florendines
and
Tarts
Pasteys

Lamb Pastey

Wild Boar Pie

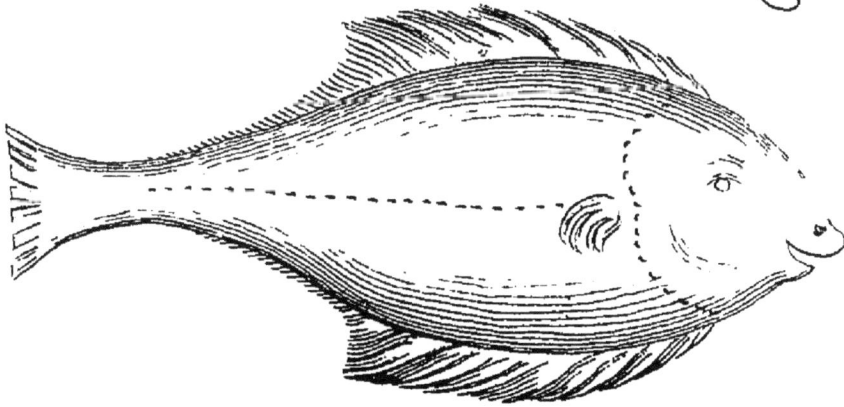

A Lamb Pie *the* German *Way.*

CUT a Quarter of Lamb in Pieces, and lard them with small Lardoons, season them with Salt, Pepper, Nutmeg, Cloves, Bay Leaf, pounded Bacon, Cives and favoury Herbs, put them into Paste, and bake them three Hours: Then draw your Pie, cut it open, take off all the Fat, pour into it a Ragoo of Oysters, and serve it hot for the first Course.

A Veal Pasty.

WE take a Quarter of a Peck of fine Flour, and a Pound of Butter, break the Butter into Bits, put in Salt and half an Egg, and as much cold Cream or Milk as will make it into a Paste : Make your Sheet of Paste, bone a Breast of Veal, season it with Salt and Pepper. Lay Butter in the Bottom of your Paste, lay in your Veal. Put in whole Mace, and a Lemon sliced thin, Rind and all ; cover it with Butter, close it up and bake it ; when it comes out of the Oven cut it up, heat some White Wine, Butter, the Yolks of Eggs and Sugar. Pour this into the Pasty and serve it up.

A Dowlet Pie.

PArboil or roast your Veal, then cut it small with Sweet Herbs, and Beef Sewet ; then put some into it seasoned with Sugar, Nutmeg and Cinnamon if you like it ; then beat as many Eggs as will wet it, then make it like Eggs, and stick a Date in the Middle of each of them, and lay them in a Pie, and put some dried Plumbs over them, and if in the Time of Year, put in ripe Plumbs,

R r r   then

then take White Wine, Sugar and Butter, and pour it in a little before you draw it; scald the Wine, and give it a Shake or two together; so serve it.

A Steak Pie, *with a* French Pudding *in it.*

SEASON your Steaks with Pepper and Nutmeg, and let 'em stand an Hour in a Tray, then take a Piece of the leanest of a Leg of Mutton, and mince it small with Sewet and a few Sweet Herbs, Tops of young Thyme, a Branch of Penny-royal, two or three of red Sage, grated Bread, Yolks of Eggs, sweet Cream, and Raisins of the Sun; work all together stiff with your Hand like a Pudding, roll them round like Balls, and put them into the Steaks in a deep Coffin with a Piece of sweet Butter; sprinkle a little Verjuice on it, bake the Pie and cut it up: Afterwards, having rolled Sage Leaves, fry them, and stick them upright in the Walls; and serve your Pie without a Lid, with the Juice of an Orange or Lemon.

Calves Foot Pie.

YOUR Calves Feet must be boiled, cut into Halves and clear'd from the Bones: That done, you are to lay a Layer of Butter in the Bottom of the Pie; then a Layer of Calves Feet; upon that, Raisins of the Sun ston'd and cut small; over those, another Layer of Calves Feet, then Raisins of the Sun order'd as before, with Currants, Orange, Lemon and Citron Peel sliced thin, a few beaten Cloves, Mace, Nutmeg, a little fine Sugar and Salt: Afterwards the Yolks of six boil'd Eggs are to be chopp'd and strew'd on the Top, with a Layer of Butter.

To

To make a Calf's Chaldron-pie.

GET a Calf's Chaldron, parboil it and set it by to cool; when 'tis cold, chop it very fine with half a Pound of Marrrow; season it with Salt, beaten Cloves, Mace, Nutmeg, a little Onion and Lemon-Peel shred small; add also the Juice of half a Lemon, and mingle all together. Then make a Piece of Puff-paste, and lay a Leaf of it in a silver Dish of a convenient Bigness; put in your Meat, cover it with another Leaf of the same Paste, and bake it: As soon as it is drawn, open it and squeeze in the Juice of two or three Oranges; stir all well together, cover your Pie again, and let it be serv'd up.

A Calf's Head Pie.

BOIL your Calf's Head, 'till you can take out all the Bones, slice it into thin Slices and lay it in the Pie, with the Ingredients for savoury Pies.

Another Sort.

CLEANSE and wash the Head well, boil it for three Quarters of an Hour, cut off the Flesh in Bits, of the Bigness of Walnuts, blanch the Tongue and slice it: Parboil a Quart of Oysters and beard them; take the Yolks of ten or twelve Eggs: Intermix some thin Slices of Bacon with Meat; put an Onion, cut small in the Bottom of the Pie, seasoning it with Salt, Pepper, Nutmeg, and Mace; lay also Butter on the Bottom, put in your Meat, close up the Pie, and put in a little Water; when it is baked take off the Lid; take off the Fat, and put in a Lear of thick Butter, Mutton Gravy, a Lemon pared and sliced,

with

with two or three Anchovies diffolved. Let them firft ftew together a little while, cut the Lid in handfome Pieces, lay it round the Pie and ferve it up.

A Lumber Pie.

GET a Pound and half of Veal, juft fcalded; mince it very fmall, with Beef Sewet the like Quantity, then take fome grated Bread, fome Mace, Nutmeg, Cinnamon, and Sugar, Rofe Water, Eggs and Currants, then fill your Pie, laying fome Marrow, Sweetmeats, and Lemon; then lid your Pie; and when it's bak'd, make a Caudle with White Wine, and the Yolks of two Eggs, and fweeten'd with Sugar. You muft be fure to put in Marrow enough.

Another Way.

HAving a Pound and an half of a Fillet of Veal, mince it with the fame Quantity of Beef Sewet; feafon it with Mace, Nutmeg, Sugar, Cinnamon and Salt; five Pippins fliced, a Handful of Spinach and a hard Lettuce, Thyme and Parfley; mix it well with a Penny white Loaf grated, the Yolks of three Eggs, a little Sack and Orange-Flower-Water, a Pound and an half of Currants, with what Preferves you pleafe, and a Caudle.

Another Way.

GET a Pound and an half of Veal, parboil it, and when it is cold, chop it very fmall, with two Pounds of Beef Sewet, and fome candied Orange Peel; fome Sweet Herbs, as Thyme, Sweet Marjoram, and a Handful of Spinach; mince the Herbs fmall before you put

them

them to the other : So chop all together, and a Pippin or two ; then add a Handful or two of grated Bread, a Pound and an half of Currants, wafhed and dried, fome Cloves, Mace, Nutmeg, a little Salt, Sugar and Sack, and put to all thefe as many Yolks of raw Eggs and Whites of two as will make it a moift Forced-Meat, work it with your Hands into a Body, and make it into Balls as big as a Turkey's Egg ; then having your Coffin made, put in your Balls. Take the Marrow out of three or four Bones as whole as you can : Let your Marrow lie a little in Water to take out the Blood and Splinters, then dry it and dip it in Yolks of Eggs, feafon it with a little Salt, Nutmeg grated, and gratted Bread, lay it on and between your Forc'd-Meat-Balls, and over that, fliced Citron, candied Orange and Lemon, Eringoe-Roots preferved, Barberries, then lay on fliced Lemon, and thin Slices of Butter over all, then lid your Pie, and bake it, and when it is drawn, have in Readinefs a Caudle made of White Wine and Sugar, and thickened with Butter and Eggs, and pour it hot into your Pie.

A Stump Pie.

WE take a Leg of Lamb from the Bones, and mince it fmall with a good Quantity of Sweet Herbs, and a good Quantity of Currants, grated Nutmeg and Salt ; feafon it to your liking, and mix it with two or three Yolks of Eggs, beat with Sack or White Wine ; then lay it clofe in the Pie, and lay on the Top either Fruit or Sweetmeats ; do not bake it too much, and when it is baked cut it up, and put in Verjuice and Sugar, or White Wine, make it hot before you put it in, then lay on the Lid, and ferve it.

An

An Umble Pie.

GET the Umbles of a Deer, parboil them, clear off all the Fat from them, take fomething more than the Weight of Beef Sewet, and fhred it together; then add half a Pound of Sugar, feafon with Salt, Cloves, Mace and Nutmeg; add half a Pint of Claret, a Pint of Canary, and two Pounds of Currants wafhed and picked, mix all well together, and bake them in Puff or other Pafte.

A Battalia Pie.

YOU muft take four tame Pigeons truffed, and four Ox-Palates well boiled, blanched and cut into fmall Pieces, alfo fix Lambs Stones, as many good Veal Sweetbreads, cut in halves and parboiled, twenty Cocks-Combs boiled and blanched, the Bottoms of four Artichokes, a Pint of Oyfters parboiled and bearded, and the Marrow of three Bones, feafoning all with Mace, Nutmeg and Salt: Afterwards lay your Meat in a Coffin of fine Pafte proportionable to the Quantity thereof; put half a Pound of Butter upon it, and a little Water into the Pie, before it be fet in the Oven: Let it ftand in the Oven an Hour and a half; then having drawn it, pour out the Butter at the Top of the Pie, and put into it a Lear of Gravy, Butter, and Lemons, and ferve it up.

Another Way.

TAKE young Chickens, fquab Pigeons, young Partridges, Quails and Larks; trufs them, and lay them in the Pie, take Ox-Palates, boil them, blanch them, and cut them in Pieces, Sweetbreads and Lamb Stones, cut
them

them in Halves or Quarters, Cocks-Combs blanched, a Pint or Quart of Oysters dredged over with grated Bread and Marrow; add Sheeps Tongues boiled, blanched and cut in Pieces, beat Pepper, Salt, Cloves, Mace and Nutmeg all together, season with this. Lay Butter on the Bottom of the Pie, and place the rest in with the Yolks of hard Eggs, Knots of Eggs, Cocks Stones and Treads and Forced-Meat-Balls. Cover up the Pie, and when you set it into the Oven, put in five or six Spoonfuls of Water, and when it comes out of the Oven, pour it out and put in Gravy.

Another Way.

YOU must take two small Chickens, two squab Pigeons, two sucking Rabbits, cut them in Pieces, season them with savoury Spice, and lay them in the Pie; add two Sweetbreads sliced, two Sheeps Tongues, a shivered Palate, a Pair of Lamb's Stones, ten or fifteen Cocks-Combs, with savoury Balls and Oysters. Lay on Butter and close the Pie. Put a Lear in it.

A Cheshire Pork-Pie.

YOU must take some salt Loin of Pork, or of the Leg, and cut it into Pieces like Dice, or as you would do for an Harsh. If it be boiled or roasted it is no Matter, then take an equal Quantity of Potatoes, and pare them, and cut them into Dice, or in Slices. Make your Pie-Crust, and lay some Butter in Pieces, at the Bottom, with some Pepper and Salt; then put in your Meat and Potatoes, with such Seasoning as you like, but Pepper and Salt commonly, and on the Top some Pieces of Butter

Then close your Pie, and bake it in a gentle Oven, putting in about a Pint of Water, just before it is going into the Oven; for if you put in your Water over Night, it will spoil your Pie.

A Devonshire Squab-Pie.

HAving sheeted a Dish with Puff-paste, put at the Bottom a Layer of sliced Pippins with some Sugar; upon that put a Layer of Mutton Steaks, cut from the Loin well seasoned with Pepper and Salt, strew some more Slices of Pippins upon that, and over them strew some Onions, shred small; repeat these 'till your Pie is full to the Top, then close it, having put in about half a Pint of Water, and bake it.

A Shropshire Pie

CUT a couple of Rabbits into Pieces, season them well with Pepper and Salt; then cut some Pieces of fat Pork, and season them in like Manner. Lay these into your Crust, with some Pieces of Butter, upon the Bottom Crust, and close your Pie. Then pour in half a Pint of Water and Red Wine mix'd, and bake it. Some will grate the best Part of a Nutmeg upon the Meat, before they close the Pie, which is a good Way. It must be served hot.

Another Way.

YOU must take Rabbits and Pork, cut and seasoned as above; then make a Farce of the Rabbits Livers, parboiled, and shred small; some fat Bacon shred small, some sweet Marjoram powdered, some Pepper and Salt,

and

and made into a Pafte, with the Yolks of Eggs beaten; and then make this into Balls, and lay them in your Pye, amongft the Meat at proper Diftances. Then take the Bottoms of three or four Aitichokes boiled tender and cut in Dice; and lay thefe likewife amongft the Meat · Put in alfo fome Cocks-Combs blanch'd; then clofe your Pye, and pour in as much Wine and Water as you think convenient. Bake it and ferve it hot.

A Venifon Pye.

WHEN you have raifed a high Pye, fhred a Pound of Beef Sewet and lay it in the Bottom, cut the Venifon in Pieces and feafon it with Pepper and Salt, lay it on the Sewet, lay Butter on the Venifon, clofe up the Pye and let it ftand in the Oven for fix Hours.

A Venifon Pafty.

LAY down half a Peck of Flour, put to it four Pounds of Butter, beat eight Eggs, and make the Pafte with warm Water; bone the Venifon, break the Bones, feafon them with Salt and Pepper and boil them, with this fill up the Pafty when it comes out of the Oven: Take a Pound of Beef Sewet, cut it into long Slices, ftrew Pepper and Salt upon it; lay the Venifon in, feafoned pretty high with Salt and black Pepper bruis'd, fet Pudding Cruft round the Infide of the Pafty, and put in about three Quarters of a Pint of Water: Lay on a Layer of frefh Butter and cover it. When it comes out of the Oven, pour in the Liquor you have made of the Bones boiled, and fhake all well together.

Another Venison Pasty.

HAving six Pounds of potted *Cambridge* Butter, rub it into a Peck of Flour, but do not rub in your Butter too small, then make it into a Paste with warm Water: Then butter your Pan well, and when your Paste is rolled out thick, lay it in the Pasty-pan, preserving only enough for the Lid. The *Cambridge* Butter is mentioned, because it is a little salt, or else, if you use fresh Butter, there should be some Salt put in the Paste. When that is prepared take a Side of Venison, and take off the Skin, as close as can be, and take the Bones out quite free from the Flesh, then cut this through length-ways, and cut it cross again, to make four Pieces of it, then strew these Pieces with Pepper and Salt, well mix'd, at Discretion. And after having laid a little of the Pepper and Salt at the Bottom of the Pasty, with some Pieces of Butter; then lay in your Pieces of Venison, so that at each Corner the Fat may be placed; then lay some Butter over it, in Pieces, and close your Pasty. When it is ready for the Oven, pour in about a Quart of Water, and let it bake from five o' Clock in the Morning 'till one, or from six 'till two in the Afternoon, in a hot Oven: And at the same Time, put the Skin, and Bones broken, with Water enough to cover them, and some Salt and Pepper in a glazed earthen Pan, into the same Oven, and when you draw the Pasty, pour off as much as you think proper, of the clear Liquor, to put into your Pasty. Serve it hot: It is properly a Dish for the Side-Board, and the Carver ought always to take the Services of the Pasty from the Corners where the Fat is, to do Honour to the Master and his Park.

A Kid

A Kid Pye.

CUT your Kid in Pieces, free from Bones, and lard it with Bacon; feafon it with Pepper and Salt, Nutmeg, Cloves and Mace, lay on Butter according to the Bignefs of your Pye, and clofe it. When it is baked, take a Quart of *Melton* Oyfters, well dry'd, and fry them brown, tofs them up in half a Pint of White Wine, the Oyfter Liquor, fome Gravy, and Barberries, thicken it with Eggs and drawn Butter; cut up the Lid, and pour it into the Pye.

A Green-Goofe Pye.

BONE two fat Green-Geefe, and feafon them to your liking with Nutmeg, Mace, Pepper, and Salt, lay them on each other, and fill the Sides with young Rabbits, bake them well, and eat them hot or cold.

A Goofe Pye.

PArboil your Goofe, and bone it, feafon it with Salt and Pepper, and put it into a deep Cruft, with a good Quantity of Butter both under and over. Let it be well baked, fill it up at the vent Hole with melted Butter. Serve it up with Bay Leaves, Muftard and Sugar.

A Giblet Pye.

LET the Goofe Giblets be fcalded and well picked, then fet them over the Fire with juft Water enough to cover them, feafoning them pretty high with Salt, Pepper, an Onion, and a Bunch of Sweet Herbs. When they are ftewed very tender, take them out of the Liquor and

fet

set them by to cool: Afterwards they are to be put into a standing Pye, or into a Pan with good Puff-paste round it, a convenient Quantity of Butter, and the Yolks of hard Eggs: Balls of Forced-Meat may also be laid over them, leaving a Hole on the Top of the Lid, to pour in half the Liquor the Giblets were stewed in, just before your Pye is set in the Oven.

A Pigeon Pye.

TRUSS and season your Pigeons with Pepper, Salt, and Nutmeg, lard them with Bacon, and stuff them with Forced-Meats, lay on Lambs Stones, Sweetbreads, and Butter, and close the Pye; pour in Liquor made of Claret, Gravy, Oyster Liquor, two Anchovies, a Faggot of Sweet Herbs, and an Onion, boil this up, and thicken it with brown Butter. This Liquor serves for several other Sorts of Meat and Fowl Pyes.

Another Way.

DRAW your Pigeons and truss them handsomely; then take their Livers, a little Marrow, a few Mushrooms, some of a Fillet of Veal, and Sweet Herbs, of which make your Forced-Meat, and stuff the Bodies of your Pigeons therewith, keeping some of it to lay under them in the Pye; then raise your Pye, set it in the Form as usual, cover the Bottom of it with the Farce, season your Pigeons and lay them upon it, cover them with Slices of Veal and Bits of Butter, lid your Pye and so bake it; when it is enough cut off the Lid and take out the Veal, pour on a Ragoo of Sweetbreads, Cocks-Combs, and Mushrooms, so serve it hot.

A Rabbit

A Rabbit Pye.

YOU muſt cut off the Heads of your Rabbits, and the firſt Joint of the Feet, lard them with middling Lardoons, and ſeaſon them with Salt, Pepper and ſome Spices, prepare your Pye, and garniſh the Bottom of it with ſcrap'd Bacon, ſeaſoned as above; cut your Rabbits in two, and place them in your Pye, being firſt ſeaſon'd as before mentioned, cover them with Slices of Veal, and Lards of Bacon; then lid your Pye and ſet it in the Oven; make a Cullis of Veal with ſome Gammon of Bacon cut in Slices, and lay it in the Bottom of a Stew-pan, together with your Rabbits Livers; ſet it over a Stove, and when the Liquor is warm take it out and pound it in a Mortar; when your Cullis begins to ſtick to the Bottom put in ſome melted Bacon with a little Flour, ſtir and moiſten it with Gravy; add a few Cruſts of Bread, and let it ſimmer awhile; then take out your Slices of Bacon and put in your Livers, mix them well in it, ſtrain it into a Sauce-pan, and keep it hot, but don't let it boil: When your Pye is baked cut up the Cover, take out the Veal Slices, and take off all the Fat; place your Pye in the Diſh, pour in the Cullis, and ſerve it.

A Hare Pye.

GET a Hare, cut it in Pieces, break the Bones, and ſeaſon it to your Taſte, and lay it in the Pye with ſliced Lemon, and Butter and cloſe the ſame.

A Chicken

A Chicken Pye.

HAving cut your Chickens in Quarters and larded them, take away the Necks, finge them and wipe them clean, and parboil them · For your Forc'd-Meat, mince fome Bacon and a little Marrow, feafoned with Pepper, Nutmeg, Salt and Parfley, and lay it about the Chickens, with a boiled young Lettuce, and when baked, ferve them with a Caudle.　About three Hours bakes it.

Another Way.

BOIL young Chickens in an equal Quantity of Milk and Water, then flea them, and feafon them with Salt, Cloves and Nutmeg.　Put Puff-pafte round, and in the Bottom of the Difh lay a Layer of Butter with Artichoke Bottoms, Veal Sweetbreads and Cocks-Combs, and over them lay the Chickens, with fome Bits of Butter rolled up in the Seafoning and fome Balls of Forced-Meat.　Lay on a Lid of Puff-pafte, the Oven muft not be too hot: While it is baking make the following Caudle: Boil a Blade of Mace in half a Pint of White Wine or Cyder, take it off the Fire and flip in the Yolks of two Eggs well beaten, with a Spoonful of Sugar, and a little Bit of Butter rolled up in Flour. Pour in this Caudle when the Pyè comes out of the Oven.

A Hen Pye.

TAKE a Hen, cut it in Pieces, feafon it with Savoury Spice, lay it in the Pye with Balls, Yolks of hard Eggs, Slices of Lemon and Butter.　Clofe the Pye, bake it, and when it comes out of the Oven, pour in a Lear thickened with Eggs.

A Turky

A Turky Pye.

LET the Turky be boned, feafon it with favoury Spice, put it in your Pye with a Couple of Capons or wild Ducks cut in Pieces to fill up the Corners: Lay on Butter and clofe the Pye. When it is baked and cold, fill it with clarified Butter as muft be done to all cold Pyes.

Another.

MAKE a good Pafte, bone your Turky and lard it with pretty large Lardoons of Bacon, feafon it with one Ounce of Pepper, two Ounces of Salt, and an Ounce of Nutmegs, if it be to be eaten cold, but if hot, with half the Seafoning before mentioned: Lay Butter in the Bottom of the Pies, lay in your Turky and put in half a Dozen whole Cloves, then lay on the reft of your Seafoning with good Store of Butter, clofe it up and bafte it over with Eggs, and when it is baked fill up with clarified Butter.

Duck Pye *to be eaten cold.*

PRepare, parboil, lard, and feafon your Ducks, with Salt, Pepper, favoury Herbs, Spice, fhred Cives, and Parfley. Having made your Pafte, roll a Sheet of it an Inch thick, and of the Largenefs you intend to make your Pye, rub a Sheet of Paper with Butter, flour a Table, lay the Paper upon it, and the Pafte upon that, raife your Pye, and then take fome minced Cives and Parfley, and pound them in a Mortar with frefh Butter, and ftuff the Bodies of your Ducks with it, cover the Bottom of your Pye with pounded Bacon, feafoned with Salt, Pepper,
Herbs,

Herbs, and Spices Lay in your Ducks, and fill up the Intervals with some of the pounded Bacon, put in one Bay Leaf and cover the whole with Bards of Bacon ; lid your Pye with a Sheet of the same Paste, rub it over with an Egg, and set it in the Oven; when it begins to grow brown cut a Hole in the Lid to give it Air, and cover it with a Sheet of Paper. Let it bake four or five Hours, then draw it, stop up the Hole you made in the Lid, and when the Pye is half cold, turn it up side down and let it stand in that Manner 'till it is quite cold. When you would serve it cut it open, place it in a Dish with a clean Napkin under it, and serve it for a second Course.

A Swan Pye, *to be eat cold.*

SKIN and bone your Swan ; lard it with Bacon, and season it with Pepper, Salt, Cloves, Mace, and Nutmeg, to your Palate, and with a few Bay Leaves powdered ; lay it in the Pye , stick it with Cloves ; lay on Butter and close the Pye : When it is baked and half cold, fill it up with clarified Butter.

A Pheasant Pye.

DRAW your Pheasants, season them with Pepper and Salt to your Taste ; then make a Forced-Meat of Veal, or the Breasts of Pullets, and stuff the Bodies of your Pheasants with it ; then having raised your Pye lay a Layer of Butter in the Bottom : Put in your Pheasants with a Layer of Butter on the Top, and some of your Forced-Meat round it that was left when you stuffed the Bodies of your Pheasants; then lid your Pye, and bake it; cut up the Cover after being drawn, and pour into it a Ragoo of Sweetbreads ; so serve it.

Minced

Minced Pies.

TA K E the beſt Part of a Neat's Tongue parboiled, peel it, cut it in Slices, and ſet it to cool: To a Pound of Tongue put two Pounds of Beef Sewet and Marrow, then chop 'em all together on a Block very fine; to each Pound of Meat put a Pound of Currants, and a Pound of ſton'd Raiſins, chopp'd or cut ſmall; then pound your Spice, which muſt be Cloves, Mace and Nutmeg; ſeaſon it as you like, with Sugar, Orange, Lemon and Citron Peel, ſhred with two or three Pippins; ſqueeze in the Juice of one Lemon, a large Glaſs of Sack, with ſome Dates ſton'd and ſhred ſmall; all theſe being mixed together very well, make your Pies and bake them, but not too much.

Another Way.

BO I L a freſh Neat's Tongue, blanch and mince it, hot or cold, then mince four Pounds of Beef Sewet by itſelf; mingle them together, and ſeaſon them with an Ounce of Cloves and Mace beaten, ſome Salt, half a preſerved Orange, and a little Lemon Peel minced, with a Quarter of a Pound of Sugar, four Pounds of Currants, a little Verjuice and Roſe Water, and a Gill of Sack, ſtir all together and fill your Coffins.

See the different Shapes and Forms of them at the End this Chapter.

Minced

Minced Pies *with* Eggs.

HAving ten Eggs boiled hard, and cold, fhred them with one Pound of Beef Sewet, feafon it with a little Salt, half an Ounce of beaten Cinnamon, a little Mace, better than a Quarter of a Pound of Sugar, half a Rind of a Lemon, fhred very fmall, fix or eight Dates fhred fmall, three Pippins chopp'd fmall, a Quarter of a Pint of Rofe Water, a Pound and a Quarter of Currants, the Juice of an Orange and a Lemon, and fome candied Citron and Orange, what Quantity you like.

A Neat's Tongue Pye.

BOIL your Tongues 'till about half done; blanch and flice them; and feafon them with Pepper, Salt, Cloves, Mace and Nutmeg, with fome Balls, fliced Lemons, and Butter, and clofe your Pye, when 'tis baked take a Pint of Gravy, with Sweetbreads, Palates, and Cocks-Combs, toffed up, and pour into the Pye.

A Lamb's Stone *and* Sweetbread Pye.

BOIL, blanch, flice and feafon them with Pepper, Salt, Nutmeg, and Mace, and lay them in the Pye with fliced Artichoke Bottoms; butter and clofe the Pye and pour in a Lear.

An Artichoke Pye.

BOIL Artichokes very well, take the Bottoms, feafon them with a little Mace, add a good Quantity of Butter. Make a Layer at the Bottom of the Pye, put in the Artichokes, ftrewing on a little Salt and Sugar, alfo

some

some Pieces of Marrow wrapp'd up in the Yolks of some Eggs, with a few Gooseberries or Grapes : Upon these lay some Dates, some Yolks of hard Eggs, Citron, large Mace, &c. then cover these with Butter: Bake it and pour in scalded White Wine.

A Pompion Pye.

WE take about half a Pound of Pompion and slice it, a Handful of Thyme, a little Rosemary, Parsley, and Sweet Marjoram slipped off the Stalks and chopp'd small; also Cinnamon, Nutmeg, Pepper and six Cloves, all beaten with ten Eggs: Then mix them, and beat them all together, and put in as much Sugar as you think fit: Fry the whole Compound like a Fraze, let it stand 'till it is cold, and fill your Pye. Afterwards, take Apples sliced thin round Ways, and lay a Row of the Fraze, and a Layer of Apples, with Curiants betwixt the Layer while your Pye is fitted; and put in a good deal of Sweet Butter before you close it: When the Pye is baked, take six Yolks of Eggs, some White Wine or Verjuice, and make a Caudle thereof, but not too thick; cut up the Lid and put it in, stir all well together 'till the Eggs and Pompions are not perceived, and so serve the Pye up.

A Potatoe Pye.

HAving boiled the Potatoes, peel them and lay them in the Pye with good Store of Marrow, whole Mace, preserved Lettuce Roots and Stalks, and Citron cut: Cover it with Butter, and when it comes out of the Oven scald White Wine and put some Sugar in, and give it a Shake or two, and send it to the Table.

FISH PIES

A Salt-Fish Pye.

GET a Side of Salt-Fish, or less, according to the Bigness of your Dish, and water it well over Night; next Morning put it over the Fire, in a large Pan of Water, and boil it 'till it is fit to eat; then throw it out into cold Water, drain it on a Colander, place it with its Back on your Kitchen-Table, take all the White of your Fish clean from the Bones, searching the Bones nicely out with your Fingers; and mince it small with your mincing Knife. You must save a square Bit of your Salt-Fish, as big as your Hand, whole with the Skin on: Then take the Crumb of two *French* Rolls cut in Slices, and boiled up with a Pint of Cream, and a Pint of Milk, break your Bread very small with a Spoon, and put to it your minced Salt-Fish, a Pound of Butter, two Spoonfuls of minced Parsley, half a grated Nutmeg, some beaten Pepper, but no Salt, except you find your Salt-Fish too fresh with the watering and boiling; if you find it too salt after you have minced it, you may put in a Quart of cold Milk, and let it lye an Hour; then throw it into a Colander, and squeeze it well from the Milk, and so stir it over the Fire with your above Ingredients: When you find it is of a good Taste and Thickness, spread it on a Dish 'till it is cold.   At the same Time prepare a raised Pye, or a Patty-pan, when it is cold, place it in with your square Piece of Salt-Fish on the Top, then cover it up as you do another Pye.   If a raised Pye, bake it two Hours, if in a Patty-pan, one Hour; When baked, cut up your Cover.   If there is any Oil,

skim

skim it off with a Spoon, then throw over it fix hard Eggs, minced fmall, pour upon it fome drawn Butter, and fhake it together. If you fee it inclines to be oily, pour round it a little hot Milk, fhake it together, and ferve it hot. You may make Ling or Stock-Fifh Pye the fame Way, only inftead of taking Yolks and Whites for the Salt-Fifh Pye, you muft take nothing but Yolks for thefe.

A Carp Pye

LARD Carps with Eels, and feafon them with Salt, Pepper, Cloves and Nutmeg, together with fome Butter; then raife your Pye, fill and lid it, bake it in a gentle Oven; when half baked pour in a Glafs of Wine, and when enough, cut up the Cover, skim off the Fat, and pour in a Ragoo of Oyfters, fo ferve it.

A Sole Pye.

YOU muft take Soles, cut the Flefh from the Bones, and feafon them with Salt and Pepper; then make a Forc'd-Meat of the Flefh of Eels, and having raifed your Pye, lay a Layer of the Forc'd-Meat in the Bottom of it, and then lay in your Soles, with a Layer of Frefh Butter on the Top; then lid your Pye, and bake it in a gentle Oven, with White Bread.

An Eel Pye.

CUT your Eels in Pieces, and feafon them with Pepper, Salt and Spices; then raife your Pye, make a Forc'd-Meat of Fifh, and lay a Layer of it in the Bottom; then lay in your Eels, put over them a Layer of Butter, lid your Pye, and bake it in a gentle Oven.

A

A Turbut Pye.

PRepare and raise your Pye, and lay a Layer of Butter in the Bottom, then season your Turbut with Salt,
Pepper and Spices, lard it with Anchovies, and so lay them
in your Pye, cover it with a Layer of Butter, lid and set
it in the Oven, when it is baked enough cut it open, skim
off the Fat, pour in a Ragoo of Crawfish; and so
serve it.

A Pike Pye.

LARD your Pike with Eels, make a Forc'd-Meat of
the Flesh of Carp, some Mushrooms, Cives and
Parsley, season'd with Pepper, Salt, Spice, a Piece of fresh
Butter, and the Yolks of two Eggs; shred all these very
small together, and put it in the Body of your Pike; raise
your Pye and garnish the Bottom of it with fresh Butter;
lay in your Pike, having cut it in two, and season it with
Pepper and Salt; then lay a Layer of Butter on the Top,
lid your Pye, and bake it in a gentle Oven.

A Trout Pye.

LARD your Trouts with Eels, and cut off their
Heads, then raise your Pye, and lay a Layer of
Fresh Butter in the Bottom of it; then make a Farce of
Trouts, Mushrooms, Truffles, Parsley, Cives, and good
Butter; season it with Salt and Pepper, the Yolks of two
raw Eggs and Spices; then stuff the Bellies of your Trouts
with it; season your Trouts with Salt and Pepper, lay
them in your Pye, and cover them with good Fresh Butter, lid your Pye, and bake it in a gentle Oven.

An

An Oyſter Pye.

HAVING a Quart of Oyſters, drain them from the Liquor, a Quarter of a Pound of Butter, one Anchovy ſhred ſmall, about a Spoonful of ſhred Parſley, a little Nutmeg and Pepper ; then make your Pye, and lay on the Bottom a Layer of Butter and the Parſley aforeſaid , then lay in your Oyſters with ſome Butter, and a ſliced Lemon on the Top , ſtrew over the Oyſters a little Pepper and Nutmeg, then lid your Pye and bake it, and when it is enough draw it , cut up your Lid, and ſqueeze in a Lemon, give it a Shake or two, and ſerve it.

Another Way.

HAVING raiſed your Pye of good Paſte, ſcald your Oyſters in their own Liquor, with White Wine, Spices, Onion and Savoury, and when they are cold put them into your Pye, with a Layer of Butter under, a Layer of Marrow and hard Eggs, a little Pepper and Salt, Nutmeg, Mace and Barberries, and lay a Layer of Butter on the Top. This Pye muſt be baked in a quick Oven, then cut up your Cover, ſcald White Wine, and pour into it, give it a Shake or two, and ſerve it.

A Salmon Pye.

MAKE Puff-paſte and lay in the Bottom of your Patty-pan; then take the Middle Pieces of Salmon, ſeaſon it high with Salt, Pepper, Cloves and Mace, cut it into three Pieces ; then lay a Layer of Butter, and a Layer of Salmon 'till it is laid all out ; then make Forc'd-Meat of an Eel, and chop it fine with the Yolks of hard

Eggs,

Eggs, with two or three Anchovies, Marrow and Sweet
Herbs, a little grated Bread, a few Oysters if you have
them; lay them round your Pye and on the Top, season
them with Salt and Pepper, and other Spices as you please.

A Lobster Pye.

WE boil Lobsters, then take them clean out of the
Shells; slice the Tails and Claws thin; season
them with Pepper and a little Mace and Nutmeg beat fine;
take the Bodies, with some Oysters well-wash'd and shred;
mix it up with a small Onion finely shred, a little Parsley
and a little grated Bread, and season it as the rest; then
take the Yolks of raw Eggs, to roll it up in Balls; lay all
into the Pye, with Butter at the Bottom and the Top of
the Fish: Bake it, and pour in Sauce of strong Gravy,
Oyster Liquor strained, and White Wine thickened with
the Yolk of an Egg: Then eat it hot.

P A S T I E S.

Marrow Pasties.

WE take the Marrow of one Bone, Cinnamon finely sifted, a little Nutmeg, Salt, and Sugar, to
your Taste; take two Yolks of Eggs boiled, and rubbed
fine, and Lemon Peel cut fine, half an Ounce of candy'd
Orange, half an Ounce of candy'd Lemon, half an Ounce
of Citron cut, but not too fine, a Quarter of a Pound of
plump Currants; mix all these well together, and make
it into Pasties, with Puff-paste; close them well up, and
fry them in Beef-dripping made very hot and a great deal:
Strow Sugar over them.

Kidney

Kidney Pasties.

FIRST take the Kidnies of Loins of Veal, with the Fat about them, and a little of the Veal; then take Beef Sewet, with the Yolks of Eggs shred all very well together, with Cloves, Mace, Nutmeg and Salt; sweeten them with Sugar and Currants to your liking; mix them all well together; then make your Pasties of Puff-paste, fry them in Hog's Lard or Butter, which you like best; let them be of a fine Colour, and yellow.

Sweetbread Pasties.

YOU must take parboiled Sweetbreads chopp'd very fine, add thereto some Marrow, or the Fat of a Loin of Veal shred with grated Bread, the Yolks of two Eggs, a little Cream, Rose Water, Sugar and Nutmeg. Then make Puff-paste with Butter roll'd in the Flour, cold Water, the Yolks of two Eggs, a little Sugar and Rose Water: Roll it out in Form of small Pasties, the Breadth of your Hand, and put in your Compound in order to be fry'd brown or baked.

Apple Pasties *to fry.*

PARE and quarter Apples, and boil them in Sugar and Water, and a stick of Cinnamon, and when tender, put in a little White Wine, the Juice of a Lemon, a Piece of fresh Butter, and a little Ambergrease or Orange-Flower-Water; stir all together, and when 'tis cold, put it in a Puff-paste and fry them.

U u u

Pasties

Pasties *for* Garnishing.

YOU must take the Kidney and Fat of a roasted Loin of Veal, shred it small and season it with Salt, Cinnamon, Sugar, Mace, a little grated Bread, a little Cream, five Yolks of Eggs, and two Whites and a little Rose Water, mix all these Ingredients well, and put them into little Pasties of Puff-paste, and fry them in good Store of Sewet or Butter. With these you may garnish your Dishes of Fish, or others.

Petit Patties *with* Gravy.

MAKE some Paste for short Crust and lay it by: Take a Piece of Veal, as big as your Fist, as much Bacon, and some Beef Sewet, cut in Bits, put it in a Stew-pan, and season it with Salt, Pepper, Sweet Herbs and fine Spice; then tofs it up, and mince all together, with some Mushrooms, and moisten it with some Cream, or Milk, and put it upon a Plate: Then roll your Paste, and having forced your Petit Patties one Inch deep, fill them with your Stuffing, and having covered them, colour them with beaten Eggs, and let them be baked. When done, open them at Top, and putting in a little Cullis and Essence of Ham, serve them up hot.

Petit Patties *of* Oysters.

GET as many Oysters in the Shells as you would make Patties, then mince the Melts and Flesh of Carps, Tenches, Pikes, and the Flesh of Eels; season all this with Pepper, Salt, pounded Cloves, and White Wine; wrap up your Oysters in it, of which only one is to be

put

put in each Patty, with a little fresh Butter. Bake them and serve them hot, either as *Hors d'Oeuvres,* or for garnishing.

Petit Patties *the* Spanish *Way.*

BLANCH a Piece of fat Bacon, a Piece of Veal, and the Breast of a Pullet, in scalding Water; and mince them very small; then season it with all Sorts of Spices. Pound it in a Mortar, adding a little Garlick and some Rocambole; so form your Petit Patties of Puff-paste, and when they are baked serve them as above.

A Patty *of* Lobsters.

YOUR Lobsters being boiled and cut in Pieces, take the small Claws and the Spawn, and pound them in a Marble Mortar; then put to them a Ladle full of Gravy or Broth, with a little of the upper Crust of a *French* Roll: When it is boiled, strain it through a Strainer or Sieve, to the Thickness of a Cream, and put half of it to your Lobsters, and save the other half to sauce them with after they are baked. Put to the Lobsters the Bigness of an Egg of Butter, a little Pepper and Salt, squeeze in a Lemon, add in half a minced Anchovy, and warm these over the Fire just so much as to melt the Butter; then set it to cool, and sheet your Patty-pan for a Plate or Dish, with good Puff-paste; then put in your Lobsters, and cover it with a Paste: Bake it three Quarters of an Hour before you want it; when it is baked, cut up your Cover and draw up the other half of your Sauce above-mentioned with a little Butter, to the Thickness of a Cream, and pour it over your Patty, with a little squeezed Lemon; cut

your

your Cover in two, and lay it on the Top, two Inches diſtant, that it may be ſeen what is under. You may bake Crawfiſh, Shrimps or Prawns the ſame Way; and they are all proper for Plates or little Diſhes for a ſecond Courſe.

A Patty *of* Calves Brains.

CLEAN the Brains very well, and ſcald them: Then blanch ſome Aſparagus Tops in a Sauce-pan, with a little Butter and Parſley. When they are cold, put them in the Patty with the Brains, the Yolks of five or ſix hard Eggs and ſome Forc'd-Meat. When it is baked, ſqueeze in the Juice of a Lemon, pour in ſome drawn Butter and Gravy, and ſo ſerve it.

L E A R S.
A Lear *for* Savoury Pyes.

IN a proper Quantity of Claret, Gravy and Oyſter Liquor, boil a Faggot of Sweet Herbs, two or three Anchovies and an Onion; thicken it with brown'd Butter, and pour it into your ſavoury Pies, when it is wanted.

A Lear *for* Fiſh Pies.

TAKE Claret, White Wine, Vinegar, Anchovies and Oyſter Liquor, put to them ſome drawn Butter, and when the Pies are baked, pour it in with a Funnel.

A Lear *for* Paſties.

YOU muſt take the Bones of the Meat of which the Paſty is to be made, cover them with Water, and bake them with the Paſty, and when it comes out, ſtrain the Liquor, and put it into the Paſty.

A Caudle

A Caudle *for* Sweet Pies.

GET half a Pint of White Wine, a little grated Nutmeg and Mace, and boil it; then beat up the Yolks of two Eggs, and put into it, with a Spoonful of refin'd Sugar, and a little Butter kneaded in Flour; shake it about and pour it in.

T A R T S.

A Peach Tart.

WE take ripe Peaches and slit them in two, pare them, and take out the Stones; put some powder Sugar in the Bottom of a Stew-pan, place your Peaches in it, put them over the Fire, stir them now and then: Make an under Crust with a Border round it, the Thickness of a Thumb, and let it be baked: When done, put it in its Dish, and your Peaches being ready and pretty well coloured, turn them upside down into a Dish, put them over your under Crust. Put a little Water in the Stew-pan where your Peaches were on the Fire, to make a little Syrup with the Sugar remaining in it; and pour this Liquor over your Peaches, placing over them their Kernels. This Tart is served up hot or cold for a dainty Dish.

Another Sort.

YOUR Peaches being ready done in Sugar, as those before, place them over the Paste prepared for an under Crust, and let them either be baked in the Oven, or under a Cover with Fire under and over. When done, you must glaze them with Sugar, by Means of a red hot

Fire-

Fire-fhovel, and ferve it up hot or cold for a dainty Difh

Another Sort.

PUT in the Bottom of a Baking-pan fome Puff-pafte for an under Cruft, with a Border round it, the Breadth of a Thumb; flit fome Peaches in two, pare them, take out the Stones, place them in your Abbefs, ftrew fome powdered Sugar over them. After which let your Tarts be done in the Oven, or under a Cover with Fire under and over. When ready, ftrew Sugar over your Tart, and glaze it with a red hot Fire-fhovel; ferve it up for a dainty Difh, either hot or cold. Apricot Tarts may be made the fame Way.

A Cowflip Tart.

GET the Bloffoms of a Gallon of Cowflips, mince them exceeding fmall, and beat them in a Mortar, put them to a Handful or two of grated Naples Bisket, and about a Pint and a half of Cream, boil them a little over the Fire, then take them off, and beat them in eight Eggs with a little Cream, if it does not thicken, put it over again 'till it does; take heed that it does not curdle. Seafon it with Sugar, Rofe Water, and a little Salt; bake it in a Difh, or little open Tarteft. It is beft to let your Cream be cold before you ftir in the Eggs.

Orange Tarts.

YOU muft take *Seville* Oranges, grate a little of the outfide Rind, fqueeze out the Juice into a Difh, throw the Peels into Water, change it very often for two Days; then fet a Sauce-pan of Water on the Fire, let it
boil

boil and put in your Oranges; boil them in two Waters to take the Bitterneſs away; when they are tender, take them out and dry them well, beat them in a Mortar very fine, then take their Weight of double refin'd Sugar, boil it to a Syrup, skimming it very clean; then put in your Pulp, and boil it all together 'till it be clear, and let it ſtand to be cold; having your Tarts ready, fill them with it, puting in the Juice; then lid and bake them in a quick Oven.

Spinach Taits.

HAving Spinach, Marrow, and hard Eggs, of each one Handful, ſome Cloves, Mace, Nutmeg and Lemon Peel ſhred fine; put in ſome Currants, and good Store of Raiſins of the Sun ſtoned and ſhreded, Orange and Citron Peel candy'd, ſweeten it to your Palate; having your Tarts ready, fill them, and bake them in a gentle Oven.

A Chocolate Tart.

WE take two Spoonfuls of Rice-Flour, ſome Salt, with the Yolks of four Eggs, and a little Milk; mix all theſe together, but don't let them curdle; then grate ſome Chocolate and dry it before the Fire, and when your Cream is boiled, mix the Chocolate well in it, and ſo ſet it to cool; make your Tart of good fine Flour, put in the Cream and bake it: When it is enough, glaze it with powder Sugar with a red hot Fire-ſhovel; then ſerve it.

An Almond Tart.

RAISE a Tart of very good Paſte, then take ſome blanched Almonds, beat very fine in a Mortar with Sack, a Pound of Sugar to a Pound of Almonds, ſome

grated

grated Bread, a little Nutmeg, fome Cream, with the Juice of Spinach to colour the Almonds green; bake it in a gentle Oven: When it is enough draw it, and ftick it with candy'd Orange and Citron.

A Chefnut Tart.

ROAST your Chefnuts and peel them, and then fheet a Difh with Puff-pafte, and between every two Chefnuts put a Lump of Marrow, rolled in Eggs, and fome Orange and Lemon Peel cut fmall, then make a Cuftard and put all over it, and garnifh with roafted Chefnuts all over.

A Tort Demoy.

GET half a Pound of blanched Almonds, beat them in a Stone Mortar in Sack, with a Quarter of a Pound of Citron, the White of a Capon, five grated Biskets, Mace, Sugar, Nutmeg and Cinnamon, Sack, and Orange-Flower-Water; then mix it with a Pint of Cream, mix'd with feven Yolks of Eggs, and two Whites well beat together; bring all thefe Ingredients to a Body over the Fire, and having a Difh covered with Puff-pafte, put Part of it into the Bottom, then put in the Marrow of two Bones, in fmall Pieces, and fqueeze on it a little Lemon Juice, and lay on the other Part of the Ingredients and cover it with a cut Lid.

Pippin Tarts.

HAving two fmall Oranges pare them thin, and boil them in Water 'till they be tender; then fhred them fmall, and pare twenty Pippins, quarter and core them,

and

and put to them fo much Water as will boil them 'till they are enough, then put in half a Pound of white Sugar, and take the Orange Peel that is fhred, and the Juice of the Oranges and let them boil 'till they are pretty thick, then fet them by to cool; make open Tarts, and put it in; fet them in the Oven moderate hot: Set them by for ufe.

Bean Tarts.

BOIL and blanch green Beans, then make Puff-pafte, and put into Patty-pans; then put a Layer of Beans, and a Layer of all Sorts of wet Sweetmeats, except Quinces, ftrow in a little Sugar between every Layer; then cover your Tarts, and make a Hole on the Top, and put in a Quarter of a Pint of the Juice of Lemon: Put in Marrow feafoned with Cloves, Mace, Nutmeg and Salt, candy'd Lemon and Orange Peel, and when they come out of the Oven, put into every Tart fome White Wine, thickened up with the Yolk of an Egg, and a Bit of Butter; and thefe Tarts are to be eat hot.

To keep FRUIT for TARTS.

Goofeberries.

TAKE Goofeberries when they are full grown, before they turn, put them into wide-mouthed Bottles, cork them clofe, and fet them in a flack Oven 'till they are tender and cracked, then take them out of the Oven, and pitch the Corks.

By this Method you may keep feveral Sorts of Fruits as Bullace, Currants, Damafcens, Pears, Plumbs, &c. only do thefe when they are ripe.

N° 32.   X x x   CUSTARDS.

CUSTARDS.

HAving two Quarts of thick fweet Cream, boil it with fome Bits of Cinnamon, and a quartered Nutmeg, keep it ftirring all the while, and when it has boiled a little Time, pour it into a Pan to cool, and ftir it 'till it is cool, to keep it from fcumming; then beat the Yolks of fixteen Eggs, the Whites of but fix, and mix your Eggs with the Cream when it is cool, and fweeten it with fine Sugar to your Tafte, put in a very little Salt and fome Rofe or Orange Flower-Water, then ftrain all through a Hair-fieve, and fill your Cups or Cruft. It muft be a pretty quick Oven; when they boil up they are enough.

Another Way.

BOIL a Quart of Cream with a Blade of Mace; beat ten Eggs, leave out half the Whites; take the Mace out, and fweeten it with Sugar, then beat in the Eggs with one Spoonful of Orange-Flower-Water; fweeten it to your Tafte, and put it into your Cuftard-Cups, and let them but juft boil up in the Oven; and if you boil the Eggs in the Cream all together, then you may put in your Cuftard-Cups over Night, and they will be fit for ufe.

Set Cuftards.

SET to boil over the Fire a Quart of Cream with fome broad Mace; when it's boiled fet it to be cold, then take fix Eggs with half the Whites, beat them very well, and put in a Spoonful of Orange-Flower-Water or Rofe Water, and put in a Pound of Sugar; harden the Cruft in the Oven, and ftuff the Corners with brown Pa-
pei,

pei, and prick the Bottoms with a fmall Pin when you fet them and fill them, and when they are enough fet them by for ufe.

Rice-Cuftards.

HAving a Quart of Cream, boil it with a Blade of Mace; then put to it boiled Rice, well beaten with your Cream; put them together, and ftir them well all the while it boils on the Fire; and when it's enough take it off, and fweeten it to your Tafte, and put in a little Rofe Water; let them be cold then ferve them.

Cheefe-Cakes.

AFTER boiling a Quart of Cream, beat the Yolks of two Eggs, and when the Cream is cold put in the Eggs, and put it on again, and boil it 'till it comes to a Curd, but not to Whey; then blanch Almonds, beat them with Orange-Flower-Water, and put them into the Cream with a little Naples Bisket, and a little green Citron, fhred fmall, Musk-plumbs ground in Sugar; fweeten it to your Tafte with good Sugar, roll it out thin, and bake them, but let not your Oven be too hot.

Another Way.

WE take two Gallons of new Milk, turn it with Runnet, that it may be a tender Curd; and when it's come and gathered, run it through a thin Strainer, and prefs out the Whey very dry; then beat the Curd with a Pound of fweet Butter very well; then put to it twelve Eggs, with the Whites of fix, feafon it with Cloves, Mace,

Cin-

Cinnamon, Nutmeg and Ginger, a little Salt and Rose Water, and what Quantity of Curiants you please, season it to your Taste with Sugar, with a Musk-plumb or two ground in it, then bake them for use.

An Almond Cheese Cake.

GET a good Handful, or more, of Almonds, blanch them in warm Water, and throw them into cold, pound them fine and in the pounding put a little Sack or Orange-Flower-Water, to keep them from oiling, then put to your Almonds the Yolks of two hard Eggs, and beat them together: Beat the Yolks of six Eggs, the Whites of three, and mix with your Almonds, and half a Pound of Butter melted, and Sugar to your Taste; mix all well together, and use it as other Cheese Cake Stuff.

Lemon Cheese Cakes.

AFTER boiling the Peel of two large Lemons, pound it well in a Mortar, with a Quarter of a Pound or more of Loaf Sugar, the Yolks of six Eggs, and half a Pound of fresh Butter, pound and mix all well together, and fill the Patty-pans but half full. Orange Cheese Cakes are done the same Way; only you must boil the Peel in two or three Waters to take out the Bitterness.

Orange Cheese Cakes *another Way.*

AFTER you have blanched half a Pound of Almonds, beat them very fine, with Orange-Flower-Water, half a Pound of fine Sugar beaten and sifted, a Pound of sweet Butter melted, that must be almost cold

before

before you ufe it; then take ten Eggs, the Whites but of four, very well beaten, two candy'd Orange Peels, or raw, with the Bitternefs boiled out; beat the Peels in a Mortar 'till as tender as Marmalade, without any Knots, then mix all well together.

For the Cruft, take a Pound of the fineft Flour, and three Ounces of refin'd Sugar, mix it with the Flour, then take half a Pound of frefh Butter, work it with your Hand 'till it comes to a Froth; then put in the Flour by Degrees, and work it together in the Yolks of three Eggs, and the Whites of two: If it be limber, put in more Flour and Sugar, 'till it's fit to roll out; then make them in what Form you pleafe. A little above a Quarter of an Hour bakes them: Againft they come out of the Oven, have fome refin'd Sugar, beat up with the White of an Egg, as thick as you can, then ice them all over, and fet them in the Oven to harden again.

C A K E S.

An excellent Plumb Cake.

WE take a Quarter of a Peck of Flour and dry it, three Pounds of Currants wafh'd and pick'd clean; fet them before a Fire to dry, half a Pound of Raifins of the Sun, wafh'd, fton'd and fhred fmall, half a Pound of blanch'd Almonds, beat very fine, with Rofe Water, a Pound of Butter melted with a Pint of Cream, but not put in hot, a Pint of Ale-Yeft, a Pennyworth of Saffron fteep'd in a Pint of Sack, ten or twelve Eggs, but half the Whites of them, a Quarter of an Ounce of Cloves and Mace, one large Nutmeg grated, a few Carraway-Seeds,

Citron

Citron, candy'd Orange, and Lemon Peel fliced; you muft
make it thin, or there muft be more Butter and Cream,
you may perfume it with Ambergreafe ty'd in a Muflin Bag,
and fteep'd in the Sack all Night. If you ice it, take
half a Pound of double refin'd Sugar fifted; then put fome
of the Sugar, and beat it up with the White of an Egg,
and beat it with a Whisk, and a little Orange-Flower-Water, but do not over wet it; then ftrew in all the Sugar by
Degrees, then beat it all near an Hour; the Cake will take
fo long a baking; then draw it, and wafh it over with a
Brufh, and put it in again for half a Quarter of an Hour.

A very good Carraway Cake.

HAving three Pounds of the beft Flour, dry it before
the Fire, then divide it into two Parts; on one Part
grate one Nutmeg, put two Spoonfuls of Rofe Water or
Sack, the Yolks of four Eggs, as much Ale-Yeft as will
make it into a Pafte, and let it lie and rife in the Warmth
of the Fire, 'till it's as light as Cork; then take the other
half of the Flower, and break into it a Pound of Butter,
very fmall, a little new Milk, luke-warm; make the Flour
and Butter into a Pafte; then take the two Paftes, and
break them together, and ftrew in a Pound of rough Carraway-Seeds and mix them well together, then make up
the Cakes, and bake it in a Hoop or Paper. Let the Oven
be not too hot, and a little more than an Hour will bake
it.

Another Plumb Cake.

GET half a Peck of Flour, half a Pint of Rofe Water, a Pint of Ale-Yeft, a Pint of Cream, boil it,
a Pound and a half of Butter, fix Eggs, leave out the
Whites,

Whites, four Pounds of Currants, half a Pound of Sugar, one Nutmeg and a little Salt, work it very well, and let it ftand half an Hour by the Fire, and then work again, and make it up, and let it ftand an Hour and a half in the Oven: Let not the Oven be too hot.

Another.

YOU muft take a Quarter of a Peck of Flour, dry'd in an Oven, put into it a little Cloves, Mace, Nutmeg and Salt, then wet it with one Pound of Butter, and one Pint of Cream, melted together; beat it very well with a Pint of Ale-Yeft, ten Eggs, leave out half the Whites, a Glafs of Sack, a little Rofe Water; mix it up very foft; then lay it by the Fire to rife; then work in three Pounds of Currants, four Ounces of Orange Peel, and Citron candy'd, three Pounds of Sugar; bake it in a Hoop, and paper the Hoop, and butter the Paper before it goes into the Oven: Ice it over with three Whites of Eggs, froth it with a Rofemary Sprig; put in half a Pound of Sugar beaten in a Mortar: Juft fet it into the Oven again to harden.

A good Seed Cake.

GET a Quarter of a Peck of Flour, two Pounds of Butter beaten to a Cream, a Pound and three Quarters of fine Sugar, one Ounce of Carraway Seeds, three Ounces of candy'd Orange Peel and Citron, ten Eggs, half the Whites only, a little Rofe Water, a Glafs of Sack, a few Cloves, Mace and Nutmeg, a little new Yeft, and half a Pint of Cream, mix it up and lay it by the Fire to rife; then bake it in a Hoop, and butter your Paper,
when

when it is baked, ice it over with the Whites of Eggs and Sugar, and set it in again to harden.

A very good Batter Cake.

YOU muſt take ſix Pounds of Currants, five Pounds of Flour, an Ounce of Cloves and Mace, a little beaten Cinnamon, half an Ounce of Nutmegs, half a Pound of Sugar, three Quarters of a Pound of Citron, Lemon, and Orange Peel candy'd, half a Pint of Sack, a little Honey-Water, a Quart of good Ale-Yeſt, a Quart of Cream, and a Pound and three Quarters of Butter melted therein; mix it well together on a Board, and lay it before the Fire to riſe; then work it up, and put it into a Hoop, with a Paper flower'd at the Bottom, and ſo bake it: Take Care not to burn it.

A Pudding Cake.

MINCE a Pound of Sewet very fine, and as much Flour, four Eggs and a Piece of Butter, mix theſe together; ſeaſon it with Nutmeg, Sugar, Cinnamon, a little Roſe Water, and Salt, work it into a Paſte with Cream, and make it up like a Cake: Butter your Diſh and bake it.

To make Diet Bread.

BEAT and dry a Pound of Loaf Sugar, then take three Quarters of a Pound of Flour dried, ſeven Eggs, Yolks and Whites; whisk your Eggs with two Spoonfuls of Orange-Flower-Water, and two Spoonfuls of fair Water, half an Hour; then ſhake in your Sugar, and beat them with a Spoon a Quarter of an Hour; and put in your
Flour

Flour, and beat it another Quarter; bake them in Tin-pans, put Paper within your Pans well floured; an Hour bakes them; put them into your Pans juft as you put them into the Oven.

Shrewsbury Cakes.

WE take to one Pound of Sugar, three Pounds of the fineft Flour, a Nutmeg giated, fome beaten Cinnamon, the Sugar and Spice-muft be fifted into the Flour, and wet it with three Eggs, and as much melted Butter as will make it of a good Thicknefs to roll into Pafte; mould it well and roll it, and cut it into what Shape you pleafe. Perfume them, and prick them befoie they go into the Oven.

Queen's Cakes.

YOU muft take a Pound of dry'd Flour, a Pound of refin'd Sugar fifted, and a Pound of Currants wafh'd, pick'd, and iubb'd clean, and a Pound of Butter wafh'd very well, and rub it into the Flour and Sugar, with a little beaten Mace, and a little Orange-Flower-Water; beat ten Eggs, but half the Whites, work it all well together with your Hands, and put in the Currants; fift over it double refin'd Sugar, and put them immediately into a gentle Oven to bake.

To make Ginger Bread.

TAKE a Pound and a half of *London* Treacle, two Eggs beaten, half a Pound of brown Sugar, one Ounce of Ginger beaten and fifted, of Cloves, Mace and Nutmeg, all together, half an Ounce, beaten very fine, Co-

Y y y   riander

riander Seeds, and Carraway Seeds, of each half an Ounce, two Pounds of Butter melted; mix all these together, with as much Flour as will knead it into a pretty stiff Paste, then roll it out and cut it into what Form you please: Bake it in a quick Oven on Tin-plates: A little Time will bake it. Of some of this Paste you may likewise make Drops

Another Sort.

HAving half a Pound of Almonds, blanch and beat them 'till they have done shining; beat them with a Spoonful or two of Orange-Flower-Water, put in half an Ounce of beaten Ginger, and a Quarter of an Ounce of Cinnamon powdered, work it to a Paste with double refin'd Sugar beaten and sifted, then roll it out, and lay it on Papers to dry in an Oven after Pies are drawn.

Dutch Ginger Bread.

MIX with four Pounds of Flour, two Ounces of beaten Ginger; then rub in it a Quarter of a Pound of Butter, and add to it two Ounces of Carraway Seeds, two Ounces of Orange Peel dried and rubb'd to Powder, a few Coriander Seeds bruised, two Eggs, then mix all up in a stiff Paste, with two Pounds and a Quarter of Treacle; beat it very well with a Rolling-pin, and make it up into thirty Cakes, put in candy'd Citron, prick them with a Fork; butter Papers three double, one White, two Brown; wash them over with the Whites of an Egg; put them into an Oven, not too hot, for three Quarters of an Hour.

To

To make Buns.

YOU muft take two Pounds of fine Flour, a Pint of Ale-Yeft, put a little Sack in the Yeft, and three Eggs beaten, knead all thefe together with a little warm Milk, a little Nutmeg, and a little Salt, then lay it before the Fire 'till it rife very light, then knead in a Pound of freſh Butter and a Pound of rough Carraway Comfits, and bake them in a quick Oven on floured Papers, in what Shape you pleafe.

To make Wiggs.

YOU muft take two Pounds of Flour, and a Quarter of a Pound of Butter, as much Sugar, a Nutmeg grated, a little Cloves and Mace, and a Quarter of an Ounce of Carraway Seeds, Cream and Yeft as much as will make it up into a light Pafte, make them up, and fet them by the Fire to rife 'till the Oven be ready; they will quickly be baked.

To make little Hollow Biskets.

AFTER having beat fix Eggs very well with a Spoon-ful of Rofe Water, then put in a Pound and two Ounces of Loaf Sugar beaten and fifted; ftir it together 'till it's well mixed in the Eggs; then put in as much Flour as will make it thick enough to lay out in Drops upon Sheets of white Paper; ftir it well together 'till you are ready to drop on your Paper; then beat a little very fine Sugar and put it in a Lawn-fieve, and fift fome on them juft as they are going into the Oven; fo bake them, the Oven muft not be too hot, and as foon as they are baked, whilft
they

they are hot, pull off the Papers from them, and put them in a Sieve, and set them in the Oven to dry; keep them in Boxes with Papers between.

To make French Bread.

GET half a Peck of fine Flour, put to it six Yolks of Eggs, and four Whites, a little Salt, a Pint of good Ale-Yest, and as much new Milk, made a little warm as will make it a thin light Paste, stir it about with your Hand, but by no Means knead it; then have ready six wooden Quart Dishes, and fill them with Dough; let them stand a Quarter of an Hour to heave, and then turn them out in the Oven, and when they are baked rasp them; the Oven must be quick.

To make the thin Dutch Biskets.

GET five Pounds of Flour, and two Ounces of Carraway Seeds, half a Pound of Sugar; and something more than a Pint of Milk, warm the Milk, and put into it three Quarters of a Pound of Butter; then make a Hole in the Middle of your Flour, and put in a full Pint of good Ale-Yest, then pour in the Butter and Milk, and make these into a Paste, and let it stand a Quarter of an Hour by the Fire to rise, then mould it and roll it into Cakes pretty thin; prick them all over pretty much, or they will blister; so bake them a Quarter of an Hour.

CHAP.

C H A P. XXV.

Of P I C K L I N G.

To pickle Walnuts.

TA K E Walnuts about *Midsummer*, when a Pin will pass through them, and put them in a deep Pot, and cover them over with ordinary Vinegar; change them into fresh Vinegar once in fourteen Days 'till six Weeks be past, then take two Gallons of the best Vinegar, and put into it Coriander Seeds, Carraway Seeds, Dill Seeds, of each one Ounce grosly bruised, Ginger sliced three Ounces, whole Mace one Ounce, Nutmeg bruised two Ounces, Pepper bruised two Ounces, give all a Boil or two over the Fire, and have your Nuts ready in a Pot, and pour the Liquor boiling hot over them, so do for nine Times.

Another Way.

YOU must take Walnuts about *Midsummer*, when a Pin will pass through them; and put them in a deep Pot, and cover them over with ordinary Vinegar; change them into fresh Vinegar once in fourteen Days, so do four Times; then take six Quarts of the best Vinegar, and put into it an Ounce of Dill Seeds grosly bruised, Ginger sliced three Ounces, Mace whole one Ounce, Nutmegs quartered two Ounces, whole Pepper two Ounces, give all a Boil or two over the Fire, then put your Nuts into a Crock, and pour your Pickle boiling hot over them; cover them close 'till 'tis cold to keep in the Steam; then have

Gallipots ready, and place your Nuts in them 'till your Pots are full; put in the Middle of each Pot, a large Clove of Garlick ftuck full with Cloves, and ftrew over the Tops of the Pots, Muftard Seed finely beaten, a Spoonful, or more, or lefs, according to the Bignefs of your Pot, then put your Spice on, and lay Vine Leaves, and pour on the Liquor, and lay a Slate on the Top to keep them under the Liquor. Be careful not to touch them with your Fingers, leaft they turn black, but take them out with a Wooden Spoon; put a Handful of Salt in with the Spice. When you firft boil the Pickle, you muft likewife remember to keep them under the Pickle they are firft fteep'd in, or they will lofe their Colour: Tye down their Pots with Leather. A Spoonful of this Liquor will relifh Sauce for Fifh, Fowl, or Fricafey.

Another Way.

WE take Nuts fit to preferve, prick them full of Holes and cut the Slit in the Creafe half through. Put them as you do them into Brine; let them lie three Weeks, changing the Brine every four Days, take them out with a Cloth, and wipe them dry, put them in a Pot, with a good deal of bruifed Muftard Seed, then have your Pickle ready, which muft be Wine Vinegar, as much as will cover them, put in Cloves, Mace, Ginger, Pepper, Salt, three or four Cloves of Garlick, ftuck with Cloves, and pour your Liquor boiling hot upon them, and keep them clofe tied for a Fortnight. Boil the Pickle again, fo do three Times, put Oil on the Top.

Mufhrooms.

Mushrooms.

WE take only the Bottoms, wash them in Milk and Water with a Flannel, put Milk on the Fire, and when it boils, put in your Mushrooms and give them four or five Boils, and have in Readiness a Brine, made with Milk and Salt, and take them out of the boiling Brine, and put them into the Milk Brine and cover them up all Night; then have a Brine with Water and Salt, boil it, and let it stand to be cold, and put in your Buttons and wash them in it. When you first boil your Mushrooms, you must put with them an Onion and Spice; then have in Readiness a Pickle, made with half White Wine, and half White WineVinegar; boil in it Ginger, Mace, Nutmegs and whole white Pepper; when 'tis quite cold, put your Mushrooms into the Bottles, and some Bay Leaves on the Sides, and strew between, some of your boiled Spice; then put in the Liquor, and a little Oil on the Top; cork and rosin the Top; set them cool and dry, and the Bottoms upwards.

Another Way.

TAKE small Buttons, cut the Dirt from the Bottoms of the Stalks, wash them with Salt, Water, and Milk, rub them 'till they are clean, then boil Salt, Water and Milk, and when it boils, throw in your Mushrooms, and when they have boiled quick and white, strain them through a Cloth, and cover them up with the rest of the Cloth, and let them cool in it: Take for the Pickle half White Wine, and half Vinegar, with sliced Nutmeg and Ginger, whole Pepper, Cloves and Mace; then stop them in Glasses.

Another Way.

SCRAPE or peel them, throw them into Water, and then take them out clear from the Water, and set them over the Fire and boil them with Salt; skim and strain them thro' a Sieve, put them in Salt and Water, made strong, and let them lie there three Hours, then put them into Beer Vinegar, and let them stand two Days, then put them into White Wine Vinegar, with an equal Quantity of Mace, Cloves, Nutmeg, White Pepper and Ginger; boil the Pickle, but not the Spice, and let it be cold before you put it to the Mushrooms.

To *pickle* Samphire.

GAther your Samphire in *May,* pick it, and lay it for two Days in Salt and Water; then take it out, and put it into a Pot and soak it well in the best White Wine Vinegar, and set it over a clear gentle Fire, cover it close 'till it is green and crisp, and put it into Pots, or Glasses, tied down close with a Bladder, or Leather.

To *pickle* French Beans.

TAKE *French* Beans, before they have any Strings, and lay them in an Earthen Pot, betwixt every Layer of Beans, a Handful of Salt, then let them stand 'till they are shrunk, and the Salt pretty well dissolved, then cover them with Vinegar: Before you boil them for use, you must steep them an Hour in Water; then hang them on the Fire, putting them in when the Water is cold: When they are boiled, let them stand 'till they are cold, and cover them with White Wine Vinegar.

Another

Another Way.

PUT them a Month in Brine very ſtrong, then drain them from the Brine; and for the Pickle, take the beſt White Wine Vinegar, a Handful of Salt, a quarter'd Nutmeg, whole Pepper, Cloves, Mace, and three Races of Ginger, boil'd together, pour it to the Beans boiling hot, keep them down cloſe two Days, and then green them over the Fire, in their Pickle 'till ſcalding hot, and green; ſtove them down cloſe, and when cold, cover them with a wet Bladder and Leather.

Another Way.

CUT off the Stalks of young *French* Beans before they are ripe, then take good White Wine Vinegar, and boil it with Pepper, Ginger and Salt, and ſeaſon it to your Palate, and let it ſtand 'till it is cold, and put the Beans in an earthen Pot, and pour in the Pickle, and cover them cloſe for three Weeks; then take the Pickle and boil it and put it to the Beans, if green, if not, boil it again: When boiling, pot and cover them cloſe, and when they are cold, they are fit for uſe. If they ſhould change Colour, let the Pickle be boil'd again, and pour'd over them ſcalding hot.

To pickle Codlings.

GAther Codlings green and near full grown, blanch them, that is, ſcald them in ſoft Water 'till the Skin will peel off, then prepare your Pickle of Vinegar and Bay Salt, about a large Spoonful of Salt to a Quart of Vinegar, three or four Cloves of Garlick, a Quarter of an Ounce of
Ginger

Ginger sliced, and as much whole Pepper; boil this in a Brass-pan, with a Piece of Allum as big as a Horse Bean, for half a Quarter of an Hour, and pour it hot upon your Codlings, covering the Mouth of the Jar with a Cloth, and let it stand by the Fire-side; boil the Pickle again the Day following and apply it as before, and repeat the same 'till your Codlings are as green as you desire, and when they are quite cold, cork them close, and set them by in a dry Place. There is one Thing that must, however, be observed in all these Picklings, which is, that if the Pickles do not come to their fine green Colour presently, by boiling often of the Pickle at first, yet by standing three or four Weeks, and then boiling the Pickle a fresh, they will come to a good Colour, and then your Pickles will eat the firmer and keep the longer when they are not too soon brought to Colour.

To *pickle* Cauliflowers.

CUT the whitest and closest Cauliflowers, before they are brown, the Length of your Finger from the Stalks, and boil them very little in a Cloth in Milk and Water, not 'till they are tender; then take them out, and let them be cold: For the Pickle take the best White Wine Vinegar, Cloves, Mace, a Nutmeg quarter'd, a little whole Pepper, and a Bay Leaf, so let these boil, and when cold, then put in your Cauliflowers. In three or four Days they'll be fit to eat.

To *pickle* Cucumbers.

WIPE your Cucumbers very clean with a Cloth, then get so many Quarts of Vinegar as you have Hundreds of Cucumbers, and take Dill and Fennel and cut

it

it fmall, and put it to the Vinegar, and fet it over the Fire in a Copper-Kettle and let it boil, and then put in your Cucumbers 'till they are warm through, but not boiled, while they are in, when they are warm through, pour all out into a deep earthen Pot, and cover it up very clofe 'till the next Day, then do the fame again, but the third Day feafon the Liquor, before you fet it over the Fire, put in Salt 'till 'tis brackifh, fome fliced Ginger, whole Pepper and whole Mace; then fet it over the Fire again, and when it boils, put in your Cucumbers: When they are hot thro' pour them into the Pot, covering it clofe, when they are cold put them in Glaffes, and ftrain the Liquor over them; pick out the Spice, and put to them; cover them with Leather.

Another Way.

AFTER having wafh'd your Cucumbers, then put them into a Pan, and make a Brine with Water and Salt, ftrong enough to bear an Egg, boil it up to skim it clean, and put it to your Cucumbers boiling hot; cover it very clofe, and let it ftand twenty Days; then take them out of the Brine, and put them into another Pot, with fome Fennel, Dill, and fome *Jamaica* Pepper, and pour into them as much boiling Vinegar as will cover them, and let them ftand feven or eight Days, and if you think they are not green enough, you muft boil up the Vinegar again, and put it to them as before. Keep them clofe ftopp'd.

To pickle Cucumbers in Slices.

YOU muft take Cucumbers at their full Bignefs, but not yellow, and flice them pretty thick; flice an Onion or two with them, and ftrew a good deal of Salt on them;

them, let them ftand to drain all Night; then pour the Liquor clean from them; dry them in a coarfe Cloth, and boil as much Vinegar as will cover them, with whole Pepper, Mace, and a quarter'd Nutmeg; pour it fcalding hot on your Cucumber Slices, keeping them very clofe ftopp'd; in two or three Days heat your Liquor again, and pour over them, fo do two or three Times more, then tie them up with Leather.

Melons *or large* Cucumbers.

TAKE the largeft and greeneft Cucumbers, cut out a Piece the Length of your Cucumbers in one of the Sides, cleanfe the Seeds from them and dry them well, then put into them fome Cloves, Mace, whole Pepper, and Muftard Seed; peel two or three Cloves of Garlick and the fame Quantity of Shalot, fome Ginger fliced thin, according to the Quantity you make, and put in a little Salt; lay the Piece in its place, that you cut out of the Side, and tie it clofe with Packthread, and lay them in an earthen Pan, and put to them as much White Wine Vinegar as will cover them, with half a Pint of made Muftard to three Pints of Vinegar and a Bay Leaf, with Salt according as you like; let them lie in this Pickle nine Days; then put them into a Brafs-kettle, and fet them over the Fire to make them green; ftop them down very clofe, and let them have but one or two Boils at a Time, take them off, but let them ftill be clofe ftopp'd, and let them ftand to green, but fet them on the Fire again, and fo order them 'till they are very green; then take them out of the Pickle, and put them into a Jarr, or Pot; boil the Pickle, and put it to

- them

them boiling hot, and tie them over with Leather, and ufe them when you pleafe.

Melons *or large* Cucumbers *another Way.*

SCOOPE them at one End and take out the Pulp clean, and fill them with fcrap'd Horfe-Radifh, flic'd Garlick, Ginger, Nutmeg, whole Pepper, and large Mace. Take for the Pickle, the beft White Wine Vinegar, a Handful of Salt, a quarter'd Nutmeg, whole Pepper, Cloves, Mace, and two or three Races of Ginger, boil'd together, and pour it to the Melons or Cucumbers boiling hot, ftow them down clofe two Days; when you intend to green them, fet them over the Fire in a Bell-Metal-Kettle, in their Pickle, 'till they are fcalding hot and green, then ftow them down clofe: When they are cold, cover them with a wet Bladder and Leather.

Afparagus.

HAving gather'd your Afparagus, lay them in an earthen Pot, make a Brine of Water and Salt, ftrong enough to bear an Egg, and pour it hot on them; keep it clofe covered: When you ufe them hot, lay them in cold Water for two Hours, then boil and butter them for the Table; and if you ufe them as a Pickle, boil them and lay them in Vinegar.

Broom Buds.

PUT your Broom Buds into little Linnen Bags, tie them up, and make a Pickle of Bay Salt and Water boiled, ftrong enough to bear an Egg; put your Bags in a Pot, and when your Pickle is cold, put it to them;

keep

keep clofe, and let them lie 'till they turn black, then fhift them two or three Times 'till they turn green, then take them out and boil them as you have Occafion for them; when they are boiled, put them out of the Bag, in Vinegar: They will keep a Month after they are boiled.

Radifh Pods.

HAving gathered the youngeft Pods, put them in Water and Salt 24 Hours, then make a Pickle for them of Vinegar, Cloves, Mace, whole Pepper; boil this and drain the Pods from the Salt and Water, and pour the Liquor on them boiling hot, put to them a Clove of Garlick a little bruifed.

Purflain Stalks.

AFTER wafhing your Stalks, cut them in Pieces fix Inches long; boil them in Water and Salt pretty quick, take them up, and drain them, and when cold, make a Pickle of ftale Beer, White Wine Vinegar and Salt, put them in and cover them clofe.

Cabbage.

YOU may do it in Quarters, or fhave it in long Slices, and fcald it about four Minutes in Water and Salt, then take it out and cool it, boil up fome Vinegar and Salt, whole Pepper, Ginger and Mace, when your Pickle is boiled and skimmed, let it be cold, and then put in your Cabbage; cover it prefently and it will keep white.

Red Cabbage is done the fame Way.

Onions,

Onions.

LET them be of a fmall Size and white; paiboil them and let them cool, make your Pickle with half Wine, half Vinegai, put in fome Mace, Slices of Nutmeg, Salt, and a little Bit of Ginger, boil this up togethei, and skim it well, then let it ftand 'till cold, put in your Onions and cover them down: If they fhould mother, boil them over again, and skim them well, and let them be quite cold before you put in youi Onions, and they will keep all the Year.

Sellery.

HAving Sellery, pick it two Inches in Length, fet them off, and let them cool; put your Pickle in cold, the fame Pickle will do as for Cabbage.

Artichokes.

YOU muft take out the Bottoms whole and firm, they muft not be above three Parts boiled, and the fame Pickle will do as above-mentioned, only inftead of Ginger put in Slices of Nutmeg; cover them clofe, and they will keep all the Year.

Ashen Keys.

HAving thofe which are young, plump and very ten- der, parboil them in a little fair Water, then take a Pint of White Wine, half a Pint of Vinegar, the Juice of a Couple of Lemons, and a little Bay Salt, and boil them together; let it ftand by 'till it is cold, then put in the Ashen Keys into the Pickle, and cover them.

Naftur-

Nasturtium Buds.

GAther your little Knobs quickly after your Blossoms are off; put them in cold Water and Salt for three Days, shifting them once a Day, then make a Pickle (but do not boil it at all) of some White Wine, some White Wine Vinegar, Shalot, Horse-Radish, Pepper, Salt, Cloves, and Mace whole, and Nutmeg quarter'd, then put in your Seeds, and stop them close: They are to be eaten as Capers.

Barberries.

WE take of White Wine Vinegar and fair Water, an equal Quantity, and to every Pint of this Liquor put a Pound of Six-penny Sugar, set it over the Fire, and bruise some of the Barberries and put in it, and a little Salt; let it boil near half an Hour, then take it off the Fire and strain it, and when 'tis perfectly cold, pour it into a Glass over your Barberries; boil a Piece of Flannel in the Liquor and put over them, and cover the Glass with Leather.

Another Way.

YOU must take Water, and colour it red with some of the worst of your Barberries, and put Salt to it, and make it strong enough to bear an Egg, then set it over the Fire, and let it boil half an Hour; scum it, and when 'tis cold strain it over your Barberries; lay something on them to keep them in the Liquor, and cover the Pot or Glass with Leather.

Lemons

Lemons.

SCRAPE twelve Lemons with a Piece of broken Glafs; then cut them crofs into four Parts, down right, but not quite through, but that they will hang together; then put in as much Salt as they will hold, and rub them well, and ftrew them over with Salt, let them lie in an earthen Difh, and turn them every Day for three Days; then flice an Ounce of Ginger very thin, and falted for three Days; twelve Cloves of Garlick parboiled, and falted three Days, a fmall Handful of Muftard Seed bruifed, and fearced through a Hair-fieve; fome red *Indian* Pepper, one to every Lemon. Take your Lemons out of the Salt and fqueeze them gently, and put them into a Jarr, with the Spice, and cover them with the beft White Wine Vinegar. Stop them up very clofe, and in a Month's Time they will be fit to eat.

Elder Buds, *or* Plumb Buds.

HAving caus'd Water and Salt to be boil'd together, throw in the Buds, and let them boil for a while, but not 'till they are tender; then ftrain them, and fet them by to cool. In the mean Time, having provided a convenient Quantity of White Wine Vinegar, boil it with two Blades of Mace and a little whole Pepper: Put your Buds into this Pickle, and let them ftand nine Days, which being expir'd, they muft be fcalded in a Brafs-kettle fix feveral Times, 'till they are as green as Grafs, taking Care to prevent their growing foft; then they are to be put into Pots and tied down with Leather. Plumb Buds may be pickled after the fame Manner.

Gerkins.

Gerkins.

PUT them into a Brine strong enough to bear an Egg, for three Days, then drain them and pour on your Pickle (as on the Melons) boiling hot, having some Dill Seeds in your Pots, cover them very close two Days, and when you green them, set them over the Fire as before.

Beet Root, or Turnips.

BOIL your Beet Root in Water, and Salt, and Spice, a Pint of Vinegar, a little Cochineal, and when they are half boil'd put in your Turnips, being par'd; when they are boil'd, take them off the Fire, and keep them in this Pickle. Carrots may be done the same Way, but without the Cochineal.

Oysters.

PArboil a Quart of *Milton* Oysters in their own Liquor. For the Pickle take a Pint of White Wine, a Pint of Vinegar, and their own Liquor, with Mace, Pepper, and Salt; boil and scum them: When 'tis cold, keep the Oysters in this Pickle.

Muscles *or* Cockles.

TAKE your fresh Muscles, or Cockles, wash them very clean, and put them in a Pot over the Fire, 'till they open; then take them out of their Shells, and pick them clean, and lay them to cool; then put their Liquor to some Vinegar, whole Pepper, Ginger sliced thin, and Mace, set it over the Fire; when 'tis scalding hot, put in your Muscles, and let them stew a little; then pour out the Pickle from them, and when both are cold, put them in

an

an earthen Jug, and cork it up clofe; in two or three Days they will be fit to eat.

Pickled Pigeons.

BONE them as whole as poffible, and ftove them in Rhenifh Wine and Vinegar, and two Slices of Lemon, feafon with Pepper and Salt, and when tender take them out; let your Liquor be cold, skim off the Fat and pour it off clear; then put your Pigeons into the Pickle, put in fome Mace, Nutmeg and a Bay Leaf

To pickle Neats Tongues.

YOU muft take white Salt and Bay Salt, of each one Pound, Salt Petre and *Sal Prunella* of each one Ounce, and a Quarter of a Pound of brown Sugar· Let all thefe be boiled together to a very ftrong Brine, and the Scum taken off clean as it rifes: When the Liquor is cold, pour it into a Tub or other Veffel, put in your Tongues and let them lie cover'd at their full Length, turn them thrice a Week, and in three Weeks they'll be fit to boil: They may be kept in the Pickle as long as you pleafe; or elfe you may rub them with Bran and hang them up in your Chimney, to be eaten cold.

Another Way to pickle Pigeons.

BONE your Pigeons, beginning at the Rump; then take Cloves, Mace, Nutmeg, Pepper, Salt, Thyme, Lemon Peel, beat the Spice, fhred the Herbs and Lemon Peel very fmall, and feafon the Infides of your Pigeons, and then few them up, and place the Legs and Wings in Order; then feafon the Outfide and make a Pickle for them.

To

To a Dozen of Pigeons two Quarts of Water, one Quart of White Wine, a few Blades of Mace, some Salt, some whole Pepper, and when it boils, put in your Pigeons, and let them boil'till they are tender, then take them out and strain out the Liquor, and put your Pigeons in a Pot, and when the Liquor is cold, pour it on them ; when you serve them to the Table, dry them out of the Pickle, and garnish the Dish with Fennel or Flowers. Eat them with Vinegar or Oil.

Beef, *or Pork,* to be salted for boiling immediately from the Shambles.

GET any Piece of Beef you desire to boil, or Pork for the same, dressing it fresh from the Shambles, or Market, salt it very well, just before you put it into the Pot ; then as soon as your Meat is salted, take a coarse Linnen-Cloth, and flour it very well, and then put the Meat into it, and tie it up close; put this into a Kettle of boiling Water, and boil it as long as you would any salt Piece of Beef of the same Bigness, and it will come out as salt as a Piece of Meat, that had been salted four or five Days; but by this Way of salting, one ought not to have Pieces of above five or six Pounds Weight. *N. B.* If to half a Pound of common Salt, you put an Ounce of Nitre, or Salt Petre, it will strike a Redness into the Beef, but the Salt Petre must be beat fine, and well mix'd with the common Salt.

Salmogundy.

MINCE very fine two boiled or roasted Chickens or Veal, which you like best: Mince also very small the Yolks and the Whites of hard-Eggs by themselves:
Shred

Shred alſo the Pulp of Lemon very ſmall; then lay in the Diſh a Layer of the minced Meat, a Layer of the Yolks, and then a Layer of the Whites of Eggs, over which a Layer of Anchovies, and on them a Layer of the ſhred Pulp of Lemon, next a Layer of Pickles, then a Layer of Sorrel, and laſt of all a Layer of Spinach and Cloves, or of Shalots ſhred ſmall: Having thus filled the Diſh, ſet an Orange or Lemon on the Top, and garniſh with ſcrap'd Horſe-Radiſh, Barberries and Slices of Lemon; let the Sauce be Oil, beat up thick with the Juice of Lemons, Salt and Muſtard. We ſerve this Diſh in the ſecond Courſe, or for a Side-Diſh, or a Middle Diſh for Supper.

To pickle Herrings, *or* Mackarel.

CUT off the Heads and Tails of your Fiſh, gut them, waſh them, and dry them well; then take two Ounces and a half of Salt Petre, three Quarters of an Ounce of *Jamaica* Pepper, and a Quarter and half Quarter of white Pepper, and pound them ſmall; an Ounce of Sweet Marjoram and Thyme chopp'd ſmall, mix all together, and put ſome within and without the Fiſh; lay them in an earthen Pan, the Roes at Top, and cover them with White Wine Vinegar, then ſet them into an Oven, not too hot, for two Hours. This is for fifteen, and, after this Rule, do as many as you pleaſe.

To pickle Smelts *to exceed* Anchovies.

FIRST waſh and gut them clean, then lay them in Rows, and put between every Layer of Fiſh, Pepper, Nutmeg, Mace, Cloves, and Salt, well mix'd, and four Bay Leaves, powder'd Cochineal, and Petre Salt, beat

N° 25.   4 B   and

and mix'd with Spice, boil Red Wine Vinegar, enough to cover them, and put to them when quite cold.

To *pickle* Pork.

GET the principal Pieces of Pork, and salt them lightly with ordinary Salt; then lay them hollow, that the Blood may drain from it, with the Fleshy Side downwards, let it lie two or three Days amongst the Salt; put some beaten white Pepper, and a few Cloves bruis'd; salt it well, and pack it very close in the Thing you keep it in, with the Rind downwards, cover it with Salt, and when it has stood near three Weeks, put in so much Salt Pickle as will cover it; and then lay a false Bottom on the Top, to keep it under Pickle. We put the ordinary and bony Pieces by themselves.

Souce *for* Brawn.

HALF Beer and half Water, and Wheat Bran and Salt boiled well together, and so strain it; and when it is cold, add more Salt, and in a Fortnight new boil it.

Liquor *for* Sturgeon.

BOIL Beer Vinegar very well, with a little Salt, and let it be quite cold; then pour it into the Fish and cover it very close.

To *keep* Anchovies.

YOU must take Anchovies, and cover them two Inches thick with Bay Salt.

To

To keep Mangoes *and* Bamboes.

MINGLE Muſtard and Vinegar and cover them cloſe.

To make Verjuice.

WE take Crabs as ſoon as the Kernels turn black, and lay them in a Heap to ſweat, then pick them from Stalks and Rottenneſs, and then in a long Trough with ſtamping Beetles, ſtamp them to Maſh, and make a Bag of coarſe Hair-Cloth, as ſquare as the Preſs; fill it with the ſtamp'd Crabs, and being well preſſed, put it up in a clean Veſſel.

Very good Vinegar.

TAKE Spring Water, what Quantity you pleaſe, put it into a Veſſel or Stone Bottle, and to every Gallon put two Pounds of *Malaga* Raiſins, lay a Tile over the Bung, and ſet the Veſſel in the Sun 'till it is fit for uſe. If you put your Water and Raiſins into a Stone Bottle, you may put it in the Chimney Corner, near the Fire, for a convenient Time, and it will do as well as if ſet in the Sun.

To diſtil Vinegar *for* Muſhrooms.

PUT to a Gallon of Vinegar an Ounce and a half of Ginger ſliced, one Ounce of Nutmegs bruiſed, half an Ounce of Mace, half an Ounce of white Pepper, as much *Jamaica* Pepper, both bruiſed, a few Cloves; diſtil this. Take Care it does not burn in the Still.

To

To make Gooseberry Vinegar.

BRUISE Gooseberries, full ripe, in a Mortar; then measure them, and to every Quart of Gooseberries put three Quarts of Water, first boiled, and let stand 'till cold; let it stand twenty four Hours, then strain it through Canvas, then Flannel; and to every Gallon of this Liquor, put one Pound of feeding brown Sugar, stir it well, and barrel it up: At three Quarters of a Year old 'tis fit for Use, but if it stand longer, 'tis the better. This Vinegar is likewise good for Pickles.

To make Rose *or* Elder Vinegar.

FIRST take Roses dried, or dried Elder Flowers, put them into several double Glasses, or Stone Bottles, and set them in the Sun, by the Fire, or in a warm Oven; when the Vinegar is out fill them up again.

To make Mushroom Powder.

WASH a Peck of Mushrooms, and rub them clean with a Flannel Rag, cutting out all the Worms, but do not peel off the Skins; put to them sixteen Blades of Mace, forty Cloves, six Bay Leaves, twice as much beaten Pepper as will lie on half a Crown; a good Handful of Salt, a Dozen of Onions, a Piece of Butter as big as an Egg, and half a Pint of Vinegar; stew these as fast as you can; keep them stirring 'till they have spent their Liquor; keep the Liquor for use, and dry the Mushrooms first on a broad Pan in the Oven; afterward put them on Sieves, 'till they are dry enough to pound all together into Powder. This Quantity usually makes half a Pound.

Another

Another Sort of Mushroom Powder.

TAKE the large Mushrooms, wash them clean from Grit, cut off the Stalks, but do not peel or gill them, so put them into a Kettle over the Fire, but no Water, put a good Quantity of Spice, of all Sorts, two Onions stuck with Cloves, a Handful of Salt, some beaten Pepper, and a Quarter of a Pound of Butter; let these stew 'till the Liquor is dried up in them, then take them out, and lay them on Sieves to dry, 'till they will beat to Powder, press the Powder hard down in a Pot, and keep it for use, what Quantity you please, at a Time for Sauce.

To make English Katchup.

WE take a wide mouth'd Bottle, put therein a Pint of the best White Wine Vinegar; then put in ten or twelve Cloves of Shalot, peeled and just bruised, then take a Quarter of a Pint of the best Langoon White Wine; boil it a little, and put to it twelve or fourteen Anchovies wash'd and shred, and dissolve them in the Wine, and when cold, put them in the Bottle; then take a Quarter of a Pint more of White Wine, and put in it Mace, Ginger sliced, a few Cloves, a Spoonful of whole Pepper just bruised; let them all boil a little, when they are near cold, slice in almost a whole Nutmeg, and some Lemon Peel, and likewise put in two or three Spoonfuls of Horse-Radish; then stop it close, and for a Week shake it once or twice a Day; then use it; 'tis good to put into Fish Sauce, or any savoury Dish of Meat; you may add to it the clear Liquor that comes from Mushrooms.

CHAP.

CHAP XXVI.

OF POTTING.

To *pot* Hare.

FIRST bone your Hare, then half lard it, and sea-son it well, then lay it in a deep Pan, put in one Pound of Sewet chopp'd, and two Pounds of Butter, cover it and bake it tender, and take out the larded Pieces and squeeze them dry; put them into your Pot again, and cover them with clarify'd Butter; beat the other very well in a Mortar, and put it in your Pot, squeeze it hard down, and cover with clarify'd Butter.

To *pot* Tongues.

LET Neats Tongues, that look red, be taken out of the Pickle; cut off the Roots and boil them 'till they may be easily peel'd: For the Seasoning, take Salt, Pepper, Nutmeg, Cloves and Mace, and rub it well into them, and set them in the Oven. When they are bak'd, take them out, and turn them into another Pot to be kept for use: At the same Time, pour off all the Butter, keep back the Gravy, and cover your Tongues with other melted Butter an Inch deep.

To *pot* Venison.

TAKE an Haunch of Venison, not hunted, and bone it; let three Ounces of Pepper, beaten, twelve Nutmegs with a Handful of Salt, be mingled together
with

with Wine Vinegar : Wet your Venison with the Vinegar, and season it ; then with a Knife make Holes on the Lean Side of the Haunch, and stuff it as you would do Beef with Parsley : Afterwards, having laid it in the Pot, with the Side downward, clarify three Pounds of Butter, put it thereon with Paste over the Pot ; let it stand in the Oven five or six Hours, then take it out, and with a Vent press it down to the Bottom of the Pot ; when 'tis cold, take the Gravy off from the Top of the Pot, boil it 'till above half be consumed, and put it in again with the Butter on the Top of the Pot.

To pot Beef *like* Venison.

CUT a large Veiny-piece of Beef into four Pieces; skin it and beat it with a Rolling-pin : Then let it be well rubb'd with *Sal Prunella* and Salt Petre powdered very fine, and laid in a Tray for two Days ; that Time being expired, take it out, and season it pretty high with Salt and Pepper ; afterwards, having cut Beef Sewet into long Slices, let them be seasoned in like Manner, and disposed of in the Bottom of a Pot ; lay your Meat over the Sewet, also two Pounds of fresh Butter broken into small Pieces on the Top, and set in to a hot Oven : When your Beef is bak'd, take it out of the Pot with a Skimmer, so as to drain it from the Gravy ; clear it from the Skins and Veins, and pound it in a Mortar with a little of the Butter that was scummed off, then put it into another Pot, and pour all the Butter over it, keeping back the Gravy   Venison may be potted after the same Manner, only you must not beat it in a Mortar, and Black Pepper is to be used instead of White.

To pot Pork.

HAving a Leg, or any fleshy Piece of Pork, skin it and cut it out in Pieces, beat it in a Mortar very fine; season it high with Salt and Pepper, shred a good Handful of Sage, a Handful of Rosemary, mix it together, and put it into a Pot to bake, with a Pound of Butter, bake it with brown Bread, and when it comes out of the Oven, take it out with Care, and drain it from the Gravy; then put it into a dry Pot, and press it down close and hard; skim off all the Butter and put to it, and clarify as much more as will cover an Inch above the Meat; then wet Paper, cover it and set it in your Cellar: In four Days cut it.

To pot Lobsters.

WE boil the Lobsters 'till they will come out of their Shells; then take the Tails and Claws, and season them with Mace, Salt and Pepper; then put them into a a Pot and bake them with sweet Butter, and when they come out of the Oven, take them out of the Pot, and put them into a long Pot, and clarify the Butter they were baked in, with as much more as will cover them very well; set them by for Use.

To pot Salmon.

HAving cut your Salmon the Bigness of your Pots you design to keep it in, then scale it, wash it, and put it in a large long Pan, and cover it over with Butter; season with *Jamaica* Pepper and Salt, and when bak'd, take it out as whole as you can and lay it in your Pot, and cover with clarify'd Butter.

To

To pot a Pike.

YOU muſt ſcale it, cut off the Head, ſplit it and take out the Chine Bone, then ſtrew all over the Inſide ſome Bay Salt and Pepper, and roll it up round, lay it in a Pot and bake it one Hour ; then pour all the Liquor from it, and cover it with clarify'd Butter, and it will be red like Salmon.

To pot Charis.

AFTER having cleans'd them, cut off the Fins, Tails, and Heads, then lay them in Rows in a long baking Pan, cover them with Butter, and ſeaſon them with All-ſpice, Salt, Mace, and three Bay Leaves, and bake them one Hour; then take them out and drain them very well and dry from that Liquor; you may put them either ſingly or two in a Pot, and cover them with clarify'd Butter; let them ſtand 'till cold.

To pot Lampreys.

SKIN them and cleanſe them with Salt, and then wipe them dry; beat ſome All-ſpice very fine, mix it with Salt, Cloves and Mace beaten, then turn them round and ſeaſon them and lay them on one another when you bake them; but when you pot them, if they be large, one will be enough for a Pot, bake them one Hour and drain them dry, and put ſome clarify'd Butter over and they will keep the Year round.

To pot Eels.

LET your Seaſoning be *Jamaica* Pepper, common Pepper, pounded fine, and Salt; ſtrew ſome of this at the Bottom of an earthen Pan, then cut your Eels and

4 C   lay

lay them over it, ſtrew ſome more of the Seaſoning upon them, and put in another Layer of Eels, and ſo in this Manner until you have put in all your Eels, and then place a few Bay Leaves on the Top of them: Pour in as much common Vinegar as you think convenient, and a like Quantity of Water; cover the Pan with brown Paper and bake them: When you take them out of the Oven, pour off the Liquor, then take as much clarify'd Butter as is proper to cover them handſomely, pour it upon them and lay by for uſe.

To pot Fowls.

LET them be pick'd clean, and bone the Breaſts and ſinge them with white Paper, and make them clean with a dry Cloth: Be ſure not to waſh them, for then they will mould, and not keep. Seaſon them well with Salt, Pepper, Cloves and Mace, and let them lay 'till the next Day; then put them in an earthen Pot, with their Breaſts downwards; then clarify as much Butter as will cover them, you may, if you will, ſtrew over them ſome whole Pepper and Mace; tie the Pot down cloſe, and bake them, if they are full grown Fowls, they will take two Hours; and after they are baked, let them ſtand an Hour; then take them out of the Butter, and drain them from the Gravy, and put them into another Pot with their Breaſts upwards and fill their Craws with good Butter, and fill the Pot an Inch with the Butter you baked them with; but be careful firſt to pour it from the Gravy; and if you have not enough, you muſt clarify ſome more.

Ducks are done the ſame Way as Fowls.

To

To pot Pigeons.

TRUSS your Pigeons and feafon them with Pepper, Salt, Mace, Nutmeg and Cloves, as high as you think fit, and put them in an earthen Pot, cover them with Butter and bake them; when enough, pour out, and drain away the Butter, and when they are cold, cover them with clarify'd Butter.

To pot Rabbits.

BONE half a Dozen Rabbits, mince them fine, and feafon them with Pepper, Salt, Nutmeg, and Mace, pretty high; then take fome Ham, and lay between each Laying of the Rabbits, and fill your Pot with Butter, and fet it in the Oven; about four Hours will do it. When you draw it, pour out the Butter it was baked with, and the Fat, and put your Meat in a frefh glaz'd Pot, and cover it an Inch thick with clarify'd Butter.

Potted Curlews.

HAving trufs'd them crofs-legg'd, cut off the Heads, or thruft them through like a Woodcock, feafon with Pepper, Salt, and Nutmeg, gut them firft, then put them into a Pot with two Pounds of Butter; cover them and bake them one Hour, then take them out, and when cold fqueeze out all the Liquor and lay them in your Pot and cover them with clarify'd Butter.

Potted Wheat Ears.

THEY are a *Tunbridge* Bird. Pick them very clean; feafon them with Pepper and Salt, put them in a Pot, cover them with Butter and bake them one Hour,

take

take them and put them in a Colander to drain the Liquor away ; then cover them with clarify'd Butter and they will keep.

To pot Mushrooms.

RUB the beft Mushrooms with a woollen Cloth, thofe that will not rub, peel, and take out the Gills, and throw them into Water as you do them ; when they are all done, wipe them dry, and put them in a Sauce-pan, with a Handful of Salt, and a Piece of Butter, and ftew them 'till they are enough, fhaking them often, for fear of burning ; then drain them from their Liquor, and when they are cold, wipe them dry, and lay them in a Pot, one by one, as clofe as you can, 'till your Pot be full ; then clarify Butter ; let it ftand 'till it is almoft cold, and pour it into your Mushrooms. When cold, cover them clofe in your Pot. When you ufe them, wipe them clean from the Butter, and ftew them in Gravy, thicken'd as when frefh.

C H A P. XXVII.
Of C O L L A R I N G.

To collar a Breaft *of* Mutton.

GET a large Breaft of Mutton, take off the red Skin, and all the Griftles and Bones, then grate White Bread, and the Yolks of two or three hard Eggs, a little
Lemon

Lemon Peel, Sweet Herbs of all Sorts, and Cives, Pepper, Salt and Spice; mix thefe all together; wafh fix Anchovies and lay them over the Meat; then ftrew your Seafoning over it, roll it hard, and bind it with Tape, and you may bake, boil or roaft it: Cut it in Pieces as thick as three Fingers, and ferve it with ftrong Gravy Sauce, and garnifh it as you pleafe, with fryed Oyfters, or Forc'd-Meat, or, if you pleafe both.

To collar Beef.

BONE a Breaft of young Beef, then make a Brine of three Gallons of Water, one Pound of Bay-Salt, two Pounds of White Salt, half an Ounce of Salt Petre; make the Brine ftrong enough to bear an Egg; then lay your Beef in the Brine nine Days; then take it out, and beat it with a Rolling-pin very well; feafon it with half an Ounce of Mace, fix Nutmegs, which is beft, fhred fine, and not pounded; an Ounce of Bay-Berries, fome dried Sweet Marjoram, powder'd fmall, two Dozen of Cloves, an Ounce of Pepper, a Handful or two of white Salt, beaten in a Mortar. Mix all your Seafonings together, and ftrew it all over the Beef; mind that the Beef be well dried, roll it up hard, and bind it well in a Cloth, and put it into a Pot that will hold it; put to it three Pints, or two Quarts of Claret, half a Pint of Vinegar, and a Quart of Water; cover the Pot with coarfe Dough, and bake it with a Batch of Bread, and let it ftand all Night: In the Morning take it out of the Liquor, and bind it fafter, and hang it up to be cold.

To

To collar a Breaſt *of* Veal.

BONE a good Breaſt of Veal, ſeaſon it with all Sorts of Spice, but take Care you don't over do it; a little Orange and Lemon Peel minc'd ſmall, with a few Sweet Herbs, and ſtrow it all over the Veal; in the thin Places put the Sweetbread, and roll it hard, and make it faſt with Tape, and ſo bake it.

Another Way to collar Beef.

HAving a Piece of Flank Beef, about three Stone, ſkin it, bone it and beat it well with a Rolling-pin and lay it in Pump-Water two Days, then take it and ſalt it with Bay Salt, and let it lie three Days, then take a Pint of Salt Petre, and boil it in a Gallon of Water, and when it is cold, pour away the bloody Brine, and put the Petre Brine to the Beef, and let it lie three Days longer, then take one Ounce of Nutmegs, half an Ounce of Cloves and Mace, one Ounce of Pepper, a Handful of Thyme, two of Sage, and one of Sweet Marjoram, one of Savoury, chopp'd together, and ſtrew'd all over the Beef; then roll it up, and ſew it in a Cloth, and bake it as you do a Leg of Beef, but fill the Pot up with Water; you may add ſome Claret: When it's bak'd, and near cold, new roll it as hard as you can.

Another Way.

YOU muſt take about three Stone of Flank Beef, ſkin and bone it, and beat it well with a Rolling-pin; lay it in Pump-Water for two Days, and then ſalt it with Bay Salt, and let it lie three Days; then take a Pint of

Petre

Petre Salt, and boil in a Gallon of Water, boil it over
Night, that it may be cold, then pour away the bloody
Brine from the Beef, and put the Petre Brine to it, then
take it out, after boiling a little Time, and drain it; take an
Ounce of Nutmeg, half an Ounce of Cloves and Mace,
an Ounce of Pepper, with Herbs, one Handful of Thyme,
one of Sweet Marjoram, two of Sage, and a little Savoury,
chopp'd all well together, and ftrow'd all over the Beef;
then roll it up as tight as you can, and few it in a Cloth,
and bake it in a Pan full of Water; when bak'd, and near
cold, new roll it: If it be kept long, you muft put in no
Herbs, nor bake it in Water, but with Beef Sewet. Let
your Rolls be fmall, two Rolls is enough in one Pot:
When they are baked, take them from the Fat hot, and fet
them by for the Gravy to run from them, then roll them up
again very tight, before they are cold; and when cold, take
off the Tape, and put them in your Pots, cover'd with
Beef Sewet. This will keep good to the *Indies.*

To collar a Calf's Head.

TAKE it in the Skin, fcald it, and cleave it down,
and boil it 'till the Bones will come eafily away;
pour over it fome Vinegar, and feafon it with Mace, Pepper and Salt, Sweet Herbs, Sage, and Lemon Peel; ftrew
all over the Infide of your Collar, and collar it as you do
Brawn; boil it in Vinegar, Salt, Water, and Spice, and
keep it in the fame.

To collar Pork.

BONE a Breaft of Pork, and feafon it with Pepper,
Salt, Cloves, Mace and Nutmeg, and a good Quan-
tity of Thyme and Parfley, fhred fine; roll it in a hard
Collar

Collar, in a Cloth, and tie it hard, and boil it in a Quart of
Water, Salt, a Quart of Vinegar, and a Faggot of Sweet
Herbs 'till 'tis tender, and when cold, keep it in this Drink

To collar Pig.

LET it be a good fat Pig, scald him, then cut off
his Head, and take out all the Bones and Gristles;
take Care to keep the Skin whole, you may make two Collars, by cutting it down the Back, or make but one, just as
you like.   Lay it in Water all Night; in the Morning take
it out, and dry it well, and season it with Salt, Pepper,
Cloves, Mace, Nutmeg, all beaten; for Herbs take Sage
Rosemary, and if you like them, a few Marygolds, and a
little Lemon Peel; roll them up hard in a Cloth, and boil
them tender.   To keep them, let your Sauce Drink be Water, Milk and Bran, and let them be cold before you put
them in, and the Drink strained.

To collar Eels.

SPLIT a large Eel and take out the Bone, and wash it,
then strew it with Cloves, Mace, and beaten Pepper,
with Salt and sweet Herbs; then roll it up, and tie it with
Splinters round it, so boil it in Water and a little Salt, and
White Wine Vinegar, and a Blade of Mace; when the
Eel is boil'd, take it up, and let the Pickle boil a little, and
when 'tis cold, put in the Eel.

Another Way.

YOU must scower your large silver Eels with Salt, and
slit them down the Back; take out all the Bones,
wash and dry them, and season them with Nutmeg, Mace,
Pepper,

Pepper and Salt, minc'd Parsley, Thyme, Sage, and an Onion; then roll each in Collars in a little Cloth; tie them close, and boil them in Water and Salt, with the Heads and Bones, and half a Pint of Vinegar, a Faggot of Herbs, some Ginger, and a little Ising-Glass: When they are tender, take them up, and tie them close again; strain the Pickle, and keep the Eels in it.

Another Way.

SKIN two large Eels, then cut them down the Back: take out the Bone, chop a Handful of Sweet Herbs and season them with Nutmeg, Pepper and Salt; strew the Herbs on the Inside of the Eel, roll them up like a Collar of Brawn; put them in a Cloth, and boil them very tender in Vinegar and Salt, and take them up, and when they are cold, put them into the Liquor for three or four Days, if too sharp, put in Water when you boil them.

To collar a Pig's Head.

TAKE the Head of a scalded Porker, with the Feet, Tongue, and Ears; soak and wash them well, boil them tender, and take out all the Bones and Gristles; then salt them to your Taste, take a Cloth, sew it tight over it, and tie each End; then roll it round with a Roller, and boil it two Hours; lay it straight against a Board, and lay a Weight upon it of five or six Pounds, 'till the next Day; then unroll it, and put it into Pickle, as Brawn.

4 D

CHAP.

C H A P XXVIII.

Of C O N F E C T I O N A R Y.

C R E A M S.

Orange Cream.

PUT to a Pint of the Juice of *Seville* Oranges, the Yolks of six Eggs, the Whites of four, beat the Eggs very well, and strain them, and the Juice together, add to it a Pound of double refin'd Sugar, beaten and sifted; set them all together on a slow Fire, and put the Peel of half an Orange into it, keep it stirring all the while, and when 'tis almost ready to boil, take out the Orange Peel, and pour out the Cream into Glasses or *China* Dishes.

Lemon Cream.

WE take five large Lemons, and squeeze out the Juice, then take the Whites of six Eggs well beaten, ten Ounces of double refin'd Sugar beaten very fine and 20 Spoonfuls of Spring-Water; mix all together and strain it through a Jelly Bag; set it over a gentle Fire, scum it very well; when 'tis as hot as you can bear your Finger in it, take it of, and, pour it into Glasses; put Shreds of Lemon Peel into some of the Glasses.

Almond Cream.

YOU must take a Quart of Cream, boil it with Nutmeg, Mace, and a Bit of Lemon Peel, and sweeten it to your Taste, then blanch some Almonds, and beat
them

them very fine; then take nine Whites of Eggs well beaten and ftrain them to your Almonds, and rub them very well through a thin Strainer fo thicken your Cream, juft give it one boil, and pour it into *China* Difhes, and when 'tis cold ferve it up.

Piftachio Cream.

GET a Quarter of a Pound of Piftachio Kernels, pound them very fine in a Marble Mortar, with a Spoonful or two of Rofe Water, and then boil them in a Pint of Cream, adding the Juice of Spinach to make it green to your Mind, thicken it with Eggs, and fweeten it to your Tafte, then fet it in *China* Bafons to cool.

Steeple Cream.

HAving five Ounces of Hartshorn, and two Ounces of Ivory, put them into a Stone Bottle, and fill it up with fair Water to the Neck, and put in a fmall Quantity of Gum Arabick, and Gum Dragant; then tie up the Bottle very clofe, and fet it in a Pot of Water with Hay at the Bottom, let it boil fix Hours, then take it out and let it ftand an Hour before you open it, leaft it fly in your Face, then ftrain it in, and it will be a ftrong Jelly; then take a Pound of blanch'd Almonds, and beat them very fine, and mix it with a Pint of Cream, and let it ftand a little, then ftrain it out, and mix it with a Pound of Jelly; fet it over the Fire 'till 'tis fcalding hot, fweeten it to your Tafte with double refin'd Sugar; then take it off, and put in a little Ambergreafe, and pour it into fmall high Gallipots fhap'd like a Sugar Loaf, when 'tis cold turn it out, and lay whipp'd Cream about it in Heaps.

4 D 2 Ratifia

Ratifia Cream.

BOIL fix Laurel Leaves in a Quart of thick Cream; when 'tis boiled throw away the Leaves, and beat the Yolks of five Eggs, with a little cold Cream and Sugar, to your Tafte, then thicken the Cream with your Eggs, and fet it over the Fire again, but let it not boil; keep it ftir-ring all the while, and pour it into *China* Difhes; when 'tis cold 'tis fit for ufe.

Rhenifh Wine Cream.

PUT over the Fire a Pint of Rhenifh, a Stick of Cin-namon, and half a Pound of Sugar; while this is boiling, take feven Yolks and Whites of Eggs, beat them well together with a Whisk, 'till the Wine is half driven into them, and the Eggs to a Syrrup, ftir it very quick with the Whisk 'till it comes to that Thicknefs that you may lift it on the Point of a Knife, but be fure you let it not curdle; add to it the Juice of a Lemon and Orange-Flower-Water; fo pour it in your Difh, and garnifh with Citron and Bisket.

Chocolate Cream.

FIRST take a Quart of Milk, a Quarter of a Pound of Sugar, and boil them together for a Quarter of an Hour, then beat up the Yolk of an Egg, put it in the Cream and give it three or four Boils: Take it off the Fire, and put Chocolate to it 'till the Cream has taken the Colour of it; then boil it again for a Minute, ftrain it through a Sieve, and ferve it in *China* Difhes: Cinnamon Cream is made in the fame Manner.

Maiden

Maiden Cream.

GET the Whites of five Eggs, whip them to a Froth, and put them into a Sauce-pan, with Sugar, Milk, and Orange-Flower-Water; set a Plate over a Stove with a little Cinnamon, and pour your Cream, when it is well beaten, into the Plate: When it is enough done, brown it with a red hot Shovel.

Whipp'd Cream.

FIRST take a Quart of thick Cream, then the Whites of eight Eggs, beaten with half a Pint of Sack, mix them together, and sweeten to your Taste with double refin'd Sugar, you may perfume it, if you please, with some Musk or Ambergrease tied in a Rag, and steeped in the Cream, a little whip it with a Whisk, and a Bit of Lemon Peel tied in the Middle of the Whisk, take the Froth with a Spoon, and lay it in your Glasses or Basons.

Blanched Cream.

HAving a Quart of the thickest sweet Cream you can get, season it with fine Sugar and Orange-Flower-Water; then boil it, and beat the Whites of 20 Eggs, with a little cold Cream, take out the Treddles, and when the Cream is on the Fire and boils, pour in your Eggs, stirring it very well till it comes to a thick Curd; then take it up and pass it through a Hair-sieve; then beat it very well with a Spoon 'till 'tis cold, and put it in Dishes for use.

Sack

Sack Cream.

TAKE a Quart of thick Cream, and set it over the Fire, and when it boils take it off, put a Piece of Lemon Peel in it, and sweeten it very well, then take the *China* Bason you serve it in, and put into it the Juice of half a Lemon, and nine Spoonfuls of Sack, then stir in the Cream into the Bason by a Spoonful at a Time, 'till all the Cream is in, when it is a little more than Blood warm, set it by 'till next Day; serve it with Wafers round it.

Currant Cream.

BRUISE ripe Currants in boiled Cream, strain them thro' a Sieve, add Sugar and Cinnamon, and so serve it up, and so you may do Rasberries or Strawberries.

Cream Croquant.

YOU must take four or five Yolks of Eggs, more or less, beat them up and pour in some Milk, by Degrees, 'till your Dish be almost full; then put in it grated Sugar, green Lemon Peel rasped, and put your Dish over a quick Fire; stir your Milk 'till it almost boils. Then lower your Fire, keep it stirring; put some of your Cream round your Dish, leaving but little in the Bottom. Take Care your Cream is not burnt, but only sticking to the Dish. When done enough, colour it with a red hot Fire Shovel: Then with a Point of a Knife loosen your Cream round the Dish without breaking it: Put it again in the same Dish it was in before, to let it dry a little more in the Oven, 'till it be much diminished and crackling.

RICE

Rice Cream.

YOU muſt take three Spoonfuls of the Flour of Rice, as much Sugar, the Yolks of two Eggs, two Spoonfuls of Sack, or Roſe, or Orange-Flower-Water, mix all theſe together, and put them to a Pint of Cream, ſtir it over the Fire, 'till it is thick, then pour it into China Diſhes.

Cream the *Italian* Way.

ABOUT a Quart of Milk take, according to the Size of your Diſh, boil it with Sugar, a ſmall Stick of Cinnamon, and a very little Salt; when it is boil'd take a large Silver Diſh and a Sieve, into which put the Yolks of four or five new laid Eggs, and ſtrain the Milk and Eggs through it three or four Times; then put your Diſh into a baking Cover, taking Care to place it very even; pour your Milk and Eggs into the Diſh; and put Fire over and under it, 'till your Cream is very thick, then ſerve it up. Obſerve that in all theſe Creams, mixing a little Cream with the Milk makes them the more delicate.

Haſty Cream.

GET three Quarts of Milk warm from the Cow, and ſet it a boiling in a Skillet: When it begins to riſe, take it off the Fire, and let it ſtand a Moment. Take off all the Cream from the Top of it into a Plate. Set your Skillet again over the Fire, and continue to do as before, 'till your Plate be full of Cream; put to it ſome Orange-Flower or other ſweet Water, and forget not to powder it well with Sugar before you ſerve it.

Cream

Cream Veloutée.

PUT to a Pint of Cream, a Bit of Sugar; then put it into a Stew-pan over the Fire; then take a Couple of Gizzards of either Fowls or Chickens, open them, and take out the Skin, wash it well, and cut it very small, then put it in a Cup, or other Veſſel, and put in it ſome of your boil'd Cream lukewarm, then put it near hot Cinders 'till it takes, then put it in your Cream, and ſtrain it off two or three Times. Put your Diſhes on hot Cinders, and lay it upon a Level, and put your Cream in it, cover it with another Diſh, with Charcoal under it. It being taken, put it in a cool Place. If you would ſerve it with Ice, in the Summer Time, you muſt put it in a Tin Mould with Ice both over and under.

Cream Veloutée *with* Piſtachoes.

TAKE a Quart of Cream and a Bit of Sugar, let it boil as aforeſaid: Take a Quarter of a Pound of ſcalded and well pounded Piſtachoes; reſerve a Dozen of whole ones to garniſh the Diſh. Take a couple of Gizzards and order them as above. Put the Piſtachoes into your Cream, and skin the Gizzards as in the Cream before mentioned, ſtrain off your Cream two or three Times, pour it into the Diſh you are to ſerve it in, and cover it with another Diſh, with Charcoal over it, and it will take preſently, then put it in a cool Place, and when you ſerve it up, garniſh your Diſh with the reſerved Piſtachoes. It may be put in Ice in the Summer, as the aforeſaid Cream. If your Cream is not green enough, blanch a little Spinach, pound, ſqueeze, and put it to it. If you would make it red, take

Cochineal

Cochineal or fome Juice of baked Beet Root. *N B* This Way of fetting Cream with Gizzards, is much better than to ufe Runnet or Thiftle.

Piftachoe Cream au Bain Marie.

PUT to a Quart of Cream or Milk, a Bit of Sugar, a Stick of Cinnamon, and a Bit of green Lemon, and let it boil a little; then put in it a Quarter of a Pound of fcalded and well pounded Piftachoes: Keep fome whole to garnifh your Difh. A Quarter of a Pound is but for a fmall Difh, you muft proportion your Quantity to the Size of your Difh. Pour your Cream of Piftachoes through a Sieve into your Difh, with the Yolks of fix Eggs, and ftrain it off two or three Times: After this put a Stew-pan full of Water over a Stove, let your Difh be bigger than the Stew-pan, fo that the Bottom of it may touch the Water: Then put in your Cream, and cover it with another Difh turned upfide down, with fome Charcoal over it. This Cream may fometimes be ferved hot for a dainty Difh in the fecond Courfe.

Sage Cream.

BOIL a Quart of Cream, boil it well, then add a Quarter of a Pint of red Sage Juice, half as much Rofe Water, and as much Sack; half a Pound of Sugar, and it will be an excellent Difh; and thus you may ufe it with any Sweet Herbs, which are pleafant and healthful.

N ⁰ 26.   4 E   Cream

Cream veloutea *with* Chocolate.

WE take a Quart of Cream, put in it a Bit of Sugar, a Stick of Cinnamon, and a Bit of green Lemon Peel, with a Quarter of a Pound of Chocolate broken in Pieces: Let it boil all together Your Chocolate being well mixed and boiled, and your Cream palatable, take it off: Then take two or three Gizzards of either Fowls or Chickens, open them, take out the Skins, wash and cut them small. Then put these Skins in a Cup or other Veffel, with a Glafs full of your luke-warm Cream, and put it near the Fire, or on hot Cinders. As foon as it is taken, put it in your Chocolate Cream, out of the Pans, and dry it in the Oven ; then put it up.

You may bake fome of the fame Batter in Tin-frames, made in the Form of Hearts, Diamonds, &c. but you muft butter the Bottom a little, or they will not come cleanly out.

Chocolate Cream, au Bain Marie.

AFTER boiling your Cream, order it as aforefaid; place your Sieve upon your Dish, and put in it fix Yolks of Eggs, with your Chocolate Cream, prepared as before. Then ftrain it through a Sieve, put a Stew-pan full of Water upon the Fire, let the Bottom of your Dish touch the Water, put your Cream in it, and cover it with a another Dish with Fire over it. Your Cream being taken put it in a cool Place, and ferve it for a dainty Dish either cold or hot.

Bailey

Barley Cream.

GET a small Quantity of Pearl Barley, and boil it in Milk and Water 'till 'tis tender, then strain the Liquor from it, and put your Barley into a Quart of Cream, and let it boil a little; then take the Whites of five Eggs, and the Yolk of one beaten with a Spoonful of fine Flour, and two Spoonfuls of Orange-Flower-Water, then take the Cream off the Fire, and mix the Eggs in by Degrees, and set it over the Fire again to thicken; sweeten it to your Taste; pour it into Basons, and when 'tis cold serve it up.

Cream *of any* Preserved Fruit.

WE take half a Pound of Pulp of any preserved Fruit; put it in a large Pan, put to it the Whites of two or three Eggs, beat together exceeding well for an Hour, then with a Spoon take it off, and lay it heap'd up high on the Dish or Salver with other Creams, or put it in the middle Bason. Rasberries will not do this Way.

J E L L I E S.

Hartshorn Jelly.

WE take half a Pound of Hartshorn, and three Quarts of Water, let it boil very slowly 'till above one Quart is consumed, the next Day, when 'tis settled, take away what is clear, put to it a Pint of Rhenish and a Gill of Sack, beat up with the Whites of five Eggs to a Froth, stir all together with refin'd Sugar, mix it and set it on the Fire, stir it well, and add to it the Juice of six Lemons and a Slice of the Peel; let it boil up, then strain it

4 E 2   through

through your Bag 'till it is extremely fine, and put it in your Glaffes.

Blanc Manger.

PUT to a couple of Calves Feet and a Handful of Hartshorn, three Quarts of Water, and let it boil flowly a long Time, 'till it jelly's, then let it ftand to be cold after being ftrained, and after that take the Fat and Settlings at Bottom clean away, then pound a Quarter of a Pound of blanch'd Almonds very fine, with a Tea Cup full of Orange-Flower-Water, then melt the Jelly over the Fire and take it again from all the Fat, then mix your Almonds in it, and a Pint of Cream, that has been boil'd, and quite cold: Then when all is mix'd and fweeten'd to your Tafte with double refin'd Sugar, ftrain it again into Bafons: And let it ftand 'till cold.

To make it red or yellow, fqueeze it through a fine Cloth, with a little Cochineal or Saffron.

Calves Feet Jelly.

GET Calves Feet, boil them in Water with the Meat cut off from the Bones; when cold, take the Fat from the Top and the Drofs from the Bottom and fweeten it as the Hartshorn Jelly, and put in the fame Ingredients.

Jelly of Currants.

TAKE four Pounds of Currants, and ftrip in the Fruit, to four Pounds of Sugar brought to its crack'd Quality, boil the Syrup to a Degree between fmooth and pearl'd till there does no Scum arife, then lay all gently on a fine Sieve, let it ftand and drain thoroughly, then boil the Jelly, fcum
it

it again well, and put it into Gallypots, and take off a thin Scum that rises upon them, to render the Liquor clear, two or three Days after cover the Pots with Paper, and keep it for Use.

Jelly of Barberries is made after the same Manner.

Jelly *of* Cherries.

HAving very good ripe Cherries, bruise them, squeeze them through a Linnen Cloth, add to the Juice the same Quantity of Sugar brought to its cracked Boiling: Strain your Cherry Juice, and pour it into the Sugar; let it boil together, keeping scumming it 'till the Syrup is brought again to a Degree between smooth and pearled: Then pour it into Glasses or Gallipots, and afterwards take off the thin Scum that will arise upon them; let the Glasses, &c. stand three Days uncovered, then cover them with Paper.

Jelly *of* Rasberries.

FIRST take six Pounds of Rasberries, then three Pounds of Currants, and seven Pounds and a half of Sugar brought to the cracked Boiling, strip in the Fruits, and let them all boil together, scumming it 'till no more Scum will rise, and the Syrup is become between smooth and pearled, then pour it out into a Sieve, set over a Copper-pan; take the Jelly that passes through, and give it another boiling, scum it well, and put it in Pots, or Glasses as before.

Jelly *of* Quinces.

FIRST bruise your Quinces, then press out the Juice, and clarify it, allow a Pound of clarify'd Sugar, boiled to a Candy height, to every Quart of Juice. Boil
them

them together, and add a Pint of White Wine, in which Plumb-Tree or Cherry-Tree Gum has been diſſolved, and this will complete it

Jelly *of* Apples, *and other Sorts of Fruit.*

CUT the Apples into Pieces, ſet them over the Fire with Water in a Copper-pan, boil them 'till they turn to a Marmalade, as it were   Then ſtrain them thro' a Linnen-Cloth or Sieve, and to every Quart of Liquor put three Quarters of a Pound of cracked boiled Sugar, boil it all to a Degree between ſmooth and pearled, taking off the Scum as it riſes.

If you would have the Jelly of a red Colour, add ſome red Wine, or prepared Cochineal, keeping it covered.

After the ſame Manner you may make the Jelly of Pears and other Fruits.

S U G A R S.

To clarify Sugar *for preſerving,* &c.

HAving firſt provided an earthen Pan of a convenient Size with Water, break an Egg or more into it with the Shell, according to the Quantity of your Sugar: That done, let all be whipp'd together with a Whisk or Birchen-Rods and pour'd upon the Sugar that is to be melted: Afterwards, ſet it over the Fire, ſtir it about continually, and as ſoon as it boils, let the Scum be carefully taken off: As the Sugar riſes from Time to Time, ſlip in a little cold Water, to prevent its running over, and to raiſe the Scum, adding alſo the Froth of the White of an Egg, whipp'd a-part, when after the Liquor has been thoroughly ſcumm'd

there

there only remains a small whitish Froth, not black and foul as before, and when the Sugar, being laid on the Surface of the Spatula or Skimmer, appears very clear, take it off the Fire, and pass it thro' the Straining-bag, by which Means the Clarification will be absolutely compleated.

Another Way for the clarifying of Sugar.

PRivate Persons, who in preserving Fruits only have occasion to use four or five Pounds of Sugar at once, may clarify it without any Loss, in the following Manner: The Sugar is to be first dissolv'd in Water, and set over the Fire, with the White of a whipt Egg, pouring in, as soon as it swells up, ready to run over, a little cold Water to give it a Check: But when it rises a second Time, it must be remov'd from the Fire, and set it by for a Quarter of an Hour, during which Space it will sink, a black Scum only settling on the Top, which you must gently take off with the Skimmer and it will be sufficiently clarify'd, tho' not all together so clear, nor so white as the former.

Different Ways of boiling Sugar.

THE common People generally judge Sugar to be boiled enough, when some Drops of it put upon a Plate grow thick or ropy, and cease to run any longer: Indeed, this Way of boiling is proper for certain Jellies, and Compotes of Fruit; but little Progress would be made in the Confectionary Business if nothing else were known: Therefore 'tis absolutely necessary to understand all the different Degrees of boiling Sugar.

These Boilings are performed by Degrees, and the following Denominations are appropriated thereto; that is to say, fay, Sugar may be boil'd 'till it becomes Smooth, Pearled, Blown, Feathered, Crack'd and Caramel. Thefe fix Degrees are alfo fubdivided with Refpect to their particular Qualities, as the lefs and greater Smooth, the lefs and greater Pearled, Feathered a little and a great deal, and fo of the reft.

The boiling of Sugar called, Smooth.

YOU muft fet the clarify'd Sugar over the Fire to boil, which has attained to this Degree when the Artift having dipp'd the Tip of his Fore-Finger into it, afterwards applying it to his Thumb, and opening them a little, a fmall Thread or String fticks to both, which immediately breaks and remains in a Drop upon the Finger When this String is almoft imperceptible, the Sugar has only boil'd, 'till it becomes a little fmooth; and when it extend itfelf farther, before it breaks, 'tis a Sign that the Sugar is very fmooth.

The Pearled Boiling

THE Sugar having boiled a little longer, let the fame Experiment be reiterated, and if feparating your Fingers, as before, the String continues fticking to both, the Sugar is come to its Pearled Quality. The greater Pearled Boiling is, when the String continues in like Manner, altho' the Fingers are quite ftretched out, by entirely fpreading the Hand. This Degree of boiling may alfo be known by a kind of round Pearls that arife on the Top of the Liquor.

The

The Blown Boiling.

WHEN the Sugar has had a few more Walms, shake the Skimmer a little with your Hand, beating the Side of the Pan, and blow through the Holes of it from one Side to the other; so that if certain Sparks, as it were, or small Bubbles fly out, the Sugar has attain'd to the Degree of boiling, termed Blown.

The Feather'd Boiling.

WHEN after some other Seethings the Artist blows through the Skimmer, or shakes the Spatula with a back Stroke, 'till thicker and larger Bubbles rise up on high, then the Sugar is become Feathered ; and when, after frequent Trials, these Bubbles appear thicker and in a greater Quantity, so that several of them stick together, and form, as it were, a Flying-Flake, then
be greatly Feather'd.

The Crack'd Boiling.

TO know whether the Sugar has attain'd to this Degree, you are to dip the End of your Finger into cold Water, set by, in a Pot or Pan, for that Purpose; then having dexterously run it into the boiling Sugar, dip it again into the Water, thus keeping your Finger in the Water, rub off the Sugar with the other two, and if it break afterwards, with a Kind of crackling Noise, it is come to the Point of boiling called crack'd.

The Caramel Boiling.

IF some Sugar reduc'd to the Condition express'd in the
preceding Article, were put between the Teeth, it
would stick to them, as it were Glue or Pitch; but when
'tis brought to its utmost Caramel height, it breaks and
cracks, without sticking in the least: Therefore, Care must
be taken to observe every Moment, when it is boiled to this
last Degree, putting the Directions just before given, into
Practice, to discover when it is crack'd, and afterwards biting
the Sugar so order'd with your Teeth, to try whether it will
stick to them, as soon as you perceive that it does not,
but on the contrary, cracks and breaks clever, remove it
forthwith from the Fire, otherwise it will burn, and be no
longer good for any Manner of Use: However, as to the
other well-conditioned Boilings, if after having preserved
any Sweet-meats, some Sugar be still left, that is crack'd for
Instance, or Feathered, and which cannot be used again in
that Condition, 'tis only requisite, to put as much Water
thereto as is needful to boil it over again, and then it may be
brought to any Degree whatsoever, and even mingled with
any other Sort of Sugar or Syrup   The Pearled Boiling is
generally used for all Sorts of Comfits that are to be kept
for a considerable Time   The Use of the other Ways of
boiling, shall be shewn in treating of several Sorts of Sweetmeats, to which they are appropriated

Sometimes Fruit may be preserved with thin Sugar, that
is to say, when two Ladles full of clarify'd Sugar are put to
one of Water, four to two, six to three; and so on proportionably to the Quantity of the Fruits which are to
be well soaked therein. To that Purpose you must heat
the

the Sugar and Water together, fome what moıe than luke-waım, in order to be poured upon them.

To preſerve Gıeen Goofeberries Liquid.

SLIT youı Goofeberries on one Side, with a Pen-knife, and take out all the fmall Graıns that aıe on the Infide, then put them ınto veıy clear Water fet oveı a gentle Fııe: As foon as they ııfe on the Top of the Water, they aıe to be removed, and fet by in the fame Liquor: When they are cool'd, let them be put into other fıeſh Water oveı a moderate Fıre, 'till they recover theır green Colour, and become very foft: Afteıwards beıng cool'd agaın ın faıⁱ Water, they are to be well drained, and put into Sugar paſs'd through the Stıaining-Bag: At that very Inftant, gıve them fourteen or fifteen Boilings, to the End, that they may thoıoughly ımbıbe the Sugar, and ſtand by 'tıll the next Day; then havıng draın'd them, ſlıp them into the Syıup boıled to the Pearl'd Degıee, and let them have four oı five covered Boılıngs, whıch will bring the whole Work to Perfection.

To preſerve Cheıries Liquid.

AFTER having cut off Part of theır Stalks, ſlip them into a Pan of Sugar, boiled to the thırd Degree, called, Blown, where they ought to have ten or twelve cover'd Boilings, before they aıe fet by. The next Day, they are to be dıained, and put into Sugar again boiled 'tıll it becomes Pearled. Then add fome Syrup of Cuı-rants of the fame Quality, to give them a finer Colour, and put them into Pots to be kept for Ufe.

Cherries *preserved dry with* Strawberries.

HAving Cherries preserved dry, out of which the Stones have been already pick'd, put in their Room as many Strawberries, likewise preserved dry: That done, let all be dry'd in the Stove, after they have been strew'd with Sugar, as well in the dressing as in the turning of them.

Cherries *in* Ears.

CHerries may be also dress'd in Ears, after the following Manner: Which is, to open and spread them joining together, so as their Skins may remain on the Outside, and the Pulp on the Inside; then another Cherry of the same Nature is to be added on each Side, the Pulp of which, is to be laid upon the Skin of the others.

Cherries *booted after the Royal Manner.*

GET *Kentish* Cherries, or others with short Stalks, and put them into Sugar boil'd to the second Degree, called Pearled. Before they are set into the Stove to dry, other Cherries preserved in Ears are also provided, which must be laid upon them cross-ways, to the Number of three, four, or six, and afterwards set into the Stove. These are commonly called, Booted Cherries.

To preserve Red Currants Liquid.

YOUR Currants being pick'd, let them be put into Pearled Sugar, and have a light covered Boiling, then they are to be scummed and the next Day strain'd through a Sieve, while the Syrup is boiled to a Degree between

tween Smooth and Pearled : Afterwards flip in the Fruit, and add as much other Pearled Sugar as is requifite to foak them : They ought alfo to have feveral cover'd Boilings between Smooth and Pearled, carefully taking off the Scum, and ftirring them 'till they are cool'd a little, to prevent their turning to a Jelly.

Currants *preferved in Bunches.*

YOU muft take a convenient Quantity of Currants tied up in Bunches, and bring your Sugar to the fourth Degree of Boiling, called, Feathered ; then fet them in Order in the Sugar, and let them have feveral covered Boilings: They are to be fpeedily fcumm'd and not fuffer'd to have above two or three Seethings, that done, let them be fcummed again and fet into the Stove in the Copper-pan ; the next Day being cool'd, drain them in Bunches, in order to be well ftrewed with Sugar, and dry'd in the Stove

To preferve Rasberries Liquid.

LET four Pounds of good Rasberries be pick'd and put into three Pounds of Pearled Sugar : Give them a fmall Boiling lightly cover'd, and ftir them from time to time Then they are to be cool'd, drain'd and dry'd as Cherries, and the Quantity of pearled Sugar augmented, to the end that there may be enough for the due foaking of the Fruit.

Rasberries *preferved dry*

YOU muft take Rasberries that are not too ripe, pick them, and put them into Sugar that has attained to its blown Quality, in order to have a cover'd Boiling . Afterwards,

terwards, being removed from the Fire, they are to be
ſcumm'd, and ſlipt into an Earthen Pan, to continue in
the Stove Twenty-four Hours, allowing as great a Quantity of Sugar as of Fruit. As ſoon as they are cool'd, let
them be drain'd from their Syrup, and dreſſed as other
Sweet-Meats, before they are ſtiewed and dried after the
uſual manner.

To preſerve Pear Plumbs, *white or green.*

TAKE the Plumbs, cut their Stalks off, and wipe
them : Then adding an equal Weight of Sugar, put
them into a Copper Pan , let them ſtand in it, and ſtew,
being cloſe cover'd, till they become tender, but they muſt
not boil   When they are ſoft, lay them in a Diſh, ſtrew
them with Sugar, and cover them with a Cloth, to be ſet
by all Night : The next Day ſlip them again into the Pan,
and let them boil a-pace, taking care that they be well ſcum-
med , when your Plumbs look clear, the Syrup will turn
to Jelly, and they are enough : If the Plumbs are ripe,
peel off the Skins before you put them into the Pan , by
which Means they'll be the better and clearer a great deal
to dry, in caſe you would have them white. Otherwiſe
for the green Colour, let them be done with the Rinds on.

Red Plumbs.

WHEN theſe Sorts of Plumbs are provided, ſuch
as Imperial or Apricock-Plumbs, Bell-Plumbs, and
Orange-Plumbs, *&c.* let them be ſlit, as it were, Apricocks, and ſtoned : Then for four Pounds of Fruit, take
the ſame Quantity of Sugar paſs'd thro' the ſtraining-bag;
put all together into a Copper-pan over the Fire, and ſtir
them

them continually, left the Skins of the Plumbs should break; let them simmer for a while, and then set them by to cool. Afterwards, they are to be drain'd on a Colander or Sieve while the Syrup is boiled smooth, slip your Fruit into the same Syrup, and give them seven or eight cover'd Boilings, carefully taking off the Scum from time to time, even when the Pan is removed from the Fire. Lastly, the Plumbs being put into Earthen Pans, must continue in the Stove all Night, so that the next Morning you may drain them as soon as they are cool'd, and dress them in order to be dry'd in the Stove upon Sieves or Slates.

Plumbs *preserved with half Sugar, and otherwise.*

LET four Pounds of Fruit be boil'd a little in the like Quantity of Sugar brought to the second Degree of boiling, call'd Pearled, and then set by 'till they have cast their Juice: Some time after, set them over the Fire again, and boil them till the Syrup becomes pearled But they must lie in Pans till the next Day, when they are to be drain'd, strewed with Sugar, and dried in the Stove The same Method may be used in preserving all Sorts of good Plumbs, and they may also be par'd when scalded in Water.

To preserve Apricocks

TAKE Apricocks that are moderately ripe, part and stone them; let them also lie a whole Night in the Preserving-pan, among Sugar laid in Lays· The next Morning put in a small Quantity of fair Water, or white Wine, and set them on Embers, so as the Sugar may be melted by Degrees. When your Apricocks are scalded a

little,

little, take them off, and let them cool; that done, set them on again, and boil them till they are tender and well coloured.

Pared Apricocks *preserved another Way.*

AFTER having neatly par'd and ston'd your Apricocks, slitting them on one Side, let them be scalded in Water almost boiling hot: When they are all equally entire and soft, they are to be put into clarify'd Sugar, and boil'd till no Scum or Froth arises any longer, which must be always carefully taken off· The next Day they are to be drain'd, while the Syrup is boil'd till it has attained to its smooth Quality, augmenting it with Sugar: Then turn the Apricocks into the Pan, and having given them a Boiling, let them be set by: On the Day following, drain them, and let the Syrup be boiled till it comes to the second Degree, call'd Pearled: Afterwards slip them into the Pan again, adding some Sugar likewise pearled, and give them a cover'd boiling, in order to be set into the Stove till the next Morning, when they are to be taken out, and put into Pots, so as they may be eaten in the same Condition, or dried at Pleasure.

Apricocks *in* Ears.

APricocks that have been ordered after this, or any other Manner, may be dress'd in Ears; to which Purpose it is only requisite to turn one of the Halves, without loosening it altogether from the other; or to join the two Halves together, so as they may mutually touch one another at both Ends, one on one Side, and the other on the other.

Apri-

Apricocks *preserved dry.*

TO dry your Apricocks at all Times, set a Copper-pan with Water over the Fire, and the Pot or earthen Pan containing the Fruit, in the Middle of the same Pan. After the Water has boil'd half an Hour, the Apricocks will be heated, and you'll have the Liberty to take them out to be drain'd; then they may be dress'd upon the Slates or Boards in order to be set into the Stove, after they have been strew'd with Sugar.

To preserve green Walnuts.

LET your Walnuts be gathered in fair Weather, before the Shell grows hard; after having boiled them in Water, to take away their Bitterness, put them into other cold Water, peel off their Rind, and lay them in your Pan, with a Layer of Sugar to the Weight of the Nuts, and as much Water as will wet it. When they are boil'd up over a moderate Fire and cool'd, do the same Thing a second Time, and set all by for use.

To preserve White Walnuts.

HAving provided Walnuts that are come to their full Growth, but before the Wood is formed, pare them neatly 'till the White appears, and throw them into fair Water: Afterwards let them boil for some time in the same Water while other Water is set over another Furnace, into which the Walnuts are to be put as soon as it begins to boil. To know whether they are done enough, prick them with a Pin from Time to Time, so that when they slip off from it, they must be removed from the Fire. To make them white, throw in a Handful of

4 G

beaten

beaten Allum, and give them one Boiling more; then they are to be forthwith cool'd by turning them into fresh Water, in order to be put into the Sugar, allowing one Ladle full of Water for every two of Sugar; after your Walnuts are well drain'd, slip them into Earthen Pans, and having caused the Sugar and Water to be heated together, pour it upon them. On the next Day, you are to clear the Syrup from the Pans, without removing the Walnuts, because they must not be set over the Fire at all: Let this Syrup have five or six Boilings, augmenting it a little with Sugar, and let it be pour'd on the Walnuts: On the second Day it must have fifteen Boilings, on the third Day it must boil till it is very smooth, between smooth and pearled, and at last entirely pearled, take Care to increase the Quantity of Sugar at every time, to the End that the Walnuts may be equally soaked in the Syrup. To bring the whole Work to Perfection, let them continue in the Stove during the Night, and the next Morning they may be put into Pots, or you may make an End of drying them in the same Stove at Pleasure, as other Sorts of Fruit.

For Walnuts preserv'd Liquid, in case you add some Syrup of Apricocks, they'll keep much better. If you have a Mind to stuff them with Lemon-peel, it may be done before they are set in the Stove. For that Purpose it would be requisite to make an Opening with the Point of an Knife, either quite through, or on the Top of the Walnut, and then the Lemon-peel issuing from thence, will appear as if it were the natural Stalk. If some Amber be also added, it will give it a Perfume very grateful both to the Taste and Smell.

To

To *preferve* Mulberries Liquid.

LET two Quarts of Mulberry Juice be ftrained, adding thereto a Pound and a half of Sugar, boil them
together over a gentle Fire, till they turn to a kind of
Syrup, then flip into your Pan three Quarts of Mulberries,
that are not over-ripe, and after they have had one Boil,
pour all into an Earthen Veffel, in order to be ftopt clofe
and kept for Ufe.

Another Way of preferving Mulberries *wet.*

BOIL your Sugar till it is a little pearled, allowing
three Pounds of it for four Pounds of Mulberries, and
give them a light cover'd boiling in the fame Sugar, gently
ftirring the Pan, by means of the Handles. That done,
remove it from the Fire, and fet it by till the next Day,
when you are to drain off the Syrup, in order to bring it
to its pearled Quality. Afterwards flip in your Fruit, adding a little more pearled Sugar, if it be requifite, and difpofe of all in Pots as foon as they are fufficiently cool'd.

Mulberries *preferved dry.*

PICK fuch Mulberries as are not too ripe, but rathe
fomewhat greenifh and tart, in the mean while,
having provided as much Sugar as Fruit, let it be clarify'd
with the Juice of Mulberries, and brought to the third
Degree of boiling, call'd Blown, then throw in your Mulberries, and give them a cover'd boiling; afterwards removing the Pan from the Fire, take off the Scum, and
leave all in the Stove till the next Day. As foon as they are
taken out and cool'd, drain them from their Syrup, and

drefs

dreſs them upon Slates, to the End that they may de dry'd in the Stove, ſtrew'd with Sugar, as the other Sorts of Fruit. Laſtly, they muſt be turned again upon Sieves, and when thoroughly dry, lock'd up in Boxes for uſe, as Occaſion may ſerve.

To *preſerve* Barberries.

GATHER the faireſt Bunches in a dry Day, and boil them in a Pottle of Claret till they are ſoft; after having ſtrained them, add ſix Pounds of Sugar, with a Quart of Water, and boil them up to a Syrup; then put your ſcalded Barberries into the Liquor, and they'll keep all the Year round.

To *preſerve* Medlars.

SCALD your Fruit in fair Water, till the Skin may be eaſily peel'd off, then ſtone them at the Head, adding to every Pound the like Weight of Sugar, and let them boil till the Liquor become ropy; at that Inſtant remove them from the Fire, and ſet them by for uſe.

To *preſerve* Green Pippins.

LET the greeneſt Pippins, gather'd in fair Weather, before they are too ripe, be par'd and boil'd in Water, till they are very ſoft: Then cut out the Cores, and mix the Pulp with the Liquid, allowing ten Pippins, and two Pounds of Sugar to a Pottle thereof: When it is come to a due Conſiſtence, put in the Fruit you would have preſerved, and let them boil till they have a greener Colour than natural.

Green

Green Apples *preserved after another Manner.*

TAKE any kind of sweet and small Apples; which are to be pared, leaving the Stalks, and slit a little, for the better soaking in of the Sugar; that done, throw them into Water, that they may be cleans'd and scalded; when cool'd, let them be brought again to a green Colour, in the same or other fresh Water; as soon as they are become very soft let them be cool'd again, drain'd, and put into clarify'd Sugar in order to have some Boilings. The next Day the Syrup is to be boil'd smooth; at another time between smooth and pearl'd, and at last very much pearled; at which Instant the Fruit is to be slipt in, that all may simmer together for some time. The next Morning give your Apples a cover'd boiling before they are taken off from the Fire to be dispofed of in Pots or Glasses, or else to be cool'd and drain'd for drying in the Stove.

To preserve Pears.

HAving provided Pears that are found, and not over-ripe, set several Rows of them in Order at the Bottom of an Earthen Pan, and cover them with Vine Leaves; put another Layer of Pears upon them, and so do till the Pot is full; then to each Pound of Pears add half a Pound of Sugar, and as much fair Water as will dissolve it over a gentle Fire : Let them boil till they are somewhat soft, and afterwards set them by for use.

Pears *preserved in Quarters, and otherwise.*

BEsides several Sorts of Pears which may be preserved whole and dry, there are others of a large Size, which can only be so order'd in Quarters as to be kept Liquid. If you are desirous to preserve pretty big Pears altogether entire, their Core, with some of their Pulp in the Middle, is to be neatly scooped out, as it were that of an Orange: They are brought to Perfection by boiling them several times in Sugar, and may also be dried.

To preserve Quinces Liquid.

HAving provided the soundest, the yellowest, and ripest Quinces, let them be cut into Quarters, clear'd from the Cores and par'd: Boil all together in a sufficient Quantity of Water; and as soon as they are become very soft, remove the Pan from the Fire; then taking up the Pieces that are to be preserved with the Skimmer, put them into fresh Water to cool, and set the rest over the Fire again, that they may have twenty other Boilings: After this Decoction being pass'd thro' the straining Bag, take two Ladles full of it, with one of clarify'd Sugar, proportionably to the Quantity of your Fruit, and turn all into a Copper Pan, with Quinces, in order to boil over a gentle Fire. Some Sugar must also be added, accordingly as the first Syrup consumes away, without pouring in any more Decoction, and the whole Mess is to be well boil'd till the Syrup becomes pearled: That done let it be cool'd, and dress your Quinces in Pots, Glasses, or Boxes, pouring the Syrup upon them, which will be very fine, and of a lively red Colour, if the Pan was cover'd in the boiling.

To

To preferve Seville Oranges *in* Quarters *or in* Sticks.

THE Oranges are firft to be turn'd, or elfe zefted, accoiding as the Defign is, either to preferve them in Zefts or Chips, or to make Faggots. Turning in this Senfe, is a Term of Art, which denotes a particular Mannei of paring Oianges and Lemons when the outwaid Rind or Peel is par'd off veiy thin and nairow, with a Knife pioper for that Purpofe, winding it round about the Fruit fo as the Peel may be extended to a very great length without breaking. To zeft, is to cut the Peel from Top to Bottom into fmall Slips as thin as it can poffibly be done. The Orange being thus prepared, may be cut into Quarteis or into Sticks at Pleafure, but the Skin in the Infide and the Juice muft be taken away : Then let them be thrown into Water, fet over the Fiie, as foon as it begins to boil, and when they are done enough, (which may be peiceived by their flipping off fiom the Pin) they aie to be cool'd and put into frefh Water, as alfo afterwaids into clarify'd Sugar, fo as to have feven or eight coveied Boilings, befoie you fet them by to cool. They muft likewife be boil'd over again, 'till the Syrup becomes almoft fmooth, and drain'd the next Day, in order to be put into Pots, while the Syiup is made peailed, which being pour'd upon your Oianges, they may be kept in that Condition, 'till it fhall be judg'd expedient to dry them.

Seville Oranges *preferved entire.*

AS you turn or zeft your Fiuit, thiow them into fair Water, and afterwaids fcald them, 'till they become very foft, and flip off fiom the Pins: Then they are to be

cool'd

cool'd and fcoop'd with a little Spoon made for that Purpofe, at a fmall Hole bor'd in the Middle, where the Stalk grew: They are ufually put into Sugar, and dry'd after the fame Manner as Quinces and Sticks of Oranges,

Faggots *of* Oranges.

THIS Term is ufually appropriated to Orange Peels, when turn'd or par'd very thin, and extended to a great length, which are often preferved, efpecially thofe of fweet Oranges, after the following Manner, *viz.* Thefe Faggots are to be firft fcalded in Water over the Fire, 'till they become very foft, and put into clarify'd Sugar, allowing them twenty Boilings: The next Morning the Syrup muft be made fmooth, and the Orange-Paring put into it, that they may have two or three Boilings. On the third Day you are to drain them, and afterwards give them a covered Boiling in Pearled Sugar, in order to be difpofed of in Pots for Ufe, unlefs you would have them dry'd at the fame Inftant: This may be effected by caufing other Sugar to be made white, rubbing it on one Side of the Pan with the Skimmer, and boiling it to the fourth Degree, called Feathered: That done, flip your Faggots into it and drefs them in Rocks.

Oranges *preferved in Zefts.*

AS your Oranges are zefting in the above-mentioned Manner, throw the Zefts or Chips into fair Water on one Side, and the Quarters on the other, to prevent their turning black: That done, heat the Water, and put your Zefts therein, to be fcalded 'till they become very foft: Then having flipt them into frefh Water, they muft be

cool'd

cool'd, and ordered with thin Sugar, putting one Ladle full of Water into a Pan, for every two of clarify'd Sugar, thus all muſt be heated over the Fire, as long as you can well endure to hold your Finger in the Liquor. In the mean time, the Orange-Chips being drain'd and ſlip'd into an earthen Pan, the hot Sugar is to be pour'd upon them 'till they are thoroughly ſoaked : The next Day they are to be drain'd thro' a Colander while the Syrup is boil'd 'till it become a little ſmooth ; afterwards this Syrup muſt be pour'd again upon the Zeſts; as alſo on the third Day : When you have brought it to its pearled Quality, and augmented it with a little Sugar, on the the fourth Day, drain your Orange-Chips again and dry them in the Sieve or Hurdles, or upon a Grate. They muſt alſo be turn'd from time to time, 'till they are very dry, and at laſt put in Boxes.

Oranges *preſerved in ſmall Slips.*

WHEN your Fruit is zeſted, cut out the Pulp into Slips, which are to be ſlit again in their Thickneſs, to render them very thin. At firſt, you are to ſcald theſe Orange Slips in Water over the Fire, 'till they become very ſoft. That done, they are to be thrown into clarify'd Sugar, newly paſſed through the Straining-bag, when it is ready to boil, in order to have twenty Boilings. The next Day having brought the Sugar to its ſmooth Quality, and put your Slips into it, let them have ſeven or eight Boilings : On the third Day you may boil your Sugar 'till it is pearled, and give them a cover'd Boiling. Some time after, they are to be put into Pots or other Veſſels and dry'd as Occaſion ſerves.

N° 27. 4 H *Note,*

Note, Lemons, Limes, and Citrons, are preserved much after the same Manner; either entire, or in Sticks, Faggots, Zests, Slips, &c.

To preserve Eringo Roots.

LET two Pounds of fair Roots, wash'd and cleans'd, be boil'd very tender over a moderate Fire; then peel off the outmost Rind, but take care to avoid breaking them. After they have lain a while in cold Water, slip them into your Pan of Sugar boil'd to a Syrup, allowing to every Pound of Sugar, three Quarters of a Pound of Roots, which having boil'd gently a short time, may be set by to cool, and afterwards laid up for use.

To ice Almonds.

BLANCH your Almonds and put them into an Ice ready prepared with the White of an Egg, powder'd Sugar, Orange or Lemon Flowers and *Seville* Orange: Roll them well in this Compound so as they may be neatly iced, and afterwards dress'd on a Sheet of Paper, in order to be bak'd in the Campagne Oven, with a gentle Fire underneath, and on the Top.

To make White Crisp-Almonds.

AFTER having scalded and blanch'd the Almonds, throw them into Sugar boil'd in the fifth Degree call'd Crack'd: That done, let all have a Walm or two together, keeping your Almonds stirr'd and turn'd, to the End that the Sugar may stick close in them.

Crisp

Crisp Almonds *of a grey Colour.*

HAving melted a Pound of Loaf, or Powder-Sugar, with a little Water, let a Pound of Almonds be boiled in it 'till they crackle: Then take off the Pan from the Fire, and stir all about incessantly with the Spatula, if any Sugar be left, heat it again over the Fire, that it may entirely stick to the Almonds, continuing to stir them without Intermission, 'till the Work be brought to Perfection.

Red crisp Almonds.

YOU must let your Almonds be ordered as before, only the Sugar being boiled 'till it becomes crack'd, add as much prepared Cochineal, as will be requisite to give it a lively Colour, and let it boil again to cause it to return to its crack'd Quality: At that very Instant, toss in your Almonds, and removing the Pan from the Fire, stir them without Intermission, as at first, 'till they are dry. The Cochineal may be prepared only by boiling it with Allum and Cream of Tartar, which Liquor is generally us'd for every thing that is to be brought to a fine Colour, as Marmalets, Jellies, Pasties, Creams, &c.

Pistachoes *in* Surtout.

HAving provided a convenient Quantity of Pistachoes, clear them from their Shells, and cause them to be made crisp after this Manner: As soon as the Sugar has attain'd to the fourth or Feather'd Degree of boiling, throw in your Pistachoes, and when they have continued a while in it, remove the Pan, stirring them well 'till they are all cover'd, but they must not be again set over the Fire: Afterwards, they are to be dipp'd into the White of an Egg, beat up with a Spoon, adding a little Orange-Flower Water: That done, take them out and roll them in dry Powder-Sugar   Laftly, having laid them in Order upon white Paper, bake them gently in a Campagne Oven, with a little Fire underneath, and more on the Top: When they are fufficiently baked, and brought to a good Colour, they may be taken out of the Oven, in order to be dry'd in the Stove.

To make clear Cakes *of* Plumbs.

WE take any Sort of Plumbs, and having fton'd them, flip them into a Jugg, fet in a Pot of boiling Water· When they are diffolved, ftrain them through a fair Cloth, and to a Pint of the Liquor, add a Pound of Sugar brought to a Candy height.   Let all be well incorporated, and boil a little, ftirring them together.   Afterwards, put your Cakes into Glaffes, and fet them in the Stove moderately heated, otherwife they will grow tough. Let them ftand fo two or three Weeks, without being cool'd, removing them from one warm Place to another: Turn them every Day, 'till they are thorough dry, and they'll be very clear.

So make a Cake *or* Pafte *of* Cherries.

STONE your Cherries, and ftew them in a Pan 'till they have caft their Juice, that done lay them in Order in a Sieve, and let them be well drain'd; afterwards they are to be be beaten in a Mortar and fet over the Fire again to be throughly dry'd: In the mean Time having allow'd a Pound of Sugar for every Pound of Cherry Pafte,

let

let it be brought to its crack'd Quality, and pour upon the fame. A little while after your Cakes may be dreffed upon the Slates with a Spoon, and fet in the Stove.

To make clear Quince Cakes.

YOU muft let a Pint of the Syrup of Quinces, with a Quart or two of Rasberries, be boiled and clarify'd over a gentle Fire, taking Care that it be well fcummed from Time to Time: Then having added to the Juice a Pound and a half of Sugar, caufe as much more to be brought to a Candy height, and poured in hot. Let the whole Mafs be continually ftirr'd about 'till it is almoft cold, then fpread it upon Plates, and cut it into Cakes of what Form or Figure you fhall think fit.

M A R M A L E T S and Q U I D D A N I E S.

Marmalet *of* Cherries.

YOUR Cherries being firft fton'd, are to be fet over the Fire, in a Copper-pan, to caufe them to caft their Juice: Afterwards, being drain'd, bruis'd and pafs'd thro' a Sieve, the Marmalet muft be put again into the Pan, to be dry'd over a quick Fire, carefully ftirring and turning it on all Sides with the Spatula, fo as no Moifture may be left, and 'till it begins to ftick to the Pan. In the mean while, boil fome Sugar 'till it be greatly Feathered; allowing one Pound of it for every Pound of Fruit or Pafte: That done, caufe all to fimmer together for a while, and put your Marmalet into Pots or Glaffes ftrew'd with Sugar, or elfe proceed to the drying of it.

Mar-

Marmalet *of* Currants.

GET a fufficient Quantity of Currants ftripp'd off from the Bunches, and foak them in boiling Water 'till they break: That done, removing them from the Fire, drain them upon a Sieve, and when cold, pafs them thro' the fame Sieve, to clear off the Grains: Afterwards they are to be dry'd over the Fire, as before, while the Sugar is brought to the fifth Boiling called, Cracked, allowing the fame Weight of it as of the Fruit: Let all be well inter-mixed together, in order to fimmer for fome time, let your Marmalet be conveniently difpofed of in Pots, &c.

Marmalet of Bell-Grapes is made after the fame Manner.

Marmalet *of* Rasberries.

WE ufually make the Body of this Marmalet of very ripe Currants, to which is only added a Handful of Rasberries, to make it appear as if it confifted altogether of the latter.

Marmalet *of* Plumbs.

IF they are fuch Plumbs as flip off from their Stones, thofe Stones are to be taken away: Otherwife fcald your Fruit in Water, 'till they become very foft; let them alfo be drain'd and well fqueezed thro' the Sieve; then dry your Marmalet over the Fire, and let it be temper'd with the fame Weight of crack'd Sugar: Laftly, having caufed it to fimmer for a while, let it be put into Glaffes or Pots, and ftrew'd with Sugar.

Marmalet *of ripe* Apricocks.

HAving provided five Pounds of ripe Apricocks, let them boil in two Pounds of pearled Sugar, 'till they have thrown out all their Scum, and then remove them from the Fire. As soon as they are cool'd, set them again over the Fire to be broken and dry'd, 'till they do not run any longer: In the mean Time, let three Pounds and a half of Sugar be brought to its crack'd Quality, in order to be incorporated with the Paste; let all simmer together for some time, and let the Marmalet, strew'd with fine Sugar, be turned into Pots as the others.

Marmalet *of* Apples.

AT first scald your Apples in Water over the Fire, and when they are become very tender, let them be taken out and drain'd; then strain all thro' a Sieve, and boil your Sugar 'till it be very much Feathered, allowing three Quarters of a Pound of it for every Pound of Fruit. The whole Mass being well temper'd and dry'd over the Fire, according to the usual Method, let it simmer together, then pour your Marmalet into Pots or Glasses, strew'd with Sugar. Marmalet of Pears is made altogether according to this Method.

Marmalet *of* Quinces, *according to the Mode of the City of* Orleans *in* France.

AFTER having pick'd out the best Sort of Quinces, cut them into Pieces, in order to be par'd and clear'd from the Cores and Kernels. In the mean while, having caus'd two Pounds of Sugar to be brought to its cracked Quality,

Quality, flip in about fix Pounds of Fruit, and let all boil together to a Pap, which you muft turn into a new Cloth to be well ftrain'd, and the Liquor that paffes thro' will ferve for the Marmalet: Let this ftrain'd Liquor be pour'd into other pearled Sugar to the Quantity of four Pounds, and as foon as the Syrup returns to the fame Degree of Boiling, let it be carefully fcummed; then removing the Pan from the Fire, take off the Scum again (if their be Occafion) and pour your Marmalet into Pots, Glaffes, or Boxes, which muft be left in the Air for fome Days before they are cover'd.

Marmalet *of* Quinces *after the* Italian *Manner.*

HAving about thirty Quinces par'd, and the Cores taken out, put to them a Quart of Water, with two Pounds of Sugar, and let all boil together 'till they are foft; then ftrain the Juice and the Pulp, in order to be boiled up with four Pounds of Sugar to a due Confiftence.

Marmalet *of* Oranges.

PARE your Oranges as thin as poffible, then boil them 'till they are foft; then take double the Number of good Pippins, cut them into Halves, core them, and boil them to Pap, fo as they may not lofe their Colour, ftrain the Pulp, and add a Pound of Sugar to every Pint: Afterwards take out the Orange-Pulp, cut the Peel, and let it be made very foft by boiling, in order to be bruifed in the Juice of Lemons, and boiled up again to a Confiftence with your Apple-Pulp, and half a Pint of Rofe-Water.

To make Quiddany *of* Pippins *of an Amber or Ruby Co-lour.*

PARE your Pippins, cut them into Quarters and boil them with as much fair Water, as will cover them, 'till they are soft, and sink in the Water: Then having strain'd the Pulp, let a Pint of the Liquor be boil'd with half a Pound of Sugar, 'till it appears a quaking Jelly on the Moulds: When your Quiddany is cold, turn it on a wet Trencher, and slide it into Boxes. If you would have it of a red Colour, let it boil leisurely close cover'd 'till it is as red as Claret Wine.

To make Quiddany *of all Sorts of* Plumbs.

BOIL your Plumbs in Apple Water, 'till they are as red as Claret: When you have made the Liquor strong of the Fruit, put to every Pint half a Pound of Sugar, and let it boil till a Drop of it will hang on the Back of a Spoon like a quaking Jelly. If you would have your Quiddany of an Amber Colour, only boil it over a quick Fire, and that will produce the desired Effect.

To make Quiddany *of* Rasberries.

HAving pick'd your Rasberries, put them into a Pot, stop it close, and set it in a Kettle of boiling Water. When they have been stewed thus almost an Hour, strain the Liquor from the Pulp, and add thereto the Weight of double refin'd Sugar, with a little Musk or Ambergreafe: That done, let all boil together over a quick Fire, for if they are long in boiling, they'll lose their Colour. Quidda-ny of Gooseberries may be made after the same Manner,

4 I   but

but they muſt boil an Hour; as alſo Quiddany of Currants which will only take up three Quarters of an Hour in boiling.

To make Quiddany *of* Apples, Quinces, Plumbs, *or any other Sorts of Fruit.*

TAKE a Quart of the Liquor of any preſerved Fruit; and put into it a Pound of the ſame Fruit raw, ſeparated from the Cores, Skins, Stones, and Kernels: Then let all boil up with a Pound of Sugar, 'till it will ſtand upon a Knife Point like a Jelly.

The P A S T E S of F R U I T.

Paſte *of ripe* Apricocks.

APricock-paſte is uſually made as the Marmalet of the ſame, or elſe the Apricocks may be only ſcalded at firſt without Sugar, but if they are not thoroughly ripe, bruiſe them as much as is poſſible, or pound them in a Mortar. Afterwards, your Fruit muſt be ſlipt into an equal Quantity of crack'd Sugar, and incorporated with it when well dry'd over the Fire: That done, having cauſed all to ſimmer, dreſs your Paſte as the others, if you are diſpoſed to dry it at the ſame Time.

Paſte *of* Plumbs.

YOUR Paſte may be made of dry Marmalet of Plumbs, putting to it ſome new Feathered Sugar, according the above-ſpecify'd Method: Or elſe your Fruit being duly prepared, *i. e.* ſtrained and dryed, cauſe it to be intermixed with crack'd Sugar: Then let all
ſimmer

fimmer together and let the Paftes be drefs'd after the ufual Manner.

Pafte *of* Apples *and* Peais.

FIRST having fcalded your Fiuit in Water, 'till they become foft, then let them be drained, paffed thro' a Sieve, and dried over the Fiie, but Care muft be taken to ftir them with a Spatula fiom time to time, both on the Bottom and round about to prevent their buining. When the Pafte flips off from the Bottom and Sides of the Pan, remove it from the Fire, and caufe fome Sugar to be gieatly feather'd or crack'd, which muft be well incoiporated with it, allowing a Pound of Fruit for the like Quantity of Sugar. Afterwaids, fet your Pafte again over the Fiie, to fimmer, and drefs it as the others in Moulds, or upon Slates, fetting all at the fame time into the Stove to be dried.

Quince-Pafte.

YOUR Quinces being pared, cut them into Quarters, and take away the Cores if you pleafe, or elfe let all be left. Then having made fome Watei boil over the Fiie throw in the Fruit, and let them continue boiling 'till they are very foft, in order to be diain'd upon a Grate or Hurdle, and pafs'd through a Hair-fieve, that done, fet the Pafte over the Fire again, to bediy'd and incoiporated with crack'd Sugar, to the Quantity of fomewhat more than a Pound for every Pound of Fruit. Laftly, your Pafte muft fimmer for awhile, and then be drefs'd as the others.

Orange

Orange Paſte.

THIS Paſte is made as Orange Marmalet, accoiding to the Method laid down in that Article, or elſe of the Marmalet itſelf, ordered as before, that is to ſay, it muſt be imbody'd with new Sugai, brought to its feather'd Quality, 'till it ſlips off from the Bottom of the Pan. Then having cauſed it to ſimmer, let it be dreſs'd after the uſual Manner, and dry'd in the Stove.

Candy'd C O N F E C T I O N S.

To candy Roſemary Flowers *in the Sun.*

LET Gum Dragant be ſteep'd for ſome time in Roſe-Water, and let your Roſemary Flowers, after they are well pick'd, be ſoak'd in the ſaid Water; then take them out, lay them upon a Paper and ſtrew fine Sugar over them; this do in the hot Sun, turning them, and ſtrewing Sugar on them, 'till they are candy'd, and ſo keep them for your Uſe.

To candy Barberries *and* Grapes.

WE take preſerved Barberries, waſh off the Syrup in warm Water, and ſift fine Sugar on them: Then let them be dry'd in the Stove, turning them from time to time, 'till they are thorough diy. Preſerved Grapes may alſo be candy'd after the ſame Manner.

To candy Eringo Roots.

LET the Roots be par'd and boil'd 'till they are ſoft, allowing to every Pound two Pounds of fine clarify'd Sugar: Afterwards, the Sugar being boiled to à due height,
dip

dip in your Roots two or three at once, and dry them in the Stove for Ufe.

To candy Elicampane Roots.

YOU muft take the Roots out of the Syrup in which they were preferved, dry them in a Cloth, and for every Pound allow a Pound and three Quarters of Sugar ; let the Sugar boil to a height, and your Roots being dipped therein, will be well candy'd.

To candy Angelica.

YOU muft boil the Stalks of Angelica in Water 'till they are tender, then peel them, put them into other warm Water, and cover them till they become very green over a gentle Fire. Afterwards, having laid them on a Cloth to dry, take their Weight in fine Sugar and boil it to a Candy height, with a little Rofe Water : Laftly, flip in your Stalks, boil them up quick, and take them out in order to be dry'd for Ufe.

To candy Orange Peels.

STEEP your Orange Peels, as often as you fhall judge expedient, in fair Water, to take away their Bitternefs ; then let them be gently dry'd, and candy'd with Syrup made of Sugar.

To candy Flowers.

GET any Sort of Flowers and cut the Stalks if they are very long fomewhat fhorter ; that done, let a Pound of white Sugar be boiled to a Clearnefs, with eight Spoonfuls of Rofe-Water : When the Sugar begins to grow

ftiff

ftiff and cool, dip your Flowers in it, take them out forth-with, and lay them one by one in a Sieve in order to be dry'd and harden'd in the Stove.

To make Barley Sugar.

HAving a sufficient Quantity of Barley boiled in Water, ftrain it thro' a Hair-fieve, and let this Decoction be put into clarify'd Sugar, brought to the Caramel or laft Degree of boiling; then take off the Pan from the Fire 'till the boiling fettles, and pour your Barley Sugar upon a Marble Stone rubb'd with Oil of Olives, but Care muft be taken to hinder it from running down: As the Sugar cools, and begins to grow hard, cut it into Pieces, and roll it out of what length you pleafe, in order to be kept for Ufe.

Several Sorts of BISKETS.

To make common Biskets.

SLIP the Whites and Yolks of fix or eight Eggs into a Bafon or Pan, beat them well with fome Sack, and a little Rofe-Water; then adding a Pound of powder Sugar with as much Flour, and half an Ounce of Coriander Seeds, mingle all together, and drefs your Pafte in Paper Cafes, or Tin Moulds, in any Form at Pleafure: After-wards, the Biskets being iced and dufted with fine Sugar, put into an Handkerchief, are to be fet in an Oven mode-rately heated, 'till they rife and come to a good Colour. When they are baked, take them up with the Point of a Knife, and let them be thoroughly dried in the Stove.

Bisket

Bisket Drops.

LET one Pound of Sugar, four Yolks of Eggs, two Whites, and a little Canary Wine be beaten well together. When the Oven is ready, add one Pound of Flour with a few Seeds, and let all be likewise well incorporated: That done, butter the Paper, lay your Drops in Order on it. Ice them with fine Sugar, and set them in a gentle Oven.

Savoy *or* French Biskets.

HAving provided a Pair of Scales, you are to put three or four new laid Eggs into one of them, as also some baked Flour into the other, so as there may be an equal Weight of both: In the mean Time, set by some Powder Sugar, of the same Weight as the Eggs, with the Whites; of which a very strong Froth is to be made by whipping them well with a Whisk: Add thereto at first some candy'd Lemon Peel grated or powdered, and then the Flour that was weighed before: All being thus mingled together, put in the Sugar, and after having beaten the whole Mass again for a while, slip in the Yolks, so as the Paste may be well tempered: That done, shape your Biskets upon Paper, with a Spoon, of a round or oval Figure, and ice them neatly with Powder Sugar: Afterwards, let the Biskets be bak'd in a Campagne Oven that is not over heated, giving them a fine Colour on the Top. When they are done enough, cut them off from the Paper with a very thin Knife, and lay them in Boxes for Use.

Lisbon

Lisbon Biskets.

LET the Whites of three or four Eggs, be beaten a little with the Yolks, and add thereto as much Powder Sugar as you can take up between your Fingers, at four or five Times, with four or five Spoonfuls of baked Flour, and some Lemon Peel When these are well imbody'd together, turn your Paste upon a Sheet of Paper strew'd with Sugar, strew the Paste likewise on the Top with the same Sugar, and set it in an Oven moderately heated. As soon as the Biskets are baked, they must be cut all at once with the Paper underneath, according to the Size and Figure you would have them to be of, and then the Paper may be gently pared off with a Penknife.

Chocolate Biskets.

WE scrape a little Chocolate upon the White of an Egg, to give it a Tincture, then work it up with Powder Sugar, and the rest of the Ingredients, to a pliable Paste: Then dress your Biskets upon Sheets of Paper, and set them in the Campagne Oven, to be baked with a gentle Fire, both on the Top and underneath.

Orange *and* Lemon Biskets.

AN experienced Confectioner may readily make up these Sorts of Biskets after the same Manner; only using a little grated Orange or Lemon Peel, with some Marmalet instead of the Chocolate. Other Biskets of the same Nature may likewise be prepared with Orange or Jessamine Flowers, beating them well before they are mingled with the other Ingredients.

Bis-

Biscotins.

GET four Spoonfuls of Powder Sugar, one of any kind of Marmalet, as of Apricocks, Quinces, Oranges, Currants, &c. and three Whites of Eggs; to these add a convenient Quantity of fine Flour, all which must be well temper'd together 'till the Paste becomes very pliable: Then proceed to make your Biscotins of various Figures, *viz.* some long, others round, others in Form of Cyphers, Love-Knots, and other Devices: They are to be bak'd with a moderate Fire, and taken out of the Oven as soon as they appear of a somewhat brown russet Colour · When they are drawn, they must be forthwith clear'd from the Paper, which may be easily done, by wetting the Sheets on the Back-side with fair Water.

M A R C H - P A N E S and M A C A R O O N S.

To make common March-panes.

TAKE a sufficient Quantity of Almonds, which are to be scalded in hot Water, blanch'd, and thrown into cold Water as they are done; then being wip'd and drain'd, they must be beaten in a Stone Mortar, and moistened with the White of an Egg, to prevent their turning to Oil. In the mean while, having caus'd half as much clarify'd Sugar as Paste, to be brought to its Feathered Quality, toss in your Almonds by Handfuls, or else pour the boiling Sugar upon them in another Vessel: Let them be well intermix'd, and the Paste continually stirr'd on all Sides. When 'tis done enough, it must be laid upon Powder Sugar, and set by to cool. Afterwards several Pieces of a convenient Thickness may be

taken

taken out, of which you are to cut your March-panes with certain Moulds, gently flipping them off with the Tip of your Finger upon Sheets of Paper, in order to be heated in the Oven only on one Side: That done, the other Side is to be ic'd over, and bak'd in like Manner: Otherwise, the Paste may be roll'd out or fqueez'd thro' a Syringe, and made curbed, or jagg'd of a round, oval, or long Figure, in the Shape of a Heart, &c.

Another Sort of Paste for March-panes.

YOUR Almonds being blanch'd, cool'd and drain'd as before, pound them well in a Mortar, and moiften them with the White of an Egg, and a little Orange-Flower-Water beaten together. Then having provided an equal Quantity of Sugar boil'd to the Feather'd Degree, flip in the Almonds, and temper all with the Spatula: That done, fet your Paste over the Fire again to be dry'd, continually ftirring the fame 'till it becomes pliable, and flips off from the Bottom of the Pan: Laftly, it muft be laid in a Bafon with Powder Sugar underneath, and made up into a thick Roll, to be fet by for awhile as the Former, fo as you may at laft fhape and drefs your March-panes after the fame Manner.

March-panes *with a Tincture of* Rasberries *or other Sorts of Fruit.*

DUring the Summer Seafon, your March-panes may be diverfify'd feveral Ways, *viz.* by tempering fome of them with the Juice of Fruit, as Rasberries, Strawberries, Cherries, Currants, &c. but if thofe Juices are made Ufe of for foaking the Almonds, when they are

pounded

pounded with the White of an Egg: The Paſte muſt be well dry'd at the Fire, or elſe with Powder Sugar.

To make Macaroons

HAving provided a Pound of Almonds, let them be ſcalded, blanched and thrown into fair Water: Then they muſt be drain'd, wiped and pounded in a Mortar, moiſtening them with Orange-Flower-Water, or the White of an Egg, leſt they ſhould turn to Oil. Afterwards, taking an equal Quantity of Powder Sugar, with three or four other Whites of Eggs, and a little Musk, beat all well to-gether, and dreſs your Macaroons upon Paper, with a Spoon, that they may be bak'd with a gentle Fire.

To make Jumbals.

LET a Pound of fine Flour, and as much white Sugar be made up into a Paſte with beaten Whites of Eggs; then add thereto half a Pint of Cream, half a Pound of freſh Butter, and a Pound of blanch'd Almonds well ſtamp'd; knead all together thoroughly with a little Roſe-Water, and cut out Jumbals into what Figure you pleaſe, in order to be bak'd in a gentle Oven.

To make Wafers.

GET as much Flour as you think fit, and mingle it with new Cream in the Evening. The next Day, when it is clear'd from Lumps, add powder Sugar, ſome-what above the Quantity of the Flour, ſo as all may be well intermix'd with a Spoon. That done, pour in more Cream, with a little Orange-Flower-Water, 'till the whole Maſs is almoſt reduced to the Conſiſtence of Milk, and

ſtir

ftir all well together: In the mean Time, the Wafer-Iron being heated and rubb'd on both Sides with fresh Butter, turn your prepared Cream or Batter upon it, which muft not exceed a Spoonful and half for every Wafer Afterwards, lay the Iron upon the Furnace, fo that as foon as the Wafer is baked on one Side, it may be turned on the other. When it is done enough, take it off from the Iron with a Knife, and roll it a little round the fame. Laftly, fpread your Wafers hot upon a Wooden Roller, to give them their due Shape, and fet them into the Stove, that they may be continually kept very dry.

White Paftils.

LET your Gum be firft fteep'd in a little Water, with the Juice of three or four Lemons, and their Zefts or Chips. As foon as the Gum is thoroughly diffolved, ftrain it through a Linnen Cloth as before, and pour it into the Mortar, with double refin'd Sugar, fifted through a fine Sieve, then throwing in a Handful of Sugar, let all be well work'd and beaten, and add another Handful, continuing to beat and temper the whole Mafs on all Sides, as it is augmenting with Sugar, 'till it comes to a very white and pliable Pafte, with which you make your Paftils with Pleafure, and dry them in the Stove.

Orange-Flower-Paftils.

THESE Sorts of Paftils are ufually prepared according to the fame Method, only fome Leaves of Orange-Flowers and Water of the fame, are to be incorporated with the Lemon Juice, in which the Gum is fteeped.

Apri-

Apricocks Paſtils.

HAving cauſed ſome Gum Arabick to be ſteep'd in Water, and ſtrain'd through a Cloth, turn it into a Mortar with Syrup of Apricocks: Then you are to temper your Compound, and augment it with Sugar at ſeveral Times, 'till the Paſte is pliable, in order to make round Paſtils, which are dry'd in the Stove, and may afterwards (if you pleaſe) be made while in the wide Pan, after the ſame Manner as Sugar Plumbs.

To make Artificial Flowers

AT firſt you are to make Paſtes of divers Colours, with Gum Dragant thoroughly ſteep'd and mingled with Powder Sugar, which is to be well tempered, and beaten in a Mortar, 'till the Paſte is become pliable For the Red, ſome prepared Cochineal may be added, for the Yellow, Gambooge; for the Blue, Indigo and Orris, and for the Green, the Juice of Beet-Leaves, which are to be ſcalded a little over the Fire, to take away their Crudity. The Paſtes being thus ordered, and rolled out into very thin Pieces, may be ſhaped in the Form of ſeveral Sorts of Flowers, as Roſes, Tulips, Wind-flowers, &c by the Means of certain Tin Moulds, or elſe they may be cut out with the Point of a Knife, according to Paper-Models. Then you are to finiſh the Flowers all at once, and dry them upon Egg-Shells, or otherwiſe. In the mean while, different Sorts of Leaves are, in like Manner, to be cut out of the green Paſte, to which you may alſo give various Figures, to be intermixed among your Flowers, the Stalks whereof, are to be made with Slips of Lemon Peel. The
Tops

Tops of the Pyramids of dryed Fruits, may be garnished
with thefe Artificial Flowers; or elfe a feparate Nofegay
may be made of them, for the Middle of your Defert; or
they may be laid in Order in a Basket, or kind of Cup,
made of fine Paftry-work of Crackling-Cruft, neatly cut
and dry'd for that Purpofe.

To make artificial Oranges *and* Lemons.

GET Moulds of Alabafter made in three Pieces: Bind
two of them together, and let them lie in the Water an Hour or two, boiling to a height, in the mean time,
as much Sugar as will fill them; the which, being poured
into the Mould, and the Lid put quickly on it, by fuddenly turning it will be hollow. You muft colour your
Sugar in boiling it, to the Colour you would have your
Fruit.

To make each Sort of Comfits, *vulgarly called,* Covering Seeds, *with Sugar.*

YOU muft provide a Pan of Brafs or Tin, to a good
Depth, made with Ears to hang over a Chafing-Difh
of Coals with a Ladle and Slice of the fame Metal; then
cleanfe your Seeds from Drofs, and take the fineft Sugar
well beaten; put to each Quarter of a Pound of Seeds, two
Pounds of Sugar melted in this Order; put into the Pan
three Pounds of Sugar, adding a Pint of Spring-Water,
ftirring it 'till it be moiftened, fuffering it to boil, and fo
from your Ladle let it drop upon the Seeds, and keep the
Bafon wherein they are, continually moving, and between
every Coat rub and dry them as well as may be; and when
they have taken up the Sugar, and by Motion are rolled
into

into Order, dry them in an Oven, or before the Fire, and they will be hard and white.

Brandy Peaches *used in Deserts.*

PUT your Peaches in boiling Water, do not let them boil, take them out, put them in cold Water, drain them in a Sieve, put them in long wide mouth'd Bottles To half a Dozen of Peaches, take a Quarter of a Pound of Sugar, clarify it, put it over your Peaches, fill up the Bottles with Brandy, stop them close, and keep them in a cool Place.

To dry Pears *or* Pippins *without Sugar.*

WIPE them clean, and take a Bodkin, and run it in at the Head-end, and out by the Stalk, and put them in a flat Earthen Pot, and bake them, but not too much. You must tie double White Paper over the Pot that they may not scorch, when they are cold drain them from the Liquor, and lay them on Sieves with wide Holes, and dry them in a hot Stove or Oven.

To dry Pears *with Sugar to keep all the Year.*

TAKE Poppering Pears, and thrust a piked Stick in at the Head of them, 'till it goes beyond the Core. Then scald them, but not too tender, then pare them the long Way into Water, and take the Weight of them in Sugar, clarify'd with a Pint and a half of Water to a Pound of Sugar; strain the Syrup clear, and put in the Pears, set them on the Fire, and boil them pretty handsomely half an Hour; then cover them with Papers, and set them by 'till the Morrow, then boil them again, and set them by

'till

'till the next Day, and then take them out of the Syrup, and boil it 'till it will draw ropy, and pack them in a Pan, and put it to them; if it will not cover them add some more Sugar: Set them on the Fire, and let them boil all over; then cover them with Paper, and set them in the Stove 24 Hours; and then take them out and let them be cold; then lay them on a Sieve to drain; then lay them on Plates, and dust them with some fine Sugar, and set them into the Stove to dry. When one Side is dry turn them upon Papers in a Sieve, and dust the other Side, and set them into the Stove again 'till they are quite dry: Then pack them up with Paper between each Laying, and keep them in a Closet.

To make red Colouring for Pippins, *or* Quince-Paste, *or* Paste Royal.

TAKE an Ounce of Cochineal, beat it very fine and put it in three Quarters of a Pint of fair Water in a Skillet, with a Quarter of an Ounce of Roach Allum, and boil it 'till you think the Water has got out the Goodness, then strain it through a Piece of fine Holland, and put it into a Vial, and put two Ounces of double refin'd Sugar to it, and keep it by you. It will keep six Months.

C H A P.

CHAP. XXIX.

Of setting out DINNERS, &c.

IN grand Entertainments, the most convenient Forms for Tables are those in the Shape of a Horse-Shoe, or of an oblong Square, open in the Middle, for at these Tables the Company being seated on the Outside, have the Pleasure of seeing one another, and being readily served without the Trouble of Waiters reaching over their Backs.

Mr. *Bradley* mentions the following Tables where five Dishes are served at a Course. These are so ordered as to save a great deal of Trouble to the Mistress of the Family, as well as the Guests, for with this Sort of Table every one helps himself, by turning what Dish he likes before him, without interrupting any body. You must have first, a large Table with a Hole in the Middle, of an Inch Diameter, wherein should be fix'd a Socket of Brass well turn'd, to admit of a Spindle of Brass, that will turn easily in it. The Table here spoken of may be five or six Feet diameter; and then have another Table-board made just so large that as it is to act on the Centre of the first Table, there may be near a Foot Vacancy for Plates, &c. on every Side. Then fix the Spindle of Brass in the Centre of the smaller Table, which Spindle must be so long, as that when one puts it in the Socket of the great Table-board, the smaller turning Table may be about four Inches above the lower Board; so, that in its turning about, no Salt, or Bread, or any thing on the Plates, may be disturb'd. These Tables have Cloths made to each of them; the upper, or fmaller Table, to have an whole Cloth faftned clofe, fo that none of the Borders hang down; and the Cloth for the under Table muft have an Hole cut in the Middle of it, for the Spindle of the upper Table to pafs through into the Brafs-Scoket; and when this is rightly order'd, and every * Cover placed on the lower Table, then the upper Table, which will turn, may be furnifhed with Meats. It remains only then, for the Lady of the Houfe, to offer the Soop; but after that, every one is at Liberty to help themfelves, by turning the upper Table about.

It is to be obferved that in fmall Entertainments and on common Days, the Soops are always firft ferved at the upper End of the Table, or Fifh if there is no Soop, and the Fifh is to fupply the Place of the Soop. The large Difh of boiled Meat again in the room of that, and the large Difh of roaft Meat at the Bottom of the Table; in the Middle is either a Pie, fomething roafted or a grand Sallad. For Tables of five Difhes and two Courfes, in every Month of the Year, fee the Plates that follow.

When the Defert is to come on, Care muft be taken to fee the Table well cleared, and the upper Table-Cloth taken off, with the Leather which lay between that and the under one. Dry'd Sweetmeats, Sweetmeats in Glaffes and Fruits, are placed in Pyramids, or otherwife, like the great Difhes of Meat. Creams and Compotes like Inter-meffes.

---

 * *N B* The Word Cover here means the Plate, Napkin, Knife, Fork and Spoon.

JANUARY

First Course

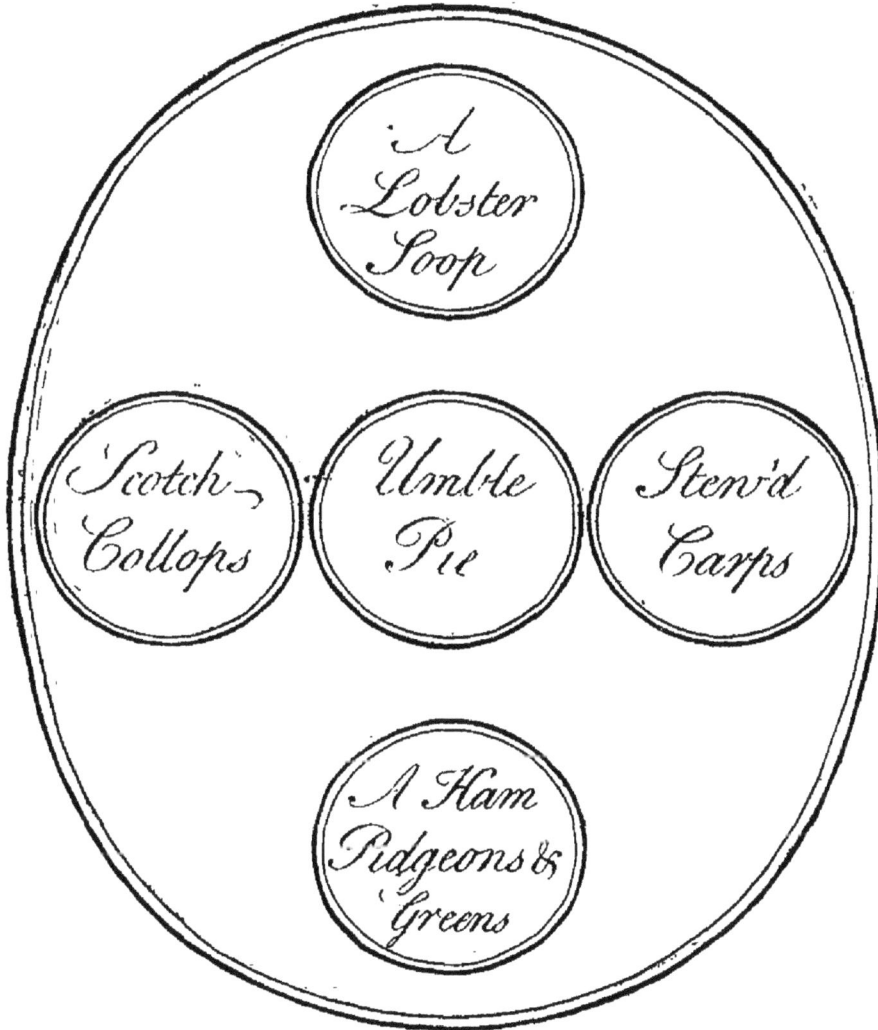

Second Course

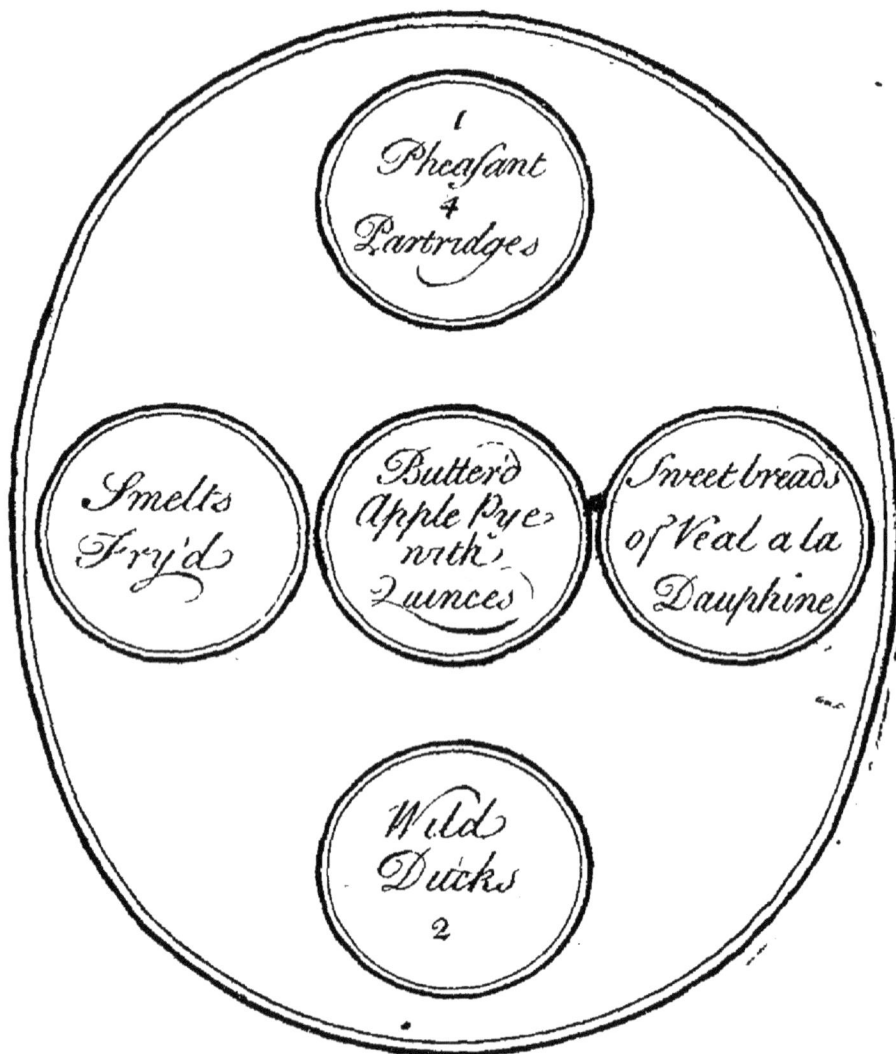

1
Pheafant
4
Partridges

Smelts
Fry'd

Butter'd
Apple Pye
with
Quinces

Sweetbreads
of Veal a la
Dauphine

Wild
Ducks
2

FEBRUARY

First Course

A
Vermicelly
Soop,
remov'd for
a Surtout
of Soals

A
Calves Head
Hash'd and
Gril'd.

A
Patty of
Chukens

A
Goose Boyl'd
with
Greens

Carps
Stew'd

Second Course

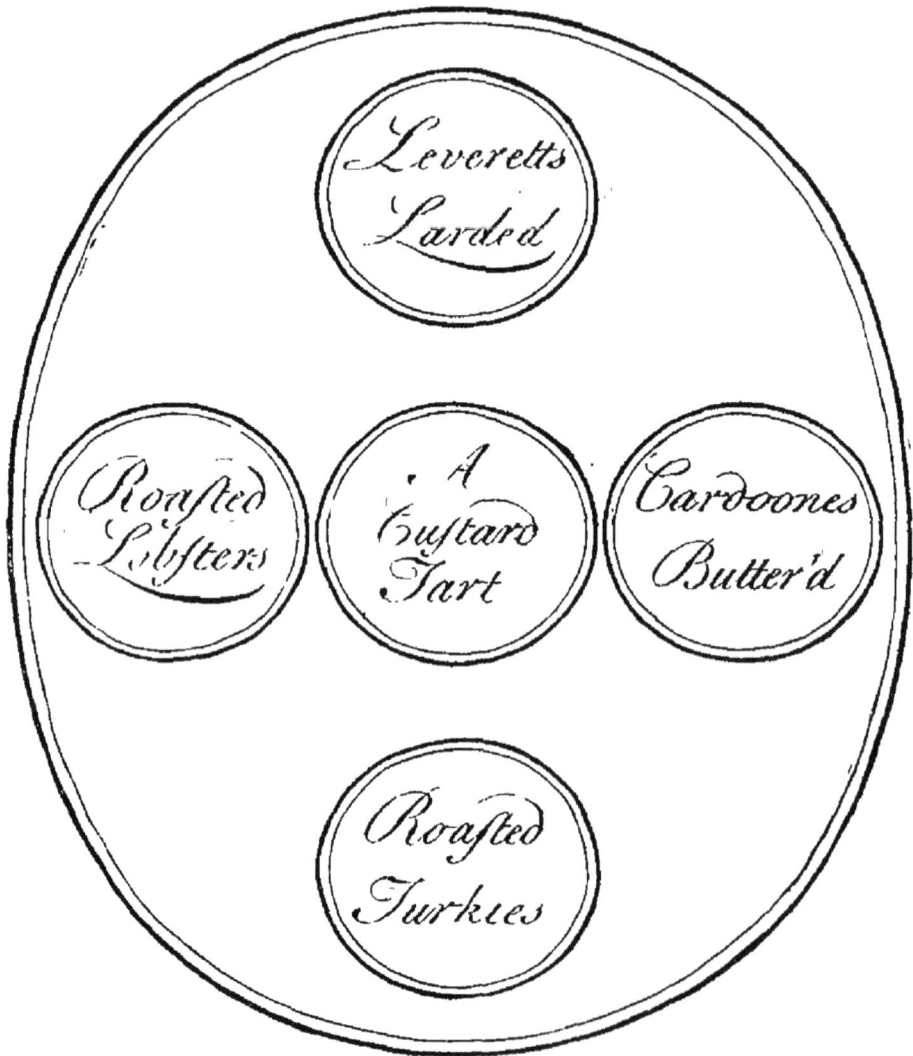

Leveretts Larded

Roasted Lobsters

A Custard Tart

Cardoones Butter'd

Roasted Turkies

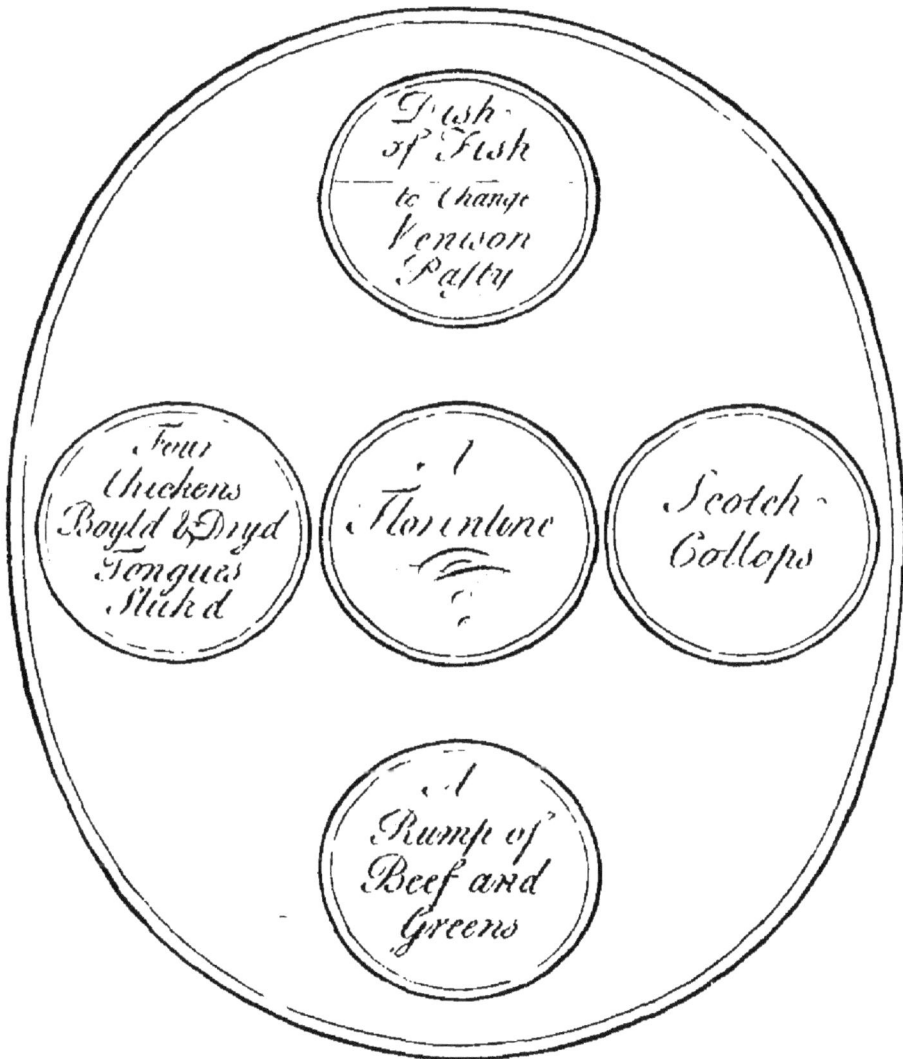

MARCH.

First Course

- Dish of Fish to Change Venison Pasty
- Four Chickens Boyld & Dryd Tongues Stuk'd
- A Florentine
- Scotch Collops
- A Rump of Beef and Greens

Second Course

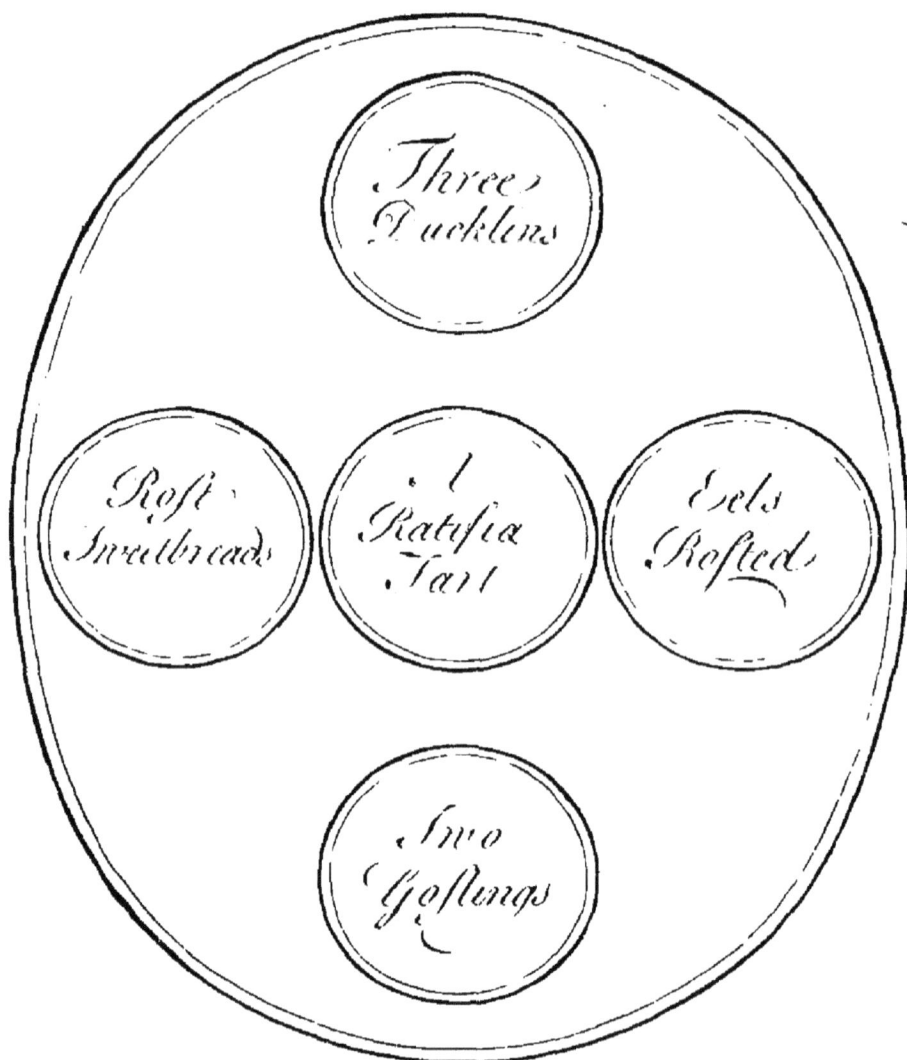

Three
Ducklens

Roft
Sweetbreads

A
Ratifia
Tart

Eels
Rosted

Two
Goslings

APRIL.

First Course

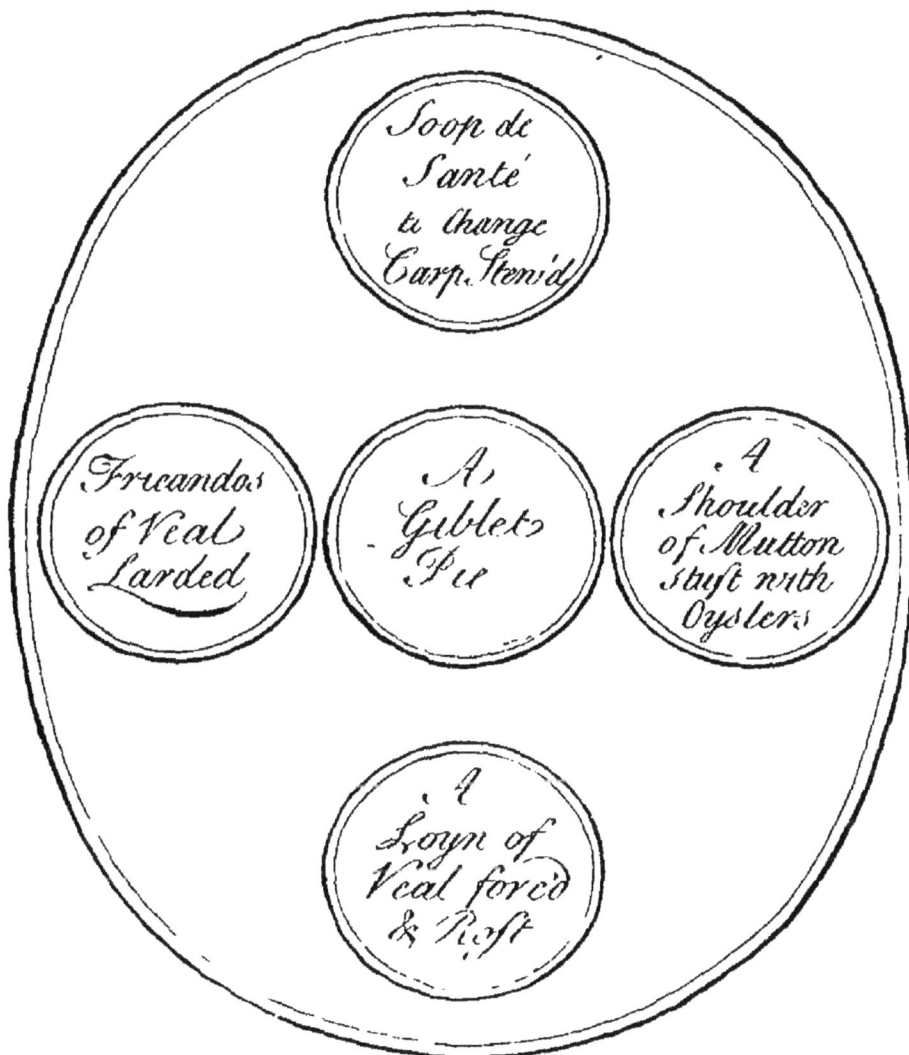

Soop de Santé
ta change
Carp. Stew'd

Fricandos
of Veal
Larded

A
Giblet
Pie

A
Shoulder
of Mutton
stuft with
Oysters

A
Loyn of
Veal forc'd
& Roft

Second Course

A Hare
2 Rabbetts
Sarded

Lambstones
Fry'd

Tamerine
Tart

Lobsters
forc'd &
Butterd

Four
Chickens with
Asparagus
in o
Sarded

9

MAY

First Course

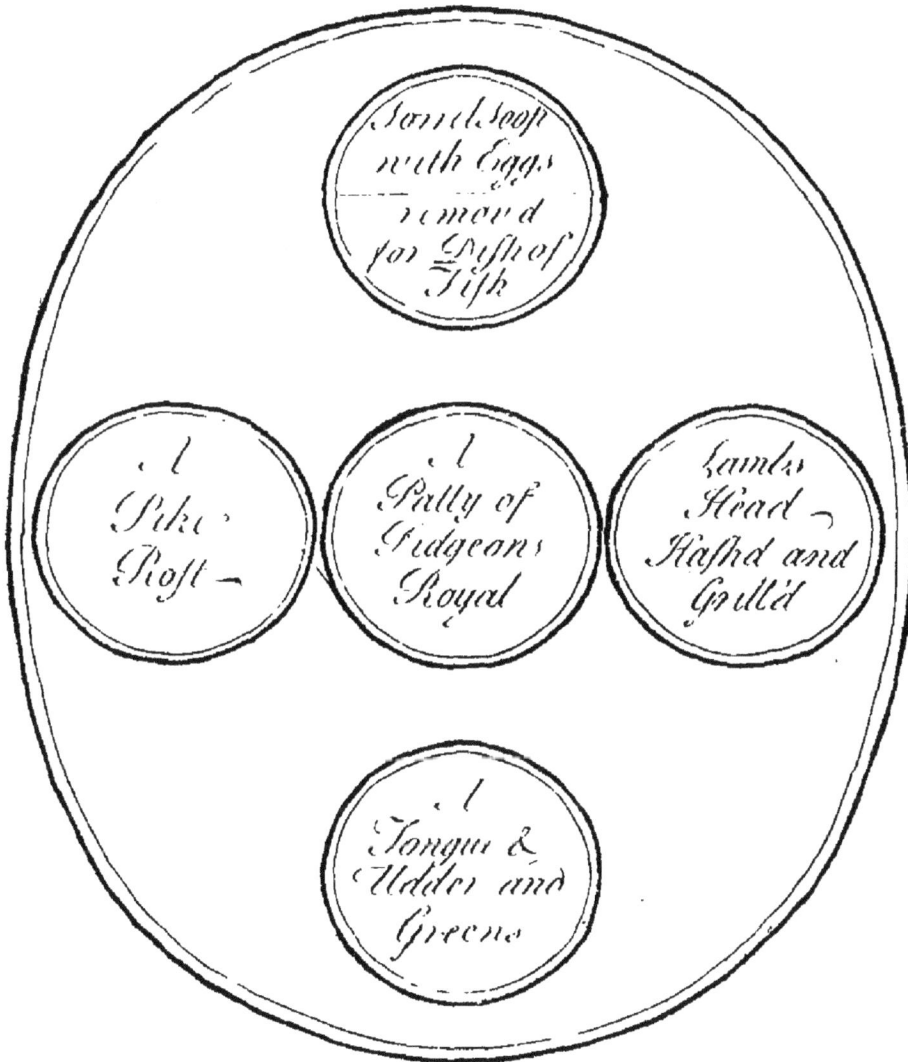

Sorrel Soop with Eggs removd for Dish of Fish

A Pike Rost

A Patty of Pidgeons Royal

Lambs Head Hashd and Grilld

A Tongue & Udder and Greens

Second Course

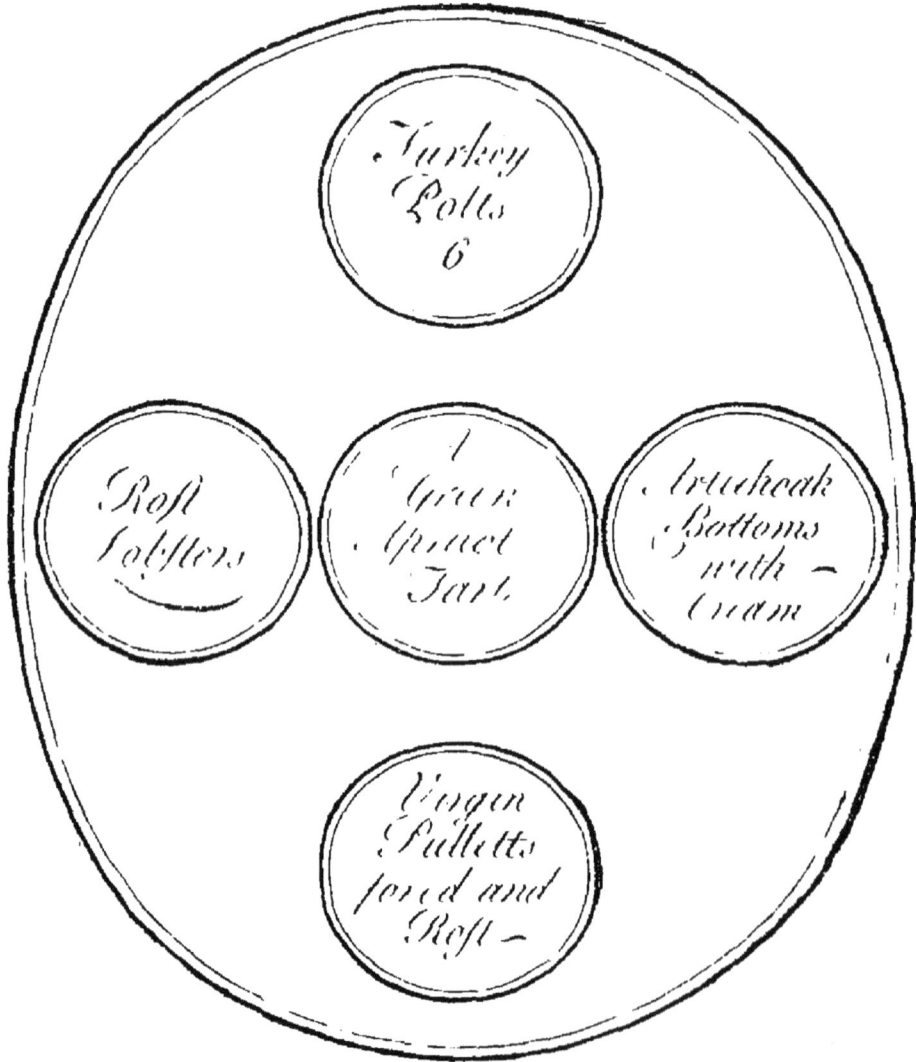

Turkey
Polts
6

Rost
Lobsters

A
Green
Apricot
Tart

Artichoak
Bottoms
with —
Cream

Virgin
Pulletts
forced and
Rost —

JUNE

First Course

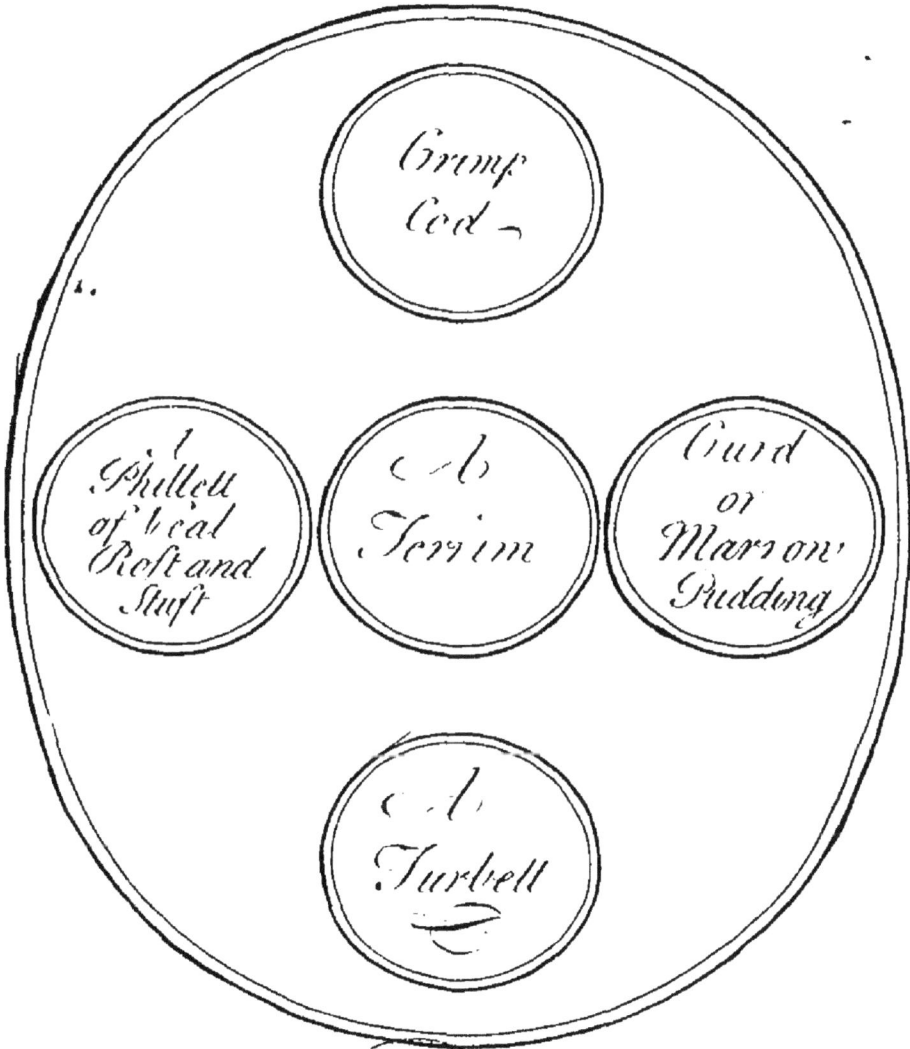

Cramp
Cod

Phillett
of Veal
Rost and
Stuft

A
Terrim

Curd
or
Marrow
Pudding

A
Turbett

Second Course

Two
Pulletts
Roast

Gray
Fish
Butter'd

Cherry
Tart

A
Ragoo of
Sweetbreads

Tame
Pidgeons
6

JULY.

First Course

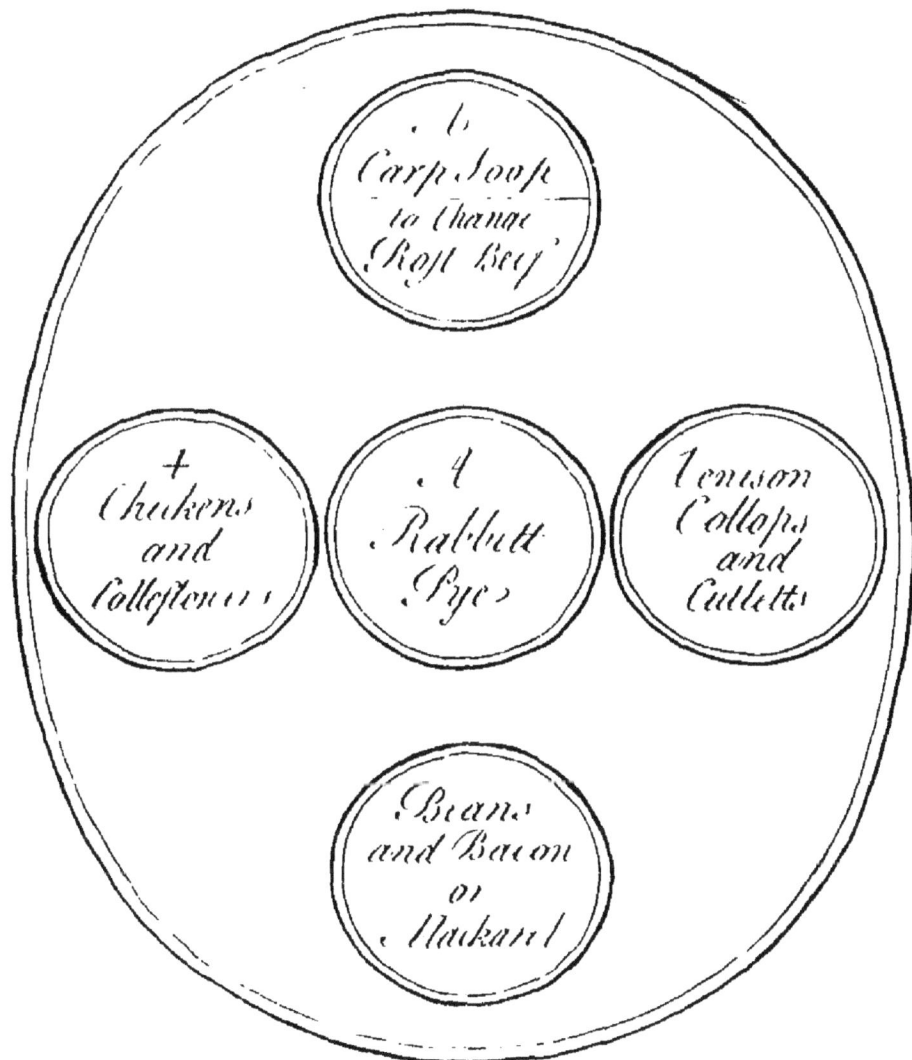

.6
Carp Soup
to Change
Roſt Beef

+
Chickens
and
Colleflowers

A
Rabbitt
Pye

Venison
Collops
and
Cutletts

Beans
and Bacon
or
Mackaril

Second Course.

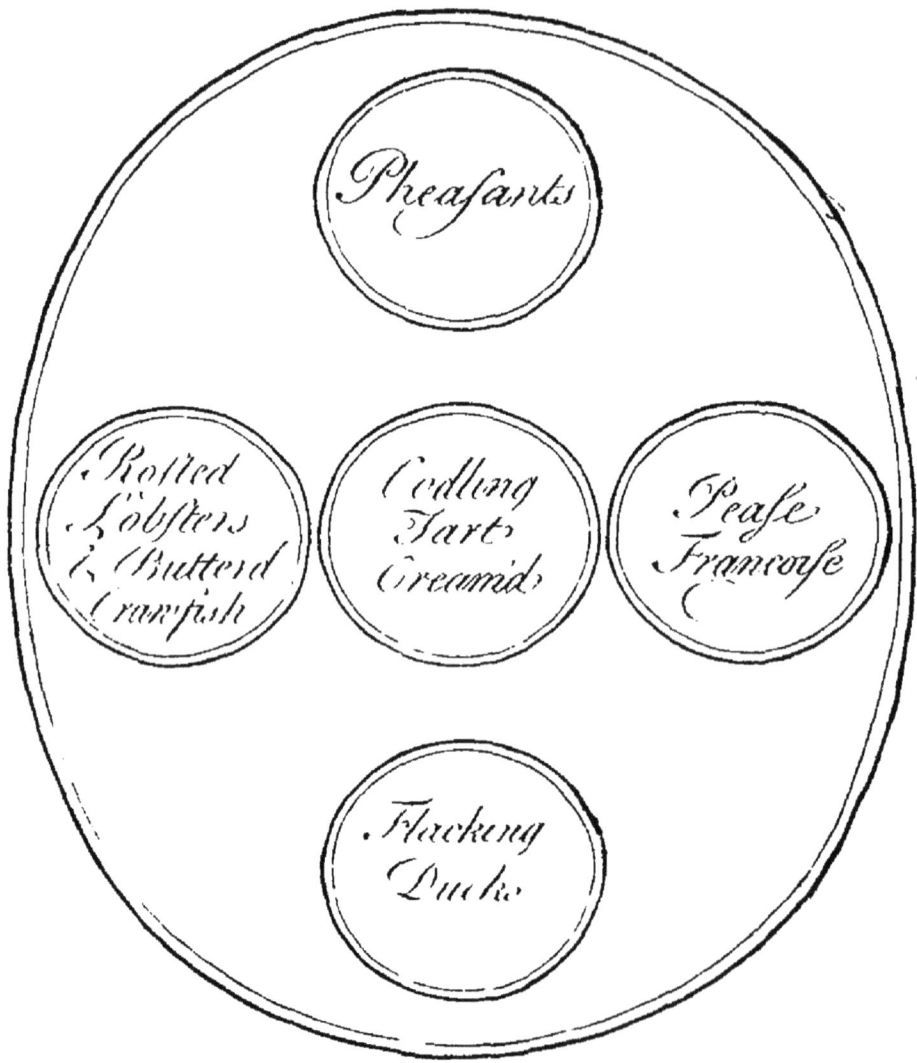

Pheasants

Rosted
Lobsters
& Butterd
Crawfish

Codling
Tart
Cream'd

Pease
Francoise

Flacking
Ducks

AUGUST

First Course

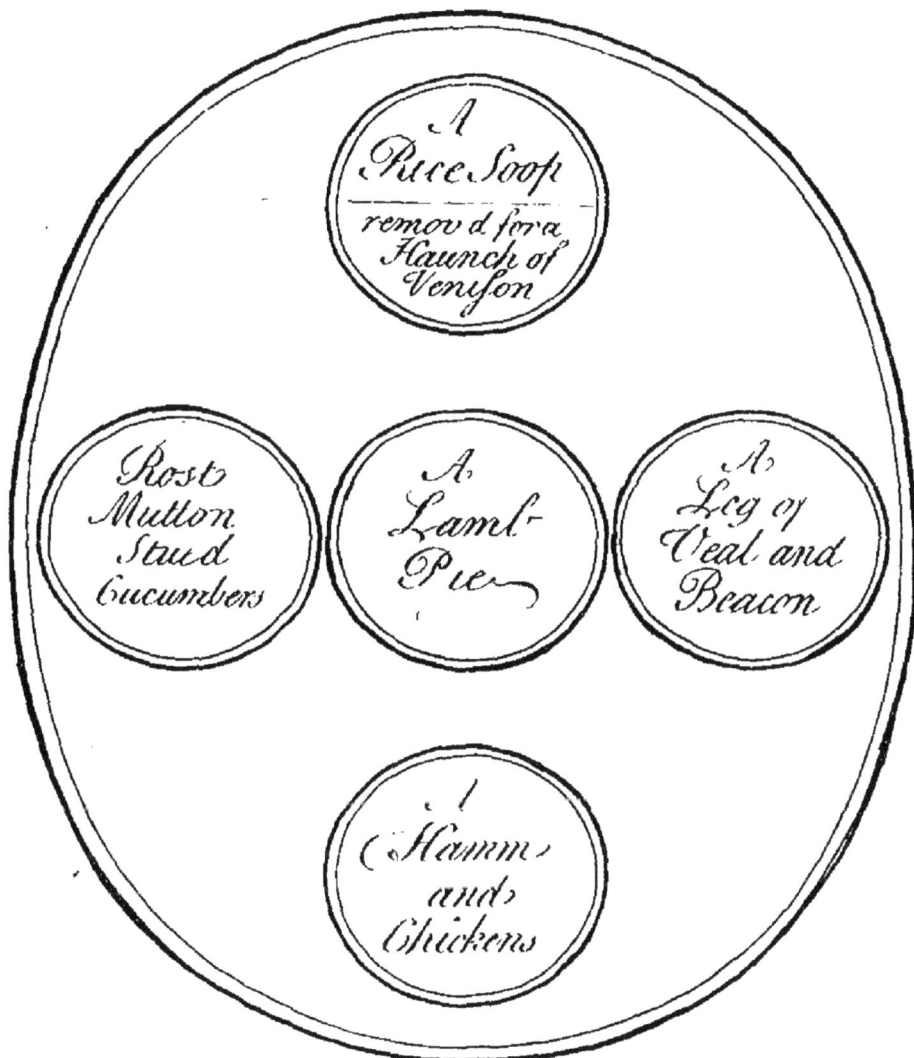

A
Rice Soop
remov'd for a
Haunch of
Venison

Rost
Mutton
Stued
Cucumbers

A
Lamb-
Pie

A
Leg of
Veal and
Beacon

A
Hamm
and
Chickens

Second Course

Two
Turkeys
Rost one
Larded

Fry'd
Artichocks

Curran
and
Cherry
Tarts

Wheat
Ears

Pot
D'Espagne

SEPTEMBER

First Course

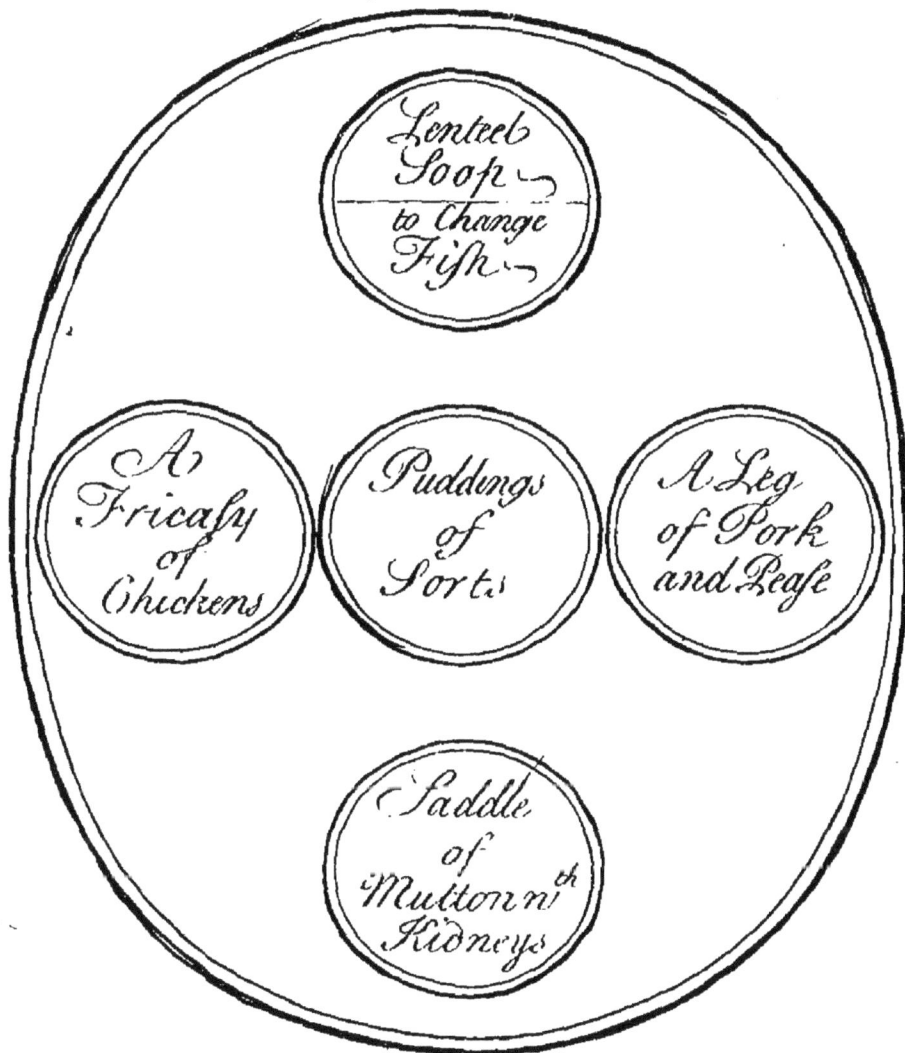

Lenteel
Soop
to Change
Fish

A
Fricasy
of
Chickens

Puddings
of
Sorts

A Leg
of Pork
and Peafe

Saddle
of
Mutton ni th
Kidneys

Second Course

Widgeons and Teale

Fry'd Cream

Butterd Apple Pie

Mushrooms Stued

Ducks Roft

OCTOBER

First Course

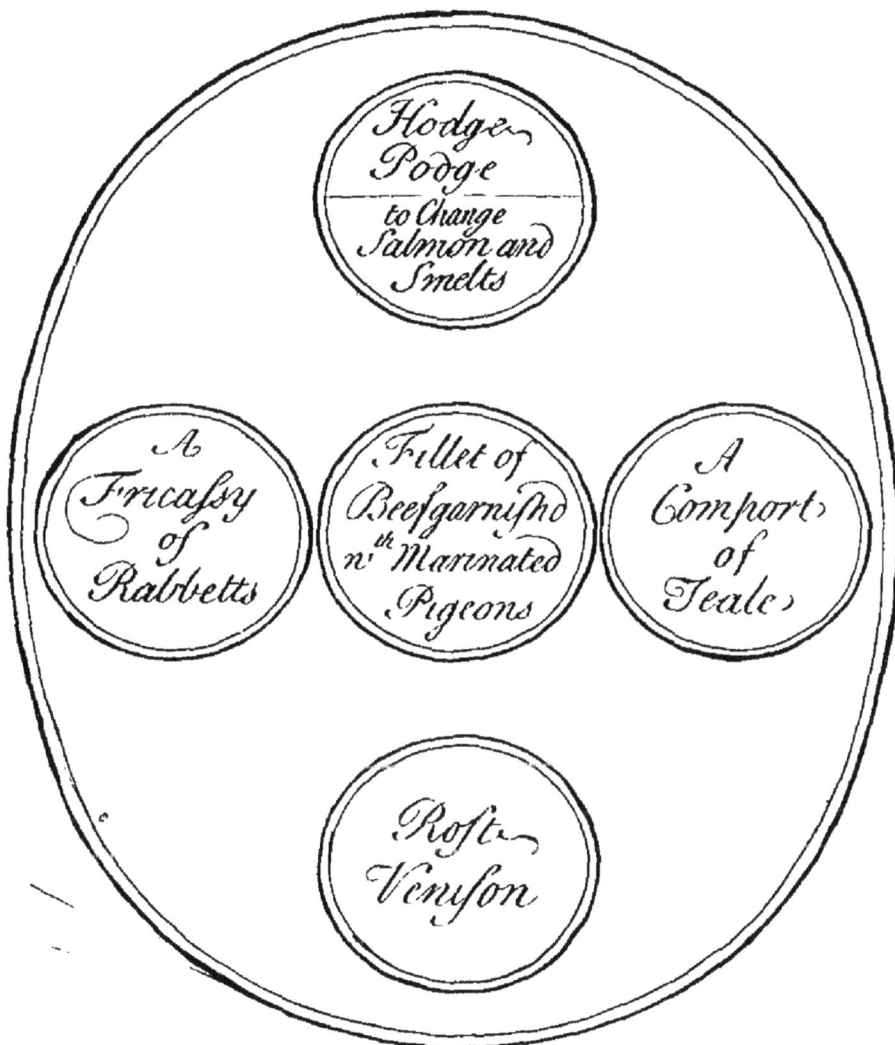

Hodge Podge
to Change
Salmon and
Smelts

A
Fricassy
of
Rabbetts

Fillet of
Beefgarnish'd
w.th Marinated
Pigeons

A
Comport
of
Teale

Roft
Venison

Second Course

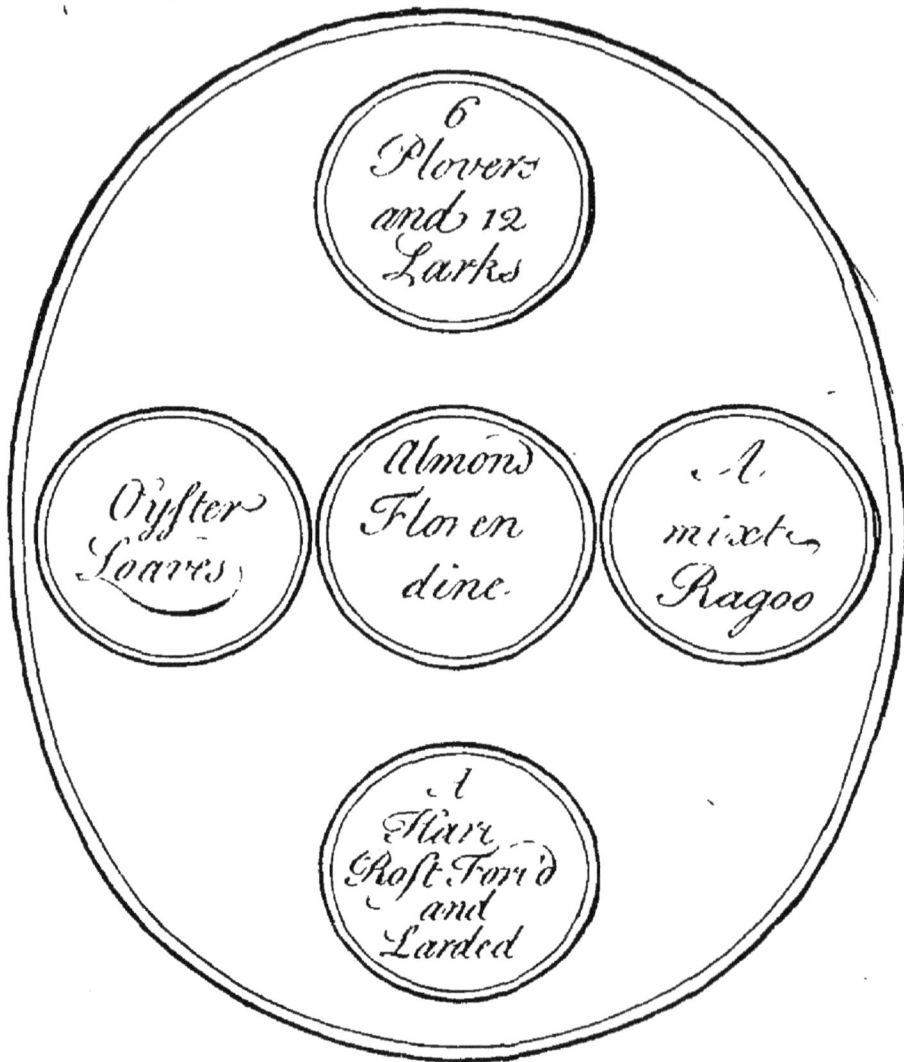

6
Plovers
and 12
Larks

Oyster
Loaves

Almond
Floren
dine.

A.
mixt
Ragoo

A
Hare
Roft-Torn'd
and
Larded

NOVEMBER

First Course

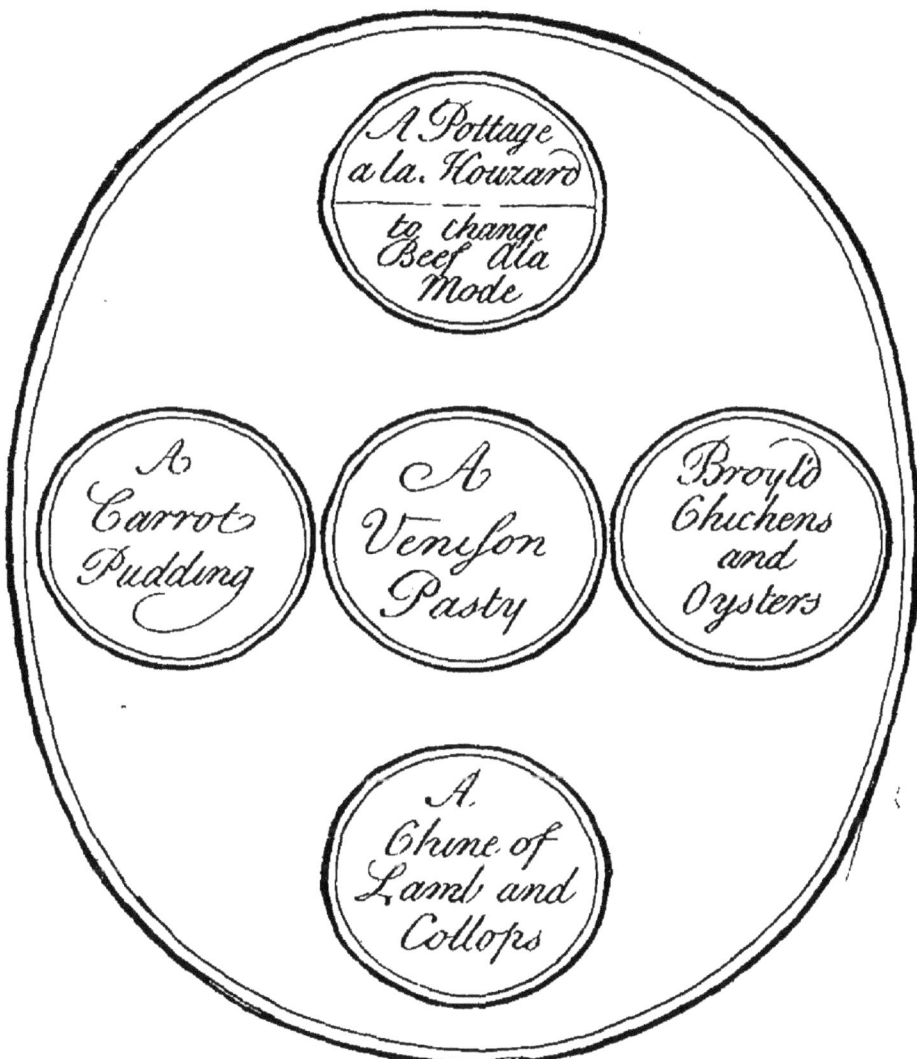

A Pottage
a la. Houzard

to change
Beef Ala
Mode

A
Carrot
Pudding

A
Venison
Pasty

Broyld
Chickens
and
Oysters

A.
Chine of
Lamb and
Collops

Second Course

A
Goose
Rost

Patties
of
Lobsters

A
Pear
Pye
Cream'd

Broyl'd
Sweetbreads

Four
Woodcocks
and four
Snipes

DECEMBER

First Course

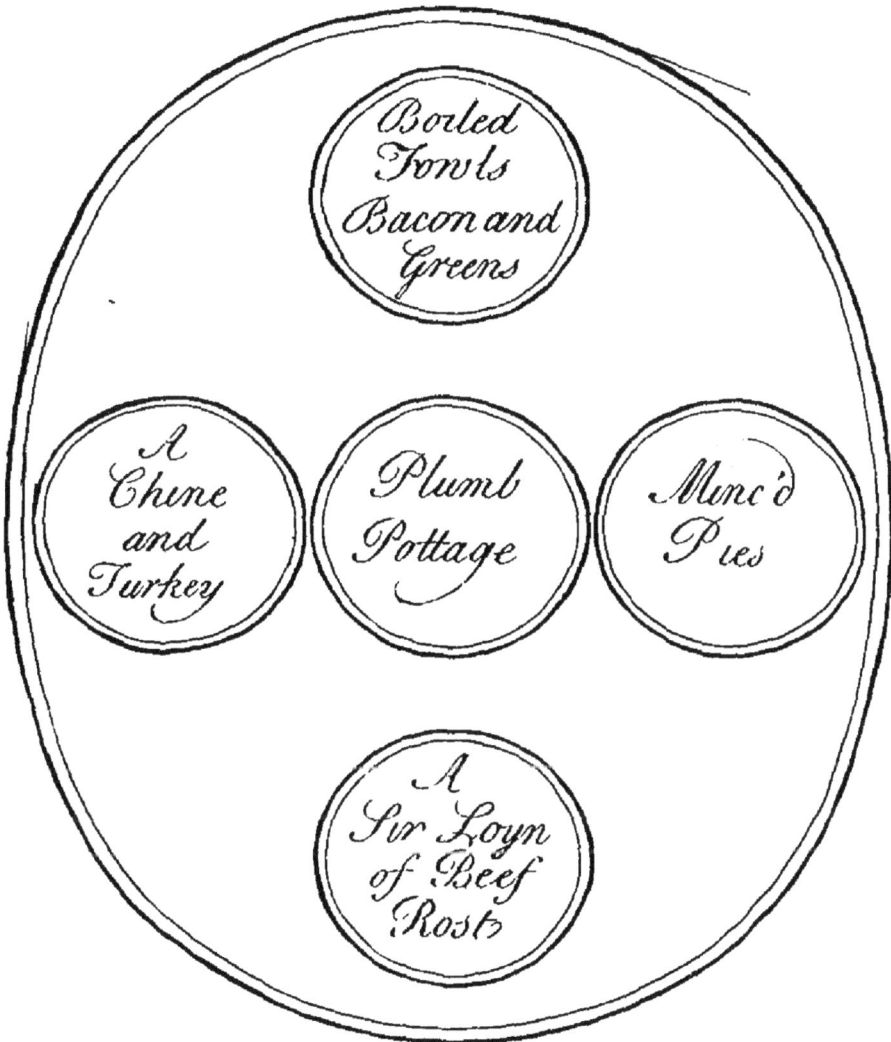

Boiled
Fowls
Bacon and
Greens

A
Chine
and
Turkey

Plumb
Pottage

Minc'd
Pies

A
Sir Loyn
of Beef
Rost

Second Course

2
Ducks
and 24
Larks

Morelles
Trouffles
and Combs
Ragoo'd

Potted
Lamprey

Sturgeon

Six
Partridges

BILLS of FARE *for every Month in the Year.*

JANUARY

FIRST COURSE DISHES

A Good Gravy, Oyster, or Craw-fish Soop
Roasted Cod's-Head
A Fricasey of Plaice.
Leg of Mutton Ham Fashion
Sir-Loin of Beef roasted with a Sal-picon
Goose Pye *à la Mode.*
Lumber Pie
A Pillaw
Tongues and Udders roasted.
Scotch Collops
Stewed Carps.
Calf's-Head Hash.

SECOND COURSE.

Pheasants and Woodcocks
Butter'd Apple Pye
Wild Ducks.
Calves Ears
Fry'd Smelts.
Collar'd Pig.
Apricock Tarts
Roasted Lobsters.
Lamb Stones and Sweetbreads
Sweetbreads of Veal *à la Dauphine.*
Lamb Stones the *Italian* Way
Grill'd Chickens with a Sauce Robart

FEBRUARY

FIRST COURSE

A Veal Soop, Barley Broth, or Lentil Soop.

Salmon boiled with Oysters and Shrimps
Surtout of Soals
Battalia Pye.
Patty of Chickens
Turkies with Eggs
Bread Puddings
Goose boiled with Greens.
Haunch of Venison.
Fricasey of Lamb
Pig Lamb Fashion
Boiled Chickens and Asparagus.

SECOND COURSE.

Fat Chickens and tame Pigeons.
Leverets
Crocant Tart.
Roast Turkies
Lamb in Joints.
Toasts with Veal Kidneys.
Fry'd Soals.
Butter'd Chardoons.
Sheep's Tongues *à la St Geran.*
Tartlets
Potted Salmon.
Potted Lamprey.

MARCH.

FIRST COURSE.

Asparagus Soop.
Boiled Turbut
Whitings fry'd
Calf's Head Pye.
Curd Pudding
Bisque of Quails.
Chickens *Chiringiate.*
Boiled Venison and Cauliflowers.
Beef *à la Mode.*

Roaſt Tongue and Udder
Rump of Beef rolled
Leg of Veal forced

SECOND COURSE

Broiled Pike
Patty of Calves Brains
Tanzy
White Fritters
Ducklings
Amulet of Aſparagus
Sturgeon
Oyſters in Shells
Spinach *Roſa Solis*
Eggs *à la Tripe*
Notts and Ruffs.
Pullets with Eggs

A P R I L

FIRST COURSE

Spring Soop, or Soop *de Santé*.
Biſque of Pigeons.
Chicken fricaſy'd with Petit Pattees
Mutton roaſted with Cutlets *à la Maintenon*
Fowls boiled with Rice
Veal Cutlets marinated
Weſtphalia Ham and Chickens.
Chine of Veal
Oxford Puddings
Grand Sallad
Ragoo of Sweetbreads
Butter'd Crabs

SECOND COURSE.

Green Geeſe roaſted.
Sucking Rabbits
Roaſt Chickens
Aſparagus.
Blanc Manger.
Pain Perdu
Souced Pig

Prauns
Lobſters
Collar'd Eels
Chocolate Tart
Fry'd Smelts,

M A Y

FIRST COURSE

Sorrel Soop with Eggs
Rice Soop
Briſcuit of Beef *a la Chalon*
Crimp'd Cod
Carp *au Court Bouillon*
Olio in a *Terrine*
Fricaſey of Rabbits
Breaſt of Veal ragoo'd.
Beans and Bacon
Mackrel
Ham and Chickens.
Roaſt Mutton, with Regalia of Cucumbers

SECOND COURSE.

Turky Polts
Green Apricock Tart
Four Chickens, two larded
Green Peaſe.
Artichoke Bottoms with Cream.
Pheaſants with Eggs.
Green Geeſe
Cheeſecakes
Lampreys potted.
Tarts
Clary with Eggs.
Morels *á la Cream*.

J U N E.

FIRST COURSE.

Green Peaſe Soop.

A Mat-

A Mattelote of Fish
Soals forced with Crawfish
Haunch of Venison roasted.
Pullets *á la St Menehout*
Mutton *à la Royale*
Fricasey of Pigeons in Blood
Quails *á la Braise*
Almond Pudding
Lamb Pye
Fillet of Veal and Collops
Pullets *à la Tartare*

SECOND COURSE

Young Pheasants
Cherry Tart
Lamb's Head and Appurtenances.
Jole of Sturgeon.
Butter'd Crawfish
Leverets larded
Souc'd Mullets
Butter'd Lobsters
Artichokes forced
Turkies roasted.
Squab Pigeons
Wild Ducks

J U L Y

FIRST COURSE

A Carp Soop
Cock Salmon with butter'd Lobsters
Venison Pasty
Chickens boiled with Bacon.
Tongue and Cauliflowers.
Orange Pudding.
Chine of Mutton
Beans and Bacon
Large Carps stewed
A Pig
White Fricasey.
A Patty Royal.

SECOND COURSE.

Partridges and Quails
Codling Tart
Squabs *en Ortolan*.
Pease *Francoise*.
Bean Tanzy
Fat Livers in Cauls.
Syringed Fritters
Crawfish
Neats Tongues cold
Fry'd Cream
Young Rabbits.
Bolognia Sausages.

A U G U S T

FIRST COURSE.

Pottage with Ducks.
Spanish Olio.
Farced Chickens.
Partridges in *Gallimafry*.
Pigeons *à la Crapeaudine*
Young Ducks with Orange Sauce
Civet of Venison
Lamb with Rice.
Turkies stuffed with Crawfish.
Forced Mutton.
Italian Pudding.
Sallad and Pickles

SECOND COURSE.

Young Pigeons.
Artichokes the *Italian* way.
Cocks Combs.
Eggs with Gravy
Roasted or potted Wheat-Ears.
Green Pease
Hogs Ears *en Gratin*.
Anchovies in *Canapè*.
Peach Tart
Potted Lobsters

Ducks Tongues
Marinated Roaches

S E P T E M B E R

FIRST COURSE

Pottage of Partridge à *la Reine*
Fried Scate with a Brown Sauce
Saddle of Mutton with Kidneys
Roast Goose
A Ragoo of Beef Palates
Boiled Pigeons with Bacon.
Marrow Pudding
Neats Tongues à *la Braise*
Stewed Tench
Umble Pye
Geese à *la Daube*
Calf's Head Hash'd and Grill'd

SECOND COURSE

Wild Fowl
Chicken Pye.
Stew'd Mushrooms.
Butter'd Apple Pye
Crawfish Loaves
Artichokes with White Sauce.
Pupton of Apples
Lobsters
Cream Tarts
Vine Leave Fritters
Mushrooms with Cream
Dutch Beef.

O C T O B E R

Vermicelli Soop.
A Pottage à *la Jacobine*
Rump of Beef à *la Royale*.
A Pottage of Chesnuts.
Loin of Veal à *la Braise*
An Esclope of Rabbits
Duck or Teal with Horse Radish.

Perch with a Cullis of Crawfish
Custard Pudding
Mutton Collops
Fricasey of Rabbits
Veal ragoo'd.

SECOND COURSE

Plovers and Larks
Chesnut Tort
Larded Hare
Oysters *au Parmesan*
Butter'd Lobsters
Pippin Fraise
Quince Pye
Fried Sweetbreads
Whitings skinned and fried in Batter.
Quail Pye.
Hash'd Partridge
Oysters à *la Daube*

N O V E M B E R.

FIRST COURSE.

Poop *au Bourgeois*
Harrico of Mutton
Hodge Podge
Barbels or Mullets
A Pig Rolliard
Broiled Chickens with Petty Patties
   the *Spanish* Way
Venison Pasty
Bisque of Pigeons.
Brawn
Chickens à *la Braise*.
P th Pudding
Fowl and Chesnuts.

SECOND COURSE.

A Chine of Salmon and Smelts.
A Pear Pye cream'd
Snipes and Woodcocks.
Salmogundy.

Larks.

Potted Hare.
Larks
Black and White Puddings
Duck Pye to be eaten cold
Ragoo of Oysters
Sturgeon
Florendine
Lamb in Joints

D E C E M B E R

First Course

Puree with Ducks
Plumb Pottage.
Chine of Mutton.
Roast Turky
Chine of Bacon
Collar of Brawn.
Roast Sir-Loin of Beef.

Minced Pies
Pullets with Oysters
Goose or Turky in Ragoo
Battalia Pye
Fore Quarter of Lamb roasted

Second Course

Roast Pheafants
Partridges
Ducks and Larks
Scollop Shells of Oysters.
Potted Lamprey
Potted Venison
Teal
Oyster Loaves
Roasted Chickens
Warden Pye
Tarts and Custards.
Jole of Sturgeon

C H A P.

C H A P XXX.

I N S T R U C T I O N S *for* M A R K E T I N G.

At the P O U L T E R E R S.

To know whether a Capon *is a true one, young or old, new or stale.*

IF he be young his Spurs are short, and his Legs smooth; if a true Capon a fat Vein on the Side of his Breast, and the Comb pale, and a thick Belly and Rump, if new he will have a close hard Vent, if stale, a loose open Vent.

A Cock *or* Hen Turky, Turky poults.

If the Cock be young, his Legs will be black and smooth, and his Spurs short, if stale, his Eyes will be sunk in his Head, and the Feet dry; if new, the Eyes lively and Feet limber. Observe the like by the Hen, and moreover if she be with Egg, she will have a soft open Vent, if not, a hard close Vent. Turky Poults are known the same Way, their Age cannot deceive you.

A Cock, Hen, &c.

If young, his Spurs are short and dubbed, but take particular Notice, they are not pared or scraped by the knavish Poulterer to cheat you, if old, he will have an open Vent, but if new, a close hard Vent; and so of a Hen for newness or staleness; if old, her Legs and Comb are rough, if young, smooth.

A Tame Goose, *Wild* Goose, *Bran* Goose, &c.

If the Bill be yellowish, and she has but few Hairs, she is young, but if full of Hairs, and the Bill and Foot red

she

she is old; if new, limber footed, if stale, dry footed, and so of a Wild Goose and Bran Goose.

Wild Ducks, and Tame Ducks.

The Duck, when fat, is hard and thick on the Belly, but if not, thin and lean; if new, limber footed, if stale, dry footed; a true Wild Duck has a reddish Foot, smaller than the Tame one.

Goodwets, Marle, Knots, Ruffs, Gull, Dotterels, and Wheat Ears.

If these be old their Legs will be rough, if young, smooth; if fat, a fat Rump, if new, limber footed, if stale, dry footed.

Pheasant, Cock and Hen.

The Cock, when young, has dubbed Spurs, when old, sharp small Spurs; if new, a fast Vent, if stale, an open flabby one. The Hen if young, has smooth Legs, and her Flesh of a curious Grain, if with Egg, she will have a soft open Vent, if not, a close one. For newness or staleness as the Cock.

Heath and Pheasant Pouts.

If new, they will be stiff and white in the Vent, and the Feet limber, if Fat, they will have a hard Vent; if stale, dry footed and limber, and if touch'd they will peel.

Heath Hen and Cock.

If young they have smooth Legs and Bill; if old, rough, for the rest they are known as the foregoing.

Partridge, Hen or Cock.

The Bill white and the Legs bluish shew Age; for if young, the Bill is black and Legs yellowish; if new a fast Vent, if stale, a green and open one: If their Crops be

full

full, and they have fed on green Wheat, they may taint theie; and for this fmell in their Mouths.

Woodcock and Snipe.

The Woodcock, if fat, is thick and hard; if new, limber footed, when ftale, dry footed; or if their Nofes are fnotty, and their Thioats muddy and moorifh, they are nought. A Snipe, if fat, has a Fat Vein in the Side under the Wing, and in the Vent feels thick; for the reft like the Woodcock.

Doves and Pigeons.

To know the Turtle Dove, look for a bluifh Ring round his Neck, and the reft moftly white; the Stock Dove is biggei, and the Ring Dove is lefs than the Stock Dove: The Dove Houfe Pigeons, when old are red legg'd, if new and fat, they will feel full and fat in the Vent, and are limber footed; but if ftale, a flabby and green Vent.

And thus of green or gray Plover, Felfare, Blackbird, Thiufh, Larks, &c.

Of Hare, Leveret, Rabbit or Cony.

A Hare will be whitifh and ftiff, if new and clean killed; if ftale, the Flefh blackifh in moft Parts, and the Body limber; if the Cleft in her Lips fpread very much, and her Claws wide and ragged, fhe is cold, the contrary if young. To know a true Leveret, feel on the Fore Leg near the Foot, and if there be a fmall Bone or Knob, it is right, if if not 'tis a Haie; for the reft obferve as in the Haie. A Coney if ftale, will be limber and flimy; if new, white and ftiff; if old, her Claws are very long and rough, the Wool mottled with gray Hairs; if young, the Claws and Wool fmooth.

At

At the FISHMONGERS.

To choose Salmon, Pike, Trout, Carp, Tench, Grailing, Barbel, Chub, Ruff, Eel, Whiting, Smelt, Shad, &c.

ALL thefe are known to be new or ftale by the Colour of the Gills, their Eafinefs or Hardnefs to open, the hanging or keeping up their Fins, Stiffnefs of their Bodies, the ftanding out or finking of their Eyes, &c, and by fmelling their Gills.

Turbut.

He is chofen by his Thicknefs and Plumpnefs, and if his Belly be of a Cream Colour, he muft fpend well, but if thin, and his Belly of a bluifh white, he will eat very loofe.

Cod and Codling.

Choofe him by his Thicknefs towards his Head, and the Whitenefs of his Flefh when it is cut: And fo of a Codling.

Ling.

For dry'd Ling, choofe that which is thickeft in the Poll, and the Flefh of the brighteft Yellow.

Scate and Thornback.

Thefe are chofen by their Thicknefs, and the She Scate is the fweeteft, efpecially if large.

Soals.

Thefe are chofen by their Thicknefs and Stiffnefs, when their Bellies are of a Cream Colour they fpend the firmer.

Sturgeon.

If it cuts without crumbling, and the Veins and Griftle give a true blue where they appear, and the Flefh a perfect white, then conclude it to be good.

4 N   *Frefh*

Fresh Herring and Mackerel.

If their Gills are of a lively shining Redness, and their Eyes stand full, and the Fish is stiff, then they are new; but if dusky and faded, or sinking and wrinkled, and Tails limber, they are stale.

Lobsters.

Choose them by their Weight, the heaviest are best, if no Water be in them: If new, the Tail will fall smart, like a Spring; if full, the Middle of the Tail will be of full hard, reddish, skin'd Meat. Cock Lobster is known by the narrow back Part of his Tail, and the two uppermost Fins within his Tail are stiff and hard; but the Hen is soft, and the back of her Tail broader.

Prawns, Shrimps and Crabfish.

The two first, if stale, will be limber, and cast a Kind of Limy smell, their Colour fading, and they slimy: The two latter will be limber in their Claws and Joints, their red Colour turn blackish and dusky, and will have an ill Smell under their Throats: Otherwise all of them are good.

Plaice and Flounders.

If they are stiff, and their Eyes be not sunk, or look dull, they are new, the contrary when stale: The best Sort of Plaice look bluish on the Belly.

Pickled Salmon.

If the Flesh feels oily, and the Scales are stiff, and shinning, and it comes in Fleaks, and parts without crumbling, then it is new and good, and not otherwise.

Pickled and Red-Herrings.

For the first, open the Back to the Bone, and if the Flesh be white, fleaky and oily, and the Bone white, or a bright Red, they are good. If Red-Herrings carry a
good

good Glofs, part well from the Bone, and fmell well, then conclude them to be good.

At the B U T C H E R S.

To choofe Lamb.

IN a Fore Quarter of Lamb, mind the Neck Vein, if it be an Azure Blue it is new and good, but if greenifh or yellowifh it is near tainting, if not tainted already. In the Hinder Quarter, fmell under the Kidney, and try the Knuckle ; if you meet with a faint Scent, and the Knuckle be limber, it is ftale killed. For a Lamb's Head, mind the Eyes, if they be funk or wrinkled, it is ftale, if plumb and lively, it is new and fweet.

Veal.

If the Bloody Vein in the Shoulder look blue, or a bright Red, it is new killed, but if blackifh, greenifh or yellowifh, it is flabby and ftale, if wrapt in wet Cloaths, fmell whether it be mufty or not. The Loin firft taints under the Kidney, and the Flefh, if ftale killed, will be foft and flimy.

The Breaft and Neck taints firft at the upper End, and you will perceive fome dusky yellowifh or greenifh Appearance ; the Sweetbread on the Breaft will be clammy; otherwife it is frefh and good: The Leg is known to be new by the Stiffnefs of the Joint, if limber, and the Flefh feems clammy, and has green or yellow Specks 'tis ftale. The Head is known as the Lamb's. The Flefh of a Bull Calf is more red and firm than that of a Cow Calf, and the Fat more hard and curdled.

Mutton.

If Mutton be young, the Flesh will pinch tender; if old, it will wrinkle and remain so: If young, the Fat will easily part from the Lean, if old, it will stick by Strings and Skins: If Ram-Mutton, the Fat feel spungy, the Flesh close grained and tough, not rising again, when dented by your Finger; if Ewe-Mutton, the Flesh is paler than Weather-Mutton, a closer Grain, and easily parting. If there be a Rot, the Flesh will be palish, and the Fat a faint whitish, inclining to yellow, and the Flesh be loose at the Bone; if you squeeze it hard, some Drops of Water will stand up like Sweat; as to newness and staleness, the same is to be observed as by Lamb.

Beef.

If it be right Ox-Beef it will have an open Grain, if young, a tender and oily smoothness: If rough and spungy it is old, or inclining to be so, except Neck, Briscuit, and such Parts as are very fibrous, which in young Meat will be more tough than in other Parts. A Carnation pleasant Colour betokens good spending Meat, the Sewet a curious white, yellowish is not so good.

Cow-Beef is less bound and closer grained than the Ox, the Fat whiter, but the Lean somewhat paler, if young, the Dent you make with your Finger will rise again in a little Time.

Bull-Beef is of a closer Grain, a deep dusky red, tough in pinching, the Fat skinny, hard, and has a rammish rank smell, and for newness or staleness this Flesh, bought fresh, has but few Signs, the most material is its Clamminess, the rest your Smell will inform you. If it be
bruised

biuifed thefe Places will look more dusky or blackifh than the reft.

Pork.

If it be young, the Lean will break in pinching between your Fingers, and if you nip the Skin with your Nails, it will make a Dent; alfo if the Fat be foft and pulpy, in a Manner like Lard, and if the Lean be tough and the Fat flabby and fpungy, feeling rough, it is old, efpecially if the Rind be ftubborn, and you cannot nip it with your Nails.

If of a Boar, tho' young, or of a Hog, gelded at full Growth, the Flefh will be hard, tough, reddifh, and rammifh of Smell, the Fat fkinny and hard, the Skin very thick and tough, and pinched up it will immediately fall again.

As for old or new killed, try the Legs, Hands, and Springs, by putting your Fingers under the Bone that comes out; for if it be tainted, you will there find it by fmelling your Finger; befides, the Skin will be fweaty and clammy when ftale, but cool and fmooth when new.

If you find little Kernels in the Fat of Pork, like Hail-Shot, if many 'tis meazly, and dangerous to be eaten.

How to choofe Brawn, Venifon, *Wheftphalia* Hams, &c.

Brawn.

BRAWN is known to be old or young by the extraordinary or moderate Thicknefs of the Rind; the Thick is old, the moderate is young, if the Rind and Fat be very tender it is not Boar Bacon, but Barrow or Sow.

Venifon.

Venifon.

Try the Haunches or Shoulders under the Bones, that come out, with your Finger or Knife, and as the Scent is fweet or rank, it is new or ftale; and the like of the Sides in the moft flefhy Parts: If tainted, they will look greenifh in fome Places, or more than ordinary black. Look on the Hoofs, and if the Clefts are very wide and tough it is old, if clofe and fmooth, it is young.

Weftphalia *Hams and* Englifh *Bacon.*

Put a Knife under the Bone that fticks out of the Ham, and if it comes out in a Manner clean, and has a curious Flavour it is fweet and good; if much fmeered and dulled it is tainted or rufty.

Englifh Gammons are tried the fame Way; and for other Parts try the Fat, if it be white, oily in feeling, and does not break or crumble, and the Flefh fticks well to the Bone, and bears a good Colour, it is good; but if the contrary, and the Lean has fome little Streaks of Yellow, it is rufty, or will foon be fo.

Butter, Cheefe, and Eggs.

When you buy Butter, truft not to that which will be given you to tafte, but try it in the Middle, and if your Smell and Tafte be good, you cannot be deceived.

Cheefe is to be chofen by its moift and fmooth Coat; if old Cheefe be rough coated, rugged, or dry at Top, beware of little Worms or Mites: If it be over full of Holes, moift or fpungy, it is fubject to Maggots. If any foft or perifh'd Place appear on the Outfide, try how deep it goes, for the greater Part may be hid within.

Eggs are to be chofen by holding them to the Light; if the White looks clear, and the Yolk floats about, it is a
good

good Egg: If cloudy, or the Yolk be funk to the Bottom, it is ftark nought.

Englifh *and* Outlandifh *Fruit.*

If the Stalk comes out eafily with the Spires belonging to it, and look rufty, the Fruit is perifh'd at the Core, or if there be a rotten Speck at the Stalk, Muftinefs is dif-cerned by the Roughnefs of their Coats, and fading of their Colour.

Oranges, Lemons, and Pomgranates are known by their Weight: If the two former be pricked, fome Spots and Specks will appear; and the laft, if it be not full, will rattle.

Things to be provided when any Family is going into the Country for a Summer.

Nutmegs, Mace, Cinnamon, Cloves, Pepper, Ginger, *Jamaica* Pepper, Raifins, Currants, Sugar Lisbon, Sugar Loaf Lump, Sugar double refin'd, Prunes, Oranges, Lemons, Anchovies, Olives, Capers, Mangoes, Oil for Salads, Vinegar, Verjuice, Tea, Coffee, Chocolate, Almonds, Chefnuts, *French* Pears, Sagoe, Truffles, Morels, Macroni, Vermicelli, Rice, Millet, Comfits, and Piftachoe Nuts.

CHAP.

CHAP. XXXI.

Of ENGLISH WINES.

Red *or* White Elder Wine.

GAther the Elder Berries ripe and dry, pick them, bruife them with your Hands, and ftrain them; then fet the Liquor by in glazed earthen Veffels for twelve Hours to fettle, then put to every Pint of Juice a Pint and half of Water, and to every Gallon of this Liquor, put three Pounds of *Lisbon* Sugar. Set this in a Kettle over the Fire, and when it is ready to boil, clarify it with the Whites of four or five Eggs; let it boil an Hour, and when it is almoft cold, work it with fome ftrong Ale Yeaft and then tun it, filling up the Veffel from time to time with the fame Liquor faved on Purpofe, as it finks by working. In a Month's Time, if the Veffel holds about eight Gallons, it will be fine and fit to bottle, and after bottling will be fit to drink in two Months, but remember that all Liquors muft be fine before they are bottled, or elfe they will grow fharp and ferment in the Bottles, and never be good for any thing.

N. B. Add to every Gallon of this Liquor a Pint of ftrong Mountain Wine, but not fuch as has the Borachio or Hogskin Flavour. This Wine will be very ftrong and pleafant, and will keep feveral Years.

We muft prepare our Red Elder Wine in the fame Manner that we make with Sugar, and if our Veffel hold about eight or ten Gallons, it will be fit for bottling in about a

Month's

Month's time; but if the Veſſel be larger, it muſt ſtand longer in Proportion, three or four Months at leaſt for a Hogſhead.

To make Palermo *Wine.*

TAKE to every Quart of Water a Pound of *Malaga* Raiſins, rub and cut the Raiſins ſmall, and put them to the Water, and let them ſtand ten Days, ſtirring it once or twice a Day; you muſt boil the Water an Hour before you put it to the Raiſins, and let it ſtand to cool; at ten Days End ſtrain off your Liquor, and put a little Yeaſt to it, and at three Days put it in the Veſſel with one Sprig of dry'd Wormwood; let it be cloſe ſtopp'd, and at three Months End bottle it off.

To make Gooſeberry Wine.

GAther your Gooſeberries in dry Wheather, when they are half ripe, pick them and bruiſe them in a Tub, with a Wooden-Mallet, or other ſuch like Inſtrument, for no Metal is proper; then take about the Quantity of a Peck of the bruiſed Gooſeberries, put them into a Cloth made of Horſe-hair, and preſs them as much as poſſible, without breaking the Seeds; repeat this Work 'till all your Gooſeberries are preſſed, and adding to this preſs'd Juice, the other which you will find in the Tub, add to every Gallon three Pounds of Powder Sugar, for *Lisbon* Sugar will give the Wine a Taſte which may be diſagreeable to ſome People, and beſides, it will ſweeten much more than the dry Powder; ſtir this together 'till the Sugar is diſſolved, and then put it in a Veſſel or Cask, which muſt be quite fill'd with it. If the Veſſel holds about ten or twelve Gallons, it muft ftand a Fortnight or three Weeks, or if about twenty Gallons, then about four or five Weeks to fettle in a cool Place; then draw off the Wine from the Lee, and after you have difcharged the Veffel from the Lees, return the clear Liquor again into the Veffel, and let it ftand three Months, if the Cask is about ten Gallons, or between four and five Months, if it be twenty Gallons, and then bottle it off. We muft note, that a fmall Cask of any Liquor is always fooner ripe and fit for drinking than the Liquor of a larger Cask will be; but a fmall Body of Liquor will fooner change four, than that which is in a larger Cask. The Wine, if it is truly prepared, according to the above Directions, will improve every Year, and laft feveral Years.

To make Currant Wine.

GAther your Currants full ripe, ftrip them and bruife them in a Mortar, and to every Gallon of the Pulp put two Quarts of Water, firft boiled and cold: You may put in fome Rafps if you pleafe, let it ftand in a Tub 24 Hours to ferment, then let it run through a Hair-fieve: Let no Hand touch it, let it take its Time to run, and to every Gallon of this Liquor put two Pounds and an half of white Sugar; ftir it well and put it in your Veffel, and to every fix Gallons put in a Quart of the beft rectify'd Spirit of Wine; let it ftand fix Weeks, and bottle it; if it's not very fine, empty it into other Bottles, or at firft draw it into large Bottles, and then after it has ftood a Fortnight, rack it off into fmaller.

To make Cherry Wine.

PULL off the Stalks of the Cherries and wash them without breaking the Stones, then preſs them hard through a Hair Bag, and to every Gallon of Liquor put two Pounds of Six-penny Sugar: The Veſſel muſt be full, and let it work as long as it makes a Noiſe in the Veſſel; then ſtop it up cloſe for a Month or more, and when it is fine, draw it into dry Bottles, and put a Lump of Sugar into every Bottle; if it makes them fly, open them all for a Moment, and ſtop them up again: It will be fit to drink in a Quarter of a Year.

Raiſin Wine.

TO every Gallon of clear Thames, or other River Water, put five Pounds of *Malaga* or *Belvedere* Raiſins, let them ſteep a Fortnight, ſtirring them every Day, then pour the Liquor off, and ſqueeze the Juice out of the Raiſins, and put both Liquors together in a Veſſel that is of a Size to contain it exactly, for it ſhould be quite full; let the Veſſel ſtand open thus 'till your Wine has done hiſſing, or making the leaſt Noiſe: You may add a Pint of *French* Brandy to every two Gallons, then ſtop it up cloſe, and when you find it is fine, which you may know by pegging it, bottle off.

If you would have it red, put one Gallon of *Alicant* Wine to every four of Raiſin Wine.

To make Orange Wine.

PUT twelve Pounds of fine Sugar, and the Whites of eight Eggs, well beaten, into ſix Gallons of Spring

Wa-

Water; let it boil an Hour, fcumming it all the Time, take it off, and when 'tis pretty cool, put in the Juice of fifty *Seville* Oranges, and fix Spoonfuls of good Ale Yeaft, and let it ftand two Days, then put it into your Veffel with two Quarts of Rhenifh Wine, and the Juice of twelve Lemons: You muft let the Juice of Lemons and Wine, and two Pounds of double refin'd Sugar, ftand clofe cover'd ten or twelve Hours before you put it into the Veffel to your Orange Wine, and fcum off the Seeds, before you put it in. The Lemon Peels muft be put in with the Oranges, half the Rinds muft be put into the Veffel; it muft ftand ten or twelve Days before 'tis fit to bottle.

To make Sage Wine.

BOIL twenty fix Quarts of Spring Water a Quarter of an Hour, and when 'tis Blood warm put twenty five Pounds of *Malaga* Raifins pick'd, rubb'd and fhred into it, with almoft half a Bufhel of red Sage fhred, and a Porringer of Ale Yeaft: Stir all well together, and let it ftand in a Tub cover'd warm fix or feven Days, ftirring it once a Day, then ftrain it off, and put it in a Runlet. Let it work three or four Days, ftop it up; when it has ftood fix or feven Days, put in a Quart or two of *Malaga* Sack, and when 'tis fine bottle it.

Birch Wine.

THE Seafon for procuring the Liquor from the Birch-Trees, is in the Beginning of *March*, while the Sap is rifing, and before the Leaves fhoot out; for when the Sap is become forward, and the Leaves begin to appear, the
Juice

Juice by being long digefted in the Bark, grows thick and coloured, which was before thin and clear.

The Method of procuring the Juice is by boring Holes in the Body of the Tree, and putting in Faucets, which are commonly made of the Branches of Elder, the Pith being taken out; you may without hurting your Tree, if large, tap it in feveral Places four or five at a Time, and by that Means fave, from a good Store of Trees, many Gallons every Day.

If you do not ufe it immediately, which is the beft Way, then in order to preferve it in a good Condition for Brewing, and that it may not turn four, 'till you have got the Quantity you want, the Bottles in which it dripped from the Faucets, muft be immediately well ftopp'd, the Corks wax'd or rofin'd.

One Method of making it is this, to every Gallon of Birch Liquor, put a Quart of Honey, ftir them well together; put in a few Cloves, and a little Lemon Peel, and let it boil for near an Hour, and fcum it well continually as it rifes, then fet it by till it is grown cool; then put in two or three Spoonfuls of new Ale Yeaft to fet it a working, and when the Yeaft begins to fettle, put it into a Runlet that will juft hold it, and let it ftand fix Weeks or longer, if you pleafe, and then bottle it, and it will be fit to drink in a Month. It will keep good a Year or two: If you have a Mind to ufe Sugar inftead of Honey, put in two Pounds to a Gallon or more, if you would keep it long. This Wine is not only very wholefome, but pleafant: It is a moft rich Cordial, good in curing Confumptions, the Pthyfick, Spleen, and alfo fuch inward Difeafes as accompany the Stone in the Bladder. And Dr. *Needham*

ham says, he has often cured the Scurvy with the Juice of Birch boiled with Honey and Wine. It is also good to abate Heat in a Fever.

Birch Wine, *as made at* Tunbridge Wells *in* Kent.

WE take the Sap of Birch fresh drawn, boil it as long as any Scum rises; to every Gallon of Liquor put four Pounds of good Sugar, and a little Lemon Peel; boil it afterwards half an Hour, and scum it very clean; when it is almost cold, set it a working with Yeast spread on a Toast, let it stand five or six Days in an open Vessel, stirring it often; then take such a Cask as the Liquor will be sure to fill, and fire a large Match dipp'd in Brimstone, and put it into the Cask and stop in the Smoak 'till the Match is extinguished.

Frontiniac Wine *imitated.*

BEFORE you put your Raisin Wine into the Vessel, add to it some of the Syrup of the White Frontiniac Grape, which we make in *England*, tho' the Season is not favourable enough to ripen that Sort of Grape; for in a bad Year, when the White Frontiniac, or the Muscadella Grapes are hard and unripe, and without Flavour, yet if you bake them they will take the rich Flavours which a good Share of Sun would have given them. You may either bake the Frontiniac Grapes with Sugar, or boil them to make a Syrup of their Juice, about a Quart of which Syrup will be enough to put to the Raisin Wine. When these have work'd together, and stood a Time, you will have a Frontiniac Wine of as rich a Flavour as the

French

French Sort, befides the Pleafure of knowing that all the an-gredients are wholefome.

Cyprus Wine *imitated.*

YOU muft to nine Gallons of Water, put nine Quarts of the Juice of White Elder Berries, which has been preffed gently from the Berries, with the Hand, and paffed through a Sieve, without bruifing the Kernels of the Berries: Add to every Gallon of Liquor three Pounds of *Lisbon* Sugar, and to the whole Quantity put an Ounce and a half of Ginger, fliced, and three Quarters of an Ounce of Cloves; then boil this near an Hour, taking off the Scum as it rifes, and pour the whole to cool in an open Tub, and work it with Ale Yeaft fpread upon a Toaft of White Bread for three Days, and then tun it into a Veffel that will juft hold it, adding about a Pound and a half of Raifins of the Sun fplit, to lye in Liquor 'till we draw it off, which fhould not be 'till the Wine is fine, which you will find in *January.* This Wine is fo much like the fine rich Wine brought from *Cyprus,* in its Colour and Fla-vour, that it has deciev'd the beft Judges. Thefe Berries are ripe in *Auguft,* and may be had at the *Ivy-Houfe* at *Hoxton.*

To make Apricock Wine.

YOU muft, to every Quart of Water put a Pound and a half of Apricocks, that are not over ripe; let them be wiped clean, and cut in Pieces; boil thefe 'till the Li-quor is ftrong of the Apricock Flavour, then ftrain the Li-quor thro' a Sieve, and put to every Quart four or five Ounces of White Sugar, boil it again, and fcum it as it rifes,

and

and when the Scum rifes no more, pour it into an earthen Pot: The Day following bottle it, putting into every Bottle a Lump of Loaf Sugar, as big as a Nutmeg. This will prefently be fit for drinking; is a very pleafant Liquor, but will not keep long.

To make Quince Wine.

GAther your Quinces when they are dry, and wipe them very clean, with a coarfe Cloth, then grate them with a coarfe Grater or a Rafp, as near the Core as you can, but grate in none of the Core, nor the hard Part of it; then ftrain your grated Quinces into an earthen Pot, and to each Gallon of Liquor put two Pounds of fine Loaf Sugar, and ftir it 'till your Sugar is diffolved; then cover it clofe, and let it ftand twenty four Hours, by which time it will be fit enough to bottle, taking Care in the bottling of it that none of the Settlement go into the Bottles. This will keep good about a Year: Obferve that your Quinces muft be very ripe when you gather them for this Ufe.

To make Cowflip Wine.

WE take fix Gallons of Water, twelve Pounds of Sugar, four Whites of Eggs; beat the Eggs very well and put them in the Water and Sugar, then put it on the Fire, in a Kettle, and let it boil three Quarters of an Hour, take the Scum off all the Time it boils, and when it's cold take a Peck of pick'd Cowflips, bruife them a little and put them in, then make a good brown Toaft and fpread it on both Sides with good Ale Yeaft, and put it in with the Cowflips; let it ftand two or three Days to work. The Night before you ftrain it off, put in two Lemons, a

Quart

Quart of Rhenish Wine, and six Ounces of Syrup of Citrons, then cover it close; the next Day strain it off thro' a Strainer, squeezing the Cowslips as hard as possible, then strain it through a Flannel Bag, and put it in your Vessel; when it has done working, stop it close for a Fortnight, or three Weeks, then bottle it off.

Damsin Wine.

HAving provided four Gallons of Water, put to every Gallon, four Pounds of *Malaga* Raisins, and half a Peck of Damsins, in a Vessel without a Head, which being cover'd, they are to steep six Days, stir them twice every Day, and let them stand as long without stirring: Then draw off your Wine, colour it with the infus'd Juice of Damsins sweeten'd with Sugar, and turn it into a Wine Vessel for a Fortnight, in order to be made fine, and afterwards dispos'd of in Bottles.

Rasberry Wine.

RIPE Rasberries being bruised with the Back of a Spoon, strain them and fill a Bottle with the Juice; stop it, but not very close, and set it by for four or five Days: Then pour it off from the Dregs, and add thereto as much Rhenish, or White Wine, as the Juice will well colour; that done, sweeten your Wine with Loaf Sugar, and bottle it up for Use.

Gilliflower Wine.

TO three Gallons of Water put six Pounds of the best Powder Sugar, boil the Sugar and Water together for the Space of half an Hour, keep scumming it as

4 P   the

the Scum rifes; let it ftand to cool, beat up three Ounces of Syrup of Betony, with a large Spoonful of Ale Yeaft, put it into the Liquor and brew it well together; then having a Peck of Gilliflowers, cut from the Stalks, put them into the Liquor, let them infufe and work together three Days, covered with a Cloth; ftrain it and put it into a Cask, and let it fettle for three or four Weeks, then bottle it.

Of CORDIALS *for the Clofet.*

Rofa Solis.

TAKE Rofa Solis, clean pick'd, four Handfuls, Nutmegs, Carraway and Coriander Seeds, Mace, Cloves Cinnamon, each half an Ounce; Ginger, Cardemums, Zedoary, Calamus, Aromaticus, each a Diam and a half; Cubebs, yellow Sanders, each half a Diam, red Sanders an Ounce, Liquorice two Ounces, red Rofe Leaves dry'd, a Handful; beft Brandy a Gallon; infufe for fome Days, and ftrain off the clear Liquor, in which diffolve White Sugar 12 Ounces.

Another.

YOU muft take Rofa Solis cleanfed, four Handfuls, Cinnamon, Nutmegs, Carraway and Coriander Seeds, each one Ounce; Cloves, Mace, Ginger, each three Drams; Cardemums, Cubebs, Zedoary, Calamus, Aromaticus, each a Dram, red Rofes, dry'd an Ounce, Liquorice two Ounces, Raifins fton'd half a Pound, Cochineal, Saffron, each one Dram, beft Brandy one Gallon; infufe for eight Days, and ftrain, to which add Loaf Sugar twelve Ounces.

Dr.

Dr. Stephens's Water.

YOU muſt take wild Cammomile, Lavender, wild Marjoram, Mint, Pellitory of the Wall, Thyme, red Roſes, Roſemary, and Sage, each two Handfuls; Anniſeeds, Fennel Seeds, Cinnamon, Galangal, Ginger, Grains of Paradice and Nutmeg, of each ſix Drams; biuiſe all theſe Ingiedients and put them into two Gallons of Canary or Claret; let them infuſe for 24 Hours, and then diſtil them off gently, the firſt and ſecond Runnings each by itſelf. Broken Leaf Gold is commonly put in this.

Aqua Mirabilis.

YOU muſt take Cloves, Mace, Nutmegs, Cinnamon, Cardemum, Cubebs, Galangals, and Melliot Flowers, of each two Ounces, Cowſlip Flowers, Roſemary Flowers, and Spear Mint, of each four Handfuls, a Gallon of the Juice of Celendine, a Gallon of Brandy, a Gallon of Canary, and a Gallon of White Wine, infuſe them for 12 Hours, and diſtil them off in a gentle Sand Heat.

Clary Water.

HAving a Quart of Borage Water, put it in an earthen Jug, and fill it with two or three Quarts of Clary Flowers freſh gather'd; let it infuſe an Hour over the Fire in a Kettle of Water, then take out the Flowers, and put in as many freſh Flowers, and ſo do for ſix or ſeven Times together; then add to that Water two Quarts of the beſt Sack, and a Gallon of freſh Flowers, and two Pounds of White Sugar Candy, beaten ſmall, and diſtil all off in a cold

Still;

Still; mix all the Water together when 'tis ftilled, and fweeten it to your Tafte with the fineft Sugar: Cork the Bottles well, and keep it cool.

Citron Water.

WE take frefh Lemon Peels, number thirty, Figs fourteen Pounds, Proof Spirits three Gallons, Water as much as is neceffary: Infufe and diftil, make it up high Proof, and dulcify with double refin'd Sugar, two Pounds and a half for Ufe.

Another.

GET beft Lemon Peel bruifed, eighteen Ounces, Orange Peel nine Ounces, Nutmegs bruifed, one Quarter of a Pound, ftrong Proof Spirits three Gallons, Water two Gallons, macerate, diftil and dulcify with double refin'd Loaf Sugar, two Pounds for Ufe.

Ratifia.

GET three Gallons of Moloffus Brandy, Nuts two Ounces and an half, bitter Almonds one Pound and a half; bruife them, and infufe them in the Brandy, adding Ambergreafe three Grains, mixed with fine *Lisbon* Sugar three Pounds; infufe all for feven or eight Days Space and then ftrain off for Ufe.

Orange Flower Brandy.

YOU muft take a Gallon of *French* Brandy, and put it in a Bottle that will hold it, then boil a Pound of Orange Flowers, a little while, and put them to the Brandy, fave the Water, and with that make a Syrup to fweeten it.

Plague

Plague Water.

WE take Rue, Rofemary, Balm, Carduns, Scordium, Marigold Flowers, Dragons, Goats Rue, Mint, each three Handfuls, Roots of Mafter-Wort, Angelica, Buttei-Bur, Piony, each fix Ounces, Scoizoneia three Ounces, Proof Spirits three Gallons: Maceiate, diftil, and make it up high Proof.

Another.

GET Roots of Mafter-Wort, Gentian, Snake Root, each two Ounces; green Walnuts bruifed 24, *Venice* Treacle and Mithridate, each one Ounce, Camphire two Diachms, Rue, Elecampane Root, each one Ounce; Horehound two Ounces, Saffron a Drachm, Proof Spirits three Gallons, Watei *q f.* diftil, and fweeten with White Sugar one Pound and a half for Ufe. *Note,* That the Saffion is beft added after Diftillation.

Epedemick *or* Plague Water.

WE take Dragons, Rofemary, Wormwood, Sage, Scordium, Mugwort, Scabius, Balm, Carduus, Tormentil with Roots, Angelica with Roots, Marigold Flowers, Centuiy, Betony, Pimpinel, Celadine, Rue, Agiimony, each half a Pound, Gentian, Zedoary, Liquorice, Elecampane, each four Ounces: Slice the Ingredients and infufe them in thiee Gallons of Moloffus Spirits; then add Spring Water two Gallons; diftil, and dulcify with fine Sugar one Pound.

Here are three Prefcriptions for compounding Plague Water, of which you may take your Choice. They are,
com-

compounded of noble and generous Alexipharmicks, and are each profitable to be taken as a Prefervative againſt all peſtilential, malign, or other contagious Diſtempers: And alſo an Antidote to expel the Malignity from the Heart, and force it towards the Circumference, there to be diſcharged by a gentle Diaphoreſis: And this they effect by the Subtilty and Tenuity of their Subſtance, whereby they divide and attenuate their Humours, ſo as to render them fine enough to paſs thro' the cutaneous Glands, by a ſenſible Perſpiration, which appears upon the Cuticle in Form of Dew, or gentle Sweat. And to this neceſſary Work we may well ſuppoſe the Nerves lend their helping Hand; for they being now invigorated by a freſh Influx of animal Spirits, communicated to them by theſe generous Cordials or Alexipharmicks, and their Waſte repaired by this timely Auxilliary, are enabled more forcibly to contract their Fibres, and ſo to ſqueeze out of the Capillaries, thoſe Humours which obſtructed the Perſpiration; or ſo to divide them by ſuch Shocks and Impulſes of the contracting Fibres, that becoming thereby more fluxile they may readily paſs out that Way, which Nature endeavours for their Excretion; which commonly terminates the Diſtemper by this critical Evacuation.

Surfeit Water.

GET a Peck of red Corn Poppies, put them in a large Diſh, cover them with another, and ſet it in an Oven ſeveral Times after Houſhould Bread is drawn; put them into a Quart of *Aqua Vitæ*, with a large Nutmeg, and a Race of Ginger ſliced, a ſmall Stick of Cinnamon, a Blade of Mace, three or four Figs, four Ounces of Raiſins fins of the Sun, ſton'd, Anniſeeds, Cardamum and Fennel Seeds of each half a Drachm beaten, of Liquorice ſliced half an Ounce, lay ſome Poppies in the Bottom of a broad Glaſs Body, then lay a Layer of the other Ingredients, and then another Layer of Poppies, and ſo continue 'till the Glaſs is full, then pour in the *Aqua Vitæ,* and cover it cloſe, and let it infuſe 'till the Liquor is very red with the Poppies, and ſtrong of the Spice: Of this you may take two or three Spoonfuls at a Time, and when it grows low you may pour another Quart of *Aqua Vitæ* to the Ingredients. You may make double the Quantity, by doubling the Ingredients, and ſo any Quantity in Proportion.

Cinnamon Water.

GET choice Cinnamon bruiſed 12 Ounces, Proof Moloſſus, Spirits rectified, three Gallons; Water one Gallon and a half; macerate them 24 Hours, and then diſtil and draw off your Spirits, and dulcify with Loaf Sugar two Pounds and a half, and make it up full Proof.

There is another Receipt for making beſt Cinnamon Water, which is by an Addition of Nutmegs to the Compoſition, and with a much larger Quantity of Cinnamon, which we ſhall here give you.

Take beſt Cinnamon bruiſed a Pound, Nutmeg bruiſed an Ounce, Bay Salt four Ounces, ſtrong rectify'd Proof Spirits three Gallons, River Water a Gallon and a half: Macerate and draw off as above directed, and dulcify the ſame with the beſt Loaf Sugar two Pounds twelve Ounces, and make them up high Proof for Uſe.

Royal

Royal Ufquebaugh *by Infufion.*

YOU mufl take Raifins ftoned two Pounds, Figs fliced half a Pound, Cinnamon two Ounces and a half, Nutmegs one Ounce, Cloves half an Ounce, Mace half an Ounce, Liquorice three Ounces, Saffron half an Ounce, bruife the Spices, flice the Liquorice, &c. and pull the Saffron in Pieces, and infufe them all in a Gallon of the beft Brandy for feven or eight Days, 'till the whole Virtue be extracted from them; then filter them, putting thereto a Quart of Canary Wine, and half a Dram of Effence of Ambergreafe, and 12 Leaves of Gold broken in Pieces, which referve for Ufe.

To make Irifh Ufquebaugh.

WE take to every Gallon of *French* Brandy one Ounce of Liquorice fliced, one Ounce of fweet Fennel Seeds, one Ounce of Annifeeds, one Pound of Raifins of the Sun, fplit and ftoned, a Quarter of a Pound of Figs fplit, two Drachms of Coriander Seeds; let thefe infufe about eight or nine Days, and pour the Liquor clear off, then add half an Ounce of Saffron in a Bag for a Day or two, and when that is out, put in a Drachm of Musk. If, when this Compofition is made, it feems to be too high a Cordial for the Stomach, put to it more Brandy, 'till you reduce it to the Temper you like. This is the fame Receipt King WILLIAM had when he was in *Ireland.*

To make Green Ufquebaugh.

WE take to every Gallon of *French* Brandy one Ounce of Annifeeds, and another of Sweet Fennel Seeds

Seeds, two Drachms of Coriander Seeds   Let thefe infufe nine Days, then take of the Spirit of Saffron one Drachms diftill'd from Spirits of Wine; mix with the reft; infufe, during this Time, fome Liquorice fliced in Spirits, one Pound of Raifins of the Sun, and filter it; put then a Quart of pure White Wine to a Gallon of the Liquor, and when all is mix'd together, take the Juice of Spinach boil'd, enough to colour it, but do not put the Spinach, Juice into the Liquor 'till it is cold.   To this put one Pound of White Sugar Candy, finely powder'd, to a Gallon of Liquor.

To make Vifney.

THIS Vifney is made of pure Brandy, and as many Morello Cherries as will fill the Bottles or Casks, with one Ounce of Loaf Sugar to each full Quart; thefe Veffels or Bottles muft be gently ftopp'd when the Cherries are put in, and ftand in a cool Cellar, for two Months before the Liquor is poured from them, and then the Liquor may be put in fmall Bottles for ufe : It is not very ftrong, but very pleafant.   The Cherries, when they are taken out, may be diftill'd, and will yield a fine Spirit.

  In fome Places, where there are Laurels grow wild, without cutting or pruning, I mean the *Lauro Cerafus*, as we find in many old Gardens, that Plant is apt to bear Berries, which in reality are Cherries, from whence it has its Name : Thefe Berries, or Cherries are ripe about *July*, and make a fine Cordial, if we infufe them in Brandy, for two or three Months with a little Sugar; this will have a Flavour of Apricock Kernels, and be of a rich red Colour.

4 Q   *A*

A philosophical Account of brewing strong O C T O B E R
B E E R.

CARE, in the firſt Place, muſt be taken that the
Malt be very clean, and when it is ground, it ſhould
ſtand four and twenty Hours at leaſt in the Sacks.

The Quantity is five Quarters of Malt to three Hogsheads
of Beer, and eighteen Pounds of Hops, unleſs the Malt be
pale dried, then there muſt be added three or four Pounds
more.

The Choice of Liquor for brewing is of conſiderable Advantage, the ſofteſt and cleaneſt Water is the beſt.

You are to boil your firſt Liquor, adding a Handful or
two of Hops to it, then before you ſtrike it over to your
Goods or Malt, cool it in as much Liquor as will bring it
to a Temper, not to ſcald the Malt; for it is a Fault not to
take the Liquor as high as poſſible, but not to ſcald.

The next Liquors do the ſame.

And, indeed, all your Liquors ought to be taken as high
as may be, that is, not to ſcald.

When you let your Wort from your Malt into the Under-Back, put to it a Handful or two of Hops, 'twill preſerve it from that Accident which Brewers call, Blink-
ing or Foxing.

In boiling your Worts, the firſt Wort boil high or quick,
for the quicker the Wort is boiled the better it is.

The Second boil more than the Firſt, and the Third or
laſt more than the Second.

In cooling, lay your Worts thin, and let each be well
cooled, and Care muſt be taken in letting them down into
the Tun, that you do it leiſurely, to the End, that as little
of

of the Fœces, or Sediment, as poſſible, may paſs with it, which cauſes the Fermentation to be fierce or mild, for,

Note, There is in all fermented Liquors Salt and Sulphur, and to keep theſe two Bodies in a due Proportion, that the Salt does not exalt itſelf above the Sulphur, conſiſts a great Part of the Art in Brewing.

When your Wort is firſt let into your Tun, put but a little Yeaſt to it, and let it work by Degrees quietly, and if you find it works but moderate, whip in the Yeaſt two or three Times or more, 'till you find your Drink well fermented, for without a full Opening of the Body by Fermentation, it will not be perfectly fine, nor will it drink clean or light

When you cleanſe, do it by a Cock from your Tun, placed ſix Inches from the Bottom, to the End, that moſt of the Sediment may be left behind, which may be thrown on your Malt to mend your Small-Beer.

When your Drink is tunn'd, fill your Veſſel full, let it work at the Bung-hole, and have a Reſerve in a ſmall Cask to fill it up, and don't put any of the Drink, which will be under the Yeaſt after it is worked over, into your Veſſels, but put it by itſelf in another Cask, for it will not be ſo good as your other in the Cask.

This done, you muſt wait for the finiſhing the Fermentation, then ſtop it cloſe, and let it ſtand 'till the *Spring,* for Brewing ought to be done in the Month of *October,* that it may have Time to ſettle and digeſt all the Winter Seaſon.

In the *Spring* you muſt unſtop your Vent-hole, and thereby ſee whether your Drink doth ferment or not, for as ſoon as the warm Weather comes, your Drink will have another Fermentation, which when it is over, let it be again well ftopped and ftand 'till *September*, or longer, and then peg it if you find it pretty fine, the Hop well rotted, and of a good pleafant Tafte for drinking.

Then, and not before, draw out a Gallon of it, put to it two Ounces of Ifing-glafs, cut fmall and beaten, to melt, ftirring it often, and whip it with a Wifk 'till the Ifingglafs be melted, then ftrain it and put it into your Veffel, ftirring it well together; ftop the Bung flightly, for this will caufe a new and fmall Fermentation; when that is over ftop it clofe, leaving only a Vent-hole a little ftopped, let it ftand, and in ten Days or a little more, it will be tranf-parently fine, and you may drink of it out of the Veffel 'till two Parts in three be drawn, then bottle the reft, which will, in a little Time, come to drink very well.

If your Drink, in *September*, be well condition'd for Tafte, but not fine, and you defire to drink it prefently, rack it before you put your Ifingglafs to it; and then it will fine the better, and drink the cleaner.

To make Drink fine quickly, there is a Way, by fepa-rating the Liquor from the Foeces, when the Wort is let out of the Tun into the Under-Back, which may be done in this Manner: When you let your Wort into your Under-Back out of your Tun, catch the Wort in fome Tub fo long, and fo often as you find it run foul, put that fo catched on the Malt again, and do fo 'till the Wort run clear into the Underback. This feems a good Method where it can be ufed, for it is the Foeces which caufe the fierce and violent Fermentation; to hinder which, is in fome Meafure, the Way to have fine Drink.

Note,

Note, That the finer you make your Wort, the fooner your Drink will be fine. Some Perfons, curious in Brewing, have caufed Flannels to be placed, that all the Wort may run thro' one or more of them into the Tun before working, by which Means the Drink has been made very fine and well tafted.

Of cleaning and fweetening Casks.

IF your Cask is a But, then, with cold Water, firft rinfe out the Lees clean, and have ready, boiling or very hot Water, which put in, and with a long Stale, and a little Birch faftened to its End, fcrub the Bottom as well as you can: At the fame time let there be provided another fhorter Broom of about a Foot and a half long, that with one Hand may be fo employed in the upper and other Parts as to clean the Cask well: So in a Hogshead or other fmaller Veffel, the one handed fhort Broom may be ufed with Water, or with Water and Sand, or Afhes, and be effectally cleans'd, the Outfide of the Cask about the Bung-hole fhould be well wafh'd, left the Yeaft, as it works over, carries fome of its Filth with it.

But to fweeten a Barrel, Kilderkin, Firkin or Pin in the great Brewhoufes, they put them over the Copper hole for a Night together, that the Steam of the boiling Water or Wort may penetrate into the Wood; this way is fuch a furious Searcher, that unlefs the Cask is new hooped juft before, it will be apt to fall in Pieces.

Another Way.

WE take a Pottle, or more, of Stone Lime, and put it into the Cask; on this pour fome Water and ftop it up directly, fhaking it well about.

Ano-

Another Way.

YOU muſt take a long Linnen Rag and dip it in melt-ed Brimſtone, light it at the End, and let it hang pendant with the upper Part of the Rag faſten'd to the Wooden-Bung, this is a moſt quick ſure Way, and will not only ſweeten, but help to fine the Drink.

Another Way.

OR to make your Cask more pleaſant, you may uſe the Vintners Way thus: Take four Ounces of Stone Brimſtone, one Ounce of burnt Allum, and two Ounces of Brandy; melt all theſe in an earthen Pan over hot Coals, and dip therein a Piece of new Canvaſs, and inſtantly ſprinkle thereon the Powders of Nutmegs, Cloves, Coriander and Anniſeeds: This Canvaſs ſet on Fire, and let it burn hang-ing in the Cask faſtened at the End with the Wooden Bung ſo that no Smoak comes out.

For a Musky Cask.

BOIL ſome Pepper in Water and fill the Cask with it ſcalding hot.

For a very ſtinking Veſſel.

THE laſt Remedy is the Cooper's taking out one of the Heads of the Cask to ſcrape the Inſide, or new ſhave the Staves, and is the ſureſt Way of all others, if it is fired afterwards within-ſide a ſmall Matter, as the Cooper knows how.

Theſe ſeveral Methods may be made uſe of at Diſcretion and will be of great Service where they are wanted. The
ſooner

sooner also a Remedy is applied the better, else the Taint commonly increases, as many have, to their Prejudice, proved, who have made use of such Casks, in Hopes the next Beer will over-come it; but when once a Cask is infected it will be a long while, if ever, before it comes sweet if no Air is used. Many therefore of the careful Sort, in case they han't a Convenience to fill their Veffel as soon as it is empty, will stop it close, to prevent the Air and preserve the Lees found, which will greatly tend to the keeping of the Cask pure and sweet against the next Occasion.

To prepare a new Veffel to keep Malt Liquors in.

A New Veffel is most improperly used by some ignorant People for strong Drink after only once or twice scalding with Water, which is so wrong, that such Beer or Ale will not fail of tasting thereof for half, if not a whole Year afterwards, such is the Tang of the Oak and its Bark as may be observed from the strong Scents of Tan-Yards, which the Bark is one Cause of To prevent then this Inconvenience, when your Brewing is over put up some Water scalding hot, and let it run thro' the Grains, then boil it and fill up the Cask, stop it well and let it stand 'till it is cold, do this twice, then take the Grounds of strong Drink and boil in it green Walnut Leaves and new Hay or Wheat Straw, and put all into the Cask, let it be full and stop it close: After this, use it for Small Beer half a Year together, and then it will be thoroughly sweet and fit for Strong Drinks; or

Ano-

Another Way.

HAving a new Cask, dig a Hole in the Ground, in which it may lie half depth with the Bung downwards; let it remain a Week, and it will greatly help this or any other ftinking mufty Cask.

Wine Casks.

THESE, in my Opinion, are cheapeft of all others to furnifh a Perfon readily with, as being many of them good Casks for Malt Liquors, becaufe the Sack and White Wine Sorts are always feafon'd to Hand, and will greatly improve Beers and Ales that are put in them : But beware of the Rhenifh Wine Cask for ftrong Drinks; for its Wood is fo tinctured with this fharp Wine, that it will hardly ever be free of it, and therefore fuch Casks are beft ufed for Small Beer: The Claret Cask will a great deal fooner be brought into a ferviceable State for holding Strong Drink, if it is two or three Times fcalded with Grounds of Barrels, and afterwards ufed for Small Beer fome Time. I have bought a But or Pipe for eight Shillings in *London* with fome Iron Hoops on it, a Hogfhead for the fame, and the half Hogfhead for five Shillings, the Carriage for a But by the Waggon thirty Miles, is two Shillings and Sixpence, and the Hogfhead Eighteen-pence: But to cure a Claret Cask of its Colour and Tafte, put a Peck of Stone Lime into a Hogfhead, and pour upon it three Pails of Water; bung immediately with a Wood or Cork Bung, and fhake it well about a Quarter of an Hour, and let it ftand a Day and Night, and it will bring off the red Colour, and alter the Tafte of the Cask very much.

To *make* Mead.

TO thirteen Gallons of Water put thirty Pounds of Honey, boil and fcum it well, then take Rofemary, Thyme, Bay Leaves and Sweet Briar, one Handful alto-gether, boil it an Hour, then put it into a Tub with two or three good Handfuls of ground Malt; ftir it 'till 'tis but Blood warm; then ftrain it through a Cloth, and put it into a Tub again, cut a Toaft round a Quartern Loaf, and fpread it over with good Ale Yeaft, and put it into your Tub, and when the Liquor is quite over with the Yeaft, put it up in your Veffel; then take Cloves, Mace, Nut-megs an Ounce and a half, of Ginger an Ounce fliced, bruife the Spice, and tie it all up in a Rag, and hang it in the Veffel, ftop it up clofe for ufe.

To *make fmall* White Mead.

GET fix Gallons of Spring Water, and having made it hot, diffolve in it fix Quarts of Honey, and two Pounds of Loaf Sugar, boil it for half an Hour, and keep fcumming it as long as any is boiling; pour it out into a Veffel and fqueeze in the Juice of eight Lemons, and the Rinds of no more than four, about forty Cloves, four Races of Ginger, a Sprig or two of Sweet Briar and of Rofema-ry: And after it has ftood in the Veffel 'till it is no more than Blood warm, fpread five or fix Spoonfuls of Ale Yeaft upon a good brown Toaft, and put it in. Put it up into a Cask fit for it, and after it has ftood five or fix Days, you may bottle it.

White

White Metheglin.

YOU muſt take Sweet Marjoram, Sweet Briar Buds, Strawberry Leaves and Violets, of each two Handfuls, of double Violets (if they are to be had) broad Thyme, Borage and Agrimony, of each two Handfuls, ſix or eight Tops of Roſemary, the Seeds of Carraways, Coriander and Fennel, of each four Spoonfuls, and ſix or eight large Blades of Mace. Boil all theſe Ingredients in ſixteen Gallons of Water for three Quarters of an Hour or better, ſcum and ſtrain the Liquor, and having ſtood 'till it is luke-warm, put to it as much of the beſt Honey as will make it bear an Egg the Breadth of a Six-pence above the Water, then boil it again as long as any Scum will riſe, and ſet it to cool; when it is almoſt cold, put in a Pint of new Ale Yeaſt; and when it has worked 'till you perceive the Yeaſt to fall, turn it up and ſuffer it to work in the Cask, 'till the Yeaſt has done riſing fill it up every Day with ſome of the ſame Liquor, ſtopping it up. Put into a Bag a couple of Nutmegs ſliced, a few Cloves, Mace and Cinnamon, all unbruiſed, and a Grain or two of Musk.

Metheglin.

WE take live Honey, which naturally runs from the Combs (that from Swarms of the ſame Year is beſt) and put ſo much of it into clear Spring Water, as both together will make up above twenty Gallons; being made ſo ſtrong with the Honey, when thoroughly diſſolved, that an Egg will not ſink to the Bottom, but ſwim up and down in it; then boil this Liquor in a Copper Veſſel (or if you have not that, a Braſs one may ſerve) for about an Hour or

more

more, and by that Time the Egg will swim above the Liquor about the Breadth of a Groat, then let it cool   The next Morning you may barrel it up, putting in an Ounce of Cinnamon, of Cloves and Mace, each an Ounce and a Quarter, all grosly pounded; for if it be beat fine, it will always float in the Metheglin and make it foul, and if the Spices be put in while it is hot they will lose their Spirits. Put in a small Spoonful of Yeast at the Bung-hole to augment its working, but it must not be left to stand too cold at first, for that would hinder its Fermentation.   As soon as it has done working, it must be stopp'd up close, and let stand for a Month and then boiled off, and if then set into a Refrigeratory, it will be a most pleasant vinous Liquor, and the longer it is kept the better it will be.

You may judge of its Strength by the floating of the Egg, and it may be made stronger or smaller, at Pleasure, by adding more Honey or more Water, and the more it is boiled, the more pleasant and more durable it will be

It is not necessary to scum the Metheglin while it is boiling, for the Scum being left behind, will help its Fermentation, and afterwards render it the clearer, it being commonly believed that it unites again.

To make Cyder.

HAving Apples so throroughly ripe that they will easily fall by shaking the Tree; the Apples proper are Pippins, Pomewaters, Harveys or other Apples of a Watery Juice; either grind or pound them, and squeeze them in a Hair-bag; put the Juice up into a seasoned Cask.

The Cask is to be seasoned with a Rag dipp'd in Brimstone ty'd to the End of a Stick, and put it in burning into

4 R 2   the

the Bung-hole of the Cask, and when the Smoak is gone, wash it with a little warm Liquor, that has run thro' a second straining of the Mure or Husk of the Apples.

Put into the Cask, when the Cyder is in, a Bit of Paste made of Flower, and ty'd up in a thin Rag; let it stand for a Week, and then draw it off from the Lees into another season'd Cask.

Some advise to put three or four Pounds of Raisins into a Hogshead, and two Pounds of Sugar to make it work the better.

To make Royal Cyder.

WHEN the Cyder is fine and past its Fermentation, but not stale, put to each Gallon of Cyder a Pint and a half of Brandy, or Spirits drawn off from Cyder, and also half a Pint of Cyder Sweets to every Gallon of Cyder, more or less, according to the Tartness or Harshness of the Cyder. The Spirits and Sweets must be mix'd together, and mix'd with an equal Quantity of the Cyder, and then they are to be put into the Cask of Cyder, and all stirr'd together with a Stick at the Bung-hole for a Quarter of an Hour, and the Bung-hole must be well stopp'd down, and the Cask rolled about ten or twelve Times to mix them well together. Let it stand for three or four Months, and you may either drink it or bottle it.

To recover any Cyder *that is decay'd, although it be quite* four.

FROM a Hogshead of pale sour Cyder draw out as much as by boiling with six Pounds of Brown Sugar Candy will make a perfect Syrup. Let the Syrup stand 'till

it

it is thoroughly cold, pour it into the Hogſhead and ſtop it up cloſe. This will raiſe a Fermentation, but not a violent one. There muſt be room in the Veſſel for the Cyder to work, and in a few Days it will be fit to drink.

To make Cyderkin, or Water Cyder.

AFTER paring half a Buſhel of Apples, core them and boil them in a Barrel of Water, 'till a third Part is conſumed, ſtrain it and put the Liquor to a Buſhel or more of ground or ſtamp'd Apples unboiled, let them ſtand to digeſt for twenty four Hours, preſs out the Liquor and put it into Casks, let it ferment, then ſtop it up cloſe, but give it Vent frequently, that it may not burſt the Cask, and when it has ſtood 'till it is fine, you may either drink or bottle it.

M U M.

The Receipt for making it according as it is recorded in the Town-Houſe of BRUNSWICK.

TAKE ſixty three Gallons of Water that has been boiled to the Conſumption of a third Part; brew it according to Art with ſeven Buſhels of Wheat Malt, one Buſhel of Oatmeal, and one Buſhel of ground Beans. When it is tunned, let not the Hogſhead be too full at firſt, and as ſoon as it begins to work, put into it of the inner Rind of Fir three Pounds, Tops of Fir and Birch one Pound, *Carduus Benedictus* three Handfuls, Flowers of *Roſa Solis* a Handful or two, Burnet, Betony, Marjoram Avens, Penny-royal, wild Thyme, of each a Handful and a half; of Elder Flowers two Handfuls or more, Seeds of Cardamum bruiſed three Ounces, Barberries bruiſed one

Ounce,

Ounce. Put the Herbs and Seeds into the Veffel when the Liquor has wrought a while; and after they are added, let the Liquor work over the Veffel as little as may be. Fill it up at laft, and when it is ftopp'd, put into the Hogfhead ten new-laid Eggs unbroken or crack'd. Stop it up clofe, and drink it at two Years End.

Englifh Brewers ufe Cardamum, Ginger and Saffafras, inftead of the inner Rind of Fir, alfo the Rinds of Walnuts, Madder, red Sanders and Elecampane. Some make it of ftrong Beer and Spruce Beer, and where it is defigned chiefly for its Phyfical Virtues, fome add Water Creffes, Brook-lime and wild Parfley, with fix Handfuls of Horfe Radifh rasp'd to every Hogfhead, according to their particular Inclination or Fancy.

Oigeatt.

TAKE two Ounces of Melon Seeds, half an Ounce of Pompion Seeds and half an Ounce of *Jordan* Almonds, blanched with fix or feven bitter Almonds: Beat the whole Compound in a Mortar, and reduce it to a Pafte, fo as to leave no Clods, fprinkling the fame now and then, with five or fix Drops of Orange Flower Water, to hinder it from turning to Oil: When your Seeds and Almonds are thoroughly ftamped, add thereto half a Pound of Sugar, which is to be likewife well pounded with your Pafte. Then flip the faid Pafte into two Quarts of Water, and let it fteep therein. Afterwards, put in about a Spoonful of Orange Flower Water, and pafs the Liquor thro' a Straining-Bag, preffing the grofs Subftance very hard, fo as nothing may be left therein; you may alfo pour in a Glafs of new Milk. Laftly,

Laftly, turn your Liquor into two Bottles and fet it by to cool.

To *make* Sherbet

HAving provided Calves Feet with Part of a Fillet of Veal, clear'd from the Fat, put them into a Pot, with a proportionable Quantity of Water and White Wine, let them boil for a confiderable Time, and take off the Scum carefully : When your Meat comes to Rags, and there is only left a third Part of the Broth, ftrain it thro' a Cloth, and skim off all the Fat with two or three Feathers. Afterwards turn the whole Mefs into a Pan, with a Stick of Cinnamon, two or three Cloves, a little Lemon Peel, and as much Sugar as will ferve to make it a pleafant Liquor. Let all boil together; clarify it with the White of an Egg whipp'd, and pafs it thro' the Straining-Bag. When this Liquor is to be kept for a long Time, it is requifite to allow two Pounds of Sugar for every Quart of Broth, or Juice of Meat, obferving for the reft, the former Directions : But at laft the Liquor is to be boiled to its pearled Degree, and put into Bottles.

Rofade.

THIS Liquor is made of pounded Almonds and Milk, to which is added clarify'd Sugar : But it will not keep very long, becaufe it's apt to grow greafy, and as it were fo unctuous that it becomes very difagreeable to the Palate.

COS-

C O S M E T I C K S, &c.

To make Pomatum.

GET two Ounces of Oil of bitter Almonds, almoft two Drams of White Wax, flice it very thin, put it into a Gallipot, put the Gallipot into a Skillet of boiling Water, and then put in four Drams of *Sperma Ceti*, and as foon as you have ftirred it together, then put in the Oil of Almonds, then take it off the Fire and out of the hot Water, and keep ftirring it 'till it is cold, with a Knife made of Bone; afterwards beat it up in Rofe Water 'till it is white: Let it be kept in Water, and the Water be changed once a Day.

To take off Freckles.

FIRST gather *May* Dew off from the Corn, then to four Spoonfuls of it add one Spoonful of Oil of Tartar newly drawn; mix them well together, wafh the Face often with it, and do not wipe it, but let it dry of itfelf. When *May* Dew cannot be had, Bean Flower Water, or Elder Flower Water will do very well.

For a pimpled Face.

HAving Roche Allum, common Salt, and live Brimftone, of each half an Ounce, of White Sugar Candy and *Sperma Ceti*, of each one Dram, pound them and fift them fine, put them into a Pint Bottle, add White Lilly Water and Spring Water, of each an Ounce and a half, and a Quarter of a Pint of Brandy, fhake them well together and fet them by for Ufe. When you go to Bed

bathe

bathe the Face well with this Wafh, fhaking the Bottle, lay a Linnen Rag dipped in it over the Face, and in a Week or Fortnight at moſt it will perfectly cure.

To make a Paſte *for the* Hands.

FIRST take half a Pound of Bitter Almonds, then blanch and pound them, and as you are pounding them, put in a Handful of ſton'd Raiſins, and pound them together 'till the Meſs is well incorporated and very fine; then add a Spoonful or two of Brandy, the ſame Quantity of Ox Gall, and two Spoonfuls of Brown Sugar, and the Yolks of a Couple of ſmall Eggs, or of one large one, after theſe have been all beaten well together, except the Almonds, let it have two or three Boils over the Fire, put in the Almonds. Put it up in a Gallipot, the next Day cover it cloſe, keep it cool, and it will keep good half a Year.

To make an excellent Lip Salve.

FIRST take half a Pint of Claret, boil it in one Ounce of Bees Wax, as much freſh Butter, and two Ounces of Alkermes Root bruiſed: When all theſe have boiled together a pretty while, ſtrain it, let it ſtand 'till it is cold, take the Wax off from the Top, melt it again, and pour it clear from the Dregs into a Gallipot, and uſe it at Pleaſure

To preſerve and whiten the Teeth.

BOIL a little Roche Allum in two Ounces of Honey, ſcum it well, add a little Ginger finely powdered; when it has boiled a little longer, take it off, and before it grows cold, put in ſome *Sanguis Draconis*, as much as will tinge it of a good Colour. Having mixed it well,

4 S   put

put it into a Gallipot and set it by for use. Rub the Teeth as oft as you please with a little of it on a Rag.

To make the Teeth *white.*

MIX a little burnt Allum, with six Spoonfuls of Honey, and two of Celandine Juice, and rub the Teeth with it.

A Powder for the Teeth.

MIX half an Ounce of Powder of Myrrh with an Ounce of Cream of Tartar, and rub the Teeth with it two or three times a Week

To cleanse foul and spotted Teeth.

AFTER winding a Bit of fine Rag about a very small End of a Skewer, cut it sharp that it may be like a Pencil for Painting, dip it into Spirit of Salt, afterwards into fair Water for a Moment, rub the Teeth with it, taking Care not to touch the Gums or Lips with it; wash the Mouth with pure cold Water, not that in which the Rag has been dipp'd. This will take off the Fur, and make them very white; but this must not be done too often, but when they are once clean, they may be easily kept so.

For Heat and Pimples in the Face.

WE take Liverwort that grows in a Well, stamp it and strain it, put the Juice into Cream and anoint your Face as often as you please. Also you may drink the Juice of Liverwort warm, to cool the Heat of the Liver.

An

An Oil *to take away the Heat and Shining of the Nose.*

YOU muſt take ſix Ounces of Gourd Seeds, crack them, take out the Kernels and peel off the Skins; blanch three Ounces of bitter Almonds and make an Oil of them, and anoint the Noſe with the Oil. The Gourd Seeds muſt weigh three Ounces when peeled.

To ſweeten the Breath.

GET the Flowers, and Tops of Roſemary, dry them; alſo Cinnamon, Cloves, Mace, and Sugar-candy; take of each a ſmall Quantity, dry them and reduce them to a fine Powder, put ſome of this Powder into a new-laid Egg, and ſup it up in a Morning faſting for ſeven Days ſucceſſively, and it will render the Breath ſweet.

To make Tincture *of* Ambergreaſe.

WE take half an Ounce of Ambergreaſe, a Dram of Musk, and a Quarter of a Pint of Spirit of Wine. Put theſe into a Glaſs Bottle, ſtop it cloſe with a Cork, tie that down with a Piece of Bladder, and ſet it for ten or twelve Days in Horſe-Dung, afterwards pour off the Tincture, and keep it in a Glaſs well ſtopp'd, then you may put the ſame Quantity of Spirit of Wine to the Ambergreaſe, and ſet it in Horſe-Dung as before, and pour off the Tincture at the End of twelve Days. The Ambergreaſe will ſerve for ordinary Uſes afterwards. This Tincture will perfume any Thing, and is alſo very good in Cordials.

To make perfum'd Wash Balls

Dissolve Musk in sweet compounded Water, then take about the Quantity of one Wash Ball of this Composition, and mix it together in a Mortar: Mix this well with your Paste, and make it up into Balls.

To make an excellent Perfume.

Cut half a Pound of Damask Rose-Buds clear from the Whites, stamp them well, and add to them two large Spoonfuls of Damask-Rose-Water, put them into a Bottle, stop them close, let them stand all Night; then take two Ounces and a half of Benjamin, beat it fine, add twenty Grains of Musk, and, if you please, as much Civet; mingle these with the Roses, beating all well together, make it up in little Cakes and dry them between Sheets of Paper.

Another extraordinary Perfume.

We take two Ounces of Juniper, the same Quantity of Storax, twelve Drops of Clove Water, twelve Grains of Musk, and a little Gum-dragant steeped in Water, beat all these Ingredients to a Paste, make it into Rolls; put each Roll between two Rose-Leaves, dry them in an Oven, and as they are burnt, they will give a most pleasant Smell.

To make the Hair black.

We take Oil of Myrtle and Oil of Costmary of each four Ounces, the Juice of green Nuts and the Juice of red Poppies, of each four Ounces, boil them together awhile, and anoint the Hair with them.

GENE-

GENERAL RULES, &c.

IN all Soops, you muſt not put in your Thickening, 'till your Herbs are very tender.

When you boil any Greens, firſt ſoak them near two Hours in Water and Salt, or elſe boil them in Water and Salt in a Copper by themſelves, with a great Quantity of Water: Boil no Meat with them for that diſcolours them.

Uſe no Iron Pans, &c. for they are not proper; but let them be Copper, Braſs, or Silver

When you fry any Fiſh, firſt dip them in Yolks of Eggs, and fry them rather in a Stew-pan over the Fire, and that will make them of a light Gold Colour.

White Sauces are now more generally uſed than Brown, which is done chiefly with Cream, and add a little Champaign or *French* White Wine, and Butter kneaded in Flower.

Parboil all your Meats that you uſe for your Fricaſeys, or elſe ſtewing them too long on the Fire will make them hard.

In roaſting or boiling, a Quarter of an Hour to every Pound of Meat, at a ſteady Fire, is the beſt Rule that can be given to do it to Perfection.

When you beat Almonds, always put in Orange Flower Water, or Roſe Water, to prevent their turning to Oil, which they are very ſubject to.

When you dreſs Mutton, Pigeons, &c. in Blood, always wring in ſome Lemon Juice, to keep it from changing

When you grill any thing, let it be over a Stove of Charcoal, rather than Sea Coal; it makes it eat ſweeter and ſhorter; turn your Meat very often.

A

An EXPLANATION *of some of the* TERMS *used in*
COOKERY.

Legumes, any Kind of Pulfe, as Peafe, Beans, &c

Cullices, are the ftrained Juice of Meat

Bifques, are Pottages or Soops in Ragoo

Farce, is a Mixture of Meat and Herbs for Stuffing

Bards of Bacon, are Slices all fat, which are often put round Birds, &c when roafted

Lardoons, are the Bits of Bacon ufed for larding any thing

To Marinate, is one Way of pickling

To Mitony, is to foak in the Dish over the Stove

Bouillon, Broth

Bouillie, boil'd Meat

A la Daube, is a Ragoo commonly eat cold

A la Braife, from *Braife*, live Coals. When you drefs Meat *à la Braife*, you muft ftop your Stew-pan clofe about the Edges with Pafte, and put Fire over as well as under

A la Poivrade, Sauce made with Pepper.

A la vinaigrette, Sauce made with Vinegar

Ravigotte, come from *ravigoter*, to brifk up, or quicken, and is commonly ufed for a Sauce in which there is Muftard

En gratin, any thing that fticks to the Bottom of the Skillet or Tofspan

Court Bouillon, is a *French* Way of drefling large Fish

Blanc-Manger, fignifies White Food A Sort of White Jelly fo called

Hors d'Oeuvres, are choice little Dishes or Plates, that are ferved in between the Courfes at Entertainments

Entremets, or *Intermeffes* are the lefs Sort of Dishes that compofe the Courfe

N B Many *French* Dishes have received their Names from Princes and Perfons of Quality who were fond of them ; as *à la Reine, à la Dauphine, à la Maintenon*, &c Some from famous COOKS, as, *à la St Menehout, à la Montizeur*, &c and fome from the Sauces ufed with them, as, *à la Poivrade*, &c.

F I N I S.